CHARLES DICKENS
AND
HIS PUBLISHERS

General Account

Charles Dickens' Ed.	3/6	457. 8. 6			
"	3/	878. 13. 6			
"	Sets	210. 12. 3			
			1546	14	3
Library Edition			583	17	5
Pickwick			24	17	.
Bleak House			29	13	9
Dorrit			24	9	2
Sketches			14	17	.
Twist			11	16	6
Chuzzlewit			25	14	9
H. Clock			19	2	6
Our Mutual			24	19	3
History of England			33	7	6
People's Edition			1287	1	4
		£	3626	.	5
Proceeds of Parts wasted			9	12	7
			3635	13	.
Advertising			280	.	.
		£	3355	13	.
Sundry Books duty		£	218	.	.
		£	3,573	13	—

Charles Dickens Esq ½ share £ 1786. 16. 6
Interest £ 81. 5. .
£ 1868 . 1 . 6

Chapman and Hall's last general account to Dickens,
1 July to 31 December 1869

CHARLES DICKENS
AND HIS PUBLISHERS

BY

ROBERT L. PATTEN

1978

OXFORD
AT THE CLARENDON PRESS

Oxford University Press, Walton Street, Oxford OX2 6DP

OXFORD LONDON GLASGOW
NEW YORK TORONTO MELBOURNE WELLINGTON
KUALA LUMPUR SINGAPORE JAKARTA HONG KONG TOKYO
DELHI BOMBAY CALCUTTA MADRAS KARACHI
IBADAN NAIROBI DAR ES SALAAM CAPE TOWN

British Library Cataloguing in Publication Data

Patten, Robert Lowry
    Charles Dickens and his publishers.
    1. Dickens, Charles – Relationship with men
    I. Title
    823'.8   PR4581   77–30164
    ISBN 0–19–812076–1

Printed in Great Britain
at the University Press, Oxford
by Vivian Ridler
Printer to the University

To
Jocelyn and Christina
with love

Acknowledgements

FOR GRANTS OR LEAVES OF ABSENCE in support of research on this book I am indebted to the generosity of the following institutions: the American Philosophical Society, Bryn Mawr College, the National Endowment for the Humanities, Rice University.

For providing me with copies of the Bradbury and Evans 'Paper and Print' ledgers, 1844–63, I am grateful to A. V. Caudery, Chairman of Punch Publications Ltd., one of the Bradbury Agnew Group of companies, and to the Librarian, Marilyn Gould.

For permission to consult Dickens's account in the ledgers of Coutts and Co. I wish especially to thank Christopher Dickens, and the Coutts Archivist, M. Veronica Stokes.

For transcripts of Bradbury and Evans's proceedings in Chancery against Dickens and Wills over the termination of *Household Words* I gratefully acknowledge the help of Jeremy Harley and the staff of the Public Record Office.

The following institutions have kindly supplied information: Bodleian Library; British Museum; Bryn Mawr College Library; University of California, Los Angeles Library; Cambridge University Library; William Andrews Clark Memorial Library, University of California; Columbia University Libraries; Dickens House; Henry E. Huntington Library; Houghton Library, Harvard University; Haverford College Library; London Library; Pierpont Morgan Library; New York Public Library, especially the Henry W. and Albert A. Berg Collection; Historical Society of Pennsylvania; Free Library of Philadelphia; Princeton University Library; Public Record Office, London; Fondren Library, Rice University; Philip H. and A. S. W. Rosenbach Foundation; John Rylands Library; The Humanities Research Center of the University of Texas, Austin; Forster Collection of the Victoria and Albert Museum; Harry Elkins Widener Memorial Library, Harvard University; Beinecke Library, Yale University.

To understand better the physical end-product of Dickens's literary labours, I had the privilege of examining the Dexter

Pickwick at the British Museum, the Gimbel Collection at Yale, and all the editions at Dickens House, including those portions of the unequalled Suzannet Collection which The Dickens Fellowship was fortunate to secure.

For counsel of various kinds, I am indebted to the following persons: Richard D. Altick, Terry Belanger, Gerald E. Bentley, Ernestine Billings, Miriam Brokaw, P. A. W. Brown, Anthony Burton, Margaret Cardwell, John Carter, James L. Clifford, Jane R. Cohen, Philip Collins, Eileen Coumont, Duane DeVries, Wilfred S. Dowden, H. J. Dyos, Oscar Dystel, Pamela Echerd, K. J. Fielding, George Ford, Charles Garside, Jr., Royal A. Gettmann, Gordon Haight, John P. Harthan, John Harvey, Howell Heaney, Joanna Hitchcock, Madeline House, E. D. H. Johnson, Sara Keith, Bruce Lively, Doris Minards, Sylvère Monod, Kathleen Murfin, Simon Nowell-Smith, Richard L. O'Keeffe, John Parish, F. H. Patten, I. G. Philip, Marjorie Pillers, John Podeschi, Edgar Rosenberg, Charles Ryskamp, Evelyn Semler, Ellen Shaffer, Peter Shillingsburg, Margaret Sobel, Brian Southam, Harry Stone, Graham Storey, John Sutherland, Lola Szladits, G. B. Tennyson, James Thorpe, Kathleen Tillotson, and Marjorie Wynne.

I owe special thanks to all those who granted permission to quote from unpublished materials: to Christopher Dickens, owner of the copyright in Dickens's letters, and to the Pilgrim Trust and the editors of the Pilgrim Edition of those *Letters*; to the Victoria and Albert Museum, owners of the Chapman and Hall and Bradbury and Evans account books; to Chapman and Hall Ltd., owners of the copyright in the Chapman and Hall account books; to the Bradbury Agnew Group, owners of the 'Paper and Print' ledgers of Bradbury and Evans, 1844–63, of the 'Bradbury Album', and of the copyright in the Bradbury and Evans account books; to Coutts and Co., owners of the ledgers recording the transactions in the account of Charles Dickens Esq., 1837–70; to the following libraries, owners of unpublished manuscripts by Dickens and others: Henry E. Huntington Library, Pierpont Morgan Library, Berg Collection of the New York Public Library, Free Library of Philadelphia, Princeton University Library, Yale University Library.

The editors of the presses and publications that follow have permitted me to quote material that originally appeared in their publications: Bantam Books Inc., for the extract from Oscar Dystel's article 'The Paperback and the Bookstore' which appeared in a special supplement of *The New York Times*; the Bibliographical Society and the author for the table from Simon Nowell-Smith's article 'The "Cheap Edition" of Dickens's Works (First Series) 1847–1852', published in *The Library*; *The Dickensian*, for tables that appeared in William Buckler, 'Dickens's Success with *Household Words*', and George Ford, 'Dickens in the 1960s'; the Nonesuch Press Ltd., for brief extracts from the Nonesuch edition of *The Letters of Charles Dickens*; Oxford University Press, for extracts from the Pilgrim edition of *The Letters of Charles Dickens*; *Rice University Studies*, for my article '*Pickwick Papers* and the Development of Serial Fiction'; and *Studies in English Literature*, for my article 'The Fight at the Top of the Tree: *Vanity Fair* Versus *Dombey and Son*'.

Philip Collins and Simon Nowell-Smith read earlier drafts of the manuscript, Robyn Swett caught many errors and inconsistencies in the final copy, and Michael Slater vetted proofs: in countless ways the argument has been strengthened by their knowledgeable assistance. Anthony Burton graciously consented to help Jennifer Brain locate and photograph appropriate illustrations.

Finally, this study has benefited from the assiduous labours of my research assistants. Throughout the winter of 1968–9 Judith Keyston verified and retranscribed my early drafts of the appendices. Over the past four summers Jean Eros has worked on every aspect of the manuscript, from typing to styling and proofing; and Beth Rigel Daugherty has recomputed each figure and revalidated each total in the account summaries. Their rigour and enthusiasm have been invaluable.

The deeper debt that I owe to my teachers—David Cowden and George Becker at Swarthmore, E. D. H. Johnson and Gerald E. Bentley at Princeton, and Kathleen Tillotson at Bedford College, University of London—is difficult to define, though easy to feel. They set an example of responsible scholarship and criticism that inspired even when it intimidated. What I have learned from them is, I hope, creditably reflected here.

Houston, Texas
24 July 1975

In whatever degree an author wishes readers of his books or buyers of his books, in that measure he rates book-sellers as partners and somewhat like kinfolk.

CARL SANDBURG

Contents

List of Illustrations

A Note on References

THE TEXT OF THE PILGRIM LETTERS is cited for all correspondence by Dickens up to the end of 1843. Thereafter I have cited the texts given in J. W. T. Ley's edition of Forster's *Life*, or that given in the Nonesuch *Letters* if not in Forster. Sources for other correspondence are identified in the footnotes. The following abbreviations appear for texts cited parenthetically:

F   John Forster, *The Life of Charles Dickens*, ed. J. W. T. Ley (New York, Doubleday, Doran, and Co.), 1928.

             Edgar Johnson, *Charles Dickens: His Tragedy and Triumph*, 2 vols. (New York, Simon and Schuster), 1953.

MS. Coutts   Account books, Messrs. Coutts and Co.

MS. B & E   Account books, Bradbury and Evans, in the Victoria and Albert Museum.

MS. C & H   Account books, Chapman and Hall, in the Victoria and Albert Museum.

N   The Nonesuch Edition of *The Letters of Charles Dickens*, ed. Walter Dexter, 3 vols. (Bloomsbury, Nonesuch Press), 1938.

P   The Pilgrim Edition of *The Letters of Charles Dickens*, ed. Madeline House, Graham Storey, and (vol. iii) Kathleen Tillotson (Oxford, Clarendon Press), 1965–.

Introduction

DESPITE ITS EXTENT, this study remains in every sense provisional. It began during 1963–4, when, on a Fulbright to Bedford College, University of London, I chanced on an entry in the Dyce and Forster Auxiliary Collection Catalogue in the Library of the Victoria and Albert Museum. Under 'Dickens, Charles', there appeared the following handwritten information: 'MSS Accounts of sales of works of C. D. Bradbury & Evans. 1845–1861. Chapman & Hall, 1846–1861 (with 3 loose letters). Chapman and Hall. 1862–1870. (with 2 letters and 1 undated acct., loose).'[1] Deposited by Fanny Crosbie, John Forster's niece, in May 1916, these accounts were added to the collection twenty-eight years after publication of the Forster Catalogue (1888). Hence it seemed to me likely that few people knew of their existence. Later I learned that several eminent Dickensians had preceded me: Gerald Grubb, John Butt, Kathleen Tillotson, the Pilgrim editors, and the editors of several of the Clarendon novels. But at the time, in my innocence, I assumed that after a few months' study of the 1,100 or so folio pages of accounts I could write a definitive essay on Dickens's publications.

Thirteen years later I know how wrong that assumption was. Even with the advice of dozens of scholars I have been unable to answer many of the questions which these invaluable documents raise, and have no doubt missed the significance of some of the facts they establish. We still lack a good deal of primary information about Dickens on which these accounts depend: a full

---

[1] Accession numbers L.307–1916, L.308–1916, and L.309–1916; press-marks F.D. 18.1, F.D. 18.2, and F.D. 18.3. Miss Crosbie, daughter of Malcolm Douglas Crosbie, Mrs. Forster's brother, executed the deed of gift on 12 May; it was recorded the next day. The three volumes, measuring $32\frac{1}{4}$–33 cm. by 20 cm., and uniformly bound in three-quarters cloth with leather spines gold-lettered, contain various-sized manuscript accounts, memoranda, estimates, and twenty-seven letters: one to Forster from Chapman and Hall, and twenty-six to Dickens: one from F. M. Evans, five from Bradbury and Evans, ten from Edward Chapman, and ten from Frederic Chapman. These accounts are quoted by courtesy of the Victoria and Albert Museum.

bibliography of his writings and of lifetime editions in England
and abroad; a stringently edited *Complete Works*; a modern
edition of his correspondence. The Clarendon Press is in the
process of issuing textual editions of the novels, and the Pilgrim
Edition of the *Letters* had, at the time this manuscript went to
press, progressed to 1843. Those first three volumes of Dickens's
correspondence comprise the most fully and carefully documented
record of his life, work, and friendship that we have ever had.
They have been used extensively in the early portions of this
narrative, and there is no page detailing Dickens's relations after
1843 that will not be modified—I trust not radically revised—by
future volumes in the series.

But even had the Dickens industry completed all its current
undertakings, our knowledge of Victorian publishing practices in
general, and of the relations between individual authors and their
booksellers, would be spotty. Despite all the books and articles of
the last fifteen years, on which this study draws heavily, we still
do not have a magisterial work on Victorian publishing. In its
absence, our emphases may favour the startling and unrepresenta-
tive.[2] What the average journeyman authors, the Margaret
Oliphants and the B. L. Farjeons, could expect in the way of
contracts and payments, how their works would be advertised,
printed, distributed, sold, translated, and reprinted, what kinds of
friendly relations, social invitations, even marital entanglements
they got into with their publishers, how their economic condition
affected their choice of medium and message—all these things are
still something of a mystery.

Throughout his career Dickens was involved socially and
familiarly as well as professionally with his printers and booksellers: he married the daughter of his superior on one paper; he
hired his father and later his son for periodicals he edited; he
produced a collection of essays for the poor widow of a publisher
he had left, and attended the funeral of another with whom he had
severed all relations; he quarrelled with Bradbury and Evans
about the publicity concerning his separation from Kate, and then

---

[2] I was fortunate indeed that John Sutherland permitted me to read in proof his
useful study of *Victorian Novelists and Publishers* (London, Athlone Press, 1976),
which begins to offer some clarification of the routine relations existing
between nineteenth-century authors and the major publishing houses. Though his
work appeared too late for me to incorporate its findings, our studies are comple-
mentary both in effort and conclusions.

saw his son marry the daughter of a man he vowed never again to speak to. Was such intimacy and tempest usual?

The more one looks at these figures, the more perplexing and revealing they become. To begin with, as I explain in Chapter 9, and at greater length in the Introduction to the Appendices, they are in fact often only approximations, despite their apparent precision. Even so, how are we to understand the magnitudes involved? How do 50,000 copies of *Nickleby* in twenty numbers over nineteen months sold in the British Isles alone during 1837-9 compare with millions of copies of *Jaws* sold in under a year in America in the 1970s? How much money in today's terms is £1,000? Depending on which authority and which conversion formula one follows, £1,000 in 1850 might represent £10,000 or $40,000 in 1968, £6,000 or $30,000 in 1960, or £4,000 or $20,000 in 'the modern monetary equivalent'.[3] And those figures are still essentially meaningless. Some things common today could not be bought at any price, while industrial or domestic labour was available for pennies an hour. Taxes were virtually non-existent on personal income, but so were programmes of social welfare and health care. In short, conversions are almost impossible because people choose to buy different things in different ages and cultures. By giving lots of comparative figures, and by indicating from time to time how Dickens chose to spend his money, I have attempted to provide some indication of his financial status as it compared to his peers and other authors.

Throughout the twenty-five years of records there seem to be reasonably constant assumptions about author–publisher relations, though equally there are hundreds of inconsistencies in details. But for the most part both firms are courteous and apparently punctilious in their correspondence, business-like in their ledger sheets, meticulous in counting up every copy sold, warehoused, or wasted, and informative about the disposition of copies and the costs of printing. Do these accounts therefore represent the usual treatment of authors by publishers, or a practice unique to Dickens? If, as I suspect, the latter, was it because of Dickens's personality,

[3] The 1968 figures were given me by Professor H. J. Dyos; the 1960 ones are derived from Gerald Reitlinger, *The Economics of Taste* (London, Barrie and Rockliff, 1961); and the third set comes from 'The Conditions of Authorship in 1820', one of William Charvat's essays posthumously edited by Matthew J. Bruccoli in *The Profession of Authorship in America, 1800–1870: The Papers of William Charvat* (Columbus, Ohio, Ohio State Univ. Press, 1968), p. 30.

or the peculiar exigencies of serial publication? With Forster and
Ouvry and Dickens scrutinizing every billing with a suspicious
eye for miscalculations and overcharges, were the publishers more
than usually scrupulous? Or were they, especially Chapman and
Hall, even under these incentives, as casual and—to the twentieth-
century eye at least—cavalier to all their authors? When the
publisher acted also as bookseller for a substantial portion of the
total sales volume, did other authors besides Dickens get paid as if
all numbers were wholesaled? Who usually received the difference
between the wholesale price of, say, 8s. for a baker's dozen of
numbers of *Chuzzlewit* and the 13s. paid by the customers? Who
customarily got the extra shilling for volumes bound from the
parts? Did any house charge a flat percentage for overhead? Did
publishers for other authors absorb regularly, as they did often for
Dickens, some of the costs of multiple revisions on the galleys and
page proofs? the extra charges when copy arrived late and the
compositors stayed all night, tearing up the heavily corrected
manuscript into short takes, and deftly setting type by guttering
candlelight in the inky shop? the postage and fees for delivering
copy to Devonshire Terrace or Broadstairs or Boulogne, to
Lincoln's Inn Fields or Lausanne? the congratulatory banquets
and the elaborate presents of money, spoons, portraits? the fees
for legal conferences, copyright disputes, contracts? Did other
authors work their copyrights as extensively as Dickens, with his
penny numbers, shilling parts, bound volumes, his Cheap, Library,
People's, and Charles Dickens editions, his translations, authorized
foreign editions, licences to print from stereos of the journals,
payments for advance sheets of the new novel, India proofs of the
illustrations to America?

It is easier to raise these questions, in the perspective of this
study, than to answer them, though whenever possible I have tried
to set Dickens's experiences next to those of his contemporaries.
At the same time that this book moves laterally from Dickens
towards his professional peers, however, it shies away from a full
exploration of his creative processes and results, deliberately
skewing such evidence as we do possess about his personal and
literary existence. John Forster and Edgar Johnson offer much
more complete pictures of Dickens the man, who was father and
husband and lover, friend, counsellor, *régisseur*, dandy, social
reformer, journalist, 'correspondent for posterity', epistoler,

editor, actor, reader, clown, and genius—all at once. But the very completeness of their approach makes it impossible to disentangle the professional author's relationships with his scores of publishers —English, American, colonial, continental—from Dickens's other roles. Concentrating on one dimension of his life distorts and limits Dickens's character, which was never so wholly calculating and professional as this perspective inescapably implies. The pressures which resulted in his glorious fictions were diffuse and diversified; one set of them concerned his need to earn a livelihood by writing, publishing, and selling books that a world-wide public clamoured to buy and read.

I

THE RISE TO FAME

You say of me;—that I would not choose to write novels unless I were paid. Most certainly I would;— much rather than not write them at all.

ANTHONY TROLLOPE TO JOHN TILLEY,
18 April 1878

I

The Professional Author

No man but a blockhead ever wrote, except for
money.

DR. JOHNSON[1]

i

FOR OVER A HUNDRED YEARS Dickens has been reproached
with having written for money. Schoolchildren on both
sides of the Atlantic are taught that his novels are so long
because he was paid by the word or the line, the implication being
that Dickens sacrificed his artistic scruples to his bank account, and
deliberately foisted on a gullible public reams of grossly padded
letterpress.[2] Literary critics have sometimes sophisticated this
myth, arguing that in order to meet deadlines or to hide the
paucity of invention, Dickens inserted into his early novels odd
scraps of tales previously written and cast aside; or that, in Ruskin's
phrase, he slaughtered characters as a butcher kills a lamb, to
satisfy the market.

Of course Dickens wrote for money. He had to. Gissing's *New
Grub Street* provides a grim reminder of the fate reserved for
writers who, like Dickens, had no prospect of inheriting or
marrying wealth.[3] Dickens's writing was his means of livelihood.
Like Trollope, when Dickens chose literature as a profession he

---

[1] *Boswell's Life of Johnson*, ed. George Birkbeck Hill, rev. and enl. L. F. Powell
(6 vols., Oxford, Clarendon Press, 1934), iii. 19; dated 5 Apr. 1776.

[2] Padding may have been even worse in three-deckers: Mrs. Samuel Carter
Hall may have tossed in 200 additional pages to *The Outlaw* (1835); and Bulwer
Lytton added twenty or more to *The Last Days of Pompeii* (1834); Royal A.
Gettmann, *A Victorian Publisher: A Study of the Bentley Papers* (Cambridge,
Cambridge Univ. Press, 1960), pp. 235–6.

[3] James Hepburn challenges the adequacy of Gissing's portrayal of New Grub
Street in *The Author's Empty Purse and the Rise of the Literary Agent* (London, New
York, and Toronto, Oxford Univ. Press, 1968), pp. 19–21.

'wished to make an income on which [he] and those belonging to [him] might live in comfort'.[4] Those who failed were legion, and their ends sordid: Laman Blanchard cut his throat, Leigh Hunt sponged, the dramatist John Poole shivered in a Parisian garret. Reading Lockhart's 'moving' account of Theodore Hook's last days in grinding poverty, Dickens observed to Miss Coutts: 'Men have been chained to hideous prison walls and other strange anchors 'ere now, but few have known such suffering and bitterness at one time or other, as those who have been bound to Pens' (P iii. 500).

Dickens's struggle to achieve some comfort, like that of many other professional writers of his time, was protracted and arduous. Despite his early popularity, he was not financially secure until more than ten years after *Pickwick*, when in the spring of 1847 he received the major share in the very large profits from the first four numbers of *Dombey and Son* (F VI. i. 464).[5] Before then, his books had chiefly enriched his publishers. Dickens's determination to succeed by his own efforts made him over-hasty in signing contracts for new works and over-sensitive to imagined or real slights. But despite quarrelsome relations with his publishers, first Macrone, then Bentley, then Chapman and Hall, and finally Bradbury and Evans, Dickens did succeed as a professional author, to a degree unmatched by any other Victorian novelist. By the late 1850s, when Thackeray's copyrights were yielding £600 a year,[6] and Trollope was getting £400 apiece for *Doctor Thorne* and *The Bertrams* from Chapman and Hall,[7] Dickens's profits on his most recent novel, *Little Dorrit* (1855–7), ran to over £11,000.

Writing for money was not only a necessity for Dickens: it was also a principle. Throughout his career he thought of himself as a professional writer, an identity which an older generation deplored. Sir Walter Scott noted approvingly Thomas Campbell's toast to Napoleon because he had once hanged a bookseller.[8]

    [4] Anthony Trollope, *An Autobiography*, ed. Bradford Allen Booth (Berkeley and Los Angeles, Univ. of California Press, 1947), p. 91.
    [5] See Robert L. Patten, 'The Fight at the Top of the Tree: *Vanity Fair* Versus *Dombey and Son*', in *Studies in English Literature*, 10 (1970), 759–73.
    [6] *The Letters and Private Papers of William Makepeace Thackeray*, ed. Gordon N. Ray (4 vols., Cambridge, Mass., Harvard Univ. Press, 1945–6), iv. 76.
    [7] Trollope, *An Autobiography*, p. 302.
    [8] Scott, *Letters*, ed. H. J. C. Grierson, Centenary edn. (12 vols., London, Constable, 1932–7), ix. 508 (14 Apr. 1826). The bookseller was Johann Phillip

Samuel Rogers grumbled that to make literature the business of life was to make it a drudgery, Coleridge advised '*never pursue literature as a trade*', and Lamb urged Bernard Barton not to give up his bank job and try to live by his writings alone.[9] With Thackeray and Carlyle, Dickens attempted in 1843 to found an authors' society, but it failed.[10] Later, he helped sponsor and direct the Guild of Literature and Art, serving as Vice-President under Bulwer Lytton and raising money for the Guild through performances of Bulwer's play *Not So Bad as We Seem*. Joined by Forster and Charles Wentworth Dilke, proprietor of the *Athenaeum*, Dickens broke with the General Committee of the Royal Literary Fund in 1864. The dissidents sought to replace the *status quo* of aristocratic patronage and amateurism by an organization which could band together and support professional writers.[11]

An ardent advocate of self-help, Dickens thought that society should reward the author for his labours just as it rewarded the factory hand or baker or navvy for his.[12] The Guild of Literature and Art was one way in which authors could unite to help themselves: it proposed insurance and pension plans, and also a select fellowship of artists and writers who would live rent-free in cottages to be built on land given by Bulwer Lytton at Stevenage (J, p. 723). Dickens believed that the Guild would 'make a revolution in [the literary man's] position which no government, no power on earth but his own, could ever effect' (F XI. iii. 821). That his own popularity rewarded him so amply was a source of justifiable pride; it was an example of the great power of the people, who had released Literature from its demeaning subservience to the whims of a wealthy patron:

To the great compact phalanx of the people, by whose industry,

Palm of Nuremberg, who was shot in 1806 for publishing a pamphlet in that year protesting French rule.

[9] A. S. Collins, *The Profession of Letters: A Study of the Relation of Author to Patron, Publisher, and Public, 1780–1832* (London, Routledge, 1928), pp. 10–12.

[10] In that year John Petheram published an interesting pamphlet giving *Reasons for Establishing an Author's Publication Society* (London, John Petheram, 1843).

[11] See *The Speeches of Charles Dickens*, ed. K. J. Fielding (Oxford, Clarendon Press, 1960), pp. 176–7.

[12] See George Ford, 'Self-Help and the Helpless in *Bleak House*', in *From Jane Austen to Joseph Conrad: Essays Collected in Memory of James T. Hillhouse*, ed. Robert C. Rathburn and Martin Steinmann, Jr. (Minneapolis, Univ. of Minnesota Press, 1958), pp. 92–105.

perseverance, and intelligence, and their result in money-wealth such places as Birmingham, and many others like it, have arisen—to that great centre of support, that comprehensive experience, and that beating heart—Literature has turned happily from individual patrons, sometimes munificent, often sordid, always few, and has found there at once its highest purpose, its natural range of action, and its best reward. . . . From the shame of the purchased dedication, from the scurrilous and dirty work of Grub Street, from the dependent seat on sufferance at my Lord Duke's table today, and from the sponging-house and Marshalsea tomorrow, from that venality which, by a fine moral retribution, has degraded statesmen even to a greater extent than authors, because the statesmen entertained a low belief in the universality of corruption, while the author yielded only to the dire necessity of his calling,—from all such evils the people have set Literature free.[13]

In addition to celebrating the financial independence that popularity yielded, Dickens sought to enhance the 'dignity and honour' of the literary profession. He commended Forster's *Goldsmith*, doubting whether any other book 'was ever written, or anything ever done or said, half so conducive to the dignity and honour of literature' (N ii. 83), and objected when anyone, by attitude or behaviour, seemed to call that dignity into question or bring it into disrepute. 'I will tell you now, candidly,' he wrote to Thackeray in January 1848, 'that I did not admire the design [of *Punch's Prize Novelists*]—but I think it is a great pity to take advantage of the means our calling gives us with such accursed readiness, of at all depreciating or vulgarizing each other.' At the same time, thanking Thackeray for his 'generous letter' of 'manly and gallant regard' with respect to *Dombey*, Dickens gently urged his own example:

I *do* sometimes please myself with thinking that my success has opened the way for good writers. And of this, I am quite sure now, and hope I shall be when I die—that in all my social doings I am mindful of this honour and dignity and always try to do something towards the quiet assertion of their right place. I am always possessed with the hope of leaving the position of literary men in England, something better and more independent than I found it.[14]

Flamboyant in manners and dress, astounding his American auditors with 'the most elegant of coats and trousers, a blaze of velvet

---

[13] *Speeches*, pp. 156–7.
[14] Thackeray, *Letters*, ii. 336–7; Dickens made similar statements to others at this time.

and satin waistcoats, golden chains and tie-pins and rings' (J, p. 360), boisterous and bohemian in relaxation, Dickens neverthe-less remained inflexible in asserting his own, and his profession's, propriety. He once refused to meet the Queen after a performance of *The Frozen Deep* because he was already in costume and make-up for the farce that was to follow; and he presided over a meeting of authors and rebel publishers at John Chapman's house in 1852 with such grave decorum and impartiality that George Eliot, watching quietly from a dark corner, was moved to comment in a letter that he filled the chair 'remarkably well, preserving a courteous neutrality of eyebrow, and speaking with clearness and decision'.[15] Writing to James B. Manson in 1858, Dickens declared: 'I have striven . . . all through my literary life—never to allow [the literary character] to be patronised, or tolerated, or treated like a good or a bad child. I am always animated by the hope of leaving it a little better understood by the thoughtless than I found it' (F XI. iii. 821 n.).

Behind all the lofty principles, accents of pride and snobbery are surely detectable. Dickens was no paragon: he did covet the power and position that wealth could secure, and towards the end of his life a note of desperation crept into his calculations, as he set the number and incapacity of his heirs against the size of his estate. Henry Crabb Robinson worried as early as 1837 that the liberality of Dickens's entertainment would bankrupt his family: 'It is to be lamented that he is ambitious of living genteely and giving dinners to the rich. With an income of three or four thousand a year, and sometimes much more, he may at length, it is to be feared, leave his children to be maintained by the public.'[16] The scurrilous New York paper *Brother Jonathan* chided Dickens during his first American tour in less friendly terms: 'If Mr. Dickens prefers dollars and cents to literary fame—selfish, sordid gratification to a position of commanding respect—and a flash waistcoat to a laurel wreath, it is his own misfortune—the result of traits inseparable from his character.'[17] And George Gissing,

---

[15] *The George Eliot Letters*, ed. Gordon S. Haight (7 vols., New Haven, Yale Univ. Press, 1954–5), ii. 23; dated 2 May 1852.

[16] *Henry Crabb Robinson on Books and Their Writers*, ed. Edith J. Morley (3 vols., London, J. M. Dent, 1938), ii. 543.

[17] Quoted in James J. Barnes, *Authors, Publishers and Politicians: The Quest for an Anglo-American Copyright Agreement, 1815–1854* (Columbus, Ohio, Ohio State Univ. Press, 1974), p. 29.

reflecting on the end of Dickens's career, lamented that 'he died in the endeavour to increase (not for himself) an already ample fortune', attributing the effort to the 'disastrous influence of his time and class'.[18]

Dickens was also capable of disguising his more materialistic motives even to himself, confessing somewhat disingenuously to his brother Frederick that 'there is not a successful man in the world who attaches less importance to the possession of money, or less disparagement to the want of it, than I do' (N ii. 11). But we must not be too hasty to condemn Dickens for enjoying the fruits of his success. '[I]t is a mistake to suppose that a man is a better man because he despises money', Trollope wrote in his *Autobiography*, in a passage that Dickens might have endorsed heartily:

> Who does not desire to be hospitable to his friends, generous to the poor, liberal to all, munificent to his children, and to be himself free from the carking fear which poverty creates? The subject will not stand an argument; and yet authors are told that they should disregard payment for their work, and be content to devote their unbought brains to the welfare of the public. Brains that are unbought will never serve the public much. Take away from English authors their copyrights, and you would very soon take away from England her authors.[19]

Dickens applied his income generously to providing hospitality for his friends and relief to the poor; he was conscientious in supporting his extensive family—parents, brothers and sister, wife, sisters-in-law, and children—and in providing for them after his death, to the detriment of his own health; and, like Micawber, 'he was a most untiring man when he work[ed] for other people', being prodigal in the expenditure of energy on behalf of publishers' widows, indigent authors, destitute orphans, and fallen women, as well as international copyright, the Society of Authors, and the Guild. And Dickens never judged others solely by economic criteria, though he was often exasperated by his family's want of prudence in managing what little money they possessed. True, Dickens wrote for money; but this fact should not be allowed to militate against him as man or novelist. So did George Eliot and Thackeray, and Trollope freely confessed: 'I write for money. Of

---

[18] *The Private Papers of Henry Ryecroft* (New York, E. P. Dutton, 1903), 'Autumn', xxii. 203.
[19] Trollope, *An Autobiography*, p. 90.

course I do;—as does he [the critic] also—It is for money that we all work, lawyers, publishers, authors and the rest of us.'[20]

ii

In the beginning Dickens received no payment whatever for his literary efforts. His first sketch, 'A Sunday Out of Town', written in his spare time while employed by his maternal uncle John Henry Barrow as a reporter for the *Mirror of Parliament*, was 'dropped stealthily one evening at twilight, with fear and trembling, into a dark letter-box, in a dark office, up a dark court [Johnson's] in Fleet Street'.[21] A few months later Dickens was overwhelmed to discover the piece, with its title 'transmogrified' (P i. 32) to 'A Dinner at Poplar Walk', 'in all the glory of print' in the December 1833 *Monthly Magazine*, 'on which occasion by-the-bye,—how well I recollect it!—I walked down to Westminster Hall, and turned into it for half-an-hour, because my eyes were so dimmed with joy and pride, that they could not bear the street, and were not fit to be seen there'.[22]

Dickens had been casting about for additional employment for some time: in June 1833 he had asked Stanley's private secretary, Richard Earle, to recommend him as a 'Short Hand Writer' if he had the opportunity; and in July John Payne Collier agreed to try to place him on the staff of the *Morning Chronicle*. The publication of his sketch delighted Dickens; he saw the prospect of following it up with further sketches, and thereby increasing his slender income.[23] Writing to his friend Henry Kolle on 3 December, Dickens spoke confidently of its being 'the first of a Series' (P i. 32). But these hopes proved premature: Dickens had in fact to pay 2s. 6d. out of his own pocket for his copy of the *Magazine*, and never received anything for the sketch, or for the eight others that appeared in the *Monthly* between January 1834 and February 1835.[24] He complained wryly to Kolle on 10 December that the

[20] *The Letters of Anthony Trollope*, ed. Bradford Allen Booth (London, New York, and Toronto, Oxford Univ. Press, 1951), no. 159; to Frederic Chapman, 1 Jan. 1862.

[21] Preface to the Cheap edition of *Pickwick*, 1847.

[22] Ibid.; F I. iv. 60; J, pp. 91–2.

[23] Edgar Johnson implies (J, p. 91) that as Captain Holland, the proprietor, had no money to pay contributors, Dickens could not have expected remuneration. But he did: see P i. 33, quoted below.

[24] P i. 32, n. 2. For the fullest listing of the publishing history of the *Sketches*, see

Monthly people were ' "rather backward in coming forward" with the needful' (P i. 33), but continued to send them new sketches well into 1835. In October of that year he told John Macrone that 'The Great Winglebury Duel' would appear in the December *Monthly*, though he later decided to withhold it, dramatizing it instead as *The Strange Gentleman* (P i. 83 and n. 2). When Captain Holland, the proprietor and editor of the *Monthly*, was negotiating to sell it early in 1836, Dickens wrote stipulating that for future sketches he receive some compensation. A few days later he told the new editor, James Grant, that he could not furnish additional sketches for under eight guineas a sheet. Captain Holland then invited himself to Dickens's new rooms at 15 Furnival's Inn, where on 20 February 1836 he, Dickens, and possibly John Macrone took a glass of grog and some oysters together (P i. 133). But because no offer of payment was forthcoming, Dickens's relations with the *Monthly* ceased (J, p. 102).

Though Dickens's contributions to the *Monthly* brought him no direct financial reward, they did start him on his career as a professional author. One of the *Monthly*'s 600-odd readers did Dickens '*the honor*' of pirating his article for the twopenny *London Weekly Magazine*, familiarly known by its earlier name, *The Thief*. The *Monthly* asked for more articles; Dickens responded with plans for two independent sketches, to be followed by a 'series of papers (the materials for which I have been noting down for some time past) called *The Parish*. Should they be successful & as publishing is hazardous, I shall cut my proposed Novel [*Oliver Twist*] up into little Magazine Sketches' (P i. 33-4). Not much came of these schemes for the moment: one of the 'two independent sketches' was probably that published in *Bell's Life*, 17 January 1836; *The Parish* came out as a series of six sketches entitled 'Our Parish' in the *Evening Chronicle*, February–August 1835, and the novel did not see print until the second number of *Bentley's Miscellany*, February 1837. But Dickens was planning and writing sketches that were likely to be published, read, and even pirated, and that, for an irrepressible young man not yet twenty-two, was enough.

In August 1834 Dickens finally did become a reporter on the *Morning Chronicle*, a paper which, under the exacting editorship

Appendix A in Duane DeVries, *Dickens's Apprentice Years: The Making of a Novelist* (London, Centenary Press, 1976).

of John Black, dared for a few years to rival Sterling's *Times*. He soon plunged into hectic excursions to Edinburgh and Birmingham, Kent, Essex, and Suffolk, reporting speeches and meetings that increased in number after William IV precipitated a crisis by dismissing Melbourne's administration in November. In addition, the *Chronicle* carried five 'Street Sketches' between September and December 1834. Dickens was paid nothing beyond his five guineas weekly wage for these papers—unfortunately, for he was 'desperately hard up'. His father was arrested for debt in November, and Dickens feared for his own freedom, possibly because he had dutifully, but unwisely, backed some of his father's bills. By 4 December he had mortgaged his salary for two weeks to pay the expenses of his family's move from Bentinck Street to cheaper lodgings. He therefore had to borrow £5 from one friend, Thomas Beard, and to beg another, Thomas Mitton, to 'advance me what you can possibly spare till Saturday . . . I am most desperately hard up, and "the smallest contribution will be thankfully received"' (P i. 49).

By January 1835 Dickens's affairs had improved. George Hogarth, the co-editor of the new *Evening Chronicle*, asked 'Boz' to write an original sketch for its first number; Dickens agreed, inquiring at the same time, in a very hesitant and apologetic manner, 'whether it is probable that if I commenced a series of articles under some attractive title for the Evening Chronicle, its conductors would think I had any claim to *some* additional remuneration (of course of no great amount) for doing so?' (P i. 55, 20 Jan. 1835.) The answer was favourable. Dickens's salary was increased to seven guineas a week, and over the next seven months he supplied the *Evening Chronicle* with twenty 'Sketches of London', including the six called 'Our Parish'. For the first time he was making some money directly from his writings. Within a few months this additional remuneration was supplemented by Vincent George Dowling, the editor of *Bell's Life*, which carried twelve of Dickens's 'Scenes and Characters' between September 1835 and January 1836 (P i. 76, n. 3). Eight years later, experienced and famous, Dickens explained to a fledgling author the pay-scale for magazine articles: 'The rate of remuneration to unknown writers, is six or eight guineas a sheet, usually. Many unknown writers, write for nothing. I wrote for the next thing to it myself, when I was one-and-twenty' (N i. 590).

From these modest beginnings Dickens rose swiftly to a commanding position in the literary and social worlds. He enjoyed an equally commanding position in the world of publishing: the history of his contracts is a history of agreements ever more favourable to Dickens, giving him increasing authority over all aspects of the issuing of his books, and an ever greater share of the profits. His principal publishers, Chapman and Hall (1836–70) and Bradbury and Evans (1844–61), learned early in their relationship that Dickens meant to have his way. On those few occasions when he found his will crossed Dickens precipitated crises which resulted in the dismissal of the offending publisher. Edmund Yates was to comment later that Dickens conducted his life 'on the *sic volo sic jubeo* principle': 'his likes and dislikes, his ideas of what should or should not be, were all settled by himself, not merely for himself, but for all those brought into connection with him'.[25]

iii

Dickens's eventual success provides a dramatic example of the changed status of the author in the nineteenth century, as compared to previous ages, and it is instructive to pause to review the historical background, before continuing with his career. In the sixteenth century the Stationers' Company virtually controlled the publishing trade: the only recognized form of copyright was the printer's entry in the company's register, which established the right to print but ignored the author. The first English Copyright Act (and the first copyright Act passed anywhere in the world[26]) was 8 Anne, c. 19 (1709). It recognized in statute law for the first time the author's right to share in his works. For works already published, the Act granted to the owner the exclusive right to print for twenty-one years from 10 April 1710; and for new books, published subsequent to 10 April 1710, the exclusive right to print was granted to the author for fourteen years, renewable for a second fourteen years if the author was still living. In practice, as the copyrights of most old books were owned by the

---

[25] Quoted in Philip Collins, 'Dickens and Punch', *Dickens Studies*, 3 (1967), 20; see *Edmund Yates: His Recollections and Experiences* (2 vols., London, Richard Bentley and Son, 1884), ii. 94.

[26] Simon Nowell-Smith, *International Copyright Law and the Publisher in the Reign of Queen Victoria* (Oxford, Clarendon Press, 1968), p. 12.

booksellers, the Act ('singularly ill-framed to secure the privilege of booksellers', according to Augustine Birrell)[27] transferred power from the printers not to the authors but rather to the booksellers, who continued to purchase what they believed to be 'perpetual copyright' from hard-pressed writers until 1774. In that year, the Lords, deciding *Donaldson* v. *Becket* on appeal, interpreted Queen Anne's Act as extinguishing an author's common-law right to his writings after publication, substituting a limited statutory right. Piracy became a matter for booksellers to prosecute, being a violation of *copy*-right only. Thus the concept of copyright in perpetuity was quashed, depriving the booksellers at last of their monopoly control, especially over valuable standard texts. Late in the reign of George III the term of copyright was extended to twenty-eight years or the life of the author, whichever was longer (54 George III, c. 156). And in 1842 Philip Henry Stanhope, Viscount Mahon, successfully introduced his amended version of the copyright bill which Serjeant Thomas Noon Talfourd had been trying to get passed since *Pickwick* days. On 1 July 1842, 5 and 6 Victoria, c. 45, received the royal assent, giving copyright for forty-two years from the date of publication, or, by Sir Robert Peel's amendment, seven years after the death of the author, whichever was longer. Though 'incomplete, often obscure, and . . . ill-expressed', Talfourd's Act survived repeated litigation for sixty-nine years.[28]

Thus in the eighteenth century booksellers dominated publishing, buying copyrights outright and 'for ever' from authors, often before the work was finished, acting as if they had a perpetual right to print the works of deceased authors (as the Tonsons were regarded as the undoubted owners of rights to Shakespeare's plays and *Paradise Lost*), and combining with other booksellers to back expensive editions and to issue lengthy works in fascicles.

---

[27] Ibid., p. 15.

[28] The description is from the report of the law commissioners (ibid., p. 13). For the often confusing history of copyright, see especially, in addition to Nowell-Smith, H. G. Aldis, 'Book Production and Distribution, 1625–1800', *The Cambridge History of English Literature*, xi. 344–79; Sir Frank MacKinnon, 'Notes on the History of English Copyright', *The Oxford Companion to English Literature*, ed. Sir Paul Harvey, 4th edn. (Oxford, Clarendon Press, 1967), pp. 921–31; Lyman Roy Patterson, *Copyright in Historical Perspective* (Nashville, Vanderbilt Univ. Press, 1968); and Ian Parsons, 'Copyright and Society', in *Essays in the History of Publishing in Celebration of the 250th Anniversary of the House of Longman, 1724–1974*, ed. Asa Briggs (London, Longman, 1974), pp. 29–60.

The greatest of these booksellers blended a keen sense of business with learning and culture, and were known equally for their counting-houses and their company. Jacob Tonson was secretary of the Kit-Kat Club, and friend to Dryden, Steele, and Pope; Samuel Johnson said that he looked on Robert Dodsley as his patron; Thomas Cadell, the publisher of Hume, Robertson, Blackstone, and Adam Smith, gave a memorable and sumptuous dinner at his house in 1788 on the completion of Gibbon's *Decline and Fall*. Pre-eminent in their trade, they were generous in their support of the more important authors, paying huge sums for copyrights and providing some writers with an unprecedented financial security: John Hawkesworth received £6,000 for his *Voyages*; Cadell paid Hume nearly £5,000 for his *History*, and gave Gibbon two-thirds of the substantial profits from his.[29]

But those so favoured were few. 'Those who have been the greatest in the practice of letters', observes A. S. Collins, 'have rarely been those to whom letters was their supporting profession.'[30] Pope may have been the first, and for a long time was the only, major literary figure who earned a comfortable income from the sale of his works, and he lived at a particularly advantageous time. The phrase 'an author by profession' seems to have gained currency about the middle of the eighteenth century,[31] although authorship did not really become a profession in England until the first decade of the nineteenth century.[32] But in the last quarter of the eighteenth century, writers were not so fortunate. Macaulay observed that Samuel Johnson 'entered on his vocation in the most dreary part of the dreary interval which separated two ages of prosperity. Literature had ceased to flourish under the patronage of the great, and had not begun to flourish under the patronage of the public.'[33] Collins disputes this assertion: 'A man who took to his pen in 1780 gave patronage scarcely a thought.'[34] Perhaps it was because there was little to expect either from private patrons or politicians: Pitt was firmly opposed to selective patronage, and

[29] Aldis, op. cit., pp. 353–5; and R. M. Wiles, *Serial Publication in England before 1750* (Cambridge, Cambridge Univ. Press, 1957), p. 133.

[30] Collins, *The Profession of Letters*, p. 8.

[31] Ibid., pp. 17–18.

[32] Charvat, *The Profession of Authorship in America*, p. 29.

[33] Macaulay, *Prose and Poetry*, sel. G. M. Young (London, Rupert Hart-Davis, Reynard Library, 1967), p. 553.

[34] Collins, *The Profession of Letters*, p. 115.

even when forced to offer it, he dispensed money so evenly that

> Left to themselves all find their level price,
> Potatoes, verses, turnips, Greek, and rice.[35]

Still, if the prospects of private patronage diminished, the potential of vast public support was not yet realized; in the fifty years following Johnson's death, only Southey lived entirely on his writings. His 'whole estate', as he put it, 'was in his ink-stand', and he succeeded because he could apply his extensive knowledge and abilities to journalism, chiefly writing reviews for the *Quarterly*. Suffering in Grub Street continued, but two outstanding counter-examples, both of whom enjoyed income from other sources besides writing, nevertheless paved the way for Victorian authors.

Some of the change in the status of publishing and of authors in the nineteenth century must be attributed to the charisma of Byron and Scott: Collins thinks 'it is hard to over-estimate the influence such popular genius as that of Scott or Byron must have had on the growth of the habit of reading'.[36] Byron was called the 'Grand Napoleon of the Realms of Rhyme'; 10,000 copies of *The Corsair*, for which he had received 500 guineas, were sold on the day of publication.[37] For *Childe Harold* Cantos I and II he received £525, but for III and IV John Murray offered nearly seven times as much, £3,500. Later he paid Moore approximately £5,000 to write Byron's biography, Moore's Memoir having been carefully burned.[38] Scott, the 'Wizard of the North', provides another dramatic instance: for several years at the height of his fame he received as much as £10,000 a year,[39] the sum that in Samuel Warren's novel of the same name set English society agog. For 'Halidon Hill', two rainy mornings' work at Abbotsford, Cadell on behalf of his partner Constable, himself nicknamed 'The Czar of the North', gave £1,000. But Scott was intimately, and

---

[35] T. J. Mathias, *The Pursuits of Literature*, 16th edn. (1812), p. 121; quoted in Collins, *The Profession of Letters*, p. 120.

[36] Collins, *The Profession of Letters*, p. 170.

[37] Samuel Smiles, *A Publisher and His Friends: Memoir and Correspondence of John Murray, with an Account of the Origin and Progress of the House, 1768–1843*, condensed and ed., Thomas Mackay (London, John Murray, 1911), p. 91.

[38] George Paston [E. M. Symonds], *At John Murray's: Records of a Literary Circle, 1843–1892* (London, John Murray, 1932), p. 9, n. 2, p. 12; cf. Gettmann, op. cit., p. 4. Moore's *Diaries* survive, and are currently being thoroughly re-edited by Wilfred S. Dowden of Rice University.

[39] Edgar Johnson, *Sir Walter Scott: The Great Unknown* (2 vols., New York, Macmillan, 1970), ii. 954.

rather carelessly, entangled in the affairs of his printers and publishers, as they were in his elaborate and heavy expenses at Abbotsford. When Constable's London agents, Hurst, Robinson and Co., failed to the extent of nearly £300,000 in the winter of 1825-6, Constable went bankrupt. Scott assumed responsibility for bills amounting to about £40,000 as well as the liabilities of Ballantyne and Co., of which he was a partner, and spent the rest of his life writing under great pressure to pay off a total indebtedness of more than £100,000.[40]

Most authors were much less intimately entangled with the business affairs of their printers and publishers than Scott. The simplest form of contract, the outright sale of copyright, was also the most common throughout the eighteenth century and well into the nineteenth. The usual payment for the manuscript of a two-volume novel in the late eighteenth century was from five to ten guineas, though manuscripts with exceptionally attractive potential, or by established authors, commanded higher prices. *The Italian* (1797) brought Mrs. Radcliffe £900; Payne and Cadell paid Fanny Burney £250 for *Cecilia* (1782); Millar bought *Amelia* (1751) from Fielding for £1,000.[41] Earlier in the century, a few authors whose works were issued in numbers had tried to retain control of their copyrights, in hopes of making a greater profit than was possible from assigning the rights to a bookseller; but in most cases those who did retain control had at best only a moderate success, and generally sold out in the end to one or more publishers or booksellers. One advantage of outright sale, they found, was that the buyer then was forced to promote the book sufficiently to recoup his investment. Another was 'ease of mind', as Coleridge put it:

the most prudent mode is to sell the copy-right, at least of one or more editions, for the most that *the trade* will offer. By few only can a large remuneration be expected; but fifty pounds and ease of mind are of more real advantage to a literary man than the *chance* of five hundred with the *certainty* of insult and degrading anxieties.[42]

---

[40] See *Sir Walter Scott: The Great Unknown*, ii. 967, 970, 1035, for the ambiguity about the actual sum of Scott's indebtedness.

[41] J. M. S. Tomkins, *The Popular Novel in England, 1770–1800* (London, Constable, 1932), p. 9.

[42] *Biographia Literaria*, ed. J. Shawcross (4 vols., London, Oxford Univ. Press, 1907), i. 112 (ch. X).

But the disadvantage to outright sale grew more pronounced as the nineteenth century wore on and the market, especially after 1815, expanded. The price was necessarily based chiefly on the success of previous works, and often bore little relation to the new book's own merits or potential. By the middle of the century, steadily selling novelists like Frances Trollope or Rhoda Broughton could expect to receive £500 or £600 a work. Disraeli, capitalizing on his double reputation as novelist and politician, sold *Endymion* to Longmans in 1880 for £10,000. But the unknown Wilkie Collins, on Dickens's advice, was content to accept £350 from Bentley in 1852 for *Basil*.[43] Moreover, though not sharing in an unexpectedly profitable work, an author was sure to suffer the consequences of a poor sale: James Fenimore Cooper saw the value of his English receipts decline from a high of £1,300 in 1831 to £100 at the end of his career in 1850.[44] And even the sum offered for copyright might be severely reduced through exigencies. Few publishers could afford to pay cash for manuscripts, so they made payment in separate bills dated at regular future intervals. To those of steady habits, temperament, or income, this arrangement was satisfactory; but to a far larger number the need for ready money became sufficiently pressing to force them to cash the bills in advance, often at a considerable discount.[45]

To compensate for the unpredictability of a work's sales and profits, some publishers wrote in an escalation clause. For Mrs. Trollope's *The Rivals*, Bentley offered £200 for an edition of 1,000 copies, £100 additional if sales reached 950, another £100 for sale of 450 in a second printing, and a final £100 if a total of 700 copies of the second printing were sold.[46] A useful modification, this kind of agreement spread out cost and sales over the whole work, but it had the disadvantage that if sales were going slowly, the publisher stopped promoting the book to save the expense of reaching the next increment.[47]

---

[43] Gettmann, *A Victorian Publisher*, pp. 76 ff., esp. pp. 79–80.

[44] Ibid., p. 102. Further, his percentage on the gross American sales declined from a peak of 45 per cent in the 1820s to 20 per cent in the 1840s; see Charvat, p. 75.

[45] Gettmann, *A Victorian Publisher*, p. 76. Bentley frequently paid by bills at four, six, or nine months' date.   [46] Ibid., p. 85.

[47] Ibid., p. 86; and James J. Barnes, *Free Trade in Books: A Study of the London Book Trade since 1800* (Oxford, Clarendon Press, 1964), pp. 86–7. The fourth

Another modification of outright sale was the sale of copyright for a specified length of time short of the copyright period; in effect, authors granted a lease of the copyright. Bentley did not use this form of agreement much, but Bulwer Lytton found it very advantageous, leasing to Routledge for ten years his copyright on nineteen already-published novels for £20,000, and subsequently extending the lease for £1,000 a year.[48]

The John Murrays preferred division of profits to outright sale: this practice distributed the cost of copyright over the edition as a whole and geared the author's payments directly to the profits of the work being published, rather than to his previous works. Many of the Murrays' authors found the arrangement advantageous: John Wilson Croker, willing to sell *Stories from the History of England* (1816) for twenty guineas, instead received £700 by 1841 as his share of the profits;[49] and Austen Henry Layard enjoyed, in lieu of the £200 he asked for *Ninevah and Its Remains* (1848-9), an annual income of around £1,500 for several years.[50] Macaulay benefited largely from the unprecedented success of his *History of England*: in March 1856 Longman paid him £20,000 on account of the profits of the third and fourth volumes.[51]

But division of profits was not universally popular. In the customary agreement, the publisher manufactured, advertised, and sold the book, made an allowance for bad debts, and, with the painful example of Scott as precedent, absolved the author of all financial liability. These costs were then set against the gross income, and, as long as some profit remained, the difference was divided equally. But half-profits meant half-losses, too, as more than one author discovered to his dismay. Richard Bentley had a profit-sharing agreement printed as early as 1831, but he seems to have used it only in doubtful cases: for works whose commercial value was unpredictable, for gentleman travellers and amateur authors not requiring immediate payment, customarily for

edition (*c.* 1835) of *The Perils of Authorship* 'by an old and popular author' warns (p. 12) that publishers will print a huge first edition, unless specifically limited, in order to avoid making an additional payment for a second edition.

48 Marjorie Plant, *The English Book Trade: An Economic History of the Making and Sale of Books* (New York, R. R. Bowker Co., 1939), p. 410.

49 Barnes, *Free Trade*, p. 87; Smiles, p. 133; and Plant, p. 410.

50 Plant, p. 410; and Paston, p. 78.

51 Harold Cox and John E. Chandler, *The House of Longman, 1724-1924* (London, Longmans, Green and Co., 1925), p. 25.

American authors, and in times of financial strain.[52] It is interesting to note therefore that Bentley published *The Memoirs of Grimaldi*, edited by Dickens, on half-profits, which were to be accumulated and divided only after he had recouped the £300 advance paid to Dickens by promissory note (P i. 663; 29 November 1837).

Professional authors distrusted the system. 'I dislike the half profit, as all writers do', observed Trollope to Colburn in March 1848.[53] Unscrupulous publishers could easily evade payment by not rendering an account, and when finally forced to a settlement could inflate the costs, depreciate the income, and so minimize the receipts to be divided. Suspicious of Bentley, Dickens insisted that several of his contracts specify that written accounts were to be submitted, and that Dickens had the right to inspect the books. Even where no dishonest intention existed, a publisher's costs could seem exorbitant to an author. James Spedding, Tennyson's friend, published at his own expense two essays raking publishers for their inability, or refusal, to state expenses and income precisely: 'upon examining such publishers' accounts as I have been able to procure,' he complained, 'I find it difficult to make out what relation the price actually received by the publisher bears to the price at which the book is advertised for sale'.[54] The situation became so acute that as early as 1845 one Mr. Joseph Jackson, 'arbitrator and accountant', announced in the *Athenaeum* that he offered his services to authors 'to adjust disputed and partnership accounts'.[55]

To replace these imperfect arrangements, a royalty system such as Spedding advocated evolved—more rapidly on the Continent, however, than in England. Not until 1885 did Bentley resort to it, with Eliza Lynn Linton's *Autobiography of Christopher Kirkland*.[56] America was more progressive; Spedding thought that H. O. Houghton of New York was the first publisher to pay authors a percentage upon the retail price of the volumes sold.[57] Routledge in the 1850s began to pay royalties on such popular works as Motley's *History of the Dutch Republic*, Russell's *Letters from the Crimea*, and Soyers's *Cookbook*, but the firm was probably motivated less by an altruistic concern for its authors than by the

[52] Gettmann, *A Victorian Publisher*, pp. 104–5.
[53] Trollope, *Letters*, no. 13.
[54] James Spedding, *Publishers and Authors* (London, John Russell Smith, 1867), p. 34.   [55] Hepburn, p. 45.
[56] Gettmann, *A Victorian Publisher*, p. 116.   [57] Spedding, pp. 23–4.

shortage of ready money for advance payments during the Crimean War, which depressed the book business severely.[58] Dickens seems never to have used a royalty system himself, and is on record to John Forster as opposing it when strictly applied, precisely because it deferred payments too long:

You and I know very well that in nine cases out of ten the author is at a disadvantage with the publisher because the publisher has capital and the author has not. . . . money is advanced by the publisher before the book is producible—often, long before. No young or unsuccessful author (unless he were an amateur and an independent gentleman) would make a bargain for having that royalty, to-morrow, if he could have a certain sum of money, or an advance of money. The author who could command that bargain, could command it to-morrow, or command anything else. For the less fortunate or the less able, I make bold to say—with some knowledge of the subject, as a writer who made a publisher's fortune long before he began to share in the real profits of his books—that if the publishers met next week, and resolved henceforth to make this royalty bargain and no other, it would be an enormous hardship and misfortune because the authors could not live while they wrote. (N iii. 490–1)

Yet another arrangement for apportioning the expenses and receipts of publication was the commission system. The author agreed to be solely responsible for all costs, and to pay the publishers a percentage, often 10 per cent of the gross receipts. Early volumes of poetry were often published by such a system, which was touted in the 1840s and 1850s by commission publishers like E. Churton and William and Frederick Cash.[59] But it was open to the familiar objection that the accounts could be doctored by inflating costs for printing and advertising. Dickens's first Christmas book, *A Christmas Carol*, was published on commission by Chapman and Hall. Prompted to its writing by pecuniary difficulties occasioned by the disappointing sales and profits of *Martin Chuzzlewit*, Dickens was dismayed on receiving the accounts on 10 February 1844 to find that the charges for the

[58] F[rank] A[rthur] Mumby, *The House of Routledge, 1834–1934: with a History of Kegan Paul, Trubner, and Other Associated Firms* (London, Routledge, 1934), pp. 65–6, 85–6.

[59] Edward Churton provides an 'estimate of a monthly work uniform with the Pickwick Papers, in 20 shilling Numbers, obtaining a sale of 10,000', which shows that on commission Dickens would have netted £2,500 (*The Author's Handbook: A Complete Guide to the Art and System of Publishing on Commission*, 3rd edn. (London, E. Churton, 1845), p. 42).

plates alone, including their design, engraving, printing, and colouring, exceeded his profits. 'I have not the least doubt that they [Chapman and Hall] have run the expenses up anyhow purposely to bring me back and disgust me with the charges', he complained to his solicitor (N i. 567; 12 February 1844).

A Victorian writer, therefore, could choose among a variety of contracts the one most suitable to his needs. As the century wore on, potential sources of income for a writer proliferated: informal, and still later formal, international copyright agreements gave him the opportunity to share in overseas receipts; lecture tours yielded substantial sums for Thackeray, Matthew Arnold, and Mark Lemon; theatrical rights or serialization in magazines or country newspapers were other possibilities.

Along with this proliferation of revenue came the literary agent: A. P. Watt, William Morris Colles, J. Eveleigh Nash, and James Brand Pinker, whose services to late Victorian and Edwardian authors, especially Conrad and Arnold Bennett, helped to establish them as successful writers.[60] John Forster served as Dickens's unofficial literary agent from the days of *Pickwick* onward. But for the most part Dickens's publishing contracts were the product of his own determination, enforced, if necessary, by cajoling, threats, and a battery of legal and financial representatives.

During his career Dickens entered into most of the kinds of agreements we have surveyed. He also combined features from several different kinds, though after 1839 the division of profits system remained the basis of all his agreements. His early contracts were not particularly advantageous to him, especially when one considers the profits which his publishers realized on *Sketches by Boz* and *Pickwick*. But then they had assumed all the risk. In 1835 Dickens had yet to publish anything under his own name or to receive any substantial payment for his fictions.

[60] Hepburn, pp. 49–66.

2

Sketches by Boz *and Macrone*

> . . . those little screws of existence—pounds, shillings,
> and pence . . .
>
> CHARLES DICKENS (P i. 57)

O N THE FACE OF IT, John Macrone's offer to a young
journalist of £100 for the copyright of sketches which
had mostly been published, and in some cases republished,
under the pseudonyms of 'Boz' and 'Tibbs', appears venturesome
in the extreme.[1] But it proved a shrewd bit of calculation. Macrone
may have become familiar with Dickens's work when from
January to September 1834 he and his partner James Cochrane
published the *Monthly Magazine*, including four of Dickens's
sketches. Further, Macrone may have corresponded with Dickens
about the proofs to William Thompson's *Two Journeys through
Italy and Switzerland*; Dickens was reading proofs for his maternal
uncle in July 1835 prior to the book's publication by Macrone in
August (P i. 69–70). Whatever the previous association, Macrone,
who went into business for himself at 3 St. James's Square in
September 1834, seems not to have met Dickens personally until
introduced, in the summer or early autumn of 1835, by Harrison
Ainsworth. Macrone had just taken over Ainsworth from Bentley,
issuing *Rookwood* in a third edition in three volumes, and planning
on a fourth edition, in one volume, with twelve etchings by
George Cruikshank, which appeared in May 1836.

---

[1] See P i. 550, where Dickens tells Mitton that he 'had, three or four days after
the publication £100'; the sum is incorrectly reported as £150 by Frederic G.
Kitton (*The Minor Writings of Charles Dickens* (London, Elliot Stock, 1900)), p. 9;
and J, p. 104. I am especially grateful to Professor Duane DeVries for his criticisms
of and suggestions for this chapter; see his *Dickens's Apprentice Years* for further
information about *Sketches by Boz*.

The idea developed of combining Dickens's closely observed sketches of London life with the illustrations of Cruikshank, the great popular favourite famous for his London street scenes. Macrone could capitalize on Dickens's growing reputation and Cruikshank's already established one. The proposed titles all emphasized the combination: 'Bubbles from the Bwain of Boz and the Graver of Cruikshank', 'Sketches by Boz and Cuts by Cruikshank', 'Etchings by Boz and Wood Cuts by Cruikshank'.[2] However, author and illustrator did not meet until some weeks after the project was first suggested to Dickens. Fortunately for Macrone, the collaborators were soon on friendly terms, with Cruikshank selecting subjects for illustrations from copies of Dickens's published pieces. The original plan was to issue the book in time for Christmas, but interruptions eventually delayed publication until the new year.

Dickens worked hard for the success of the venture. He looked forward to the money, as he and Catherine, who had already had to cancel plans to marry in December 1835, hoped at last to be married the following spring. Moreover, he was on such friendly terms with Macrone that he asked him to serve as best man; and Macrone reciprocated by presenting Catherine with Milton's *Poetical Works* in six volumes, 'with the sincere good wishes of her Friend, the Publisher' (P i. 81, n. 1). Throughout the last two months of 1835, letters flew back and forth between Furnival's Inn and St. James's Square, as Dickens and Macrone alternately congratulated each other on their progress and fretted over unexpected delays. Dickens wrote two new sketches of which he was especially proud, 'A Visit to Newgate' and 'The Black Veil'; he inserted in the *Morning Chronicle* a restrained 'puff', even though he found the practice of extravagant self-advertising offensive (P i. 123–4); he arranged for favourable reviews from friends; and he

---

[2] P i. 82, and n. 1. Some discussion took place in January 1836 about changing the title, but by then the headlines had been printed, so Dickens let it stand rather than cancelling the whole impression, as it was 'both unaffected and unassuming— two requisites which it is very desirable for a young author [not] to lose sight of' (P i. 115). The different versions of the original title indicate some uncertainty as to whether Cruikshank would supply engravings or designs for woodcuts; eventually he did etchings on copper faced with steel, the only serial illustrations ever done on copper, according to John Harvey (*Victorian Novelists and Their Illustrators* (New York, New York Univ. Press, 1971), p. 182). For the complex history of Dickens's revisions of the *Sketches*, see John Butt and Kathleen Tillotson, *Dickens at Work* (London, Methuen, 1957), ch. 2.

solicited the attention of Lord Stanley in a letter that consorts strangely with his later denunciation of patronage:

> The wish of the authors to place their works in the hands of those, the eminence of whose public stations, is only to be exceeded by the lustre of their individual talents, is, and always has been, so generally felt, even by the greatest Men who have ever adorned the Literature of this Country, that I hope it may be pardoned when it displays itself in so young, and so humble a candidate for public favor, as
>
>
>
> My Lord
> Your Lordship's most obedient,
> Humble Servant
> Charles Dickens
>
>
> (P i. 127)

It is clear from the surviving correspondence that Dickens recognized the gamble Macrone was taking, and was doing all in his power to ensure its success. Despite his annoyance with Cruikshank in the autumn of 1835 over various delays, by the beginning of February 1836 Dickens wrote 'I need not say that I am most delighted with the Plates you have done, and rejoiced to find that we have so nearly approached the termination of our labours in Boz's cause' (P i. 122). Evidently one decision to expedite the publication of the book, which had been announced in *The Times* as early as 11 January as 'nearly ready', was to cut out four illustrations, issuing each volume with eight instead of ten plates. The suggestion came up over Christmas 1835 but remained unresolved five weeks later (P i. 112). Thus the 6 February 1836 *Athenaeum* announcement specifies twenty illustrations, while that for 5 February in *The Times* has already reduced the number to sixteen. Finally, on 8 February 1836, the day after Dickens's twenty-fourth birthday, *Sketches by Boz*, First Series, appeared, in two volumes bound in dark green cloth for a guinea. It received favourable notices in many periodicals; Dickens was especially pleased by George Hogarth's in the *Morning Chronicle* for 11 February, and that in the *Morning Post* for 12 March (P i. 140). The subscription and private sales went well; Macrone was able to pay Dickens £50 on 5 March, and the balance five days later. The sales continued to mount, a second edition ('by Mr. Charles Dickens') being announced at the end of July, and a third in February 1837, no doubt given fresh impetus by the success of *Pickwick*. But meanwhile, the gamble had paid off handsomely;

Dickens and Macrone, both eager to cash in on the spirited reception, agreed to go forward with a Second Series in two volumes, for which Dickens was to receive £150, or 50 per cent more than the price for the First Series.

On 9 May 1836, about the same time as the agreement for the Second Series, Dickens wrote a letter that would cause bitter disagreement later in the year:

My Dear Macrone.

I shall have great pleasure in accepting from you, the sum of *Two Hundred Pounds* for the first Edition of a Work of Fiction (in Three Volumes of the usual size) to be written by me, and to be entitled *Gabriel Vardon, the Locksmith of London*: of which, not more than *one Thousand Copies* are to be printed.

I also agree to your printing an extra number of copies, if it should appear desirable; on condition that the profits thereon, all expenses being first deducted, be divided between us.

I also understand that the before-mentioned Two Hundred Pounds, are to be paid by you, on delivery of the entire Manuscript—on or before the 30th. day of November next, or as soon afterwards, as I can possibly complete it—by your acceptances, at such dates as may be agreeable to both of us—

(P i. 150)

There are several points worth noting about this publishing agreement. Macrone was committing himself to pay double what he had offered for the copyright of *Sketches*, First Series, a half-year earlier, but on the other hand Dickens was to supply an original work of fiction in three volumes, rather than collecting previously published sketches in two. Some allowance was made for an unexpected success: the outright sale of copyright was limited to an edition of 1,000 copies, on which Macrone would probably clear about £100.[3] Thereafter, profits were to be divided equally between Dickens and Macrone. Thus Macrone would take the risk, should the book not sell out its first edition, while Dickens was to share in the profits, should the sale exceed 1,000. This agreement guaranteed Dickens payment on delivery of the manuscript, though payment was to be effected by means of bills 'at such dates as may be agreeable to both of us'. Dickens thus would not get cash—Macrone seems to have been very short of ready money, having started his business on borrowed capital (P i. 81,

---

[3] Marjorie Plant, *The English Book Trade*, p. 413.

n. 1), and probably could not have afforded to pay Dickens outright before the receipts from the sales came in—but Dickens
could, if pressed, arrange to cash Macrone's bills at a discount.
Moreover, since the *Pickwick* format had not established its
potency by May 1836, the agreement specifies 'Three Volumes of
the usual size'. Finally, all the provisions of the contract depended
on Dickens's delivering the manuscript to Macrone, and though
30 November was mentioned as the date for delivery, in fact no
deadline was established. Nor was anything said about the priority
of *Gabriel Vardon* over existing or future publishing commitments. In short, the agreement bound Macrone to publish *Gabriel
Vardon* on certain terms, and guaranteed Dickens £200, but it did
not commit Dickens to writing the book in a hurry, or to writing
it prior to any other work.

For the moment all went well. Macrone sent Dickens a draft
for the first of July, probably £100 towards the Second Series;
four weeks later, Dickens arranged for his brother Fred 'to be
initiated into business habits' in Macrone's 'Counting House'.[4] At
the beginning of August Dickens closed with the new editor of
the *Carlton Chronicle* for 'a series of short sketches . . . which I have
consented to do, once a fortnight, as they will be very short, and
the terms long; the Carlton club being as liberal as need be' (P i.
160). He hastened to assure Macrone that publication in the *Carlton
Chronicle* would not affect the sale of the Second Series of *Sketches*:
'The circulation I believe is a small one. So much the better—
Fewer people will see the Sketches before they are collected. It is
all among the nobs too—Better still. They'll buy the book.' He
then went on to consult Macrone about a title that would advertise the forthcoming Second Series: 'LEAVES/FROM AN UN-
PUBLISHED VOLUME/BY BOZ/ (which will be torn out,
once a fortnight)'. Only two new sketches ever appeared; trouble
quickly developed because the *Carlton* pirated sketches previously
published. One wonders just how happy Macrone was to find out
that Dickens was selling his copyright a second time over.

Although he was already 'over head and ears in work' (P i.
178), Dickens agreed to complete for £100, 'by Christmas next',

<hr>

[4] P i. 157. This was not the last time Dickens was to find openings for relatives
in the offices of his publishers. However, from what happened to Macrone subsequently it is doubtful that Fred learned much about 'business', unless it was 'how
not to do it'.

a child's book for Thomas Tegg 'to be called *Solomon Bell the Raree Showman* (unless we should hit upon some other title, which we should consider a more catching one)'.[5] And on 22 August he signed an Agreement with Richard Bentley to furnish 'a Novel, the Title of which is not yet determined, to form three Volumes of 320 pages each and 25 lines in each page' (P i. 648). This Agreement, the first of nine with Bentley, reveals how much more experienced a publisher Bentley was than Macrone, only three years older than Dickens. Dickens got Bentley to raise the price from £400 to £500 on 'the great probability of it's having a very large sale (we are justified in forming our judgment upon the rapid sale of *everything* I have yet touched)' (P i. 165). Bentley's offer was two and a half times Macrone's, but was for outright sale of copyright, and contained two important restrictive clauses: first, 'no other literary production shall be undertaken by the said Charles Dickens Esqre until the completion of the above mentioned novel', and second, Dickens agreed to offer his next novel to Bentley on identical terms (P i. 649). Dickens's affairs were now becoming very complicated. He was obligated to write three new works, and by the terms of his latest contract he could not honour the two earlier ones. Obviously 'Solomon Bell' must have been cancelled by this date, and Dickens may have thought himself released from the second with Macrone.

Publication commitments continued to pile up. Colburn, then Bentley, took *The Village Coquettes*, Dickens having turned down Macrone's offer to publish at half profit, and having sold the music, of which he had half rights, to Cramer & Co. 'for a good round sum' (P i. 170). John Braham, tenor and theatrical speculator, gave £30 for *The Strange Gentleman*, Dickens's two-act farce based on 'The Great Winglebury Duel', and it was published by Chapman and Hall in the winter of 1836–7 (P i. 171). On 4 November Dickens entered into his second Agreement with

[5] P i. 163. Dickens never wrote it; Tegg's son told John Eckel that all the negotiations were cancelled (*The First Editions of the Writings of Charles Dickens: Their Points and Values*, rev. and enl. (New York, Maurice Inman, Inc.; London, Maggs Bros., 1932), p. 208). But see Tegg's advertisement, in the *Athenaeum* for 1 Dec. 1838 and thereafter, of *Sergeant Bell and His Raree-Show*, one large volume square 16mo embellished with 100 cuts by Cruikshank, Williams, *et al.*, neatly bound for only 7s. 6d. Albert M. Cohn (*George Cruikshank: A Catalogue Raisonné* (London, Office of 'The Bookman's Journal', 1924)), believes the letterpress to have been written by George Mogridge (Cohn, no. 569), as do the Pilgrim editors (P i. 163, n. 2).

Bentley, to edit 'The Wits' Miscellany', a ninety-six-page demy 8vo monthly, for £20 a month, to supply 'an original article of his own writing, every monthly Number, to consist of about a sheet of 16 pages . . . for which the said Richard Bentley agrees to pay him at the rate of twenty guineas per Sheet of 16 pages', the copyright then reverting to Bentley; and to contract not to 'enter into any arrangement to conduct or write for any other periodical publication whatever', excepting his agreements with Chapman and Hall for *Pickwick* and its sequel (*Nicholas Nickleby*) (P i. 649–50).

As of November 1836 Dickens faced seven or eight publishing commitments: *Pickwick* monthly to November 1837; *Sketches*, Second Series (published 17 December 1836); *The Village Coquettes* (published for 2s. as a sewn pamphlet of seventy-two pages on 22 December 1836); *The Strange Gentleman* (late December 1836 or early January 1837); an original sixteen-page article monthly, commencing January 1837; at the conclusion of *Pickwick*, a sequel in the same format; possibly *Gabriel Vardon* for Macrone; and a novel for Bentley, which was to be written prior to any other literary production.

Dickens's affairs had reached a perilous state. He was falling behind with his *Pickwick* instalments, for which he fulsomely apologized to Chapman and Hall, at the same time assuring Bentley that he was perfectly satisfied that editing and writing for the new magazine 'will not interfere with Pickwick' (P i. 189). Simultaneously, he wrote to John Easthope, proprietor of the *Morning Chronicle*, promising that sketch number five in the 'New Series', long delayed by his cold, would be forthcoming immediately.

Dickens had vastly overextended himself, and could no doubt see the probability of defaulting on one or more of his obligations in the near future. The second Bentley contract guaranteed him a monthly income for at least a year, to be added to his regular stipend from *Pickwick*, so on the day after signing it he sent in his resignation to the *Morning Chronicle*, only to become embroiled in an unpleasant altercation with Easthope, who charged Dickens with receiving six guineas for three original sketches (including the promised number five) never submitted (P i. 195–7). Dickens saw another way of reducing his commitments: he would write to Macrone and confirm the cancellation of the agreement for

Gabriel Vardon, and transfer that long-awaited novel to Bentley. Thus he would satisfy the Agreement of 22 August to produce a three-volume novel for Bentley, indefinitely postpone the date on which the manuscript was due beyond the 30 November deadline mentioned in Macrone's agreement, and increase his future profit from £200 to £500 *for the same novel*.

Understandably, Macrone was unhappy. Dickens was milking his *Sketches* for every penny they could bring, getting paid by the *Morning Chronicle* or the *Carlton Chronicle* and Macrone, for the same copyrights, and adapting one sketch as a farce, which was then sold for £30 and published separately. Moreover, though Macrone had offered half-profits, Dickens's comic opera, *The Village Coquettes*, had gone elsewhere. He had gambled twice on Dickens: once in buying the previously published *Sketches*, and again in May 1836 (when *Pickwick* was a dismal failure, selling fewer than 500 copies per number), in contracting with Dickens for an original work of fiction. Now that he was a success Dickens wanted to be relieved of one of these agreements, as he could command better terms elsewhere. Macrone wrote angrily to Dickens, accusing Bentley of dishonourable behaviour, and when Dickens's reply proved unsatisfactory, he asked Ainsworth's advice. On 12 November Ainsworth observed that to lose Dickens would be 'a serious misfortune', and two days later he urged Macrone 'to place the matter between Mr. Dickens and yourself *immediately* in legal hands. Your reply to him ought simply to have been—"My Dear D., In reply to your note, I beg to state that I shall hold you to your agreement." Nothing more.'[6]

Meanwhile, Dickens had fallen severely behind in producing copy for the Second Series of *Sketches*, so that Macrone, who had advertised a forthcoming two volumes in October, finally decided to issue only one volume and get it out in time for the Christmas trade. On 3 December he announced that the Second Series would be ready 'In a few days'. Hastily assembling text and illustrations, the binders sometimes gathered up 'Vauxhall Gardens by Day' twice, first as frontispiece and second opposite page 216 in place of 'Mr. Minns and his Cousin' which should have appeared opposite page 263.[7] By 17 December it was out, one volume 'very

[6] S. M. Ellis, *William Harrison Ainsworth and His Friends* (2 vols., London, John Lane, The Bodley Head; New York, John Lane Co., 1911), i. 305–7.
[7] John C. Eckel, *The First Editions of the Writings of Charles Dickens and Their*

handsomely bound' for 15s., just in time for the Christmas trade, as the Preface was at pains to explain:

With these few words, [the author] gives a modest tap at the door of the public with his Christmas Piece, when, perhaps, he may imagine the following dialogue to ensue, founded on the well-known precedent of the charity-boys and the housemaid.

Publisher (to author.)—*You* knock.

Author (to publisher.)—No—you. [Here the publisher seizes the knocker, and gives a loud rap at the door.]

Public (suspiciously, and with the door a-jar.)—Well; What do *you* want?

Publisher.—Please, will you look at this Christmas Piece; me and the other boy goes partners in it.

Public.—Go away; we have so many knocks of the same kind, at this time of year, that we are tired of answering the door. Go away.

Publisher (pushing it.)—No; but do look at it, please. It's all his own doing, except the pictures; and they're capital, let alone the writing. [Here the public gradually softens, and takes the Christmas Piece in; upon which the Publisher makes a bow, and retires]—while the author lingers behind, for one instant, to repeat an old form with much sincerity; and to express his hearty wish that his best friend, the Public, may enjoy 'a merry Christmas, and a happy new year.'[8]

Not until 7 January 1837 did Macrone list the contents, and the number of 'capital' illustrations by George Cruikshank remained unspecified.[9] A 'new and improved' second edition of the Second Series was announced in February, with two additional plates, 'The First of May' and 'The Last Cab-driver', and with the earlier confusions corrected. But in March Macrone was still advertising that the second edition of the Second Series would soon be out.

Despite the jovial and friendly references to 'the Publisher' in the Preface, dated 17 December 1836, Dickens and Macrone were at this time not speaking. Macrone appointed a deputy, his printer

Values: A Bibliography (London, Chapman & Hall, Ltd., 1913), p. 16; this point has been deleted from the revised edition of 1932. Duane DeVries has described for me the Hersholt copy in the Fales Collection of the New York University Library: it contains no list of illustrations; 'Vauxhall Gardens' only as frontispiece, although 'Vol. III, p. 217' is engraved under the title; and 'Mr. Minns' facing p. 263.

8 With the exception of the first set, the brackets are part of the original text.

9 In the Commin copy described by Eckel (rev. edn., p. 12), 'the lower half of the second page of contents [ordinarily the list of plates] was blank'. Thus in the first issue of the first edition of the Second Series, the number of plates, and even perhaps their order, was still undecided.

Thomas C. Hansard, to negotiate; Hansard acted so strongly on behalf of his friend that Dickens afterwards 'supposed *him* to have been a pretty considerable sharer . . . in the profits of my works' (P i. 549–50). Macrone must have known that going to law would only exacerbate their relationship, and would be futile, since how could one force an author to write a book? He tried instead to be firm about *Gabriel Vardon*, while conciliating Dickens by offering him £100 for the second edition of the First Series, and an additional £100 for the entire copyright of both Series, having previously bought copyright only for the first editions (P i. 203; J, p. 184). This offer Hansard took to Dickens in Furnival's Inn on Thursday morning, 1 December; within an hour Dickens was penning his reply.

Aware that since the letter of 9 May 1836 was not actually cancelled, Macrone could at least try to claim damages against him, Dickens sought room to manœuvre. He would take £250 for the copyrights of the two Series of *Sketches*, plus the £100 for a second edition of the First Series, and the £50 owing on the Second. But he insisted on knowing whether Macrone planned to 'continue to advertize a novel by me, and to retain possession of a letter of mine [the agreement of 9 May 1836], respecting which, a misunderstanding has arisen between us' (P i. 203). Macrone didn't want to get the successful *Sketches* mixed up with the unhappy negotiations over *Gabriel Vardon*; Hansard remonstrated that the two issues should be kept separate. Dickens disagreed, but consented to sign two combined agreements respecting the *Sketches*, while refusing to enter into any other negotiations with Macrone until his dispute over the letter was settled.

Macrone was anxious to secure copyright to the *Sketches*, which were selling well, and to get out a second edition of the First Series quickly. He tried to force Dickens to keep the agreement of 9 May by continuing to advertise *Gabriel Vardon* as 'in the course of publication' (P i. 209, n. 1). He sent such copy to Chapman and Hall for the January *Pickwick* Advertiser just after receiving the last corrected proofs of *Sketches*, Second Series; Dickens had to warn them, and Bentley, not to accept any such notices (P i. 209).

The ambiguity of the 9 May letter encouraged compromise rather than a lawsuit. Bentley may have approached Macrone directly, offering to buy back the letter, since he was eager to secure a Dickens unfettered by other publishing commitments.

Dickens doubted that Bentley's offer would be accepted, and was right (P i. 213). Finally, Dickens and Macrone settled the matter between themselves. Macrone agreed to cancel the 9 May letter; in return, Dickens sold, for only £100, 'the entire copyright of the first and second series of . . . "Sketches by Boz" . . . without any reserve whatever'.[10]

Thus Dickens received a total of £450 for *Sketches by Boz*: £100 each for the first and second editions of the First Series; £150 for the first edition of the Second Series; and £100 more for the copyright of both Series. He was never a partner in the work, and never shared in the profits from it. This was in a way fortunate, for after Macrone's sudden death in September 1837 Hansard applied through his solicitors to Dickens as a 'partner' in *Sketches* for payment of £150. 3s., the cost of the two editions of *Sketches* that Hansard printed, for which he had evidently never been paid (P i. 550, n. 1). Dickens's heated rejoinder to his solicitor Mitton seems to have put an end to the claim: 'I never was a partner, I never signed any agreement to be a partner, I never claimed or received one six pence as a partner, in the publication of that work' (P i. 550).

Had he shared in the profits from the *Sketches*, Dickens would certainly have done better than £450. He estimated that Macrone cleared £4,000, before selling the copyrights back to Chapman and Hall for £2,000 plus allowance for stock in June 1837.[11] Macrone, who seems to have been more enterprising than provident, was not content with this large return. He decided to milk his copyright further by cashing in on the success of *Pickwick*. He would issue *Sketches* in the same format, twenty monthly numbers, with the same green wrappers; he even went so far as to commission Cruikshank to draw up a wrapper design. When Dickens heard about this plan, he was livid:

My dear Forster.
    I heard half an hour ago on authority which leaves me in no doubt about the matter (from the binder of Pickwick, in fact) that Macrone

---

[10] Receipt dated 5 Jan. 1837 (P i. 647); printed in A. S. W. Rosenbach, *A Catalogue of the Writings of Charles Dickens in the Library of Harry Elkins Widener* (Philadelphia, privately printed, 1918), p. 2.

[11] Dickens's estimate (P i. 550) seems wildly high. Macrone might have made as much as £2,000, but sales (and profits) in volume form were more limited than in numbers, as Chapman and Hall proved. Macrone could not have been too flush, or surely he would have paid his printer.

intends publishing a new issue of my sketches in monthly parts of nearly the same size and in just the same form as the Pickwick papers.

I need not tell you that this is calculated to injure me most seriously, or that I have a very natural and most decided objection to being supposed to presume upon the success of the Pickwick, and thus foist this old work upon the public in its new dress for the mere purpose of putting money in my own pocket. Neither need I say that the fact of my name being before the town, attached to three publications at the same time, must prove seriously prejudicial to my reputation.

As you are acquainted with the circumstances under which these copyrights were disposed of, and as I know I may rely on your kind-feeling, may I beg you to wait upon Macrone, and to state in the strongest and most emphatic manner, my feeling on this point. I wish him to be reminded of the sums he paid for these books—of the sale he has had for them—of the extent to which he has already pushed them—and of the very great profits he must necessarily have acquired from them. I wish him also to be reminded that no intention of publishing them in this form was in the remotest manner hinted to me, by him, or on his own behalf, when he obtained possession of the copyright. I then wish you to put it to his feelings of common honesty and fair-dealing whether after this communication he will persevere in his intention.

I feel it necessary to add—not as a hasty threat but as my deliberate and well-considered determination—that if this new issue does appear, I shall advertize in all the Newspapers that it does so—not only without my sanction, but in opposition to my express request; that it is of no advantage whatever, to me; and that I most earnestly and emphatically entreat all my friends and supporters to abstain from purchasing it. Wherever he advertizes the work, I will advertize this statement.

I have only to add that in case you should be met with the assertion that the preparations he has made have involved him in great expence already, and that this is a reason for his persisting in his design, Chapman and Hall, knowing my feeling on the subject are ready and willing to buy the copyrights, and to consider this circumstance in settling the amount of the purchase money.

If you will undertake this mission you will confer a lasting obligation on

My Dear Forster
Yours most faithfully
CHARLES DICKENS
(P i. 269–70)

The injured tone cannot disguise the fact that Dickens hadn't a leg to stand on. He had parted with the copyrights 'without any

reserve whatever' six months earlier, and had no further legal
claim against their rightful owner. The concern that having his
name attached to three publications at the same time might prove
prejudicial rings very hollow in the light of Dickens's eagerness to
agree to new ventures. The ulterior motive for his opposition, as
he confessed to Bentley, was that Macrone stood to make a lot
more money through a format Dickens had revitalized in *Pickwick*,
while Dickens got nothing: 'I unfortunately parted with these
valuable copyrights (as I have done with others) without advantage or reflection.' (Considering the prolonged negotiations of
December and January, that statement was hardly the whole
truth, though he obviously had not considered the possibility that
Macrone would exploit the monthly numbers.) 'In the high tide
of my popularity and success I feel that I must no longer act with
the same thoughtlessness, and that it is quite time that I should
seek to derive some permanent advantage from works from which
booksellers derive so much present gain' (P i. 272). Dickens's
indignation reveals itself even in the rhetoric, 'booksellers' having
become, by the late 1830s, a term of disparagement.[12]

Macrone was not disposed to give up his scheme, from which
he anticipated further large profits. Dickens was in a fever of
anxiety to settle the issue. In this impasse Chapman and Hall came
forward, agreeing to purchase the copyrights to *Sketches* back from
Macrone. But John Forster, who was by now acting as Dickens's
adviser, was appalled at the sum—£2,000—which Macrone asked
for copyrights for which he had paid £100 six months earlier: 'so
wide a mouth was opened . . . that I would have no part in the

---

[12] So used by Dickens: cf. to Chapman and Hall, 27 July 1837: 'It is indeed a pleasure to be connected with such men (I was going to say booksellers) as you' (P i. 288);
and to Leigh Hunt, 19 July 1842: 'he is *not* a bookseller; and therefore comes within
the pale of human sympathies', a comment made with respect to the dispute with
Colburn over *The Pic Nic Papers* (P iii. 273). Dickens is not consistent in using
'booksellers' disparagingly, however: cf. *Oliver Twist*, ch. 14, written in August
1837, a portion of which—the exchange where Oliver says he would like to be
a bookseller—was inscribed on the end fly-leaf of a first-edition *Pickwick* and
presented to Chapman and Hall in November 1839 (P i. 601). It is also employed
neutrally as description, as 'Messrs. Chapman and Hall, booksellers' (P iii. 278).
    One hundred and forty years later publishers still complain about authors'
propensity to break contracts. Recently Erwin Glikes, president of Basic Books,
proclaimed that 'If an author is allowed to resell a book he has worked on with
one publishing house to another house because the book has become increasingly
valuable since the original contract was made, then that is the end of editorial
publishing in the U.S.' (*Newsweek*, 86 (4 Aug. 1975), 67.)

costly process of filling it' (F II. i. 87). At this juncture Richard
Bentley stepped in, hinting to Hansard that he might bid 'for
these apples of discord' (P i. 272). (The presence of so many rivals
for the *Sketches* copyright shows what a valuable property
Dickens's writings had become.) Armed with this alternative,
Macrone and Hansard waited upon Chapman and Hall the next
morning, Saturday 17 June, determined to accept nothing less
than the £2,000. After calculating the probable profits upon the
sale in numbers, William Hall could not dispute the justice of
Macrone's figures. The partners then requested a few hours'
delay, and hurried over to 48 Doughty Street to consult with
Dickens. If the *Sketches* were going to be issued in monthly
numbers, could not they, with their *Pickwick* machinery already
set up, hope for even larger profits than Macrone? No other mode
of publication would repay such a large expenditure for copyright,
but Chapman and Hall were willing to undertake the responsibility, and to have Dickens explain in an address that they were
forced into that mode of publication. Further, they would make
Dickens an equal partner, so that the profits would be shared, and
they would advance him his half share of the purchase price to be
deducted from the profits. All Dickens's objections at once gave
way, and unable to consult Forster, who was out, he consented
(P i. 273; from F II. i. 87–8).

A week later Macrone turned over his unsold stock, 100
volumes of the First Series, and 750 of the Second, along with
Cruikshank's twenty-eight copper plates, in return for £300
cash and bills for the remainder.[13] Cruikshank enlarged twenty-
seven of the designs he had done for the volume editions, and
added to them thirteen new ones. The design he had drawn on
commission from Macrone for the front wrapper had been translated into a woodcut by L. Schönberg, but Chapman and Hall, or
Dickens, evidently didn't like it, so Cruikshank produced a second
design, which was engraved by Jackson and printed on flimsy pink
covers. The different colour was chosen in all probability to
distinguish the previously published *Sketches* from the original
serial novels in green; and the second cover design exploited
both Cruikshank's long interest in ballooning and Dickens's

---

[13] Bills for £200 each were at three, four, five, six, seven, and eight months
from 22 June, and for £250 each at nine, ten, and eleven months (P i. 273, nn. 3
and 4, and the contract, i. 653).

prefatory metaphor in the first edition, First Series, about the 'pilot balloon' in which he and Cruikshank were embarking.

Beginning in November 1837 and running without interruption until June 1839, *Sketches by Boz* was issued in twenty monthly numbers without a final double one. To accommodate the letter-press, the text was run on from month to month without any concern for stopping at a natural division like a chapter end, and the last two numbers were enlarged beyond the customary twenty-four pages, to fifty-six and thirty-eight pages respectively. The serial edition was printed by Charles Whiting, who had printed the First Series of *Sketches* for Macrone and parts of the three-volume *Oliver Twist* for Bentley, and who was eventually to serve as printer of Dickens's last periodical, *All the Year Round*. The individual parts, in their crisp newness, must have borne some resemblance to the book Doctor Marigold describes:

> Whiting's own work, Beaufort House to wit, thrown off by the steam-ingine, best of paper, beautiful [pink] wrapper, folded like clean linen come home from the clear-starcher's, and so exquisitely stitched that, regarded as a piece of needlework alone it's better than the sampler of a seamstress undergoing a Competitive Examination for Starvation before the Civil Service Commissioners.[14]

None the less, there were those who complained that the monthly numbers of *Sketches* contained one-quarter less material than the numbers of *Pickwick* and *Nickleby*, yet cost the same amount. The publishers responded in an address printed on the penultimate page of the Advertiser for Part II. This was not the address Dickens mentioned in his letter to Forster describing the terms of Chapman and Hall's June 1837 purchase of the copyright; then the idea had been for Dickens to explain that '*they*, who may be fairly put forward as the parties [Dickens was to be a silent partner], have been driven into [parts publication] or the copyright would have been lost'. Now it was not the format which needed defending, however, but the *price*:

ADDRESS

SOME Complaints have reached the Publishers of this Work, that, although each Number contains a smaller quantity of matter than the PICKWICK PAPERS, it is charged at the same price. *The price of the*

---

[14] 'Doctor Marigold's Prescriptions', *All the Year Round*, Extra Christmas Number (7 Dec. 1865), p. 9.

three volumes, which are embodied in this edition, is One Pound Sixteen Shillings; and the whole of their contents, with the addition of many expensive Illustrations, are now publishing in Twenty Numbers, for One Pound. The Work having had a great sale in an expensive form, and being still in demand when this issue was undertaken, its present Proprietors were induced to give a very large sum for the copyright, which no further reduction of price could possibly cover. The expenses of the work in its present form being unusually heavy, and the Public having it in their power, notwithstanding, to purchase this edition at a very reduced price, as compared with any former edition, it will be apparent to any one who considers the subject, that the quantity of matter in each number cannot be increased; and that even in its present shape nothing but a very large circulation of the work can remunerate the Proprietors for the great outlay already incurred.

At its conclusion, the *Sketches* once again made an appearance in a different dress; this time both Series were bound in a single volume, demy 8vo, encased in brown cloth, and sold for a guinea. In forty months, the *Sketches* had gone through five editions of two Series, into twenty numbers, and back into bound form. The 'pilot balloon' had proved remarkably buoyant: it had risen fast, stayed aloft a considerable period of time, and yielded substantial remuneration to all participants.

It is pleasant to record that Dickens's relations with the Macrones did not end on an acrimonious note. Macrone fell ill in the summer of 1837, and died at Duppa's-hill, Croydon, on Saturday, 9 September. 'Mr. Macrone was much respected by all who knew him, and his death will be sincerely lamented by his friends and acquaintances', noted the obituaries.[15] His widow and two surviving children were left destitute, so Dickens and Ainsworth (who had left Macrone for Bentley earlier in the year) determined to get up a volume of papers to help them. This scheme materialized as *The Pic Nic Papers*, three volumes post 8vo (1841), edited by Dickens alone, published by Henry Colburn, and illustrated by Cruikshank, Browne, and R. J. Hamerton.[16] Publication was

[15] *The Times*, 12 Sept. 1837, p. 5.
[16] For the collection Dickens promised to write an original story of at least two sheets (thirty-two printed pages) and a preface, and also agreed to furnish free two suitable etchings by Cruikshank and two by Browne. He eventually collected two volumes' worth of material. To make up the requisite third volume, Colburn, acting on his own, included Joseph Neal's *Charcoal Sketches*, plates and all. Dickens

often postponed; even in the summer of 1841 Colburn had to retract previous notices that the book would appear on the first of August, explaining that publication had been unavoidably delayed by the plates. And Dickens's relations with Colburn turned sour over Colburn's insistence on exercising editorial prerogatives. Dickens finally 'damned his eyes (by implication and construction) . . . and declined to hold any further correspondence with him, on any subject' (P iii. 274). By 7 August the volumes were at last ready, and Mrs. Macrone eventually received £450 towards the maintenance of her family.[17]

casually alluded to this addition in his 'Introduction', noting that the third volume was 'appended from an American source'.

In their *American Book Circular* (1843), Wiley and Putnam, responding in part to Dickens's attack during his American tour on United States piracies, pointed out that the unacknowledged borrowing of texts was not all that one-sided, and instanced the Neal case, particularly damning since it appeared in a book under Dickens's nominal editorship. Dickens fumed to Carlyle that the *Athenaeum* gave publicity to a variety of such statements, and charged that Wiley and Putnam 'lie consumedly—after the true American fashion of smartness'. (See the *Athenaeum*, 1 Apr. 1843, p. 307; Richard D. Altick, 'Dickens and America: Some Unpublished Letters', *The Pennsylvania Magazine of History and Biography*, 73 (1949), 328–9; and P iii. 474.)

17 P i. 371, n. 3, and the contract, i. 664–5, dated almost a year after Macrone's death, 10 Aug. 1838. Fewer than 2,000 copies were sold, or Mrs. Macrone would have received another £50.

3

Pickwick Papers *and the Development of Serial Fiction*

If I were to live a hundred years, and write three
novels in each, I should never be so proud of any of
them, as I am of Pickwick, feeling as I do, that it has
made its own way . . .

CHARLES DICKENS (P i. 189)

THOUGH SKETCHES inaugurated Dickens's career, *Pickwick*
made it.[1] Dickens's first continuous fiction—many would
deny that it is a novel—ushered in the age of the novel,
which critics looking backward from the perspective of the
eighties and nineties thought either the glory or the curse of the
Victorian era.[2] The success of the flimsy shilling parts, issued in
green wrappers once each month from April 1836 to November
1837, was unprecedented in the history of literature. The lion's
share of credit for that success has always, and properly, gone to
the pseudonymous 'Boz', a twenty-four-year-old shorthand
writer with a quick eye, a fluent pen, and an inexhaustible,
buoyant, and loving imagination. Critics from 1836 onwards
have tended to slight the part played in the runaway reception of
the book by its unusual format; yet subsequent to Dickens's
success with *Pickwick*, parts publication became for thirty years
a chief means of democratizing and enormously expanding the
Victorian book-reading and book-buying public.

[1] Portions of this chapter reflect arguments I have developed elsewhere,
especially in my Introduction to the Penguin English Library edition of *Pickwick*
(1972, revised, fourth printing 1976); in a slightly different form, the entire
chapter appeared as '*Pickwick Papers* and the Development of Serial Fiction' in
Studies in English, Rice University Studies, 61 (winter 1975), 51–74.
[2] Guinevere L. Griest, *Mudie's Circulating Library and the Victorian Novel*
(Bloomington and London, Indiana Univ. Press, 1970), *passim*.

Dickens and his publishers discovered the potential of serial publication virtually by accident. Even though in the half century after *Pickwick* most of the novels appeared 'compact in three separate and indiwidual vollumes' as Mr. Omer describes David Copperfield's maiden effort, and were not bought but borrowed from the great circulating libraries like Mudie's and W. H. Smith's, serial publication opened up a new reading and buying public that subsequent publishers and formats did then exploit in a variety of ways. Furthermore, serial publication yielded profits hitherto thought impossible for any publisher or author, and transformed Dickens, Chapman, and Hall from minor figures in Victorian letters to titans. What forces made that format suddenly possible, and how the changes in publishing converged in 1836 and were connected by two shrewd, courageous, and lucky booksellers with the one man who could write letterpress for *all* the people, needs to be understood more fully than it has been so far. The prodigious success of *Pickwick* in parts signals a revolution in publishing.

i

The Pickwick Papers stands at the end of a long, complex, and accelerating series of developments. Piecemeal publishing was well established by 1740.[3] Early serial publications were generally of five kinds: fascicle issue, cheap part reprints, newspapers and magazines, instalment fiction, and series. Most visible, though probably not most common, were long, expensive books—dictionaries such as Johnson's, encyclopedias such as Chambers's, histories such as Smollett's, atlases such as Moll's, scientific and religious works—issued in fascicles. Sheets, or alternatively sewn gatherings of the volumes, were issued periodically as printed to subscribers or to booksellers for retail sale. The first leaf of each gathering, or the dust-wrapper, would have the special signature of that fascicle. A part might end in mid chapter, mid paragraph, even mid sentence, the catchword for the next part dangling below the final line. When all the gatherings were printed and distributed, the subscriber or customer would take the fascicles to his bookseller or bookbinder to be appropriately encased. Some customers were likely to be wealthy, and to have their own

[3] Wiles, *Serial Publication in England before 1750*, p. 3.

binding styles for their libraries. But others were less affluent: number books sold for as little as a farthing a part. The advertisements repeatedly insist that 'the Design of publishing Books in this manner Weekly is to lighten the Expence of them'.[4]

Though the relationship between cheap books and a wider reading public is undoubtedly reciprocal, there is no doubt that the availability of number books encouraged reading. 'This Method of Weekly Publication', the *Grub-Street Journal* declared on 26 October 1732, 'allures Multitudes to peruse Books, into which they would otherwise never have looked.'[5] This mode of publication made it possible, even easy, for middle- and lower-class Englishmen to buy and read books, and the range of their interests was enormous: biographies, translations, collections of songs, treatises on mathematics, topography, astronomy, architecture, officinal herbs, painting, calligraphy, even jest books. Prior to 1725 only a score of books were issued in consecutive parts; the boom began around 1732, and continued throughout the rest of the century.

For the publishers, who sometimes combined into 'congers' to bear the costs and share the profits of a particularly expensive work, the rewards could be enormous. The *Grub-Street Journal* of 19 September 1734 reported 'that the Knaptons were expected to clear between eight and ten thousand pounds by their publication —first in monthly and then in weekly numbers—of Rapin's *History of England* in the English translation by Nicholas Tindal, in spite of the fact that a rival translation by John Kelly was at the same time being published in numbers by J. Mechell'.[6] Seldom did the authors or translators benefit from these huge profits, however; most had sold their copyrights outright, or were already dead, and the booksellers and publishers engaged in production and distribution reaped the substantial rewards.

After 1732, publishers tended to the weekly, rather than monthly, issue, lowering costs and increasing cash flow. Regularity of purchase, a key to the success of serial publication, was encouraged by every possible means. On those rare occasions when some unavoidable delay occurred, proprietors usually inserted an elaborate notice in newspapers, or carried some announcement within the shop or at the window. Advertisement was an integral

---

[4] Ibid., p. 10. [5] Ibid., *half-title*, p. 2, and p. 260.
[6] Ibid., p. 5.

part of selling serials: the copy had to be enticing. The most dramatic features of the work were stressed, as in John Wilford's announcement of the third number of *Select Trials at the Sessions-House in the Old Bailey* (1734), issued in sixpenny fortnightly numbers:

> This Number . . . contains the remarkable Trials of George Duffus for Sodomy; Mary Harvey and Ann Parker for privately stealing Money from Dr. Cassel; Butler Fox for robbing Sir Edward Lawrence on the Highway . . .; Christopher Kraft for ravishing Sarah Pearse; George Nicholas for forging a Bank Note; James Shaw and Richard Norton for Robbery and Murder, &c.[7]

Descriptive details of the contents were often set forth in eye-catching type on the covers or dust-wrappers; sometimes the whole prospectus was reproduced. Anything that would bring the potential customer into the store to buy the first few numbers might be tried: there is an apocryphal story that over 20,000 copies of Smollett's *History of England* were sold because the publisher tipped every parish clerk in the kingdom a half-crown to scatter prospectuses in the pews.[8]

But not all serial publications were as vulgar as the *Select Trials* nor as dubiously promoted as Smollett's *History*. Though parts publication was sometimes 'a paltry money-grubbing enterprise undertaken by a handful of book pirates on the outer fringes of the publishing business',[9] there were also eminently respectable publishers, and fine editions of important works in all sorts of fields, which were made available to a vastly larger and more geographically diversified reading public than would have been discovered had the books been issued only as completed volumes. Herman Moll's *Atlas Geographus*, the first number book compiled expressly for publication in monthly parts, extended to five volumes and took nine years to complete, 1708–17. The subscribers to the venture included Michael Johnson, Bookseller, in Lichfield and Alexander Pope, Gent.

A second kind of serial, created by publishing or republishing standard works—notably the Bible and *Pilgrim's Progress*—in cheap part reprints, for sale or even free distribution by various

[7] Wiles, p. 207, from *The Daily Advertiser* for 11 May 1734.
[8] Richard D. Altick, *The English Common Reader: A Social History of the Mass Reading Public 1800–1900* (Chicago and London, Univ. of Chicago Press, 1957), p. 56 and n. 68.   [9] Wiles, p. 4.

organizations, was immensely popular in the later eighteenth and early nineteenth centuries. These works, often crudely printed and with clumsy woodblock cuts sometimes picked at random from the printer's stock, were distributed weekly or monthly, chiefly to the lower middle and lower classes, for whom they supplied instruction in reading and writing, moral and religious training, political propaganda, and entertainment. Illustrations, particularly coloured plates, made a strong appeal. John Kitto, the Biblical scholar, and Thomas Carter, in his *Memoirs of a Working Man*, both record the powerful effect which illustrations produced, exciting their imagination, and stimulating them to become book purchasers.[10] Trade in these items was especially brisk in the provinces; Edward Baines of Leeds sold over 20,000 copies of *History of the Wars of the French Revolution* by reprinting it in sixpenny parts and distributing it through hawkers.[11] By the first decades of the nineteenth century, provincial distribution networks were doing a lively business in improving tracts, like Hannah More's, political propaganda, like Cobbett's, and the first spate of self-help books. Number reprints were often, like fascicles, discrete divisions only in a bookmaking sense; flimsy and cheap, they were seldom bound, and only infrequently preserved.

Magazines and newspapers are a third form of serial publication, differing from serials (which have sequential page numbering and a consecutive narrative) by repeating the pagination in each issue and keeping the contents of each separate.[12] In the early eighteenth century, bona fide newspapers often swelled their contents by instalment printing of books, sometimes pirated. This practice may have related to a loophole in the Act (10 Anne, c. 19) which allowed publishers to avoid much of the stamp tax if they printed a sheet and a half of letterpress rather than a single sheet. However,

---

[10] Altick, *English Common Reader*, pp. 265–6 and n. 15.

[11] Ibid., p. 264 and n. 13.

[12] For instance, Roger L'Estrange's *Poor Robin's Memoirs* came out weekly, beginning 10 December 1677; for a penny one got a badly printed single half-sheet of narrative about Robin's *Life, Travels, and Adventures*. Each part is a complete, independent unit, and the seventeen 'tomes' are not, strictly speaking, fascicles at all; but the instalments have a cumulative effect, and the contents seem more fiction than reportage. On the other hand, Henry Care's compilation, *The Weekly Pacquet of Advice from Rome*, 1678 ff., was paginated continuously throughout its eventual 240 numbers or five volumes, and a preface and title-page to each was printed after the final number in that volume, but it is, by content, more closely related to newspapers than books (Wiles, pp. 75–8).

fiction in instalments must have been popular, for it was often featured on page one, and the practice continued even after the tax anomaly was corrected in 1725 (11 George I, c. 8).

Fiction in journals was cheaper than the same fiction in book form. Some novels were pirated almost as soon as they came off the press; most were sub-literary; almost none were written or translated expressly for instalment printing. While the newspaper itself was discrete bibliographically, the stories were not. They were considered filler, and stopped at any point necessary to fill the issue, even in mid sentence.[13] After 1725, publishers devised further ingenious schemes to avoid taxes; repeated efforts by Parliament to curtail these schemes led to the passage in 1743 of 16 George II, c. 26, which put teeth into the statutes respecting stamped papers by specifying stiff penalties for their violation.[14]

Since 'news' was defined as anything original or of immediate interest, including the first publication of a novel, publishers began to circumvent the 1743 prohibitions through magazines which reprinted extracts from the daily and weekly papers. So long as the magazine was not published more often than once a month, and did not contain original material, it was not taxable. After a corpus of fiction developed, standard reprints in magazines became popular: *The Novelist's Magazine*, and *The New Novelist's Magazine*, twenty-five volumes together, 1780–7, reprinted Fielding, Richardson, Smollett, and others, accompanying the text with fine plates by Stothard, Burney, and Corbould. Printed in 8vo double columns and stitched into small numbers retailing for 6*d.* each, *The Novelist's Magazine* achieved a sale of some 12,000 copies every week.[15]

The widespread publication of original essays and short stories and the reprinting of standard literature and Gothic fiction in numbers were encouraged by 60 George III, c. 9 (1819), which redefined a periodical in ways that made it possible for monthly magazines to begin publishing new material without paying stamp duty, and also exempted from duty all part issues of works originally published in book form.[16] Captain Marryat's *Metropolitan Magazine* (1831–50) was the first to make a regular feature

13 See the example facing p. 50 in Wiles.   14 Wiles, p. 53.

15 A. S. Collins, *The Profession of Letters*, p. 58.

16 Graham Pollard, 'Serial Fiction', in John Carter, ed., *New Paths in Book Collecting* (London, Constable, 1934), p. 257.

of original serial stories; by the 1840s these stories were often the most important feature of the half-crown monthly magazines.[17] From 1832 onwards the penny weeklies built large circulations; by the end of that year Charles Knight's *Penny Magazine* was selling at the rate of 200,000 copies in weekly and monthly parts, eclipsing *Chambers's Edinburgh Journal* ($1\frac{1}{2}d.$) by providing illustrations. Pictures were an essential part of Knight's concept, as Richard Altick explains:

> Knight . . . went to great trouble and expense to obtain good woodcuts. Like the publishers of number-books, he seems to have consciously intended this emphasis upon pictures as a means of bringing printed matter to the attention of a public unaccustomed to reading. Even the illiterate found a good pennyworth of enjoyment in the illustrations each issue of the *Penny Magazine* contained. And these, perhaps more than the letterpress, were responsible for the affection with which many buyers thought of the magazine in retrospect.[18]

Dickens was an avid reader of the lower range of such publications as a boy, consuming the *Penny* and *Saturday* magazines and later recalling that

> I used, when I was at school, to take in the *Terrific Register*, making myself unspeakably miserable, and frightening my very wits out of my head, for the small charge of a penny weekly; which considering that there was an illustration to every number, in which there was always a pool of blood, and at least one body, was cheap.
>
> (F I. iii. 43–4 n.)

Closely related to newspapers and magazines, original prose fiction in parts constitutes a fourth form of serial fiction. Reprints of fiction in parts occur as early as Richard Bentley's fifty 'modern novels', begun in 1692 in serial instalments; in the 1720s the *Monthly Amusement* ran a novel in each shilling number.[19] Edward Ward's *The London Spy*, eighteen parts beginning November 1698, was a 'Monthly Journal' recounting in the first person what purported to be actual experiences of the author. The instalments ran to four sheets each, for 6d.; and an 'essential continuity is easily perceived in the well sustained sprightliness of style and the consistent point of view.' But each part is separate,

[17] Ibid., pp. 258–9.
[18] Altick, *The English Common Reader*, p. 335. For a further discussion of the penny magazines, see Margaret Dalziel, *Popular Fiction 100 Years Ago: An Unexplored Tract of Literary History* (London, Cohen & West, 1957).
[19] Altick, *English Common Reader*, p. 55.

with distinctive signature and pagination. None the less, '*The London Spy* is just as much a "book" as *The Pickwick Papers*, which was issued in much the same way 140 years later', R. M. Wiles concludes.[20] If Ward's work is the first number fiction, it did not spawn many successors; before 1750, virtually nothing of importance in prose fiction was published in numbers. Except for a few fictitious and usually salacious autobiographies, original prose fiction in serial parts virtually disappeared until Smollett published *Sir Launcelot Greaves* in his *British Magazine* between January 1760 and December 1761. Smollett's novel broke new ground in several ways: it was the first large piece of original fiction written expressly for publication in a magazine; it was conceived and written for instalment publication—the beginning having been printed before the end was written; it was a new work by a novelist of established reputation; it marks the pinnacle of achievement for miscellany fiction from 1740 on; and in composing it Smollett paid marked attention to the requirements of serial publication, notably the organization of chapters.[21]

However, Smollett's novel appeared in a magazine; though original, it was not issued in independent parts. And afterwards, novel publication flourished only at a low level of achievement. J. M. S. Tompkins begins her book with the observation that 'During the years that follow the death of Smollett . . . the two chief facts about the novel are its popularity as a form of entertainment and its inferiority as a form of art.'[22] Sub-literary species abounded, in magazines, reprints, and cheap editions; Gothic fiction appeared in bound volumes. But original fiction of good quality issued in parts disappeared from view.

The 'series', hard to distinguish from other kinds of serials, was employed for works that could be contained within one or two gatherings. In the eighteenth century, plays came out weekly or monthly in quarto series produced by William Feales, Jacob Tonson, and Robert Walker. Each play would be complete, sometimes with specially engraved frontispiece and all prologues and epilogues; and the publisher would run through a playwright's entire canon, issuing, say, one of Shakespeare's plays

[20] Wiles, p. 81.
[21] Robert D. Mayo, *The English Novel in the Magazines 1740–1815: With a Catalogue of 1375 Magazine Novels and Novelettes* (Evanston, Northwestern Univ. Press; London, Oxford Univ. Press, 1962), pp. 277–82.
[22] *The Popular Novel in England, 1770–1800* (London, Constable, 1932), p. 1.

every Thursday.[23] Newgate series were similarly issued piecemeal; sermons and lecture series were less successful. By the 1830s, series such as Chapman and Hall's *The Library of Fiction* existed for original as well as reprinted stories, but the main impetus toward the publication of novels in series was not original work in parts, but reprint series like Bentley's and Colburn's.[24]

The publication of *Pickwick Papers* was shaped by yet another influence, derived in the first place not from the letterpress, but from popular illustrations. Since Hogarth, there had been a market, especially in the city, for series of prints which told stories, on the order of *Marriage à la Mode* or *A Rake's Progress*. The strip narrative, often a progress, became popular in Europe as well as England, and series were done by such well-known artists as Chodowiecki, John Hamilton Mortimer, James Northcote, George Morland, and Johann Heinrich Ramberg.[25] Instead of supplying a set of six or eight plates, post-Hogarthian caricaturists, appealing to a less affluent audience, often went back to an earlier, more demotic tradition of multiple scenes in a single illustration. Even though the resulting spaces were cramped, these cheap prints seem to have been more successful than the post-Hogarthian 'high art' progresses. Cruikshank worked extensively in this mode in the first two decades of the nineteenth century, composing plates of from one to six divisions, and progresses of six and eight plates. The well-known shops of such print-sellers as Hone, Tegg, Fairburn, and G. Humphrey were decorated with caricatures and progresses, which the populace of London scrutinized with care and relish; it is clear that the response was lively and widespread from the various places in which reference to these prints would turn up—from Mayfair drawing-rooms and the Commons to Billingsgate and cheap fiction.[26]

In 1820 Pierce Egan hit on a scheme for issuing coloured plates, etched by the Cruikshank brothers, along with letterpress leading

[23] Wiles, pp. 19–21.

[24] Michael Sadleir, *XIX Century Fiction: A Bibliographical Record* (2 vols., New York, Cooper Square Publishers, Inc., 1951; rpt. 1969), ii. 91–104, 112–22.

[25] David Kunzle, '*Mr. Lambkin*: Cruikshank's Strike for Independence', in Robert L. Patten, ed., *George Cruikshank: A Revaluation* (Princeton, Princeton Univ. Library, 1974), pp. 169–87; and *The Early Comic Strip: Narrative Strips and Picture Stories in the European Broadsheet from c. 1450 to 1825; History of the Comic Strip*, vol. i (Berkeley, Los Angeles, and London, Univ. of California Press, 1973).

[26] Louis James, 'An Artist in Time: George Cruikshank in Three Eras', in *George Cruikshank: A Revaluation*, ed. Robert L. Patten, pp. 157–68.

up to the big scene, once a month, until the story of *Life in London; or, the Day and Night Scenes of Jerry Hawthorn, Esq., and his Elegant Friend Corinthian Tom, Accompanied by Bob Logic, the Oxonian, in their Rambles and Sprees through the Metropolis* was completed in twelve monthly numbers (October 1820 to July 1821). Whether the lively plates, the flash letterpress, or the mode of publication was responsible is difficult to determine, but the combination proved irresistible, and Tom and Jerry's adventures were widely purchased, imitated, dramatized, plagiarized, and extended in sequels.

Over a century of experience with serials of various kinds had taught English publishers many lessons. Cheapening books enlarged the potential audience and pool of customers. Serial issue could substantially lower the costs even of expensive, illustrated works. Periodical issuance of books in progress recirculated a publisher's cash flow: each part financed the next.[27] Advertising was a key to success, and regularity of publication a key to establishing the customer's all-important habit of coming to his bookseller every week or month. Provincial distribution networks could be highly profitable adjuncts to urban trade. Illustrations often more than recouped their cost by inducing readers to buy. Resourcefulness in circumventing tax laws could lead to profitable innovations in publishing and distribution. Magazine fiction became a staple of many households, and could establish the habit of reading early in life. Reprints of standard works of fiction whetted the appetite for more. Works that exploited contemporary events and settings, like Newgate series or political caricatures, found a sure audience among city-dwellers. Cheap series persuaded many middle-class households to buy the complete works of an author, even copies of otherwise uncommercial books. But though these and other lessons had been learned in specific circumstances, no one had put all of them together in a form of writing, publishing, and distributing that would take full advantage of the potential mass market.

ii

Technological innovations, proceeding alongside the development of parts publication, assisted in the revolution that was to

27 Guinevere Griest is somewhat mistaken in saying (pp. 44, 217) that the profit on part issue depended on large sales.

come. The first thirty-five years of the nineteenth century introduced more radical changes in book production than the preceding 350.[28] It may be true that 'the most original aspects of
printing since 1800, both from the design and technical standpoints, are seen in jobbing and periodical printing',[29] among the
firms which produced the countless forms, advertisements, letter-
heads, and government documents that the rapidly expanding
bureaucracies demanded. But several improvements in printing
and book production had important effects on the manufacture of
cheap fiction.

A major stumbling-block to producing mass inexpensive literature was the supply of paper. Until 1803 it was impossible for any
paper-making process to yield more than a few thousand sheets
at any one time. Publishers could not issue large editions, nor
could they be ready quickly for huge reprints, since it took the
paper-makers five to six weeks to manufacture a new order. In
1803 Gamble and Donkin completed a prototype of the Fourdrinier cylindrical paper-making machine, for endless web production.[30] By 1837, the Fourdrinier process was perfected and
established commercially; what it meant to one large-scale
publisher of inexpensive books is described by Charles Knight, in
a statement to a committee of the House of Commons in that year:

> The supply [from these machines, 280 of them at six miles of paper
> each made 1,680 miles of paper in one day] is such as to enable one with
> perfect ease to meet the demand, however large, without keeping any
> stock in hand: for example; I use about 1,500 reams of paper per month;
> unless this machine had been invented, I could not have gone into the
> market with the certainty of purchasing 1,500 reams of paper for the
> month's consumption; and I should have been obliged to have kept
> two or three months' consumption to have insured a regular periodical
> supply; that amounts to a large saving to a person engaged in publi-
> cation.[31]

The new paper-making processes also produced larger paper
sizes, enabling printers to impress thirty-two pages rather than

---

[28] John Carter, *Books and Book-Collectors* (Cleveland and New York, World
Publishing Co., 1957), p. 158.

[29] Michael Twyman, *Printing 1770–1970: An Illustrated History of Its Uses and
Development in England* (London, Eyre & Spottiswoode, 1970), p. 2.

[30] Carter, *Books and Book-Collectors*, p. 157; Philip Gaskell, *A New Introduction
to Bibliography* (New York and Oxford, Oxford Univ. Press, 1972), p. 216.

[31] Quoted in Plant, *The English Book Trade*, pp. 329–30.

sixteen at one time. There was an additional saving since taxes were assessed per sheet, regardless of the number of printed pages that sheet yielded. So doubling the size of the sheet halved the printing time and the taxes.[32]

Printing also speeded up. In the eighteenth century, before the introduction of the Stanhope press, 'the only machinery in use', as Balzac notes at the start of *Illusions perdues*,

was the primitive wooden invention to which the language owes a figure of speech—'the press groans' was no mere rhetorical expression in those days. Leather ink balls were still used in old-fashioned printing-houses; the pressmen dabbed the ink by hand on the characters, and the moveable table on which the form of type was placed in readiness for the sheet of paper, being made of marble, literally deserved its name of 'impression-stone.' . . . Séchard had been in his time a journeyman pressman, a 'bear' in compositors' slang. The continued pacing to and fro of the pressman from ink-table to press, from press to ink-table, no doubt suggested the nickname. The 'bears', however, make matters even by calling the compositors monkeys, on account of the nimble industry displayed by those gentlemen in picking out the type from the hundred and fifty-two compartments of the cases.[33]

At the turn of the century Stanhope's iron printing press was being tested at Bulmer's, and in 1804 the first book printed by his stereotype process appeared.[34] In 1811 Friedrich Koenig patented a steam-powered cylindrical press, 'an invention', according to *The Times*, 'only second to that of Gutenberg himself'.[35] Whereas printing *The Times* on a large iron hand press yielded only 150 copies per hour, by 1816 Koenig's double-cylinder steam press produced six times the quantity, effecting a dramatic saving. The evolution of Stanhope's machine was much more rapid and its adoption more widespread than was the case with Church's composing machine, patented in 1822. Because labour was cheap and hand-compositors vehement in their opposition to machinery, and because the early composing machines were not particularly efficient (lines still had to be justified and type distributed by hand), mechanization of composition did not advance much until later in the nineteenth century.

[32] Plant, pp. 331–2.
[33] Honoré de Balzac, *Lost Illusions*, trans. Ellen Marriage, in *The Novels of Balzac*, Centenary edition (Philadelphia, John D. Morris and Co., n.d.), vi. 2.
[34] Carter, *Books and Book-Collectors*, p. 157.
[35] Quoted in Percy Muir, *Victorian Illustrated Books* (London, B. T. Batsford Ltd., 1971), p. 4.

Now that the printers could get larger supplies of paper faster, and print more quickly, they had the technical capacity to issue much larger editions. Larger in both senses, since the iron presses could print over a much bigger surface. But long works, and large printings, were still expensive, especially if the standing type had to be kept for possible reprintings. Stereotyping had long been known as a solution to this and other problems, but not until the nineteenth century did it become economically attractive. Moulds for type existed as early as the sixteenth century, and in the late eighteenth additional improvements were patented. Earl Stanhope, Andrew Wilson, Applegarth, and Brunel worked on stereotyping in the early nineteenth century; and the most considerable alteration occurred in 1846, when papier mâché was substituted for plaster to make the moulds. The restrictive practices of the Stationers' Company hindered the use of stereotypes until the 1800s, but by 1828 Clowes had nearly 800 tons of stereotype plate, worth £200,000, and this stock more than doubled during the next fifteen years. Still, even in 1840 stereotyping was not profitable except for large printing orders; but it was just the answer to the peculiar demands of serial publication, where big initial printings might be followed, after many months, by reprints of the individual parts as the publishers made up completed runs to bind and sell in volume form. Moreover, once stereotype was made, the printers need only press enough copies to meet the immediate demand. The movable type could be distributed, yet the warehouse need not be filled with huge advance printings. Printers tied up less of their capital but retained flexibility to respond to anticipated sales. Of course, the use of stereotype plates led to bibliographical nightmares; editions, issues, and states become formidably complicated to distinguish.[36] The leisurely world of eighteenth-century printing (leisurely, at least in retrospect) fades, and the hand-made quality of books disappears; in their places emerges a dynamic, high-pressure, increasingly mechanized, quickly responsive commercial enterprise.

Photographic processes were first used in making illustrations as early as 1826, but not until the second half of the nineteenth century did collotype, photo-etched line-blocks, half-tone, and

[36] Peter L. Shillingsburg, 'The First Edition of Thackeray's *Pendennis*', *Papers of the Bibliographical Society of America*, 66 (1972), 35–49.

photogravure become perfected and commercially viable.[37] Illustration, in the first half-century, was largely done by hand, with the assistance of a few instruments like the roulette which produced an endless series of parallel lines. Bewick perfected and sophisticated wood-block engraving—that is, cutting into the end-grain of the wood block with a graver, following an outline either drawn directly on a thin wash of Chinese white, or chalked on the block by tracing it over transfer paper. Under Bewick's hands, and in those of his successors John Jackson and William Harvey, wood engraving achieved a high state of development and art. But it was comparatively an expensive and time-consuming process. In London in 1827 there were no more than twenty woodcutters; they were artists, receiving artists' wages, so that it cost more than £200 for the illustrations to Charles Knight's *Library of Entertaining Knowledge*.[38] Copperplate was even more costly, and could be used only on expensive books.

Alternatives were being explored in the early 1830s. In *Sketches by Boz* Cruikshank used copper plates faced with steel; Seymour and Browne struggled with polished steel plates, whose surfaces, in the first numbers of *Pickwick*, had a tendency to break down early in the printing. The steel-plate process, though patented in 1810, was not used commercially until the 1820s.[39] It was never possible during Dickens's lifetime to discover a metal plate that would hold up through a substantial printing run; consequently duplicate steels were the rule after the ninth number of *Pickwick*. Woodblocks were used for *Master Humphrey's Clock*; though they could withstand up to 100,000 impressions, as they were cut (on the whole skilfully) by a hand other than the designing artist's, they lacked the character and freedom of the original. Electrotyping,[40] glyphography, and lithography were other methods tried out for large-scale printings, though they were little used in Dickens's works. It is interesting to speculate what would have been the appearance of Dickens's work twenty years earlier,

---

[37] Carter, *Books and Book-Collectors*, p. 158.

[38] Charles Knight, *The Old Printer and the Modern Press* (London, John Murray, 1854), p. 244; Plant, p. 311.

[39] Gaskell, p. 267, n. 5.

[40] Ibid., pp. 266–7; electrotyping was not common in England until the late nineteenth century, but at Harpers in New York all blocks were electrotyped in the forme with the type by 1850.

when woodblock and copperplate were the only processes perfected. There is no question that the mechanical advances and
limitations in block-making significantly affected the shape of his
serial fiction.

Hand-printed books published in small editions for the urban
middle class and the country gentry did not require elaborate or
sophisticated commercial establishments. But as the market grew,
the need for capital grew too: inventory, warehousing, distribution, and advertising all became more significant items in the
expenses of book production. Most important, the introduction of
machinery required capital, and its efficient use required that books
be printed in larger numbers and more frequently. In the decades
on either side of the turn of the century, partly prompted by disruptions to the competition on the Continent during the Napoleonic Wars, certain English booksellers began to amass sufficient
capital to bear independently a larger proportion of the total risk.
Murray, Cadell & Davies, Blackwood, and Constable all began
publishing on their own, instead of dividing into congers.[41] At
the same time, the amalgam of activities in which the eighteenth-
century bookseller might have been engaged—publisher, printer,
stationer, retailer, financier, print seller, agent, editor, newspaper proprietor, and public relations director—began to be
subdivided. The nineteenth century ushered in the age of the
specialist publisher, who initiated, financed, produced, advertised, wholesaled, and accounted for his works, but who did not
necessarily print, bind, or retail them.[42] Printing and binding,
publishing newspapers, and selling stationery or books became
separate businesses, and the capital that had once been spread over
all aspects of book production gradually became consolidated
in specialized areas. This concentration generated momentum,
complications, and advantages which will become apparent as we
trace Dickens's career.

Several other critical developments not directly related to
printing have been sufficiently detailed in Richard Altick's
masterly study of *The English Common Reader*. The sheer
increase in population; the rise of urban centres, real wages, the
middle (and especially professional) class; the steady spread of
literacy; the impulses to self-improvement, both spiritual and
material; the expansion of leisure time; the rapid improvement in

[41] Ibid., p. 297.   [42] Carter, *Books and Book-Collectors*, p. 158.

transportation, yielding wider markets, first within England and, by mid century, around the world: all these forces converged to create a rapidly expanding reading and book-buying public. Book-*buying* is, of course, the key: it is far preferable from many standpoints, though the readership is the same, to have fifty copies of a book sold, with two readers apiece, than one copy in a library which can be read by a hundred. And *buying* is the key to serial fiction, for whereas three-deckers were designed for the convenience of circulating libraries, serial fiction put the ownership of novels within the means of the middle class. Dickens was the first English novelist really to *belong* to the people of England, and they loved him all the more because he was, so to speak, a resident in their homes.

iii

When Edward Chapman and William Hall joined together in the early months of 1830 to start a bookselling establishment, they undoubtedly knew, at least in a general way, something of the history of publishing which I have summarized. Chapman, son of a Richmond solicitor, was 'a quiet and retiring man . . . full of information, and had such a broad, just mind that it was a great privilege to hear his judgment upon any subject'. One of his daughters described him as 'truth and sincerity'.[43] Perhaps something of his breadth of view and knowledge is contained in the firm's first venture, *Chat of the Week; or, Compendium of all Topics of Public Interest, Original and Select*, a sixpenny weekly of extracts with 'no limits as to subject',[44] which began on 5 June 1830. Hall, on the other hand, was universally characterized as 'brisk, and a good business man'; he could run up figures like lightning, and all 'the young men they employed stood in awe of him'.[45] He would have perceived instantly the advantageous location which was available in the Strand, at No. 186: a pleasant, double-fronted house, it was close to the publishing and printing worlds on an attractive and busy street along which hundreds of potential

---

[43] Arthur Waugh, *A Hundred Years of Publishing: Being the Story of Chapman & Hall, Ltd.* (London, Chapman & Hall, Ltd., 1930), pp. 4–5; and letter of Mrs. Gaye, daughter of Chapman, to Waugh, facing p. 4.

[44] Ibid., p. 10; see facsimile of Chapman and Hall's first announcement of *Chat*, facing p. 10.

[45] Ibid., p. 5.

customers would pass each day. And so the lease was taken, and Chapman and Hall began business.

Initially they were booksellers only, and their early ventures outside retailing were, according to John Forster, 'ingenious rather than important'.[46] By midsummer, as we have seen, they had inaugurated a weekly periodical, hoping no doubt that the customers who entered the shop each Saturday for *Chat* might be lured into further purchases. Obviously someone (Hall?) recognized early the value of serials in establishing a habit of buying, for they also connected themselves quickly to a current serial publication, Gorton's new *Topographical Dictionary*, which was scheduled for forty-two monthly parts, each consisting of forty pages of 'closely printed' letterpress and a quarto map, 1s. plain, 1s. 6d. coloured.[47] Chapman and Hall's first publication ventures, then, involved two of the kinds of serials we have already discussed, and were taken up in association with other booksellers, so that they prudently avoided the whole risk. The printer, in each case, was the same Charles Whiting, in Beaufort House, Strand, near by, who printed the serial issue of *Sketches*; whether he was a relative of Chapman's future wife is unclear.

Arthur Waugh's account of the early years of the firm says little about the period between 1831 and 1834, when the first *Athenaeum* announcement for a Chapman and Hall book appears. This silence is not surprising, for in 1831 one of the periodic depressions that hit the book trade must have affected the fledgeling entrepreneurs. Caused by the death of George IV, the fall of Wellington's government, tight money, agitation over the Reform Bill, industrial depression, agricultural distress, an epidemic of cholera, and a widespread distrust of potentially inflammatory printed matter, the depression in the book trade was both severe and general. Dibdin uses as epigraph to his *Bibliophobia. Remarks on the present languid and depressed state of literature and the book trade* (1832) this description: 'FEAR is the order of the day. To those very natural and long-established fears of bailiffs and taxgatherers, must now be added the fear of *Reform*, of *Cholera*, and of BOOKS.'[48] In London six hundred printers were

[46] Ibid., p. 10; F I. v. 74.

[47] Ibid., p. 11, and facsimile of advertisement, facing p. 11.

[48] Thomas Frognall Dibdin [pseud. Mercurius Rusticus], with notes by R. Heber [pseud. Cato Parvus] (London, Henry Bohn, 1832), title-page, p. 6.

jobless because publishers were holding back on long-promised books, while in Scotland, according to Wordsworth, 'the Book-selling Trade was in a deplorable state, and . . . nothing was sale-able but newspapers on the Revolutionary side'.[49] Still, the very appeal made to the masses by such newspapers and political pamphlets as Cobbett's encouraged literacy, and as the effects of the temporary civil, political, and economic dislocations of 1830–1 moderated, booksellers began once again to issue new works. Prudently contracting to the retail end for the duration of the slump, by 1834 Chapman and Hall were once more publishing, as well as retailing, such perishable commodities as *Scenes and Recollections of Fly-Fishing* and *The Book of Science*, which came complete with 200 engravings on wood, bound in embossed cloth with gilt edges, for 8s. 6d.

In the following year Chapman and Hall issued *The Squib Annual*, a glossy book for the Christmas trade illustrated by the popular Robert Seymour, political caricaturist and humorous illustrator. In the course of discussion about that book, Seymour broached the idea of drawing plates for a series of cockney sport-ing scenes, to be issued with accompanying letterpress written to order.[50] Accepting the suggestion, Edward Chapman urged that the plates come out monthly. Seymour agreed, and Chapman and Hall then attempted, without success, to find someone to compose the text. The commission was hardly a flattering one. While comic plates with letterpress were eminently commercial in the 1830s, credit and cash most often went to the illustrator, not the author, who usually took his direction from plates already designed. In March 1836 Thackeray, readying his first separate publication, a series of lithographed caricatures, told his publisher John Mitchell, 'I do not know whether you propose to publish any letter-press with the drawing, will you allow me to see it, before its appearance'.[51] If a fledgeling artist like Thackeray, desperately hard up, can have taken such a casual attitude towards

[49] Gettmann, pp. 10–11; Wordsworth, *The Letters of William and Dorothy Wordsworth: The Later Years*, ed. Ernest de Selincourt (3 vols., Oxford, Clarendon Press, 1939), ii. 583–4.

[50] For a fuller account of these deliberations, and the Seymour family's subse-quent claims, see Robert L. Patten, ed., *The Pickwick Papers*, pp. 11–16, 919–22. Seymour had already approached several other publishers with his idea, and been turned down.

[51] Thackeray, *Letters*, i. 300.

the letterpress of his maiden venture, then clearly no ambitious writer, with a strong sense of his own priorities, was likely to be eager to accept such a menial assignment.

After trying out several other authors, William Hall approached Dickens. Writing about the origins of *Pickwick* for the Cheap edition in 1847, Dickens confessed that at the time of Hall's proposal he dimly recalled 'certain interminable novels in [serial] form, which used . . . to be carried about the country by pedlars, and over some of which I remember to have shed innumerable tears, before I served my apprenticeship to Life'.[52] Apart from *Launcelot Greaves*, which Dickens knew, the literary merit of those works was negligible. But the public was getting used to buying these serial instalments of brightly illustrated escapades, whether concerning portly butchers or young scapegraces. *Tom Cringle's Log*, by Michael Scott, had recently appeared in parts, along with various works by Theodore Hook which viewed with amusement the pretensions to gentility of a harassed and rising middle class.[53]

Surprisingly, Dickens did accept the firm's offer to provide a sheet and a half of letterpress, monthly, 'for a book illustrative of manners and life in the Country' (P i. 648). Though ambitious and possessing a strong sense of his own priorities, Dickens was also poor, eager to get married, and energetic. Hall's offer of nine guineas a sheet or £14. 3s. 6d. for the sheet and a half (slightly more than Captain Cuttle's famous savings of £14. 2s.), payable on publication day each month, would provide a regular stipend, permit him at last to marry, and offer a vehicle for mounting a further assault on the reading public. Caught up in his own visions of future glory, Dickens did not hear very clearly Hall's references to Robert Seymour, who, in priority and fame, was the senior partner in the proposed venture. To Catherine, Dickens reported: 'They [Chapman and Hall] have made me an offer of £14 a month to write and edit a new publication they contemplate, entirely by myself' (P i. 128–9). What 'write and

[52] Preface to the Cheap edition of *Pickwick*, 1847. In 1859 Dickens told Edward Walford, journalist and editor, 'that it is hardly well to rest anything connected with the origin of the Pickwick Papers on a vague "it is said", when their origin has been for some years exactly described by my own hand, and before the Public, in the preface to the Cheap Edition of that work' (N ii. 776).
[53] Sylvère Monod, *Dickens the Novelist* (Norman, Univ. of Oklahoma Press, 1968), p. 70, n. 18.

edit' means is not clear, either: Dickens was addicted at this time to legal-sounding double phrases, like 'devise and bequeath', which he absorbed in Parliament and had copied over and over again as a clerk at Ellis and Blackmore's. Perhaps he had in mind something like the monthly *Library of Fiction*, which contained original and reprinted material, or like the future *Bentley's Miscellany*, for which he was to 'write and edit' ten months later. Or perhaps he had already planned to appear in the guise of an 'editor' of the *Posthumous Papers*, like Carlyle in *Sartor Resartus* which ran in *Fraser's* from November 1833 to August 1834.

In any case, Chapman and Hall were thinking in terms of yet another serial publication wedding hack letterpress to humorous plates. A monthly periodical of twenty-four pages, with four plates plus a coloured wrapper design, would have to sell around 2,000 copies to yield a profit. Fixed costs included Dickens's stipend of £14. 3s. 6d. plus Seymour's remuneration (variously estimated at £6 or £20) for the plates and wrapper design. A sizeable proportion of the total expenses, perhaps as much as half, would come from the illustrations (including the special paper for the plates and the cost of the steels); the venture was undoubtedly conceived by the publishers as a partnership between an illustrator who sold them copyright in the plates and a writer who sold them copyright in the text. In both cases Chapman and Hall owned the copyright outright, bore all the expenses of publication, guaranteed the contributors their monthly stipends regardless of the profit and loss statements, and expected to reap whatever gains might be forthcoming from a large sale. Seymour's name was good among the London public, and Boz was an increasingly popular cognomen, so the prospects seemed favourable. If a great success was achieved, Chapman and Hall promised Dickens in writing 'to increase the amount in a proportionate degree' (P i. 648). The adjective was deliberately vague; the details were left to be worked out during the serial run.

Thus the three participants, Seymour, Dickens, and Chapman and Hall, all with slightly different conceptions of their joint project, went on with preparations for its commencement. Dickens finally finished writing the first two numbers; asked, and received, a slight advance on his stipend so that he could get married; and went off to Chalk on his honeymoon. Chapman and Hall prepared an initial press-run of 1,000 copies of Part I, and placed advertisements which were as detailed, explicit, and enticing as Dickens could make them, in *The Times*, the *Athenaeum*, and the *Morning Chronicle*. Cautious men, who may have detected a certain reluctance on the part of booksellers and the general public to subscribe in advance for this new periodical, they ordered the bindery to process only 400 copies, which Mr. Aked, the foreman, did one evening after the rest of the staff had left. Seymour laboured away at the illustrations, getting into difficulties over the tendency of the steel surfaces to crumble, and hastily etching a duplicate set of plates when all his efforts to rebite and repair the original ones failed to halt their disintegration.

It was not an auspicious beginning. Despite polite notices, sales were so poor that the printing run for Part II was reduced to 500 copies. Then Seymour committed suicide, and the surviving participants had to decide on a future course of action. Here was a new firm, lately returned to publishing on its own account after weathering a severe depression in the book trade, faced with a losing serial from which the more important contributor had just violently resigned. It is to their eternal credit and fame that, inspired by Dickens's runaway enthusiasm, they decided to continue, on an 'improved plan' of thirty-two pages of letterpress and two illustrations per month. At a single stroke something permanent and novel-like (Chesterton called *Pickwick* 'something nobler than a novel')[54] was created out of something ephemeral and episodic: with sixteen pages between pictures, Dickens could expand his scenes and amplify his characterizations in ways he could not when he had to invent a new comic climax every six pages. And the costs of production radically shifted in favour of the author and away from the illustrator: two plates could be printed on a single sheet and later be divided, there were half as many steels to provide, and illustrators of less repute than Seymour could settle for less (R. W. Buss, who unsuccessfully illustrated Part III, received only £6. 10s.). Dickens, on the other hand, asked for a rise, not only to include the extra letterpress, which would bring him to eighteen guineas for two sheets monthly, but also a general rise of two additional guineas, to £21. And the publishers, deciding that they might as well be hanged for a sheep as for sheepishness, agreed.

[54] G. K. Chesterton, *Charles Dickens: A Critical Study* (New York, Dodd Mead, 1906), p. 79.

8120761   D

Something had to be done about sales, which, even with Number III, where the print number was restored to 1,000, were still too anaemic to support the costs. Charles Tilt, a neighbouring bookseller and publisher, suggested sending copies out to provincial booksellers 'on sale or return'. From this suggestion we can infer that up to 1836 Chapman and Hall had not acquired a very extensive network of regional booksellers to help in working off their stock. Tilt's idea was a good one, as it turned out, but the initial results were unpromising: out of 1,500 copies dispatched, an average of only 50 per number were sold. Thus Chapman and Hall recouped none of the cost of reprinting the numbers, an expense which only added to what must have been a deficit balance. On the other hand, sales in the suburbs around London may have been brisker; years later Charles Knight recalled one pedlar who, though taking undue credit for *Pickwick*'s success, exemplifies the kind of salesmanship that must have rescued many cheap works from disaster:

> There was an old man of the name of Knox who used to carry about new periodical works to suburban shops, and by this means, at a time when there was far less activity amongst small retail booksellers, he would in some degree force a sale of a new serial work. Three or four numbers of the 'Pickwick Papers' had been published when the pedestrian dealer, who saved the little shop-keeper the trouble of going to the Row on a Magazine-day, shewed me a large bundle of shilling parts which he had just purchased of Messrs. Chapman and Hall. With a pardonable vanity he ascribed much of the success of 'Pickwick' to his own indefatigable exertions, for he was not content with providing a supply for the first of the month, but went again and again the round of the suburbs from Whitechapel to Chelsea. Mr. Dickens's first great venture was very soon beyond the necessity of any extra trade exertion, to command a sale much larger than any work of fiction had previously attained; not even excepting the Waverley Novels in their cheaper form.[55]

By the end of *Pickwick*'s run, people in Edinburgh or Glasgow, or even in a remote hamlet like the one where Mary Russell Mitford was virtually imprisoned, were reading *Pickwick* at the same time as people in London. The lag between the city and the country was eliminated, and *Pickwick* parts—more, I suspect, even than

[55] Charles Knight, *Passages of a Working Life During Half a Century: With a Prelude of Early Reminiscences* (3 vols., London, Bradbury & Evans, 1864–5), iii. 37.

Scott's or Byron's new works—achieved an instant island-wide circulation. (Visiting in Ireland, Emily Jephson had not heard of *Pickwick*, more than half-way through its initial run, so perhaps in publication as in other things Ireland was still neglected.) Though there are only a few indications of the procedures which Chapman and Hall used to maintain this network of dealers, its importance in contributing to Dickens's popularity and profitability must not be underestimated.

Three advantages of serial publication rapidly became apparent, as, after the fourth number, sales began to rise. The first is the familiar one of habit. Chapman and Hall were careful to insert notices in the newspapers and journals towards the end of each month reminding the public that the next instalment was forthcoming. When, after Mary Hogarth's death on 7 May 1837, Dickens found that he could not finish his instalment for June, notices were sent out everywhere, an announcement was included in the June *Bentley's Miscellany*, and the July *Pickwick* (XV) contained a further explanation, intended to scotch rumours that Dickens was mad or dead.

Second, original serial fiction encouraged multiple reviews, which in turn stimulated more buyers.[56] How could a reviewer do more than comment in a general way on the progress of the story, and excerpt a few choice passages, until the novel was completed? And so, month after month, journals commented briefly on Dickens's story, and month by month more people were drawn to buy the flimsy paper parts. It became topical matter, almost like news; people asked themselves, 'What were the Pickwickians doing last month?' and hastened to their booksellers to find out.

Third, the very periodicity of the serial made it appropriate, like a newspaper or magazine, for advertising. As early as the third number, Chapman and Hall were inserting notices of their other publications, and permitting other advertisers, possibly for a small fee, to have their printed circulars stitched in. In *Pickwick* IV appears the first *Pickwick* Advertiser, a four-page quarto insert extolling the publications of Charles Tilt, John Macrone, John Murray, and Richard Bentley. In time, this Advertiser swelled to a maximum of twenty-four pages, and there were other inserts as

[56] For multiple reviews of a serial, see Philip Collins, ed., *Dickens: The Critical Heritage*, pp. xv–xvi.

well, the largest number (seven, totalling twenty-six pages) occurring in the July 1837 number, and probably representing backlog caused by its postponement at Mary's death. The relation of the Advertiser to sales is not exactly constant; merchants tended to take space in certain seasons (Christmas, for instance) and not in others (August). But the phenomenal popularity of *Pickwick* did contribute to the coffers of Chapman and Hall.

The consequences of this success had to be worked out month by month. At first, Chapman and Hall found the expenses of printing the next month's instalment, while reprinting the earlier numbers (twenty times in the first eighteen months), so great that they could not afford to pay Dickens until after the receipts for the current number came in. At the same time, Dickens found himself committed to multiple deadlines, and fell repeatedly behind in submitting his copy. Both problems were resolved by the end of 1836: as the current numbers sold more largely, Chapman and Hall's cash flow improved; and they renegotiated their agreement with Dickens so as to pay him on the 8th of the succeeding month, rather than on publication day. That helped a lot. Dickens promised to reform himself, and though he was signing agreements with Bentley to 'write and edit' the *Miscellany* at the very same time he was apologizing to Chapman and Hall about his tardiness, he did at last work off some of the galling obligations.

By the turn of the year it was clear that *Pickwick* was a gold mine. Beginning with Part IX, the instalments had to be printed from stereotype as well as movable type. By Part X, Hablot Knight Browne ('Phiz'), the third and final illustrator, had to make duplicate steels, as one set would not hold up under the increased press runs. Sales were at 14,000 copies in February 1837, 20,000 in May, 26,000 in September, 29,000 in October, and reached nearly 40,000 within a few weeks of the novel's completion in November. On the numbers alone, Chapman and Hall cleared £14,000.

iv

Such magnitude of success causes problems, especially when it is unprecedented. The initial agreement between Chapman and Hall and Dickens provided for outright purchase of copyright in return for a specified rate of pay per printed page. Anticipating some increase in sales, the publishers had mentioned the possibility of a rise in that rate of payment if the venture proved successful; moreover, when the amount of letterpress was increased, they did increase Dickens's pay scale, by a guinea a sheet. But as *Pickwick* continued, it proved more and more lucrative. There was no legal obligation on Chapman and Hall's part to give Dickens further increases, though he had hopefully anticipated additional rises in proposing the new rate of twenty guineas per number in April 1836: 'If the Work should be very *successful*, after the period I have mentioned, I apprehend you would have no objection to go a little further' (P i. 148).

But if no legal obligation prevailed, there certainly were sound business reasons for keeping Dickens happy. He was, after all, still in mid book. The future success of *Pickwick* depended on his continuing in a pleasant frame of mind. So in March 1837, anticipating the first anniversary of the novel, Chapman and Hall presented Dickens with a bonus of £500, and in early April they gave him a celebratory banquet. Further, Chapman repeatedly urged Dickens, who had extensive financial obligations to his wife, new child, sister-in-law, and occasionally to his mother, father, and brother, to look upon him as his banker whenever he was short. This offer was accepted on more than one occasion, especially when Dickens found himself hard pressed to meet funeral expenses after Mary's sudden death. Chapman and Hall continued to behave thoughtfully and generously towards their prodigy; in July Dickens received from them a set of Pickwickian punch ladles. This last instance of their regard prompted him to write: 'It is indeed a pleasure to be connected with such men (I was going to say booksellers) as you, and I do most unaffectedly and sincerely assure you that my whole endeavours at this moment are directed to perpetuating our most pleasant and friendly association' (P i. 288).

Admirable sentiments, but not entirely candid, as both parties knew. Dickens was very much embroiled in Bentley's affairs, and had repeatedly demonstrated over the past eighteen months a propensity for seeking the most favourable contract, regardless of sentiment. Looking ahead to the termination of *Pickwick* in November, Chapman and Hall were eager to secure Dickens's written agreement for a new serial, of the same kind, to begin shortly afterwards. As early as October 1836 Chapman and Hall had discussed with Dickens a sequal to *Pickwick*.[57] After all, they had hit upon a very successful formula, their printing and distribution machinery was all geared up, and it made sense to capitalize right away on Boz's phenomenal popularity and their equally phenomenal format. So in August 1837 they instructed counsel to draw up papers giving Dickens £2,000 for *Pickwick*, a substantial further rise which brought his remuneration from the initial £14. 3s. 6d. to £100 per part. In return, Dickens was to agree to furnish them with copy for a new novel right away.

One evidence of the good feeling then existing between Dickens and his publishers was his 'semi-business Pickwickian celebration' (P i. 325) held at the conclusion of the novel's serial run. Dickens asked John Francis Degex, Swiss immigrant landlord of the Prince of Wales Hotel in Leicester Place, to supply the feast, and began planning for it as early as 30 October when he wrote to invite Ainsworth. Guests at the dinner, postponed from 14 to 18 November, included Talfourd, who served as Vice-Chairman of the evening, Forster, by now Dickens's literary adviser, Ainsworth, with whom Dickens was shortly to project a book 'to illustrate ancient and modern London in a Pickwick form' (P i. 358, n. 5), Jerdan, Browne, Samuel Lover, Chapman, Hall, John Dickens, and Macready, who noted in his diary that 'We were detained long for dinner, but the day was interesting.'[58] Thomas Hill and George Cruikshank couldn't attend; Hicks, foreman for Bradbury and Evans, and the two partners of the printing firm probably rounded out the guest list. Dickens himself took the chair. Jerdan mentioned (inaccurately) 'the pleasant and uncommon fact . . . that there never had been a line of written agreement', that all participants had proceeded on 'simple verbal assurances', and that 'there had never arisen a word to interrupt or prevent the complete satisfaction of everyone'. Just before Talfourd's toast after a capital dinner, Degex brought in his *chef d'œuvre*, 'a glittering temple of confectionery', topped by a canopy under 'which stood a little figure of the illustrious Mr. Pickwick'. Talfourd then 'proposed Dickens's health in a very good speech',

[57] See Clause 6 in the Agreement with Richard Bentley for 4 November 1836 (P i. 650).

[58] Macready, *Diaries*, i. 426; and P i. 324–31; see also the letter from William Harrison Ainsworth to James Crossley, 22 Nov. 1837, in Ellis, *William Harrison Ainsworth and his Friends*, i. 330–1.

according to Macready, and 'Dickens replied—under strong emotion—most admirably'. Chapman and Hall presented their author with a set of silver 'Apostle' spoons, with characters from *Pickwick* substituted for the apostles on the handles. The evening ended in high spirits and uniform good feelings, which were dissipated neither by the bill of £41. 7s. which Dickens subsequently paid, nor by the terms of the two contracts which had been hammered out that very day.

An additional advantage of serial publication became apparent shortly after the final double number was issued. Since each part had more or less financed the next, when the final part was published and sold, the book was virtually paid for. Thereafter, any sales were almost pure profit. Further, many people wanted back parts to make up complete sets; and others simply wanted the novel in bound form. Thus *Pickwick* continued to have a strong sale even after its serial run was completed. Because of the nature of their original agreement with Dickens, Chapman and Hall were the sole beneficiaries of this additional remuneration; once Dickens completed the text for the twentieth part, he had no more financial interest in *Pickwick*'s sales. And yet, in all fairness, it was his genius which created that demand, and it was in the publishers' interest to keep him with the firm. What could be done?

Indeed, the kind of economic potency that *Pickwick* developed, and the relationship in that novel of process to end, necessitated the reworking of publisher–author arrangements. Was the copyright the right to the text, in whatever form it was published, or was it more narrowly restricted to copyright of the serial edition and editions bound from serial numbers? If stereotypes are made, how does one determine or limit the size of the edition for which copyright is sold? One solution to these problems is to make the author share in the work, and this is the solution which Chapman and Hall reached regarding *Pickwick*.

The contract, witnessed by William Chapman acting for the firm and Charles Molloy acting for Dickens, and finally signed two days after the *Pickwick* banquet, was a complex instrument which attempted to deal with some of these issues. Dickens confirmed that he had previously assigned to Chapman and Hall 'the exclusive licence of printing and publishing for their own use the said Work during the term of Five years from the first day of

November' 1837;[59] 'the gains and profits which can or may be made' by the publication and sale of *Pickwick* belonged, during this period, to Chapman and Hall exclusively. At the same time, Dickens confirmed that he had given Chapman and Hall 'two thirds of the whole Copyright'. In fact, Chapman and Hall were giving Dickens one-third copyright, after five years. The provisions for Dickens's buying in after 1 November 1842 were spelled out in detail: he was then 'at liberty if he [or if his executors, administrators, or assigns] shall think fit so to do to purchase one third part of the stock and printed Copies of the said Book or Work and of the Engravings published therewith'. (Clearly Chapman and Hall believed that they had the rights to Seymour's, Buss's, and Browne's plates too.) Chapman and Hall were compelled to sell this stock to Dickens at cost price. Should either party wish to dispose of his share in the copyright, he must first offer it to the other party at a price which, if necessary, would be arbitrated by a third party. Two other provisions were important. So long as they owned the two-thirds of the copyright, Chapman and Hall retained the right to publish the book, and should 'be allowed and receive all such charges as are justly and usually made by and allowed to the publishers of Works according to the custom of the trade of Publishers'. In effect, that meant that they were allowed to recoup all their costs, and to take a commission on sales, before any division of profits. (The division of profits did not begin of course until Dickens came into his share of the copyright, and had paid for his share of the stock.) The second provision somewhat limited their freedom to publish, and was directly inspired by the success of the format in which *Pickwick* had first appeared: Chapman and Hall would automatically forfeit their copyright if they printed the book 'in any other form or at any less price than the form and price in and at which the same has hitherto been published and sold', or if they printed, published, or sold any selection or abridgement, without the previous consent in writing of the author. Dickens had obviously learned from the Macrone episode. When, ten years later, he first considered publishing the Cheap edition, this clause suddenly assumed special importance.

In effect, Dickens leased back to Chapman and Hall for five years the one-third interest in the copyright of *Pickwick* which

59 The contract, quoted *passim* in the following discussion, appears in P i. 655-8.

they had given him. He was not originally a partner in the venture; had it lost money, he would not have been liable. On the other hand, even with the two-thirds of the copyright Chapman and Hall retained permanently there were constraints on their movements. They might sell the novel in a more expensive format (and they did, binding the parts in cloth for 21s., half morocco for 24s. 6d., or full morocco with gilt leaves for 26s. 6d.) but not a less expensive one. They were thus encouraged to work their copyright only within the existing formats, since at the time there seemed no point in bringing out a freshly printed *de luxe* edition.

Making Dickens a partner in the copyright entangled him in his publishers' affairs, and created the need for elaborate contracts spelling out how each was to sell out to the other should one side wish to dissolve the relationship. Potentially, such agreements could involve Dickens in losses, as well as gains, although with *Pickwick* only profits were divided. Ownership of a third of *Pickwick* was, in this case, both a recognition of Dickens's contribution to its success and a bribe, for above all Chapman and Hall wanted him to write another block-buster. Had the consideration been for *Pickwick* alone, Hall might well have urged that in law they had no further obligation to their author beyond paying him his stipend per sheet, and giving him some 'proportionate' increase as sales mounted. But on the horizon loomed the promise of another rainbow, and another pot of gold; and only Dickens could lead them to it. The contract for *Nickleby* was tied to that executed at the termination of *Pickwick*; Dickens's signature on it could not be obtained until he was happy about the completed work.

Thus accidentally in *Pickwick* Dickens and Chapman and Hall hit upon an arrangement for issuing original works of fiction in serial parts that revolutionized nineteenth-century publishing, distribution, bookselling, author–publisher relations, copyright provisions, and of course fiction itself.[60] There are many instances of other authors such as Lever, Surtees, and Thackeray specifying a contract similar to *Pickwick*'s, or being told that they could earn much more money if they would issue their next book in serial instalments like those of Dickens.[61] The thirty-two-page,

[60] Pollard, 'Serial Fiction', p. 261.
[61] John R. Harvey gives examples of contracts or agreements based on the *Pickwick* model (p. 13).

two-illustration part became a standard to which the public rapidly became accustomed; when *Sketches by Boz* came out in the same format, but with fewer pages, the public was outraged. It is ironic, in view of later events, that there never was a formal contract for *Pickwick*; the arrangements were worked out through the serial run, apparently in each instance to the satisfaction of all parties concerned. But shortly Dickens realized by how far even the *Pickwick* agreement fell shy of fairly remunerating him for the extensive and protracted popularity which his fiction and format obtained. He determined to do better, to share even more largely in the publication and profits of his serials.

4

Dickens and the Burlington Street Brigand

If the name [Bentley] be never whispered in Heaven
(as I should think it never was) it is no doubt muttered
very often in the other place, and it is a great relief to
be free of it.

CHARLES DICKENS (P ii. 200)

DICKENS'S 'THREE-YEAR DUEL' with Richard Bentley
repeats the pattern with Macrone: early friendship,
exchanges of family news, convivial times spent at each
other's homes, minor disagreements patched over but continuing
to rankle, inflammatory demands resolved after long hours of
conference through intermediaries, cold correctness, and finally
an explosion producing total rupture.[1]

Two major areas of friction can be distinguished. First, Dickens
found Bentley's interference in the editorial policy of the *Miscellany*
annoying. Dickens's duties as editor were defined by the second of
nine Agreements with Bentley[2] made on 4 November 1836: to
correspond with contributors, read all submissions and 'give his
judgment upon their eligibility', revise and correct all articles
accepted, furnish the printer with enough matter for six sheets
demy 8vo by the twenty-fourth of every month, and correct
proof. Bentley retained the right to veto the insertion of any
article, and this he gradually extended into co-editorship. A little
over two months after the Agreement was signed, Dickens was

---

[1] Dickens's relations with Bentley are fully discussed by Edgar Johnson, Ch. 4,
and by Kathleen Tillotson in '*Oliver Twist* in Three Volumes' (*The Library*, ser. 5,
18 (1963), 113–32), and her Introduction to the Clarendon edition of the novel
(1966).

[2] The agreements are printed in P i. 648–51, 654–5, 662–4, 666–80; ii. 471–5.

already remonstrating: 'I must beg you once again, not to allow anybody but myself to interfere with the Miscellany' (P i. 223–4). (Someone else, probably Bentley's older brother Samuel, the printer of the *Miscellany*, had tampered with the proof of Lover's *Handy Andy*.) On seeing the April 1837 issue in final form, Dickens wrote a terse note to Bentley: 'I am very sorry to say, that the alterations which have been made in the contents of the Miscellany very greatly injure it—in my opinion at least.'[3]

In September, on returning from his Broadstairs holiday, Dickens was incensed to discover that his arrangements for the October 1837 number had been countermanded, and new articles set up in proof to replace those that he had accepted. 'By these proceedings I have been actually superseded in my office as Editor of the Miscellany; they are in direct violation of my agreement with you, and a gross insult to me',[4] he thundered, making 'a stand upon his Editorial Right', as Cruikshank put it (P i. 308, n. 1). By the fourth Agreement, drafted 28 September 1837, Bentley actually gained editorial ground, becoming explicitly responsible for all arrangements with the contributors for payment, and reserving 'the power if he wishes of originating 3 Articles in every number' (P i. 654). By December, Bentley's exercise of his editorial prerogatives had become so habitual that Dickens, in an uncharacteristically resigned mood, wrote:

My Dear Sir.

Order the Miscellany just as you please. I have no wish or care about the matter.

I merely wish to set myself right with you on two points.

First, I do not choose Captain Marryatt [*sic*] to suppose that *I* pillage his articles from American papers, and advertize his name as a contributor to the Miscellany. I shall write him a line to that effect tomorrow, in my own justification.

---

[3] P i. 243–4. In his 'Retrospective Sketch of Mr. Bentley's connection with Mr. Dickens' (MS. Berg), Richard Bentley alleges that Dickens's 'inexperience' in conducting the *Miscellany* and 'his limited acquaintance with literary men which he was free to admit' forced Bentley to play an active role in procuring contributors and in arranging and choosing articles. 'Mr. Dickens gladly availed himself of this cooperation', Bentley alleges, and 'the most perfect good understanding subsisted' until the end of June 1837.

[4] P i. 308. In his 'Retrospective Sketch' Bentley explains that he had an article set up in type in case Dickens carried out his threat to Cruikshank not to supply an instalment of *Twist*, and Bentley had cancelled one or two other pieces, as he had a right to do, because Dickens refused to consult with him about the *Miscellany*'s contents.

Secondly, I cannot and will not bear the perpetual ill will and heart-burnings and callings and writings consequent upon my accepting papers which are never inserted. In future therefore I would much rather forward you my opinion of the papers I receive, towards the close of every month, and leave you to make out the Notices to correspondents as you think proper. (P i. 339–40)

Relations unaccountably improved in the new year. Bentley was invited to join Dickens and Hullah in a visit to Hampton Court and a ride by the Thames, and by and large their meetings to 'settle the Miscellany' went off amiably enough.

Even though Dickens had threatened to resign on account of editorial principles in September 1837, the rupture with Bentley that resulted in Dickens's giving up the editorship as of 31 January 1839 was primarily caused by money. Some friction developed over Dickens's desire to share materially in the success of the *Miscellany*, but renegotiated agreements appeared to satisfy him on this point: from March 1837 (Agreement signed 17 March) Dickens was to receive £10 for each monthly number selling 6,000 copies, and £5 more for each succeeding 500 copies; and from October (Agreement signed 28 September) Dickens was paid £30, rather than £20, for his editorial duties. The provision for bonuses on sales of 6,000 or more copies of any monthly issue of the *Miscellany* was confirmed four times, on 28 September 1837, 22 September 1838, 27 February 1839, and 2 July 1840. For the January 1838 number Dickens received £25 extra (indicating sales of over 7,500), for the February number an extra £10 (the sum being deposited on 28 April), and on 7 August he appears to have deposited another £10 bonus.[5] The real source of trouble was Dickens's agreement for books.

It will be recalled that on 22 August 1836 Bentley had secured Dickens's agreement to write two novels, each extending to 'three Volumes of 320 pages each and 25 lines in each page' (P i. 648). For the entire copyright of each Bentley was to pay £500 in instalments of two notes for £200 due at six and nine months' date from the delivery of manuscript, and a final £100 if sales

---

[5] See P i. 402, n. 3, and MS. Coutts. The February sales are confirmed in the June 1837 *Miscellany*. Gettmann (p. 143) and P i. 369, n. 3, imply that in Jan. 1839 sales were at 7,500. That figure may be high, and it may incorporate sales at cut prices for export (chiefly to India), which did not count toward Dickens's income.

reached 1,450.[6] In addition, by the Agreement of 4 November that year Dickens committed himself 'to furnish an original article of his own writing, every monthly Number, to consist of about a sheet of 16 pages'. For this, Bentley agreed to pay £21. Dickens's rate of remuneration for original material had risen from nine to twenty guineas per sheet in less than nine months. After a false start with a paper in the genre of *Sketches*, 'Public Life of Mr. Tulrumble', Dickens embarked on *Oliver Twist*, not a series of unconnected humorous articles, but a novel, and an increasingly sombre one at that. The third Bentley Agreement, signed 17 March 1837, extended Dickens's term as editor to five years and set up the bonus provisions for copies sold at trade price (2s. each, 26 as 24). There was no mention made of the Agreement for the novels, and when Forster raised the issue, Dickens replied that although he had no copy of the Agreement of 22 August 1836, he feared Bentley had his second novel on the same terms as the first (P i. 271).

From Calais, where he had gone with Kate and Browne, Dickens wrote to Bentley on 2 July 1837 to propose revising their novel Agreement; he appealed to Bentley's oft-repeated desire 'to treat me "with the utmost liberality" ' (P i. 282), and asked him, in view of the increased popularity of his works since the first Agreement was signed, to consider on what altered footing they should proceed. Bentley went up to London to see Dickens, but as he had no distinct proposition to offer, Bentley suggested that Dickens should go down to Brighton when he had firm proposals. On 14 July Dickens wrote to Bentley at 98 King's Road, Brighton, explaining that he had fallen so behind that he could not go out of town even for a day, and stating what he desired as alterations to their agreements: £600 'for permission to publish 3000 copies of my first Novel Barnaby Rudge' (*né Gabriel Vardon*; P i. 283), with manuscript to be delivered by 1 March 1838, and £700 for 'the same number of copies of my second Novel *Oliver Twist*' (P i. 284), with payments for portions printed in the *Miscellany* deducted. The finished manuscript for this book was promised for 'Midsummer next'. Bentley put off answering as long as possible; after a second letter from Dickens on 7 August he

---

[6] Bentley had originally offered £400 apiece; Dickens persuaded him to raise the figure by a letter of 17 August 1836, but Bentley shrewdly made the concession contingent on substantial sales (P i. 164–5 and n. 2).

finally consented to come up to Doughty Street on Saturday, 12 August:

> I approached him in the usual friendly manner, but was met on his side with an air of coldness and restraint. In reference to his proposition I observed that although he must be well aware that the Agreement entered into between us was a deliberate act & like all contracts mutually binding, & that had his own popularity declined I could have had no claim whatever for a reduction in the consideration I had agreed to pay him—nevertheless I was willing to *present* him with the additional Sums which he specified for the two novels, but that I could not consent to take a limited interest in these two novels, the entire copyright of which I had already agreed for. Moreover I objected to 'Oliver Twist' being considered as his 2nd. novel on the ground that portions of that work had appeared in the Miscellany and the Copyright had therefore become my property as far as was already published. Upon this he exhibited considerable irritability, threatening amongst other intemperate expressions that he would not write the novel at all. His object was evidently to provoke me, failing in which attempt he proposed to refer the matter to the arbitration of Mr. Serjeant Talfourd. (P i. 292–3, n. 5)

In the skirmish that followed, Dickens threatened to withdraw altogether, so Bentley, realizing that a 'sullen editor and a reluctant novelist were worse than none' (J, p. 238), surrendered, conceding to Dickens almost everything he demanded, and in some ways going beyond Dickens's original proposal. By the Agreement outlined and signed on 28 September, *Oliver Twist* was to be continued in the *Miscellany* until Midsummer 1838, when Bentley was to receive the completed manuscript in return for £500 and a three-year assignment of copyright, with the stipulation that it was not to be published in the Standard Novels, or in numbers or parts. *Miscellany* payments were *not* to be deducted from this price. Thereafter, half the copyright was to revert to Dickens, and further editions were to be published on joint account. *Barnaby Rudge*, due by the end of October 1838, and thus the *second* novel, was to be published on the same terms, Dickens receiving for it £700.

Dickens's victory is significant. Not only did he once again increase the price of *Barnaby*, this time by £200, not only did he succeed once again in making one work serve two functions, *Oliver Twist* counting both as his *Miscellany* contribution and as a novel, but also he gained at last a share in his copyrights. If his behaviour at times was touchy and high-handed, it must be admitted that the agreements he wrested from his publishers did not ruin them: he seems to have asked for a share in the profits which they could afford to give.

But, favourable as this Agreement was, Dickens was still not satisfied. Edward S. Morgan, Bentley's chief clerk and accountant, believed with Bentley that Dickens's 'feeling of discontent so pertinaciously exhibited was to be attributed to the meddling agency of some person by whose advice Mr. Dickens allowed himself to be swayed'—i.e. John Forster (P i. 223-4, n. 3). Others have had harsh words for Forster, who could be bullying, over-bearing, and stubborn. He was also a loyal friend, and may well have felt it his obligation to point out to Dickens that he was undervalued and overcommitted. Whether Forster was the instigator of this new request or not, Dickens applied to Bentley for yet another alteration in their agreements: could *Barnaby* not follow *Oliver* in the *Miscellany* first, and then be published in three volumes (P i. 369)? As in the previous cases, Dickens wanted one work to fulfil two obligations. He appealed to the pathetic example given in the last volume of Lockhart's *Life*, just out: 'The conduct of three different stories [*Nickleby*, *Barnaby*, and the monthly *Miscellany* instalment] at the same time, and the production of a larger portion of each, every month, would have been beyond Scott himself' (P i. 370). But the appeal was disingenuous: Dickens had just finished *Grimaldi* for which Bentley had paid £300,[7] and twelve days later he agreed to complete a new comic work, 'Boz's Annual Register and Obituary of Blue Devils', for Chapman and Hall before Christmas.

Bentley did not want to agree; having conceded just this point on *Oliver Twist*, he was now faced with it again. The wrangling continued for months; it concluded, as usual, with Bentley's surrender. The Articles of Agreement executed on 22 September 1838, the sixth with Bentley, confirmed in detail the provisions of earlier covenants, except that the price for a three-year lease on *Oliver Twist* was reduced to £400. Further, it stipulated, in the seventeenth and eighteenth of twenty-five articles, that *Barnaby Rudge* would run in the *Miscellany* in eighteen monthly parts, for

---

[7] Bentley's promissory note payable at three months, given to Dickens on 29 Nov. 1837, was credited to his account on 3 Mar. 1838 (MS. Coutts).

which Dickens would receive £21 per sheet, and an additional £422 on completion of the manuscript, or £800 in all. *Barnaby* was to begin in the month following the conclusion of *Oliver Twist*. Two days before signing these articles, Dickens inscribed a cautiously cordial letter to his publisher, apologizing that the long postponement

has greatly chafed and irritated me, and so led to expressions of feeling on my part which I should be hurt if I supposed likely to give you any pain. Let me assure you with real sincerity that in our future inter-course all proposals emanating from you in a spirit of fairness and candour will be most cheerfully and cordially responded to by me; and that it will be my endeavour as I feel it will henceforth be yours to make our connection a source of mutual pleasure and advantage. (P i. 436)

The rhetoric smacks of a wary neutrality, which may have been favourably altered by the dinner which Dickens proposed for the Wednesday after the signing of the agreements, 'to put a less formal termination to our differences'.

By January 1839 war had been declared once more. Dickens was disheartened both by Bentley's continued editorial interference, and by the contrast between the profits from *Oliver* enjoyed by Bentley and 'the paltry, wretched, miserable sum it brought to me (not equal to what is every day paid for a novel that sells fifteen hundred copies at most)' (P i. 493). This is an exaggeration: Dickens actually received almost £800 for *Oliver*, a sum nearly equal to that Bentley had given Maria Edgeworth in 1834 for an edition of 3,000 copies of *Helen*, and considerably above Bentley's average offer of slightly more than £250 for an edition of 1,000.[8] On the other hand, Bentley was certainly imprudent not to offer Dickens some additional stipend; Chapman and Hall were far more generous over *Pickwick*. In the *Miscellany* alone, the sales of *Oliver* sometimes exceeded 6,000. Dickens had proposed 3,000 as the total printing in book form; that was probably reduced for the 1838 three-volume edition to somewhere around 2,000. Of that edition, 528 were immediately subscribed, all in cloth for

---

[8] Gettmann, p. 139. The £400 for the final manuscript was paid in bills of four and six months' date from delivery of the manuscript, and credited to Dickens's account on 23 Feb. and 23 Apr. 1839 (MS. Coutts), thus confirming Tillotson's speculation that the date of delivery was two or three days after 20 Oct., the time stipulated in the 27 Feb. 1839 Agreement (see her Introduction to Clarendon *Twist*, p. xxiii; and P i. 677). The 27 Feb. Agreement says that £500 'has been paid'. I find no deposit for the remaining £100.

18s. 3d., 25 as 24, except 62 as 57 in quires at 16s. 9d.[9] A Dublin bookseller ordered 100 bound copies, testimony that Dickens had at last arrived across the Irish sea.[10] Yet Bentley had tried to shave the price for a three years' lease on copyright by £100 in September 1838. And his niggardliness had been carried to the extent of deducting the half pages by which Dickens fell short of his contracted sixteen, though after Dickens irately reminded him that he was often forced to cut his manuscript in order to accommodate other matter, some of it inserted by Bentley, the publisher apparently restored full payment. 'The consciousness that I have still [in January 1839] the slavery and drudgery of another work on the same journeyman-terms', Dickens complained to Forster,

the consciousness that my books are enriching everybody connected with them but myself, and that I, with such a popularity as I have acquired, am struggling in old toils, and wasting my energies in the very height and freshness of my fame, and the best part of my life, to fill the pockets of others, while for those who are nearest and dearest to me I can realise little more than a genteel subsistence: all this puts me out of heart and spirits: and I cannot—cannot and will not—under such circumstances that keep me down with an iron hand, distress myself by beginning this tale until I have had time to breathe; and until the intervention of the summer, and some cheerful days in the country, shall have restored me to a more genial and composed state of feeling. There —for six months *Barnaby Rudge* stands over. And but for you, it should stand over altogether. For I do most solemnly declare that morally, before God and man, I hold myself released from such hard bargains as these, after I have done so much for those who drove them. This net that has been wound about me so chafes me, so exasperates and irritates my mind, that to break it at whatever cost—*that* I should care nothing for—is my constant impulse. But I have not yielded to it. I merely declare that I must have a postponement very common in all literary agreements; and for the time I have mentioned—six months from the conclusion of *Oliver* in the *Miscellany*—I wash my hands of any fresh accumulation of labour, and resolve to proceed as cheerfully as I can with that which already presses upon me. (P i. 493–4)

9 Tillotson, Introduction to Clarendon *Twist*, pp. xxiv–xxv; and John Carter, *Binding Variants in English Publishing, 1820–1900* (London, Constable; New York, R. R. Smith, 1932), pp. 107–8. Thirty-nine of those in quires went to Richardson, who dealt mainly with India.

10 See Tillotson, '*Oliver Twist* in Three Volumes', p. 121 and n. 2. The thirty-five booksellers and libraries who initially subscribed paid £463. 16s. 9d., according to Frederic G. Kitton, *The Novels of Charles Dickens: A Bibliography and Sketch* (London, Elliott Stock, 1897), p. 32.

As Edgar Johnson rightly observes, Dickens, determined to have his own way, found that 'Bentley's every way of doing things rasped him' (J, p. 247). Once again, he was disingenuous in his complaint: the desire for six months' rest cannot be squared with his recent agreements to edit the *Pic Nic Papers* for Colburn, and to write 'Boz's Annual' for Chapman and Hall in addition to *Nickleby*. Bentley saw the opening and took advantage of it. Although finding 'no clause under our Agreement [of 22 September 1838] which entitles you "to require a postponement of six months"', he will agree, *provided that* the contract is continued by six months beyond its stipulated date of expiration, and *provided that* Dickens suspend all his other labours, excepting *Nickleby* (P i. 495, n. 2). He won the point, but lost the debate. Dickens was furious:

I do *not*, and will not receive it as a favour or concession from you—
. . . I will *not* consent to extend my engagements with you for the additional term of six months— . . . if you presume to address me again in the style of offensive impertinence which marks your last communication, I will from that moment abandon at once and for ever all conditions and agreements that may exist between us, and leave the whole question to be settled by a jury as soon as you think proper to bring it before one. (P i. 495–6)

Two days later, on 28 January 1839, despite Bentley's conciliatory offer of £40 a year just for the use of his name, Dickens made it clear he was resigning as editor; that evening he asked Ainsworth to succeed him at once. All through February solicitors for both sides hammered out two more agreements, and on the 27th Dickens signed both documents, the first confirming his resignation and the provisions concerning bonuses and *Oliver Twist*, whose price was restored to £500, and the second renegotiating *Barnaby Rudge*. It would not appear in the *Miscellany* now, but instead was to be completed by 1 January 1840. Dickens agreed not to commence or write another work, besides *Nickleby*, the 'Annual', and the *Pic Nic Papers*, until it was finished. And for it, Bentley agreed to pay £2,000 down (in bills at four, six, and eight months), £1,000 in bills of like date if sales reached 10,000, and another £1,000 in bills if sales reached 15,000.

Dickens did not start work on *Barnaby* until October. Throughout the spring and summer of 1839 he was busy on *Nickleby*, having 'stiff work' to finish the double number for October in time, and 'sending Hicks the last 20 pages of MS by the Night coach' from Broadstairs (P i. 581). On the third of October he told Cruikshank, who was to illustrate it, that he was 'going forthwith tooth and nail at Barnaby, and shall have MS by the middle of the month for your exclusive eye' (P i. 589). At the end of the month, Kate was delivered of a third child, Kate Macready Dickens; to accommodate his growing family and rising income, Dickens entered into 'the agonies of house-letting, house-taking, title proving and disproving, premium paying, fixture valuing, and other ills too numerous to mention' (P i. 603), which concluded in his taking Devonshire Terrace from December 1839 until 1851. Despite these distractions he continued to work at *Barnaby*, which moved 'not at racehorse speed, but yet as fast (I think) as under these unsettled circumstances could possibly be expected' (P i. 605). He realized he couldn't complete the novel by 1 January, but hoped to get an extension, and to finish it as speedily thereafter as possible, so as to take up his new project, *Master Humphrey's Clock*, the proposals for which had been signed by all parties on 15 October.

On Saturday afternoon, 14 December 1839, Dickens happened to glance at the *Morning Herald*, and saw there an announcement from Bentley that *Barnaby Rudge* was 'preparing for publication'. Having told Cruikshank that he was not prepared to finish *Barnaby* by the January deadline, and having assumed that Cruikshank would so inform Bentley, Dickens was touched to the quick by the repetition of the same kind of pressure Macrone had tried to put on him three years earlier. He instructed his solicitors, Smithson and Mitton, to inform Bentley through his agents that Dickens was willing for Bentley to avail himself of the final clause in their 27 February Agreement: if any other work is written or published or advertised to be written or published before *Rudge* then Bentley 'shall be at liberty to put an end to this Agreement if he shall think so fit but not otherwise' (P i. 675). This clause, inserted because earlier contracts had given Bentley no suitable recourse if Dickens defaulted, was now turned against the publisher, as Dickens declared himself willing to sacrifice the £2,000–£4,000 to be quit of Bentley once and for all.

Dickens complained further to Smithson and Mitton about the manner of Bentley's advertising, which coupled his name with other books and hawked them about 'in a manner calculated to do me serious prejudice' (P i. 617). Bentley was known as a puffer, a practice to which Dickens and Forster objected.[11] But the more immediate source of irritation, if cause for complaint were needed at all, was to be found in Bentley's treatment of *Jack Sheppard*, Ainsworth's Newgate novel published at 25*s*. on 15 October. Bentley had done what he could to associate Ainsworth's work with Dickens's, announcing it as 'uniform in size and price with *Oliver Twist*', and reissuing it from December 1839 in fifteen weekly parts.[12] Feeling that he had no protection against Bentley's using his new work in a similar way, and unwilling to 'arm Mr. Bentley with such a powerful engine of annoyance and injury to [his] own reputation, as a new work . . . would assuredly become in his hands just now', Dickens declared that when the specified time came he would not be prepared with the manuscript.[13] In a covering letter to Mitton, however, he hinted at compromise: 'you must use entirely your own discretion as to the prospect you hold out of their having the MS at some *un*stipulated time' (P i. 618).

The acrimonious exchanges that followed on Mitton's transmission of this letter to Bentley's solicitor Gregory are recounted by Johnson in detail; it was indeed 'War to the knife and with no quarter on either side . . . with the Burlington Street Brigand' (P i. 619). Macready offered to mediate, though he confided in his diary that he thought Dickens's case indefensible: 'He makes a contract, which he considers advantageous at the time, but subsequently finding his talent more lucrative than he had supposed, he refused to fulfil the contract.'[14] Expert legal counsel told Bentley that he could not obtain an injunction restraining Dickens from writing the *Clock*, as no Court of Equity could compel him to write *Barnaby*, and would therefore 'not give partial relief by enforcing the negative stipulation' (P i. 621, n. 8). After threats issued from both sides, and printed notices arguing the case appeared in the papers, negotiations finally got under way,

[11] See Forster's attack on puffing in his long, censorious review of *Jack Sheppard* in the *Examiner*, 3 Nov. 1839.

[12] Despite Dickens's fears, some reviewers were able to distinguish clearly between his novel and Ainsworth's; see the *Athenaeum* review, 26 Oct. 1839.

[13] P i. 617–18. Both Bentley's attorney Gregory, and his son George Bentley, considered Dickens's charge trumped up. George Bentley concluded that 'Dickens was a very clever, but he was not an honest man' (P i. 618, n. 2). See also his letter to *The Times* recounting Dickens's relations with his father, written 7 Dec. 1871.

[14] *Diaries*, ii. 45–6.

Forster for Dickens and William Jerdan for Bentley.[15] The ninth
and last Agreement, signed on 2 July 1840, severed all relations.
Dickens paid £1,500 for *Oliver Twist* and for the surrender of
Bentley's claims on any of his writings, past and future, and also
purchased the Cruikshank plates for *Twist*, and the remaining
stock, 1,002 copies of the 1840 edition in quires, for £750.
Bentley received the right to buy prints of the illustrations at 4s.
per hundred. Chapman and Hall agreed to deduct £2,250 from
the £3,000 they would pay Dickens for the licence to issue *Rudge*
in numbers, and also in book form 'for six months after the
publication of the last number' (P ii. 93–4; 94, n. 2). That ill-fated
novel, of which only two chapters were yet written, had risen in
value in less than four years from £200 for outright copyright to
£3,000 for a six months' lease. At the same time, Dickens had
consolidated all his publications with one firm, Chapman and
Hall, 'my trusty friends'.[16]

In Edgar Johnson's view, the heart of the breach with Bentley
was a conflict between two radically opposed, equally stubborn
temperaments. Bentley at every stage had the law on his side,
though he used this advantage very clumsily. Finding legal
redress unsatisfactory, he gave in so grudgingly, and continued to
indulge in such petty annoyances, as to inflame Dickens further.
On Dickens's side was the inescapable fact that it was his talent
alone which had achieved such spectacular profits for his publishers, and so little for himself. No contract without an escalation
clause can adequately remunerate an author for an unexpected
success; it was Dickens's misfortune to enter the publishing world
before such clauses were standard, as it was in part his achievement to make them a regular feature of later agreements (P i.
164–5, n. 1).

One cannot help feeling, however, that Dickens behaved out-
rageously at times.[17] And yet, while deploring his methods, it must
be conceded that his grievance was real. Granted that a publisher

[15] See P ii. 31–3, for Dickens's reaction to Bentley's Feb. 1840 notices, and ii.
85, n. 2, for Jerdan's account of negotiations on behalf of Bentley.

[16] P i. 601–2; William Chapman, a Richmond solicitor serving as counsel to his
younger brother Edward, insisted that something further be done to secure
Chapman and Hall against the loss of their £2,250, leading to a temporary
estrangement.

[17] J. W. T. Ley thinks that Dickens hadn't 'fair play on his side' in the disputes
with either Macrone or Bentley (F II. i. 98, n. 101).

takes the risk, in buying a manuscript, that he may lose some, or all, of his initial investment, and therefore deserves the whole profits from a successful venture. But keeping a remunerative author depends upon much more than merely fulfilling the letter of a contract: had Bentley been less backward in additional compensation, more like Chapman and Hall, some of the trouble might have been avoided. On the other hand, Dickens was not above holding a stick over his 'trusty friends' either, urging them, through Forster, to do 'something handsome—even handsomer perhaps than they dreamt of doing' (P i. 562). It was not altogether inconvenient to have the examples of Macrone and Bentley to reinforce his argument.

5

'The Best of Booksellers
Past, Present, or to Come'

'How should you like to grow up a clever man, and write books?' said the old gentleman.

'I think I would rather read them Sir' replied Oliver.

'What! Wouldn't you like to be a book-writer?' said the old gentleman.

Oliver considered a little while, and at last said he should think it would be a much better thing to be a bookseller; upon which the old gentleman laughed heartily, and declared he had said a very good thing, which Oliver felt glad to have done, though he by no means knew what it was.

Vide Oliver Twist in which the old gentleman does *not* say, though I *do* that Chapman and Hall are the best of booksellers past, present, or to come; and my trusty friends. Which I give under my hand for the benefit of Edward Chapman, his book, this fourteenth day of November 1839.

Witness   CHARLES DICKENS[1]
Boz

DICKENS'S QUOTATION OF A PASSAGE from *Oliver Twist* inscribed on the endpaper of a bound first edition of *Pickwick*, presented to Edward Chapman at the successful conclusion of *Nicholas Nickleby*, conveniently draws together the major publishing enterprises since 1835. The steady cordial relations between Dickens and his 'best of booksellers' which had commenced in February 1836, and had been repeatedly ratified since, contrasted vividly with the erratic, frustrating, and eventually hostile associations with Macrone, Bentley, and Colburn.

[1] P i. 601–2; facsimile reproduced in Waugh, facing p. 44.

After the early numbers of *Pickwick*, Chapman, Hall, and Dickens had settled into a routine; John Forster was growing into a deeply trusted adviser to all three;[2] and the printing firm of Bradbury and Evans, accustomed to Dickens's particular handwriting and demands, were coping easily with the special pressures of serial publication. Despite some hitches—Browne's illness postponed the plates to XIV for one month, and Dickens was perennially late with copy—*Nickleby* went so smoothly that an account of its issuance provides an opportunity to examine some details of Dickens's publishing arrangements passed over in earlier chapters.

Dickens approached the writing of his new work in good spirits, though he complained in January 1838 that his 'month's work has been dreadful' (P i. 359). He finished *Grimaldi* for Bentley and *Sketches of Young Gentlemen* for publication anonymously by Chapman and Hall, got through his budget of editing for the *Miscellany* and his instalment of *Oliver Twist*, and suffered with fair humour the birth and subsequent nocturnal disruptions of his first son, Charles Culliford Boz Dickens. He was eager to clear his desk so that he might travel with Browne to Yorkshire at the end of the month to look into cheap boarding-schools whose abuses he thought of exposing in his new book. There was some urgency in getting started: by a contract signed on the same day as the Deed of Licence, Assignment, and Covenants for *Pickwick*, the manuscript of the first number was due on 15 March.

Dickens's agreement for *Nickleby*, to which we have already referred, called for a work 'of similar character and of the same extent and contents in point of quantity' as *Pickwick*, which Chapman and Hall promised to publish in the identical format (P i. 659). The manuscript of each part was to be delivered on the fifteenth day of the month.[3] On delivery of each month's instalment Chapman and Hall were to pay Dickens £150, for a total of £3,000; in return, they were granted a lease on the copyright for

[2] Waugh gives this description of Forster: 'Of all the counsellors and literary advisers who have helped the firm of Chapman & Hall during its hundred years of existence, John Forster was undoubtedly the most influential; for in his generation he occupied a practically unique position. It is not, perhaps, too fanciful to say that, in his fashion, he bridged the gulf between the Patron of the eighteenth century and the Literary Agent of the twentieth' (pp. 27–8).

[3] Monod has erred in stating that *Nicholas Nickleby* I 'was to be published on March 15, 1838' (p. 139).

five years, to be computed from the day on which the last number was published.[4] Thereafter, the copyright reverted entirely to Dickens. This was the first time Dickens could look forward to owning a work of his own hand outright. Three other provisions, to some extent similar to those in the *Pickwick* deed, allowed Dickens at the expiration of the five years' lease to buy the unsold stock and the 'engravings' at cost,[5] guaranteed both sides the right of first refusal should either side wish to sell, and stipulated that Dickens's written permission must be secured before the novel could be published in any other form or at a lesser price than *Pickwick*, or issued in an abridged version.

But rumour exaggerated Dickens's financial status. *En route* to Yorkshire, Dickens chanced while waiting for the York coach on Saturday morning, 3 February, to read in the 26 January *Durham Advertiser* a brief biography by Dr. Robert Shelton Mackenzie, whose later *Life* is famous for advancing Cruikshank's claim to have originated *Twist*. Mackenzie instanced a string of false statistics to show 'the uncertainty of literary remuneration': Chapman and Hall,

having with some difficulty, been persuaded to become the Pickwick publishers, agreed to give him ten pounds a month for each number, or £120, for the whole work. After the second number, the sale became so immense as to induce the publishers to give him £70 a month; and since number 10, he has had one half of the profits, including those of the first numbers. By the Pickwick Papers alone he will net between £2000. and £3000.

(cited in P i. 367, n. 2)

Further, Mackenzie reported that Dickens was now in receipt of £3,000 a year, and that Bentley allowed him £1,000 a year to edit the *Miscellany*. Dickens dashed off a hasty contradiction, which the editor duly printed on 9 February, and Dickens found Mackenzie's subsequent letter of explanation 'quite satisfactory' (P i. 375).

Dickens's popularity had also encouraged Grub Street imitations and cheap theatrical plagiarisms. *Pickwick* and *Oliver* were on the boards after twelve instalments, *Nickleby* after eight, with tableaux

---

[4] Determining the date of publication was another small wrinkle in serial issue. Did the statutory copyright period commence for each part on the day it was published, or only when the book was published as a bound volume and deposited in the British Museum?

[5] Chapman and Hall were entitled to retain 500 'copies'.

arranged after Browne's plates. In an effort to forestall such adaptations, which Dickens complained tended 'to vulgarize the characters, to destroy or weaken in the minds of those who see them the impressions I have endeavoured to create, and consequently to lessen the after-interest in their progress' (P i. 463), he wrote an exuberant 'Proclamation' for the March number of *Sketches by Boz*, which Chapman and Hall had set up in a riot of type-faces impossible to reproduce here:

[SB, Pt. V,] [1 March 1838] [elaborate caps]
Proclamation. [b.l.]

═══════════

Whereas [b.l.] we are the only true and
lawful "BOZ." [b.l.]

And Whereas [b.l.] it hath been reported to us, who are commencing a New Work, to be called —THE

LIFE & ADVENTURES

OF

NICHOLAS NICKLEBY

THAT some dishonest dullards, resident in the by-streets and cellars of this town, impose upon the unwary and credulous, by producing cheap and wretched imitations of our delectable Works. And Whereas [b.l.] we derive but small comfort under this injury, from the knowledge that the dishonest dullards aforesaid, cannot, by reason of their mental smallness, follow near our heels, but are constrained to creep along by dirty and little-frequented ways, at a most respectful and humble distance behind.

And Whereas, [b.l.] in like manner, as some other vermin are not worth the killing for the sake of their carcases, so these kennel pirates are not worth the powder and shot of the law, inasmuch as whatever damages they may commit, they are in no condition to pay any.

THIS IS TO GIVE NOTICE

[elaborate caps, b.l.]

FIRSTLY,

TO PIRATES.

THAT we have at length devised a mode of execution for them, so summary and terrible, that if any gang or gangs thereof presume to hoist but one shred of the colours of the good ship NICKLEBY, we will hang them on gibbets so lofty and enduring, that their remains shall be a monument of our just vengeance to all succeeding ages; and it shall not lie in the power of any Lord High Admiral, on earth, to cause them to be taken down again.

SECONDLY

TO THE PUBLIC.

THAT in our new work, as in our preceding one, it will be our aim to amuse, by producing a rapid succession of characters and incidents, and describing them as cheerfully and pleasantly as in us lies; that we have wandered into fresh fields and pastures new, to seek materials for the purpose; and that, in behalf of NICHOLAS NICKLEBY, we confidently hope to enlist both their heartiest merriment, and their kindliest sympathies.

THIRDLY,

TO THE POTENTATES OF PATERNOSTER-ROW.

THAT from the THIRTIETH DAY OF MARCH next, until further notice, we shall hold our Levees, as heretofore, on the last evening but one of every month, between the hours of seven and nine, at our Board of Trade, Number ONE HUNDRED AND EIGHTY-SIX in the STRAND, LONDON: where we again request the attendance (in vast crowds) of their accredited agents and ambassadors. Gentlemen to wear knots upon their shoulders; and patent cabs to draw up their doors towards the grand entrance, for the convenience of loading.

> GIVEN [b.l.] at the office of our Board of Trade aforesaid, in the presence of our Secretaries, EDWARD CHAPMAN & WILLIAM HALL, on this Twenty-eighth day of February, One Thousand Eight Hundred and Thirty-eight.

(Signed)   *Boz.*

The 'dishonest dullards' were not dissuaded, however; Michael Slater has discussed the 'cheap and wretched imitations' that plagued Dickens during *Nickleby*'s serial run, even audaciously parodying the *Nickleby* Proclamation itself![6] But the public's appetite was, if anything, whetted by all the publicity; vast crowds did attend the levee, patent cabs did draw up with their doors towards the grand entrance, for the convenience of loading; nearly 50,000 copies of Number I were spirited away from the Strand in, at most, a few days' time (F II. ii. 109; confirmed IV. ii. 302). As Sylvère Monod observes, the success of *Nickleby* I 'was the supreme and striking confirmation of *Pickwick*'s triumph'.[7]

The pressures of his other work made it impossible for Dickens to adhere strictly to his contractual agreements to have his *Nickleby* copy ready for the fifteenth of the month; with *Oliver* until 22 October and the *Miscellany* until February 1839, plus other small projects like 'The Lamplighter' which he hoped (in vain) Macready would produce, and the usual round of parties, holidays, and domestic worries, he was nearly always late, and was never able to get a month or two ahead. The first number probably reached the printer in time;[8] indeed, Dickens sent in on 22 February the first chapter 'to print as soon as you like' (P i. 379). Sometime in mid March the whole first number was reset, Dickens returning virtually uncorrected proofs for that purpose (P i. 389). Throughout *Nickleby*'s run, and subsequently, Dickens used galleys the way we use a typist: to translate foul copy into a fresh, clean text, which could then be evaluated for length, proportion, and effect, even though authors' manuals of the period emphatically chastised authors who corrected their manuscripts only in proof.

[6] *The Composition and Monthly Publication of Nicholas Nickleby* (Menston, Yorkshire, The Scolar Press, 1973).

[7] *Dickens the Novelist*, p. 141.

[8] There is a good deal of confusion about this, Forster inaccurately reconstructing the events (II. iv. 124). The Pilgrim editors conjecture that about 100 slips were needed to fill thirty-two pages in the 1837–9 period (P i. 547, and n. 2); by the end of *Nickleby*, that seems to have been cut nearly in half, since Dickens thought not more than 105 would be needed for the fifty-two printed pages of text in the final double number (P i. 580). If Forster is correct in recalling that twenty-eight slips were written by 21 Feb., then the twenty-four additional slips composed on 8 and 9 Mar. (P i. 385) would, with a few intervening ones, finish the third chapter and the first number, not just the chapter alone as P i. 385, n. 3 says.

But if the first number was written on schedule, the others were frequently not. On 20 May he had finished but one chapter for June (III), he only began Number V on 10 July, he had not done the last chapter of Number VII by 20 September, and fell even further behind in November, doubting for a time whether there would ever be a December number.[9] After freeing himself from the *Miscellany* at the end of January 1838, Dickens looked forward to an easier time, but alas, he faced February. On 9 February he was mulling plans; by the eighteenth he was fuming about 'this fraudulent month of February, which for the sake of periodical Writers should be blotted from the calendar, although I was born in it, or made a reasonable length' (P i. 509–10). He finished the March instalment late on the evening of the twenty-first, and hoped to plunge right into the next one, having no other tasks to intervene. But the hopeful promise to Evans and his foreman-printer, Charles Hicks, that at last he would be mending his ways was broken: writing to Forster on 5 March from Exeter, where he was fixing up a cottage for his parents, Dickens requested that the printers be informed 'how it is that they will not get the copy for the next No. as soon as I promised' (P i. 521). He had reached only the second chapter ('I think Mrs. Nickleby's love scene will come out rather unique' (P i. 527)) by the fifteenth; and then Bradbury and Evans grew nervous because Easter week-end fell on the last days of the month. Hard at work on 22 and 23 March, Dickens was correcting proof three days later (P i. 528, 529, 533). 'Nicklebeian fetters' kept him in check in April, too, as he was 'doing the Snail at present—not the Railroad' (P i. 542, 540). In May things improved suddenly: Dickens hoped 'to get on like a house on fire' and to come up from Petersham, where he was staying at Elm Cottage, to correct the last chapters of the June number (XV). Exultantly he asked Hicks what Evans would think 'when he gets the copy on the 10th' (P i. 549). Alas, next month copy went astray and had to be redone, and on 11 July Number XVII for August was 'yet an infant' (P i. 556, 561). September was devoted almost entirely to the difficulties of winding up 'so many people *in parts*, and mak[ing] each part tell by itself' (P i. 561). Dickens was thinking about the end on 4 September, and from the fifth to the twentieth his Diary entries specify 'work'.

---

9 P i. 400, and n. 3; i. 413 and 633; i. 437, the chapter he hopes will make twelve printed pages being 22; i. 457 and 459.

The Preface was completed on 15 September, and on Friday afternoon the twentieth he wrapped up 'the last little chapter' in a parcel and posted it to Bradbury and Evans from Ramsgate (P i. 642). Chapman and Hall, who served regularly as middlemen on the illustrations, had already brought down Browne's sketches for the final illustrations, so there would be no unpleasant surprises as with *Oliver*.

His recurrent tardiness with *Nickleby* caused Dickens some small loss of income from a source that was later very lucrative, namely, American publishers. On 14 June 1837 Henry Charles Carey, managing partner of the Philadelphia firm of Carey, Lea, and Blanchard, wrote for the first time to 'Mr. Saml. Dickens' to offer him £25 in the form of a four months' draft on the firm's Liverpool bankers, W. and I. Brown and Co., for the parts of *Pickwick* which the firm had already printed (P i. 652). Carey had published Dickens's earlier works in somewhat unfamiliar guises: the First Series of *Sketches by Boz* was 'transmogrified' into *Watkins Tottle, and other sketches, illustrative of every-day life and every-day people* (1,250 copies of two volumes published in May 1836); the Second Series appeared in February 1837 as *Sketches by Boz . . . Being a continuation of 'Watkins Tottle, and other sketches'* (1,250 copies of one volume). On 1 June 1837 *The Tuggs's at Ramsgate*, published separately six months earlier, in an edition of 1,000, was combined with the Philadelphia Second Series of *Sketches* and *The Pantomime of Life* in a new edition of 1,000 copies. And in April 1837 Carey, Lea, and Blanchard had brought out 2,000 copies of a two-volume edition containing the *Public Life of Mr. Tulrumble* and other tales and sketches from *Bentley's Miscellany* and *The Library of Fiction* in Volume I, and *Oliver Twist* plus other matter in Volume II.[10] For none of these works had the firm offered Dickens anything. Nor were they obliged to, either in law or equity, since no reciprocal copyright agreement existed between England and the United States.

Still, it must have been clear to the firm, which had by June 1837 printed several thousand copies of Dickens's works, that he was a coming author, whose goodwill it might be useful to secure. Carey had begun publishing *Pickwick* in November 1836: 1,500 copies of the text of the first four numbers had been bound

[10] David Kaser, ed., *The Cost Book of Carey & Lea, 1825–1838* (Philadelphia, Univ. of Pennsylvania Press, 1963), *passim*.

up in boards with paper labels in one volume, duodecimo, to retail at 45 cents.[11] Each succeeding four parts were similarly printed and sold; to June 1837 Carey had issued three editions of I, two of II, and one of III, totalling 5,000 copies of each volume.[12] The money, he explained, 'we beg you will accept not as a compensation, but as a memento of the fact that unsolicited a bookseller has sent an author, if not money, at least a fair representative of it' (P i. 652). He then went on to explain how little margin there was in his publication, and to inquire about the possibility of arranging for early proofs of Dickens's forthcoming novel *Barnaby Rudge*.[13] Dickens did not reply until 26 October,

[11] Henry C. Lea, *American Literary Gazette*, 15 May 1867, printing an open letter to G. W. Childs dated 10 May; quoted in an appendix to R. Shelton Mackenzie's *Life of Charles Dickens*, 'The Dickens Controversy' (Philadelphia, T. B. Peterson and Bros., 1870), pp. 5–6; and in Eugene Exman's *The Brothers Harper: A Unique Publishing Partnership and its Impact Upon the Cultural Life of America from 1817 to 1853* (New York, Harper & Row, 1965), pp. 58–9; cf. W. Glyde Wilkins, 'Dickens and his First American Publishers', *Dickensian*, 9 (1913), 258; and P i. 322, n. 2.

[12] The complete printing history of the Philadelphia *Pickwick* is as follows: *Pickwick Papers*.

Part 1.	Nov. 1836	1,500	[first edition]
	Dec. 1836	1,500	second edition
	31 May 1837	2,000	third edition
	[Sept.–Nov.] 1837	750	fourth edition
	[Sept.–Nov.] 1837	500	[fifth edition?]
		6,250	
Part 2.	Dec. 1836	2,500	[first edition]
	May 1837	2,500	[second edition?]
	[Sept.–Nov.] 1837	1,000	[third edition?]
		6,000	
Part 3.	May 1837	5,000	[first edition]
	[Sept.–Nov.] 1837	500	[second edition?]
		5,500	
Part 4.	[Sept.–Nov.] 1837	5,000	[first edition]
Part 5.	Dec. 1837	5,000	[first edition]

See Kaser, *passim*.

[13] P i. 652, n. 3 notes that in the one-volume 1838 illustrated *Pickwick* the costs were completely covered by the sales of the first 1,600 copies out of an edition of 5,000, and that all the rest was pure profit. But that of course was published in Jan. 1838, six months after Carey's letter referring to the close margins on the five-volume unillustrated *Pickwick*, of which only three volumes had yet been issued. The Pilgrim note differs significantly from that in Kaser, pp. 234–5. According to Barnes (*Authors, Publishers and Politicians*, p. 52), Carey and Lea were the first American firm to make a systematic effort toward paying foreign authors an

when he expressed his 'great pleasure to hear of the popularity of the Pickwick Papers in America—a country in which . . . I take a high interest, and with which I hope one day to become better acquainted' (P i. 322). Declining the money, he asked instead for a copy of the work. When he later saw the 1838 one-volume edition he thought the illustrations by Onwhyn and Crowquill vile (P i. 414 and n. 2). As *Barnaby* was not yet settled, he declined to enter into any discussion about it, but offered hope for the continuation of *Oliver*: 'I shall be very happy to enter into any arrangement with you for the transmission of early proofs' (P i. 322). The result of that carrot was that Carey sent Bentley £60, and Dickens £50, for the manuscript of the 'latter portion' of *Oliver* (chapter 44 to the end).[14]

At the conclusion of *Pickwick*, Carey forwarded £50 to Dickens via a bill on his agent John Miller, 'in acknowledgement of the success of [Dickens's] work' (P i. 322, n. 2). The draft was deposited in Dickens's account on 9 May 1838 (MS. Coutts). Carey followed up with a letter offering to purchase advance proofs of *Nickleby*. In doing so he was trying to steal a march on his competitors, but in a way fully recognized by them. Before the signing of international copyright agreements, American publishers attempted, in the words of Henry Holt, 'a brief realization of the ideals of philosophical anarchism—self-regulation without law'.[15] To temper the ruthlessness of competition for manuscripts not protected by copyright, they developed and maintained an informal but fairly effective system of 'trade courtesy'. In order to establish the right to print such a book a publisher took out a trade announcement. Even if no actual arrangement for publishing the work had yet been made, a notice that the book was 'in press' would secure it to the house, with one exception, pertinent for our story. *If* another publisher had contracted for advance proofs, that contract took precedence over the 'in press' claim. Generally speaking, the firms that

honorarium for advance sheets, although he also notes (pp. 53–65) that from 7 Apr. 1835 Bulwer got £50 per volume from Harper's for advance sheets of his works.

[14] The textual consequences of the arrangement have been analysed by Kathleen Tillotson in '*Oliver Twist* in Three Volumes' and the Introduction to Clarendon *Twist*.

[15] Quoted in J. Henry Harper, *The House of Harper* (New York and London, Harper and Brothers, 1912), p. 110.

observed 'trade courtesy' tried to settle all disputes 'on the highest plane of equity'.[16] So by obtaining early proofs, Carey hoped to forestall all rivals, and could have looked to his fellow publishers for support in defending his claims. He commissioned his agent, Miller, to treat with Dickens on the matter, but evidently Miller either never received his instructions or failed to act upon them. *Nickleby* began its serial run in England without any agreement. Concerned, Carey wrote directly to Dickens, who replied on 18 July 1838:

> I have never seen your Agent Mr. Miller upon the subject of Nicholas Nickleby, but if I had I should have been unable to have sent you early proofs of any Number that has yet appeared, as I have been rather behindhand than in advance and have only completed each Number a day or two before its publication.
>
> I shall be glad to hear that Nicholas is in favor with our American friends.[17]

In subsequent years Dickens was able to keep far enough ahead to contract for advance proofs; we will cite those agreements in their places. But for *Nickleby* the last-minute pressures were unrelenting and inescapable. For Chapman and Hall, something seems to have gone awry, too, for instead of paying Dickens on the fifteenth of every month, their payments were regularly deposited on the first, at publication (MS. Coutts). It is inconceivable that they were trying to punish Dickens for his lateness, hard to believe that they felt it necessary to withhold payment in order to make certain that he got the number written, and unlikely that they were short of cash, since payments were made before the receipts came in. So we must conclude that the altered practice was mutually satisfactory, for some unknown reason.

Certainly the sales of and profits from *Nickleby* were satisfactory—highly so. The contemporary reception was far more enthusiastic than the current one. Forster asks, 'Who that recollects the numbers of *Nickleby* as they appeared can have forgotten how each number added to the general enjoyment? All that had given *Pickwick* its vast popularity . . . had here the advantage of a better

[16] J. Henry Harper, *The House of Harper*, p. 111.

[17] P i. 417. Dickens's American friends were now also acquainted with his work on *Bentley's Miscellany*, for from 1837 to 1841 William Lewer, and afterwards his widow Jemima, later Mrs. Joseph Mason, reprinted the monthly issues (Barnes, *Authors, Publishers and Politicians*, p. 33).

laid design, more connected incidents, and greater precision of character' (F II. iv. 121). By September 1838 Sydney Smith, who had held out against Dickens's humour as long as he could, confessed himself conquered, judging *Nickleby* '*very good*' (F II. iv. 125-6). Sales held up remarkably; in December Dickens crowed 'I don't know where [*Nickleby*] is going to stop' (P i. 480). Evidently the initial circulation of 50,000 copies was nearly maintained; and the profits upon the numbers alone equalled those from *Pickwick*: £14,000 (P i. 570). Ten years later, the *Athenaeum* in a review of the Cheap edition of the novel called it 'perhaps the best of Mr. Dickens's works'.[18]

As Dickens approached the end of his *Nickleby* labours he turned his mind towards his next venture. When *Barnaby* was finished, supposedly by the beginning of 1840, he would be entirely free, not only of Bentley, but also of Chapman and Hall. On 14 July 1839 he therefore instructed Forster to open negotiations with the latter: first, determining what they planned to do at the conclusion of *Nickleby*; second, urging them that if they did something handsome they would find Dickens 'tractable', and third, reminding them

That I have had straightforward offers from responsible men to publish anything for me at a pr. centage on the profits, and take all the risk. But that I am unwilling to leave them, and have declared to you, that if they behave with liberality to me I will not on any consideration, although to a certain extent I certainly and surely must gain by it. [In short,] if they wish to secure me and perpetuate our connection, now is the time for them to step gallantly forward and make such proposals as will produce that result. (P i. 562)

It is worth pausing here to remark that Dickens knew he had no legal claim on Chapman and Hall for any compensation for *Nickleby* beyond his £3,000. To share more largely in its profits, therefore, he had Forster put before them his 'rough notes of proposals for the New Work'. Thus the additional compensation he sought from his latest work once again depended on their eagerness for the next. Dickens's pattern of committing himself to a future work in order to obtain some present concession continued into the early 1840s, with unfortunate results, for it was as a consequence of a similar agreement that trouble first arose with Chapman and Hall.

[18] 3 June 1848, p. 554.

On Tuesday, 23 July, Dickens went up to London from Elm Cottage, Petersham, to spend the day with Forster, Chapman, and Hall. The negotiations concerned *Nickleby* and *Master Humphrey's Clock*; for the moment, we will look only at the former. Chapman and Hall agreed to pay Dickens £1,500 more for *Nickleby* (P i. 570). He already had received £500 in two instalments, £300 deposited on 3 January 1839, and £200 credited, along with his April stipend of £150, on 26 March. The remainder was paid into his account on 11 October (MS. Coutts). It is clear from Dickens's tone that he thought his 'trusty friends' had indeed come through handsomely.

There remained only the final number of *Nickleby*, completed on 20 September, the Dedication to Macready, a copy of which Dickens sent to him on the twenty-first, and the *Nickleby* banquet, held at the Albion in Aldersgate Street on Saturday evening, 5 October. In addition to the printers and publishers, Dickens invited 'one or two intimate friends'; those attending included Forster, Macready and his brother Captain Edward Neville Macready, Thomas Hill, John Pritt Harley, Thomas Beard, William Jerdan, and a host of artists: Clarkson Stanfield, George Cattermole, Sir David Wilkie, Browne, and Daniel Maclise whose portrait of Dickens, commissioned as a gift from the publishers, adorned the room.[19] 'We sat down to a *too* splendid dinner', Macready records in his *Diary*. 'I had to begin what the Duke of Sussex terms "the business" of the day, by proposing Dickens's health.' In spite of having spent all morning at home trying to think of something to say, Macready thought he 'did not get through well'. He spoke of Dickens 'as one who made the amelioration of his fellow-men the object of all his labours—and whose characteristic was philanthropy', and compared his interest in 'little details and minute feelings' to Wordsworth's.[20] If this was not particularly scintillating, neither was Dickens: 'Not so good as he usually is. He stated that the *Nickleby* had been to him a diary of the last two years: the various papers preserving to him the recollection of the events and feelings connected with their production.' Dickens then went on to eulogize his publishers, and little Hall, in response, gave a 'very sensible and genuine' reply,

[19] Macready gives all but Beard, who was invited, and whom Forster places among the party (*Diaries*, ii. 25; F II. iv. 127; cf. P i. 590, n. 1).
[20] Michael Slater quoting Sir David Wilkie (*Composition*, p. 41).

with which Macready 'was quite touched'. The aura of good feeling expanded over port and cigars: Wilkie compared Dickens's parts publication to that of Richardson, who issued *Clarissa Harlowe* in single volumes, and was deluged with advice from readers; Macready replied to his health by declaring that the friendship of such a man as Dickens increased his—that is, Macready's—self-respect. Those must have been heady words indeed from the most eminent actor of the day to a young man of twenty-seven, unknown four years earlier! More drinking, smoking, and mutual congratulating ensued; and the party finally broke up 'very late'.[21]

Some additional measure of Dickens's popularity may be obtained from the history of the *Nickleby* portrait. Thackeray thought Maclise's painting, exhibited at the Royal Academy in 1840, amazing, as faithful as a reflection in a mirror, and praised it in *Fraser's Magazine*.[22] William Finden, the engraver, reproduced it for the *Nickleby* frontispiece; by 9 November 1839 it was available for sale separately in quarto size on plain paper for a shilling, and in folio on India paper for 2s. So great was the demand by a public that knew Dickens's heart and mind, but not his features, that the plate deteriorated. A replica, technically inferior and containing minor alterations, was rushed out.[23] Meanwhile, the bound edition of *Nickleby* was ready by the end of October, for sale as usual, in cloth for 21s., half-morocco for 24s. 6d., and full morocco, gilt, for 26s. 6d. By 1863, in book form alone, sales exceeded 100,000.[24]

At the close of *Nickleby*, Dickens broke the rhythm and habits of the last three and a half years. There was to be no new monthly serial to follow the last part, nor was any contemplated for the future. Instead, Dickens proposed to try a different format altogether. And though he eagerly anticipated the commencement of a weekly periodical totally under his control, he also regretted the termination of that regular monthly intercourse with his public. The Preface to *Nickleby* expressed that sense of loss in very personal terms:

It only now remains for the writer of these passages, with that feeling

[21] Macready, *Diaries*, ii. 25–6.   [22] 22 (1840), 113.
[23] Frederic G. Kitton, *Charles Dickens by Pen and Pencil* (3 vols., London, Frank T. Sabin, 1890–2), i. 29.
[24] 'The Circulation of Modern Literature', supplement to *Spectator*, 3 Jan. 1863, p. 17.

of regret with which we leave almost any pursuit that has for a long time occupied us and engaged our thoughts, and which is naturally augmented in such a case as this, when that pursuit has been surrounded by all that could animate and cheer him on,—it only now remains for him, before abandoning his task, to bid his readers farewell.

"The author of a periodical performance," says Mackenzie, "has indeed a claim to the attention and regard of his readers, more interesting than that of any other writer. Other writers submit their sentiments to their readers, with the reserve and circumspection of him who has had time to prepare for a public appearance. He who has followed Horace's rule, of keeping his book nine years in his study, must have withdrawn many an idea which in the warmth of composition he had conceived, and altered many an expression which in the hurry of writing he had set down. But the periodical essayist commits to his readers the feelings of the day, in the language which those feelings have prompted. As he has delivered himself with the freedom of intimacy and the cordiality of friendship, he will naturally look for the indulgence which those relations may claim; and when he bids his readers adieu, will hope, as well as feel, the regrets of an acquaintance, and the tenderness of a friend."

With such feelings and such hopes the periodical essayist, the Author of these pages, now lays them before his readers in a completed form, flattering himself, like the writer just quoted, that on the first of next month they may miss his company at the accustomed time as something which used to be expected with pleasure; and think of the papers which on that day of so many past months they have read, as the correspondence of one who wished their happiness, and contributed to their amusement.[25]

[25] (London, Chapman and Hall, 1839), pp. ix–x.

II

THE ANXIOUS FORTIES

Annual income twenty pounds, annual expenditure
nineteen nineteen six, result happiness. Annual income twenty pounds, annual expenditure twenty
pounds ought and six, result misery.

WILKINS MICAWBER, *David Copperfield,*
Chapter 12

6

Master Humphrey's Clock: *'wind, wind, wind'*

I learn that the Society for the Diffusion of Useful Knowledge are in want of a Publisher, and that my publishers, Messrs. Chapman and Hall of the Strand, aspire to that distinction. I do assure you, My Lord, that there are not in London two persons so well calculated by their high respectability, their perfect integrity, and thorough knowledge of their business, for such a situation.

CHARLES DICKENS (P ii. 374)

ENERGY, ENTHUSIASM, and a willingness to be shaped by Dickens's plans were useful qualities to possess when dealing with him. These Chapman and Hall had exhibited from the time of their first overtures about *Pickwick*, and they once again generously deferred to Dickens's proposal for a radically new venture, though Hall at least seems to have retained doubts about abandoning monthly numbers. Dickens was fearful, Forster tells us, that the public might tire of the old twenty numbers over again; further, he had 'the hope, that, by invention of a new mode as well as kind of serial publication, he might be able for a time to discontinue the writing of a long story with all its strain on his fancy, or in any case to shorten and vary the length of the stories written by himself' (F II. vi. 139). Moreover, Dickens wanted a more advantageous financial arrangement; he even thought, until March 1840, that he might be able to enjoy the profits of a continuous publication without having to write all of it (P ii. 46). Finally, he told George Cattermole that his 'object' in turning to '*weekly* parts at three pence *and* monthly parts at a shilling' was 'to baffle the imitators and make it as novel

as possible' (P ii. 7). W. T. Moncrieff's dramatization of *Nickleby*,
which opened on 20 May 1839, had been particularly galling,
because Moncrieff anticipated a major revelation in the novel by
making Smike Ralph's son.[1] 'I am always most intensely mortified
and very much aggravated by having my stories anticipated in
their course; and . . . I think the state of the law which permits
such things, is disgraceful to England', Dickens wrote to the
adapter of *Barnaby*, Charles Selby (P ii. 332-3).

Though Dickens was not able to enjoy the profits without
having to provide all the copy until *Household Words* ten years
later, Chapman and Hall tried to meet his requirements, responding with alacrity and openness to his 'rough notes of proposals
for the New Work' (P i. 562), communicated via Forster in July
1839. Dickens there predicted that its chances of success were
'almost beyond calculation' (P i. 565); Chapman and Hall, after
calculating, agreed they were very good. On 23 July, when they
settled on the amount of the *Nickleby* bonus, they also established
the preliminary terms for the *Clock* (P i. 569-70), which were later
incorporated into Proposals for Agreement signed in the autumn
(P i. 681), and finally set forth formally in an Agreement dated
31 March 1840 (P ii. 464-71). Dickens was to receive a weekly
salary to conduct the work, out of which he could hire assistance
if he chose, and to share equally in the net profits, while Chapman
and Hall paid all expenses. The printers and publishers estimated
that an average weekly sale of 26,000 would be needed to break
even. 'By this arrangement,' Dickens explained to Mitton, 'upon
a sale of 20,000 copies they get nothing; upon a sale of 40,000,
they get half the profit upon the additional 20,000 and I add the
other half to my £50—you understand? If the work went on for
two years, and were to sell 50,000 (which Bradbury and Evans
think certain, but which I confess I do not, though there is a good
chance of it) my profits would be between ten and eleven thousand pounds, and theirs five thousand' (P i. 570). If it did sell so
well, Dickens concluded, he might make 'a decent thing out of
some one of my works yet'.

Proposals for the *Clock* were signed by the partners, and witnessed by Forster, on 15 October. For 'a weekly periodical of One
Sheet Royal Octavo to sell for three pence a number; each
number to contain twelve pages of Original Literary matter and

[1] See Michael Slater, *Composition*, pp. 33-4.

four pages of Title and Advertizements', Dickens was to receive £50 weekly 'to supply the literary matters'. Chapman and Hall contracted to manage the publishing, to account for all the numbers sold at 2*d*. each, allowing 13 as 12, to receive 5 per cent for 'Management', and also to allow the usual commissions and charges to 'Agents'. An account was to be made up and delivered to Dickens within three months following each 30 June and 31 December, and the profits remaining after all expenses of printing, illustrating, advertising, sale, agency charges, and Dickens's weekly stipend were deducted were to be divided equally. Dickens committed himself for five years, but Chapman and Hall retained the option to discontinue the *Clock* after twelve months. The copyright of the work was owned jointly.

These provisions were confirmed and elaborated in the formal Agreement worked out by William Chapman for his brother and Charles Smithson for Dickens. The revenue expected from advertising was for the first time included, to be accounted for at the rate of £6 per page; Chapman and Hall charged nine guineas per page for the weekly numbers, and eight for the monthly, the difference covering their expenses.[2] The cost of insuring the stock, drawings, and engravings against loss or damage by fire was also allowed, for the first time. To help cut Dickens's potential losses, Smithson and Mitton stipulated on 3 March 1840 that each number be accounted separately (P ii. 47–8, n. 4; 467 and n.). Thus if the receipts on any particular number did not meet the expenses, the publishers bore the loss, which was not carried over in the accounting for the succeeding number. William Chapman endorsed the corrections made to the original draft on 13 March 'Subject to the alterations in blue ink'—the sentence pertaining to the accounting by number was stricken through. Dickens evidently stuck by the clause, for on 20 March William Chapman wrote to Smithson and Mitton:

The clause you contend for is so opposed to all my notions of what is right, not only abstractedly, but as fairly arising out of the proposals made by Mr Dickens himself & assented to by my clients, that as a matter of business to be settled by us professionally *I* never could agree to it. The question must be decided by the parties themselves. I shall

[2] Weekly advertisements were not continued in the monthly numbers, for which separate arrangements had to be made.

forward your letter to Messrs. Chapman & Hall & request them to settle the point as they think proper. (P ii. 47–8, n. 4)

Edward Chapman and William Hall deferred to Dickens, requesting only that an additional sentence be inserted specifying that charges like advertising not attributable to any one number be distributed equally over the whole of the half-yearly volume. That was accepted, the previous sentence was stetted, and the full Agreement was signed on 31 March.

This Agreement, which sets forth in detail for the first time how the accounts were to be drawn up, established many of the features of Chapman and Hall's later semi-annual reports to Dickens. The terms of the sale contained provisions for the usual discounts, commissions, and agency charges,[3] though the 5 per cent allowance for 'Management' seems low to cover the cost of overheads.[4] The specification of the dates on which the semi-annual accounts were due (within three months of 30 June and 31 December) reflects a long-standing difficulty Dickens had experienced, with several of his publishers, in getting paid. Macrone could not pay Dickens for *Sketches*, First Series, until a month after publication. Bentley was repeatedly tardy in making up the accounts of the *Miscellany* sale, from which Dickens would determine what he was to receive in the way of extra payments. Chapman and Hall had not always found it easy to make payments on time either. Once Dickens wrote to Chapman, 'Will you mention to your book-keeper, that in case he should meet a Fair Copy of our accounts, walking about anywhere, I shall be glad if he will give her my compliments, and say she may rely upon a welcome, whenever she is disposed to come towards this end of the town.'[5]

---

[3] Plant, pp. 404–5; Wiles, pp. 180, 186–7.

[4] In 1908 John Murray estimated that overheads ran 16⅔ per cent of the gross turnover; today, it is figured at 20–30 per cent; see Gettmann, *A Victorian Publisher*, p. 127.

[5] P i. 625. The headnote, citing the 1882 edition of Dickens's letters where this extract is dated 27 Dec. 1839, argues for 'roughly the same period; reference to accounts would support end of year'. A fair copy of the half-year's accounts would not be available anywhere near 27 Dec.; for 1 July to 31 Dec. the account would be ready around the middle of the following March at the earliest. And as Dickens had no share in the profits of any volume published by Chapman and Hall up to the end of 1839, he had no reason or right to expect an accounting; therefore, this passage must have been written after March 1840, when he became a partner in *Master Humphrey's Clock*.

The contract for the *Clock* addressed itself to this problem. Dickens received a regular weekly payment of £50, generally in the form of a four weeks' advance of £200, and at six-monthly intervals he would receive a half-share of the net profits. Though there was a delay of three months between the end of the accounting period and the date on which the accounts were due, to enable Chapman and Hall to inventory their stock and assemble all bills, only seven days were allowed between the time all parties audited and signed the accounts and the date by which the publishers had to pay Dickens his due.[6] In time, as Chapman and Hall had to report not only on the sales of current ventures, but also on back sales of previous ones in which Dickens had a share, the half-yearly accounts of all Dickens's work came to be standard practice.

As the day appointed for the *Clock* to strike one approached, the hopes of all concerned soared higher and higher. Bradbury and Evans had thought nine months earlier that a sale of 50,000 was certain, though Dickens was more cautious, but by the middle of March the printing order had been advanced to 60,000. Even this was exceeded by some 10,000, as Forster told a jubilant Dickens at Birmingham on 4 April (F II. viii. 158); the news prompted the Dickenses, Forster, and Alfred to extend their holiday by visiting Stratford and Lichfield, an excursion which so straitened their resources that Alfred was forced to pawn their gold watches. On his return to London, Dickens told Macready that if the demand for the *Clock* was sustained at its present pitch, it would be worth £10,000 a year to him.[7] He also reassured Hall that copy for Number 6 would be forthcoming shortly, hoping thereby 'to put Mr. Chapman at rest (pro tem at least, for he will be an unquiet spirit always, and a thorn in my side, I know)' (P ii. 50–1). He could not resist crowing about his success:

The Clock goes gloriously indeed. What will the wiseacres say to weekly issues *now*? And what will they say to any of those ten thousand things we shall do together to make 'em wink, and stagger in their shoes? Thank God for this great hit. I always had a quiet confidence in it, but I never expected *this*, at first. (P ii. 50)

[6] Gerald Grubb is wrong in asserting that 'The "June" accounts were frequently based on estimates' ('Some Unpublished Correspondence of Dickens and Chapman and Hall', *Boston University Studies in English*, 1 (1955), 103, n. 10).

[7] Macready, *Diaries*, ii. 56.

Macready, rereading Number 1, thought it might be 'too good for so wide a circulation',[8] and he was right, for sales of subsequent numbers fell off by almost one-third. Thackeray reported to his mother in May 1840 that 'Dickens is sadly flat, with his Old Clock: but still sells 50000.'[9] Even before the first number appeared, however, Dickens was uneasy about the miscellaneous nature of his new periodical; and the public's disappointment in not getting a continued story for their weekly 3*d.* reinforced his instinct to jettison the *Clock* machinery and expand the 'little child-story' scheduled for Number 4 into a full-length continued narrative. The declining sales precipitated a discussion, perhaps at the time of the long-scheduled Easter Tuesday dinner, 21 April, and with his publishers' concurrence Dickens then began working on a new novel, *The Old Curiosity Shop*, expanding the hints contained within the 'little child-story' set up for publication 25 April.[10] There was no panic or haste in Devonshire Terrace or the Strand; Nell and her grandfather did not reappear until midway through Number 7, issued 16 May. Eventually, their pilgrimage sent the sales of the *Clock* above anything previously reached; the circulation of the last chapters of the *Shop* reached 100,000.[11]

In America, too, Nell's wanderings were followed with feverish intensity: crewmen and passengers on sailing packets were met at the New York docks by urgent queries about her fate. Dickens wrote to Lea and Blanchard on 22 November 1839, notifying them of the desire of Chapman and Hall and himself 'to treat with you for the transmission (at such times as will enable you to publish in America on the same day as we publish in England) of a complete cast of each number of my new work in parts, including the plates' (P i. 604). The letter did not reach them until 5 February 1840, however; in the meantime, their London agent John Miller had independently arranged for early proofs of each

---

[8] Macready, *Diaries*, ii. 56.

[9] Thackeray, *Letters*, i. 444. The footnote states that the reference is to the second number, but by the beginning of May four numbers had been issued, and a fifth came out on 2 May.

[10] For further details of this sequence of events, which significantly revises Edgar Johnson's account (p. 298), see Robert L. Patten, ' " The Story-Weaver at His Loom": Dickens and the Beginning of *The Old Curiosity Shop*', in Robert B. Partlow, Jr., ed., *Dickens the Craftsman: Strategies of Presentation* (Carbondale and Edwardsville, Ill., Southern Illinois Univ. Press; London and Amsterdam, Feffer & Simons, 1970), pp. 44–64.

[11] Kitton, *The Novels of Charles Dickens*, p. 64.

number at £2. 10s., or £112. 10s. for the entirety of the *Shop*, and £107. 10s. for *Barnaby*. Lea and Blanchard were willing to authorize a much larger payment—£300—but had hoped for the sheets thirty days in advance (P i. 604–5, n. 6). Finding the weekly numbers impossible to imitate, they issued the *Clock* instead in twenty monthly parts, 1840–1. Dickens also contracted for early proofs to Germany, where there was considerable interest in his works as a result of the simultaneous appearance in 1839 of translations of *Sketches*, *Oliver*, and *Nickleby* (P ii. 7; 43, n. 2). Chapman and Hall sent out stereotypes of the *Clock* plates to Calcutta, but ended up many years later having to pay £2. 3s. 6d. 'Freight and other charges' for their return, 'no profit having being [*sic*] derived from the Sale of the Work in India'.[12]

Such sales should have ensured a large return to Dickens— thousands of pounds at least—which would have been some comfort for the unceasing labour of writing in weekly instalments: 'Mr. Shandy's Clock was nothing to mine—wind, wind, wind, always winding am I; and day and night the alarum is in my ears, warning me that it must not run down' (P ii. 106). That the *Clock* did not prove such a gold-mine can largely be attributed to the unexpectedly heavy costs for the woodcuts. Dickens knew they would be 'very expensive', but by the 1840s 'the most influential novelty' for weekly periodicals, especially newspapers, was 'the growing emphasis upon illustrations'.[13] Wood engraving was widely used in the first half of the nineteenth century, having been perfected by Bewick and his students. Following a tracing, the engraver cut the desired image into the end grain of a section of boxwood with a gouge and graver. The block was then inked and wiped, and impressions were produced by intaglio printing.[14] Browne and Cattermole supplied the majority of designs for the *Clock*, with Samuel Williams and Daniel Maclise supplying one cut apiece for the *Shop*. Browne at first traced some of Cattermole's designs, as well as his own, on to the blocks, which were cut by such expensive and accomplished engravers as Charles Gray, Vasey, Williams, Ebenezer Landells, and the brothers

[12] MS. C & H. In 1843 Dickens briefly considered entering into arrangements for the republication of his works in India, but nothing seems to have come of it (P iii. 523–4).

[13] P i. 570; Altick, *English Common Reader*, p. 343.

[14] Muir, *Victorian Illustrated Books*, p. 5.

Dalziel (P ii. 8–9, nn. 7 and 8). The process of woodcutting also took time; Browne, writing to Dickens for 'some notion of the sort of design' he wanted for the frontispiece to *Clock* II, and already faced with two other blocks to complete within three days, urged Dickens to suggest 'something nice and *light*' which would 'be best adapted to my *palette*, and prevent an excess of perspiration in the relays of wood-cutters'.[15] Adjusting the type to surround the illustrations, and adjusting the contents of the number to fill up twelve pages exactly, added further to the costs.

The financial results of the *Clock* must have been disappointing to everyone. One hundred pounds from Chapman and Hall deposited to Dickens's account on 4 September may be approximately what was owed him on the half-yearly accounts to 30 June (MS. Coutts). The *Clock* had been running for only a few months then, and there may have been hopes of a better reckoning next time; but by October it was evident that there would be little of those thousands of pounds to share. Macready recorded that on the seventeenth of that month, 'Dickens told me of the heavy expenses of *Humphrey's Clock* eating up so very much of the profits.' A more pleasant consumption took place on the twentieth, the *Clock* dinner to celebrate the publication of Volume I: 'A very cheerful day', Macready noted.[16] But Dickens was hard pressed for cash. The Midsummer's Day balance showed him £27. 2s. overdrawn; in October he was running 'very near indeed' (P ii. 133); by December he was forced to request from Chapman and Hall a £500 advance, which was paid into his account in two instalments, £200 on 29 December 1840, and £300 on 11 January 1841 (P ii. 175, and MS. Coutts). The new year proved no better than the old. In June 1841 his balance was £36. 11s. 5d. (MS. Coutts). Dickens had to borrow from Chapman and Hall again and again, eventually running up a debt of at least £769. 9s. 5d. by the end of July,[17] even though the publishers deducted £50 from each month's advance. The complications of his account with Chapman and Hall at this time make it difficult to ascertain exactly which deposits relate to the half-yearly *Clock*

[15] Quoted in Fred[eric] G. Kitton, '*Phiz*' (*Hablot Knight Browne*): *A Memoir* (London, George Redway, 1882), p. 23; cf. P ii. 218, n. 3.

[16] *Diaries*, ii. 90.

[17] P ii. 345; William Chapman thought it higher, 'about £1000' by 12 June (P i. 488). Dickens borrowed £50 on 6 March, and another £50 on 28 June (P ii. 312, n. 2).

profits, but the following entries are probable, if Chapman and Hall paid at the stipulated times:

11 March 1841	for the half-year ending 31 December 1840	£235 6 7[18]
28 August 1841	for the half-year ending 30 June 1841	£264 13 7
10 December 1841	for the half-year ending 4 December 1841	£468 0 10

These may not be the right payments, and even if they are, they may be net of cash Dickens drew separately. But if they, plus the £100 deposited in September 1840, approximate a half-share of the *Clock* profits, then Dickens's hopeful estimate that his 'profits would be between ten and eleven thousand pounds' was ten times too high. Including his £50 stipend for each of the eighty-eight numbers, he would have cleared £5,468. 2s., but in profits alone only £1,068. 2s. to 31 December 1841.

There were other pecuniary difficulties. John Dickens was forging his son's signature to bills, which were then presented for payment at Devonshire Terrace, his bankers', or his publishers'. Dickens had Mitton insert a notice on 8 March 1841 in all London morning and evening papers warning creditors that he would not honour any bills so executed, and at the same time asked Mitton to inform John that if he would emigrate, take Augustus with him, and allow Dickens's mother £40 per annum support should she not choose to go with them, then and only then would he settle his father's debts and supplement his pension.[19]

But the major source of irritation and disappointment stemmed from the old disputes about *Barnaby Rudge*. It will be recalled that in June 1840 Richard Bentley finally sold out to Dickens all his remaining stock in *Oliver Twist* for £750, and surrendered his claims on any Dickens writing, past, present, or future, for an additional £1,500. Chapman and Hall advanced the money out of the £3,000 they agreed to pay for *Barnaby Rudge*, which was to 'contain literary matter or composition which shall be equal to ten numbers each containing two Sheets of letter press' exactly similar to those for *Pickwick* and *Nickleby*.[20] The publishers were 'at liberty to divide and publish in fifteen smaller numbers if you

---

[18] Dickens sent Mitton 'the C & H accounts' on 19 Mar. (P ii. 239).

[19] P ii. 224–6, and nn. 8 (224–5), and 1 (225).

[20] P ii. 476; the Agreement, signed at the end of July 1840, is printed on pp. 475–7.

think fit', Dickens acknowledged on 2 July (P ii. 93–4). Two chapters were already in hand; the rest was to be written 'within some convenient time to be agreed upon between us'. If Dickens should not complete *Barnaby* within five years, Chapman and Hall were granted a lien in the amount of £2,250 on Dickens's 'property' then in their hands (copyrights and stock), and were made beneficiary of an Insurance policy on Dickens's life for £1,500. Since the remainder of the advance was for the purchase of stock, Dickens believed that the publishers would not require further surety on it. Dickens's 'property' at the time included 'a certain *contingent* interest' (P ii. 482) in *Sketches by Boz*, half-profits on which reverted to him after the £1,125 Chapman and Hall had advanced in 1837 was paid off. He also could expect one-third of the profits on *Pickwick* after November 1842, all the profits on *Nickleby* after October 1844, all profits on *Twist*, and half-profits on the back numbers of the *Clock*. Dickens retained his right to the £50 weekly stipend free of the lien. Despite five years of unremitting labour, he had precious little in the way of expectations from the sale of back numbers to show for it. And his total indebtedness, until *Barnaby* was written, amounted to £3,000-odd, assuming that *Sketches* was not paying off too rapidly.

Dickens explained these understandings in his 2 July 1840 letter, which provided Chapman and Hall with security only in equity. At the same time, he wrote to Edward Chapman a private letter, expressing what he felt; namely, that he 'had a strong sense of the ready and kind way in which you had come forward with the money, and of the personal interest you had shewn in the matter—this made it in my eyes something of a more pleasant nature than a mere matter of business' (P ii. 349). William Chapman, concerned to protect his brother's interest and aware that Dickens's letter was not security in law, proposed to Smithson and Mitton that a more formal security for the £2,250 advance be executed. At the same time (25 July 1840) he forwarded a draft of the *Barnaby* Agreement, which was signed shortly thereafter. Nothing further was done on the security, and by November new arrangements about *Barnaby* and the loan were being negotiated. On 28 October William Chapman sent Smithson and Mitton a copy of Dickens's July letter; at 1 p.m. on 30 October the lawyers began preliminary discussion. Ten days later, in Forster's chambers, the principals held another meeting, at which Forster himself 'minuted down' the 'understanding' later given 'bodily form' by Mr. James Bacon (P ii. 487). *Barnaby Rudge* was to succeed the *Old Curiosity Shop* in the *Clock*; for it Dickens would receive £50 per instalment plus half-profits, and since the novel would appear in the *Clock*, Dickens was by the *Clock* Agreement owner of half the copyright once again. That arrangement 'virtually superseded' the 2 July 1840 letter. Now Chapman and Hall were in effect paying for *Rudge* twice—in weekly instalments of £50, plus whatever they risked of their £2,250 advance against the £3,000 they no longer owed Dickens. They were willing to forgo exclusive rights to *Rudge* in numbers and book form if Dickens would provide some kind of legal assignment of copyrights as security; Forster's memorandum refers to 'a lien in the nature of a Mortgage'.[21] Mitton as well as Forster was present during this meeting, but somehow Dickens was left with the impression that his 2 July 1840 letter was sufficient guarantee. After all, both parties had always behaved honourably, whatever the experience elsewhere, both had profited largely from Dickens's 'abilities and powers of perseverance and application' (his 'only Bank'), and both looked forward to future profitable transactions (P i. 348–9).

Free at last of Bentley's shackles, and of *Barnaby* separate from the *Clock*, Dickens determined by the end of November 1840 to follow the *Shop* immediately with the new work. From a three-volume novel, it had gone prospectively to a sequel to *Oliver* in *Bentley's*, then into ten monthly numbers or fifteen smaller ones, and finally was to appear in weekly instalments. Though the notice about *Barnaby* was written by 24 November 1840 (P ii. 153), it was held up while Dickens plotted the end of the *Shop*. In this connection, he composed his first known number plans, distributing the remaining material over the remaining numbers to the forty-fifth, where the *Shop* was to close.[22] The announcement that *Barnaby* was to follow finally appeared in Number 41, 9 January, and on 13 February 1841 *Master Humphrey's Clock* began Number 46 with the first chapter of *Barnaby Rudge*, most

<hr>

[21] P ii. 487; letter from William Chapman to Smithson and Mitton, 12 June 1841, citing Forster.

[22] See P ii. 167, n. 3, and Robert L. Patten, 'Plot in Charles Dickens' Early Novels, 1836–1841' (Ph.D. dissertation, Princeton University, 1965).

of which had been written sixteen months earlier as the opening of a three-decker for Richard Bentley.

Meanwhile, of course, Dickens was borrowing more and more from Chapman and Hall, and nothing was being done about legal security for the £2,250 advance. Eventually Bacon seems to have drafted a deed based on William Chapman's of 25 July 1840, and forwarded it to Smithson and Mitton around the middle of May 1841. Smithson opened the parcel, and, according to Dickens's account of Smithson's testimony, 'could not refrain from expressing to those who were about him, at the moment, his unbounded surprise at the conditions it recited'. On 25 May Smithson expressed his surprise to William Chapman that Bacon ' "came to hit upon the present mode" ' (P ii. 487)—namely the 'most hard, stringent, and overbearing' deed (P ii. 349)—and urged that Chapman and Hall be dissuaded from pursuing their course. William Chapman replied that the deed was part of the arrangement made during the meeting the preceding November at Forster's. Meanwhile, Smithson told Mitton, who seemed astonished at the whole proceeding, and urged Dickens to borrow the money elsewhere and pay off his debt to Chapman and Hall rather than sign the deed. Dickens, after reading the document, declared that he would not sign it, and instructed Mitton to return it. William Chapman consulted with his brother and Hall, replying to Dickens's solicitors on 12 June with a long recapitulation of the agreement reached at the meeting in Forster's chambers the preceding November, pointed out how shaky his clients' security was, refused to qualify his opinion of the propriety of the deeds prepared by himself and Bacon, but, acting on his clients' instruction—reluctantly, it appears—offered to compromise: a bond, a fresh letter to replace that of 2 July 1840, and a Life Insurance policy would now be sufficient. 'As the least offensive way of putting me into double irons,' Dickens subsequently explained to his publishers, 'Mr. Mitton recommended the bond' (P ii. 350). Mitton wrote to William Chapman on 15 June urging that if the bond was signed the old letter ought to suffice (P ii. 488–9). No reply was drafted until 10 July, the principals being out of town in the intervening period. William Chapman disagreed, but enclosed a copy of the letter modified to suit the altered circumstances. Infuriated, 'disgusted with the whole course of proceeding and thoroughly sick at heart' (P ii.

350), Dickens signed the bond on 31 July (P ii. 489–90). Chapman and Hall having loaned him a total of £3,019. 9s. 5d. by that date, could call in, on or after 2 July 1845, any balance left after Dickens's share in the profits of the back numbers of the *Clock* and *Oliver Twist* had been applied to its reduction. The outstanding balance was to be interest-free, and was further secured by Britannia Life Assurance Company Policy No. 2251 for £2,000. Dickens coldly summarized the understanding in a letter of the same day, and then wrote a second time demanding the return of the private letter of 2 July 1840 to Edward Chapman thanking him for the original advance. Afterwards he went straight down to Broadstairs, where on 3 August he received a full and effective apology from the firm, which caused his sentiments to undergo 'a complete change', and to make him look forward once again to their negotiations about the new undertaking. Chapman had said, among other things, that the firm could do without the bond; Dickens replied: 'As you think you can trust me without the bond, I would rather you threw it into the fire with your own hands,—for I can trust you to do it' (P ii. 351). The restoration of good feelings prompted Dickens to recommend the firm to the Society for the Diffusion of Useful Knowledge, and to share, in buoyant good spirits, the celebrations occasioned by Edward Chapman's marriage in late September.

Master Humphrey's Clock appeared in a bewildering variety of formats: the partners certainly worked the copyright within the limits imposed by the Agreement. There were eighty-eight weekly threepenny numbers in white paper covers, running from 4 April 1840 to 4 December 1841. The four or five numbers per month were also collated and sold in twenty monthly parts, stitched in a green wrapper, for 1s. or 1s. 3d. At half-yearly intervals the *Clock* numbers were collected into volumes: I (15 October), bound in cloth with marbled edges for 8s., II (by 10 April), for the same price, and III (15 December), somewhat longer, for 10s. 6d. On the same day as Volume III appeared, the *Shop* and *Barnaby* were issued separate from the *Clock*, as the 'Original Edition', bound in cloth for 13s. each, or by January, elegantly bound by Hayday ('the slowest man in England', Dickens called him (P ii. 266)), in calf with gilt edges for 18s. The sheets containing the miscellaneous stories at the *Clock*'s commencement Dickens cancelled 'at some loss, merely because I considered that they injured the effect of the two long stories . . . They *sold* as well as the rest, but they did not please me; and therefore I disposed of them to the four Winds.'[23]

Though heavily in debt and exhausted, Dickens had finally, with *Barnaby*, worked off the last of the commitments so hastily entered into in the heady days of 1836. In five years he had written or edited and published sixteen books, pamphlets, or plays, and risen from an obscure journalist to world-famous author, whose health was 'a subject of grave discussion', as he facetiously but accurately put it in a cancelled passage to the Preface of *Clock* I, 'in England, Ireland, Scotland, America, Germany, France, and the East and West Indies' (P ii. 126, n. 2). Unhappily, the reports of his wealth continued to be greatly exaggerated; he still paid his publishers better than he paid himself, and had almost daily to decline assistance to begging letter writers: 'Fame's Trumpet should blow a little more of the wealth arising from the circulation of my works, into the Booksellers' pockets, and less into my own', he complained (P ii. 416). Despite the precariousness of his financial position, he needed a rest from his labours, a change of pace and scenery, a chance to increase his stock of impressions. In order to gain the respite, he had to mortgage his future even more heavily.

[23] P iii. 445; the consequences of cancelling the opening sheets of *The Old Curiosity Shop* are explained in my article on ' "The Story-Weaver at His Loom" '. But see Appendix A, *Master Humphrey's Clock*, where Chapman and Hall continue to account in the full eighty-eight numbers.

7

Trouble in Eden: American Notes *and* Martin Chuzzlewit

Is it not a horrible thing that scoundrel-booksellers should grow rich here [the United States] from publishing books, the authors of which do not reap one farthing from their issue, by scores of thousands? And that every vile, blackguard, and detestable newspaper,—so filthy and so bestial that no honest man would admit one into his house, for a water-closet door-mat—should be able to publish those same writings, side by side, cheek by jowl, with the coarsest and most obscene companions, with which they *must* become connected in course of time, in people's minds? Is it tolerable that besides being robbed and rifled, an author should be *forced* to appear in any form—in any vulgar dress—in any atrocious company—that he should have no choice of his audience—no controul over his own distorted text—and that he should be compelled to jostle out of the course, the best men in this country who only ask to *live*, by writing? I vow before High Heaven that my blood so boils at these enormities, that when I speak about them, I seem to grow twenty feet high, and to swell out in proportion. 'Robbers that ye are' —I think to myself, when I get upon my legs—'Here goes!—'

CHARLES DICKENS (P iii. 230)

C HAPMAN'S LETTER OF APOLOGY and explanation concerning the hateful Deed had 'done more to awaken the feelings which have so long subsisted and should always subsist between us', Dickens wrote, 'than whole years of

uninterrupted good understanding without any allusion to this
theme, could have effected' (P ii. 351). Dickens went on in a similar vein to assure the firm 'that in the negociation of our new undertaking, you will find me as ready to respond to you in a frank and
cordial spirit, and as earnestly desirous to meet you on all points
with a liberal construction, and a confidence, founded on mutual
[knowledge] and esteem as I ever have been at any period of our
intercourse'. The *Clock* was not making money, and its sale had
fallen to 30,000 copies; there was not a single project in mind to
follow the conclusion of *Barnaby* in November. No wonder that
Hall picked up the reference to 'our new undertaking', and wrote
back quickly urging Dickens when he was next up to London to
dine with him and Chapman, 'as they wish to talk about the new
story' (P ii. 360). Dickens was having a glorious holiday at
Broadstairs, enjoying the sparkling sun and the sea, writing easily
and effectively, and he longed for an extended break. But *Oliver*
was not selling well enough in its 'Third Edition' to pay off much
of the £3,000 in loans and advances which Dickens owed
Chapman and Hall. If the *Clock* stopped in November, there
would be no more monthly stipends; and half his *Clock* profits
were pledged as repayment for that much abused bond signed
only a few days earlier, and still morally, if not legally, in force.

Hall was recommending that Dickens return to the familiar
monthly numbers, and prepare for a new serial to commence, like
Pickwick and *Nickleby*, in April, a date which would allow Dickens
time at the conclusion of *Barnaby* to get a few months ahead, if he
plunged immediately into writing the new work. After visiting
Mitton in London on Saturday, 21 August, Dickens, finding
himself early for the meeting with Chapman and Hall at Forster's,
walked about Lincoln's Inn, revolving possibilities. If he switched
suddenly to monthly parts, would not the public take the change
as an admission that the weekly numbers had failed? What
circulation could he expect the new work to achieve? Was the
pause between publications sufficient? Scott seemed a pertinent
and ominous example of a writer whose best works had failed to
sell '*because he never left off*'. Was Dickens not spoiling the sales of
his own works by too frequent appearances? (He had already
hurt the sales of Bulwer, Marryat, and others by his 'great
success'.) And did he not encourage the plagiarists and imitators,
who deluged 'the town with every description of trash and rot',

thus tiring his potential audiences more? If only he had foreseen these consequences, and made better bargains for his earlier works. But, Dickens reasoned, if his position now was strong, and his reputation as good as money, why not use that reputation to gain the year's respite, and then return before the public 'with a complete story in three volumes—with no cuts or any expense but that of printing—and put the town in a blaze again'.

Satisfied that he was right, Dickens walked straight up to Forster and said, 'Now will you in my presence say to Chapman and Hall for me after dinner to day . . . what I am going to tell you?' 'What is it?' Forster asked apprehensively.

I see, I said, as in a clear bright glass that if I go to the monthly parts next March, I do so at a great hazard. Scott's life warns me that let me never write so well, if I keep on writing, without cessation, it is in the very nature of things that the sale will be unsteady, and the circulation will fall. The Clock shews us this, every week, for it started at 70,000, and is now 30,000—and this, notwithstanding that the Curiosity Shop made, without doubt, a greater impression than any of my other writings. I am doing what every other successful man has done. I am making myself too cheap. And although I still command a sale wholly unprecedented and unknown, even in Scott's case, that sale is *shaky*, and trembles every day. Propose this to Chapman and Hall. That the notice I have written be cancelled directly—that we contemplate no monthly parts at all—that we finish the Clock on the 27th. of November, and advertize for that day twelve months a new book in three volumes. And say to them this:—if Mr. Dickens is willing to let you have one half of the Copyright of that book, what can you afford, and what do you propose to give him for it, over and above Two Thousand Pounds which is to be paid to him in quarterly payments, for his subsistence through the year during which he retires from public notice?[1]

Forster agreed, and bided his time. After dinner, little Hall, his pockets bulging with papers containing estimates for new works, proposed a toast: 'Success to our new undertaking'. Thereupon Forster laid out Dickens's plans, warmly supporting all Dickens's reasoning, and supplying on his own such additional inducements as the effect which a year's silence might have on the back sales of other works, pledged to help reduce Dickens's debts.

[1] P ii. 365-7: Dickens's letter to Mitton (23 Aug. 1841), from which the account of Dickens's deliberations is taken.

Chapman and Hall were stunned into silence. Two weeks
before they had almost lost Dickens, trying to obtain some sort of
legal security for the enormous sums they had loaned him.
Turning themselves inside out to accommodate him, they had
agreed to abandon the very document which had cost them so
much pain, feeling that the restoration of perfect confidence
between them and their only major writer was essential to the
well-being of the firm. On the strength of that confidence, they
had approached this meeting, having prepared ahead of time
several calculations of the profits to be expected from a new serial
to duplicate the phenomenal success of the previous monthly
novels. Now they were being asked, because of that perfect
confidence, to forgo all hopes of a new novel for at least a year, to
subvent Dickens in the meantime to the tune of £2,000 *beyond
what they had already given him*, and to receive in return, for some
further unstipulated payment, half copyright, not of a monthly
serial, but of a three-decker.

Struggling to meet the occasion, Chapman admitted that 'he
did believe', if one took the long view, 'that the effect of the year's
silence would be tremendous'. (Did he also, silently, consider his
own case—pledged to be married a month later to a young
Quaker lady whose father disapproved and might have protested
even more strongly if the fiancé were to be declared bankrupt
because he had lost his major publishing asset?) Hall, whom
Dickens considered 'morally and physically feeble though perfectly well intentioned' (P ii. 367), chimed in, 'Yes—he thought
so too' (P ii. 366). But he wondered whether it would not be
better to break the silence with monthly numbers. No, Forster
and Dickens replied. It would be better to try the new form; it
was a cheap form, not requiring pictures; and besides, after a
three-decker, it was still open to Dickens to return to numbers.

Well, the partners replied, they had never meant to press
Dickens into burning himself out; it was true that his reputation
was great and might be enhanced by the pause; and, on the whole,
they were willing to go along with whatever their author and
their literary adviser recommended. Though they put a brave
face on it (Dickens thought their reception 'quite triumphant'),
Chapman and Hall must have been sick at heart.

A week later, Dickens went up to London again, to settle final
details for his year's vacation. He proposed that he receive £150

a month during the year off, and that he not be bound by any restrictions on other activities during the interim. Weighing further the merits of three volumes against monthly parts, he concluded that he should reappear in the familiar green wrappers, as promising a three-decker at the end of the year would in effect pledge him to writing another novel during his so-called leave. On 1 November 1842 the new work would commence, and during its serial run Dickens would receive £200 for each instalment. In addition, he was to receive three-quarters of the profits, from which the year's advance of £1,800 was to be repaid (P ii. 372–3). Dickens gave these proposals to Chapman and Hall on Saturday, 28 August; the firm considered all the calculations and returned a favourable answer, along with Dickens's notes, which he then forwarded to Mitton for incorporation in a formal Agreement. Dickens stipulated that, in order to avoid any interference from William Chapman, Forster should adopt the phrasing and provisions of Mitton's copy of the *Clock* contract in drawing up the new one (P ii. 375).

Excluding Chapman's lawyer and his own from the conference, Dickens, Forster, and the publishers spent the whole of Tuesday afternoon and evening, 7 September, minutely examining the Agreement for a new novel-to-be, 'in form size and price, precisely similar to the Pickwick Papers and Nicholas Nickleby'.[2] The arrangements for the *Clock* were left as prescribed on 31 March 1840. For the new publication, the arrangements were as Dickens proposed: £200 a month for copy, to be delivered 'in time' (no more demeaning specifications as to the day of the month); Chapman and Hall to pay all expenses, to account for all numbers sold at the rate of 8s. per dozen, counting 13 as 12 (a standard discount), to receive a 5 per cent commission on all units sold, and to allow agents the usual commissions.

For the monthly serial, the *Clock* advertising policy was modified. In the three pages of the wrapper not occupied by the cover design, Chapman and Hall were responsible for a net return of no less than £10; whatever they made beyond that, or from the inserted advertising sheet, or whatever they lost, was to apply exclusively to them. One supposes that the disappointing experience with the advertisements for the *Clock* determined

---

[2] See P ii. 478–81 for the Memorandum of the Agreement, written entirely by Forster.

Dickens to insulate himself against a similar experience with the new periodical, while at the same time the offer of all insert advertising profits to Chapman and Hall partially compensated them for a less favourable split in the net profits from the numbers. For Dickens was to receive three-quarters of the profits, Chapman and Hall only a quarter; Dickens's £200 monthly was to be accounted a publication cost, not a down-payment on his share of the net proceeds; and each number was in so far as possible to be balanced separately, with Chapman and Hall making up all deficits, rather than carrying them on to the next month. Similarly, at the half-year accountings, if by reason of such charges as could not be apportioned to any one number, but were spread over the whole six months, the balance was in the red, again Chapman and Hall were to absorb the whole deficit.

Six months *after*—not before, as the Pilgrim editors have it— the publication of the last number, Chapman and Hall could buy from Dickens one-quarter of the stock in the numbers and volumes then on hand, and thereafter be entitled to one-half of the copyright and profits.[3] Provisions for arbitrating disputed valuations of copyright and stock, limitations on the licence to print constraining Chapman and Hall from issuing the novel in any other form or price, and procedures for selling out either party's share all replicated previous contracts.

So far so good—in fact, excellent. Dickens was to be paid to fill thirty-two printed pages what he had been receiving on account of the *Clock* to fill forty-eight; he had the lion's share of the profits for the richest portion of the novel's circulation; he was insulated against loss; he retained at least half copyright. It was a better contract than any for *Pickwick*, in which he shared only after November 1842 to the extent of one-third; it was better than *Nickleby*, of which he owned nothing until October 1844, when he received full rights; it was better than *Oliver Twist*, where to secure to himself the novel well after its initial appearance as a serial and in bound volumes he had to pledge a huge sum of money which still had not been worked off; it was better than *Sketches by Boz*, where a similar debt had been incurred to buy half copyright in material that had been widely disseminated; and by one-quarter of the profits it was better than the Agree-

---

[3] Error, based on Forster's awkward phrasing, appearing in P ii. 372, n. 5.

ment for the *Clock*. Dickens was certainly using his reputation as if it were money.

But—and it proved a momentous 'but'—he was broke, tired, restless, and heavily in debt. The provisions entered into in connection with the Agreement for the new novel that related to these facts seemed equally favourable, but were to prove galling and injurious. For the year's break Dickens was to receive £1,800 in equal instalments, to be repaid, with 5 per cent interest, out of his three-quarters share of the net profits commencing with the first number of the new work, and the interest was to be figured separately on each monthly instalment and to stop at the commencement of the monthly serial. Thus, on the £150 advanced in November 1841, Dickens would owe interest for twelve months; but on that advanced in October 1842, he would owe interest for only one month, the serial commencing on 1 November 1842. The repayment of this advance was not to interfere with his stipend of £200 per part, however. Out of Dickens's three-quarters share of the net proceeds, two-thirds (or in other words one-half of the undivided net profits) were to be applied to the repayment of the £1,800 advance, and one-third (or one-quarter of the undivided net profits) was to be applied to the £3,019. 9s. 5d., which was also being reduced by the profits from the back numbers of the *Clock* and *Oliver*. Thus in reality Dickens could look forward to little, until May 1844 (when the final double number of the new novel would be issued), beyond his monthly stipend of £150, rising to £200 on 1 November 1842. Unless the new serial reaped fabulous rewards, and his advances and loans were paid off before the end of the run, his three-quarters share in the profits was, as current income, illusory.

There were two other provisions for securing to Chapman and Hall their repayments. If after the first five numbers were issued, the amount of Dickens's share of the profits set aside to repay the £1,800 advance was not likely, by the end of the serial run, to effect repayment, then 'on and after the publication of the sixth number' Chapman and Hall could deduct £50 a month towards that debt. Second, if the whole of the £1,800 and interest had not been repaid by the end of 1844, when Chapman and Hall came in for half-profits and half copyright, then one-half of Dickens's moiety (one-quarter of the undivided net profits) was pledged to the reduction of that debt, and the other portion to the other debt.

When the £1,800 advance was repaid, then Dickens's whole share of the net proceeds was to be applied to the other debt.

In other words, to gain the year's respite, Dickens pledged himself to repay, out of the profits of what was to become *Martin Chuzzlewit*, both debts: the advance of £1,800 and the loan of £3,019. 9s. 5d. He could not receive any of the profits until both debts were liquidated, and though all parties hoped that would be a speedy process, the Agreement made provision for a period extending to the end of 1844 and beyond. The brilliance of the contract as it related to Dickens's present prospects (Mitton was 'quite aghast last night at the brilliancy of the C. & H. arrangement', Dickens told Forster (P ii. 376)) was enhanced by the cloud of previous unsatisfactory ones. Dickens's indignation at the tendency of his publishers to enrich themselves at his expense may seem exaggerated and unfair; but when one examines his position in 1841, mortgaged on all sides and possessing scarcely any copyrights of present value, it must be conceded that he had hardly emancipated himself financially, despite his staggering successes and overwhelming public receptions.

The *Chuzzlewit* Agreement is a remarkable document. It certainly attests to the strength of all parties. Dickens commanded from his publishers the sum of £4,000, plus three-quarters of all profits excluding all losses, for their one-quarter interest plus a reversionary one-quarter interest in a book to be written from twelve to thirty-two months in the future. On the supposition of all parties to the Agreement that this as yet unwritten book would more than meet its expenses, the publishers further advanced Dickens £1,800 in twelve instalments so that he could take off for a year and do anything he wanted—not even excluding contracting to write a book for someone else. And though that money was to earn interest, the interest was not discounted at the beginning but applied at the end, and was levied on any month's advance only until Dickens began writing. During the period of *Chuzzlewit*'s serial run the advance was interest free!

Chapman and Hall were equally potent. Past were the days when they could not pay Dickens £14 for his instalment until the receipts from the current number came in. Now they could lend him up to £3,000 one year, tear up the bond promising repayment, and a few weeks later sign an Agreement to lend a further £1,800, pay out £4,000 for a future book, and absorb any losses should it prove unpopular. They also stopped the *Clock* without a murmur, though technically—unenforceably—Dickens was bound for five years had they elected to continue.

Equally, the contract reveals their weaknesses. Dickens had nothing to live on apart from money for future writings, and even that was largely pledged to past debts. He had no investments beyond life insurance policies, one taken as security on a loan; and it was hardly conducive to a sense of financial well-being to know that it would pay off to Chapman and Hall, not to his family, and only when he was dead! He owed a large mortgage for his Devonshire Terrace house. His monthly expenses ran high. He had to have a break, and he had to pressure his publishers into financing that break.

If Dickens needed Chapman and Hall, they also needed him. How else were they to recoup the purchase money for Bentley's stock and copyrights, or the loans they had already made? What other literary property did they have that promised to be even half so profitable? And what means did they possess to bind Dickens to them productively beyond being agreeable and trying to adjust his desires and needs to their practical ones? If Dickens objected to the firm's solicitor, what could they do but accede, and kick William out? So the two parties, brought together through their mutual adviser Forster, met without counsel to work out an Agreement that recognized their respective strengths and weaknesses by tying them all together inextricably in a bold bet on one man's future creativity.

Forster had his doubts, too, despite his warm advocacy of Dickens's proposals. He did not doubt the popularity of Dickens's new serial—no one seriously considered that it would not sell hugely. What he feared was the use Dickens might make of the year's leisure, and his disquiet was intensified by a letter from Broadstairs a week after the signing reporting that Dickens was 'in an exquisitely lazy state, bathing, walking, reading, lying in the sun, doing everything but working. This frame of mind is superinduced by the prospect of rest, and the promising arrangements which I owe to you.' Bad enough, but the next sentences were still worse: 'I am still haunted by visions of America, night and day. To miss the opportunity would be a sad thing. Kate cries dismally if I mention the subject. But, God willing, I think it *must* be managed somehow!' (F II. xii. 194–5; P ii. 380–1.)

The idea of a visit to America appeared in the earlier proposals to Chapman and Hall concerning the *Clock*; it had been sporadically revived by correspondence with Washington Irving who predicted a triumphant welcome; now it became an obsession. A day after the letter to Forster, Dickens drafted one to Hall, combining instructions about *Barnaby* with questions about the wisdom of running over to America in February for four or five months and returning with a one-volume account, 'a ten and sixpenny touch' (P ii. 383). Dickens asked Hall to look into fares, quietly, as he did not want his plans 'blabbed about' before they were settled, and he closed with a plaintive question: 'Don't you conceive that it would be, on every account, an excellent employment of a part of the interval?' Five days later he had decided, as he told Forster with double underlining for emphasis (and release): 'I HAVE MADE UP MY MIND (WITH GOD'S LEAVE) TO GO TO AMERICA—AND TO START AS SOON AFTER CHRISTMAS AS IT WILL BE SAFE TO GO' (F III. i. 197; P ii. 386).

Chapman and Hall returned a satisfactory answer, saying they expected Dickens to go, as he had been talking so about it, and Dickens began a flurry of preparations, including a successful campaign to persuade Kate to join him and leave the children behind. He wrote and rewrote the Address which finally appeared on 9 October in the *Clock*, announcing his plans; he told Irving; he reserved a cabin on the *Britannia*; he took out yet another life insurance policy, having heard from 'a great City man' that both his Argus and Britannia policies were doubtful (P ii. 404, 414, 424). On returning to London at the beginning of October Dickens was stricken with an increasingly painful fistula, which was eventually repaired by surgery without anaesthetic. During his convalescence he dictated correspondence to Kate, forced himself to give up his graveyard plot adjoining Mary's to inter her maternal grandmother, Mrs. Thomson, and complained jocularly about his continued weakness to Miss Coutts, saying that he feared he 'was about to go through life on Two pillars of jelly, or tremulous Italian cream' (P ii. 411). The insurance policies cost extra to cover America; the house was let to General Sir John Wilson; there were a thousand details to attend to. Lea and Blanchard heard the great news, and set to work instantly preparing a reissue of all Dickens's works in twenty parts, 'EMBELLISHED WITH A PORTRAIT OF THE AUTHOR DONE

ON STEEL', to retail for twenty-five cents per part.[4] They also wrote immediately to Dickens, inviting him to be their guest in Philadelphia; he replied by putting off more formal arrangements until he arrived 'on your side of the Atlantic' (P ii. 425). He postponed his promised contribution to Lady Blessington's book; he arranged through Edward Marjoribanks for a Letter of Credit on Coutts's New York correspondent bank for £800 (P ii. 442–3). To back it, he requested and received from Chapman and Hall an advance of £800. At the same time he acknowledged receipt of £885 on account of the new book (*American Notes*), which was to be deducted from the receipts after its publication. In addition, he instructed his publishers to pay to Frederick certain sums while he was abroad, and to treat him as Dickens's agent in authorizing expenditures. 'Having disposed of the business part', Dickens concluded, 'I should not feel at ease on leaving England, if I did not tell you once more with my whole heart, that your conduct to me, on this and on all other occasions, has ever been honorable, manly, and generous; and that I have felt it a solemn duty, in the event of any accident happening to me while I am away, to place this testimony upon record. It forms part of a Will I have made for the security of my children;—for I wish them to know it, when they are capable of understanding your worth and my appreciation of it' (P iii. 1–2).

We shall skip over Dickens's trip to America, except for two or three points. He found the prices for rooms '*enormously* dear' (P iii. 70): a fortnight's bill, for lodging alone, came to £70; on another occasion Dickens was charged $9 a day board for Philadelphia rooms unoccupied because Kate's indisposition kept the whole party in New York! (P iii. 123). The American trip put a considerable strain on his budget; and his speaking out on behalf of International Copyright strained his relations with press and public. The precarious financial state of the nation, its fierce and licentious journals, its hypocrisy about slavery, the crudeness of the culture, the unrestrained curiosity about Boz all contributed to Dickens's discomfort. Although he formed many abiding friendships, he concluded in disappointment, 'This is not the Republic I came to see. This is not the Republic of my imagination' (P iii. 156). As the time for departure approached, he

---

[4] William Glyde Wilkins, *First and Early American Editions of the Works of Charles Dickens* (1910; rpt. New York, Burt Franklin, 1968), pp. 20–1.

was 'FEVERED with anxiety for home. . . . Kiss our darlings for us. We shall soon meet, please God, and be happier and merrier than ever we were, in all our lives. . . . Oh home—home—home—home—home—home—HOME!!!!!!!!!!!' (P iii. 248).

After a round of reunions and parties, and Charley's recovery from violent convulsions caused by being 'too glad' to see his parents, Dickens got down to the business of writing up his journal, borrowing the letters he had written to Forster and others to supplement his entries. Gradually the book swelled from one volume to two; half-way through the first at the end of July, Dickens prepared to go to Broadstairs for two months, to finish it up for an anticipated October or November publication date. He was facing the deadline of 1 November for the first part of the new monthly serial, so there was little time to spare. And the accounts were not healthy: the Midsummer balance was only £119. 8s. 9d., to which was added in July nearly £541 from Chapman and Hall, settling up for the preceding six months (MS. Coutts).

The writing of *American Notes* went easily, with no more than the usual ups and downs. A forged letter widely circulated in the American papers gave Dickens and his friends distress; he wrote several letters explaining that 'the cross of every t, and the dot of every i', was 'a most wicked and nefarious Forgery' (P iii. 327). Despite this interruption, he ploughed ahead, discovering happily that he had written by the beginning of September more than enough for the first volume: 'Chapman and Hall, and Bradbury and Evans opine that I was doing too much for the money' (P iii. 319). By now it was clear that the opening of the new novel must be delayed a few months; apparently Dickens's £150 monthly stipend was continued, the additional £300 either coming out of his profits from the *Notes* or being added to his debt.[5] On 16 September Dickens directed Edward Chapman to prepare advertisements announcing the publication of the *Notes* on 20 October (P iii. 325); on the fourth of that month he finished the penultimate chapter (F III. viii. 283); two days later Longfellow arrived and Dickens burst into an exhilarating round of entertainments.

---

[5] The Coutts accounts for the second half of 1842 are full of deposits from Chapman and Hall which I cannot with certainty identify; there are payments of £150 from Chapman and Hall credited 29 Oct. (for ?Nov.) and 1 Dec.

Public interest in Dickens's travel notes was high on both sides of the ocean. Trade orders for Chapman and Hall's edition exceeded 3,000 one week before publication on 18 October, 'much larger than have ever been known since Scott's time', Dickens told his sister Fanny (P iii. 344). Several copies were given to Longfellow to take back to American friends when he left via the *Great Western* from Bristol two days later. There was no arrangement with Lea and Blanchard about advance proofs, Dickens having decided on principle to have nothing more to do with American republications until the law on copyright was altered.[6] Consequently, he hoped that Longfellow would have the first copies to appear in America. Dickens's plan evidently succeeded; as soon as the *Great Western* docked, the sheets went to the *New World* and *Brother Jonathan*, which on 7 November 1842 both published the entire text for twelve and a half cents (P iii. 346, n. 2). 'The Notes had an enormous sale', Dickens reported to Longfellow (P iii. 407). The *New World* distributed 24,000 copies in twenty-four hours, and it is said that nineteen hours after receiving copy the *New York Herald* had the book printed, selling 50,000 copies in two days. In Philadelphia 3,000 copies changed hands in half an hour.[7] Harper and Brothers issued their edition as an 8vo pamphlet, 92 double-column pages in brown wrappers, retailing for twelve and a half cents. Hitherto they had respected Lea and Blanchard's rights, but the flood of newspaper competition, and the generally depressed state of publishing, were eroding the ground rules of the previous decade.[8] The Lea and Blanchard edition, a modest effort of 5,000 copies hastily printed and offered with portrait for twenty-five cents and without for half that price, was attached as 'No. 21' of the collected edition prepared for Dickens's visit. Though it apparently sold out, it was

[6] P iii. 258: 'I have resolved that I will never from this time enter into any negociation with any person for the transmission, across the Atlantic, of early proofs of any thing I may write; and that I will forego all profit derivable from such a source.' His resolution held for ten years; on 2 Apr. 1844 he wrote to Lea and Blanchard refusing 'to break my determination in your favor' (Altick, 'Dickens and America', p. 330).

[7] See Wilkins, *First and Early American Editions*; Peter Bracher, 'The New York *Herald* and *American Notes*', *Dickens Studies*, 5 (1969), 81–5, and 'The Lea & Blanchard Edition of Dickens's *American Notes, 1842*', *Papers of the Bibliographical Society of America*, 63 (1969), 296–300; Meade Minnegerode, *The Fabulous Forties, 1840–1850: A Presentation of Private Life* (New York and London, G. P. Putnam's Sons, 1924), p. 284.

[8] Eugene T. Exman, *The Brothers Harper*, p. 163.

aimed not at the customers who could buy more cheaply the huge New York printings, but at a local market and old customers.[9] Although the critical reception was violently mixed in both countries, sales held up, even in England, where the Chapman and Hall printing ran through 'Four large Editions' (P iii. 411) by the end of the year, netting Dickens £1,000 and thus more than repaying his advance.[10]

On the heels of Longfellow's departure, Dickens joined Forster, Maclise, and Stanfield for a hurried trip to Cornwall, where he thought of opening his new book, due in two months, 'in some terrible dreary iron-bound spot' (F III. viii. 279). Back in London, he set to work, abandoning this idea, and concentrating instead on the theme of selfishness. In an attempt to keep his structure firmly under control, Dickens shut himself up 'obstinately and sullenly in my own room for a great many days' (P iii. 367), plotting and contriving his new work, before writing a word. Among other things, by the end of the year Dickens had declined Lea and Blanchard's offer of around £100 for the *Notes* and 'double the price that had been paid' for early sheets of the *Clock* for *Martin Chuzzlewit*.[11] That hurt, because without an advance of £100 from Chapman and Hall credited 23 December he could not have purchased the Maclise picture of Georgina Hogarth as *A Girl at a Waterfall*, as he had 'not more than £20 at Coutts's, in all' (P iii. 401 and n. 3; MS. Coutts). He had considered, and rejected, Leech's application to join in the illustration of the new work. He had finally devised a title. And he had at last got the first number into print.

The routine during the composition and publication of *Chuzzlewit* in numbers was similar to that established for the previous monthly serials. The first half of each month was devoted to writing the new instalments, the second half to correcting proofs. Subjects for the plates were supplied as early as possible, usually by the tenth (P iii. 439); several were detailed and explicit. Dickens reported at the opening of March that he was 'in great health and spirits, and powdering away at Chuzzlewit, with all manner of facetiousness rising up before me as I go

9 Bracher, 'The Lea & Blanchard Edition', p. 300.
10 John C. Eckel, rev. and enl. edn. (1932), p. 108.
11 P iii. 404–5; J, p. 449; and R. Shelton Mackenzie, Appendix, quoting Henry C. Lea, p. 6.

on' (P iii. 452). A few days later he received the Chapman and Hall accounts to December 1842. After reviewing them, and finding the balance still heavy against him, Dickens instructed Mitton to defer purchase of a freehold in Highgate. There was nothing, apart from his monthly stipend of £200, coming in. In May a £100 deposit may have been borrowed against that income; the 24 June Midsummer's balance showed a scant £8. 7s. 1d. credit, and the July Chapman and Hall desposit was reduced to £100 (MS. Coutts).

Meanwhile, *Chuzzlewit,* though according to Forster 'much the most masterly of his writings hitherto' (F IV. ii. 302), was not selling particularly well, about 20,000 parts per month: 'I shall be glad to hear of any improvement in Chuzzlewit', Dickens told Chapman and Hall on 2 March, as he awaited word on the sales of Number III (P iii. 450). Many reasons have been given. The first number was slow, uneven, and unfocused. The change to weekly issues in the last two works had encouraged a different habit of buying, and perhaps gained Dickens large numbers of readers from a class which could ill afford the shilling monthly numbers. The temporary withdrawal to America may have been unfavourable 'to an immediate resumption by his readers of their old and intimate relations' (F IV. ii. 302). Perhaps his year's silence had cost him his pre-eminence in the public eye. Or it might be, as Ada Nisbet has argued, that combined with the lukewarm response to *Barnaby Rudge,* the widespread and hearty condemnation of the *Notes* blemished Dickens's prestige and disillusioned his public.[12] The sales figures do not entirely support a conclusion that the *Notes* were a failure; travel books in two volumes for a guinea a copy appealed to a much more limited audience than fiction for 3d. a week. But there is much truth to the argument that the hostile—or, even worse, condescending—critical reception of the book affected the public's feeling about Dickens. And some truth, perhaps, to Forster's attribution of the disappointing sales of *Chuzzlewit* to a capricious lull in popular taste.

There is, however, one additional and important reason for the

[12] 'The Mystery of "Martin Chuzzlewit" ', in *Essays Critical and Historical, Dedicated to Lily B. Campbell,* English Studies: I (Berkeley and Los Angeles, Univ. of California Press, 1950), pp. 201–16, *passim,* esp. p. 216. The Pilgrim editors believe this argument 'cannot be sustained', and also cite as a contributing factor 'the continuance of the trade depression of 1842' (P iii. 516–17, n. 4).

comparative failure of *Chuzzlewit*. Both in England and America, publishing had been in the doldrums for some time, adversely affected by financial uncertainties, political unrest, and the sort of general depression that feeds upon itself to intensify its effects. As early as 1839 John Murray II had written to Horace Twiss 'that the publishing of books at this time involves nothing but loss, and . . . I have found it absolutely necessary to withdraw from the Printers every work that I had in the press'.[13] Murray attributed this state to the importation of pirated editions from the Continent and America, and to 'those parasytical Weekly Publications that extract everything that is required by the great mass of readers, viz., sufficient to supply them with conversation in Society'.[14] No longer could he afford to offer thousands of pounds for a poem or a cookery book; instead he reverted to simple profit-sharing agreements, offering little if anything in advance for copyright. People wanted food, not books; and those authors they had been so fond of were mostly dead—Austen, Shelley, Mrs. Radcliffe, Byron, Hazlitt, Scott, Coleridge, Lamb, Godwin—or silenced—Maria Edgeworth, Wordsworth.

Over the next three years, the depression intensified. John Murray III returned every manuscript in the house. R. H. Barham reported that only one novel in three was paying its way, and in 1843 *Bentley's Miscellany* dropped in circulation by two-thirds, forcing Bentley to sell stock to Thomas Tegg, who had made a fortune out of cheap reprints, advertisements, and remainders.

If anything, the situation in America was worse: 'Real and personal property is diminished greatly in value, and the confidence which promotes success in the dealings of men seems to have fled', Philip Hone, ex-Mayor of New York and diarist, noted in his journal. 'Here, in the city of New York, trade is stagnant. Local stocks are lower than ever. Real estate is unsalable at any price; rents have fallen and are not punctually paid, and taxes have increased most ruinously.'[15] Journalists took advantage of this plight, hawking cheap, scandal-laden papers for pennies and driving the respectable publishers out of business. In retaliation, the major publishing houses waged aggressive campaigns

---

[13] Paston, p. 25. [14] Ibid.
[15] *The Diary of Philip Hone, 1828–1851*, ed. and intro. Allan Nevins (2 vols., New York, Dodd, Mead and Co., 1927), ii. 579. An excellent discussion of the American depression is contained in Barnes, *Authors, Publishers and Politicians*.

of their own: Harper's printing of *American Notes* in such an inexpensive form indicates the extremities to which they were forced. Gone were all gentlemanly agreements about respecting another's authors and 'forthcoming' notices. 'The year 1842 was one of the darkest in Cliff Street [Harper's office] since the panic of 1837. Only thirty-six new books were published, and these moved out slowly; some works that were announced as in press in January were still there in March, sluggish as the icy waters of the Hudson.'[16] Two years later, the recession had eased slightly, but the gentlemanly world of the 1830s was gone for ever. Harpers now aggressively sought business at every level: *Chuzzlewit* was issued without any arrangement in seventeen weekly numbers at six cents apiece, January to July 1844, and was distributed by armies of insistent newsboys.[17]

The pressures building on Parliament to provide some relief for the publishing industry may have been increased by Dickens's statements; certainly his remarks on International Copyright and the piratical 'Paul Joneses' were timely. The 1842 Copyright Act, which Talfourd's friends at last succeeded in getting through a reluctant House, prolonged the copyright term to forty-two years, or seven years after the author's death, which gave some security to writers, but not so much as the French laws, where copyright passed to the widow for her life and to the author's children for twenty years thereafter. Yet there was no reciprocity between the two countries only twenty miles apart: a French author in England was governed by the English standard, and an English author in France by the French one.[18] The importation of foreign reprints of British books into England or her colonies was also forbidden by the new Act; and some not very successful attempts were made to exploit the colonial market by producing inexpensive series in London and shipping them out.[19] The failure of Chapman and Hall's efforts to open up the Indian market with the *Clock* stereotypes indicates how undeveloped as yet the colonial market was for London booksellers. The market only gradually improved; writing in the *Journal of the Statistical Society* in 1843, G. P. R. James observed that 'there is no author

[16] Exman, p. 151.
[17] Harper, p. 77; Exman, p. 163.
[18] Nowell-Smith, *International Copyright Law*, pp. 23, 40.
[19] Paston, p. 25; Nowell-Smith, *International Copyright Law*, pp. 22–40.

now living in this country who could obtain 500 *l.* per volume for any prose work; and the general rate of remuneration to British authors, as compared with those of France is about one to five'.[20]

Yet Dickens was receiving £4,000 for *Chuzzlewit* for a quarter share of the copyright, making the total rights theoretically worth £16,000, astronomically high given the temper of the times. There was little he could do to further stimulate sales among the 15,906,589 inhabitants of England and Wales. He certainly appealed through the title of his travel book—*American Notes for General Circulation*—to contemporary interest in defaulting banks, journalism, plagiarism and imitations, and travel accounts (one of the few categories of book whose sales held up, as we can see from Melville's works). The suppressed motto would have reinforced the association with banknotes, and even perhaps recalled Cruikshank's famous 'Bank Restriction Note' of 1819:

In reply to a question from the Bench, the Solicitor for the Bank observed, that this kind of notes circulated the most extensively, in those parts of the world where they were stolen and forged.—*Old Bailey Report.* (F III. viii. 283)

At Forster's insistence (P iii. 310, n. 3), the motto was omitted; but the advertisement on the last page of the *Brother Jonathan* piracy included a lithograph facsimile of an American $50 note.[21] To encourage further *Chuzzlewit* circulation, and to vindicate his *Notes,*[22] Dickens sent Martin to seek Eden in America, episodes which he fit into that novel's many forgeries and inversions of pastoral. Though he certainly hoped to attract to the novel the attention still being given to *American Notes*, he was not particularly successful; the maximum monthly circulation of *Chuzzlewit* was only about 23,000 copies (F IV. ii. 302). On such sales, Chapman and Hall could expect a profit of around £400 a number after printing expenses were all deducted. Then there was Dickens's £200 monthly stipend, and their 5 per cent commission, and their quarter share of the remainder to be subtracted. That left very little towards reducing any of the debts.

By midsummer, just before the July number came out, Hall

---

20 G. P. R. James, 'Some Observations on the Book Trade, as connected with Literature, in England', *Journal of the [Royal] Statistical Society*, 6 (1843), 53.
21 Nisbet, p. 209 and n. 34; Wilkins, *First and Early American Editions*, p. 23.
22 See comments by the Pilgrim editors, iii, p. xv.

was fretting about the state of affairs. According to the Agreement, if after the fifth number Dickens's projected share of the profits on the remaining numbers seemed likely to be inadequate to repay the £1,800 advance, a further £50 monthly should be deducted from his stipend. Hall had overridden Forster's objections to this clause when the contract was being hammered out precisely because he felt that it was important to secure to the firm repayment of that advance out of the current *Chuzzlewit* income. After all, there was no arrangement whatever for anything after the present novel, and no very great chance that back sales would quickly diminish the outstanding sum, interest free after 1 January 1843. He felt that he had to speak to his partner about the advisability of invoking the clause, and Chapman reluctantly consented. Hall broached the subject as gently as possible to Dickens on 27 June; but it was as lighted match to tinder.

'I am so irritated, so rubbed in the tenderest part of my eyelids with bay-salt, by what I told you yesterday,' Dickens wrote to Forster the following morning, 'that a wrong kind of fire is burning in my head, and I don't think I *can* write. . . . I am bent upon paying Chapman and Hall *down*. And when I have done that, Mr. Hall shall have a piece of my mind' (P iii. 516–17). Dickens insisted that the monthly £50 be henceforth deducted from his payments, and it was, commencing with the September number. But it was a disagreeable principle to enforce. On 22 July he had to ask Mitton to draw for him £70 against a bill deposited at Mitton's bankers, to tide him over until the first of September; 'I needn't say why I will not exceed by sixpence the reduced monthly of C and H.' Further, he didn't want to be overdrawn at Coutts's at just the moment when Miss Burdett Coutts was 'exerting herself in behalf of Alfred'.[23] On 10 August Dickens told Mitton to let his life insurance policies lapse, unless they were for Chapman and Hall, as the accounts were still shy, and the debt not 'wiped off to the extent we had looked for'.[24]

[23] P iii. 525. *Martin Chuzzlewit* was eventually dedicated to her, 'with the true and earnest regard of the author'.

[24] P iii. 539. The Britannia policies were held by Chapman and Hall, and the £5,000 Eagle policy written two months before his American trip remained in force. The Eagle's actuary, Henry Porter Smith, became a good friend to Dickens and godfather to his son, Sydney Smith Haldimand. At Dickens's death the company paid £6,337. 7s. 1d. to the beneficiaries. (See William J. Carlton, 'Dickens's Insurance Policies', *Dickensian*, 51 (1955), 133–7.)

Smarting from Hall's remark, galled by the continual pressure
to lighten his indebtedness, Dickens instructed Forster immediately afterward to 'propound from me the one preliminary
question to Bradbury and Evans'. During the autumn of 1841
the printer Clowes had urged Dickens to give him a hearing if he
should ever think of changing publishers; now Dickens reasoned
that 'A printer is better than a bookseller, and it is quite as much
the interest of one (if not more) to join me' (P iii. 517). Since he
was literary adviser to Chapman and Hall, Forster was placed in
an awkward position; besides, Dickens might simmer down after
a few days, and if he did not, the fetters in which he would have
to place himself to get free of Chapman and Hall could prove
as close as those now binding him. Forster did propound the
one preliminary question, and received such an unenthusiastic
response that he was able to persuade Dickens to suspend proceedings until after his Broadstairs holiday. Meanwhile, sales
were inching up, and Dickens scrabbled for money wherever he
could, urging an Amsterdam author and translator to treat with
his publishers for early proofs, and hinting that there was no
incentive like a financial one: 'I believe there are difficulties and
objections in the way of such an arrangement, unless it were
attended with a certain profit to' Chapman and Hall.[25] He could
not, at this moment, afford to pass up any chance to increase his
income.

  [25] P iii. 566. There had been a Dutch translation of *Pickwick* printed at Amsterdam in 1840 in two 8vo volumes bound in blue boards, and *Martin Chuzzlewit* had
appeared in the Netherlands in five parts, 1840–2.

8

The Break

... with every one of his publishers Dickens—under
Forster's influence generally, I think—demanded
more than his share of the bargain and called the
other parties to the contract hard names if they asked
for no more than their bare share.
                    J. W. T. LEY (F IV. ii. 318, n. 262)

BRADBURY AND EVANS'S cool reception of the proposition
that they should publish Dickens temporarily checked his
ardour. He had known and respected both men ever since
the opening days of *Pickwick*, and gradually there had grown up
a considerable intimacy among the families, which extended also
to Charles Hicks, their foreman. One of Dickens's better-known
verses was that penned to Hicks at the completion of the August
1837 *Pickwick*:

> Oh Mr. Hick
> —S, I'm heartily sick
> Of this sixteenth Pickwick
> Which is just in the nick
> For the publishing trick,
> And will read nice and slick,
> If you'll only be quick.
> I don't write on tick,
> That's my comfort, Avick!
>   (P i. 287)

During the serialization of *Nickleby* Dickens canvassed votes for
Hicks for the position of Beadle to the Stationers' Company: 'I
have recommended him most warmly myself, and know him to
be a man of very high character and deserts' (P i. 389). Hicks lost
the election; but Dickens continued his friendship, inviting him to

the *Nickleby* banquet, and apparently keeping up social intercourse with his widow into the forties.[1]

Like Chapman and Hall, Hicks's principals exhibited two quite different personalities, which had proved compatible enough to build up a very good printing business. William Bradbury, born at the turn of the century in Bakewell, Derbyshire, had begun as a printer in Oxford Arms Passage, St. Paul's, and was known as 'the keenest man of business that ever trod the flags of Fleet Street, and the founder of a dynastic line nearly as long and eminent as that of John Murray himself'.[2] The senior partner of the firm was tall, imposing, and astute. Frederick Mullet Evans, on the other hand, was a jovial, Pickwickian figure, known to the staff of *Punch*, which they had begun publishing in 1841, as 'Pater'. His rotund figure, shining spectacles, and good-humoured countenance endeared him to the members of the firm, and provided both Leech and Thackeray with good 'copy' for their own versions of a convivial Victorian paterfamilias.[3] Evans left a Southampton printing business to come up to London, where he joined with Bradbury in 1830, first on Bouverie Street, and later, in July 1833, on Lombard Street, Whitefriars (P i. 397, n. 2). The partners secured the printing business of Edward Moxon, then Chapman and Hall, and gradually rose to a commanding position in London printing. By Dickens's death they had founded *The Field* and *The Army and Navy Gazette*, and printed such periodicals as *The Family Herald* and the *London Journal*, as well as their own *Daily News*.[4] Although not directly associated with Dickens until 1844, they still were sociable, attending the *Nickleby* and *Clock* dinners, and commencing, before 1839, the annual custom of presenting the Dickens household with a gigantic Christmas turkey. On one occasion the astonishing bird held out until New Year's Day, having furnished seven grills, one boil, one or two cold lunches, and a breakfast (P ii. 1). Dickens reciprocated the good feeling, and wrote a letter of condolence to Bradbury on the death of his daughter in the spring of 1839 (P i. 515). Bradbury in turn was deeply moved by the passages describing the death of Nell, for it brought back to mind his own bereavement, as his

[1] See P i. 583 and 215, n. 6.
[2] M. H. Spielmann, *The History of 'Punch'* (London, Paris, and Melbourne, Cassell, 1895), p. 36.
[3] Ibid., pp. 36–8.   [4] Ibid., p. 38.

had brought to Dickens's mind the death of Mary Hogarth. This chain of associations bound Dickens to Bradbury and Evans apart from their business relationship, which, barring occasional disputes caused by frequent compositors' errors and the temporary bad feeling over the *Daily News*, was until 1858 trouble free. Having printed *Pickwick*, *Nickleby*, the *Clock*, *American Notes*, and *Chuzzlewit*, as well as most of Dickens's minor writings, the firm was known to be generally quick, efficient, and accommodating.

But their notions of what they could do for Dickens if he chose to break with Chapman and Hall were decidedly timid. They knew little about publishing books until 1844, when they issued Douglas Jerrold's *Story of a Feather* (P iii. 517, n. 2), and they had no experience in the complicated business of advertising and distributing new serial works. Thus they feared that branching out into new territory might injure the valuable printing business which they had carefully built up. Lacking confidence in their ability to promote new work successfully, they recommended instead a collected edition of all Dickens's writings in a cheap form. Dickens thought that idea premature: 'I am sure if it took place yet awhile, it would damage me and damage the property, *enormously*. It is very natural in them to want it; but, since they do want it, I have no faith in their regarding me in any other respect than they would regard any other man in a speculation. . . . I don't see what I gain, in such a case, by leaving Chapman and Hall', Dickens told Forster in conclusion (P iii. 587). Or, Bradbury and Evans suggested, since they had experience with *Punch*, and Dickens with *Bentley's Miscellany* and the *Clock*, they would be willing to invest any amount of money in a magazine or periodical which Dickens would edit. But Dickens was

afraid of a magazine—just now. I don't think the time a good one, or the chances favourable. I am afraid of putting myself before the town as writing tooth and nail for bread, headlong, after the close of a book taking so much out of one as *Chuzzlewit*. I am afraid I could not do it, with justice to myself. I know that whatever we may say at first, a new magazine, or a new anything, would require so much propping, that I should be *forced* (as in the *Clock*) to put myself into it, in my old shape

—that is, to write what would amount to a new serial.[5]

[5] P iii. 587–8, based on F IV. ii. 304–5, from which the following account is taken.

Instead of changing publishers, at the end of his holiday Dickens told Forster that in the summer of 1844 he would 'fade away from the public eye for a year, and enlarge my stock of description and observation by seeing countries new to me'. At the conclusion of *Chuzzlewit* he would claim his share of the subscription money for the volume edition, and tell Chapman, Hall, Bradbury, and Evans that he would make no new arrangement until his return. Deeply in debt, Dickens would find it difficult to manage: the house would have to be rented again, and this time he planned to have his family and two or three servants accompany him to some place 'which I know beforehand to be CHEAP and in a delightful climate, in Normandy or Brittany'. As relaxation and change of pace, he would travel through Switzerland, France, and Italy, collecting impressions for a new travel book and writing them to Forster. At the same time he could 'turn over the story I have in my mind, and which I have a strong notion might be published with great advantage, *first in Paris*'.

'All very well,' Dickens imagined Forster to grumble, 'if you had money enough.' 'Well, but if I can see my way to what would be necessary', he countered, 'without binding myself in any form to anything; without paying interest, or giving any security but one of my Eagle five thousand pounds; you would give up that objection. And I stand committed to no bookseller, printer, moneylender, banker, or patron whatever; and decidedly strengthen my position with my readers, instead of weakening it, drop by drop, as I otherwise must. Is it not so?' Dickens pleaded, 'and is not the way before me, plainly this?'

The problem was, quite simply, that now Dickens *was* writing 'on tick'. Once upon a time his booksellers had offered to serve as his bankers; now they were his money-lenders as well; and the alternative of converting his printers into booksellers, bankers, and money-lenders all in one hardly simplified matters or alleviated the strain. It would eventually be necessary to reconsider Bradbury and Evans's propositions, and in fact each of their suggestions was tried. But at the moment all Dickens could think about was rest.

Forster was appalled, though somewhat inclined to attribute Dickens's desperation to overwork. He argued strenuously for more consideration, and when Dickens remained adamant, he suggested a limited vacation of two or three months as a compromise.

'But it is not rest enough', Dickens replied. 'It is impossible to go on working the brain to that extent for ever. The very spirit of the thing, in doing it, leaves a horrible despondency behind, when it is done; which must be prejudicial to the mind, so soon renewed, and so seldom let alone.'[6] The spectre of Scott continued to haunt him. Dickens did not lack confidence in himself; in fact, he felt *Chuzzlewit* 'immeasurably the best of my stories'. Had he his health, he could hold his own against any new competition. If he wrote for appreciative friends, like Forster, instead of a fickle public which viewed unremitting productivity with suspicion, he could go on without ceasing. But since he felt weary, not well, and since his public appeared to be tiring of his constant performances, he needed escape; and the more Dickens thought of it, the more it seemed certain that a travel book, composed from his letters home, 'would cost me very little trouble; and surely would go very far to pay charges, whenever published.' After that, perhaps another novel.

Forster temporized; Dickens became more impatient. Perhaps if he could not use printers or publishers as bankers, he could obtain relief from a patron who would lend him money on the security of his future successes. He turned to Mitton, who broached the subject of a loan to his former partner, Charles Smithson. Smithson had seemed sympathetic about the 'Deed' two years before, and might be flush, as Mitton had just bought out the partnership. But Smithson was apparently surprised by this application for money, telling Mitton that he assumed Dickens was comfortably off, and was not certain he had the money (around £3,000) to spare.[7] Mitton conveyed these sentiments to Dickens, who in turn wrote on 14 December directly to Smithson to set the record straight. 'Don't believe all you hear', he warned. The large debt likely to be owing at the conclusion of *Chuzzlewit* came from Chapman and Hall's eagerness to 'wrest' the copyright of *Twist* from Bentley and release Dickens from his editorial chains. His publishers had more benefit from the loan than he,

---

[6] P iii. 591. Evidently the Pilgrim editors are following the text of the 1872–4 edition of Forster.

[7] An understatement at the least; at his sudden death a few months later it was discovered that his affairs were in terrible shape, his family almost destitute.

Dickens charged, but he would have been greatly injured in his income had Bentley flooded the town with *Oliver* in numbers, so his hand was forced.

The *Clock* was unprofitable, 'not from any onesidedness in the agreement, but because every calculation made by Chapman and Hall (who are preposterously ignorant of all the essentials of their business) was wrong'. Dickens admitted that the *Pickwick*, *Oliver*, and *Nickleby* contracts had been of his own making, but they had all turned out unsatisfactorily from the standpoint of money. 'It was a consequence of the astonishing rapidity of my success and the steady rise of my fame that the enormous profits of these books should flow into other hands than mine.'

Finally, Dickens explained that he preferred to ask Smithson for a loan rather than to apply to 'The Trade', even though he knew Bradbury and Evans 'would bring to my house £3,000 to-morrow morning', simply because he wished to free himself by his own exertions. He thought 'that if you had the money to put out at all, you would as soon advance it for a short period to one in whose energy and honor you could confide, as you would employ it in any other way. If you haven't got it to spare—you can't send it', Dickens concluded (P iii. 599–600). While that negotiation was being pursued, Dickens was pressuring Forster to help him resolve the impasse: 'do, my dear fellow, do for God's sake turn over about Chapman and Hall, and look upon my project as *a settled thing*. If you object to see them, I must write to them.'[8]

Meanwhile, other irons were heating. Early in October, after a trip to Manchester, Dickens began writing a little Christmas book 'with but the special design of adding something to the *Chuzzlewit* balance'.[9] The idea of issuing books in time for the Christmas trade was certainly not new, nor was it unfamiliar to Dickens, who had tried to get *Sketches* ready in time for the holidays on both occasions (1836 First Series and 1837 Second Series). Nor was the notion of a book on a Christmas subject especially novel: the January 1837 *Pickwick* recounted the Pickwickians' Christmas

[8] P iii. 595. Starting with Dec. 1843 the monthly deposits from Chapman and Hall are reduced a further £50, apparently in an attempt to speed up repayment (MS. Coutts).

[9] F IV. i. 299. Michael Slater, in the 'Introduction to *A Christmas Carol*', in his edition of the *Christmas Books* ((2 vols., Harmondsworth, Penguin Books, 1971), i. 33–4), argues persuasively that the plight of poor children was also preoccupying Dickens at the time he began composing the *Carol*.

at Dingley Dell, including the Clergyman's 'Christmas Carol', and Dickens had twice before contemplated writing books especially for the Christmas trade: 'Solomon Bell and the Raree Showman' for Tegg and 'Boz's Annual Register and Obituary of Blue Devils' for Chapman and Hall. But this little book, which he directed Chapman and Hall to publish on commission, soon exercised a 'strange mastery' over him. Into it he poured all his present anxieties and concerns, his perplexities about money, time, gifts (like the Christmas turkey), love, ambition, social injustice, reformation, spiritual conversion, life, death.[10] He 'wept and laughed and wept again, and excited himself in a most extraordinary manner' (N i. 553).

Nothing but a lavish format would satisfy him. The binding was to be 'Brown-salmon fine-ribbed cloth, blocked in blind and gold on front; in gold on spine; in blind on back. . . . All edges gilt.'[11] Several versions of the title-page were run off: in red and green dated 1844, then later in red and blue dated 1843. 'The title page I have had materially altered', Dickens told Mitton on 6 December. 'They always look bad at first' (P iii. 605). Dickens was eager to get green into his book. It was a colour for which he declared 'a natural partiality' (N i. 676), it was happily associated with the 'green leaves' of his monthly numbers, and it agreed with the principal ornamental device on the title-page, a sprig of holly. He tried to shade the end-papers to complement the ink, but the hand-applied colouring dusted off and smudged, and a yellow stock had to be substituted. Moreover, the green ink turned miserably drab ('about as festive as a stale olive'[12]) which matched neither the provisional green endpapers nor the final yellow ones. Forced to choose another shade, Dickens opted for blue, though that colour bore no relation to the shade of the endpapers, or to the holly. And there was trouble with other parts of the volume: getting the four etchings by John Leech—who had finally secured a commission to illustrate a Dickens book—coloured in time; making press corrections to bring 'STAVE I' into conformity with 'STAVE TWO'; adjusting the title-page date to indicate that

[10] See Robert L. Patten, 'Dickens Time and Again', in *Dickens Studies Annual*, 2 (1971), 163–96.

[11] Sadleir, *XIX Century Fiction*, i. 104.

[12] Philo Calhoun and Howell J. Heaney, 'Dickens' *Christmas Carol* After a Hundred Years: A Study in Bibliographical Evidence', *Papers of the Bibliographical Society of America*, 39 (1945), 298.

the book was for Christmas 1843, not 1844; and correcting the text, which shows signs of many press errors.[13] Altogether, the volume was sumptuously arranged, produced much too expensively and elaborately to retail at 5s., the price Dickens specified.

These facts were not yet apparent as Dickens and his publishers anticipated publication. Mitton saw advance proof, and was enthusiastic. 'I am extremely glad you *feel* the Carol', Dickens replied. 'For I knew I meant a good thing. And when I see the effect of such a little *whole* as that, on those for whom I care, I have a strong sense of the immense effect I could produce with an entire book.' In Dickens's mind, the idea of appearing before the public all at once, in three volumes, was far from dead; his dissatisfaction with serial publication remained. 'Bradbury predicts Heaven knows what', he continued. 'I am sure it will do me a great deal of good; and', he added practically, 'I hope it will sell, well' (P iii. 605).

According to the 'Form of Requiring Entry of Proprietorship', publication day for *A Christmas Carol* was 19 December 1843.[14] Responding to Charles Mackay, a 'sub-editor' on the *Morning Chronicle* which enthusiastically reviewed the *Carol* on publication day, Dickens reported that 'the Subscription was large, and the demand great' (P iii. 610). By Christmas Eve sales had reached 6,000, with orders still 'coming in fast from town and country' (P iii. 616). But the more astonishing aspect of the *Carol*'s reception is the sale *after* Christmas, *after* Boxing Day, on into the summer of 1844. More copies were printed and sold between January and April of that year than during the Christmas season of 1843. No wonder Dickens told Macready on 3 January that the little book 'has been a most prodigious success—the greatest, I think, I have ever achieved' (N i. 557). Orders from the trade nearly exhausted the 2,000 printing of the second edition by publication day, 6 January, and a third, fourth, fifth, sixth, and seventh were machined, pressed, bound, and sold by May.

[13] The bibliography on the bibliography of the *Carol* is itself extensive: I have followed Calhoun and Heaney, and Richard Gimbel, 'The Earliest State of the First Edition of Charles Dickens' *A Christmas Carol*' (*Princeton University Library Chronicle*, 19 (winter 1958), 82–6), taking note of the eight variant copies of the first edition in the Parrish Collection at Princeton. Calhoun and Heaney identify thirty-nine textual changes for the second edition (p. 285).

[14] Gimbel, facsimile facing p. 85.

Meanwhile, relations with Chapman and Hall degenerated. Dickens learned at the beginning of the month that Chapman and Hall had failed to place advertisements in the December issue of most of the monthlies; and though their publicity campaign was in fact rather extensive, amounting to nearly 20 per cent of the total costs of the first edition, including unusually elaborate notices with ornamental type for the title inserted in the monthly number of *Martin Chuzzlewit* and in the *Athenaeum* for 9, 16, and 23 December, still Dickens was enraged. 'Bradbury would not believe it when I told him', Dickens reported to Mitton, incidentally revealing how customary it had become for him to seek solace from his printers (P iii. 605). He wrote a very forceful letter to his publishers, telling them to make no response in writing or person, 'but simply to do what I have ordered'.[15] His frustration was increased by his financial troubles: it was the holiday season, but he was overdrawn on his Coutts's account despite his resolution to the contrary, Kate was once more expecting, his insurance premiums were due again, his December and January incomes were already committed, and he chafed at the repeated but unpredictable financial demands made by his father and other 'blood-petitioners' (P iii. xvii). The only thing to do was to borrow another £200 on a bill from Mitton, which Coutts's as a favour to Dickens discounted 'without the acceptance of a banker or large mercantile house' (P iii. 606), and then to stave off creditors until the *Carol* profits were in.

Additional cause for grievance was the publication, on the same day as the second edition of the *Carol*, of Number 16 of *Parley's Illuminated Library*, price 2*d.*, which contained the first half of *A Christmas Ghost Story*, supposedly 're-originated' and 'anylitically condensed' from Dickens's book. Dickens received a copy between three and four o'clock on Saturday afternoon, 6 January; by Sunday night he had written Mitton instructing him first to register the copyright of the *Carol* (done Monday morning) and second to consult with someone about filing for an injunction. The bills of complaint were written by the same James Bacon who had been involved in the hateful Deed of 1840–1; a preliminary injunction was granted by one of the vice-chancellors,

---

[15] P iii. 604. He may have ordered the more elaborate notice appearing in the *Athenaeum* on 9 Dec.; an earlier advertisement, on 25 Nov., was more modest in size and type design.

Sir J. Knight Bruce, Talfourd appearing for Dickens and winding up his appeal with a quotation from Sheridan: 'You use my ideas as Gipsies do stolen children; they steal children, disfigure them, and then make them pass for their own.' Subsequent litigation supported Dickens's contention that the *Christmas Ghost Story* was a flagrant imitation, that its sale should be permanently barred, and that Dickens should proceed with a suit for damages for infringement of copyright. Prematurely, as it turned out, Dickens rejoiced: 'The Pirates are beaten flat. They are bruised, bloody, battered, smashed, squelched, and utterly undone' (F IV. iii. 321). But though he won the legal battle, he lost the financial one. The defendants were gazetted bankrupts at the end of February. Talfourd hoped he could find 'some means ... to deliver [Dickens] from the penalty which will await on success—the payment of his own costs of an action against Bankrupt Robbers'. But he failed. The costs to Dickens were heavy, as each of the five defendants had to be named in a separate suit; Dickens's total bill came to £700, and he was still paying 'Law Charges' in the amount of £207 in June.[16]

Vexed, harassed, cheated, and in debt, Dickens put all his hopes on the gilt-edged *Carol* accounts. Chapman and Hall were instructed to forward them as soon as possible. Dickens anticipated at least a clear £1,000. By February he could already foresee that legal costs would run to several hundred pounds, and there was Mitton's bill to be provided for shortly. On Saturday, 10 February, Chapman and Hall presented the promised accounts; when they arrived, Dickens tore open the seal and saw something resembling the following:[17]

[16] MS. Coutts; for the full story of Dickens's proceedings against the pirates, consult E. T. Jaques, *Charles Dickens in Chancery* (London, Longmans, Green and Co., 1914), and S. J. Rust, 'At the Dickens House: Legal Documents Relating to the Piracy of *A Christmas Carol*', *Dickensian*, 34 (1938), 41–4. Lee and Haddock, the defendants, filed an affidavit on their behalf citing precedent for their piracy: Henry Hewitt had analysed, abridged, reoriginated, and published upwards of 70,000 copies of *The Old Curiosity Shop* and *Barnaby Rudge* in *Parley's Library*.

[17] A reconstruction based on F IV. ii. 315 and Arthur Waugh, pp. 66–7, sales figures estimated from the practice in subsequent accounts, and letters. For the explanation of discrepancies between this version of the accounts and Forster's, see text. In 1844, a total of 9,000 more copies were printed, and because the charge for drawing and engraving the plates had already been paid, and the advertising was reduced, these sold at a slightly higher margin:

A CHRISTMAS CAROL
First Edition: 6,000 Nos.

Publishers' Account
December, 1843

Sales

	£	s.	d.
6,000 less approximately 103 gift, library, and press copies, sold 26 as 25 in cloth for 3s. 6d. each.	992	5	0

Expenses

	£	s.	d.
Printing	74	2	9
Paper	89	2	0
Drawing and Engravings	49	18	0
Two Steel Plates	1	4	0
Printing Plates	15	17	6
Paper for Plates	7	12	0
Colouring Plates	120	0	0
Binding	180	0	0
Incidentals and Advertising	168	7	8
Commission to Publishers (C & H) [15 per cent on £992. 5s. 0d.]	148	16	9

	£	s.	d.
TOTAL EXPENSES	855	0	8
Balance of account to Mr. Dickens's credit	137	4	4

(*Footnote 17 cont.*)

Second to Seventh Editions, making 7,000 copies:
January–April 1844

Sales

	£	s.	d.
7,000 less approximately 227 in cloth, 337 in quires, unsold (N i. 599); sold 40 as 39 in quires at 2s. 10½d. each, and 26 as 25 in cloth for 3s. 6d. each.	1069	19	0

Expenses

	£	s.	d.
Printing	58	18	0
Paper	103	19	0
Printing Plates	17	10	0
Paper [for Plates]	8	17	4
Colouring Plates	140	0	0
Binding	199	18	2
Incidentals and Advertising	83	5	8
Commission	107	18	10

	£	s.	d.
	£720	7	0
Balance of account to Mr. Dickens's credit	£349	12	0

By the end of the year, all the remainder of the seventh edition (or sixth, since Forster says 'five' editions following the first), plus 1,930 more copies, had been sold, yielding a further £189. 11s. 5d. to Dickens's credit. Thus by 31 December 1844, the accounts stood as follows:

Printed 15,000 copies
Sold 14,930 copies

Dickens's profits		£	s.	d.
	to 31 Dec. 1843	186	16	7
	to 30 Apr. 1844	349	12	0
	to 31 Dec. 1844	189	11	5
	TOTAL	£726	0	0

He tried to go to sleep, to put the bitter disappointment out of his mind until the morning. But it was no use. 'Such a night as I have passed!' he told Forster:

I really believed I should never get up again, until I had passed through all the horrors of a fever. I found the *Carol* accounts awaiting me, and they were the cause of it. The first six thousand copies show a profit of £230![18] And the last four will yield as much more. I had set my heart and soul upon a Thousand, clear. What a wonderful thing it is, that such a great success should occasion me such intolerable anxiety and disappointment! My year's bills, unpaid, are so terrific, that all the energy and determination I can possibly exert will be required to clear me. . . . I am not afraid, if I reduce my expenses; but if I do not, I shall be ruined past all mortal hope of redemption. (F IV. ii. 314)

Though Dickens got over the initial shock in a few hours, he continued to sleep 'as badly as Macbeth' (N i. 567). He blamed Chapman and Hall for mismanaging the book, and accused them of running 'the expenses up anyhow purposely to bring me back and disgust me with the charges'. He recognized that the plates contributed significantly to the costs, more than equalling his profit (£194. 11s. 6d. for all charges connected with illustrations), and reflected that for *Sketches of Young Couples*, 'a poor thing of little worth published without my name', he had received £200. Unwilling to acknowledge that both price and elaborate format were his own choices, dictated to publishers who were instructed not to answer or drop by, but only to do as they were told, Dickens wrote a stiff letter of response. He may have cut their commission from 15 to 10 per cent, as he informed Mitton, 'I have adhered to the strict business percentage', and saw 'the shadow of war' before him. If so, Chapman and Hall apparently responded promptly to Dickens's peremptory letter, and were conciliatory, for another cheque from the firm for £49. 12s. 3d. was deposited to Dickens's credit two days later, 14 February (MS.

---

[18] Either Forster has misread Dickens's hand, and copied '£230' for '£130' (the actual figure being £137. 4s. 4d.), or Dickens includes in his computation of profit in addition to his balance two-thirds of Chapman and Hall's 15 per cent commission, that is £99. 4s. 6d., making a total of £236. 8s. 10d. The other 5 per cent of the commission was returned to Dickens, increasing his profit to the £186. 16s. 7d. shown by Forster (IV. ii. 315), and reducing Chapman and Hall's net to exactly 10 per cent of the wholesale sales. They may, of course, have made additional profit from retail sales, but as Dickens was no partner in the book-selling enterprise, he would not be concerned about that profit.

Coutts), bringing his profits to £186. 16s. 7d., and reducing their commission to the £99. 4s. 6d. shown in Forster's account.

But Dickens was not to be mollified. Even as he sent off his stiff letter to his former 'trusty friends', he was planning to inspect the books minutely before signing them. Hall's allusion to the American book rubbed the wrong way. True, *Chuzzlewit* was beginning to turn the corner in profits, and contribute at last to the reduction of his debts; but Chapman and Hall were finished, 'past and over. Nothing can remedy that' (N i. 568).

Angry as he was, Dickens took precautions to see that his disappointment was not revealed at large. He instructed Mitton, to whom he sent three letters and the accounts on Monday the twelfth, not to 'talk of this to anyone'. He went on, 'I shall not tell Bradbury & Evans, as I think it highly important not to dash the triumph of the book' (N i. 568). Not only was he concerned not to damp the enthusiastic reception (Thackeray calling it a 'national benefit'), but also he wanted to appear before his printers in the strongest possible light, now that he was determined to separate from Chapman and Hall before summer.

Mitton returned the accounts and a copy of Dickens's letter to Chapman and Hall the same day, and expressed the hope of seeing Dickens before dinner to reconsider his actions. But Dickens was still worked up. He anticipated—incorrectly, as it turned out—an impertinent reply, and still felt 'not only on my beam-ends, but tilted over on the other side. Nothing so unexpected and utterly disappointing has ever befallen me'. Shades of the sponging house, the bailiff, the Marshalsea, all the old terrors of poverty, ignominy, hunger stirred up once again. The £200 note must be repaid from the scanty *Carol* balance, and the 'rest must be worked round somehow. I wish I could say that I see how (I am thunderstricken by the amount), but I have been on the other side with you often', he concluded to Mitton, 'and you must do your best for me' (N i. 568). Two days later, Thomas Beard asked to have William Beard McCabe, Dickens's former colleague in the Reporters' Gallery, introduced to Chapman and Hall; Dickens declined, explaining confidentially that his relations with the firm were 'not perfectly agreeable', and that a 'vague kind of barrier has arisen between us'. He added, 'and I do not entertain the least desire to throw it down' (N i. 568-9).

Negotiations started almost immediately to disentangle Dickens from his publishers. Meanwhile, he went on a triumphant tour to the Midlands, speaking at institutions in Liverpool and Birmingham. There were some abortive discussions with John Easthope about writing letters from abroad for the *Morning Chronicle* for pay; it was nice revenge for previous mistreatment, but the proposition was turned down (F IV. iii. 325). By the beginning of March, Chapman and Hall sent in the accounts for the half-year ending 31 December 1843, and these were encouraging. 'The half year's account is GOOD', Dickens told Mitton. 'Deducting £50 a month from Chuzzlewit up to the end, the [whole] debt is reduced to £1900. There will then be the half year's profits to deduct, and the whole subscription [to the novel in volume form]. So please God it will have come down bravely by the time I start' (N i. 578). Still, the shoe pinched occasionally; once, quite sharply, in mid April, forcing Dickens to apply to Mitton once again: 'I am very much and pressingly in want of a hundred pounds until June. Though the time is short, my father's debts, two quarters income tax etc., coming all at once, drive me, sailing so near the wind by not drawing any profits from C and H, into a most uncomfortable corner. Can you oblige me with this or devise any means of doing so?' (N i. 594). Once again Mitton, who had just come back from Yorkshire after attending the funeral of his former partner Smithson, devised the means of supplying 'the one thing needful'; on 19 April £100 was deposited in Dickens's account (MS. Coutts).

Prospectively at least, the situation was eased by the conclusion of discussions with Bradbury and Evans on 25 April. Dickens's determination to leave Chapman and Hall, and to take a year off to rest and travel principally in Italy, had not wavered; all his plans now tended in that direction. There was therefore no point, and some potential danger and embarrassment, in waiting until he returned to settle up the accounts and transfer from one publisher to the other, so Bradbury and Evans, somewhat reluctantly it might be supposed, agreed to take him on, on his own terms. They planned to pay off all the Chapman and Hall balance, and to consolidate into their own firm as much as possible of the stock on hand of books in which Dickens retained a share. Chapman and Hall were therefore instructed to prepare 'the necessary statements' with 'all dispatch', and copies of all agreements with them were requisitioned from Mitton, with a view to determining precisely what Dickens's share was, and whether the copyrights were sufficiently unencumbered to permit Bradbury and Evans to publish a cheap edition. 'I must of course give them an Interest in throwing every possible kind of alacrity into the business working of books old, and book new', Dickens confided to Mitton (N i. 595). The results were communicated to the printers on 8 May (N i. 598–600).

First, Dickens anticipated that the balance due to Chapman and Hall on all his debts would be reduced to £1,500 by the end of the serial run. In addition, he would require £1,500 for his year's expenses, with the right to draw up to £500 more, and he was already in their debt to the amount of £500. Towards this certain total of £3,500, he would apply £500 from the sales of *Chuzzlewit* in book form, leaving an advance of £3,000, or £3,500 should he require the extra money, to be repaid.[19]

Dickens then proposed four means of repayment:

First, the reissue of the *Carol*—nearly 2,000 more copies were sold between May and December 1844—and the publication of a 'new Carol' for Christmas 1844. Clearly in the April meeting Dickens had volunteered to attempt to repeat his previous triumph.

Second, the publication of a magazine or journal. 'I would suggest that it should be commenced within six months, certainly, after the expiration of my year's retirement.' All his objections to another periodical had given way.

Third, there was 'the question of other new books by me' (N i. 598). Dickens had told Felton back in January that he wanted to go away for a year, 'next midsummer, bag and baggage, little ones and all—' and then come out 'with *such* a story, Felton, all at once, no parts, sledge-hammer blow' (N i. 554). Perhaps the notion of writing a three-decker was also attractive to Bradbury and Evans, who would thereby not have to cope with creating a distribution network for parts.

And fourth, there was 'the best working of the Copyrights in existence'. Of these, *Oliver Twist*, the *Carol*, and *American Notes* were free: *Twist* and *Carol* Dickens owned unconditionally, and for the American book, he had written Chapman and Hall giving them a quarter share. As no agreement had been made, he felt at

---

[19] His actual debt to Chapman and Hall, paid 21 June 1844, was only £640. 19s. 6d. (MS. Coutts).

liberty to withdraw his gift.[20] On the other books, various complicated arrangements remained in effect. *Sketches* was held by Chapman and Hall 'in trust', as Dickens put it, until March 1845, with all profits until then being put towards repaying the £2,250 which Chapman and Hall had given Macrone; at that time, Dickens could buy half the copyright and stock, if he paid half the outstanding balance. Dickens's interest in *Pickwick* was one-third, and so long as Chapman and Hall retained two-thirds he thought that he had no power to appoint another publisher. In November 1844 the five-year lease on the *Nickleby* copyright expired but, as with *Pickwick*, if he wished to sell Dickens was obliged to offer the copyright to Chapman and Hall first. Of the *Clock*, Dickens had half copyright. There was no distinct clause, he explained to Bradbury and Evans, making Chapman and Hall always the publishers, 'but I apprehend the stipulation that they shall not alter the form or price without my consent, implies that.' Finally, for *Chuzzlewit* Dickens had a three-quarters interest during serial publication and for six months thereafter, subject to repayment of loans. And in December 1844 Chapman and Hall, on paying a fourth of the cost of the stock on hand, came into half the copyright. Again, if either side wished to dispose of its interest, the other side had right of first refusal. In short, in all these ventures in which they shared the copyright, Chapman and Hall had the right to buy Dickens's if he wished to sell.

Therefore, Dickens suggested two alternatives: to publish the three books owned outright with a new publisher in a cheap form, or 'to break ground with Chapman and Hall, for a general serial Edition of *all* the books in Volumes', under the auspices of Bradbury and Evans. 'This Edition I should propose to embrace new prefaces, and here and there a note, by me, and in short anything I could think of, to increase its interest.' What finally eventuated three years later was a combination of the two—a cheap edition of all the works, in weekly numbers, monthly parts, and volumes, with new prefaces and revised texts.

In addition, Dickens gave his printers an account of some of the current stock in hand, excluding that for *Sketches* and for *Pickwick*

---

20 But he evidently was not. There is an unpublished A. L. S. to Chapman and Hall dated 28 June 1844 which requests that the stock and plates for *Twist* and the *Carol* only be delivered to Bradbury and Evans (the Pierpont Morgan Library, MA 2707).

'(which is preparing), but as [Chapman and Hall] were moving me not long ago towards a new issue of this book, I suppose it is not very large'.[21]

Oliver Twist: 27 in cloth, 583 in quires

American Notes: 61 in cloth, 168 in quires

A Christmas Carol: 227 in cloth, 337 in quires

Master Humphrey's Clock: 208,753 numbers. 'This of course has to be divided by the *number of numbers* in the two stories [*Shop* 45, *Barnaby* 43]. The miscellaneous papers were reserved for wasting; and of them there are on hand 99,250.'

Dickens concluded his lengthy summary of 'business details' with the proviso that he would like his money on the first of June, or shortly thereafter, and that he and Forster were ready to wait upon them when they had considered these matters. An Agreement was signed on 1 June 1844; on the same day, £2,000 from Bradbury and Evans was deposited in Dickens's account, along with Chapman and Hall's final payment for the last Dickens serial the firm would publish for twenty years (MS. Coutts). For the £2,000, and three possible further payments (a £1,000 draft on 'Smith & Co.' deposited on the 15th, and advances of £500 on 17 January 1845 and £300 on 17 March (MS. Coutts)), Dickens assigned to Bradbury and Evans a quarter share in everything he might write over the next eight years, to 31 May 1852. There was no interest on the advance to accrue at any time or in any event. There was an understanding that Dickens would write a successor to the *Carol* to be ready by Christmas 1844, and that some sort of magazine might be started. And there was a stipulation that if Dickens was 'only partially editor or author' of the journal, his share would be reduced to two-thirds. But no further commitments—not even to a travel book or a cheap edition or a reissue of previous works—were made, and none demanded. And the money was not even a loan, since repayment was secured by the publishers' putative share in the profits of future works, not by promissory notes which might attach Dickens's share. The only security offered were the two Britannia life insurance policies, and possibly the Eagle one for £5,000 (N ii. 398).

Once again, the generosity of the new publishers contrasted sharply with the supposed miserliness of the old. And for the first

[21] Dickens paid £81. 9s. 8d. for his share of the *Pickwick* stock in Apr. 1844 (N i. 671).

time, Dickens's future was not heavily mortgaged. A 'Printers' Party' to celebrate the new alliance, with *Punch* contributors Gilbert A'Beckett, John Leech, and editor Mark Lemon, as well as Mrs. Hicks, the Bradburys, the Evanses, members of Dickens's family, and Forster, was held shortly afterwards to cement the good feelings. A more subdued celebration marked the conclusion of *Chuzzlewit*; Lord Normanby presided at a dinner at Greenwich during the 'dog days', as Carlyle called them; Clarkson Stanfield brought along the ageing J. M. W. Turner, who sat next to Forster without saying much, quietly enjoying himself by gazing at the changing lights on the river that sultry summer afternoon.

III

FORTUNE WITH FAME

Literature has become a profession. It is a means of subsistence, almost as certain as the bar or the church. The number of aspirants increases daily, and daily the circle of readers grows wider. That there are some evils inherent in such a state of things it would be folly to deny; but still greater folly would it be to see nothing beyond these evils. Bad or good, there is no evading the 'great fact', now what is so firmly established. We may deplore, but we cannot alter it.

'THE CONDITION OF AUTHORS IN ENGLAND,
GERMANY AND FRANCE',
Fraser's Magazine, March 1847

9

With Bradbury and Evans

Carlyle said of Dickens that . . . he had a remarkable faculty for business; he managed his periodical[s] skilfully, and made good bargains with his book-sellers.[1]

SETTLED AT LAST by the end of July in a 'lonely, rusty, stagnant old staggerer of a domain' (F IV. iv. 330), the Villa di Bella Vista, Albaro, outside Genoa, Dickens began to turn his thoughts towards the promised Christmas book. His desk, with paper, pens, and mementoes tidily arranged, was placed in the best bedroom under a window which afforded a peaceful yet cheerful view of sea, mountains, washed-out villas, vineyards, and 'blistering white-hot fort' (F IV. iv. 334). But the shabby villa was clearly unsuitable for the winter; at the end of September, after a visit from Fred, the Dickens entourage moved from the Pink Jail to the *piano nobile* of the Palazzo Peschiere in Genoa. There, after being driven nearly mad with vexation and giddiness by the bells of Genoa, 'pouring into his ears, again and again, in a tuneless, grating, discordant, jerking, hideous vibration' (F IV. v. 346), he finally got down to writing the promised sequel to the *Carol*, informing Forster of his title in a letter of a single sentence: 'We have heard THE CHIMES at midnight, Master Shallow!' (F IV. v. 346). By the end of October, despite interruptions, the first section was written, and Dickens forwarded it with the outline of the rest of the book. He missed the streets of London, but still got on well: 'my steam very much up', 'in regular, ferocious excitement with the *Chimes*', 'in stout heart' (F IV. v. 350 and 353). On 3 November, at half past two in the afternoon, he wrote 'The End'; already he was planning to go to

---

[1] Sir Charles Gavan Duffy, *Conversations with Carlyle* (London, Sampson Low, Marston, and Company, 1892), p. 77.

London to read it to a select circle of friends at Forster's, and to supervise this first of Bradbury and Evans's publications through the press (F IV. v. 354–5). Unable to handle the distribution of copies on their own, they had to call in Chapman and Hall for help. Conciliatory once again, Dickens's old publishers agreed to co-operate, with the result that though the book was published by Bradbury and Evans, title-page and advertisements carried the name Chapman and Hall.

Dickens first saw designs for the illustrations in the Piazza Coffee House, Covent Garden, on 1 December; he found one of Leech's drawings, and one of Doyle's, 'so unlike my ideas, that I had them both to breakfast with me this morning,' he told Kate on the 2nd, 'and with that winning manner which you know of, got them with the highest good humour to do both afresh' (N i. 647). He spent two solid days at the printer's reading proof and nervously superintending the production of his book, but finished in time to depart for Italy on Sunday night, 8 December, eight days before the *Chimes* was published.

On 14 April 1845, Dickens was able to report good news to Mitton concerning its sales and profits: Bradbury and Evans

make *the Profit* on the first 20,000, from fourteen to fifteen hundred pounds. And they add that if they had charged only their own small commission, and had not been obliged to employ Chapman and Hall, the profit would have been from £150 to £200 more. C and H's accounts make a profit of £726 only, on a sale of 15,000 of the Carol. So that supposing it had sold 20,000, the gross profit would have been about £1,000. This is a slight difference! Think of the difference too, in the appearance and production of the two books—and I think you will agree with me that Bradbury and Evans are the men for me to work with. (N i. 671)

In all fairness to Chapman and Hall, it must be said that the *Chimes* was a cheaper book to produce, Dickens having abandoned coloured illustrations rather than raising the price above the *Carol*'s five shillings. Nevertheless, it was a handsome book, a foolscap 8vo bound in bright red horizontal fine-ribbed cloth, blocked in blind and gold, with gilt edges, yellow endpapers, and vignette title on steel.[2] The Whitefriars printers were very anxious to please Dickens. The 'Paper and Print' Ledgers of the firm set forth neatly the details of the first 20,000 copies, 19,916

Edward Chapman

Frederic Chapman

William Bradbury

F. M. Evans

DICKENS'S PUBLISHERS

Receipt for *Pickwick Papers*, 4 February 1837

From *Sketches by Boz*, Part I, November 1837

CHAPMAN AND HALL

From Richard Doyle's journal, 16 April 1840, showing customers at
186 Strand with copies of *Master Humphrey's Clock*, No. 3

Advertisement for books sold by Chapman and Hall,
from *Martin Chuzzlewit*, Part I, January 1843

CHAPMAN AND HALL

New Work in Monthly Parts,
By Mr. CHARLES DICKENS.

On the First of October,

(To be completed in Twenty Monthly Parts, uniform with " MARTIN CHUZZLEWIT," *&c.)*

Price One Shilling,

THE FIRST NUMBER

OF

Wholesale, Retail, and for Exportation.

EDITED BY " BOZ."

WITH ILLUSTRATIONS BY "PHIZ."

LONDON:
BRADBURY & EVANS, WHITEFRIARS.

AGENTS—J. MENZIES, EDINBURGH ; J. MACLEOD, GLASGOW ; J. M'GLASHAN, DUBLIN.

Advertisement for *Dombey and Son*, from inside wrapper of *Oliver Twist*, Part IX, September 1846

THE BREAK

Advertisement for the Cheap Edition, from Chapman and Hall's *Catalogue of Books* of June 1847

THE BREAK

MS. account, Bradbury and Evans, July to December 1846, showing profits on
Dombey and Son, Parts I–IV

BRADBURY AND EVANS

Little Dorrit N.1

1855

Nov 30 Printing 1 Sheet D. Demy   N. 32000
        Composition 5.15.6   Cor.d Machinist 3/1   8 15 6
        Stereos 4.0.0   Machine 64 th. £4 24.16.0   28 16 —
        Reeping 64 th. of 6.8.0   Postage 1.15.0   8   3 —
        Casual.d Matter   17   6 6
        32000 Wrappers   11 11 —
        Elect.l T. page   4 casts   4   —
        Paper — Text 64 th. & Demy c 32/   102   8 —
        —   Wrappers 16 — c 23/   18   8 —
        —   Additional 64 th. c 24/   83   4 —
        —   Plate 64 Rem c 16/   52   —
        Print 32000 Plate c 32/ 8.0.0 High Net 74/   90 10 —
        Drawing & Etching   22 17 —
        —   Duplicate   8 18 6
        Printing Additional 5000. 32/1/   11   6 —
        Plate 27/. Working off Plate 14/   2   1 —

        Reprinting   3000
        Paper, Machine. Press & Wrapper   16 18 6
        Reprint Additional 10.0.0   Plate 14.0.0   24 10 —

        Reprinting   3000
        Paper, Machine, Press & Wrapper   16 18 6
        Plate & Paper   10 10 —
        Stitching 36780 c 24/   48   1 4
        Sundry Bill £ —   15   2 5
                                                                    612 5 3

        Carr.d forward   612 5 3

Notice regarding the discontinuance of *Household Words* and the commencement of *All the Year Round*, from *The Bookseller*, 23 April 1859

Advertisement for books sold by Bradbury and Evans, from *Bleak House*, Part XII, February 1853 (including 257 allowed as the thirteenth book) of which had been sold as 18,873 at 3s. 6d. by 31 December, yielding £3,302. 15s. 6d. The net profit, after deducting all expenses including £49. 10s. 11d. commission to agents and a 10 per cent or £330. 5s. 6d. commission to publishers, was £1,420. 10s. 11d., shared three-quarters or £1,065. 8s. 2d. to Dickens, and £355. 2s. 9d. to Bradbury and Evans. Dickens's response indicates their eagerness to solicit his approval. 'They were very anxious to know what I thought of their management in general, under the disadvantageous circumstance of having C and H in the business at all. I wrote and told them that I was greatly pleased, and that I was quite certain it couldn't have been better done, as I am' (N i. 671). He may well have suggested doing another Christmas book for the coming season in the same letter. Mitton did not agree that Bradbury and Evans had done all that well, but Dickens was hot to defend them: 'I don't think you quite understand that the little book is in a very expensive form—that you remember it is not sold [wholesale] at five shillings [but at 3s. 6d.] . . .' (N i. 677)

By the spring of 1845, Chapman and Hall had rendered their accounts to Forster, for the period from April 1844 through December. These accounts were 'not so bad either':

	£	s.	d.
Chuzzlewit [Nos. XVIII–XX, ¾ share]	611	12	4
Humphrey's Clock [½ share]	24	2	3
Pickwick [⅛ share]	50	2	4
Carol	189	11	5
Oliver Twist	54	0	10
German Bookseller for proofs [Tauchnitz]	5	10	0
	934	19	2[3]

[3] N i. 671. Since Dickens owed Chapman and Hall a few pounds for purchases charged against his profits, the net balance was reduced to £928. 14s. 2d., paid into his Coutts account 24 May 1844. Tauchnitz published an 'Edition Sanctioned by the Author' of the *Carol*, possibly printed from the earliest English proofs of the book, as well as of *The Chimes* and subsequent works by Dickens; I do not know if Dickens received any payment for the former, but it would be likely, as he wrote to Tauchnitz on 3 Oct. 1843: 'if you will favour me with any distinct proposition . . . I shall be happy to give it *immediate* consideration' (P iii. 579). See J. Y. Southton, 'Authorised Leipzig Edition of Dickens', *Dickensian*, 8 (1912), 181–3. Tauchnitz's 'Collection of British Authors', published for continental circulation only and prohibited from importation into England or any British colony, began in 1841 with *Pickwick* and Bulwer's *Pelham*, and reached its 500th volume in 1863, its 2,000th in 1881. See Tighe Hopkins, ' "The Tauchnitz" Edition: The Story of a Popular Publisher', *The Pall Mall Gazette*, 25 (Oct. 1901), 197–208.

Though the Bradbury and Evans advances had been substantially reduced, it would be an exaggeration to say, as Edgar Johnson does, that there 'was certainly no longer any need to worry about money' (J, p. 556). The publishers had not yet recouped their investment, and Dickens's expenses still ran high. His Midsummer 1845 balance was healthy—£1,104—but a year later it had fallen to only £121 (MS. Coutts). None the less, as a consequence of the good news, Dickens ordered a rather liberal redecorating scheme for Devonshire Terrace.

Before leaving Genoa in June, he began considering schemes for publishing a book of travels similar to *American Notes*. But somehow the letters to Forster and others didn't seem very appropriate material. 'I cannot for the life of me devise any plan of using them to my own satisfaction, and yet think entirely with you that in some form I ought to use them', he told Forster on 7 June 1845 (F IV. vii. 372). He was also revolving in his mind plans for the periodical, which it was suggested in his letter of 8 May 1844 should commence 'within six months, certainly, after the expiration of my year's retirement'. He inclined to a weekly, at three-halfpence, with papers both original and extracted from other journals, notices, and reviews, and

Carol philosophy, cheerful views, sharp anatomization of humbug, jolly good temper; papers always in season, pat to the time of year;[4] and a vein of glowing, hearty, generous, mirthful, beaming reference in everything to Home, and Fireside. And I would call it, sir—

THE CRICKET
A cheerful creature that chirrups on the Hearth.
Natural History.

(F V. i. 378)

Forster was against the plan, and it was soon abandoned; but the name survived in Dickens's mind as a 'delicate and beautiful fancy for a Christmas book, making the Cricket a little household god—silent in the wrong and sorrow of the tale, and loud again when all went well and happy' (F V. i. 379–80). By 6 August he

---

4 Another indication of Dickens's sensitivity to 'seasonal relevance'. Cf. David M. Bevington, 'Seasonal Relevance in *The Pickwick Papers*', *Nineteenth-Century Fiction*, 16 (Dec. 1961), 219–30.

was busy getting together estimates for Bradbury and Evans on the cost of running a daily paper, despite Forster's grave misgivings (N i. 691); five days later he told them that 'Rather a good notion in connexion with the Cricket has occurred to me this morning. A decided chirp!' (N i. 693), indicating that Whitefriars was also alerted to the forthcoming Christmas book.

Meanwhile, Dickens was entangled in producing *Every Man in his Humour*, with an amateur company that included Stanfield, Frank Stone, and many of the *Punch* people: Douglas Jerrold, Lemon, A'Beckett, Leech. At the same time, social and personal relations with the *Punch* publishers remained warm. In the midst of 'Managerial agonies', Dickens arranged for Bradbury and Evans to work the copyright of *Oliver Twist*, which belonged solely to him, by issuing it in ten monthly numbers similar in format to *Pickwick* and *Nickleby*, with twenty-four illustrations and a new cover by Cruikshank.[5] By the first of October he was also preparing his illustrators for the third Christmas book, which 'we intend publishing earlier than usual this year' (N i. 706), perhaps because of the *Daily News*, perhaps also because he had decided to cash in on the inevitable dramatizations by arranging with Robert Keeley for a Lyceum Theatre production to open on the night of publication. One hundred pounds paid after opening night secured an advance copy of the story from which the play was adapted.[6] Obligations snowballed, and Bradbury and Evans were dragged into the mêlée, printing ordinary tickets and programmes, as well as 'White satin Play Bills' for Prince Albert, who planned to attend a performance of *Every Man* at St. James's Theatre on 15 November.

A major preoccupation for Dickens and his publishers during the last months of 1845 was the founding of the *Daily News*. It used to be argued that Dickens's abortive venture into newspaper editing was prompted by his spite at John Easthope and the *Morning Chronicle*, and that his resignation only a few weeks after the paper began publication was yet another instance of his irresponsibility and capriciousness. Gerald Grubb laid these

---

[5] Parts II, III, IX, and X had three illustrations each; there was no final double number. Cruikshank was paid £24 for retouching the plates, and £10 for the wrapper design (MS. B & E).

[6] See N i. 698 and 785; payment for the *Cricket* was made on 23 Dec. 1845, and for *Battle* on 24 Dec. 1846 (MS. Coutts). Dickens was 'bothered to death' by the dramatization of the latter (N i. 821).

allegations to rest in the early 1950s through a series of articles on 'Dickens and the *Daily News*';[7] supplementing his account by more recent scholarship, we can see how and why Dickens entered into, and quickly departed from, Fleet Street.

There always was a journalistic streak in Dickens; he never completely abandoned the role of reporter, and in the 1840s in particular he contributed a number of articles on current affairs to various journals. In the summer of 1842, just after he returned from America, Dickens contemplated establishing a new Liberal evening paper by buying up the premises, type, and stock of the recently merged *Courier*. Soliciting the financial support and influence of leading Liberals, Dickens assured Lady Holland that

if I threw my small person into the breach, and wrote for the paper (literary articles as well as political) I could command immediate attention; while the influence I have with Booksellers and Authors would give me a better chance of stamping it with a new character, and securing for it, after a reasonable trial, good advertisements, than almost any other man could possess. (P iii. 262)

But Stanley advised Dickens that the Liberals could not afford to back the paper, and so the scheme quickly fell through. A plan for associating himself with a newspaper resurfaced during the spring of 1844, first with the *Morning Chronicle* discussions about his Italian papers, then with the Bradbury and Evans negotiations.

However, the idea for the *Daily News* did not, as it happens, originate with Dickens or his new publishers.[8] In the earliest days of the printing firm of Bradbury and Evans, they had produced for Joseph Paxton, gardener to the Duke of Devonshire, a monthly

7 'Dickens and the *Daily News*: The Origin of the Idea', in Hill Shine, ed., *Booker Memorial Studies: Eight Essays on Victorian Literature in Memory of John Manning Booker* (Chapel Hill, Univ. of North Carolina Press, 1950), pp. 60–77; and three articles on 'Dickens and the "Daily News"' in *Nineteenth-Century Fiction*, sub-titled 'Preliminaries to Publication' (6 (1951–2), 174–94); 'The Early Issues' (6 (1951–2), 234–46); and 'Resignation' (7 (1952–3), 19–38).

8 The evidence so far published does not seem to support David Paroissen's view that Dickens was involved with the *Daily News* for twenty-eight months, that is, from the February 1844 meeting with Andrew Doyle, editor of the *Morning Chronicle*, until May 1846 (*Pictures from Italy*, ed. Paroissen (London, André Deutsch, 1973), p. 21). Forster says that in the council he had with Dickens, Bradbury, and Evans concerning Dickens's writing travel letters from abroad for the *Chronicle* lay 'the germ of another newspaper enterprise he permitted himself to engage in twelve months later' (F IV. iii. 325), but there is no indication that Dickens was consistently involved in the planning of any daily publication until the summer of 1845.

gardening paper called the *Horticultural Register*.[9] Paxton and Bradbury soon became friends; Bradbury helped to introduce the young man, then under thirty, to London literary circles, and in return Paxton advised Bradbury on business and showed him how to invest in railway shares. As Paxton's fortune increased, so did his ambition: he built more and more elaborate structures at Chatsworth, he invested widely and shrewdly in railway shares, he supervised the reorganization of the Duke's affairs, and he expanded his botanical publications to include the *Magazine of Botany* which he edited and the weekly *Gardeners' Chronicle* which he founded.[10] In the summer of 1845 the time seemed ripe for the founding of a daily newspaper, and by the first of July it is likely that Paxton had broached the subject to his old friend, now a leading London printer with the experience of printing and publishing the successful weekly magazine *Punch*. Bradbury in turn seems to have asked Dickens for advice, since Dickens considered that he had been, during his *Mirror of Parliament* days, 'as well acquainted with the management of [a newspaper] . . . as an Engineer is, with the Steam engine' (P iii. 265–6). Dickens, in turn, asked the experienced journalist Thomas Beard questions about the cost of running a newspaper.

Several months of negotiations ensued, with the consequence that Dickens's role imperceptibly enlarged from 'actively assisting' to editing. On 3 November he wrote to Bradbury and Evans formally declaring that he was, despite Forster's opposition, prepared to accept the post of editor at £2,000 a year. Included in his duties would be

the Publication of the series of Italian letters, with my name—my frequently writing for the paper from day to day—my constantly exercising an active and vigilant superintendence over the whole machine. When I am there, or after I have left the office, I shall, (as the custom is) have a Sub-Editor to whom I can, with perfect confidence, hand over the practical management for the time being. The head and leading principle of the thing I am willing to become on these terms. (N i. 714)

Dickens was not himself to be a shareholder; financial backing came from Paxton and his friends. On the very day he wrote his proposal, unhappily, there 'was a failure of a great Broker in the

---

[9] Violet R. Markham, *Paxton and the Bachelor Duke* (London, Hodder & Stoughton, 1935), p. 36. [10] Ibid., p. 165.

city ... which so affects two of my principal people that the Paper *cannot be*, on any proper footing', he told Beard the next day. 'They will have to pay some five or six Thousand Pounds for engagements made. I shall take nothing but my leave' (N i. 715).

Dickens continued to give this same advice to his publishers after consulting with Forster. 'So far as I am personally concerned, the heart of the enterprise is broken and dead. If I could do such violence to myself as to resume it tomorrow,' he told them, 'I should have no faith in it. It would always oppress me as a doomed thing; and every new engagement we might make, would fill me with new fear and wretchedness.' He was equally discouraging about the project as a scheme apart from himself. Paxton wanted to patch things up and go forward, but Dickens believed that the spirit had gone out of the enterprise, and that there was no way out except to 'look the utmost present loss, steadily in the face; ... meet it; and pay the utmost of the money; and turn the leaf down on which the amount is written, and look at it no more' (N i. 716). He was distressed to think of all those who had risked their present incomes to join the project, but repeatedly urged abandoning it. Macready had already expressed forcibly to Forster his objections, sensing that Dickens was 'rushing headlong into an enterprise that demands the utmost foresight, skilful and secret preparation and qualities of a conductor which Dickens has not'.[11]

But Paxton, not to be dissuaded, talked Bradbury and Evans into putting up nearly one-quarter of the reconstituted capital of £100,000.[12] They soon were seeing to the practical furnishing of the carpeted rooms next door at 90 Fleet Street, hired for the paper's offices: 'an ordinary office table and armchair, a stained-wood reading desk, six leather-bottomed chairs, a small bookcase, and a black horsehair sofa'.[13] While they were taken up with

[11] *Diaries*, ii. 309.
[12] Markham, p. 168, cites a memorandum of partnership dated 17 Nov. 1845 that gives the initial capital contributed by each partner: Paxton—£25,000, Bradbury and Evans jointly—£22,500, Richard Wright—£2,500. Later Sir William Jackson and Sir Joshua Walmsley doubled the capital, either by themselves or with the help of other parties (Grubb, 'Dickens and the "Daily News"', *Nineteenth-Century Fiction*, 6 (1951–2), 182).
[13] Justin McCarthy and John R. Robinson, *'The Daily News' Jubilee, A Political and Social Retrospect of Fifty Years of the Queen's Reign* (London, 1896), p. 8, quoted in Grubb, 'Dickens and the "Daily News"', *Nineteenth-Century Fiction*, 6 (1951–2), 193.

their new commitment, Dickens sent out a flurry of correspondence about the *Cricket* illustrations, which the publishers wanted to be as extensive and costly as those in *The Chimes*. He also finished the text by 1 December, and then bustled down to Fleet Street to arrange the paper's affairs, zealous to make it a commercial and journalistic success: 'I am regularly in harness now, and we are getting on vigorously and steadily', Dickens told Paxton (N i. 724). The steadiness and gallantry of the printers during the dark days of November impressed him strongly; writing at that time, he assured them 'in a truly earnest and affectionate spirit . . . that I esteem and honor you the more for what I have known of you since these occurrences. I hope and believe that a long course of mutual confidence and friendship and mutual usefulness, is open to us' (N i. 718).

The *Cricket*'s chirp was met by an angry blast from *The Times*, whose writer may have been aroused by the impending appearance of an 'independent newspaper of liberal politics' under Dickens's editorship.[14] But the public flocked to Dickens's latest work in greater numbers than ever before; the habit of his Christmas books—'as regularly expected as a pantomime'—had caught on, and Forster reports that at the outset *Cricket* sales doubled those of its predecessors.[15] From the office of the *Daily News*, on New Year's Day 1846, Dickens told C. C. Felton that the *Cricket* was a tremendous success, beating his 'other Carols out of the field, and . . . going, still, like wildfire' (N i. 730).

These accounts exaggerate. By 31 December 1845 the entire first edition was sold out, but the print order for it had been reduced from *The Chimes*'s 20,000 to 16,500. A second edition of 8,500 was then produced, and of the two 20,617 (including 358 allowed as the thirteenth book) as 19,449 had been sold, certainly

[14] J, p. 579. Forster believed *The Times* to be motivated by jealousy, as did Macready, who noted on 27 Dec. that the 'most *savage* attack on Dickens and his last book' looked to him 'like the heavy and remorseless blow of an enemy, determined to disable his antagonist by striking to maim him or kill if he can, and so render his hostility powerless'. Forster told Macready on that day of his fears that the *Daily News* would greatly injure Dickens, who was unqualified to direct it, but that 'Dickens was so intensely fixed on his own opinions and in his admiration of his own works (who could have believed it?) that he, Forster, was useless to him as a counsel, or for an opinion on anything touching upon them, and that, as he refused to see criticisms on himself, this partial passion would grow upon him, till it became an incurable evil' (*Diaries*, ii. 316).

[15] F V. i. 380. The quotation, from the 27 Dec. *Mirror of Literature*, is used by Michael Slater in his Introduction to *The Christmas Books*, ii. 10.

not 'double' the circulation of *The Chimes*. The profits were almost identical with the preceding book: £1,363. 0s. 6d., of which £1,022. 5s. 5d., Dickens's share, was added to £200 of other Bradbury and Evans revenue and deposited to his account on 29 April (MS. Coutts). Interest was undoubtedly quickened and sustained by the seventeen different dramatizations that appeared within a month after the *Cricket*'s publication. Between January and June 3,074 more copies were sold as 2,945 at 3s. 6d. each, bringing Dickens's three-quarters share of the profit on the book just for that six-month period to £294. 6s. 5d.

Meanwhile, at the beginning of 1846 the monthly numbers of *Oliver Twist* went on sale, encased for the most part in the familiar green wrappers, with Cruikshank's admirable cover of eleven vignettes.[16] A modest advertising campaign had been launched—200,000 16mo bills, 32,000 quarter-sheet demy notices, 1,000 show cards, 100 advertising cards, and fifty post 8vo circulars were printed—but only £69. 4s. 6d. worth of advertising in journals was taken during the first six months. The expectations were decidedly *not* great: only 5,000 copies of each number were printed, and the amount stitched into wrappers declined from all 5,000 of Number I to 4,000 of III and IV, 3,750 of V and VI, and 3,250 each of the remainder. Even this proved too sanguine. Of the 35,000 copies of Numbers I–VII issued by 1 July, only 23,836 were sold, at 8s. 6d. for a baker's dozen.[17] Dickens's half-share of the profits, £81. 7s. 3d., was exceeded by Bradbury and Evans's commission, £84. 8s. 5d.

The truly earnest affectionate spirit, the mutual confidence and friendship, of the preceding November, was being eroded. Everyone connected with the *Daily News* laboured to scoop *The Times* on covering Peel's speech attacking the Corn Laws at the reconvening of Parliament on 20 January; John Dickens ran a veritable relay between the Commons and Fleet Street as his staff of reporters took their turns transcribing the debate. But at

---

[16] A few blue wrappers of Part I exist (Thomas Hatton and Arthur H. Cleaver, *A Bibliography of the Periodical Works of Charles Dickens: Bibliographical, Analytical, and Statistical* (London, Chapman & Hall Ltd., 1933), p. 216).

[17] Customarily both Bradbury and Evans and Chapman and Hall include the July number in the Midsummer accounts (to 30 June), and the January number in the Christmas accounts (to 31 Dec.), since publication day was the last day of the preceding month. The accounts are always given in bulk figures; it is seldom possible to determine the exact sales of an individual part.

Whitefriars, some printers got drunk and blunders ensued. Paxton reported to his wife Sarah that 'all our efforts were nearly ... floored at 4 o'clock this morning, and it was only by exertion, almost superhuman, that it was got out at all'.[18] Incompetent printing was exasperating, but temporary and remediable. Dickens himself 'sat at the stone, and made it up' with his own hands (N i. 733). More serious was the familiar problem of editorial interference. Bradbury, 'a prey to worrisome fidget' (J, p. 583), and temperamentally akin to Bentley and Hall, repeatedly interposed between Dickens and his subordinates, refused to pay a minor employee hired by Dickens, acted discourteously towards Dickens's father ('than whom there is not a more zealous, disinterested, or useful gentleman attached to the paper') (N i. 738), and otherwise criticized or arbitrarily altered Dickens's arrangements.

Dickens was moreover concerned about the paper's editorial freedom. Since its principal backer, Paxton, had made a fortune in railway shares, Dickens feared that it would not be possible to maintain strict neutrality concerning railway matters. He asked Forster to dine with him on 31 January, as he wanted to have a long talk: 'I have been revolving plans in my mind this morning for quitting the paper and going abroad again to write a new book in shilling numbers' (F V. i. 387). As the attraction of another foreign excursion increased, Dickens's interest in and patience with the paper waned. By 9 February Forster seemed in 'very low spirits', reporting to Macready 'that no one could be a worse editor than Dickens'.[19] On 9 February Dickens formally abdicated the editorship, refusing at the same time to address himself any longer to the firm, but corresponding solely with Evans. 'I am not in that state of feeling with reference to your partner, which would render a personal negociation with him agreeable to me', Dickens wrote. 'Of Mr. Bradbury separated from the newspaper, I entertain my old high opinion. I hold him, as separated from the newspaper, in my old regard. But I cannot separate him from it sufficiently, at this time, to affect a cordiality which ... I do not feel' (N i. 738–9).

The quarrel was patched up quickly. A little over a fortnight later, on 16 March, Dickens was addressing the firm once more, 'Dear Sirs'. The problem of finding an illustrator for *Pictures from*

[18] Markham, p. 171.   [19] Macready, *Diaries*, ii. 321.

Italy, now running in the *Daily News* and scheduled for publication by Bradbury and Evans in volume form in May, was taxing. Clarkson Stanfield agreed to do about twelve designs for woodcuts to be transferred to the block by his brother George and engraved by whomever the printers recommended as 'the best engravers on wood of landscape and architectural subjects, with small figures' (N i. 737). But these plans were never executed, perhaps because Dickens's anti-Catholicism offended the Catholic artist.[20] In any event, Dickens applied at Colnaghi's for 'any clever young artist or student who has been in Italy, and has brought home a portfolio of such sketches as I want' (N i. 741–2). The successful candidate proved to be Samuel Palmer, visionary, disciple of Blake, and one of the greatest Victorian painters. Though the commission hardly contributed to his artistic reputation, the twenty guineas he received for the five designs and four plates kept starvation at bay during one of the leanest years of his life.[21] The sum was larger than the average price at which he sold forty-five works, including oil paintings, in the decade from 1843.[22]

At the same time as he was arranging for an illustrator, Dickens asked his printers 'how soon after June, you think we might, safely, and with real effect, begin a story in monthly numbers—so that it should not commence at a dead time of the year' (N i. 742). One of the minor secrets of serial publication to which Dickens's experience had given him access was determining the appropriate season for launching a new serial. It was essential to ensure a great sale of the first number. Spring and winter were especial favourites: *Bleak House*, March; *Pickwick Papers*, *Nicholas Nickleby*, *Master Humphrey's Clock*, *Edwin Drood*, April; *David Copperfield*, *Our Mutual Friend*, May; *Sketches by Boz*, November; *Little Dorrit*, December; *Martin Chuzzlewit* and *Oliver Twist* in numbers, January. The summer months were to be avoided—no serial was ever commenced in June, August, or September, and *Tale of Two Cities* was issued in July only because it was running

[20] See David Paroissien, '*Pictures from Italy* and its Original Illustrator', *Dickensian*, 67 (1971), 87–90; and his edition of *Pictures from Italy*, pp. 247–9.

[21] Carlos Peacock, *Samuel Palmer: Shoreham and After* (London, John Baker, 1968), p. 50.

[22] A. H. Palmer, *The Life and Letters of Samuel Palmer, Painter and Etcher*, new edn., intro. Raymond Lister, preface Kathleen Raine (London, Eric and Joan Stevens, 1972), p. 85.

then in *All the Year Round*.[23] In general, Dickens's practice with
his serials followed conventional publishing wisdom for all works
of fiction and religion; the *Spectator* reported in 1863:

> The flow of this vast stream of literature is very unequal; sometimes
> rapid like a mountain torrent, and at other periods slow as a caravan
> creeping through the desert. There is, however, a constant rise and fall
> of the tide, returning with annual regularity. It is high water at Christ-
> mas, and neap tide during the greater part of the summer and autumn;
> but the ordinary flood sets in about the beginning of September, and
> lasts far into the new year. . . . Unlike fiction and religion, the current
> of science, law, and commerce continues its course in perennial order.[24]

In the case of *Dombey*, it was decided by mid May not to risk
beginning before October.

Finding it difficult while in England to disentangle himself
completely from the *News*, which Forster was now editing,[25]
Dickens decided to write his new serial from Europe; Kate could
not bear to return to Genoa, where she had often been ill, so
Dickens settled on Lausanne, where he rented the little doll's
house Villa Rosemont for £10 a month beginning in June. There,
in a study 'something larger than a Plate Warmer', he began
contemplating 'terrific and tremendous industry': the new book
in monthly numbers, advertised as early as 18 April in the

---

[23] *Oliver Twist* began in February, but the *Miscellany* was launched in January.
Barnaby Rudge began in February at the conclusion of *The Old Curiosity Shop*, but
the *Clock* started in April. We can conclude that February was not a propitious
time for launching a new serial either. Its awkward shortness brought the beginning of the next month, with its demand for another part, too quickly for comfort.

[24] 'The Circulation of Modern Literature', p. 16.

[25] Payments from Bradbury and Evans of £300 were deposited on 31 Dec.
1845 (for Jan.–Feb. 1846) and 6 Mar. (for ?Mar.–Apr. 1846), implying that
Dickens did not entirely sever his relations with the paper until the end of April
(MS. Coutts). Not knowing of those payments, Gerald Grubb could only say that
for 'some reason, no longer clear', Dickens continued, through April, to feel some
responsibility toward the enterprise ('Dickens and the "Daily News"', *Nineteenth-Century Fiction*, 7 (1952–3), 29). Evidently Dickens took full advantage of
the clauses entitling him to use a sub-editor to whom he could, 'with perfect
confidence hand over the practical management'. His refusal to leave town until
the paper's future was resolved supports the hypothesis that he still considered
himself obligated (see N i. 744–5), as do the articles he wrote and published during
the weeks following his 'resignation' as editor. There is a letter in the 'Bradbury
Album' of Messrs. Bradbury, Agnew & Co., dated 5 Mar. 1846, which confirms
this supposition. Therefore Dickens's remark to Mme De La Rue ('I straightway
stopped my Letters and walked bodily out of the concern' (N i. 744)) should be
seen as another instance of Dickens's touching up the facts a little, in this case to
appear dramatically decisive.

Athenaeum, and the Christmas volume, whose 'small red face' he hardly knew by sight yet (N i. 758–9). But he was beset by anxiety concerning the publication of the new serial. The printing of it would go all right, if Bradbury and Evans put their minds to it.[26] But would they be able to handle the publicity and the distribution effectively? Would they not be so totally involved in guiding the faltering *Daily News* as to have no resources left over for the new work? Moreover, they were going to do Thackeray's new novel in monthly numbers as well, and had scheduled it to begin in May 1846, though the opening was delayed until January 1847. Finally, Dickens found it injurious, indeed unacceptable, for his new book to be issued from the 'Office of the Daily News', the legend which had been painted over the door in Fleet Street at the time *Pictures from Italy* was published. 'Pray explain to Bradbury and Evans that I do not make this a matter of complaint against them', Dickens told Forster:

> I am most anxious that they should (as I now hope they will) recover their loss and turn the enterprise to good account. But the question whether it is proper that a book of mine should be published at a newspaper office, is quite another thing; and that it is not advisable that it should be published at their place in Whitefriars, I take for granted. (N i. 759)

There were apparently three objections to having his new serial issued from the newspaper office. First, on personal grounds, Dickens did not wish to have any further connection with the paper from which he had just 'succeeded in detaching [himself] ... by a great wrench' (N ii. 26). Second, it would undoubtedly 'lower' the serial, still in some minds a cheap and tawdry mode of publication, associating it with Grub Street and the evanescent, the quotidian, the speciously sensational. Third, the book might be attacked because of the paper's editorial policies, or find its fictions localized and identified with a particular party, faction, or political philosophy, whereas Dickens always strove to avoid just this kind of reduction of symbol to allegory, this limiting of applicability to one time and place. As he explained to Peter

---

[26] Grubb believes that the firm's constant printing blunders became, with *Household Words*, 'an almost constant source of irritation to Dickens' ('Dickens and the "Daily News"', *Nineteenth-Century Fiction*, 6 (1951–2), 237). Dickens's irritation over compositors' errors was easily aroused, and for the most part it quickly subsided.

Cunningham in denying that *Hard Times* was inspired by the Preston strike:

> The mischief of such a statement is twofold. First, it encourages the public to believe in the impossibility that books are produced in that very sudden and cavalier manner (as poor Newton used to feign that he produced the elaborate drawings he made in his madness, by winking at his table); and secondly in this instance it has this bearing: it localizes (so far as your readers are concerned) a story which has a direct purpose in reference to the working people all over England, and it will cause, as I know by former experience, characters to be fitted onto individuals whom I never saw or heard of in my life. (N ii. 546)

Though unwilling to raise any new matters of difference between his printers and himself, and eager to allow the old ones to fade away, Dickens's concern was so great that he told Forster to ask them 'whether it would not be better—whether it is not positively necessary, as matters stand, for them to arrange with Chapman and Hall, for Chapman and Hall being the publishers of the new book in monthly numbers'. There was, after all, a great deal at stake:

> There will be the beginning of the new book, and there will be the Christmas Book, close on each other's heels. There is all the preliminary announcement to be considered and arranged, and the board to be made quite clear and clean for the playing out of a very great stake; and I do not think—not because I will not, but because I cannot—that Bradbury and Evans's arrangements, so thoroughly unsettled and so sweepingly changed by the newspaper, are so capable of the undertaking as Chapman and Hall's. (N i. 759–60)

That Dickens should have considered a return to his former publishers so shortly after their separation is significant in at least two ways: it confirms, first, that pecuniary pressures shortened his temper, and second, that serial publication was a very special kind of venture. The experience of Chapman and Hall in developing monthly numbers to their present commercially successful heights was important to future success; 'the machinery is as familiar to them, as the ticking of their own watches' (N i. 759). Though Bradbury and Evans had themselves been reluctant to undertake such a venture a few years earlier, they had now heavily invested in Dickens's name, and rejected his suggestion, no doubt resolving that they would vigilantly and energetically

prosecute *Dombey*'s affairs. Indeed, one suspects that Dickens's
true motive in writing thus to Forster was to redirect Bradbury
and Evans's attention to his new work, and that he may not have
expected, or even wanted, them to concur in making the transfer
to Chapman and Hall.

One other request in this important letter of 25 June must be
noted. 'Will you remember', Dickens asked Forster, 'in about
a month or five weeks from the 21st of this month, to have
accounts from Bradbury and Evans and Chapman and Hall, and
to adjust and settle them?' These accounts, heretofore rendered
erratically as the occasion demanded, now became a regular
feature of Dickens's professional life. Every six months, from 1846
onwards, his publishers drew up detailed statements of the cost
and sales of the works in which they were partners. These statements fall into three general categories: statements on the individual works, a cash account showing the balance for or against
Dickens, and, on occasion, a list of the books Dickens ordered and
charged against his six months' balance. These accounts conform
to no single type of record as recommended by contemporary
handbooks on the keeping of publishers' accounts. Rather, they
summarize information that would be found at greater length and
precision in the Day Book, Trade Ledgers (recording sales and
discounts), the Author's Ledger, the Stock Ledgers, the Miscellaneous Publications Book (recording copies sent out for review,
gratis, and to the statute libraries, and those jobbed off or still for
sale), the Copyright or Plant Ledger (recording the valuation of
copyright, stereos, plates, and so forth), Advertising Books, the
Petty Cash Book, and the Cash Sales Book (especially as used to
record sales of books to Dickens, the cost of which was to be set
against his profit). Bradbury and Evans's 'Paper and Print'
Ledgers for this period survive, and they contain much of the
information summarized for Dickens in the accounts, which
conform most closely to models of 'Author's Ledgers'.[27]

There was generally a lag of two or three months between the
end of the accounting period—30 June and 31 December—and the

[27] See Clarence E. Allen, *Publishers' Accounts* (London, Gee & Co., 1897); *The
Author's Printing and Publishing Assistant* (2nd edn., London, Saunders and Otley,
1839); and *A Manual of Book-keeping for booksellers, publishers, and stationers . . . by
a bookseller* (London, Simpkin and Marshall, 1850). The Appendices contain
summaries of the sales, printing history, and profits of Dickens's works, and a
further discussion of the Account Books themselves.

rendering of the accounts themselves, an understandable delay, since inventory had to be taken and bills received and paid, and one provided for in earlier agreements.[28] From the covering letters which accompany some of the accounts we can see that the earliest dates on which we know they were forwarded were 25 July 1846 (for the June 1846 Chapman and Hall accounts) and 18 February 1848 (for the December 1847 Bradbury and Evans accounts).[29] In general, as the number of different books increases, and the range of customers expands to include India, Australia, and America, the accounts arrived later.

The accounts were sent to Dickens, or to Forster, who looked them over often, customarily when Dickens was out of the country. Sometimes Mitton saw them; Dickens gave him a summary on a number of occasions. Eventually Dickens endorsed them, after querying doubtful figures and verifying the computations—not always accurate—and instructed the publishers to pay the balance due to him into his Coutts's account. Sometimes he drew against this prospective balance at regular intervals, usually during the months a new serial was being published; at other times the entire balance was paid off only after he had approved the accounts. Where large sums were involved, payment was often effected through a combination of cash and bills due four, five, even six months later.

Comparisons between the two publishers' figures can only be approximate. Differences in accounting procedure over the years by the same firm—Chapman and Hall changed clerks at least ten times between 1846 and 1870—and between firms make figures only roughly comparable. For example, Chapman and Hall usually include discounts and allowances in computing the gross sales receipts, and they subtract commissions separately as a cost. But Bradbury and Evans more often than not subtract all commissions, discounts, and allowances in figuring the gross receipts. On identical sales, therefore, Bradbury and Evans's figure for gross sales receipts might be as much as 10 per cent below Chapman and Hall's. In some cases where the accounts are deficient, estimated figures have been supplied—especially in the cases of

---

[28] The June accounts were *not* 'frequently based on estimates', as Grubb has stated in 'Some Unpublished Correspondence', p. 103, n. 10.

[29] See Grubb, 'Some Unpublished Correspondence', *passim*, for many of these letters.

Bradbury and Evans's commissions on small sales. Occasionally the accounts themselves are out of balance; when they exhibit computational errors they have been corrected only where the evidence is conclusive that the publishers were aware of the error. Sometimes multiplicity of contractual arrangements led to mistakes. Thus in the December 1865 accounts, Chapman and Hall's clerk, trying to simplify procedures, carried the profits and deficiencies of all books forward to the final balance sheet, and there divided the net equally between the firm and Dickens. But for *The Uncommercial Traveller*, Dickens should have been credited with *all* the profit, less only a 5 per cent publishers' commission. Moreover, the books are manipulated to make the balance favourable wherever possible: for example, since the publishers were responsible for absorbing debit balances on *Master Humphrey's Clock*, if withholding the warehousing and insurance costs on the unsold stock for another six months will bring the current account into favourable balance, they do not hesitate to do so. Likewise, if a book is reprinted during an accounting period, but does not sell enough copies to repay the printing expenses, the charges may be withheld for six months until the profits make up the deficiency. Nevertheless, though only approximate, these figures are not out significantly, and can be used with confidence to indicate the order of magnitude of Dickens's publishing ventures.

They are not easily used. Nothing could be more awkward than the mixture of arithmetical bases with which the poor clerk had to contend in drawing up the accounts. The monthly serials, published as twenty parts in nineteen, were sold from month to month in quantities of a baker's dozen; when the novel was concluded, the back numbers were still sold in the same bulk quantity. A sale of fifty dozen numbers would mean 50×13 or 650 numbers; assuming an equal distribution of all parts, that would give thirty-two *and a half* complete novels. Agents' allowances and publishers' commissions were usually figured in decimal percentages of pounds, shillings, and pence; the cost of stitching a number was calculated in shillings and pence per thousand. Thus the hard-pressed clerk might have to figure $7\frac{1}{2}$ per cent of £143. 17s. $8\frac{1}{2}d.$, or determine the cost of binding 24,833 numbers at 23s. per thousand. Reckoning the gross sales receipts could be a nightmare. The June 1866 gross from the Library edition totalled £1,639, a straightforward enough sum, but it comprised the receipts of 600 volumes in quires to Lippincott at 2s. 8d.; 1,200 volumes in cloth to Lippincott at 3s.; 2,400 in cloth to Ticknor and Fields at the same price, and an equal number in quires at a considerable discount, 2s.; 600 volumes in quires to Little, Brown for yet a fourth price, 2s. 6d.; 100 as 96 (probably bound) to Scribner at 4s. 6d.; 960 volumes in cloth to Johnstone for Australia at 3s. 6d.; 120 copies free; 900 as 864 (that is, 25 as 24) sold at 5s. 4d. each; and 1,050 as 1,008 (25 as 24) sold at 5s. 8d.

The method of making up the accounts is also singularly awkward. At the end of each six-month period the inventory of stock on hand was totted up, the difference between this total and the beginning figure carried over from the last account representing the number sold. From July to December 1852 the stock of back numbers of *David Copperfield*, which sold comparatively briskly, though the novel had a disappointing initial sale, was reduced by 6,012. But which of the twenty numbers sold? All are lumped together. The only way to gauge the sales of an individual part is to check the charges for reprinting, and even these are not always sufficiently explicit. As for determining the number of complete copies sold, that is almost impossible.

Let me give another example to illustrate the difficulties for all parties. *Little Dorrit* I was issued on the last day of November 1855, and II on the corresponding day in December. As the parts carried the date of the succeeding month, we have the anomaly that the January number appears in the preceding December's accounts. By the end of 1855, 63,393 parts had been sold, and 215 given away to journals, the statute libraries, and as presentation copies. (In reporting sales figures, I have included only those copies given as a discount for bulk purchases.) Though only one Part bears the date 1855, in fact the sales of 63,393 includes two Parts. To arrive at the sales of Part I, a key index to the reception and probable future of the serial, should we therefore halve the figure for total sales? On the face of it, that procedure seems incorrect—after all, the second number had only been on sale a single day. How then does one apportion the sales? Three other figures help. The accounts show, number by number, the cost of printing each monthly serial: 32,000 parts of *Little Dorrit* I were ordered, and during the course of December two reprintings of 3,000 each required. Thus the maximum number of Part I that could have been sold by 1 January 1856 is 38,000. But though 38,000 copies of the text were in print (give or take a few for spoilage), lesser quantities of the advertising insert or the plates might have been printed. After all, printing copies of the Advertiser beyond the circulation base ate into profits for the publishers, and as the plate paper cost more than the text paper, it was correspondingly more expensive to overprint the illustrations. In the case of *Little Dorrit* I, the illustrations seem to have kept pace with the text through both reprints. But we cannot be sure, since the charge for 'Plates & Paper' for the second reprint, ten guineas, is exactly what the charge to 'Reprint Advertisements' is in the first reprint, while there is no mention of reprinting the advertisements a second time. And to reprint the plates the first time cost £14, not ten guineas. There is a third figure which often helps: the number of copies of any one Part stitched into wrappers. To keep down expenses, Bradbury and Evans only wrappered those copies they expected to sell; the others were not wasted but kept aside to be sewn into wrappers on demand, or stitched into covers at the conclusion of the monthly run. Only 36,280 of I were put in wrappers. So taking all the figures together—63,393 of I and II sold by 1 January, 38,000 of the text of I printed, probably an equal number of illustrations and possibly only 35,000 Advertisers, and 36,280 copies stitched into green wrappers—it is possible to conclude that upwards of 36,000 copies of *Little Dorrit* I were sold in the first month, and that in the first day Part II sold around 27,000. Moreover, rare book dealers and collectors might note that the absence of an Advertiser may not indicate later issue, but only unexpectedly heavy demand.

In response to Forster's request, Chapman and Hall forwarded their accounts, 'which we trust you will find correct and satisfactory',[30] on 25 July. The works still in their hands were the *Sketches*, for which no account appears, *Pickwick*, *Oliver Twist* in three volumes, *Master Humphrey's Clock*, *Martin Chuzzlewit*, and *American Notes*. *Pickwick* had sold 2,379 parts (183 dozen), *Oliver* 25 as 24 copies, the *Clock* 6,305 various numbers, computed as 485 dozen, *American Notes* 12 copies, and *Chuzzlewit* had sold 1,378

---

[30] MS. C & H. The correspondence of Dickens's publishers included within these accounts has been published by Grubb in 'Some Unpublished Correspondence'; I have silently corrected many inaccuracies, and have not noted each of the times when his annotation is wrong. For instance, he frequently mixes up the various editions of *Oliver Twist* and those of the Christmas Books.

parts (106 dozen). The sales of individual parts are not given, and the awkwardness of this bulk accounting system is compounded by the discounts, 26 as 25, 25 as 24, and 13 as 12, which correlate neither with the monthly base (20 parts in 19) nor the weekly (*Clock* in 88 numbers). The wholesale price of the monthlies before commission was 8s. per dozen; for the weekly, 2s. per dozen; for the three volumes of *Oliver*, 18s. 3d., and for the two volumes of *American Notes*, 15s. It is difficult, as James Spedding complained, 'to make out what relation the price actually received by the publishers really bears to the price at which the book is advertised for sale'.[31] Ignoring for the moment that a monthly serial novel might appear at five or more different advertised retail prices (1s. per month, 20s. for the nineteen parts, 21s. bound in cloth, 24s. 6d. in half morocco, and 26s. 6d. in full morocco with gilt edges), there were at least six other prices below retail: the 'trade price', at least 25 per cent under retail paid by booksellers and favoured individuals like the author; the 'trade sale price', or 'subscription price' paid for orders prior to publication; the 'discount price' for bulk orders, which allowed free books (26 as 25, 25 as 24, 13 as 12, or 7 as 6½) and for colonial markets, often running as high as 25 to 30 per cent; the 'unbound price', for stock in quires; the 'remainder price', received for jobbed-off lots of unsold stock; and the 'publisher's price', the amount he accounts for to the author, which in the case of these records would be net of allowances and commissions.[32] Dickens was entitled to half the profits from *Oliver*, the advance by now having been paid off, to three-quarters of those from *American Notes*,[33] to half profits from the *Clock* and *Chuzzlewit*, and to one-third profits from *Pickwick*. In addition to sales, in this accounting period Tauchnitz had paid £30 for the right to reprint the *Clock*, of which Dickens received one-half. The total due him, £95. 0s. 6d., was less than the combined total of Chapman and Hall's

---

[31] *Publishers and Authors*, p. 34; see ch. 1, p. 25.

[32] See Spedding, *passim*; John Chapman, *Cheap Books and How to Get Them* (London, John Chapman, 1852), p. 209; Leonard Huxley, *The House of Smith Elder* (London, printed for private circulation, 1923), p. 163; John Carter, *Binding Variants*, pp. 33–4; and Simon Nowell-Smith, *International Copyright*, p. 88. My terminology is only approximate, as various combinations of price reduction were variously denominated.

[33] He did not finally withdraw from Chapman and Hall their quarter share, as he contemplated doing in May 1844.

commissions (£13. 8s. 3d.) and share of the profits (£94. 18s. 6d.), because on the largest-selling work, *Pickwick*, the publishers received 10 per cent commission instead of 5, and two-thirds of the profits. The sums are not great, though Dickens's share was half again as much as his six months' rent at Lausanne; but the fact that in spite of ever more favourable publishing contracts he was still not sharing equally in his most profitable ventures lends some additional support to his persistent complaints that his books were enriching everybody but himself. Deducting the cost of a gilt frame for a portrait by W. Walton, and the wholesale price of a complete run of his Chapman and Hall publications, the publishers paid the balance, £89. 13s. 10d., into Coutts's bank on 12 August.[34]

The 'Midsummer 1846. Bradbury and Evans. Account.' which Dickens received and endorsed towards the end of August was more promising. Though Dickens's publishers only since 1844, as his current firm they enjoyed the profits of all new ventures, which were usually substantially greater than back sales. And being governed by more recent agreements, these publications returned to Dickens a more favourable share of the profits. These works were the three Christmas books and *Pictures from Italy* in which Dickens had a three-quarters share, and the monthly numbers of *Oliver Twist*, which he shared equally with Bradbury and Evans. On 4 December 1845, Chapman and Hall had delivered up their *Carol* stock: 469 copies in quires, and 42 in cloth; the following February Bradbury and Evans reprinted 1,000. At 2s. 10½d. (40 as 39) in quires, and 3s. 6d. (654 as 619) in cloth, the sales (£113. 18s. 8d.) had exceeded the costs (£76. 2s.) sufficiently to leave a profit of £37. 16s. 8d. *The Chimes* was not so fortunate: the cost of reprinting 3,000 copies on 18 January 1845 had exceeded the revenue from 667 copies sold as 617 at 3s. 6d. over the succeeding eighteen months, leaving Dickens with three-quarters of the deficit, £93. 11s. 6d. The *Cricket*, being most recent, was most profitable: 3,074 copies sold as 2,945 at 3s. 6d. brought in net to Dickens £294. 6s. 5d. As we have already seen, *Oliver* was not terribly successful; Dickens's half-share amounted only to £81. 7s. 3d. But *Pictures from Italy*, though the expectations were modest, turned a nice profit:

34 MS. Coutts. The Chapman and Hall proceeds for the half-year ending 31 Dec. 1845 had been £166. 13s. 7d., paid on 14 Mar. 1846.

				£	s.	d.
Sales: 4,911 as 4,715 @ 4s. 2d.				982	5	10
Costs:	£	s.	d.			
Printing 6,000 copies	121	2	6			
Paper, 105 reams double foolscap	136	10	0			
Binding 5,251 copies	97	2	11			
Illustrations						
to Palmer for drawings	21	0	0			
engraving	22	10	0			
Advertising	63	6	0			
Commissions and Allowances						
to Country agents	11	12	6			
to Publishers, on £982. 5s. 10d.	98	4	7			
Paid for copying letters	4	10	0			
				575	18	6
Profit				406	7	4
¾ to Mr. Dickens				304	15	6[35]

The total balance due to Dickens from Bradbury and Evans to 30 June 1846 was £629. 0s. 7d., down from the preceding period's £1,222. 5s. 5d., when the bulk of the Christmas book profit had been made. This does not tally, however, with Dickens's letter to Mitton, written 30 August 1846, in which he says the account 'for the half year is £1100 and odd, of which £500 was paid on account of the *Pictures from Italy*, before I left England, and the remainder is just now paid in'.[36] Dickens misunderstood his publishers, for they had charged the £500 advance (deposited with the July–December 1845 receipts on 29 April 1846) against a separate account. Thus *Pictures* had not paid off any advance, and the profits were as stated, and not as Dickens inflated them. In any event, Dickens was pleased: 'They certainly keep a very active eye upon the expences and profits' (N i. 783).

[35] Tauchnitz paid £17 for rights, which was credited on 7 Nov., and included in the Dec. 1846 accounts. Customarily Bradbury and Evans treated such payments as part of gross receipts; thus Dickens did not by any means receive the whole payment.

[36] N i. 783. It was actually paid in, along with £100 on account of the new serial, a month later, 1 Oct. (MS. Coutts).

10

Dombey and Son, *'the greatest success'*

Although Literature as a profession has no distinct status in England, I am bound to say that what I experience of its recognition, all through Society, in my own person, is honorable, ample, and independent. I find that to make no exacting assertion of its claims, on the one hand—and steadily to take my stand by it, on the other, as a worthy calling, and my sole fortune,—is to do right, and to take sufficient rank. Go where I will, in out of the way places and odd corners of the country, I always find something of personal affection in people whom I have never seen, mixed up with my public reputation. This is the best part of it, and makes me very happy.

CHARLES DICKENS (N ii. 102–3, to D. M. MOIR)

DICKENS BEGAN *DOMBEY* ON 27 JUNE and determined the title of his Christmas book, *The Battle of Life*, by 3 July (N i. 760, 762). He felt anxious to forestall premature disclosure of his monthly title—'an odd one, and therefore a good one' (N i. 783)—urging Forster on 18 July to 'impress on B. & E. the necessity of the closest secrecy. The very name getting out, would be ruinous' (F V. iii. 405). But this injunction may be only another indication of Dickens's nervousness about his new publishers; for he had already told Thomas Chapman the title, and by the end of August it was being widely advertised.[1] Reports from England were en-

---

[1] N i. 762; see the *Athenaeum* of 29 Aug. 1846, p. 874, where 'the title is at last divulged' (Alan Horsman, ed., *Dombey and Son* (Oxford, Clarendon Press, 1974), p. xiv).

couraging; Browne, 'who is generally the most indifferent fellow in the world, couldn't help writing' a long letter to Dickens praising the first number (N i. 783). There was great difficulty fitting that first number into its allotted thirty-two pages; Dickens finally had to consider lengthening the page by two lines to get in the revised matter.[2] By 5 August he had started Part II, and seemed to be writing easily, but a battle was shaping over the *Battle of Life*. It was too difficult to begin two books simultaneously; Dickens was forced to cancel the opening of the first scene—'which I have never done before' (F V. v. 425); he missed the streets of London, the noise and bustle and people. On 26 September he told Forster that there might not be a Christmas Book: 'I am sick, giddy, and capriciously despondent. I have bad nights; am full of disquietude and anxiety; and am constantly haunted by the idea that I am wasting the marrow of the larger book, and ought to be at rest' (F V. v. 426). Four days later, having gone to Geneva in search of more congenial surroundings, Dickens asked Forster to tell Bradbury and Evans about his earlier letter. But he wanted to go on with the story, if possible: 'I shall not have abandoned it until after a most desperate fight' (F V. v. 427). Three days after that he was in better spirits, and believed that the Christmas Book would be finished in due course.

In addition to all the other causes of worry which Dickens listed, the unsettled feelings at the end of September may have been aggravated by the impending appearance of *Dombey* I; 'I am all anxiety and fever to know what we are starting *Dombey* with', he confessed to Forster in mid August (F V. iv. 414 n.). It was fifteen months since the last new green leaf had appeared on the bookstands—the longest hiatus yet. Dickens's last serial had not sold well—certainly not up to expectations—and neither *Pictures* nor *Oliver* had achieved a large circulation. The *Daily News* venture had proved a fiasco. And Bradbury and Evans, who had gambled a great deal of money, and were insisting on handling the distribution themselves, had also agreed to issue Thackeray's new novel, in the same format, and almost concurrently. Finally, the place of publication was, in spite of Dickens's objections, Whitefriars. True, Forster and Browne were enthusiastic; the little circle in Lausanne had listened to Dickens read the first number with

[2] F VI. ii. 474. Instead, Dickens and later Forster made extensive, and not altogether helpful, cuts; see Horsman, pp. xv–xvii.

gratifying attention (F V. v. 424). But would it sell, sell widely, sell enough to repay his debts and reconfirm his popularity?

The publishers conducted an extensive advertising campaign. By 29 August they had printed 160,000 demy 8vo bills; within three weeks another 60,000 rolled off the presses.[3] On 5 September, 5,000 double royal posting bills were prepared, and in October two more printings doubled the total; in December a third printing sported green ink. In Exeter, Edinburgh, Glasgow, Coventry, Bath, and London, bill stickers posted the broadside announcements of Mr. Dickens's new work, while salesmen eagerly distributed 300 cards announcing the terms for advertising, and 3,000 red and black show cards with specially designed and engraved lettering. In the journals to 31 December Bradbury and Evans took £163 worth of advertising, twice what they spent stimulating the public to buy their Christmas Book, but five pounds less than Chapman and Hall had spent on the *Carol*. Another expense partly attributable to advertising was the cost of Browne's wrapper design, which Dickens thought 'very good: perhaps with a little too much in it' (N i. 787). By 19 September it had been engraved for £9. 15s., more than the eight guineas Browne received on publication day for his design. For each plate, he received six guineas, the publishers supplying the steels, and for duplicates he was paid double. Robert Young got £6 a number for biting in the steels. However, for lithographic transfers, over which Browne and Young exercised no supervision, there was no additional remuneration.

Advance orders from advertisers began to come into Whitefriars, some a bit tardily, resulting in a one-guinea night-work charge. Dickens told Mitton that the firm of E. Moses and Son, whose publicity was noted for its delightful verses, 'has taken one page of the wrapper, all through'.[4] Eventually, the *Dombey and Son* Advertiser for Part I ran sixteen pages, cost £60. 10s. to print, brought in £124. 7s. 9d., and produced for the printers £27. 17s. 4d. in commissions.[5]

[3] MS. B & E, and 'Paper and Print' Ledgers, Bradbury and Evans.

[4] N i. 783; for an amusing account of these poetical effusions, and the other advertisements in Dickens's serials, see Bernard Darwin, ed., *The Dickens Advertiser: A Collection of the Advertisements in The Original Parts of Novels by Charles Dickens* (London, Elkin, Matthews & Marrot, 1930).

[5] Advertising contained in inserted bills yielded an additional £10. 10s. for Part I; this category will be included with the Advertiser in subsequent figures.

As *Chuzzlewit* sales had not exceeded 23,000, the printers began *Dombey* with a press-run of 25,000. The cost of composition, printing, stitching letterpress and plates came to £284. 18s. 1d.; this included £8. 10s. for 'Corrections & Composition in Old Type to save time', necessitated by the many revisions to the first number, and £2. 15s. 11d. for postage, principally no doubt to Dickens in Lausanne. On Thursday, 1 October 1846, Bradbury and Evans opened their doors for business. Within hours, the entire stock was sold out. Hastily, ten more reams of double demy were bought, machined, prepared, and printed; 5,000 more wrappers were readied; the plates were reprinted; 2,000 more advertising inserts were run off. The whole was stitched together and issued before the tenth. By 7 November, another edition of 2,000 was called for, and yet another of the same size printed by the twenty-first. When the presses were not busy with reprints of the first part, they were turning out the second, third, and fourth. The pace was frantic: charges for 'Night & Sunday work' on Part I alone suggest that the printers billed at least ninety hours of overtime.

On 5 October Dickens wrote to Miss Coutts: 'I hear that the Dombey has been launched with great success, and was out of print on the first night' (N i. 796). By the eleventh, with the second printing well on its way to selling out, Dickens could gloat to Forster: 'The *Dombey* sale is BRILLIANT! I had put before me thirty thousand as the limit of the most extreme success, saying that if we should reach that, I should be more than satisfied and more than happy; you will judge how happy I am!' (F VI. ii. 477). Bradbury and Evans raised the initial press-run of the second part to 30,000, but by mid November sales of Part I were nearing 32,000, and by the 21st 2,000 more of II, as well as I, were reprinted. Thus *Dombey* had outstripped *Chuzzlewit* by 10,000 copies (F V. vi. 431). 'Dombey is a prodigious success', Dickens told Beard, 'Enthusiastic bulletins reach me daily' (N i. 800). Macready was warm in its praise; Jerrold gave it a fine notice in his *Weekly Newspaper*.[6] At the end of November, sales were still rising: 'Dombey is doing wonders. It went up, after the publication of the second number, over the thirty thousand. This much is a very large sale so early in the story, that I begin to think it will

[6] Cf. Macready, *Diaries*, ii. 353, 358, 359, covering Jan.–Mar. 1847; and N i. 802, 803.

beat all the rest' (N i. 816). For the third and fourth numbers, December 1846 and January 1847, the printing was raised to 32,000.

On the last day in December, the sales of the first four numbers reached 122,035. Of the 130,000 printed, there remained on hand only a little over 7,000, the balance having been sent to the depository libraries, to town and country newspapers for review, or to Dickens for presentation to his friends and family. The gross receipts totalled £4,106. 19s. 2d., and the proceeds from advertising added another £556. 17s. 6d. After deducting all expenses, Dickens received three-quarters of the profit, just short of £1,500, or as he calculated himself on the cash account sheet, almost £375 on each number, while Bradbury and Evans got a 10 per cent commission on sales, £466. 7s. 8d., plus one-quarter of the profits, £499. 8s. 2d. With the profits on the other Bradbury and Evans books, Dickens's share came to £3,005. 19s. or the six months ending 31 December 1846. 'B and E's accounts had just reached Forster', Dickens told Kate on 20 February 1847. 'They are exactly what I supposed, and will leave me, thank God, £2000 clear, to put away.'[7] Deducting £500 paid in instalments from October to January (and thereafter throughout *Dombey*'s serial run), he was still owed £2,488. 19s., which the publishers paid in three instalments, £500 on 1 March, £1,500 on 11 March, and the balance the next day.[8] These sums 'were so much in excess of what had been expected from the new publishing arrangements,' Forster reports, 'that from this date all embarrassments connected with money were brought to a close. [Dickens's] future profits varied of course with his varying sales, but there was always enough, and savings were now to begin' (F VI. i. 464). On 20 April Dickens purchased £600 worth of Consols, the first of many such investments that appear in the Coutts records from this time forward. And on 24 June 1847, anticipating a favourable Midsummer's Day balance, he withdrew £1,200, leaving £737. 17s. 10d. For a couple of weeks he looked around for a suitable investment, notifying Mitton on 4 July that he had 'twelve or fifteen hundred pounds, now lying idle' (N ii. 40). But nothing

7 *Mr. and Mrs. Charles Dickens: His Letters to Her*, ed. Walter Dexter (London, Constable, 1935), p. 128.
8 MS. Coutts. The missing £17 was credited to Dickens from Tauchnitz, for rights to *Pictures from Italy*.

attractive turned up, so the £1,200 went back into the account on 10 July, and were not invested until 20 October, when £2,000 were put in 3¼ per cents, then discounted to 85⅜ per cent of their face value.

All Bradbury and Evans's other books made profits, too. The Christmas Books continued to sell a few hundred copies; *Pictures from Italy* sold just over 500; *Oliver Twist* was completed, with press runs of 5,000, stitching runs of 3,250, sales of 15,363 numbers, and a reprint of 1,000 copies of Part I. And the *Battle of Life*, despite some hostile reviews, including one in *The Times* which Macready thought 'a most savage but most malicious and, I think, innoxious attack on Dickens and his book',[9] 'shot far ahead of its predecessors' (N ii. 11): 24,448 copies to the public at 3s. 6d. less discounts—23,000 of them on the first day (N i. 822)—plus one in quires for £4 for reprinting at The Hague. Dickens's three-quarters share came to £1,281. 15s. 4d. In comparison, Thackeray's first Christmas Book, *Mrs. Perkins's Ball*, issued at the same time, sold only 1,500 copies, a fact which Thackeray reported ruefully to his mother: 'Mrs. Perkins is a great success—the greatest I have had—very nearly as great as Dickens. that is Perkins *500* Dickens *25000* only that difference!'[10] *Tait's Edinburgh Magazine* complained that sales of the Christmas Books were in inverse relation to their quality:

The [*sic*] Christmas Carol, the first and the best, has reached only a *tenth* edition. The Chimes was said to be inferior to its predecessor, and is up to the twelfth edition. The Cricket on the Hearth had the worst character of the three, and has, therefore, attained its twenty-second edition. The facts merely show that book-buyers and reviewers do not always entertain similar opinions. . . . On the ratio of increase in the previous publications, the Battle of Life will run into forty-four editions.[11]

All in all, for the six months ending 31 December 1846, Dickens's works for Bradbury and Evans had earned him over £3,000, and his printers £1,067 as their share of the profits, plus £942. 3s. 3d. in commissions. In the same period, the Chapman and Hall books yielded £105. 7s. 4d. for Dickens, £131. 17s. 4d. for the publishers, and £21. 10s. 6d. in commissions. Paltry though the amounts were, Dickens scrutinized the accounts rigorously: 'My Dear Sir,' he wrote Chapman on 28 April 1847, 'There seems

---

[9] *Diaries*, ii. 353.   [10] *Letters*, ii. 258.   [11] 14 (Jan. 1847), 55.

to me to be some mistake in the "American Notes" item of the accounts to Christmas last.—advertising, £7..7..8, against sales to the amount of £9..15..0. Surely this is not correct? Is it?'[12] Unhappily, it was. Nevertheless, in the year 1846 Dickens earned more than £3,800 by his writings.[13]

Dombey maintained its sales. After Paul's death in Number V, the press run was increased 1,000 to 33,000;[14] it dropped back to 32,000 five months later, but rose again to 33,000 following Edith's flight, and to 34,000 for Numbers XVII and XVIII. The final double number appeared in April 1848, 35,000 copies being printed, of which 32,000 were stitched into wrappers. By June of 1847, 4,000 more of I, and 2,000 each of II and III, had been reprinted; the accounts to June 1848 show all twenty parts reprinted, in runs from 1,500 to 3,000 each, in preparation for the volume issue. Over 40,000 copies of Part I, and 35,000 of Parts XIX and XX, were in print by this date. The sales and profits to the end of June 1848 can be summarized in tabular form.

Sales and Profits of *Dombey and Son* by half-years, 1846–8

(a) *Sales*

	Gross Sales Numbers	Gross Sales			Advertising Gross		
		£	s.	d.	£	s.	d.
Dec. 46	122,035	4,106	19	2	556	17	6
June 47	197,110	6,633	10	5	593	4	6
Dec. 47	188,940	6,358	11	0	525	19	0
June 48	159,274	5,360	3	6	351	0	0
	667,359	22,459	4	1	2,027	1	0

(b) *Profits*

	Profits, Dickens			Profits, B & E			Commission, B & E		
	£	s.	d.	£	s.	d.	£	s.	d.
Dec. 46	1,498	4	8	499	8	2	466	7	8
June 47	2,773	19	9	924	13	2	722	13	6
Dec. 47	2,635	2	11	878	7	7	688	9	0
June 48	2,258	4	6	752	14	10	571	2	4
	9,165	11	10	3,055	3	9 +	2,448	12	6 =
	9,165	11	10		5,503	16	3		
	Dickens			Bradbury & Evans					

[12] Grubb, 'Some Unpublished Correspondence', p. 104.

[13] His deposits for the year total less, because of the usual quarterly delay in receiving profits.

[14] Paul's death was planned months before the first number appeared, and though the event was subsequently transferred from the fourth to the fifth number, it was neither conceived nor executed with any eye towards sales. None

By contrast, *Vanity Fair* sold fewer than 5,000 copies per number and brought Thackeray no profits beyond his £60 per number stipend.[15]

Gratifying though the results were, they were not achieved without effort. Fatigued from the double labours on *Battle* and *Dombey*, Dickens went to Paris in November 1846, then dashed over to London in time for the publication of his Christmas Book. While home, he helped the Keeleys stage the *Battle of Life* at the Lyceum, and settled with Chapman and Hall about a Cheap edition of his works on 19 December, then returned to Paris for Christmas and January, and tore back to London on 18 February, because his March *Dombey*, over which he had laboured to 'transfer to Florence, instantly, all the previous interest' (F VI. ii. 482), was making less in type than he expected: 'I have a terrible apprehension that there will not be copy enough for the number!' (F V. vii. 453 n.). No sooner was he back in Paris than word reached him that Charley, just enrolled at Eton, was ill with scarlet fever. Back to London with Kate he hurried, took a temporary house at 1 Chester Place, and then tried to get to work on the next number. But by 9 March he had not yet begun his month's agonies (N ii. 17).

Beleaguered by house-hunting and moving, Dickens was further unsettled by the sudden death of William Hall on 7 March 1847. He communicated immediately with Chapman, saying he wished to attend the funeral, and on 15 March wrote Browne an account of the event: 'He lies in the Highgate Cemetery, which is beautiful. He had a good little wife, if ever man had; and their accounts of her tending him at the last, are deeply affecting. Is it not a curious coincidence, remembering our connexion afterwards, that I bought the Magazine in which the first thing I ever wrote was published from poor Hall's hands? I have been thinking all day of that'.[16]

At the end of March, the first number of the Cheap edition of

---

the less, as the *Athenaeum* put it in its 22 July 1859 review of David Masson's *British Novels*, 'It is scarcely an exaggeration to say that the death of Little Dombey caused a national mourning' (p. 107).

[15] For a further comparison, see Patten, 'The Fight at the Top of the Tree', and for the sales and profits of *Dombey* 1848–70, see Appendix A, below.

[16] N ii. 20; the recollection found its way into the Cheap edition Preface to *Pickwick*, dated Sept. 1847.

Dickens's works went on sale.[17] This project, first broached by Bradbury and Evans in 1843, and settled with Chapman and Hall during Dickens's December 1846 visit to London, once again anticipated a new development in publishing. Margaret Dalziel, referring to the Parlour and Railway Libraries, notes that 'in 1847 there began the first successful attempts at really cheap reprints of novels in volume form (as distinct from the novels published as serials in the early cheap periodicals, or in penny parts)'.[18] By issuing the Cheap edition in several different formats, Dickens and his publishers tapped several different markets among 'the English people' to whom the series was dedicated, 'in whose approval, if the books be true in spirit, they will live, and out of whose memory, if they be false, they will very soon die'. The March *Dombey* carried a Prospectus, announcing that the edition would be published in weekly numbers at 1½d., the price he had originally suggested for the *Cricket* journal, and in monthly parts, sewn in a wrapper, at 7d., beginning on Saturday, 27 March. Each number consisted of one sheet (sixteen pages) printed in double columns, the text running on from number to number without interruption. Even novels were run-on in the same monthly part: *Pickwick* sharing with *Nickleby*, *Nickleby* with the *Shop*, and so on. In effect, having experimented with two other kinds of serial publication, Dickens now revised publication in fascicles: these so-called 'numbers' and 'parts' bear no relation to the self-contained units in which his monthly novels first appeared. The original intention was to issue the monthly part after the four weekly numbers, as had been done with the *Clock*, but after May 1847 this plan was altered, the monthly part coming out with the first number, rather than the last.

The mixture of motives which resulted in this edition, 'unprecedented, it is believed, in the history of Cheap Literature', is revealed in Dickens's Address, issued first in the Prospectus, and

---

[17] Simon Nowell-Smith, 'The "Cheap Edition" of Dickens's Works [First Series] 1847–1852', *The Library*, 5th Series, 22 (1967), 251, offers the table appearing on p. 191.

[18] Dalziel, p. 2. Bulwer copied Dickens in issuing a Cheap edition of his works through Chapman and Hall starting 30 Oct. 1847. In the 'Advertisement by the Author', he declared his long-standing desire to issue such an edition, and went on to state that 'The recent example of my illustrious contemporary (Mr. Dickens) did not, therefore, suggest, though it undoubtedly has served to encourage, the present enterprise.'

TABLE TO NOTE 17 ON PAGE 190

Title and title-page date	1½d. Numbers	7d. Parts	Months of issue of Parts	Complete volumes				
				Publication date	Prices¹		Frontispieces	
					Wrappers	Cloth	Artist	Engraver
Pickwick, 47	1–31	i–viii (3)	i–viii Apr.–Sept. 47	8 Oct. 47	4s. 6d.	5s.	C. R. Leslie	J. Thompson
Nickleby, 48	32–63	viii (4)–xvi (3)	ix–xvi Oct. 47–May 48	27 May 48	4s. 6d.	5s.	T. Webster	T. Williams
O.C.S., 48	64–85	xvi (4)–xxii (1)	xvii–xxi June–Oct. 48	28 Oct. 48	3s. 6d.	4s.	G. Cattermole	T. Williams
B. Rudge, 49	86–109	xxii (2)–xxviii (1)	xxii–xxvii Nov. 48–Apr. 49	28 Apr. 49	3s. 6d.	4s.	H. K. Browne	W. T. Green
Chuzzlewit, 50	110–141	xxviii (2)–xxxvi (1)	xxviii–xxxv May–Nov. 49	8 Dec. 49	4s. 6d.	5s.	F. Stone	T. Bolton
O. Twist, 50	142–160	xxxvi (2)–xl (4)	xxxvi–xl Dec. 49–Apr. 50	13 Apr. 50	3s.	3s. 6d.	G. Cruikshank	T. Bolton
Am. Notes, 50	161–172	xli–xliii	xli–xliii (?)May–July 50	13 July 50	2s.	2s. 6d.	C. Stanfield	T. Bolton
Sketches, 50	173–192	xliv–xlviii	xliv–xlviii (?)July–Nov. 50	16 Nov. 50	3s.	3s. 6d.	G. Cruikshank	—
Christmas Books, 52	193–209	xlix–lii	xlix–lii June–Sept. 52	? Sept. 52	—	3s. 6d.	J. Leech	G. Dalziel

¹ L. A. Kennethe, *Dickensthe*, xxxix (1943), 113, says that 'the books in bound form were originally priced as four shillings for [*Pickwick, Nickleby and Chuzzlewit*], half-a-crown for the *Sketches* and *Oliver Twist*, three shillings for [*Old Curiosity Shop* and *Barnaby*], and eighteenpence for *American Notes*'. These prices pertained, however, not to bound volumes but to sets of unbound numbers. Volumes were also offered 'in half-morocco, marbled edges', at 2s. 6d. above the price in cloth.

reprinted with minor alterations inside the front wrapper to the first monthly part:

It is not for an author to describe his own books. If they cannot speak for themselves, he is likely to do little service by speaking for them. It is enough to observe of these, that eleven years have strengthened in their writer's mind every purpose and sympathy he has endeavoured to express in them; and that their re-production in a shape which shall render them easily accessible as a possession by all classes of society, is at least consistent with the spirit in which they have been written, and is the fulfilment of a desire long entertained.

It had been intended that this CHEAP EDITION, now announced, should not be undertaken until the books were much older, or the Author was dead. But the favour with which they have been received, and the extent to which they have circulated, and continue to circulate, at five times the proposed price, justify the belief that the living Author may enjoy the pride and honour of their widest diffusion, and may couple it with increased personal emolument. . . .

To become, in his new guise, a permanent inmate of many English homes, where, in his old shape, he was only known as a guest, or hardly known at all: to be well thumbed and soiled in a plain suit that will bear a great deal, by children and grown people, at the fireside and on the journey: to be hoarded on the humble shelf where there are few books, and to lie about in libraries like any familiar piece of household stuff that is easy of replacement: and to see and feel this—not to die first, or grow old and passionless: must obviously be among the hopes of a living author, venturing on such an enterprise. Without such hopes it never could be set on foot. I have no fear of being mistaken in acknowledging that they are mine; that they are built, in simple earnestness and grateful faith, on my experience, past and present, of the cheering-on of very many thousands of my countrymen and countrywomen, never more numerous or true to me than now;—and that hence this CHEAP EDITION is projected.

CHARLES DICKENS

Moreover, Dickens took care to see that the sales of back stock of his novels in parts were as little affected as possible: each volume in the Cheap edition contained a frontispiece from a design by a well-known artist—C. R. Leslie, T. Webster, Cattermole, Browne, Frank Stone, Cruikshank (two), Stanfield, and Leech—but none of the original illustrations.[19] Supplementary fascicles of plates,

19 These frontispieces were not altogether satisfactory to Dickens, as his correspondence with Chapman and Hall edited by Grubb reveals. Dickens dis-

wrappered to resemble the monthly parts, were issued with Dickens's 'approbation', but these contained new subjects, and after *Barnaby*, the attempt to compete with the multitudes of unauthorized extra plates seems to have been abandoned. The new prefaces, issued with the final numbers, gave Dickens an opportunity to reflect on his career and the fortunes and receptions of his works, while the new setting of text allowed revisions.

The initial expectation seems to have been for a sale of some 75,000 numbers a week, but by the close of *Pickwick* this press run had been reduced to 40,000, and in 1848 it was further reduced in stages to 20,000. Chapman and Hall had estimated that at three-halfpence per number it would take sales of 10,000 to break even, and that thereafter profits would range from over £23 on 20,000 to nearly £211 on 100,000. In fact, during 1847 the sales diminished from 62,338 for the first number of *Pickwick* to 31,263 for the last, and for *Nickleby* declined from the opening sales of 25,505, itself a drop of nearly 6,000 from *Pickwick*, to 18,735 by 25 December. Through the year, 727,155 numbers, and 164,190 parts (each part containing four numbers, or 656,760 more numbers), were sold, an average weekly sale of better than 30,000. By Chapman and Hall's estimate, such a circulation should have netted around £2,000, but in fact by 31 December 1847 the total profits had reached only £265. 2s. 7d. of which Dickens got half. Dickens asked Chapman for the June 1847 accounts on 6 August, 'as I am anxious to look over them with a view to the cheap Edition',[20] but

liked C. R. Leslie's grisaille painting of Mrs. Bardell fainting in Pickwick's arms, comparing it as a work of art unfavourably with 'a Bank of England sketch for the same amount', but recommending to Chapman that 'if he has the least reason to think it is to be purchased, pray do nothing but pay him for it, as I am not *very* particular on the subject in as much as a collection of Sketches would be incomplete without this one' (Grubb, 'Some Unpublished Correspondence', p. 105). Dickens also thought Thompson's woodcut 'dear and not very satisfactory'. Leslie's painting fetched £137. 11s. at the sale of Dickens's effects in 1870. Learning from this mistake, Dickens cautioned Thomas Webster to make his painting for *Nickleby* 'in colours and presentable in order that I might purchase it afterwards'; Webster's design, which Dickens bought for £12. 12s., he thought *most admirable*', and it fetched a much higher price in 1870: £535. 10s. (both quotations, p. 106). And Dickens may have tried unsuccessfully to get Frith's painting of Dolly Varden engraved for the frontispiece to *Barnaby*; eventually W. T. Green engraved a design by Browne of the same subject. (See pp. 108–9, n. 33.) There were also delays over Frank Stone's plate for *Chuzzlewit*, and questions about who should illustrate *Oliver Twist*, discussed below.

[20] Grubb, 'Some Unpublished Correspondence', p. 104.

Chapman replied that they could not yet be made out, probably because the cost of printing still exceeded receipts from sales. At the end of August Chapman sent the accounts of the other books to Dickens at Broadstairs. He replied on 31 August: 'My chief interest in the past half-year's accounts, was with the accounts of the re-issues. But if they cannot be made out now, there is no help for it, and I must wait until they can be. Meantime my interest will by no means decay, but quite the contrary.'[21] Pressing for information, Dickens renewed his request for Cheap edition accounts on 4 October, suggesting to Chapman

that it would be satisfactory and convenient to make out the accounts of the Cheap Edition, by the works, and not by the half-yearly periods. Thus—as soon as it can be conveniently done after the Pickwick subscription, to make an account taking in all Pickwick. To make out the next, at the same period after the close of Nickleby, and so on. If you should discry no particular objection to this it would give me a clearer view of the matter, certainly.[22]

But Chapman did discry objections: it might be difficult to separate out the sales by title inasmuch as the monthly parts sometimes contained more than one book, and to take inventory other than half-yearly would be disruptive and confusing, especially to booksellers handling stock on consignment. So Dickens had to wait until the spring of 1848.

When he finally rendered the accounts on 23 March, Chapman regretfully admitted that they 'do not present so favorable an aspect as I could have wished. The times have been much against the class of purchasers we depended on & the advertizing [£1,108. 9s. out of a total expense of £5,576. 5s. 5d.] has much exceeded what I thought it would be.' The sale of *Pickwick* complete, he concluded, could be estimated by taking the minimum sale on the stock list (31,263); of this number, about 6,000 'have been sold since its completion', which augured well for the future.[23]

Meanwhile, *Dombey* was going from strength to strength.

---

[21] Grubb, 'Some Unpublished Correspondence', p. 104; from the balance for the half-year, £75. 14s. (not £75. 4s., as Grubb reports), Chapman and Hall deducted the cost of nine books Dickens had ordered, paying the remainder, £72. 9s. 10d., into Coutts's 'as usual' on 4 Sept. (MS. Coutts).

[22] Ibid., p. 105.

[23] Ibid., pp. 106–7. Between famine in Ireland and revolution on the Continent, the times were indeed adverse to cheap fiction.

Almost 200,000 parts were sold from January to the end of June 1847, bringing in £6,633. 10s. 5d.; with the addition of the revenue from advertising, the gross receipts reached £7,226. 14s. 11d., the net profit was £3,698. 12s. 11d., and Dickens's share came to £2,773. 19s. 9d. Bradbury and Evans sent the accounts to Dickens at Broadstairs on 1 September, and the next day Dickens wrote to Forster that 'The profits of the half-year are brilliant. Deducting the hundred pounds a month paid six times [29 January, 1 and 30 March, 30 April, 4 and 30 June], I have still to receive two thousand two hundred and twenty pounds, which I think is tidy. Don't you?' (F VI. i. 464). And three days later he was still gloating over his success: 'The profits, brave indeed, are four hundred pounds more than the utmost I expected' (F VI. i. 465). For the six-month period, each number of *Dombey* was now netting him over £460. Bradbury and Evans could not cope with such large sums all at once: the amount owing to June 1847 was paid in instalments: £1,000 on 21 September, another £500 on 1 October, and the remaining £720. 14s. 11d. on 20 December 1847 (MS. Coutts).

The Christmas 1847 Bradbury and Evans accounts were equally satisfactory. There was no Christmas Book to swell the coffers, Dickens having doubted, as early as 19 September, that he could produce it and *Dombey* too, though he was 'very loath to lose the money. And still more so to leave any gap at Christmas firesides which I ought to fill' (F VI. i. 466). *Dombey* held up well, bringing nearly £440 a number to Dickens; deducting six £100 payments made at the end of every month, he was still owed £2,060. 1s. 10d. when he received the accounts on 18 February 1848 (MS. Coutts). But there was one dark spot in the picture: the £500 lent on 29 April 1846 on account of *Pictures from Italy* still had not been repaid. Now Frederick Evans wrote asking what Dickens wished to be done about it, and offered to call personally on the morning of the nineteenth to receive Dickens's instructions.[24] Dickens conceded that the amount was due his publishers, and directed that it be taken from his Christmas balance. Accordingly, he received £1,000 on 2 March, and £518. 4s. 10d. on 17 March, which cleared all debts (MS. Coutts).

The final account including *Dombey* receipts covered the last

[24] MS. B & E.

five numbers, January to April 1848, and arrived at the beginning
of September. Despite heavy reprintings for a volume issue that
never sold very briskly, there was still a substantial sum owed
Dickens, £2,258. 4s. 6d. less £400 advanced in February and April
for the last four numbers (the January one having been paid for
on 31 December 1847) and plus a few pounds for *Oliver* in parts
and some of the Christmas Books. The final numbers thus netted
over £451 apiece. This balance again was divided into staged
payments: £1,000 on 1 September, and three instalments of
£295. 6s. deposited on the twenty-seventh of January, February,
and March 1849 (MS. Coutts).

At the conclusion of *Dombey*, Dickens involved himself once
again in amateur theatricals, *Every Man in His Humour* being
supplemented with a new production of *The Merry Wives of
Windsor*. Proceeds were to endow a Shakespeare House curatorship for Sheridan Knowles; the cast included such prominent
Shakespearians as Peter Cunningham, treasurer of the Shakespeare
Society, and Mrs. Cowden Clarke, compiler of the Shakespeare
Concordance, who played Mistress Quickly to Mark Lemon's Fal-
staff. The initial performances at the Theatre Royal, Haymarket,
were so enthusiastically received that the company was soon tour-
ing the provinces, playing at Manchester, Liverpool, Birmingham,
Glasgow, and Edinburgh, and raising over £2,500 which Knowles,
having received a pension from the government which rendered
the curatorship unnecessary, received directly.

After *Dombey*, Dickens did very little writing in 1848: Edgar
Johnson estimates his output at only about 14,000 words in nine
short *Examiner* articles. Partly this may be attributed to diminish-
ing creativity, although it is easy to exaggerate that facet of
Dickens's career. But partly, too, this period of frenzied relaxation
reflects the fact that, for the first time, Dickens was not dependent
on a current serial for all of his current income. Reviewing his
situation in a letter to the physician and author D. M. Moir
('Delta') on 17 June 1848, Dickens exhibits a mellower mood than
in former years. Just before the passage quoted as epigraph to this
chapter, he confesses:

I am not rich, for the great expenses of my position have been mine
alone from the first, and the Lion's share of the great profits has been
gorged by the booksellers. But I have changed all that, within these
three years or so,—have worked back half of all my copyrights which

had gone from me before I knew their worth—and have got, by some few thousand pounds (I could count the thousands on one hand) ahead of the world. Dombey has been the greatest success I have ever achieved.[25]

[25] N ii. 102. *Dombey* was a best seller in America, too, where its sales, above 175,000 in various editions, placed it in company with such diverse works as Whittier's *Poems* and a handful of Harper's favourites, including *Jane Eyre*, *Wuthering Heights*, and *Vanity Fair*. See Exman, p. 281, citing Frank Luther Mott, *Golden Multitudes*.

11

David Copperfield *and the* *Cheap Edition*

This is indeed a great age for great authors. Dickens
told a friend of mine, that he had made *four thousand
guineas* by his last year's Christmas book—(The
Battle of Life)—a five shilling publication, (!) which
everybody abused, and which, nevertheless, everybody read. Eighteen thousand copies of his present
Christmas book (The Haunted Man) were 'subscribed for' by the booksellers, before publication.

WILKIE COLLINS[1]

EXCEPTING THE FIVE NEW MONTHLY SERIALS and his
share of *Household Words* and *All the Year Round*, after 1847
Dickens's significant earnings for his writing come from the
four reprint series: the 'Cheap', 'Library', 'People's', and 'Charles
Dickens' editions. The first year's gross from the Cheap edition,
over £5,700, was nearly all used up in expenses, but from 1848
to the end of 1853, though the income was less, the profits were
substantially higher, yielding Dickens more than £400 annually,
and over £834 in 1848. On 15 April 1848 Edward Chapman sent
Dickens an 'estimated a/c' of the profits on the Cheap edition to
Midsummer 'which I think you will find more satisfactory than
the last' estimate. 'My hope', he continued, 'is that it will turn out
even a little better for I have endeavoured not to *exceed* the probability, but at the same time not to fall much below it.'[2] To publish
32,000 each of Numbers 46 to 72, plus commissions, would cost

---

[1] W. Wilkie Collins to R. H. Dana, 12 Jan. 1849, in M. L. Parrish and Elizabeth
V. Miller, *Wilkie Collins and Charles Reade* (London, 1940, rpt. New York, Burt
Franklin, Bibliography and Reference Series No. 186, 1968), p. 10.
[2] Grubb, 'Some Unpublished Correspondence', p. 107.

£1,773; proceeds from the sale of 634,000 numbers (including 80,600 bound in parts) would produce over £2,712, and the resulting profit would be £939. 15s. 8d., over £227 more than the original estimate at the time the edition was first planned. These figures reassured Dickens, and were confirmed when the Mid-summer accounts came out that autumn. Though the press run was gradually reduced—30,000 for 46 to 49, 28,000 for 50 to 57, and 24,000 for 58 to 73—and though sales reached only 601,848 numbers (83,967 in parts), profits at £925. 7s. 1d. were less than £15 under Chapman's guess.[3] Dickens's share was of course one-half the net. In addition to sending the revised estimate, Chapman had a question to pose: 'Is "Curiosity-shop" to be next, or would you recommend "Barnaby" in consequence of Mr. Tappertit bearing somewhat upon the present times.'[4] Dickens chose not to capitalize on revolution, selecting Nell's pilgrimage over the burning of Newgate; and the *Shop* began appearing with Number 64 in June 1848.

Once again Dickens itched to see the ledgers long before they were ready.[5] On 27 July he asked Chapman to forward the Mid-summer accounts to him at Broadstairs, but he did not receive them until 10 September. On books other than the Cheap edition, the results were dismal: nothing on *Oliver* (the three-volume Bentley 'third edition'), piddling sums on the others, total under £40. If it were not for the Cheap edition, which netted £462.13s. 7d. as Dickens's half share, his receipts would have been scant indeed. 'The times are no doubt very much against us', he acknowledged, a phrase that was repeated often in the years to come. Nevertheless, profits had been increased by bringing the press runs more into line with sales: Dickens was 'glad to see the preposterous mistake of over-printing, that was made in the commencement, set right'.[6]

He noticed too that in the general account there was no mention of *Nickleby*. 'Oliver Twist is quoted there, although there is no

---

[3] Grubb (ibid., n. 26) is off by £4 on the estimated account.

[4] Ibid., p. 107.

[5] There is an undated A.L.S. to Chapman on paper watermarked 1847 informing him that Dickens wants to talk about 'the cheap Edition accounts', and that he will call on Chapman that day at 2 p.m. (Maggs Bros. Ltd. Catalogue 965, spring 1975, item 32).

[6] The following account is taken from Grubb, 'Some Unpublished Correspondence', p. 108.

sale; but Nickleby is not mentioned at all.' Chapman replied that
Nickleby had not been mentioned in earlier accounts, and explained
something further that satisfied Dickens. 'I knew of course that
Nickleby had not made its appearance in the past accounts; but as
that involved no very logical reason why it should never appear
in the present or future accounts, I stood in need of the explanation
you have given me', he reported three days later. What that
explanation was can only be surmised: the copyright of *Nickleby*
belonged wholly to Dickens after 1 October 1844, and at that time
he had the right to purchase from Chapman and Hall all remaining
stock excepting 500 copies. Since he was sole owner, and the
accounts were of partnership arrangements, Chapman and Hall
would not include *Nickleby*. I have not found any record of
Dickens's buying from them the remaining unsold stock in 1844;
perhaps they were selling copies of the parts or bound volumes
until their purchase price was reached. Undoubtedly sales were
slow, and when *Nickleby* appeared as the second title in the Cheap
edition, they probably came to a standstill, as there is no account
of that novel for another ten years.

But Dickens's troubles over the June 1848 Chapman and Hall
accounts were not over. He asked Chapman to pay his balance,
£500. 3s. 11d., into his account 'at your convenience'. Two
weeks later, on 26 September, a portion was paid in: £300 (MS.
Coutts). October and November passed without any further
word. On 6 December Dickens nudged Chapman in a terse one-
sentence note: 'I shall be glad to receive the balance due on the
last halfyear's accounting, at your convenience.' It was still not
convenient. Dickens finally received the remainder on 29 December, acknowledging its receipt the following day. By then, it was
nearly time for the next accounting.

Further questions about the Cheap edition arose towards the
end of *Barnaby* (Numbers 86–109). The advertised order of the
series placed *Sketches* third and *Chuzzlewit* last. This had already
been altered to move up the *Shop* and *Barnaby*, Dickens instructing
Chapman on 15 February 1848 'that we must go on, in the Cheap
Edition, with the stories, and not take the sketches yet'.[7] To
adhere to his promise that a very considerable period would elapse
before republication in the Cheap edition, Dickens should have
kept back *Chuzzlewit* to the end. But on the other hand, inter-

[7] Grubb, 'Some Unpublished Correspondence', p. 106.

rupting the series of novels seemed bad policy. Writing to Chapman on Wednesday night, 21 March 1849, Dickens said:

I feel it rather early to take Chuzzlewit, but I feel convinced that—in poor times especially—the Sketches would make a dangerous break in the continuity of the Sale, and perhaps damage what followed. Under the circumstances I think 1, it would be best to take Chuzzlewit next, 2, then Oliver, then 3, The American Notes and lastly the Sketches and so to alter the announcement on the cover, putting this line after the last or Sketches, *with which the Cheap Edition will terminate.* But if you have any other suggestion to make, *I should very much like to have the benefit of it before we finally decide.*[8]

Chapman had nothing better to suggest, so the order of Dickens's letter was followed, and the announcement printed on the wrappers to Part XXVIII (April 1849) and thereafter.

In the same letter, Dickens remarks that the 'accounts will be welcome when they come, as I am anxious to know how they stand', especially with regard to the Cheap edition. Nine days later, on 30 March, Chapman replied, sending the December 1848 accounts, 'which I regret to say are not quite so good as they should be. I was in hopes that the amount of last half [to 30 June 1848] would have been maintained steadily for a long time, but that apparently is not to be—at least for the present.'[9] The printing order, reduced to 20,000 for Numbers 74 to 89, was raised 1,000 for Numbers 90–7; 459,199 numbers (52,754 in parts) had been sold; Dickens's half share of the profits came to £371. 9s. 9d., nearly £100 under the preceding half-year. They were never to rise to such heights again, though in the sixties large quantities, sold at big discounts, pushed profits up over £300 semi-annually for a short time. In December 1849 J. Gilbert of the Newsvendors' Institution suggested to Dickens that he reduce the price of the Cheap edition still further, but Dickens argued in reply that he couldn't, and that his twenty-number books contained about three times the matter of an ordinary novel (N ii. 192). As Forster remarks, the success of the Cheap edition 'was very good, but did not come even near to the mark of the later issues of his writings'

---

[8] N ii. 148. It became standard practice in the case of three-deckers to issue a cheap one-volume reprint after about a year (Griest, p. 53). Any shorter span between original publication and reprint cut into the three-volume sale and hurt the lending libraries, who counted on the high original price to discourage buyers and encourage borrowers.

[9] Grubb, 'Some Unpublished Correspondence', p. 109.

(F V. vii. 448). Dickens, disappointed but not discouraged on seeing the Christmas 1848 figures, admitted that 'The result is certainly not what I had wished, or even what I had expected, but the times have no doubt been against us.' The balance due him after deducting just over ten guineas for books ordered and charged against his account, £304. 13s. 4d., was received on 20 April, and acknowledged the next day.[10]

The other major contributor to Dickens's income in 1848 was his fifth and last Christmas book, *The Haunted Man*. Settled at Broadstairs in September after the summer theatricals and his sister Fanny's death, he began 'a mentally matooring of the Christmas book' (F VI. iv. 507), elaborating the 'ghostly and wild idea' first recorded in July 1846 about which he composed a few slips in September of the following year.[11] Although 5 October found him frowning at a blank quire of paper, at the end of that month he read Leech the beginning and saw John Tenniel about a frontispiece. In November his old friend Frank Stone contributed some very satisfactory designs for the second and third parts; and on 1 December he dispatched manuscript of the third part to Whitefriars. Time was pressing as usual, and Dickens's letter on that day to Bradbury contains a flurry of instructions: a note for Leech about subjects in Part III; ditto to Stanfield, for Bradbury to deliver in a cab; Stone's third subject; and information about the copy of the third part kept back to read to Mark Lemon, but to be sent the next day. There were also directions about proofs: 'My proofs of the first two parts, you shall have by Lemon to-morrow.

[10] Grubb, 'Some Unpublished Correspondence', p. 109, and MS. Coutts; he reiterated 'the times' excuse in confirming receipt of the balance.

[11] When Dickens decided not to issue any Christmas Book in 1847, Bradbury asked Samuel Warren, author of £10,000 a Year who was considered by himself and others a rival, perhaps even greater than Dickens, to step into the breach. Bradbury predicted that Warren's effort might net £600–£700. Before Warren could reply, John Blackwood countered on behalf of *Maga* with the offer of a £500 advance and £500 on delivery of the manuscript. (See Mrs. Oliphant, *Annals of a Publishing House: William Blackwood and his Sons: Their Magazine and Friends* (2 vols., Edinburgh and London, William Blackwood and Sons, 1897), ii. 403–4.) On second thought, Blackwoods issued *Now and Then* as a separate publication, 'One Thick Volume, royal, post 8vo. half-bound morocco', for a guinea. There were several other competing Christmas Books for 1847 that imitated Dickens's format, binding, and price: for example, Hans Christian Andersen's *A Christmas Greeting* from Bentley, portions of which Dickens enjoyed 'with the most unspeakable pleasure' (N ii. 65), and two from Parry & Co., G. P. R. James's *The Last of the Fairies*, and Charles Rowcroft's *The Triumph of Woman*.

My corrections had better be made and then the fresh proof go to Mr. Forster for the usual corrections. I will arrange with him for their being immediately done, as I have promised Tauchnitz of Leipzig proofs by Tuesday or Wednesday next' (N ii. 134). Publishing is seldom leisurely, but it is useful to be reminded of how very swiftly Dickens and his publishers did work to put out his new books.

Even before the official publication date, word had leaked out concerning the nature of Dickens's new story, as he learned from the manager of the Adelphi Theatre, where Mark Lemon was preparing an authorized stage version. Dickens immediately 'instituted a searching investigation at the Printers where my suspicion mainly lies, notwithstanding that we enforce the greatest caution throughout the establishment' (N ii. 135). Four days before publication, subscriptions for 16,000 copies were in hand; when issued on the nineteenth, 18,000 were sold, Dickens told Wilkie Collins and Thomas Beard.[12] Forster likewise paints a glowing picture, saying it 'sold largely, beginning with a subscription of twenty thousand' (F VI. iv. 507). To account for the copies of the first printing still remaining unsold by the last Christmas of Dickens's life, John C. Eckel supposes the printing to have been a large one.[13] In fact, it was not so large as that for *Battle*. The accounts show that out of 20,000 printed, on 31 December there were still 2,008 copies on hand, 1,282 in quires and 726 in cloth. Of the remainder, the fate of 125 sent out to agents had not been reported, ninety-one were distributed free to the statutory libraries and as presentation and review copies, one in cloth was sold for £5 to New York for reprinting there, and 17,775 were sold. Dickens's three-quarters share of the profit amounted to £793. 5s. 11d. Clearly the year's break between Christmas books had interrupted the habit of buying Dickens's offerings and allowed others to garner a share of the market. Sales were down by more than 6,000 from the *Battle of Life*, and profits were nearly £500 shy of the earlier total. An additional £100 came in from the Managers of the Adelphi Theatre (N ii. 141). But there was no disguising the fact that, despite Dickens's early enthusiasm, the *Haunted Man*, though profitable, was not especially successful, either in 1848 or subsequently. When Bradbury and Evans turned over their stock of the

---

[12] See epigraph to this chapter and N ii. 136.
[13] Rev. and enl. edn. (1932), p. 124.

first edition to Chapman and Hall in 1861, there were still 1,270 in quires, and 294 bound, unsold, and these were not entirely worked off by Dickens's death nine years later. In forwarding the Christmas accounts on 15 March 1849, the printers tactfully refrained from comment, only sending their 'good wishes for the future'.

Impending was the commencement of his next serial in monthly numbers, *David Copperfield*. Dickens's 'favourite child', it was notwithstanding one of his less successful serials from a commercial point of view, and the story of its publication from month to month reads very differently from that of its predecessor, *Dombey*. The origins of *Copperfield*, and Dickens's planning of it, have been so well told by others, that while necessarily retracing some of that ground we can concentrate on Dickens's relations with White-friars rather more than on his struggles to compose the text.

Publication was still governed by the eight-year contract Dickens had signed in 1844, assigning Bradbury and Evans a quarter share in anything he might write over the period. Out of his own share of the profits, during the months *Copperfield* was being issued, Dickens took a monthly stipend of £100; and from the spring of 1850 onwards, he also enjoyed approximately £500 a year salary from *Household Words*.[14] But the monthly serial was still a principal source of income for Dickens, and when his green leaves were not being issued, his income was drastically reduced. For example, in 1849 his publishers paid Dickens £3,044. 15s. 11d.; in 1850, £4,434. 18s. 6½d.; but in 1851, when no serial was forthcoming, Dickens received only £784. 2s. 8d.[15]

Thus the pressing economic need of earlier years had somewhat abated. But even without the stimulus of a specific contract appointing a specific deadline, Dickens continued to find it necessary to write for his living. The subject of his next serial developed out of Forster's casual inquiry in the spring of 1847 about an incident in Dickens's remote past; in reply Dickens was prompted to write an autobiographical fragment.[16] Later, when he was

[14] J, p. 702; payments of £40 a month commenced on 1 Apr. 1850 (MS. Coutts).

[15] All figures exclusive of *Household Words* and *All the Year Round*, the records of which are not a part of these accounts.

[16] Horsman, Introduction to *Dombey and Son*, pp. xxiv–xxv, points out that as early as Nov. 1846 Dickens refers to his 'life in MS.' as if it were already at least partly written. In June 1845 while staying at Geneva Dickens told Forster for the

revolving plans for a new work, Forster again contributed to its shape by suggesting 'that he should write it in the first person, by way of change' (F VI. vi. 522). Dickens's earlier attempt at this point of view in *Master Humphrey's Clock* had been speedily abandoned when he found it too restricting for the expanded narrative he wanted to write. It is a mark of his rapid artistic maturation that less than ten years later he could handle the confinement of this perspective so easily.

In January 1849 Dickens, accompanied by Leech and Mark Lemon, visited Norwich and Stanfield Hall, stopping along the way at Yarmouth, which Dickens told Forster was 'the success of the trip . . . Yarmouth, sir, . . . is the strangest place in the wide world: one hundred and forty-six miles of hill-less marsh between it and London. More when we meet. I shall certainly try my hand at it' (F VI. vi. 523). In Brighton in February, Dickens reported that his mind was running, 'like a high sea', on names (F VI. iii. 496)—always an early consideration when starting a new work. In 'Deepest despondency, as usual, in commencing' (F VI. vi. 524), he spent six days, from 23 to 28 February, trying out alternative titles, beginning with the idea of '*Mag's Diversions*'—that is, mischief—;[17] he experimented with various readings of the explanatory sub-title, 'the personal history of MR. THOMAS MAG THE YOUNGER, Of Blunderstone House', and finally discarded '*Mag's Diversions*' in favour of '*The Copperfield Survey of the World as it Rolled*', which Kate, Georgy, and Forster all picked out as the best (F VI. vi. 524-5). Though this served provisionally, Forster tells us that as late as 19 April, just a few days before Part I was to be issued, another alteration occurred, as Dickens, determined to reject 'everything not strictly personal', expunged the '*Survey*' and added a last parenthetical clause, which resulted in the final wrapper title: *The Personal History, Adventures, Experience, & Observation of David Copperfield the Younger, of Blunderstone Rookery: (Which He never meant to be Published on any Account.)*. Forster is misinformed on the date. Dickens decided on this title

first time about his early theatrical ambitions, so perhaps the autobiography can be traced that far back.

[17] A 'mag' ('magg' or 'meg') was also used throughout the British Isles to denote a small sum, usually a halfpenny. Did Dickens hope his readers would associate the book's title with its cheapness, especially in view of the rising impact of penny magazines and other inexpensive publications? Could this secondary meaning of 'mag' help to explain the change from Thomas *Mag* to David *Copper*field?

at least as early as the end of March, for it appears in Bradbury and Evans's *Athenaeum* announcement on the thirty-first.[18] The advertising campaign began over a month earlier; Bradbury and Evans had printed 80,000 crown 8vo announcements by 24 February, before Dickens had thought of his title, and by the beginning of March were advertising a new work by Dickens.[19] Another 80,000 bills of the same size in green and blue were printed at the end of the month. In addition to the bills, 5,000 double crown posters were run off, and for the pay of a shilling for every twenty-five, eager hands posted 2,200 of these across London by May, and another 750 by the beginning of June. The remainder were sent around the country. Two thousand colourful red and black show cards were provided, as well as 1,000 window slips. The design for the wrapper cost the usual eight guineas; and the engraving, the usual £9. 15s. By the end of June 1849 nearly £150 worth of advertising had been taken in magazines and journals, and the total cost of promotion to that date was £247. 5s. 1d.

Comparing Bradbury and Evans's second campaign with their first reveals some differences. For the four numbers of *Dombey* issued to the end of 1846, £163 had been spent on advertisements, £13 more than for *Copperfield*'s three. But the total spent on promotion for *Dombey*, £347. 0s. 5d., is almost exactly £100 more than for *Copperfield*; this difference is attributable largely to the enormous number of posters and bills printed for *Dombey*: 220,000 bills and 10,000 posters, at a cost of £114. 10s., compared with 160,000 bills and 5,000 posters, costing £57. 6s. for *Copperfield*. Subsequent promotional campaigns tended to follow the latter example, indicating that for their first original Dickens serial Bradbury and Evans may have overextended their advertising in their anxiety to do well.

Meanwhile, Dickens was getting on slowly. 'My hand is out in the matter of *Copperfield*', he told Forster while working on Number I. 'Though I know what I want to do, I am lumbering on like a stage-waggon. . . . the long Copperfieldian perspective looks snowy and thick, this fine morning' (F VI. vi. 525–6). Dickens's discomfort at getting started is not, however, reflected

---

[18] Furthermore, the only *Athenaeum* notice which includes the 'Survey' is that for 21 Apr., two days after Dickens is supposed to have expunged it.

[19] Cf. *Athenaeum*, 3 Mar. 1849, p. 240.

in the number itself, which Sylvère Monod calls 'masterly . . . one that gives an impression of splendid ease'.[20] Eventually, the manuscript was sent off to Whitefriars, where a press run of 25,000 was ordered for the text and the *Copperfield* Advertiser, swollen to thirty-two pages because of the popularity of *Dombey* and the general expectation of continued success. This insert cost £101. 10s. to produce, £5. 15s. 6d. for duty, and approximately £6. 11s. 4d. for commissions; it brought in £205. 17s. 6d., thus furnishing a modest profit of £92. 0s. 8d.[21]

On publication day sales went well, and soon a reprint order for 5,000 more copies was necessary. But this commercial success was quite moderate in contrast to the enthusiastic reception of *Dombey*; only 26,000 of the 30,000 copies of Part I were wrappered by the end of June, the press run for the second and third numbers was reduced to 24,000, of which 20,000 of II, and 19,000 of III, were sewn into covers, and the *Copperfield* Advertiser shrank to twelve pages, its revenue below £90. A total of 59,218 copies were sold to 30 June, just under 20,000 per number.

Evans himself brought the accounts down to Bonchurch in the middle of September; they showed Dickens's profits on the first three numbers to be £611. 14s. 5d., slightly above £200 a number. A chastened Dickens wrote to Forster:

The accounts are rather shy, after *Dombey*, and what you said comes true after all. I am not sorry I cannot bring myself to care much for what opinions people may form; and I have a strong belief, that, if any of my books are read years hence, *Dombey* will be remembered as among the best of them: but passing influences are important for the time, and as *Chuzzlewit* with its small sale sent me up, *Dombey's* large sale has tumbled me down. Not very much, however, in real truth. These accounts only include the first three numbers, have of course been burdened with all the heavy expenses of number one, and ought not in reason to be complained of. (F VI. iv. 509)

To some extent, Dickens is right. The reputation earned by any of his novels seemed to work on the next. Wilkie Collins, in

---

[20] *Dickens the Novelist*, p. 279.
[21] When an additional 5,000 copies of Number I were printed, a like number of additional Advertisers was run off, at a cost of £16. 10s. That brings up an interesting question: were the fees for advertising set on a sliding scale according to the number of parts sold, or were they fixed at so much per page, half-page, and so on? If the latter, then Dickens and his publishers lost money whenever an especially heavy sale necessitated a reprint, since they had to bear the entire cost of reprinting the Advertiser.

marginalia on his copy of Forster's *Life*, says that the 'latter half of "Dombey" no intelligent person can have read without astonishment at the badness of it, and the disappointment that followed lowered the sale of the next book, "Copperfield," incomparably superior to "Dombey" as it certainly is'.[22] Likewise, *Copperfield*'s critical reception sent sales of *Bleak House* even above those of *Dombey*. Dickens's other excuse, that the first account is always burdened with extra charges, is also true. The custom of charging the majority of advertising expense against the profits of the first accounting period, and the necessity of reprinting the first number, often several times, usually inflated the costs and depressed the profits of early numbers. For instance, 30,000 of Number I cost £450, 24,000 of II only £297. In subsequent months, though sales rose only slightly, the charges were kept down, so that Dickens averaged close to £300 a number, rising to nearly £400 for the last months. But as the disappointing sales of *Chuzzlewit* had indirectly led to the *Daily News*, so the modesty of *Copperfield*'s reception turned Dickens's thoughts towards a periodical: '. . . it is clear to me', he continued to Forster, 'that the Periodical must be set agoing in the spring; and I have already been busy, at odd half-hours, in shadowing forth a name and an idea' (F VI. iv. 509). Within a few days, the notion was 'growing into form',[23] and by 7 October Dickens was able to write Forster concrete suggestions (F VI. iv. 510–11). Six months later, on 30 March 1850, *Household Words* commenced; from the time of receiving the Bradbury and Evans accounts in September 1849, *Copperfield* shared Dickens's attention with this developing project.

Although *Copperfield*'s sales fell short of *Dombey*'s, Evans told Dickens that the firm had 'but one opinion repeated to them of *Copperfield*, and they feel very confident about it. A steady twenty-five thousand, which it is now on the verge of, will do very well. The back numbers are always going off.' But alas, *Copperfield* did not even sustain 25,000.[24] With Number VI, the press run dropped to 22,000, where it remained throughout the rest of the publication, while the binding order, the most accurate index of monthly sales, inched up: 19,000 (III, IV), 19,300 (V, VI, VII), 19,700 (VIII, IX, X), 19,800 (XI, XII), 20,000 (XIII), 20,100 (XIV–

XVII), 20,200 (XVIII), 20,300 (XIX and XX). From time to time sheets of the back numbers were bound up for sale, but with the exception of Number I no initial printing order was exhausted during *Copperfield*'s publication, and as late as 1861, when Bradbury and Evans transferred their stock to Chapman and Hall, only Numbers I–V had been issued in more than 25,000 copies. At that time, the numbers of *Dombey* in print exceeded those of *Copperfield* by 212,500, or over 10,000 complete copies. There were, in addition, the usual foreign issues: Tauchnitz published a three-volume edition set up from proofs, John Wiley and G. P. Putnam shared in the American part issue set from the English one, and in Russia the market for all Dickens's work had been widened by Wredenskii's translation of *Dombey*, reported 'to inspire with enthusiasm the whole of the literary Russia'.[25] But none of these brought Dickens any income, or increased his reputation in England.

Happily, Dickens kept his spirits up through *Copperfield*; there was no break with Whitefriars over the limited sales, and he remained in good heart about his writing, in spite of minor irritations and press blunders. In one case, Dickens learned by letter that Bradbury and Evans had altered some phase of the customary procedure in issuing his books. On 5 May 1849, he chided Evans: 'I think it excessively injudicious if there be any departure on your part from the old course of my books' (N ii. 152). But when Evans seemed deeply troubled about the rebuke, Dickens was quick to soothe him, and to assure him that he did not need to inquire into the matter further. He reiterated that he disapproved of the change, however: 'The saving is a great and tempting one, but that is no proof of the wisdom of the alteration. We might save as much again, I dare say, by doing something that would nevertheless be very impolitic and ill-advised' (N ii. 152). And to Bradbury, recovering from a prolonged illness, he sent on 28 July from the Isle of Wight a letter full of high good humour and affection.

As for the writing itself, after a slow beginning it went exceedingly well. Dickens was 'quite confident in the story' by June, and could already see his moves through the September number.[26]

[25] F VI. iv. 510; see N ii. 172 and 240–1; and Gaskell, Appendix C 2, pp. 384–91.

[26] F VI. vi. 536, misdated 1850 in N ii. 218.

'I am wonderfully in harness, and nothing galls or frets', he told
Forster on 17 November (F VI. vi. 536); chapters 23 and 24, for
the December number, were composed within four days,[27] and
Dickens thought the whole 'smashing'.[28] He frequently over-
wrote, and had to devise means for getting all the matter in, in one
case placing the beginning of chapter 5 at the bottom of page 46
instead of at the top of 47. And on the top of the first page of proof
for Number IX, Forster revolted against the tyranny of inflexible
printing limits, writing, 'The overmatter must be got in somehow
—by lengthening the page.'[29] The pages of Part I each contain
forty-nine lines, those in Parts II to VIII, page 254, fifty lines, but
page 255 contains fifty-one, and Part IX has fifty-one throughout.
On the other hand, *Copperfield* XVI was underwritten by one
entire page.[30]

The praise of friends buoyed him, in spite of the continuing
sluggish sales. In December 1849 he told W. F. de Cerjat 'that
Copperfield is a great success. I think it is better liked than any of
my other books' (N ii. 194). On the other side of the coin, Dickens
spurred Evans in February to an early accounting of the preceding
half-year: 'I shall be glad to have the Copperfield accounts as soon
as they are ready—for I am poor' (N ii. 206). A month later, the
firm sent him £500 on account, and when the books were finally
drawn up there was still owing to Dickens's credit £662. 11s. 6d.
All told, from 1 July to 31 December 1849, 121,888 numbers of
Copperfield were sold, and Dickens's proceeds from it and the
other Bradbury and Evans books reached £1,737. 9s. 5d. In the
preceding period the stock on *Dombey* had been miscounted; to
correct it meant Dickens owed £14. 17s. 11d. The £500 March
advance, and the six £100 monthly payments, made up the
balance. The succeeding two accounts showed very similar nets
for Dickens: £1,767 to Midsummer, and £2,017 to Christmas
1850.

As *Copperfield* drew to a close in the autumn, the favourable
comments increased. 'Every one is cheering David on, and I hope
to make *your book* a good one', Dickens told the Hon. Richard
Watson on 3 July 1850; 'I like it very much myself, thoroughly
believing it all, and go to work every month with an energy of
the finest description' (N ii. 221). Ten days later, he reported to

[27] Monod, p. 286.   [28] F VI. vi. 536, misdated 1850 in N ii. 246.
[29] Monod, p. 288.   [30] Ibid., p. 294.

the Revd. James White that 'there seems a bright unanimity about Copperfield' (N ii. 223). Thackeray thought the book excellent, speculating that Dickens might have learned something from *Vanity Fair*,[31] and Bulwer complimented Dickens handsomely, remarking that some hitherto deficient qualities might be observed (N ii. 224). Dickens knew from the first that he could not hope to maintain his pre-eminence by repeating old formulas: 'The world would not take another Pickwick from me now,' he told Dudley Costello just before *Copperfield* I was issued, 'but we can be cheerful and merry, I hope, notwithstanding, and with a little more purpose in us' (N ii. 150). That 'unity of drift or purpose', as Forster observed, 'is apparent always, and the tone is uniformly right' (F VI. vii. 554). Forwarding the Midsummer 1850 accounts on 26 August, Evans remarked parenthetically '(By the way, what a pity that there should be any necessity for finishing at No 20; there will be one general feeling of regret.)' (MS. B & E). Easy, more naturally plotted, less melodramatic, with gentle humour, wide-ranging character, and sure command of style, *David Copperfield* earned Dickens high critical praise: he never again 'stood so high in reputation' (F VI. vii. 547).

Dickens's other literary ventures continued to supply some income. Chapman and Hall's accounts for 1849 were substantially lower than for the previous year: Dickens's shares were £322. 13s. to June, and £314. 16s. 1d. to December. Sending the Midsummer accounts on 2 October, Edward Chapman once again apologized: 'I . . . am sorry to say they have not come up to the former mark. The beginning of the half year promised very well but the last half fell off in business sadly.'[32] On 6 October Dickens replied from Broadstairs, notifying Chapman that he had examined and certified the accounts. 'I could wish the profits were larger, but the times have not been such as to justify any sanguine expectations in that regard.' To improve profits, Dickens again suggested bringing press runs more into line with sales. 'It seems to me, however, that the stock on hand is too large. Would it not be advisable to reduce the Numbers printed?'[33] The stock on hand 30 June 1849 was certainly great: 800,496 numbers in quires not folded, 288,612 folded, and 24,825 in parts (99,300 numbers).

[31] *Letters*, ii. 531.
[32] Grubb, 'Some Unpublished Correspondence', p. 109.
[33] Ibid., p. 110.

Chapman took the hint, and reduced the press run still further, to 18,000 per number.

Early in the new year, Chapman had inquired who was to design the frontispiece to *Oliver*, already in the process of publication in weekly numbers, and scheduled to conclude in April with front matter inserted in the final number. 'George Cruikshank, by all means', was Dickens's unhesitating reply. Whatever estrangement had led to the cancellation of plans for Cruikshank's illustrating *Barnaby* had by now dissipated in the brisk winds of theatrical barnstorming; and within a few months Dickens had commissioned from the illustrious George a second frontispiece, for *Sketches*.

Although Dickens had loaned T. J. Thompson £975 around the end of 1849,[34] by February he was once again concerned about his financial affairs, probably because he counted on larger *Copperfield* receipts than were actually coming in. In February, as we have noted, Dickens spurred Evans to produce the Christmas 1849 accounts; on 9 March he wrote in a similar vein to Chapman, requesting also 'in all future accounts, to have a *separate abstract* of the results of Oliver Twist, *as* I have sharers in my interest in that book'.[35] Dickens thought about *Twist* repeatedly during the early months of 1850, not only in connection with the frontispiece and the accounts, but also with respect to its political and social assertions. Stung by Sir Peter Laurie's speech to the vestry of Marylebone parish on Saturday, 9 February, asserting that Jacob's Island existed only in the pages of *Oliver Twist*, he retorted brilliantly in a new Preface for the Cheap edition. Having finished it, Dickens decided to use it to advertise the Cheap edition *Twist* by inserting it in the next number (XII, April 1850) of *Copperfield*. But where? He consulted Evans. 'Facing the last page? We ought to keep the place between the illustrations and the first page, for [advertising] Household Words' (N ii. 211). Two days later, he concluded 'that the Oliver Preface ought decidedly to be a Bill at the end' (N ii. 211). And thus it appeared, following the text, as

---

[34] At least, there are two cheques to Thompson—£200 on 23 Nov. and £775 on 4 Jan. 1850—and a letter to Mitton of 13 Nov. discussing 'on what terms the thousand pounds are required' (N ii. 184).

[35] Grubb, 'Some Unpublished Correspondence', p. 110; his explanatory n. 39 is incorrect: the 'sharers' were Bradbury and Evans who, it will be recalled, by the June 1844 Agreement received for eight years a quarter share in anything Dickens published. At the time of that Agreement, Dickens was sole owner of *Twist*.

a separate two-page insertion, along with an eight-page insert touting the virtues of Cassell's publications and Kaye's Wordsell's Pills, another insert of similar length announcing the 'Exhibition of Industry of all Nations', and a single slip extolling the virtues of a 'Visit to the Exhibition of Ancient and Medieval Art' and 'Part III. of the Ladies' Companion'.

On 9 April 1850 Chapman forwarded the accounts, with a separate statement for the Cheap edition *Twist*. To December 1849, 18,000 copies each of eight numbers had been issued (142 to 149), and 57,616 (including 6,071 parts) sold, leaving a small deficit of £27. 18s. 6d. 'I have had a separate a/c made out of Oliver Twist as you wished', Chapman wrote, 'by which you will perceive that the balance is a little on the wrong side—this of course will be changed next time—when also its share of advertizing will be charged.'[36] Though the account is succinctly and legibly presented, the balance is incorrectly figured, being off a shilling, and Dickens as usual was exasperated by Chapman and Hall's way of keeping records.[37] Sending on to Evans both the accounts and Chapman's letter, he grumbled that 'there will be no profits on Oliver Twist until next half year. I suppose it is all correct. I never understand his accounts. The other books are all paying very well.'[38] In forwarding the Midsummer 1850 accounts, delayed until the middle of October, Chapman suggested another method of rendering the *Oliver Twist* Cheap edition accounts, to which Dickens agreed, promising on 18 October to 'arrange the matter with my partners, according to those just and reasonable considerations you explain' (N ii. 239). Whatever they were, they precluded Chapman from making out a separate account to 30 June 1850, although he had predicted in his earlier letter that by Midsummer even after its share of advertising was charged *Oliver* would be in the black. And the Christmas 1850 accounts, submitted in the succeeding April, likewise lacked the separate *Twist* accounts. So the comedy played itself out once again, Dickens requesting a separate account ('I shall be much obliged . . . if you will, like my friend Captain Cuttle, "Make a note of it"

---

[36] Grubb, 'Some Unpublished Correspondence', p. 110.

[37] The next accounting also contained an error of £3 which was corrected before the balance was deposited in Coutts's.

[38] N ii. 213. Dickens must be referring to the other Cheap edition books, his net profit for the half-year on them being £300. 5s. 2d. despite *Oliver*'s deficit. Back sales of original editions continued sluggish, netting only £14. 10s. 11d.

for the future'[39]), and two days later sending on the freshly prepared *Twist* account to Evans complaining, 'I don't understand it.
Perhaps you will. At any rate, if you will make it all square to this
time, either with his assistance or without, I shall be glad to know
. . . what I have to pay you, and to have your demonstration of
the labyrinth' (N ii. 302). Thereafter, Chapman evidently complied with Dickens's request, except that in Midsummer 1853 the
reprints were so heavy 'that the cost of the half year exceeds the
sales consequently I have not rendered a separate a/c'.[40] June 1851
shows a profit on *Oliver* of £52. 0s. 8d.; June 1852 shows
£72. 12s. 2d. But several accounts are missing, including that for
December 1851—possibly because Dickens sent them on to Evans
for him to make 'all square'.

[39] Grubb, 'Some Unpublished Correspondence', p. 111.
[40] Ibid., p. 112.

Bleak House *and the*
Literary Croesus

> It is, perhaps, not considered through how many
> hands a book often passes, before it comes into those
> of the reader; or what part of the profit each hand
> must retain, as a motive for transmitting it to the
> next.
>
> SAMUEL JOHNSON[1]

*B*LEAK HOUSE, coming almost exactly in the middle of
Dickens's career, affords an opportunity to pause and compare its publishing history both with others of Dickens's
serials, and with the works of his contemporaries. Its critical
reception was mixed. Forster cites *Bleak House* as the 'book in
which some want of all the freshness of his genius first became
apparent', though he admits that in construction the novel is very
nearly perfect (F VII. i. 562). Sydney Dobell and Dean Ramsay
were greatly moved, while Miss Mitford, Mrs. Oliphant, and
Henry Crabb Robinson all began to lose interest in Dickens's
work after 1850. George Ford thinks that Dickens's wide-
sweeping criticism of society alienated liberal and conservative
alike, and that political partisanship had much to do with the less
favourable reviews Dickens received after mid century, and with
the constant refrain that he should go back to the happier vein of
Pickwick.[2] Philip Collins agrees that *Bleak House* stands at a
turning-point in Dickens's reputation, but emphasizes that the 1853

---

[1] Samuel Johnson to the Revd. Dr. Nathan Wetherell, 12 Mar. 1776, in *Boswell's Life of Johnson*, ii. 425.
[2] *Dickens and His Readers: Aspects of Novel-Criticism Since 1836* (Princeton, Princeton Univ. Press, 1955), p. 100.

reviews were less hostile than those in later years, when, after the publication of *Hard Times* and *Little Dorrit*, it became apparent that Dickens's vision was darkening and that his concern with social questions was increasing.[3] But the popular success of *Bleak House*, measured by sales rather than reviews, was markedly greater than that of any of the monthly serials written during the 1840s. Furthermore, *Bleak House* inaugurated a sustained increase in Dickens's circulation. *Little Dorrit* opened with 38,000, *Our Mutual Friend* with 40,000, and *Edwin Drood* reached 50,000. These sales confirmed Dickens's reputation as England's most popular novelist, and encouraged all sorts of exaggerations about his prosperity. Though the rumours were frequently wide of the mark, they were essentially correct in perceiving Dickens as far and away more successful than most of his peers.

i

Late at night on 21 February 1851 Dickens sat down at his desk and, as a dying fire cast flickering shadows about the room, wrote that 'the first shadows of a new story' were 'hovering in a ghostly way' about him (N ii. 274). For a time nothing was done to concretize these shadows. There were domestic upsets—Kate, ill, was taken to Malvern for its 'cure' (N ii. 290); John Dickens died unexpectedly at the end of March; Dora Annie succumbed two weeks later. And there were other distractions, principally occasioned by getting up Bulwer's *Not So Bad as We Seem*, a series of performances designed to benefit the Guild of Literature and Art, which opened in May at Devonshire House. From May until November Dickens rented Fort House, Broadstairs, to which he retired whenever he could get rest from his multiple activities as actor, *régisseur*, and editor. There, in August, thoughts of a new book once again pressed upon his consciousness, and the usual violent and intolerable restlessness that accompanied such thoughts assailed him.

Fitting up his new residence at Tavistock Square, Frank Stone's old house, further delayed the start of the new serial. Wider and a storey higher than Dickens's residence in Devonshire Terrace, it would more comfortably accommodate his large family. But Tavistock House was 'in the dirtiest of all possible conditions'

[3] *Dickens: The Critical Heritage*, pp. 272–3.

(J, p. 746). Dickens determined to have it thoroughly modernized and redecorated before moving in, and, preoccupied with these arrangements, with knocking down walls and throwing up book-cases, improving the garden and the kitchen and the bathroom and the study, he found it impossible to settle down to writing. 'I am wild to begin a new book,' he told Thomas Beard on 6 October, 'and can't until I am settled' (N ii. 348). Several other letters of this period convey his manic frustration: 'Oh! if this were to last long; the distraction of the new book, the whirling of the story through one's mind, escorted by workmen, the imbecility, the wild necessity of beginning to write, the not being able to do so, the, O! I should go—O!' (N ii. 349).

Tavistock House not only prevented his starting to write (or provided the excuse he subconsciously needed), it also encouraged Dickens to put his business affairs in order, as the alterations were expensive. Not having received Bradbury and Evans's accounts as late as 24 September, he wrote to Evans from Broadstairs: 'A remarkable circumstance has occurred here, in which I think you will be interested. A voice, apparently proceeding from the Ocean, continually utters these words, in a voice indescribably forlorn "No accounts yet." What is your opinion of this prodigy?' (N ii. 344). The accounts were immediately dispatched. Since there was no current book, and no account on two of the Christ-mas books, it is hard to understand the delay. But as the balance was skimpy, perhaps the firm was just trying to postpone the evil day when Dickens would see them. The only bright spot was *Copperfield*: back numbers went off more rapidly and consistently than any other of Dickens's serials. Between January and June 1851, for example, 6,811 parts, the equivalent of more than 340 complete copies, were sold. But reprints of VI, VII, and IX cut into profits, leaving only £146. 19s. 4d. as Dickens's share in all their joint copyrights. If he was to pay for Tavistock House and have anything left over, he would have to start his new book soon. 'Clearly a magnetic fact!' Dickens replied to Evans two days later. 'The voice is now silent. I guessed the balance within £6. Please to pay it in to Coutts's.[4] It won't be there long; for I find my new house so remarkable for nothing as for its Drainage[5]—which is of

---

[4] Deposited on 1 Oct. (MS. Coutts).

[5] Dickens's brother-in-law Henry Austin, architect and sanitary engineer in charge of the alterations, had discovered the drains needed work. And Dickens's

a most powerful description. . . . Wait till I get rid of my workmen and get to my work, and see if we don't raise the (East)
wind!' (N ii. 344).

Dickens's last reference indicates that Evans had already received
some notion of the subject for *Bleak House*, and perhaps even had
seen the dozen titles Forster lists as having been successively proposed, three of which refer to the East wind.[6] However, with his
customary reluctance to reveal the new title prematurely, Dickens
did not include the name of his serial in the text of the announcement that he sent to Evans on 12 October (see N ii. 351–2). Also
unspecified in this preliminary notice is the date for the first
number; since Dickens could not 'get a moment's respite from the
convulsions incident to my present severe attack of Tavistock
House', the most he was willing to commit himself to was that
'the first number will appear early in the new year. . . . I hope by
vigorous exertions to get settled in three weeks or so', he assured
Evans, 'and then go at it Ding Dong' (N ii. 351–2). Caution prevailed in Bouverie Street, to which the firm had moved a short
time previously, and no date whatever was promised in the preliminary announcement. But on another matter of importance
there was no doubt: Browne had agreed to illustrate the book, and
his name was included in the notice. 'Diffuse the bill as widely as
possible', Dickens counselled. And so, before a single chapter was
written, the public learned that 'A New Work' by Charles Dickens
was in preparation.

ii

During the next two years, Bradbury and Evans conducted their
customary advertising campaign for a twenty-part serial. That
campaign compares interestingly with the sort of promotional
effort usual for novels, and thus emphasizes once again the specialized nature of serial publishing. The targets of serial promotional
literature were not always those aimed at by novel publishers. To

personal situation reflected a national one: recent agitation over sanitary reforms
was a topic of several cartoons in the Aug. 1851 issues of *Punch*.

6　For further discussion of Dickens's alternative titles, see George H. Ford, 'The
Titles for *Bleak House*', *Dickensian*, 65 (1969), 84–9. In the number plans for the
first seven chapters, the title is *Bleak House and the East Wind*; cf. H. P. Sucksmith,
'Dickens at Work on *Bleak House*: A Critical Examination of His Memoranda
and Number Plans', *Renaissance and Modern Studies*, 9 (1965), 66–7.

begin with, many of Dickens's customers would be unlikely to read *The Times* and the *Athenaeum*. Further, though I have not discovered direct evidence on this point, it is my supposition that the great lending libraries, often accounting for up to 90 per cent of a three-decker's sales, did not purchase the parts.[7] Finally, part of the advertising was directed at potential clients of the *Bleak House* Advertiser, an insert running from eight to thirty-two pages bound in before the text in every number. One reason for announcing the novel so early was to line up potential advertisers; the first notice for the serial's buyers appears in the *Athenaeum* on 14 February 1852, two weeks before Part I was issued.

To reach the vendors, 250 cards, costing the small sum of 10s. 6d. to print, were run off.[8] How effective an advertising medium serial parts were is difficult to determine. Several clients, like E. Moses, were regular customers of Dickens's, and many firms that have survived into the twentieth century announced their wares between the green leaves: Heal's bedsteads, Mappin and Webb's best electro-silver plate and cutlery, Colman's mustard, Bryant and May's matches, Pears' soap.[9] What was the basis for buying space in the Advertiser? Sales of the preceding novel? If so, then sales for *Bleak House* should have been small, as *Copperfield* in parts had not done particularly well. Whatever the publisher's representative could generate in the way of enthusiasm for the

[7] John Carter told me that he had seen one copy of *Edwin Drood* bound from the parts with a lending library ticket, but no others. Since *Drood* is a special case, even this evidence tends to support the hypothesis that lending libraries did not deal extensively with serial novels. In a list of the most popular novels at Mudie's, printed in the *Spectator* in 1863, only one was originally issued in serial parts, and that was *Vanity Fair*, whose sale in bound form was considerably stronger than usual. See 'The Circulation of Modern Literature', pp. 17–18; and Patten, 'The Fight at the Top of the Tree', p. 770. Sara Keith in her Checklists of Mudie's Catalogues indicates that the Leviathan stocked Dickens in Cheap, Library and Charles Dickens editions, but not usually in the first edition bound from the parts.

[8] Though I have not seen a schedule of charges for a Dickens novel, I have seen a memorandum of the terms for advertising in Ainsworth's *Tower of London* (13 monthly parts in 12, Bentley, 1840), showing that the nominal rate for a page was three guineas, and for ten lines 7s.; separate bills, printed by the client but sewn in by the publisher, cost £2 for two pages, three guineas for longer ones. Bentley's chief clerk and accountant, E. S. Morgan, told Cruikshank that this was the rate in *Bentley's Miscellany* as well, and added that 'it is however rarely that the nominal price is paid; abatements from 10 to 20 PC! are made according to circumstance' (MS., Cruikshank Collection, Princeton University Library, quoted by permission).

[9] Darwin, esp. pp. 197–208.

forthcoming one? Then the lack of announced title before mid
February might have been hampering. The author's critical reputation? Hardly. The largest number of trade inserts appear in *Our
Mutual Friend*. The season? December numbers usually contained
more advertising than August ones, but many vendors contracted
for the run of the serial, not just for an individual part.

For whatever reasons, advertisers flocked to *Bleak House* in
record numbers, taking a total of 264 pages in the Advertiser, the
front wrappers inside and the back wrappers inside and out, and
printing eighty-two separate trade inserts, totalling 318 pages.
There were, if one includes the wrappers, more pages of advertising than text. And these advertisements brought in considerable
revenue: £2,167. 15s. 4d. gross, £731. 0s. 1d. net.[10] Such profits
constitute a sizeable additional inducement to publishing in parts.

To reach the general public Bradbury and Evans again relied
heavily on posters. At a cost of £3. 2s., 210,000 16mo bills
and 4,000 broadsides were pasted on to walls, fences, and lamp
standards. Two thousand extra wrappers, and 1,100 plates, were
printed for display in booksellers' windows. On the other hand,
their campaign in journals was modest, especially when compared
with the magnitude of the gross sales receipts. From October 1851
to the end of December 1853, Bradbury and Evans spent only
£260. 6s. 1d. on magazines and newspapers, under £10 a month.
The total cost of promoting *Bleak House*, including the cost of
designing the wrapper (eight guineas) but excluding the cost of
review copies of each part, came to £322. 2s. 8d. That may seem
high. The cost of advertising a new novel around 1850 usually
ranged between £20 and £150, though sums of £200 or £300
were reached quite often.[11] Some publishers relied more on press
ballyhoo than others. A generation earlier Constable assured
Joseph Robinson of Hurst, Robinson that 'advertisements in the
ordinary way, in newspapers, you may depend on it, *always pay*.
You may think otherwise, and be told otherwise; but I say—
advertise judiciously and you will never fail to reap the benefit.'[12]
Colburn and Bentley, assiduously puffing their books in the years
of their partnership, 1829–32, spent £27,000 advertising 149 ordi-

[10] Expenses comprised £763. 2s. 3d. for paper, £629. 6s. 6d. for printing and
binding, and £71. 6s. 6d. for duty (MS. B & E).

[11] Plant, p. 408.

[12] Thomas Constable, *Archibald Constable and his Literary Correspondents* (3 vols.,
Edinburgh, Edmonston and Douglas, 1873), iii. 341 (25 Jan. 1825).

nary works and forty-six titles in the cheap series, an average of just under £140 per title. Separated, in the single year 1852 they spent £5,000 each.[13] Sometimes, of course, no amount of advertising helped; though Bentley took £180. 12s. worth of advertisements for LeFanu's *Uncle Silas* in 1864, he sold only 847 copies. For Bradbury and Evans the strategy was to build up the largest possible sale of Number I. Thereafter, most of the advertising came from reviews of the parts as they appeared, and from word of mouth; notices were placed to remind customers that a new part was about to, or had just, come out. The habit, once formed, was usually strong enough to sustain upwards of 80 per cent of the initial sales.

A considerable factor in the expense of advertising was the duty, 3s. 6d. when imposed in 1815. Though reduced to 1s. 6d. in 1834, it still yielded substantial sums to the government: over £65,000 in 1850.[14] This duty was levied each time the advertiser's name was displayed in a notice. Thus four books advertised at one time would be dutiable at 1s. 6d. the lot, or 4½d. per title, but four separate notices would cost 6s. Figured as a percentage of the sales price, the duty weighed unfairly on cheap books, and discouraged publishers from chancing new formats or unusual topics which might require heavy promotion to succeed. 'Why are novels, narratives of voyages and travels, and indeed nearly all the most entertaining books—no matter what their natural or actual length —either spread out into the most ludicrous state of attenuation, or remorselessly cut down, as the case may be, in order to fit them for the publisher's Procrustean bed of three volumes post octavo?' John Chapman asked in 1852. 'Simply because the said publisher knows that books of this class *will* be had at almost any price by the few; and in face of the difficulties he has to encounter from the high price of paper and advertising, he finds it easier and more profitable to sell 500 copies of a work at a guinea and a half per copy, than 5000 at half a crown, or 50,000 at a shilling. Mr. Bentley's "Library of Standard Novels" was an exceptional experiment in the right direction, but to make it known efficiently he had to spend three thousand five hundred pounds!'[15] Chapman,

---

[13] Chapman, p. 7; Gettmann, p. 122.   [14] Chapman, p. 5.
[15] Ibid., p. 8. Gettmann (p. 122) says Bentley spent an average of £76 a volume, figuring that a series, once launched, is usually self-advertising, each title recommending all the others. The table that follows in the text comes from Chapman, p. 11.

mounting a campaign for the abolition of paper and advertising duties, gives examples of the effect of the latter tax on four books:

	Tax			Total advertising cost			Total production cost			Profit		
	£	s.	d.	£	s.	d.	£	s.	d.	£	s.	d.
1.	36	19	9	73	19	9	615	9	6	120	7	4
2.	30	10	7	61	1	2	444	11	4	−138	11	4
3.	29	7	8	58	15	4	176	15	10	50	17	6
4.	11	14	8	23	9	4	109	0	10	59	14	2

In one case the tax is just under 20 per cent of the profit; in another, it is nearly 50 per cent; and in a third, it constitutes about 22 per cent of the total loss. Caught between the need to promote a book in order to recoup costs, and the cost of promotion itself, publishers preferred to take their chances on works with a large sale price and familiar format. (In the light of that economically determined preference, the discovery of a new format in *Pickwick* takes on additional significance.) The advertising duty worked even more inequitably for individuals than for commercial firms, as Dickens pointed out to Macready: 'The advertisement duty has this preposterous anomaly, that a footman in want of a place pays as much in the way of tax for the expression of his want, as Professor Holloway pays for the whole list of his miraculous cures.'[16]

[16] N ii. 374. Nevertheless, Dickens did not support Charles Knight's campaign against the 'taxes on knowledge'—stamp, paper, and advertising duties. He thought the stamp duty 'some protection to the public against the rash and hasty launching of blackguard newspapers' (N ii. 373). And he told Knight that he feared with respect to the paper duty that he 'could hardly find the heart to press for justice in this respect, before the window-duty is removed. [The people] cannot read without light. They cannot have an average chance of life and health without it' (N ii. 205). As part owner of *Household Words*, however, Dickens's opinion of the paper duty began to change; in February 1851 he joined the publisher John Cassell and Thomas Crompton, owner of the Farnsworth paper mills at Bolton, Lancashire, and a fierce opponent of the paper duty, in a deputation to the Chancellor of the Exchequer demanding repeal. This duty, levied at four guineas a ton, produced in 1850 revenue in the amount of £852,996. 13s. 10d. But like the advertising duty, it fell unevenly. If a book manufactured from one pound of paper was sold for 10s., the duty amounted to 1¼ per cent, but if its price was 2s. 6d., the duty amounted to 5 per cent (Chapman, p. 2). Further, the red tape involved in affixing the duty was galling, delaying, and expensive; Edinburgh paper manufacturers estimated that the duty of 1½d. in the pound obstructed manufacturing to the extent of another ½d. (ibid.). But Dickens thought that removing the paper duty, while reducing his manufacturing costs, would

Thus only if a book was commercially very successful did the advertising duty become negligible. In the happy instance of *Bleak House*, the entire cost of advertising, duty and all, amounted to only about $2\frac{1}{4}$ per cent of the net profits, or $2\frac{1}{2}$ per cent of the total expenses. Dickens's serials sold by themselves, without extravagant advertising campaigns.

iii

While Bradbury and Evans were gearing up their efforts, Dickens was busy writing. Settled at last in Tavistock House, and eager to begin, he gave a general order to the servants that he was not to be disturbed during working hours. But a few days later he learned to his vexation that his order had inadvertently excluded Bradbury, who had come by to pay a call. He quickly dashed off a note of apology. Gradually the routine was established, and *Bleak House* proceeded apace; by 7 December Dickens had 'only the last short chapter to do, to complete No. 1' (N ii. 362). Exasperation with his printers, who had set 'Dark' for 'Deep' in the Christmas number of *Household Words*, temporarily interrupted his writing: 'I declare before God that your men are enough to drive me mad! . . . I don't know where there is a beastly unstamped newspaper in London in which such a flagrant and unpardonable mistake would be made. I am so disgusted by it, that I throw down my pen in an absolute despair, and could as soon paint an historical picture as go on writing' (N ii. 363). A more dispassionate observer might have remarked on the increasing difficulty of reading Dickens's hand, and praised the compositors who, often working under considerable pressure, late at night by inadequate light, managed to decipher the heavily corrected foul papers with so few

make little difference to the public, as its effect on the per copy cost of *Household Words* would be too minute to permit him to reduce its price, and he doubted Knight's argument that marginal journals would be aided. He told the Chancellor, in fact, that he 'could not honestly' argue in favour of abolishing the paper duty 'as against the soap duty, or any other pressing on the mass of the poor' (N ii. 374). Gradually in the next few years these objectionable duties were removed. Dickens and Bradbury and Evans breached the stamp duty at the end of 1851 when in the Court of the Exchequer they won the right to issue the monthly *Household Narrative of Current Events* unstamped (Simon Nowell-Smith, *The House of Cassell: 1848–1958* (London, Cassell, 1958), p. 28); the advertising duty was abolished in 1853; and the abolition of the paper duty, rejected by the Lords in 1860, was effected the next year, saving Cassell around £10,000 per annum (ibid., pp. 56–7).

substantive errors.[17] Perhaps even Dickens, in a quieter moment, realized that the error was comparatively trivial. In any event, all was amiably resolved, publishers and author both completed their jobs, and on 28 February 1852 the first instalment of *Bleak House* went on sale.

Gauging by *Copperfield*, which had maintained a circulation of under 22,000, Bradbury and Evans ordered an initial printing of 25,000 copies. The paper for Part I cost £171. 17s. 6d., and was of four kinds: fifty reams of double demy at 32s. per ream for the letterpress; twelve and a half reams of the familiar green paper for the wrappers, at 23s.; fifty reams of cheaper stock for the advertisements, at 21s.; and heavy stock, of a size to take two upright plates on each leaf, for the illustrations, fifty reams costing 10s. each. Printing and stereotyping the letterpress cost £40. 18s., the wrappers cost £9. 5s. to print, and the plates added another £67. 5s. 2d. to expenses. With night work and postage included, the charges for the first part, including the Advertiser, came to £329. 14s. 8d. Of this sum roughly 52 per cent is accounted for by paper, and another 20 per cent by the cost of printing the illustrations. Though people bought the parts in order to read the story, the cost of printing the letterpress and the Advertiser together came to less than one-eighth of the total. By printing such a large quantity Bradbury and Evans kept their charges down: whereas it was usual in 1850 for the printing expenses for an edition of 1,000 to average three-quarters of the total cost,[18] with 25,000 thirty-two-page parts, and a twenty-four-page Advertiser, Bradbury and Evans charged less than the cost of the paper for all the printing expenses. They kept a sharp eye on other expenses too: they were still paying for their paper stock exactly what they had for *Dombey* six years earlier, despite the acute shortage of rags which had forced paper manufacturers to introduce rag substitutes and to produce inferior papers for superior prices.[19]

No one was prepared for the reception *Bleak House* received. At the end of the first day in March, the first edition was exhausted, and Bradbury and Evans 'were obliged to go to Press again' (N ii. 381). The staff turned to with a will to machine and press 5,000 more texts, wrappers, and plates, and 2,000 additional copies

[17] The publishers' account books note 'night work very heavy' for several parts of *Bleak House*.
[18] Plant, pp. 339–40.   [19] Ibid., p. 333.

of the Advertiser, some staying well into the night.[20] On 4 March Dickens replied to his father-in-law's note praising the part by saying that 'It has been a very great success, and is blazing away merrily' (N ii. 382). Three days later, sales were at 30,000 (F VII. ii. 568), and yet another printing, this time of 3,000, was required. And the circulation continued to rise: by the end of June, 38,500 copies of *Bleak House* I had been printed. The press run for the second number, for April, was raised to 32,000, but even that proved insufficient, and two more reprintings, of 2,000 each, were done before July. Number III started at 34,000, and required another 1,500; Numbers IV and V began at 35,000. The stitching runs likewise crept up: 34,043 of the first 35,000 of Number I, 30,000 of II, 33,000 of III, 34,000 of IV and V, and 14,329 of various numbers, accounting by the end of June for all but 628 of the 180,000 numbers printed.[21] 'It is a most enormous success', Dickens told de Cerjat on 8 May, 'all the prestige of Copperfield (which was very great) falling upon it, and raising its circulation above all my other books.'[22]

Of these 180,000 copies of Numbers I–V, one of each part went to each of the five depository libraries, the British Museum, the Bodleian, University Library Cambridge, the National Library of Scotland, and Trinity College Dublin; 835 parts (an average of 167 of each) were given to reviewers and friends, and 15,855 remained unsold. The rest, 163,285 parts, were sold at the usual discount, thirteen for 9s., bringing in a gross of £5,652. 3s. 9d., plus £636. 15s. 11d. in gross advertising revenue. Against this total were set expenses of printing (£2,234. 13s. 5d.), advertising and duty (£272. 7s. 6d.), a 10 per cent commission to agents, who were responsible for £1,876. 10s. in sales (£187. 13s.), and Bradbury and Evans's straight 10 per cent on all sales (£628. 18s.). After all these deductions, the net profit for the first five numbers

[20] See charge of 10s. for night work. The work week for compositors and pressmen in London in 1850 ran around sixty hours; the pay averaged 30s. a week; thus 10s. for 'night work' represents some twenty additional hours' labour, perhaps less if overtime was paid. See *Great Britain, Parliamentary Papers*, vol. 89 (1887), 580, 583, 584; vol. 68 (1890), 632–3; and Ellic Howe, ed., *The London Compositor, 1785–1900* (London, The Bibliographical Society, 1947), pp. 184–5.

[21] Johnson's account somewhat exaggerates even this striking success: 'it soon sold thirty-five thousand copies every publishing day, and there is no estimate of how many in back sales or spread out through the month' (p. 752).

[22] N ii. 394. Dickens's awareness of the influence of the preceding serial on sales of the succeeding one confirms Ada Nisbet's speculation in 'The Mystery of "Martin Chuzzlewit" ', pp. 210–16.

was still handsome: £2,965. 7s. 9d. Dickens's three-quarters share amounted to £2,224. 0s. 9d., or £444. 16s. per number. And these were not the best figures of the run: his profit for the next six months rose to £3,106. 13s. 6d., better than £517 a number. Included was Dickens's share of Harper's payment of £20 each for advance sheets of the monthly parts.

Dickens continued to measure his success by comparisons to *Copperfield*. To the Hon. Mrs. Richard Watson, recently widowed owner of Rockingham Castle, model for Chesney Wold, he wrote in November 1852: 'You ask Catherine a question about Bleak House. Its circulation is half as large again as Copperfield!' (N ii. 430). And nine months later, on the day he completed the novel, he returned to the subject: 'To finish the topic of Bleak House at once, I will only add that I like the conclusion very much and think it *very pretty indeed*. The story has taken extraordinarily, especially during the last five or six months, when its purpose has been gradually working itself out. It has retained its immense circulation from the first, beating dear old Copperfield by a round ten thousand or more. I have never had so many readers' (N ii. 483). The last sentence figures also in the Preface, probably written on the same day. Dickens could not resist letting his readers know how popular he was, and he concluded, 'May we meet again!'

The final double number was issued on the last day in August 1853. By the end of that year, a total of 714,250 parts had been printed, ranging from a high of 43,500 of Number I to a low of 34,000 for Numbers XI–XX. Of this total, 686,853 had been sold, the equivalent of 34,342 complete novels, although apparently the actual number of completed runs was under 34,000. Despite Dickens's statement that the story had taken extraordinarily during the last five or six months, there is a steady decline in the press run, and also a decrease in the initial stitching order, from 34,000 for Number IV to 31,500 for Numbers XVII–XX. And profits fell slightly below expectations too, as Dickens explained to Catherine on 9 September:

The half year's accounts have appeared, and are two hundred pounds behind Evans's estimate; the sum I have to receive, being £2,300. I have made up my mind, for this reason and considering the cost of my trip, not to have any party at Christmas but the children's—the rather as the house will just have been got into good order again.[23]

23 *Mr. and Mrs. Charles Dickens*, p. 174.

Nevertheless, to have sustained such readership over such a long period of time is a signal achievement.

iv

Just how signal that achievement was can be clarified by comparing Dickens's sale with that of his contemporaries. Most of Richard Bentley's agreements between 1830 and 1850 stipulated an edition of 1,000 copies; John Murray III told Gladstone in 1852 that he usually printed 1,000 copies of the first edition of a new book.[24] Often, of course, sales didn't even exhaust that printing: Longmans sold fewer than 700 copies of Trollope's *Warden* over five years, though the novels that followed, including *Barchester Towers*, *Doctor Thorne*, and *Framley Parsonage*, were well received by critics and public alike. *Vanity Fair*, Thackeray reported wryly to his mother, did 'everything but sell; and appears really immensely to increase my reputation if not my income'.[25] By 20 August 1848 it had sold 1,500 copies in volumes, an unusually high post-serial sale.[26] In 1852 an edition of 1,000 copies was probably still standard for many works, and two years the minimum amount of time needed to work off the edition.[27] First printings of yellowbacks ranged between 1,000 and 5,000 copies; occasionally there was an order for 7,500 or 10,000, but the numbers rarely if ever exceeded the latter figure.[28] In such contexts, the 34,000 copies of *Bleak House* in parts indicates striking popularity.

Dickens's earnings from the novel are equally striking. Gerald Grubb has said that these accounts 'show that Dickens' income was very great, but not fabulous, as sometimes hinted, that he had the touch of Midas in but one of his hands, so to speak'.[29] However, Grubb was basing his statements on the accounts of Chapman and Hall rather than those of Bradbury and Evans, though the latter firm was between 1846 and 1860 the source of the greater part of Dickens's publishing income. The total profit on *Bleak House* in parts reached £14,750. 11s. 1d. by June 1870. Of this total,

[24] Quoted in Barnes, *Free Trade in Books*, p. 82.   [25] *Letters*, ii. 318.
[26] Ibid. ii. 420. By 1863 Mudie's listed it as one of their 'most popular novels' ('The Circulation of Modern Literature', pp. 17–18).
[27] Barnes, *Free Trade in Books*, p. 53.
[28] Michael Sadleir, 'Yellow-Backs', in John Carter, ed., *New Paths in Book Collecting: Essays by Various Hands* (London, Constable, 1934), p. 150.
[29] Grubb, 'Some Unpublished Correspondence', p. 100.

Dickens received £10,984. 13*s.* 3½*d.* This figure does not include *Bleak House*'s share in the profits of subsequent editions, either; it is only for the novel in parts.[30] Bradbury and Evans, entitled to one-quarter of the net profits, also received a 10 per cent commission on sales which nearly doubled their take: to the end of 1853, their share of the profits came to £3,386. 5*s.* 4*d.*, and the commission amounted to £2,606. 7*s.* 1*d.* To Dickens's death the publishers cleared in profits and commissions on the parts of *Bleak House* a halfpenny under £6,526. And the individual booksellers, getting better than 3½*d.* per copy, together amassed a gross profit of over £12,000.

How does Dickens's profit compare with the usual earnings on novels at this time? Spectacularly well. According to *Fraser's* in 1847, 'Novels, when by popular authors, are paid for at prices varying from 100*l.* to 500*l.*; and, in one or two instances, to 1500*l.*'[31] The average Grub Street annual income approximated £300.[32] A diligent worker like Mrs. Trollope, when lucky, could make more: she received £800 for *The Domestic Manners of the Americans* (1832) and £650 from Bentley for *The Ward* (1840). At first her son Anthony did much worse. His second novel sold 140 copies and lost £63. 10*s.* 1½*d.*, which he split with Colburn; eventually it earned £123. 19*s.* 5*d.*, according to the table in his *Autobiography*.[33] *The Warden* and *Barchester Towers* between them produced £727. 11*s.* 3*d.* over twenty years. Novels published in numbers or in the pages of a journal usually fetched higher prices;[34] in 1856, after Bentley had sold his *Miscellany*, Bulwer told him that the price of his next novel would be beyond the reach of any publisher who could not profit from both periodical and book publication.[35] But serial rights were not always munificent, especially for first novels by unknown novelists. George Eliot

[30] It does include profits from sales of parts bound up in volume form at the end of the serial run and sold subsequently for 21*s.* and up. The publishers always account for this volume sale in numbers.

[31] 'The Condition of Authors in England, Germany, and France', 35 (1847), 290.

[32] Ibid., p. 286.   [33] p. 302.

[34] Marryat, who serialized many of his novels in his own magazine, and who certainly wrote partly for the money, got as much as £1,300 for one novel, *Snarleyyow* (1836–7), but that was evidently his high point; see Donald Hawes, 'Marryat and Dickens: A Personal and Literary Relationship', *Dickens Studies Annual*, 2 (1972), 39–68.

[35] Gettmann, p. 143.

received £443 from John Blackwood for serial and first edition rights to her *Scenes of Clerical Life*, issued in 1,050 copies in January 1858, and £200 more for a second edition of 1,500 copies, required in August 1859.[36] Lewes tried to get *The Mill on the Floss* into shilling numbers, having heard that 10,000 copies would produce £5,000 profit.[37] He failed, but Eliot's value continued to rise, until it reached its height with George Smith's offer of £10,000 for the entire copyright of *Romola*. Smith proposed to shore up lagging sales of the *Cornhill* by running Eliot's new work immediately after the conclusion of the popular *Framley Parsonage*.[38] Trollope too fared better in his serials: the *Cornhill* paid £1,000 for *Framley Parsonage* in 1860 and £2,800 for *The Claverings* in 1866–7, the 'highest rate of pay that was ever accorded to me', he reports.[39] He had been paid higher sums before, but for longer works: for *Orley Farm*, issued in twenty monthly numbers by Chapman and Hall in 1861–2, with woodcuts by John Everett Millais, Trollope received £3,135, and for *Can You Forgive Her?* (1864) he was paid £3,525, but Trollope considered these the equivalent of five post 8vo volumes, so that his *rate* of pay for them never exceeded £700 a volume, whereas for *The Claverings* it came to £933. For *The Last Chronicle of Barset* George Smith gave £3,000, plus half-profits from the cheap edition; it was issued in thirty-two sixpenny weekly numbers from December 1866 to July 1867, and illustrated by George Housman Thomas, but it was not wholly successful. Virtue tried the same experiment with *He Knew He Was Right* (1868–9), using Dickens's illustrator and friend Marcus Stone, but after *The Duke's Children* (1880), which lost £120, Trollope found the value of his copyrights declining.[40] All in all, between 1862 and 1874 his annual income averaged £4,500, of which he saved about a third, but this total includes his salary as well as his income from writing.

Thackeray provides an even closer parallel. For *Vanity Fair* he received £60 a month, while Dickens was making between six and seven times as much per number of *Dombey*. Smith, Elder

[36] Thomas A. Noble, *George Eliot's* Scenes of Clerical Life, Yale Studies in English, vol. 159 (New Haven and London, Yale Univ. Press, 1965), p. 16, n. 9; cf. Gordon S. Haight, *George Eliot: A Biography* (Oxford, Clarendon Press, 1968), pp. 246–7.   [37] Haight, p. 317.
[38] Ibid., pp. 355–6.   [39] *An Autobiography*, p. 164.
[40] Cf. Gordon N. Ray, 'Trollope at Full Length', *Huntington Library Quarterly*, 31 (1968), 313–40; and *An Autobiography*, pp. 302–3.

increased the stipend to £1,000 a year for *Pendennis*; Dickens made
over twice that on *Copperfield* in 1849, and over three and a half
times as much in 1850. *The Newcomes* began shortly after *Bleak
House* concluded, and for it Bradbury and Evans, already associated with Thackeray through *Punch*, gave £3,600, plus £500
from Harper in New York and Tauchnitz in Leipzig, for a work
in twenty-four numbers like *Pendennis*. 'It's coining money isn't
it?' Thackeray crowed.[41] He was supposed to get £300 a month
for *The Virginians*, but only drew £250 as it did not sell 'so very
well as we expected'.[42] With the editorship of the *Cornhill* in the
1860s, Thackeray at last came into his own financially. For the one
or two novels serialized in the magazine in twelve portions each
equal to a monthly number, and for rights to publication in
volume form afterwards, Smith offered £350 a month; for a
familiar essay, twelve guineas a page; and for the editorship,
£1,000 a year, doubled when the first number sold 120,000 copies.
Thus Thackeray was enjoying receipts of close to £600 a month,
£7,200 a year.[43]

Dickens's closest continental counterpart, Balzac, began his
career on a royalty basis, getting two francs per volume for every
copy printed, or about 8,000 francs (£320) per work. But as his
fame and sales extended, he changed to selling his copyrights outright, in an interesting reversal of the English trend, and by 1843
he could command 30,000 francs or more (£1,200 and up) for one
volume post 8vo, the same sum *Henry III* brought Dumas.[44] However, *Fraser's* reported four years later that Balzac by his own admission 'has a hard task to make 300l. a-year', partly because in
France rates for magazine articles were less than half what they
were in England, partly too because outright sale of copyright left
Balzac with no rights to residual sales.[45]

Perhaps the most famous offers made for works of fiction during
the Victorian period came to Disraeli. In 1868 E. S. Dallas offered
him £10,000 for an as yet unnamed novel.[46] Two years afterwards, *Lothair*, eventually published by Longmans on a royalty

[41] *Letters*, iii. 280.   [42] Ibid. iv. 65.
[43] Gordon N. Ray, *Thackeray: The Age of Wisdom, 1847–1863* (New York,
Toronto, and London, McGraw Hill Book Co., 1958), pp. 293–6.
[44] Chapman, pp. 37–8, quoting G. P. R. James in the *Journal of the Statistical
Society* for 1843.
[45] 'The Condition of Authors', p. 286.
[46] Cox and Chandler, p. 32.

basis of 10s. in the pound,[47] was the talk of the season. 'There is immense and most malevolent curiosity about Disraeli's novel', Lord Houghton wrote to Henry Bright. 'His wisest friends think that it must be a mistake, and his enemies hope it will be his ruin.'[48] Speculation raged as to the actual sum paid for copyright; upon hearing the figure £10,000, Trollope disputed it hotly, and bet Lord Houghton £10 that it could not be so much. 'Twelve years ago—not to talk of twenty-two [reference had been made to an 1848 offer]—novels were worth almost double what they are now', he lamented, 'but I think that no novel has ever been sold for £10,000, and no novel would be worth it, except by Dickens, whose prices, by-the-bye, are much more moderate.'[49] But as Houghton knew the exact sum Dallas had offered, Trollope conceded. Forwarding payment, he argued still that as Dallas went bankrupt very shortly afterwards, it could not be regarded as a genuine business offer; and he went on to analyse the gloomy economics of book publication:

I know fully well the value of these articles in the market, and I think that I know that no novel would be worth £10,000 to a publisher by any author: no house could afford to give such a sum. Dickens's last novel [*Edwin Drood*] (which, I do not hesitate to say, is worth three times the value of 'Lothair' in a simply pecuniary view) has been sold for a considerably less sum—not indeed the entire copyright, but the immediate publication, and half-copyright afterwards. I have heard you quote as to other works sums reputed to be paid, but which were fabulous. For a novel published as 'Lothair' is published, and sure of a large circulation, a publisher could offer to give an author about 10s. a copy for all copies sold by him at the cost price, nominally 31s. 6d., for which he gets about 17s. 6d. The other 7s. 6d. would pay the cost, the advertising, and give the publisher a small profit. —— told me the other day that 6,000 copies had been sold—that would make £3,000 for the author; and the market has been so glutted with the work, that the publisher cannot hope to sell above another thousand. Where could he possibly recoup himself in an expenditure of £10,000?[50]

Fortunately, a furious controversy sparked by Professor Goldwin Smith, formerly at Oxford and later at Cornell, who thought he saw himself abused in Disraeli's parasitical 'Oxford Professor',

[47] Robert Blake, *Disraeli* (New York, St. Martin's Press, 1967), p. 734.
[48] T. Wemyss Reid, *The Life, Letters, and Friendships of Richard Monckton Milnes, First Lord Houghton*, 3rd edn. (2 vols., London, Cassell, 1891), ii. 223.
[49] Ibid. ii. 224.   [50] Ibid. ii. 225–6.

kept up public attention and sales. In fact, by 1876 Disraeli had netted £6,000, plus £1,500 more from America; and when one figures in the royalties and copyrights for the ten-volume collected edition which Longmans brought out in 1870 to capitalize on the public interest generated by the novel, it is not exaggeration to say that Disraeli earned on *Lothair* at least £10,600 by 1877.[51]

Three years later Montague Corry, Lord Rowton, Disraeli's private secretary, conducted secret negotiations with Thomas Norton Longman about *Endymion*. On 4 August 1880 Rowton left his seat in the House of Lords for a few minutes, and then returned with a note for Disraeli, who was waiting to reply to the Duke of Argyll's speech on the Compensation for Disturbance Bill:

> There are things too big to impart in whispers! so I leave your side, just to write these words—Longman has today offered *Ten Thousand Pounds* for *Endymion*.
>
> I have accepted it![52]

Unfortunately, though the book sold moderately well, it looked for a time as if it would not turn a profit for the publishers: 10,500 copies were printed and about 8,000 sold, but Mudie's on the basis of their experience with *Lothair* heavily over-ordered, and Norton Longman feared a loss of some £5,500.[53] Four months after publication Disraeli offered to cancel his contract and return to the royalty he had received on *Lothair*, but Longman refused. By issuing the cheap 6s. edition quickly, he recouped his investment by April 1881, and ultimately obtained a modest profit.[54] Once again it becomes clear that serial publication, which spreads both costs and receipts over the extended period of publication, possesses important advantages over outright purchase of copyright prior to publication. 'The outright purchase of the copyright can seldom be a fair arrangement either to author or publisher', Philip Wallis writes; 'one side is bound to be the loser, and . . . all too often publishers are so dazzled by a great name that they are persuaded to pay above the odds.'[55]

[51] Blake, pp. 519–20.

[52] Quoted from the original MS. by Annabel Jones, 'Disraeli's *Endymion*: A Case Study', in Asa Briggs, ed., *Essays in the History of Publishing*, p. 149.

[53] Philip Wallis, *At the Sign of the Ship: Notes on the House of Longman, 1724–1974* (London, Longman Group Ltd., printed for private circulation, 1974), p. 26. See also the full story of the publishing of *Endymion* by Annabel Jones, op. cit.

[54] Blake, pp. 734–5; Griest, pp. 200–1.   [55] p. 27.

Dickens was a publishing phenomenon in America as well as England, and there *Bleak House* enjoyed notable success. The editor of the *International Monthly Magazine*, Rufus Wilmot Griswold, tried to forestall *Harper's* in securing the rights to *Bleak House* by sending one of the publishers to London to offer $2,000 for advance sheets. The unfortunate representative went to Bradbury and Evans, who told him that Dickens was wrapped up in private theatricals and contemplated no new novel, so he left empty-handed. *Harper's*, on the other hand, sent a representative directly to Dickens, and so secured an agreement for the price of £360 ($1,728).[56] Serialization began in April 1852; within a year, 118,000 copies a month were being sold. At the same time it was issued in monthly numbers, and at its completion in two volumes. Henry C. Carey calculated that no fewer than 250,000 copies of *Bleak House* were 'supplied to American readers, through newspapers and magazines, and in the book form'.[57]

Rumour vastly exaggerated even these considerable sales and receipts. At the time of *American Notes* and *Chuzzlewit*, Dickens's profits were alleged to approach £30,000 (P iii. xvii). Readers of *Fraser's* learned that 'Dickens received 3000l. for one of his tiny Christmas stories, whereas Eugène Sue only received 4000l. for the ten volumes of his *Juif Errant*'.[58] And according to 'one of the journals of the day' quoted by Henry C. Carey, *Bleak House* 'had so wide a circulation' in monthly numbers 'that it became a valuable medium for advertising, so that before its close the few pages of the tale were completely lost in sheets of advertising which were stitched to them'. The article went on to tot up Dickens's probable income:

The lowest price for such an advertisement was £1 sterling, and many were paid for at the rate of £5 and £6. From this there is nothing improbable in the supposition that in addition to the large sum received for the tale, its author gained some £15,000 by his advertising sheets. The *Household Words* produces an income of about £4,000, though Dickens, having put it entirely in the hands of an assistant editor, has nothing to do with it beyond furnishing a weekly article. Through his talents alone he has raised himself from the position of a newspaper reporter to that of a literary Croesus.[59]

[56] Exman, p. 310.

[57] *Letters on International Copyright* (Philadelphia, A. Hart, late Carey and Hart, 1853), p. 59.

[58] 'The Condition of Authors', p. 286.   [59] Carey, p. 37.

The damage which Dickens sustained from such irresponsible journalism, which encouraged begging letter writers of all descriptions and depreciated his concern with the quality of all his work, probably cannot be assessed, but it is no wonder that he occasionally exhibited irritation at these exaggerations. They lent comfort to a point of view expressed by *Fraser's* in its review of 'The Condition of Authors in England, Germany, and France':

Literature should be a profession, not a trade. It should be a profession, just lucrative enough to furnish a decent subsistence to its members, but in no way lucrative enough to tempt speculators. As soon as its rewards are high enough and secure enough to tempt men to enter the lists for the sake of the reward, and parents think of it as an opening for their sons [the reviewer is peculiarly blind to the professional accomplishments of women authors in the Victorian period], from that moment it becomes vitiated. Then will the ranks, already so numerous, be swelled by an innumerable host of hungry pretenders.[60]

Whether Dickens vitiated the profession by his success, or encouraged mothers' sons to think of writing as a means of livelihood, or caused the ranks to swell with hordes of hungry pretenders, his sale of 34,000 copies of *Bleak House* in parts and his profit of nearly £11,000 demonstrate that he had found literature lucrative enough to furnish a more than decent subsistence. This return was not made from an expensive edition with elaborate binding and inflated price; it came from thousands upon thousands of individuals, putting down their shillings month after month in exchange for another thirty-two pages of tightly-packed letterpress—nearly 20,000 words—and two illustrations.[61] And these shillings were not transferred directly into Dickens's pocket—not by any means. The bookseller paid 9s. to the publisher for every twelve copies, receiving a thirteenth free. Thus he made 4s. on every thirteen sold, or just over $3\frac{1}{2}d.$ a copy. Agents received 10 per cent on their sales, and the publishers got 10 per cent on all sales. The printers charged for their materials and operating costs, though not for overheads, and each one of the suppliers made a profit on what he sold the printers. The government extracted duty on paper and advertisements. And after all these expenses had

---

[60] p. 285.
[61] Except in Number IX, where in one plate Phiz mistakenly introduced Grandmother Smallweed instead of Judy. After 6,000 had been printed, the plate was withdrawn, and a corrected one issued with the two new ones for Number X.

been deducted, one-quarter of what was left of the buyer's shilling went to the publishers outright. Dickens's £11,000 was actually accumulated out of the small share remaining to him from each of the 768,000 shillings put down for a monthly part of *Bleak House*, the pennies piling up, one by one, until at his death there were over two and a half million of them.

13

Working the Copyrights

... the works of Dickens ... are [as] sure to be sold
and read as the bread which is baked is sure to be sold
and eaten.

The Economist, 3 April 1852[1]

DICKENS SUSTAINED HIS HECTIC LITERARY PACE
throughout the 1850s. In one decade, he published two
novels in shilling parts, two novels in weekly parts, and
a three-volume *Child's History of England*, conducted nineteen
volumes of *Household Words* and two of *All the Year Round*, issued
a second series of the Cheap edition, inaugurated a new and expensive Library edition, devised, performed, and published five different readings, and wrote a substantial number of occasional pieces.
And this list excludes his dramatic performances, his readings for
charity, his work on Urania Cottage for Miss Coutts, his strenuous
holidays, the move to Gad's Hill, his separation from Kate and
liaison with Ellen Ternan, and half a dozen other activities that
would have absorbed all the energy of ordinary men. Dickens's
frenzy was not altogether healthy; he was more and more deeply
troubled, and began to fear for the survival of his artistic vitality,
even for his sanity, as Forster reports: 'he had frequently a quite
unfounded apprehension of some possible breakdown, of which
the end might be at any moment beginning' (F VIII. ii. 637).

The variety of formats and publishing projects which issued
from Dickens during the fifties may evidence this turmoil, may
even seem to suggest that he was not sure of his craft and direction.
At the end of the decade the final and most spectacular eruption
of his professional life occurred, simultaneously with, and as a
result of, his marital unhappiness. But underlying the apparent

[1] pp. 363–4.

changes of direction, from history to contemporary social comment, from monthly numbers to weekly parts to volumes, from
Devonshire Terrace to Tavistock House to Gad's Hill, from Bradbury and Evans to Chapman and Hall and from Kate to Ellen, are
continuities that extend Dickens's past into his future. It is a decade
of transition not only for Dickens but also for Victorian publishing; strains develop at the pinnacle of success, and new directions
must be sought for a viable future.

i

Early in its run *Household Words* began instalments of *A Child's
History of England*, which Dickens dictated occasionally to Georgina. It appeared from time to time between 25 January 1851 and
10 December 1853; the later parts were perfunctory, and the last
chapter, running less than two columns, managed to cover everything from 1688 onwards. Clearly Dickens got bored. And
there was little incentive to continue from the balance sheet of the
volume issue. Published in time for the Christmas trade each year,
the square 16mo volumes, retailing at 3s. 6d. each, never sold more
than a few thousand copies. Every volume lost money during its
first accounting period; the greatest profit reached in any six
months came to £58. Possibly Dickens learned some lessons from
this experience. The next time he wrote something extended for
Household Words, he wrote fiction, not history, he wrote it quickly,
he published it in consecutive instalments over a few months, and
he counted on an extra payment for the manuscript, plus additional
profits from increased sales of the journal, instead of post-serial
volume sales.

Throughout these years, Chapman and Hall kept on with the
Cheap edition and other books remaining to them. Between June
1851 and December 1853 Dickens's biannual half-share of the
profits ranged between £229 and £283, but despite general prosperity, bookselling was becoming increasingly competitive and
cut-throat. In 1852 Dickens joined John Chapman, whose bookselling ticket had been forfeited for selling American imports
below established retail prices, Richard Bentley, Bradbury and
Evans, and others in combating restrictive practices in publishing.[2]

[2] Barnes, *Free Trade in Books*, p. 31.

At the end of April John W. Parker and Son posed the following question to various eminent Victorian authors:

If a retail bookseller, of ascertained credit and respectability, applies to your publisher for copies of any book in which you are directly or indirectly interested, which he is ready to purchase on the terms at which the publisher has offered them to the trade at large, but with the avowed intention of retailing his purchases at a smaller profit than that provided for between the wholesale rate and the retail price fixed for single copies, do you consider the intention to sell at a low rate of profit a good and sufficient reason why the publisher should refuse to supply him with books which he is ready to purchase and to keep in stock at his own risk?[3]

Granted, the question is slanted; but among the 'no's' numbered Carlyle, Darwin, R. H. Horne, Charles Kingsley, G. H. Lewes, J. S. Mill, Herbert Spencer, Tennyson, and W. H. Wills. Dickens's answer was one of the briefest: 'No; most certainly not.' A few days after this reply, on 4 May, Dickens chaired a meeting at Chapman's house, and declared that he 'was, on principle, most strongly opposed to any system, in any commercial direction, of exclusion or restriction. He held that every man, whatever his calling, must be left to the fair and free exercise of his own honest thrift and enterprise.'[4] Charles Knight 'made a wise and telling speech which silenced one or two vulgar, ignorant booksellers', George Eliot told the Brays.[5] Tom Taylor, Richard Owen, and George Cruikshank ably supported Chapman. The Booksellers' Association eventually relaxed its strictures, with important consequences for Dickens in the 1860s; but meanwhile, the book trade was confused, uncertain, and divided.

The next blow to routine came from the Crimean War, which sharply curtailed book buying. Edward Chapman anticipated this development in the note he wrote on the last day of March 1854 to accompany the Christmas 1853 accounts: 'I fear the war will tell upon the next'.[6] He was right. From £273. 13s. 1d. for December 1853, Dickens's share of the profits declined over 50 per cent, to £126. 19s. 10d. for June 1854, and another 50 per cent for December 1854, to £60. 5s. 10d. This figure of £10 per month

[3] *The Opinions of Certain Authors on the Bookselling Question* (London, John W. Parker and Son, 1852).
[4] *Speeches*, p. 142.   [5] Haight, *George Eliot*, p. 110.
[6] Grubb, 'Some Unpublished Correspondence', p. 112.

on back sales is the lowest in the twenty-four years of accounts. It accords well, however, with the experience of other publishers at the time. Bentley found himself in such serious difficulties that he tried every way he could think of to dispose of his stock; one shift was to offer Dickens the remaining copies of the *Village Coquettes*.[7] Routledge apologetically turned down the manuscript of Samuel Smiles's *Self-Help* (a decision they surely regretted later): 'We were in hopes that we should have been able to publish it, but trade continues so dull that we find it will be quite impossible.'[8] But Dickens's sales were during these years as at other times somewhat protected against the most severe effects of recession. His December 1854 profit is low partly because of the cost of heavy reprintings to build up stock. The sales, Chapman pointed out, 'are better than the last. I have been compelled to reprint so many numbers that the outlay has been nearly up to the receipts.'[9] Chapman had indeed been busy; 4,000 each of fifty-four numbers of the Cheap edition had been run off from stereos, 216,000 numbers costing over £400. Although 10,481 dozen numbers and three dozen parts had been sold for £514. 15s., when the charges for reprinting, the allowances to agents, and the publishers' commission were deducted, Dickens's half-share came to only £31. 19s. 6d.

The year 1855 was indifferent. The June accounts, 'which', Chapman wrote, 'I am glad to see are much better than the last',[10] showed that Chapman and Hall owed Dickens £123. 16s. 1d., mostly as a result of the Cheap edition sales. 'I am glad to see that we suffer less from this sad war than might have been expected', Dickens returned (N ii. 694). One hundred and ninety-two numbers of the Cheap edition went to the battlefield; 936 volumes were sold in New York at half-price. But Chapman grumbled that the discounts and allowances demanded by foreign booksellers cut into his already small profit. December 1855 figures were not so favourable; again, good sales had made it necessary to reprint heavily. The next year, 1856, was one of the best in a long time. Reprints were low, sales were steady, the net profit on all Chapman and Hall books rose to £768. 18s. 1d. Dickens was happy to

---

[7] Gettmann, p. 130.
[8] Mumby, *The House of Routledge*, p. 89.
[9] Grubb, 'Some Unpublished Correspondence', p. 112.
[10] Ibid., p. 113.

find the state of the accounts so much improved, and told Chapman on 8 May 1857 that he shared the hope that the improvement would prove lasting.[11] It didn't last. The next year was once again adversely affected by reprintings, though sales of the Cheap edition reached 23,000 numbers, 'better than they have been since December 1853', Chapman reminded Dickens.[12]

ii

Twenty years earlier, an annual income of £242, Dickens's share from Chapman and Hall for 1857, would have seemed far more significant; now Dickens's expenses were running between £8,000 and £9,000 a year. His substantial revenues derived from two Bradbury and Evans projects: *Household Words* and his original serial fiction.[13] The contract for *Household Words*, signed on 28 March 1850, gave Dickens an undivided half of the net profits (or losses), and distributed the other half among Bradbury and Evans (one-quarter), Forster (one-eighth), and Wills (one-eighth). For editing, which Dickens performed with meticulous vigilance, he received £500 a year, and Wills as sub-editor got £416, both charged as expenses of publication and not deducted from their respective shares. Dickens was to be paid additionally for articles, but Forster was expected to earn his share by contributing occasional pieces without further remuneration. Bradbury and Evans were to be publishers and printers, and to manage the Commercial Department, which included all accounting, advertising, and warehousing. To review and settle the accounts, there were to be half-yearly meetings (the half-year ending 30 September and 31 March); any proprietor could call a special meeting on seven days' notice. Three out of four proprietors (the firm counting as one) constituted a quorum, and disputes were to be settled by a vote. As with Dickens's other ventures, provisions were made for offering to the other partners first if one wished to sell out.[14]

[11] Unpublished letter, Free Library of Philadelphia, C7-5-1-1-000.

[12] Grubb, 'Some Unpublished Correspondence', p. 113.

[13] For full recent discussions of Dickens's editorial practices and other matters relating to *Household Words*, see Harry Stone, ed., *Charles Dickens' Uncollected Writings from Household Words, 1850–59* (2 vols., Bloomington and London, Indiana Univ. Press, 1968), and Anne Lohrli, comp., *Household Words* (Toronto, Univ. of Toronto Press, 1973).

[14] R. C. Lehmann, ed., *Charles Dickens as Editor: Being Letters Written by Him to William Henry Wills His Sub-Editor* (New York, Sturgis & Walton Co., 1912), pp. 19, 196–7; and K. J. Fielding, 'Bradbury *v.* Dickens', *Dickensian*, 50 (1954), 75.

Issues were dated each Saturday, though in fact they came out the preceding Wednesday; the first number bore the date 30 March 1850. Weekly numbers cost 2*d*., or 3*d*. stamped for post; the journal also appeared in monthly parts for 11*d*., and in volumes, cloth boards, for 5*s*. 6*d*.

Writing in 1934, Graham Pollard could assert that *Household Words* was the first twopenny weekly to contain original work, and that the penny papers of the forties and fifties 'were almost wholly devoted to reprinted fiction'. The *London Journal* sponsored Charles Reade's *White Lies* in 1856, Pollard notes, 'but the experiment was not a success'.[15] Margaret Dalziel, in her more recent (1957) study of *Popular Fiction 100 Years Ago*, shows that original and sensational stories constituted a large part of the Salisbury Square fiction of Edward Lloyd during the forties, and that periodicals like the *London Journal* and the *Family Herald* combined the merits while avoiding the defects of the really cheap publications. *Chambers's Journal* and *Cassell's Illustrated Family Paper* included articles on scientific, historical, and geographical subjects, while *Eliza Cook's Journal* addressed itself to 'social conditions, specially so far as they affected women and children'.[16] Thus Dickens's achievement in *Household Words* was not unique; but it answered the plea of Hepworth Dixon in the *Daily News* for a moral and elevated inexpensive periodical literature. The *Athenaeum* and the *Examiner* supported Dixon; Reynolds and others tried to tone down their style and subjects and to conform to higher standards, and 'Dickens accepted the implicit challenge to provide better cheap literature'.[17] Initially *Household Words* seemed to have much in common with *Eliza Cook's Journal*:

Both were weeklies a little more expensive than those designed for the very poor (*Household Words* cost twopence, *Eliza Cook's Journal* a penny-halfpenny); both were bent on exploiting a well known name in their struggle to attract readers; and there was considerable similarity in their contents. Both spurned the facile attractions of riddles, puzzles, illustrations, correspondence columns, and so on. Both were keenly interested in social problems, and in emigration as a solution for them. Both gave less space to fiction than to articles and sketches.[18]

The difference lies in the quality of Dickens's journal. He worked hard to keep it interesting, to produce articles on social and

[15] 'Serial Fiction', p. 264.   [16] Dalziel, p. 57.   [17] Ibid., p. 46.   [18] Ibid., p. 60.

scientific subjects that were informed, sprightly, personal, and conveyed an impression of immediacy and closeness to the subject: 'matters of passing interest in the liveliest form that could be given to them', as Forster put it (F VI. iv. 512). Above all, fancy was to be mixed with fact, the people to be amused as well as instructed. One main object of the periodical, Dickens explained in his first issue, was

to show to all, that in all familiar things, even in those which are repellant on the surface, there is Romance enough, if we will find it out:—to teach the hardest workers at this whirling wheel of toil, that their lot is not necessarily a moody, brutal fact, excluded from the sympathies and graces of imagination; to bring the greater and the lesser in degree, together, upon that wide field, and mutually dispose them to a better acquaintance and a kinder understanding—is one main object of our Household Words.

Within two weeks of its inaugural issue, *Household Words* had settled down to an average weekly sale of some 40,000 copies.[19] That was not extensive, compared with the *Family Herald*'s 300,000, the *London Journal*'s 450,000, or *Reynolds' Weekly Miscellany* at 200,000,[20] but then Dickens appealed to a higher class of readers, both more educated and more affluent, and his venture was accordingly capitalized and produced to yield a profit at that circulation. Moreover, in adhering to higher standards of writing, it established a new benchmark for respectable journals, and thus indirectly supported and enlarged the audience for his serials. He explained all these factors to Miss Coutts on 12 April 1850:

The Household Words I hope (and have every reason to hope) will become a *good property*. It is exceedingly well liked, and 'goes', in the trade phrase, admirably. I daresay I shall be able to tell you, by the end of the month, what the steady sale is. It is quite as high now, as I ever anticipated; and although the expenses of such a venture are necessarily very great, the circulation much more than pays them, so far. The labor, in conjunction with Copperfield, is something rather ponderous; but to establish it firmly would be to gain such an immense point for the

19 William E. Buckler says 950,000 copies weekly, which is way out ('Dickens's Success with *Household Words*', *Dickensian*, 46 (1950), 198–9, n. 6). Johnson believes that 'during its very best years' *Household Words* sold 40,000 copies per week (p. 946). Calculating from profits I would estimate a steady sale of 38,500 plus.

20 Dalziel, p. 23, quoting Charles Knight's 1854 estimates.

future (I mean my future) that I think nothing of that. It is playing havoc with the villainous literature.[21]

However, even Dickens's success augured ambiguously. Lowering the price and raising the quality of periodical fiction didn't stop with twopenny weeklies; first the penny weeklies tried to improve their fare, and then in the 1860s the big shilling monthlies like the *Cornhill* began competing all too successfully with the shilling parts.[22] From 1854 to 1869 Dickens published more of his novels in weekly parts (three) than in monthly (two); his Christmas stories and occasional pieces also appeared first in *Household Words* or *All the Year Round*. Though his relations with his publishers concerning these two journals were sustained on a relatively even keel, with one spectacular exception, and thus do not figure prominently in the succeeding narrative, it is essential to keep in mind that day in and day out from 1850 to 1870 Dickens, Bradbury, Evans, and later Edward and Frederic Chapman were editing, printing, publishing, selling, and accounting for upwards of 40,000 copies of a journal per week, a minimum of 2,080,000 each year, not counting the extra Christmas number which sold 80,000 or more copies (N ii. 615). And it is equally important to recall that Dickens's profit of from £700 to £1,000 per annum cushioned the sharp fluctuations in his income from current serials.

Dickens's contract with Bradbury and Evans for original fiction was also renegotiated in the early fifties. During the course of *Bleak House*, the eight-year Agreement running from July 1844 expired, never once having been challenged by either party. It had clearly taken account of all the important features of serial publication, and disposed of the costs and profits in a way that all partners found satisfactory. Amiable relations between Dickens and his publishers overcame their difficulties with the *Daily News*, and occasional flares of temper over printers' errors, insufficient secrecy, or inefficiency. When things were going well, Dickens could treat the odd lapses with good humour. For instance, when he found out that two of those he had designated on his 'free list',

[21] Edgar Johnson, ed., *The Heart of Charles Dickens* (New York, Duell, Sloan and Pearce; Boston, Little, Brown and Co., 1952), no. 116.

[22] See Spencer L. Eddy, Jr., *The Founding of* The Cornhill Magazine, Ball State Monograph No. 19, Publications in English, No. 13 (Muncie, Indiana, Ball State Univ., 1970).

Frank Stone and Carlyle, missed their complimentary numbers of *Bleak House*, Dickens prodded the firm gently, urging them to inquire into the matter, 'as a porter, judiciously ringing the changes on his Delivery-list, and pocketing twenty numbers or so a month, may perhaps be making himself comfortable at our expense and casting an appearance of carelessness on our business too' (N ii. 444–5).

In the high tide of *Bleak House*'s success, a new agreement was quickly reached, even more advantageous to Dickens than the last. By it, Bradbury and Evans continued to receive a quarter of the net profits, but agreed to cease charging the publishers' 10 per cent commission on gross sales. In addition, Dickens reserved the right to withdraw whenever he pleased (F VII. ii. 570).

These arrangements did not apply to past or current works, however; they were put into effect with the volume publication of *Hard Times*, issued in August 1854. As with so many other of Dickens's writings, this one originated in part with bad news from Fleet Street. The profits of *Household Words*, which had been running between £900 and £1,300 per half-year, dropped suddenly to £527. 15s. 10d. by 30 September 1853.[23] When the partners assembled to review the situation and verify the accounts, they urged Dickens to begin a story that would run serially in the magazine for some time, and prophesied that such a course would arrest the declining sales. Dickens must have been reluctant at first, recalling how he chafed under the peculiarly constricting and exacting conditions of weekly serialization during *Master Humphrey's Clock*. But as he rushed around getting the Christmas theatricals set up at Tavistock House, the idea of a new story, about capital and labour and strikes, about parents and children, about education, and about the importance of fancy or imagination, grew in his mind, and he decided to write it forthwith. 'My purpose is among the mighty secrets of the World at present,' he told Miss Coutts in January 1854 before setting out to see for himself the unhappy conditions fostered by the long strike at Preston, 'but there is such a fixed idea on the part of my printers and co-partners in Household Words, that a story of me, continued from week to week, would make some unheard of effect with it that I am going to write one' (N ii. 537). The profits of

23 Buckler, p. 198. For the bi-annual profits of *Household Words* and *All the Year Round*, see Appendix D.

the journal to 31 March 1854 fell lower than ever before, to £393. 7s. 2d., giving new importance to Dickens's serial. By the beginning of March, Dickens had settled on a title, *Hard Times*, and the length: his story was to run weekly for five months, beginning with the issue of 1 April which would go on sale 29 March, and it was to be as long as five numbers of *Copperfield* or *Bleak House*.[24] After he started planning the novel, Dickens decided to issue it in one inexpensive volume at the conclusion, and laboured to shape it so that it would be all of a piece, concise and uniform in pace and tone. As he approached the end of his writing, he asked Carlyle if he might dedicate the story to him: 'I have constructed it patiently, with a view to its publication altogether in a compact cheap form. It contains what I do devoutly hope will shake some people in a terrible mistake of these days, when so presented' (N ii. 567). On the same day, writing from Boulogne, Dickens sent Wills the text for the notices advertising the 'compact cheap form'. He objected to the 'hideous placard all askew, invented in Whitefriars for Hard Times', and preferred 'the plain, good, sensible bills . . . that we had at the office' (N ii. 572). The proposed announcement merely stated that

On such a day will be published complete in

One Volume, price five shillings,

HARD TIMES,

By Charles Dickens.

(N ii. 567)

By the time the notice appeared in the 29 July *Household Words*, Dickens had made up his mind to take advantage of the necessity of resetting the type from column to book format to make what Monod and Ford term 'significant' revisions in the text,[25] so the wording was changed to include 'carefully revised and wholly reprinted'. Since both weekly serial and one-volume publication

---

[24] According to George Ford and Sylvère Monod, the actual number of words is 'approximately 117,000' (Introduction to *Hard Times*, Norton Critical Edition (New York, W. W. Norton, 1966), p. vii). By Dickens's estimate, then, *Copperfield* and *Bleak House* would run to four times as many words; that is, approximately 468,000. Ford and Monod, however, give 350,000 words as the length of those twenty-part serials; and Edgar Johnson estimates 380,000 (J, p. 757).

[25] 'A Note on the Text' of *Hard Times* (Norton Critical Edition), p. 229.

were strange to Dickens, to ground himself in familiar settings he used the old monthly number format for memoranda and calculations, and then divided his one-volume novel into three books.[26] In these ways as in others, we can observe the strain of transition.

Not a great deal was expected from this volume sale, especially after the disappointing results of the *Child's History*. Most readers would have seen the novel in *Household Words*, the circulation of which rose dramatically on its appearance.[27] The September 1854 net receipts rose 237 per cent; a similar profit was recorded in May 1855. As Graham Pollard observes, magazines can capitalize on the popularity of original fiction, even after serialization.[28] In addition to increased profits, Dickens was supposed to receive £1,000 for his story, in two payments at the beginning and end of the serial run. It vexed him to learn that neither payment got sent into Coutts's on time, causing Dickens in April and again in August to overdraw his account.[29] The large sale which produced these returns seemed likely to use up most of the demand, so the publisher ordered only 5,000 volumes printed. Happily they underestimated public interest, and by 26 August reprinted another 3,000 copies: 'Your account on Bradbury authority of the Volume is capital', Dickens told Wills two days after the book went on sale 7 August (N ii. 578). To the end of 1854, 5,616 copies were sold, 25 as 24 at 3*s*. 6*d*. each, yielding gross £943. 12*s*. Deducting the cost of printing all 8,000, and binding 6,068, the modest charge for advertising of £42. 1*s*., and the commissions to agents and allowances for export, £38. 14*s*. 3*d*., there remained £277. 14*s*. 7*d*., of which Dickens received three-quarters. Thus when everything was added in, *Hard Times* swelled Dickens's coffers by nearly £1,500. After 1854 its sales and profits were not particularly significant; in June 1855 back numbers of *Bleak House*, *Copperfield*, *Dombey*, even the *Child's History*, outsold it.

[26] See Butt and Tillotson, *Dickens at Work*, pp. 202–5.

[27] Forster says it doubled (VII. i. 565); so does Percy Fitzgerald, *Memories o Charles Dickens* (Bristol, J. W. Arrowsmith; London, Simpkin, Marshall, Hamilton, Kent, 1913), p. 161; Buckler thinks the low must have been multiplied four or five times to yield the greater profits (p. 200, n. 6); cf. J, p. 797.

[28] 'Serial Fiction', p. 263.

[29] See letters of 12 Apr. 1854 (N ii. 550) with £500 credited on the 13th; and 23 Aug. 1854 (N ii. 583), with £500 credited on the 24th (MS. Coutts). This £1,000 appears neither in Appendix C, because it was paid directly to Dickens by the other partners in *Household Words*, nor in Appendix D, which merely records the profits of the journals.

iii

Sometimes small errors at the printing-house caused Dickens great trouble, especially when they had to do with estimating over- or under-matter for a part. One of the more prolonged and irritating battles with Whitefriars occurred in connection with Mrs. Gaskell's *North and South*, which followed *Hard Times* in *Household Words*. On first receiving the manuscript, Dickens saw that it would need judicious pruning and division if it were to run weekly; not content with his own estimate, he sent eighteen pages, randomly selected, to be cast off by the printers. This amount, he explained to the author,

would make a weekly No. On *about* this calculation, the MS I have, would divide at the good points I have mentioned, and pretty equally. I do not apologize to you for laying so much stress on the necessity of its dividing well, because I am bound to put before you my perfect conviction that if it did not, the story would be wasted—would miss its effect as it went on—*and would not recover it when published complete*. The last consideration is strong with me, because it is based on my long comparison of the advantages and disadvantages of the periodical form of appearance. (N ii. 562)

The printer's estimate exactly accorded with Dickens's. But when the time came to start printing, Dickens, relaxing in Boulogne after finishing *Hard Times*, began to have doubts about the novel's length. 'I am alarmed by the quantity', he told Wills. 'It is not objectionable for a beginning, but would become so in the progress of a not compactly written and artfully devised story. It suggests to me (but I may be wrong) that the Whitefriars casting-off was incorrect' (N ii. 580). In accordance with Dickens's instructions, Wills took the key which Dickens enclosed, opened the drawer of the round writing table in the study at Tavistock House, got out a bunch of keys, found one that fitted another writing table, opened the third drawer from the top on the fireplace side, and retrieved the slip of Dickens's rough notes of the serial division, along with Will's memorandum of the Whitefriars estimate. The next day proofs arrived, with altogether too much of *North and South* crammed in, especially in the second chapter which was unaltered despite Dickens's understanding that Mrs. Gaskell was to make considerable excisions. Forster offered to help, but Dickens told Wills to keep him out of it; relations between

Forster and Wills thereafter degenerated. Mrs. Gaskell was slow in returning proof; they would have to divide the manuscript and go to press without her alterations. Dickens remained calm, but he was 'unspeakably vexed by all this needless trouble and bewilderment. There is no more reason for it, than there is for a calomel pill on the top of the Cross of St. Paul's' (N ii. 584). Although earlier he had told Mrs. Gaskell that the agreement between his and the printer's estimate gave him 'no doubt of its correctness', he now put all the blame on his partners:

The real difficulty is in the reckless casting-off at Whitefriars, and upon this point I must beg you to make, from me, a grave representation that it is impossible to proceed if such tricks are played with us. When I read the beginning of this story of Mrs. Gaskell's, I felt that its means of being of service or disservice to us, mainly lay in its capacity of being divided at such points of interest as it possesses. Rejecting my own estimate on that subject, I referred it to them, the Printers (of course) for a correct one. A statement was furnished to me in reply, which turns out to be entirely wrong. If I had known how it was to turn out, and that when they said in Whitefriars 'white,' they meant 'black,' or when they said 'Ten' meant 'Twenty,' I could not, in my senses, have accepted the story. I want to know what the Masters in Whitefriars say to this mode of doing business. It is a matter of perfect indifference to me what anybody else says. *They* enter into a certain agreement with us, upon their fidelity and exactness in discharging which, we rely. I want to know what they say to not discharging it and to shirking and shuffling it off, anyhow. And *I* say to them that I am perfectly convinced there is not another house in the trade to which I could refer a question so vital to a periodical, who would lazily mislead me altogether. (N ii. 583)

This was not, alas, the end of the story. Mrs. Gaskell's text continued to make more than an average instalment of *Hard Times*, and the sale of the journal dropped noticeably. Dickens was 'not surprised', he told Wills in October. 'Mrs. Gaskell's story, so divided, is wearisome in the last degree. It would have scant attraction enough if the casting in Whitefriars had been correct; but thus wire-drawn it is a dreary business' (N ii. 598). Even when it was concluded in February of the following year, some difficulty arose over final payment for serial copyright. Still, Dickens could separate the firm from his friends, and write with genuine warmth and sympathy to Bradbury when he was prevented from joining Dickens, Wills, and wives for a seaside holiday at Boulogne in September. And in December 1855 Forster, Evans, and Mark Lemon joined Dickens at a hilarious evening at the Bradburys:

We had a dinner, without pretension, but the very best cooked dinner I ever sat down to in my life. Afterwards we played at Vingt-et-un, and Lemon and I made a Bank against the company in the wildest manner. Mrs. Bradburys account of Bradbury's setting fire to the Bed on the occasion which has become historical, was wonderful, and we made all sorts of ridiculous superstructures upon it. It seems that, she being hat Brihteen hat the time, he kept the secret of what had happened until she came home. Then, on composing that luxuriant and gorgeous figure of hers between the sheets, she started and said, 'William, where his me bed?—*this* is not me bed—wot has append William—wot ave you dun with me bed—I know the feelin of me bed, and *this* is not me bed.' Upon which he confessed all.[30]

iv

Early in 1855 Dickens began planning *Little Dorrit*, the penultimate twenty-number serial, and the last published by Bradbury and Evans. Though challenged by other cheap forms of serialization, shilling monthly parts continued through the fifties to hold their own. The Crimean War gave impetus to publishing more contemporary and political kinds of writing in numbers. *Bleak House* and *Little Dorrit* offer some testimony to that trend, and further evidence is supplied by Routledge's advice to the great *Times* war correspondent, William Howard Russell. On the strength of the success he enjoyed with the first volume of his history of the war, Routledge's proposed that he compose an expanded history:

The form we should suggest should be Demy Octavo like Dickens's works, to appear in shilling monthly parts, with illustrations either from photographs or from artists who have been there. But this you can decide; we merely suggest what we think would be the most popular form, and for remuneration we should propose that you should receive a certain sum per copy. This in all cases when a large sum is expected is the best for the author, it being a property so long as the book sells.[31]

Dickens had, therefore, no reason to expect *Nobody's Fault*, as the new novel was provisionally titled, to fare worse than his other monthly efforts.

[30] *Mr. and Mrs. Charles Dickens*, pp. 241–2.   [31] Mumby, p. 87.

But he no longer found writing so easy as in the early years, when he could dash off (not without complaining) instalments of two different novels in the same month. This time, the preliminary planning itself took months, and in the course of publication (December 1855 to June 1857) he lost much of the lead with which he began. The first two weeks in March saw him 'writing and planning and making notes over an immense number of little bits of paper', as he devised 'a new tree with the old green leaves, afar off' (N ii. 638, 639). As usual, he was 'in the wandering-unsettled-restless uncontrollable state of being about to begin . . . . At such a time', he told Leigh Hunt, 'I am as infirm of purpose as Macbeth, as errant as Mad Tom, and as ragged as Timon' (N ii. 658), and this condition persisted into early May. By July he had got under way with Number I; but it did not progress rapidly. He shut himself up every day from nine until two, then walked out by himself until five (N ii. 686); yet despite this admirable regularity, the third number was not finished until mid September. On the fifth of that month Dickens's publication arrangements were sufficiently far advanced for him to alert Tauchnitz, who in addition to publishing the novels regularly from advanced sheets, served *in loco parentis* to Dickens's sixteen-year-old son in 1853 when Charley went to Leipzig 'to obtain a scholarly knowledge of German and French' and to enjoy 'the advantages of cheerful and good society'. By 8 October Tauchnitz had returned his offer, which Dickens found satisfactory: 'It is a pleasure to me to renew our former terms, and to have any dealings with one whom I so highly esteem.'[32] In the middle of October, the English public finally learned that a new serial work by Dickens was in preparation, and on the last day of November Bradbury and Evans offered the first number for sale.

Once again, their estimate of Dickens's popularity proved conservative. An initial printing of 32,000 was ordered, 2,000 less than the final numbers of *Bleak House*. But this stock was quickly exhausted, and two more reprintings of 3,000 each were required by the end of the year. Dickens was 'overjoyed', telling Forster that it 'has beaten even *Bleak House* out of the field. It is a most tremendous start' (F VIII. i. 624). In mid December Dickens

---

[32] [Kurt Otto], *Der Verlag Bernhard Tauchnitz, 1837–1912* (Leipzig [Tauchnitz], 1912), pp. 52–3. For a full discussion of Dickens's as well as other English authors' relations with Tauchnitz, see 'Continental: Mainly Tauchnitz' in Nowell-Smith, *International Copyright Law*, pp. 41–63.

reported to Catherine that '*Little Dorrit* is still going amazingly', and added that the extra Christmas number of *Household Words*, containing *The Holly-Tree Inn*, 'seemed to have an enormous sale, thank God'.[33] The printing order for the second number of *Little Dorrit* was advanced to 35,000 copies, all of which were sold by New Year's Day (F VIII. i. 624). Three hundred and ten thousand bills and 4,000 posters had been printed by 31 December, despite Dickens's scepticism that bills did any good at all (N ii. 573). Otherwise, the advertising campaign was on the scale of White-friars' other efforts. Sales and profits just of the first two numbers presaged enormous success: out of 73,000 numbers printed by the end of the year, 69,393 had been sold at the usual discount for £2,194. 7s. 9d., and another 215 had been given out as review and presentation copies. The net came to £1,187. 11s. 11d., or for Dickens £890. 13s. 11d., better than £445 per number, with the second number on sale only a day when the accounts closed. Brad-bury and Evans received £296. 18s., about £165 less than if they had still been charging a commission of 10 per cent on gross sales.

Little Dorrit continued to hold its own throughout the run. By 8 February the first number had gone to 40,000 (N ii. 741), and by the time the double number was issued a total of 43,000 of *Little Dorrit* I were in print. The second, third, and fourth numbers started at 35,000, but 2,000 more of II and 1,500 of III were soon needed, so the initial order for V and VI was raised to 36,000. Thereafter, the press run declined to 31,000 for XV–XX, and the stitching order traces a similar curve, going from a high of 36,280 for I to around 29,000 for the closing double number. Profits held up well. Dickens made just over £600 per part for Numbers III–VIII, £542 each on Numbers IX–XIV, and again just over £600 each on the remaining parts. These are the best figures of his career. In addition, Harper's is reported to have paid £250 for advanced sheets.[34] Dickens's pleasure with the success of *Little Dorrit* was shared with his readers, to whom he wrote:

In the Preface to Bleak House I remarked that I had never had so many readers. In the Preface to its next successor, Little Dorrit, I have

---

[33] *Mr. and Mrs. Charles Dickens*, p. 240.

[34] See 'The Dickens Controversy', an appendix to Mackenzie, *Life*, p. 3; confirmed in MS. B and E, except that the payment was *included* with other gross income derived from the monthly sale of and advertisements in the serial, and the net divided three-quarters to Dickens, one-quarter to his publishers. Thus the figure of £600 per number incorporates Dickens's share of the Harper payments.

still to repeat the same words. Deeply sensible of the affection and confidence that have grown up between us, I add to this Preface, as I added to that, May we meet again!

Although receipts from *Little Dorrit* exceeded those from *Bleak House* by more than £1,000, 40,000 fewer parts were sold, and the gross revenue was £1,400 less. This seeming discrepancy is explained by the new publishing contract: whereas for *Bleak House* the publishers received about two-fifths of their revenue from commissions, for *Little Dorrit* they were entitled to only a quarter of the net, so their income diminished from close to £6,000 to just under £3,900, and Dickens's proportionately rose.

It was pleasant to have this additional income, because Dickens was once again engaged in the heavy expense of changing residence. He decided to buy the freehold of Gad's Hill for £1,790, and wanted to fit it up properly, telling Forster that 'The changes absolutely necessary will take a thousand pounds; which sum I am always resolving to squeeze out of this, grind out of that, and wring out of the other; this, that, and the other generally all three declining to come up to the scratch for the purpose' (F VIII. iii. 651). One of the 'thises' and 'thats' was Bradbury and Evans, who increased his monthly payment against *Dorrit* profits from £100 (December 1855 and January 1856) to £200. On 12 February Dickens asked Evans if the sum might be augmented: 'if it should be convenient to you even to increase upon the £200 monthly payment, it will suit me perfectly well. The circulation being so large, I do not care how much you pay in every month, or by how large a sum you so diminish the half yearly balance. It will be as useful to me in six large portions and a moderate lump, as in six small portions and a great lump. All that I care for, is, that it should always be the same appointed sum. I address this to you, as you are the currency man and as you spoke to me on the subject; but of course I refer the point to B. and E. Let me know how you propose to proceed' (N ii. 745). Dickens's bank account shows that Bradbury and Evans began February with a payment of £140, £100 for the novel and £40 for *Household Words*. On 23 February an additional £150 for *Little Dorrit* was deposited, and thereafter £290 appears at the first of every month during the serial run, £540 for Numbers XIX and XX (MS. Coutts).

In his letter Dickens made another request of his usually compliant publishers. Would they 'be so good as to make up the last half year's account with as little delay as you can, because, having this purchase to make I am glad just now of all the money I can get. I know that the usual time has not yet arrived, but you may perhaps be able to anticipate it a little, knowing my desire' (N ii. 745). Within a fortnight, the December 1855 accounts were forwarded; they showed that of the £1,065. 9s. 7d. owing to Dickens on all his books, only £200 had been paid in equal sums at the beginning of December and January. Dickens acknowledged receipt from Paris on 24 February, informing Bradbury and Evans that 'all your arrangements are most convenient and satisfactory'. (The extra £150 had been deposited the day before.) 'But', he continued,

> looking over the balance-sheet of the accounts, there seems to me to be a mistake in it, which will unnecessarily embarrass the present half-year [.] I take the profits on the 2 first Nos. to extend in this account, only to the last Day of 1855. Then I think you should not charge to my debit in this account, £100 paid on the 1st. of January 1856. Would it not be best to alter the balance and the balance sheet, so as to put that hundred pounds into the half-year to which it belongs?
>
> If you think so, we can make the alterations in these figures when I come to town next month and bring the accounts with me. (N ii. 747)

But Bradbury and Evans did not think so; the payments were really made on publication of the monthly instalment, and thus related to earlier arrangements in which Dickens was paid on delivery of the manuscript or on publication day. Therefore the £100 paid on 1 January was applied to the January number, published 31 December and therefore part of the December 1855 accounts, confusing though that seems. A year later the publishers moved back the date on which payment was credited to Dickens to the last day of the month, publication day, although the deposits continue to show up at Coutts's on the first day of the next month.

Throughout *Little Dorrit*, the partners remained cordial. In July 1856, Dickens wrote a letter introducing to Carlyle 'my printers and old friends, Messrs. Bradbury and Evans', who wished to join in the proposed collected edition of Carlyle's works:

> Now, they have not only printed my books from the first page thereof to this hour, but have been closely associated with me in matters of trust and confidence. And I believe that when I assure you they are not only the best and most powerful printers in London, but have in all our transactions won my affectionate esteem and regard, you will believe that you cannot do better than entrust your Edition to

them. I am perfectly sure you will never repent it, or have a moment's dissatisfaction with them. I cannot say too much for them, and no man could say anything for them out of a closer knowledge of them than mine is. (N ii. 793)

v

At the end of *Little Dorrit*, another project began to form in Dickens's mind. John Forster suggested that his copyrights were not being fully exploited. There were stereotype reprints of the novels in parts, but none of the novels after *Chuzzlewit* had been included in the Cheap edition, and there was no 'quality' edition for the rich.[35] At first Dickens did not agree, but the more he considered the matter the more he came round to Forster's opinion, and to the realization that publishing his novels in a dignified and handsome edition might elevate their place.[36] Having come to a decision, he broached the matter to Evans, who returned a number of suggestions and pointed out the difficulty of publishing a complete edition of Dickens's works when the copyrights were shared with different publishers.[37] On Tuesday, 15 September, Dickens, still on his lazy tour of two idle apprentices with Collins, responded from the Angel Hotel, Doncaster:

I like your notion of the Edition, and as soon after next Monday (when I return), as you please, let us have a quiet day at Gad's Hill and go into the 'facts and figures.' In the meantime I have begged Forster to see Chapman, and so to pave the way as that you and Chapman shall have the road open for making all arrangements. I have told Forster that Bradbury and Evans's name must be on all the series as well as Chapman's and that I must have B and E in all the accounts and all the business, and must have (and will have) no Chapman delays and shortcomings from first to last, but must wholly extinguish the same. (N ii. 883-4)

While negotiations were being carried on for what was to become the Library edition, a seemingly unrelated development

[35] Had Forster approached Chapman with this idea earlier? Dickens replied to some Chapman proposal in 1854: 'Generally speaking I like alterations of form very little, and imitations of anything still less. But I will consider your suggestion between this present year 1854 and the good time coming (perhaps) when the peaceful arts shall be heard of again' (N ii. 606).
[36] Unpublished letter, Dickens to Evans, 6 Sept. 1857, Free Library of Philadelphia, E9-2-1-4-000.
[37] Frederic Ouvry eventually collected transcripts of all copyrights in order to sort out Dickens's affairs; see N ii. 897.

was taking place in Dickens's household. The incompatibility of temperament between husband and wife, apparent even during their engagement, had worsened over the years. At last Dickens could find no relief save in action, and so determined to sever all but the outward marital forms. He converted his bathroom into a dressing room, ordered a small iron bedstead placed there, and directed that the doorway communicating to Mrs. Dickens's room be 'fitted with plain white deal shelves, and closed in with a plain light deal door, painted white' (N ii. 890). Dickens wanted the break to be clean, simple, unemotional.

By 20 October, arrangements had been made for the commencement of the Library edition. It was to be issued in 6s. monthly volumes, 'a far more convenient form, at once for present perusal, and for preservation', than any previous format.[38] Outstanding details still had to be resolved with Chapman and Hall, but Dickens planned to draft a prospectus when he met with Evans at the *Household Words* office (N ii. 892). One of the principal decisions already reached was that Chapman and Hall, using Bradbury and Evans for their printer, would publish the books they controlled, and Bradbury and Evans would do likewise for theirs. Thus the series appears under the imprint of both firms, and their varying methods of keeping records add further confusion.

Working his copyrights in yet another way, Dickens found an opportunity to cash in on continuing French interest in his works. From the time of Mme Niboyet's 'freely translated' 1838 *Aventures de Mr. Pickwick*, there had been a steady succession of translations: Barba published Mme Niboyet's versions of *Nicholas Nickleby* (1838) and *Oliver Twist* (1841); *Martin Chuzzlewit* ran serially in *Le Moniteur*; *David Copperfield*, translated by Pichot, appeared in the *Revue britannique* and also as a book published by Perrotin; *Oliver Twist* had been imitated without acknowledgement by Molé under the title *L'Escroc du grand monde*; and *Hard Times* had been imitated by Léon de Wailly in *L'Illustration*.[39] In an 1854 catalogue of Hachette's Railway Library (la Bibliothèque des Chemins de fer) are listed two of the Christmas Books, *La Battaile de la Vie* and *Le Grillon du Foyer* (*The Cricket on the Hearth*). The

---

[38] Advertisement for the Library edition.
[39] For this and much of the succeeding information on Dickens's French translations the most recent authority is Jean Mistler, *La Librarie Hachette de 1826 à nos jours* (Paris, Hachette, 1964), pp. 155–62, whose discussion I follow here.

only common feature of these translations, Jean Mistler observes, published by different firms with different translators and formats, was their 'infidélité'. Moreover, several important works, including *The Old Curiosity Shop* and *Bleak House*, were not translated at all. The recent signing of a reciprocal copyright agreement between England and France provided an opportunity for Hachette to issue a new and faithful translation of all Dickens's novels, and to pay him accordingly.

Dickens spent from October 1855 to May 1856 in Paris. Towards the beginning of December, Hachette wrote to him at 49 Champs Élysées proposing such an edition, intended originally to comprise part of a fourth section of the Railway Library called 'La Collection des Romans Étrangers'. Texts would be printed in tightly-packed 18mo pages of forty-eight lines of sixty characters, bound in orange-coloured cloth, and sold for one franc each. This series, which included American authors like Harriet Beecher Stowe, English writers like Bulwer, Thackeray, Disraeli, and Charlotte Brontë, and Germans, Russians, Italians, and Spaniards, was the fundamental vehicle for the dissemination of English literature in France during the middle decade of the century.

Dickens replied to 'Messrs de la Hachette et Cie' asking for further details of their proposal and noting (in French) that he had authorized no French translation of his books, although all foreigners paid him the flattering honour of regarding his writings as public property (N ii. 713). The head of the office, É. Templier, answered on the 10th. Under what conditions would Dickens grant Hachette the exclusive rights to translate his works? Templier noted the legal distinction between those novels published before the international treaty and those which came after; technically no payment was necessary in the former cases, but in fairness and as confirmation of a twenty-year-old policy, Hachette would offer 500 francs per volume for the old books, and 1,000 francs each for the more recent ones.

Dickens crossed the Channel for Christmas; when he got back to Paris he met with Louis Hachette on 7 or 8 January, sent him on the 10th a list of novels comprising eighteen volumes to begin with *The Old Curiosity Shop* and to end with *Little Dorrit*, and on the 14th he followed up with some corrections and additions —*Oliver Twist*, *Hard Times*, The Christmas Books (N ii. 729–30)— making a total of eleven novels and the five Christmas Books. Dickens, in return for 11,000 francs paid in monthly instalments of 1,000 francs beginning 1 April, ceded to Hachette 'the sole and exclusive right of making a translation authorised by me, of these books, into the French language' (N ii. 730). Before signing a contract, Dickens forwarded to Tauchnitz the proposed terms, which also included Hachette's right to future novels at 1,000 francs the volume, and to other writings at half that sum. When the German publisher replied that they seemed fair, Dickens was satisfied, reporting to Miss Coutts that it 'will be a pleasant thing to have done in one's lifetime'.[40] His introductory address 'to the great French people, whom I sincerely love and honour' was carried both in English and in French.

On 9 April, Louis Hachette signed a contract with his old friend Paul Lorain to direct the Dickens translations. The fifty-seven-year-old Lorain had once been rector of the Lyon division of the University of France, but he had resigned in protest against the policies of Louis Philippe at the time of the *coup d'état*. Since then his friendship with Hachette had been of considerable value in protecting him from government reprisals. Lorain and Hachette set up minutely detailed procedures for the translations: each translator signed a contract specifying delivery date, agreed to write only on the recto of each page and to leave a half-page margin for corrections, and was paid directly by the publishing house, so that Lorain dealt only with the literary side of things. In addition, on disputed points, doubtful idioms, and unfamiliar allusions, Lorain and his fellow translators regularly consulted Fleming, who had published with Hachette in 1853 *L'Interprète français-anglais*. The result, at least in prospect, pleased Dickens, who observed of the still incomplete translations in his 'Address' that they had 'been made with the greatest care, and [the] many difficulties have been combated with unusual skill, intelligence and perseverance. [The translation] has been superintended, above all, by an accomplished gentleman, perfectly acquainted with both languages, and able, with a rare felicity, to be perfectly faithful to the English text, while rendering it in elegant and expressive French.'

The first volume, *Nicholas Nickleby*, prepared by Lorain, got the series off to a brisk start in May 1857 by selling 100,000 copies in a short time.[41] Dickens estimated that he would net by the venture

---

[40] *Heart of Charles Dickens*, no. 228, 10 Jan. 1856.
[41] So asserted in F VII. v. 619–20 n., and 622, n. 427; the figure is not repeated by Mistler.

between £300 and £400 (N ii. 722, 726–7, 831); the nine bills actually deposited from June 1857 (payments for April and May were cashed in France) amount, after charges for conversion, to just over £350.[42]

At this time the readings were also being expanded, and changed from benefiting charity to benefiting Dickens directly. Bradbury and Evans also published five reading editions, of which the first, that for *A Christmas Carol*, appeared in December 1857. They began with a printing of 2,500 on 5 December; the public reception was good, and the first edition was soon sold out, necessitating a further printing of 3,000 copies. By the end of the year, 4,158 had been sold to retailers at 8s. 6d. for thirteen, a price so low that though 75 per cent of the stock had been purchased there was still a net loss of £3. 12s. 2d.

By July 1858, 3,000 more *Carols* had been printed, 2,740 sold, and the ledger showed a favourable net balance of £29. 16s. 2d., three-quarters of which was Dickens's. The four other readings were printed in this period; *The Cricket on the Hearth*, 4,000 printed, 2,058 sold, loss of £19. 9s. 6d; *The Chimes*, 4,000 printed, 1,988 sold, loss of £20. 9s. 9d.; and *The Story of Little Dombey*, 4,000 printed, 2,252 sold, which, because longer yet sold at the same price, sustained a larger loss, £29. 7s. 3d. The fifth reading edition, *The Poor Traveller: Boots at the Holly-Tree Inn: and Mrs. Gamp*, though first printed in June, did not appear in the accounts until December 1858, by which time it made a small profit of £22. 7s. 2d. on a printing of 8,000 and sales of 6,175 copies. The low wholesale (thirteen for 8s. 6d.) and retail (1s.) price and limited circulation combined to prevent these reading editions from ever becoming substantial money-makers. The *Carol* did best: by 1870 there were 23,500 copies in print; the 'eleven dozen of one title' that 'sold out in ten minutes'[43] at one performance probably were of the *Carol*, consistently the public favourite. None of the others came even close to this figure. And the profits were equally modest, seldom going above £10 per accounting period. Net

[42] MS. Coutts; Mistler, p. 160. In June 1856 Hachette sent his son Alfred to Dickens for suggestions of other English authors who might appear in the series, along with letters of introduction.

[43] John D. Gordan, 'Reading for Profit: The Other Career of Charles Dickens: An Exhibition from the Berg Collection', *Bulletin of the New York Public Library*, 62 (1958), 431.

receipts from the actual performances, on the other hand, amounted to £3,964 in 1858 alone.[44]

Chapman and Hall launched the Library edition in the spring of 1858, printing 4,000 copies of *Pickwick* (two volumes) and 2,000 copies of *Nickleby*, *Chuzzlewit* (both two volumes) and the first volume of the *Shop*. They supplied special American title-pages and vignettes for Ticknor and Fields, who purchased 3,500 volumes at 2s. each, half the wholesale price. Of the remaining 14,500, one hundred and forty-nine were given away, and 7,800 were sold as 7,488 (25 as 24) for 4s. 2d. each. But the expense of publication outweighed the receipts, leaving a deficit of £305. 12s. 9d.; 'The Library Edition is in arrear', Edward Chapman wrote on 15 September 1858, 'but I trust the next a/c may set it right.'[45] In the second half of 1858, 2,000 copies of the second volume of the *Shop* which included *Reprinted Pieces*, of the two volumes of *Barnaby Rudge*, in the second of which *Hard Times* appeared, and of *Sketches by Boz* were printed; Ticknor took 2,000 volumes at 2s.; yet far from being set right, the deficit increased to £727. 17s. 6d. The following year the debt fell slightly, to £661. 3s. 6d. ('The Library Edition goes slowly', Chapman remarked),[46] and in 1860 further sales brought it down to £547. 7s. But three years after it was launched Chapman and Hall's share of the Library edition was still deeply in the red.

Bradbury and Evans followed Chapman and Hall, printing 2,000 copies of *Oliver Twist* in November, on which they sustained a loss of £194. 4s. 6d. by the end of the year, and 2,000 copies of *Dombey and Son* Volume I in December, on which they lost £133. 1s. A like number of Volume II was printed in January of 1859, followed by 2,000 each of the two volumes of *Copperfield*, of the one-volume *Pictures from Italy* and *American Notes*, and of the two volumes of *Bleak House*. *Little Dorrit* appeared in two volumes in July and August, and the Christmas Books came out at the end of September, the twenty-second volume and the last in the series. Ticknor took 500 copies of each volume, and the rest were sold under the same arrangements as to cost, with publishers in both cases receiving a 5 per cent commission on sales. In 1858, their portions of the edition sustained a debt of £327. 5s. 6d., and in

[44] MS. Coutts. Cf. letter to Beard, 14 Oct. 1858 (N iii. 63).
[45] Grubb, 'Some Unpublished Correspondence', p. 114.
[46] Ibid., p. 116.

1859 they lost a further £845. 16s. 8d. However, because they were his principal publishers, Bradbury and Evans could charge the whole of a year's losses against Dickens's greater accumulated profits, wiping out the debt immediately. Thus after the first appearance most of their Library edition volumes show a small profit, whereas Chapman continues to apologize for deficits year after year. Moreover, as well as apologizing, Chapman and Hall carried the whole of the debt, three-quarters of which properly belonged to Dickens, without charging any interest.

Forster's other point, that the Cheap edition ought to be brought more nearly up to date, led Bradbury and Evans in the spring of 1858 to issue a second series of Cheap editions, selling for 3s. 6d. wholesale, 5s. retail, and including *Dombey and Son* (6,000 printed in April and 3,000 more printed before the end of the year), *David Copperfield* (5,000 in July), and *Bleak House* (5,000 in November). These sold modestly, *Dombey* reaching 7,947, *Copperfield* 8,264, and *Bleak House* 5,531 copies to 31 June 1861, when they were taken over by Chapman and Hall. And the profits were accordingly modest: for Dickens, who received a half share, £189. 3s. 1d. for *Dombey*, £63. 14s. 9d. for *Copperfield* (a reprint of 2,000 in June 1861 leaving a deficit of nearly £50), and £126. 10s. 9d. for *Bleak House*.

Thus under Forster's prodding Dickens was, in the winter of 1857–8, vigorously working his copyright. He had arranged for the first quality edition of his works, brought the Cheap edition up to 1853, contracted for French rights, issued texts of his readings, and in general brought Bradbury and Evans into a large number of new projects. Whereas in December 1857 eight ledger sheets sufficed for the account, a year later it took almost double the number. Dickens's income did not rise correspondingly, however, because of the increased costs; indeed, it fell from £440 in December 1857 to £132 in December 1858, to minus £329. 10s. in June 1859, and back to £3. 19s. 7d. in December.[47]

vi

Meanwhile, the simple, clean break with Kate, that apparently unrelated separation of the preceding autumn, had grown into an

[47] In the J58 accounts, Bradbury and Evans's commission on old works was cut from 10 to 5 per cent, but for the first time this percentage was allowed on *Hard Times* and *Little Dorrit* as well.

incubus that blighted all Dickens's affairs. Early in 1858 Dickens decided that it would be better to live apart from his wife; discussions about the legal terms of a separation began in May; a formal deed was drafted and signed before the end of the month, Forster having represented Dickens, and Mark Lemon his wife. Rumours of the separation circulated about London, becoming more fantastic, scandalous, and prejudicial with every retelling. Conscious that his mode of publishing had always demanded the greatest frankness and mutual trust between himself and his public, Dickens decided to issue a personal statement in *Household Words*, and to cause it to be distributed to other journals as well. Delane, editor of *The Times*, supported Dickens's resolve, in contrast to many of his friends who urged silence;[48] and the statement first appeared in the 7 June edition of *The Times*, followed a few days later in the 12 June number of *Household Words*. K. J. Fielding, whose account, based on new material, is followed here, thinks that there is 'no doubt that it generally had a good effect at the time; although Dickens has often been blamed subsequently, largely because the results have been confused with those of the "Violated Letter," published by the *New York Tribune*'.[49]

One of the journals Dickens confidently expected to publish his defence was *Punch*, edited by his old friend Lemon and published by Bradbury and Evans. But the publishers declined. Some tension had already developed over the choice of Catherine's trustees. 'Pater' Evans had refused at first, then consented at Dickens's insistence, and then found himself vetoed at the last minute for reasons that remain obscure.[50] As for Lemon himself, having acted for Catherine with good taste and discretion throughout the long hours of negotiation, he may have thought it improper to publish in a journal under his editorship a letter of explanation by the other party, even though it was endorsed by Catherine and Charley. In any case, Bradbury and Evans never considered

---

[48] Henry Crabb Robinson had a 'very friendly chat' with Miss Coutts and Mrs. Brown 'about Dickens's unwise advertisement of domestic calamities. Miss Coutts is satisfied there has been nothing criminal—nothing beyond *incompatibilité d'humeur*—to require a separation, which should have been done quietly. Miss Coutts is friendly with both husband and wife' (*Books and Their Writers*, ii. 778).

[49] Fielding, 'Bradbury *v*. Dickens', p. 74.

[50] Arthur A. Adrian, *Mark Lemon: First Editor of Punch* (London, New York, and Toronto, Oxford Univ. Press, 1966), p. 133.

inserting 'statements on a domestic and painful subject in the inappropriate columns of a comic miscellany'.[51]

When *Punch* appeared on Wednesday, 16 June, Dickens eagerly scanned the pages for his letter. Its omission infuriated him, and he told a friend, who communicated the information to the publishers, that he was determined to sever all connections. It was difficult for the publishers to understand or credit Dickens's fury. In the negotiations that followed, they expressed doubt that 'this was the sole cause of Mr. Dickens's altered feelings towards them'. They repeatedly pressed Forster upon the point, and repeatedly got the same answer: 'they were assured that it *was* the sole cause, and that Mr. Dickens desired to bear testimony to their integrity and zeal as his publishers, but that his resolution was formed, and nothing would alter it'.[52] Some light on Dickens's motivation may be shed by a letter he wrote to Evans when he was contemplating the first personal reading tour in March 1858:

would such an use of the personal (I may almost say affectionate) relations which subsist between me and the public and make my standing with them very peculiar, at all affect my position with them as a writer? Would it be likely to have any influence on my next book? If it had any influence at all, would it be likely to be of a weakening or a strengthening kind? (N iii. 12)

Dickens looked upon his publishers as partners in a very complex and sensitive venture. They too had a stake in his public reputation, and everything to do with it; the accuracy of an illustration, even the address from which a book was published, might affect the value of their copyrights. Thus Dickens did not see their decision from the standpoint of the inappropriateness of the letter to *Punch*, but from the vantage of their joint partnership in past, present, and future serials. And from that standpoint it was essential that his publishers publicly support his position. Their declining to do so might appear an act of criticism. And if it did, the criticism would be levelled not only at the most sensitive part of Dickens's own life, but also at the core of his philosophy, the image of the happy hearth which for Dickens and his public seemed almost to constitute a new myth of the Golden Age.[53] How much of this reasoning

[51] 'Mr. Charles Dickens and His Late Publishers', *Once a Week*, 1 (1859), 3.
[52] Ibid., p. 4.
[53] See Robert L. Patten, ' "A Surprising Transformation": Dickens and the Hearth', in *Nature and the Victorian Imagination*, ed. Ulrich C. Knoepflmacher

Dickens consciously performed we cannot know; I hypothesize, to account for the apparently unreasonable and inflexible stand Dickens took. Dickens worried about how his 'peculiar' standing with the public would be affected by *any* action, and he believed that such concern was essential to maintaining his personal and affectionate relations which were the foundation of his great success. Bradbury and Evans's insensitivity on this point struck him as a potentially fatal flaw.

Nothing could be done until he completed his reading tour, however; it is doubtful if Dickens wanted the publicity about his quarrel during the months of barn-storming. A few days before his tour ended, Dickens wrote on 9 November (which happened to be the half-yearly audit day for the periodical) asking Bradbury and Evans to convene a meeting of all partners in seven days, to consider a resolution he would submit.[54] He refused to attend himself, executing a power of attorney for Forster, who along with Wills proposed and voted in favour of the following motion:

That the present partnership in Household Words be dissolved by the cessation and discontinuance of that publication on the Completion of the Nineteenth Volume.[55]

But the dissolution of the partnership was not to be so antiseptically surgical. No provision existed in the contract for winding up when the partners disagreed, and Bradbury and Evans emphatically disagreed, 'Believing the resolution to be contrary to the conditions of the deed of partnership and therefore illegal'.[56] The dispute eventually wound up in court, where Bradbury and Evans not only lost *Household Words*, but also Dickens apart from the journal, and all the stock in the works they had jointly issued. It was as messy, and as decisive, a break as the one with Catherine.

and Georg B. Tennyson (Berkeley and Los Angeles, Univ. of California Press, 1977), pp. 153–70, and Alexander Welsh's chapter 9, 'The Hearth', in *The City of Dickens* (Oxford, Clarendon Press, 1971), pp. 141–63.

[54] Fielding, 'Bradbury *v.* Dickens', pp. 75–6.

[55] Ibid., p. 76.

[56] Quoted in ibid.

IV

MAN OF THE WORLD

And how did authors and publishers earn a living
when about 40 books a year weren't written about
Dickens?

CAPTAIN PETER DICKENS,
11 June 1971

14

Return to Chapman and Hall

... we are anxious to prove that it is not gain alone
that we have at heart in being your publishers.

FREDERIC CHAPMAN TO CHARLES DICKENS,
2 March 1860[1]

i

THE SWITCH BACK TO CHAPMAN AND HALL turned out
to be very complicated, taking three years to complete.
Dickens attempted through Forster on 27 November to
buy out Bradbury and Evans's share in *Household Words*. The
publishers countered on 9 December with a suggestion that
Dickens purchase their share in all his works. Forster was offended
by both the tone and the substance of their reply; Dickens re-
offered for the journal alone; the publishers again intimated their
desire to be quit of all their Dickens ventures. On 14 December
Dickens made a final offer of £1,000 for their interest in the copyright, plus the stock on hand at a valuation, but Bradbury and
Evans declined to accept. Then Dickens proceeded with his
arrangements to wind up *Household Words* with the 28 May 1859
number, the end of Volume XIX, so informing his partners by
written notice on 22 December. At the start of the new year, he
turned his attention to the new journal. By the end of January he
had hit upon a title; shortly thereafter he asked Wills to check
with Ouvry about the legality of advertising *All the Year Round*,
to start a full month before *Household Words* terminated. Ouvry
was of the opinion that a prospectus could be issued, but not
in the pages of *Household Words* without Bradbury and Evans's

[1] Grubb, 'Some Unpublished Correspondence', p. 115.

permission, which was Dickens's most audacious plan. The separately issued 'Address' announced that 'On Saturday, 28th May, 1859, Mr. Charles Dickens will cease to conduct "Household Words," that Periodical will be discontinued, and its Partnership of Proprietors dissolved.'

That did it. Bradbury and Evans, hitherto patient, filed a Bill of Complaint in Chancery on 21 March, praying that the partnership be dissolved and wound up under the direction of the Court, that Dickens be restrained by injunction against issuing any advertisement announcing the discontinuance of *Household Words* or the substitution of any other journal, that the copyright of *Household Words* be sold as a going concern, and that Dickens pay the costs of the suit.[2] On the same day Bradbury and Evans warned Chapman and Hall not to issue any of the half-million disputed notices until a decision was rendered. Three days thereafter, the printers filed their lengthy affidavit rehearsing the provisions of the original Agreement of 28 March 1850, the history of the magazine's publication and of the current dispute (including the agitated correspondence of the previous November and December), and the complaint that publication of the notice to the press and the trade 'would be very injurious to us the plaintiffs and if not restrained will seriously diminish the value of the Copyright'.[3] In his brief reply filed the next day Dickens affirmed that he had duly executed a Power of Attorney authorizing Forster to act on his behalf, denied that he had 'endeavoured to deprive the plaintiffs of any part of their share or interest in Household Words or to appropriate the benefit of the Copyright of that Publication' to himself, stated that it would have been 'a serious loss' if the plaintiffs had succeeded in stopping the distribution of his notice, and concluded, with that characteristic note of touchy pride, that he stood to lose much more if the Copyright was injured, but that 'it concerns not only my pecuniary interests but my honour and reputation that my name should not be erroneously associated with any Publication which I have ceased to conduct'.[4] The case came before the Master of the Rolls the following day; he refused the injunction, required Dickens to make clear in any future Addresses that *Household Words* was only discontinued by him,

2 PRO, C. 15. 596/B–76. X/K 2107.
3 PRO, C. 31. 1392/1608. X/K 2107.
4 PRO, C. 31. 1392/1635. X/K 2107.

and reserved any decision on costs until the partnership property was sold. Both sides tried to claim the victory, but Bradbury and Evans had the worst of it. 'I suppose Whitefriars to be, as Mr. Samuel Weller expresses it somewhere in Pickwick, "ravin' mad with the consciousness o' willany",' Dickens told Edmund Yates (N iii. 98).

The only remaining difficulty was the journal itself. An order for sale was issued on 28 April,[5] and an auction at Hodgson's held on 16 May. Forster had relinquished his eighth share in 1856, so between them, Dickens and Wills owned three-quarters of the copyright. Thus they had only to pay one-quarter to secure the whole, while Bradbury and Evans would have to pay three times the amount, and for a journal whose conductor had defected. To prevent the bidding's running too high, Dickens employed a subterfuge: Frederic Chapman put in bids up to a point; the 'Whitefriars gang', represented by a certain Joyce, kept pace with their supposed rival; and in between Arthur Smith, Dickens's reading manager, noisily related anecdotes to Joyce and Shirley Brooks and Frederick Evans. Suddenly Smith put in a bid '—as it were accidentally—to the great terror and confusion of all the room' (N iii. 104). The result was further triumph. Smith, on behalf of Dickens, got *Household Words*, lock, stock, and copyright, for £3,550. The stock Dickens valued at £1,600, making the copyright worth £2,000. Thus in reality he paid £500, one-half of what he had offered Bradbury and Evans for their quarter share a few months before. Nor was this the end of the dealing. Dickens incorporated the name *Household Words* into his new journal (thereby deftly appropriating Wills's share), and sold the back stock to Chapman and Hall for £2,500.[6] He was clear of the rival journal and several hundred pounds richer to boot. In another gesture of independence, he ran in the final number 'A Last Household Word', pointing out that 'He knew perfectly well, knowing his own rights, and his means of attaining them, that it *could not be* but that this Work must stop, if he chose to stop it. He therefore announced, many weeks ago, that it would be discontinued on the day on which this final Number bears date. The Public have read a great deal to the contrary, and will observe that it has not in the least affected the result.'

---

[5] PRO, C. 33/1058.
[6] See, for most of this account, K. J. Fielding, 'Bradbury *v*. Dickens'.

ii

Simultaneously with the winding up of *Household Words*, both
Bradbury and Evans and Dickens were working on their new
journals. Whitefriars planned to bring out *Once a Week* as a 3*d.*
weekly illustrated periodical, 'a miscellany of literature, art, science,
and popular information'. They laid much stress in the preliminary announcement on 'the modern department of Pictorial Illustration', to be supervised by John Leech. On the other hand, no
editor was announced—Samuel Lucas eventually served in that
capacity—no political party or bias was to be supported, no clique
of writers predominated. The proprietors added 'that there appears
to be ample scope for this project without trespassing on the
province of any existing periodical', a distinct slap at Dickens's
advertising, which attempted to depreciate *Household Words* by
making *All the Year Round* as near an imitation as legally possible.[7]
Further, they continued in another dig at their rival, 'The Pro-
jectors seek only to sustain their own conception of the requisite
standard of Popular Literature, under the impression that it has
yet to be realised by themselves or others; and they expect popular
support only in proportion to their success.' It is customary to
declare that Bradbury and Evans did not receive that support. But
the journal did continue for twenty years; it carried its share of
significant Victorian fiction; if the payment of £2,000 a year to
Tennyson for contributions is any standard, its rate of pay was far
higher than either of Dickens's periodicals;[8] and its stable of illustrators included Tenniel, Millais, Browne, and Charles Keene. A
study of the contents of the journal, in conjunction with whatever
records survive in the publishers' archives, might yield more precise information on Bradbury and Evans's success at publishing on
their own, and throw additional light on the extent to which other
journals, like Dickens's and the *Cornhill*, owed their popularity to
a well-known editor-in-chief.[9]

[7] But they were not above imitating Dickens's successful formula themselves:
'What fools they are!' Dickens told Wills. 'As if a mole couldn't see that their
only chance was in a careful separation of themselves from the faintest approach or
assimilation to All the Year Round!' (N iii. 108–9).

[8] Arthur A. Adrian, *Mark Lemon: First Editor of Punch* (London, New York,
and Toronto, Oxford Univ. Press, 1966), p. 70.

[9] Lionel Stevenson notes that George Smith of Smith, Elder, proprietors and
publishers of the *Cornhill*, 'adhered to a theory accepted among London publishers

One of the first items of business in starting up *All the Year Round* was the contract. To correct what had turned out to be a troublesome mistake in his earlier periodical contract, Dickens excluded Chapman and Hall from any share in the ownership of the copyright or stock: 'there is no publisher whatever associated with All the Year Round', Dickens told Bulwer; 'therefore implicit reliance may be placed in the journal's proceedings' (N iii. 194). Dickens and Wills became co-proprietors, entitled respectively to three-quarters and one-quarter of the profits, and obligated for a similar share of any losses.[10] As editor, Dickens received £504 a year; as sub-editor and general manager in control of the commercial department, Wills received £420. Should he retire, his share of the profits would drop to one-eighth, while Dickens's would rise to seven-eighths. The title and the goodwill belonged exclusively to Dickens. When Wills complained about this point, Dickens put him down flatly: 'But as to the Title, I must be quite positive and immoveable, and place myself at once beyond the possibility of mistake with you. My design is, and always has been (I have purchased the experience on which I formed it, rather dear) that if I chose to abolish the thing it is abolished, and that the Title is *Mine*. Nothing would induce me to depart from this' (N iii. 113). The familiar firm of Charles Whiting in Beaufort Street did the printing; Chapman and Hall were the exclusive agents, outside London, receiving a 12½ per cent discount from list price and six months' credit;[11] but the magazine was published from the Office of *All the Year Round*, No. 11 (after April 1860 it was No. 26) Wellington Street, Strand. To an extent unusual, perhaps unprecedented, Dickens was his own publisher. He had taken his assertion of his own rights and the exercise of his own power as a writer about as far as they could possibly go. The evolution of the author to pre-eminence was complete.[12]

—that the success of a popular magazine depended chiefly upon a famous literary personage in the editorial chair. The routine work could be done by subordinates, but a great name must decorate the title page', *The Showman of Vanity Fair* (New York, Charles Scribner's Sons, 1947), p. 357.

[10] *Charles Dickens as Editor*, p. 261.

[11] 'Office Letter Book' of *All the Year Round* at the Huntington Library, quoted by Grubb in 'Some Unpublished Correspondence', p. 117, n. 72.

[12] Sutherland has an enlightening discussion of 'Dickens as Publisher' in chapter 8 of *Victorian Novelists and Publishers*; he argues, in contrast to most critics who

iii

To give the new journal a good send-off, Dickens decided to write an original story. His thoughts had been tending towards another book for a year, ever since he acted in Wilkie Collins's *The Frozen Deep* in the summer of 1857. During the refitting of Gad's Hill in January 1858 he complained to Forster that 'Growing inclinations of a fitful and undefined sort are upon me sometimes to fall to work on a new book. Then I think I had better not worry my worried mind yet awhile. Then I think it would be of no use if I did, for I couldn't settle to one occupation' (F IX. ii. 729). Three days later he returned to the theme: 'If I can discipline my thoughts into the channel of a story, I have made up my mind to get to work on one: always supposing that I find myself, on the trial, able to do well' (F IX. ii. 729). He hoped to have the 'neck' of 'the anxious toil of a new book . . . well broken' before beginning to publish, say in October or November. But the manifold distractions from which he sought relief crowded in upon him: readings, new editions, Kate, the break with his publishers. In November he once again thought of a new book, perhaps growing out of the paper he had written for the Christmas number of *Household Words*, as it involved 'such an odd idea—which appears to me so humorous, and so available at greater length—that I am debating whether or no I shall . . . make it the Pivot round which my next book shall revolve' (N iii. 74–5). After settling on a name for the journal in January, Dickens tried to settle on a name for his story, trying out BURIED ALIVE ('Does it seem too grim?'), THE THREAD OF GOLD, and THE DOCTOR OF BEAUVAIS.[13] On 11 March, he solved the problem:

This is merely to certify that I have got exactly the name for the story that is wanted; exactly what will fit the opening to a T. A TALE OF TWO CITIES. Also, that I have struck out a rather original and bold idea. That is, at the end of each month to publish the monthly part in the green cover, with the two illustrations, at the old shilling. This will give *All the Year Round* always the interest and precedence of a fresh

think Dickens neglected his editorial duties on the new journal, that 'a case can be made that in the early years of the magazine Dickens presided over something like a truly co-operative novel-publishing venture, that *All the Year Round* offered, for a while at least, a glimpse of the ideal in publisher–novelist relationships' (p. 170).

[13] F IX. ii. 729, dated Mar. 1858 but possibly 1859, as it connects with the next; missing from N iii.

weekly portion during the month; and will give me my old standing with my old public, and the advantage (very necessary in this story) of having numbers of people who read it in no portions smaller than a monthly part. (F IX. ii. 729–30)

Once again Dickens sought some way of combining periodical with serial publication, this time avoiding both the unillustrated one-volume form of *Hard Times* and, at least for some of his audience, the disadvantages of reading the story in what Carlyle called 'Teaspoons' (N iii. 119). In the December 1856 accounts there appears a 'Statement of loss on one and a half sheet numbers at ᵈ6 [sixpence] with one plate: compared with two sheet numbers at ˢ1/- [one shilling] with two plates'. The net loss on an impression of 32,000 copies Bradbury and Evans calculated to be £225. That seemed unsatisfactory. Then along with the December 1858 accounts, which Chapman and Hall must have sent to Dickens in late March or early April 1859 (the balance was deposited to Dickens's account on 7 April (MS. Coutts)), his new publishers provided a new 'Estimate of the cost of producing 30,000 copies of the Monthly Serial to sell at one shilling'. The total, £133. 19s., is one-third of Bradbury and Evans's cost for 31,000 impressions of a number of *Little Dorrit*, but it does not include the cost of binding, the wrapper (paper, printing, or design), or the Advertiser. In the end, *A Tale of Two Cities* appeared in eight as seven shilling numbers with all the usual appurtenances, a good wrapper design by Browne printed on blue paper, and an eight-page Advertiser in each part.

Since Dickens was his own publisher, he could not pay himself extra for the inclusion of a long story, as Bradbury and Evans had done for *Hard Times*. But to compensate he worked his copyright thoroughly. For one thing, there were foreign payments to collect. Simon Nowell-Smith reminds us that 'before the days of international copyright, although an author might enter into a contract with a foreign publisher, he could not sell the foreign rights in his book, for he had none; and for many years after the first international conventions an author might well remain unaware that he now had foreign rights to sell'.[14] Trollope's agreements as late as 1857 made no mention of foreign rights; but after 1858, when he assigned 'the copyright and all rights attaching thereto at home

---

[14] *International Copyright Law*, p. 52.

and abroad' to Chapman and Hall, he became more aware of possible foreign income. Dickens seems to have been particularly quick off the mark in exercising his 'rights', whatever their legal standing. Beginning with the 22 December 1855 issue of *Household Words*, his journals carried the assertion that '*The right of Translating Articles . . . is reserved by the Authors*'. The next year he negotiated his agreement with Hachette, which also covered future novels. Perhaps Dickens taught Chapman and Hall, who then passed the word on to other authors like Trollope.

In another direction, American interest in Dickens continued to grow, and out of that interest a complex set of lucrative agreements emerged. One was the payment by the *New York Ledger* of £1,000 for the story 'Hunted Down' (F VIII. v. 677). Another developed out of meetings with Thomas Coke Evans, an American essayist and journalist, who went to London in January 1859 armed with letters of encouragement from prominent persons assuring Dickens of a warm welcome, to talk him into an American reading tour. At first Dickens was tempted; then other business interfered and he began to learn something of Evans's own situation. Warning Bulwer against taking up a similar offer from Evans in August, Dickens reported that

I have made some private enquiries respecting him in America, and have ascertained that he has no capital whatever, though there seems to be nothing against his character. I have reason to believe that if you made any agreement with him, he would take it to New York, and sell it to the highest bidder there. He is a kind of unaccredited agent, and seeks to live upon what such transactions would yield in the way of profit. (N iii. 115)

Dickens had learned these facts as a result of the other proposition Evans put forward: that Dickens grant him the right to publish *All the Year Round* in America. A verbal agreement was reached before 11 March; on that date, at the conclusion of Dickens's other news about his novel and its appearance in the journal and shilling numbers, he added, 'My American ambassador pays a thousand pounds for the first year, for the privilege of republishing in America one day after we publish here. Not bad?' (F IX. ii. 730). This arrangement seemed so satisfactory that Dickens turned down an alternative proposal from Frederic Chapman (N iii. 96) on 18 March, the day after he signed a contract witnessed by Wills and Wilkie Collins (it is interesting that Forster seems to have taken no part in these negotiations) stipulating the following conditions:

One. Evans has the sole privilege of publishing *All the Year Round* in the United States simultaneously (not 'one day after') with its publication in England, for one year.

Two. Dickens is required to ship one set of stereotype plates, varied as to date and imprint to make them applicable for American publication, and if possible by a different ship one printed copy, of each number at least two weeks before the date of publication in England.

Three. Dickens binds himself to publish in the periodical a continued story to extend over six months.

Four. Evans agrees to pay the cost of plates, printed copies, and shipping each half year, the first payment becoming due on 30 October 1859.

Five. Evans agrees to pay Dickens £1,000 in two instalments, half one month after returning to the States and the other half seven months thereafter.[15]

At first all went swimmingly. Evans, on his return home, dispatched the requisite payment; Wills in turn made arrangements for shipping the stereos on a regular basis.[16] Evans asked for the plates to be sent a week earlier than the contract specified, but Wills could not comply. None the less, Evans went ahead with his arrangements, and correspondence remained friendly until he returned to England in July. But in the meantime Dickens had learned that Evans, lacking capital, had been forced sometime in April 1859 to sell his contract to J. M. Emerson and Company of New York, who thus became, and continued to serve as, the publishers of the Authorized American edition. Thus Dickens could tell Bulwer as part of his warning that Evans had sold his rights to the journal but did not know Dickens knew of it.

By the autumn Evans was having great difficulty meeting the financial terms of his agreement with Dickens, partly because the

[15] See Altick, 'Dickens and America', pp. 331–4.
[16] Gerald G. Grubb, 'Personal and Business Relations of Charles Dickens and Thomas Coke Evans', *Dickensian*, 48 (1952), 106–13, 168–73 *passim*, is the principal source for much of this story, but additional facts are offered in his note on 'The American Edition of "All the Year Round" ', *Publications of the Bibliographical Society of America*, 47 (1953), 301–4, and by Philip Collins in 'The *All the Year Round* Letter Book', *Victorian Periodicals Newsletter*, 10 (Nov. 1970), 23–9.

journal was not selling well. On 28 October Evans owed £589. And its poor sales may be explained in part by another contract into which Dickens entered in the spring. Notwithstanding Evans's exclusive right to publish the journal, Dickens got him to execute another agreement on 1 April permitting Harper's to publish the story simultaneously with its appearance in the journal. A contract ratifying that arrangement was executed by Dickens and Sampson Low and Son, Harper's London agent, on 7 April; it specified that proof sheets were to be delivered to Sampson Low one month in advance. In return, Harper's promised to pay £1,000 in eight instalments beginning 1 May.[17] So Evans, who had stipulated in his contract with Dickens that there should be a continued story in the periodical, knowing that it would be the chief selling point, lost his exclusive rights to it, and could not get Wills to forward stereos to him more than two weeks in advance, though Harper's London agents were to get proof sheets four weeks ahead. In the end, even though Dickens and Wills seem to have considered renewing the agreement for a second year despite some arrears in payments, Evans succumbed to the competition and his own lack of capital, and sold out to Emerson, who negotiated new agreements with Wills that converted the American edition of the journal from January 1860 to a monthly. And Dickens, if all the bills got paid as scheduled, received £1,000 for the journal for the first year, and another £1,000 for his story in the journal.[18]

Whatever their fate in America, both *All the Year Round* and *A Tale of Two Cities* prospered in England. Wills reported to Evans on 19 March that 'Our success here exceeds the most sanguine expectations. One hundred and twenty thousand of No. I have already been sold. We are settling down to a steady current sale of one hundred thousand.'[19] Sales continued to hold up well,

[17] See 'Agreement', in Yale University Library.

[18] Compare Dickens's calculations of the possible profits Bulwer could realize from serializing *A Strange Story* in *All the Year Round*: £1,500 in ready money from the journal, £1,200 from 'an unimpeachable publisher' for the right to republish the instalments in a collected form for two years, beginning a week or two before the end of the serialization, and £300 for early proofs to America for simultaneous publication there (N iii. 194).

[19] Grubb, 'Personal and Business', p. 113 n. Collins ('Letter Book', p. 25) quotes a letter of 28 Apr. 1859 from Wills to Dickens reporting on the sale of the first number (dated Saturday the 30th but on sale the preceding Wednesday, the 27th):

and there was a demand for back numbers which in June reached 35,000 (F IX. ii. 730). Dickens told Forster on 9 July that 'The run upon our monthly parts is surprising', but the figures for those parts are not startlingly large. In fact, it is difficult to account for the poor quality of the plates, none of which was duplicated. Hatton and Cleaver suppose the cause to be 'large initial print-ings',[20] but only 15,000 of I, 10,000 of II, 7,000 of III, and 5,000 of the rest were originally published. More probable cause can be found in Browne's carelessness, Young's failing skill in biting in, or Whiting's unfamiliarity with the whole business of producing serial parts. Perhaps there was additional time pressure as a result of the American contracts. Dickens complained that his poor health and other 'irksome botheration' kept him from getting ahead more than his 'old month's advance' (F IX. ii. 730).

'Nothing but the interest of the subject, and the pleasure of striving with the difficulty of the form of treatment', Dickens told Forster at the end of August, '—nothing in the mere way of money, I mean,—could else repay the time and trouble of the incessant condensation' (F IX. ii. 730). In the way of mere money, he was doing quite well. The first quarter's account showed that *All the Year Round* was able to repay him 'with five per cent. interest, all the money I advanced for its establishment (paper, print &c. all paid, down to the last number), and yet to leave a good £500 balance at the banker's!' (F VIII. v. 672).

On the novel in parts Dickens received quarterly reports from Frederic Chapman, whose firm received bills from Whiting's for the printing and sold and accounted for all copies in return for a commission stipulated at 10 per cent of the sales. All net profits belonged exclusively to Dickens. In the first quarter, of the first

Sold at the office	20,000 odd
To Smith	6,500
Chapman & Hall	22,000—but these *may* be reduced by returns
Wanted for parts (say)	20,000
For Volumes (do.)	5,500
	74,000

say 70,000 because I think your shilling book [*A Tale of Two Cities*] will hit the part sale to that [words illegible]. So you see the 100,000 will hardly be enough to last out the month even if A.Y.R. sells no more than H.W. 1st number did. We are *sure* to sell 20,000 more in numbers . . .

[20] *A Bibliography of the Periodical Works of Charles Dickens* (London, Chapman and Hall, 1933), p. 334.

three numbers, 15,691 were sold by 23 August, and Dickens netted
£145. 13s. 8d.[21] In the next quarter, of the remaining five numbers
16,406 were sold by the end of November, netting £254. 10s. 3d.[22]
On 2 March 1860, Frederic Chapman forwarded the third-quarter
reports to the end of February, explaining as he did so a number
of adjustments which had been made to permit the balance sheets
to look good: 'No 4 to 8 were reprinted in February but I have
not brought in the expenses—they will be charged in the next.
These numbers were also reprinted in August last and are charged
in the present account.'[23] The balance due to Dickens was the
largest yet, £350. 5s. 6d.[24] In addition to sustaining a heavy
reprinting charge, this account is the first to have Chapman and
Hall's commission deducted for the sales in all three quarters,
£141. 8s. 11d. Chapman drew Dickens's attention to one feature
of this deduction: 'You were so good as to say that you would
allow us a commission of 10 per cent, but on referring to the
account you will find that we have made it 7½ per cent as we are
anxious to prove that it is not gain alone that we have at heart in
being your publishers.'[25] That sort of treatment from Dickens's
old firm must have gone far to remove any lingering doubts about
the wisdom of his switch, and to efface any lingering resentment
of the late Mr. Hall's niggling over a few pounds.

iv

The firm to which Dickens returned in 1859 was very different
from the one he had left, at least in so far as current projects were
concerned, in 1844. Then a small outfit chiefly concerned to promote Dickens's interests, it had become a large and prosperous
firm with many other authors to satisfy.

   Almost immediately after their break with Dickens, Chapman
and Hall had tried to capitalize on the discovery of the power of
serial fiction by issuing 'ORIGINAL WORKS OF FICTION
AND BIOGRAPHY' in a monthly series, each work appearing

[21] Deposited 30 Aug. (MS. Coutts).
[22] Deposited 20 Jan. 1860 (MS. Coutts).
[23] Grubb, 'Some Unpublished Correspondence', p. 115.
[24] Deposited 14 Mar. 1860 (MS. Coutts).
[25] Grubb, 'Some Unpublished Correspondence', p. 115. A reprint of 1,000
copies cut the balance due to Dickens on 29 June 1860 to only £32. 18s. (MS.
C & H).

in four monthly parts of 160 pages each costing 3*s*., or the equivalent of a three-decker in two volumes for 12*s*., or bound in cloth for 14*s*. 'This SERIES OF BOOKS is undertaken with the belief', their Prospectus declared,

that while the taste for WORKS OF FICTION has in late years greatly increased, high prices and inconvenient forms of issue have so restricted their sale, that, as well with reference to authors as to readers, a change in the manner of submitting them to the public is generally called for.

Messrs CHAPMAN & HALL acted on this belief nine years ago, when they commenced the publication of the works of a distinguished writer in monthly parts. In the present undertaking it is intended to apply similar resources of issue, on an enlarged scale, to a more extended series.[26]

The effort began bravely enough with novels by Mrs. S. C. Hall and Mrs. Anne Marsh; Thackeray's *Life of Tallyrand* was announced but not apparently issued, although between 1843 and 1846 Chapman and Hall published his two travel books and several Christmas Books; and other biographies and novels appeared. But by September 1846 Chapman and Hall announced the first in a series of strategic withdrawals, abandoning part issue and increasing by 2*s*. each the price of the cloth-bound volumes. Eventually the attempt to break the conventional price and format of the three-deckers was doomed to a 'melancholy' but 'inevitable' defeat, but the venture brought the firm in touch with writers like G. H. Lewes, Marmion W. Savage, and Geraldine Jewsbury. *Alton Locke* and *Mary Barton* were published in the same format and binding, but without any connection to the monthly series. Other authors found their way to the Strand: Charles Lever, Thomas Carlyle, Robert and Elizabeth Barrett Browning, Arthur Hugh Clough, Ainsworth, Mrs. Gaskell, and, in 1858, Anthony Trollope. The firm, as Percy Fitzgerald has observed, 'was infinitely more suited' to Dickens than Bradbury and Evans, whose publishing, as opposed to printing, efforts lay more in the direction of periodicals and journals than literature. Chapman and Hall 'were more flexible, more literary in their *entourage*, and they were always inclined to further [Dickens's] wishes'.[27] But not all of the firm's '*entourage*' were especially happy to hear of Dickens's decision; Lever complained that 'the return of Dickens to C. & H. will make them so entirely *his* as to leave no margin to attend to any other interests'.[28]

About the time of Dickens's break with Bradbury and Evans, Chapman and Hall were reorganizing. Edward Chapman, a product of the country who had never mastered the finer points of book-keeping and general office procedure, had been assisted since Hall's death by his cousin, Frederic. Edward's daughter, later Mrs. Gaye, used to wonder what he did at the office, since whenever she and her mother went to 193 Piccadilly, 'Papa was standing with his back to the fire, and Frederic [was] writing at a table in a big book in the same room'.[29] Gradually Frederic assumed more and more responsibility. On 24 December 1858 the *Bookseller*, 'the leading organ of the publishing trade of Great Britain',[30] carried an announcement that the 'firm of Messrs. Chapman & Hall has been strengthened by the admission of Mr. Frederic Chapman, who has for some years taken an active part in the management'. By 1860 he was listed as equal to Edward in a contract for *Orley Farm*.[31] In the next few years, his ascendancy increased. Edward began talking about building himself a place in the country, at Tunbridge, and retiring from all the harassing details of office work;[32] finally in 1864 he did.

Frederic, on the other hand, relished publishing. 'An excellent fellow', according to Percy Fitzgerald, he was

somewhat blunt and bluff, but straightforward and good-natured. On his shoulders, even when Edward Chapman was alive, lay the burden. He was a tall, burly, rubicund man, and had good business instinct. He had a small but delightful house in Ovington Square, to which some one had added a billiard-room, which he turned into a charming dining-room. What tasty Lucullus-like dinners were given there! I cannot say how he managed the firm, but when Dickens was alive he tried to meet his wishes in every conceivable way.[33]

[27] Percy Fitzgerald, 'Boz and His Publishers', *Dickensian*, 3 (1907), 159.
[28] Lionel Stevenson, *Dr. Quicksilver: The Life of Charles Lever* (1939; reissue New York, Russell and Russell, 1969), p. 238.
[29] Transcription from facsimile of letter in Waugh, facing p. 4.
[30] 'The Circulation of Modern Literature', p. 16.
[31] Nowell-Smith, *International Copyright Law*, p. 53.
[32] Waugh, p. 116.
[33] 'Boz and His Publishers', p. 128.

Frederic brought others into the firm to assist in special ways: Meredith joined in 1860 at under £250 a year as a reader, gradually replacing Forster as literary adviser;[34] and in 1868 Henry Merivale Trollope entered into partnership with Chapman when his father Anthony with £10,000 bought for him a third interest in the firm.[35] Frederic also moved the stock much faster than Edward, offering sizeable discounts for bulk orders, expanding the overseas customers, jobbing off lots to remainder houses, and devising new ways to sell old books. At times Dickens got exasperated with his way of doing business; he complained to Lever in January of 1860 that Frederic 'seems to me to be making holiday one half of his life, and making mistakes the other half, and making money (I suppose) in spite of himself, always' (N iii. 144). But the complaint is embedded in a humorous context, in which Dickens apologizes to Lever for some slip-up about a book, calling Chapman a 'Monstrous Humbug'. He could hardly think ill of a man who voluntarily cut his commission by one-quarter in order to prove that gain was not all he had at heart.

Within a year, Dickens decided that Chapman and Hall should have the opportunity to be his exclusive representatives. Hitherto, he had not acted on Bradbury and Evans's repeated offer to sell their share in his other works, but in the spring of 1861 he instructed the Chapmans to explore the terms, estimating 'the utmost value of the whole of the Copyrights, stereotypes, illustrations, stock, etc., at £10,000'.[36] The Whitefriars gang replied that they considered the value of Dickens's copyrights to be greater to Dickens than to anyone else, and thus that they were entitled to ask more from him than they might get on the open market. Another 'wide mouth' had been opened, but this time Dickens determined to fill it, offering £3,000 for their fourth share. 'We certainly think this a handsome sum', Chapman and Hall concluded, 'and are too glad to find the great value of Mr. Dickens's Copyrights.' Bradbury and Evans agreed after further haggling; the deal was concluded; and then Dickens sold Chapman and Hall this quarter share for £3,250, 'in order that you may be equally interested in the whole issue of my books' (N iii. 217–18). Chapman and Hall paid in

---

[34] Waugh, p. 142.   [35] Trollope, *Letters*, no. 420.
[36] Chapman and Hall to Bradbury and Evans, in Charles J. Sawyer and F. J. Harvey Darton, *Dickens v. Barabbas, Forster Intervening: A Study Based Upon Some Hitherto Unpublished Letters* (London, Charles J. Sawyer, 1930), p. 74; misdated 1867.

three bills, which Dickens held on the understanding that they would be taken up when convenient, and earn interest of 5 per cent payable half-yearly, until then.[37] The bills were not paid during Dickens's lifetime; instead £81. 5s. appears as a credit in the accounts every six months (MS. Coutts). Thereafter half the profit on any Dickens book belonged to the firm; on new serials, however, Dickens reserved to himself the option to make such arrangements as seemed appropriate at the time (F VIII. v. 670).

Between the close of *Little Dorrit* and the sale of all their stock to Chapman and Hall, Bradbury and Evans had done comparatively little business with Dickens. Of the more than £43,000 which Dickens had earned on their joint publications, only about £1,200 came between 1 July 1857 and 31 December 1861; in June 1859 he actually owed them £329. 10s. for the only time in the entire history of their association. Winding up their relations was therefore not terribly difficult—the only current project was the marginally successful Library edition—but it did take time to count up the stock of every single book under Bradbury and Evans's supervision, a total of twenty-six which included original and cheap editions of the serials and Christmas Books from *The Chimes* to *Little Dorrit*, the reading editions, their volumes of the Library edition, and a few others. The accounts were closed on 31 May 1861, but inventory and the balance due to Dickens were not rendered until the new year.[38] Some time before the end of December, however, the stock on hand was transferred to Chapman and Hall, who re-inventoried it and found significant shortages, 251 8vo quires of *Dombey* numbers, 86 of *Bleak House*, 174 of *Copperfield*, and others, as well as overages, including 210 extra numbers of the parts issue of *Oliver Twist* and twenty-six additional volumes of the Library edition. The net shortage amounted to £103. 10s. at wholesale prices less discounts; subtracting Bradbury and Evans's quarter share, Dickens owed £77. 12s. 6d. which Chapman and Hall deducted from his balance. The figures in themselves are unimportant, and the total is not large. Nor is it surprising that there should be such mistakes in stock-taking, considering all the difficulties of accounting for every stray unsold copy at every distribution point and preventing any error in

---

[37] See unpublished letter to Ouvry, 15 Oct. 1862, Huntington Library.

[38] Bradbury and Evans gave the cheque for £102. 1s. 4d. to Wills, who paid it to Dickens's account on 30 Jan.; see N iii. 284, MS. B & E, and MS. Coutts.

reckoning or pilferage or wastage in two different warehouses and during transfer. What the discrepancy does reveal, however, is the extent to which all the inventories in these accounts, so apparently precise, are in fact only approximate, and constantly shifting. There are a few places where the total stock for a particular title remaining in one accounting period does not tally with the stock on hand at the beginning of the next, but the transfer to Chapman and Hall is the most substantial instance of these ever-present discrepancies. Even the most exact figures in the accounts must be used with caution.

Frederic Chapman's ability to dispose of large quantities at a time certainly complicated stock-taking. In the late 1850s the Cheap edition sailed along: 215,000 numbers sold in 1858, 285,000 in 1859, and 315,000 in 1860. Reprints for stock were correspondingly heavy, but every half-year showed a profit. In 1861 the book market was again disturbed, this time by the Civil War, and as a consequence the profit on the Cheap edition fell to a scant £138. 10s. 2d.: 'The Cheap Editions did not sell at all up to their average during the half year', Frederic Chapman reported to Dickens in a letter of 10 October accompanying the Midsummer accounts, 'and this in consequence of the wretched state of trade'. Sales in the first half were more than 50 per cent off the previous year's pace, but they picked up somewhat in the second half, to reach 193,000 for the year.

The Library edition, on the other hand, appeared an incorrigibly feeble product. The publishers' records do not bear out Walter Dexter's contention that it was 'a great success; the comparatively slim volumes were more easily handled than the bulky original editions, and the print was considerably larger and clearer. So great was the success, that in February, 1861, it was decided to publish a monthly issue containing all the original illustrations'.[39] On the contrary, by the end of 1860 only 17,400 volumes, or about 791 complete sets, had been sold in England and America; of these, Ticknor paid for 5,700 volumes with special American titles and vignettes, but may not have retailed them at all.[40] So

---

[39] 'The "Library," "Peoples," and "Charles Dickens" Editions', *Dickensian*, 40 (1944), 186.

[40] James T. Fields tried to get Dickens to come to America under his auspices when it looked as though Evans's proposal would fall through (N iii. 112–13); Dickens postponed acting on the idea until it was too late—America was in turmoil over the election of 1860 and the resulting Civil War. Thus Ticknor and

during the spring of 1861 Frederic Chapman tried a new expedient. He reprinted *Pickwick*, *Nickleby*, and *Chuzzlewit*, each in
two volumes, and for the first time printed the plates from the
original editions. He then bound up 6,550 volumes, better than
1,000 sets of the six books, and sold them for 4s. 2d. to New York,
5s. 4d. otherwise, 25 as 24, and for 7s. 6d. each retail. He took
a considerable risk: including the deficit of £545. 7s. carried
forward from the last account, his expenses for the six months
amounted to £1,527. But the reward was greater: 'The Library
Edition has paid off its debt', he told Dickens, 'and left a balance
of £113'.[41] All but 100 of the volumes had been taken, and though
there were heavy expenses in subsequent years reprinting the
volumes and making up the plates (some of which were newly
designed for the issue), the illustrated Library edition continued
in the black throughout Dickens's lifetime.[42] Sales consistently ran
better than 5,000 volumes per year; and after 1864 they rose into
the tens of thousands. Concurrently, the wholesale price per
volume, especially to America, dropped further and further, to
1s. 7d. in the late 1860s. On a volume of 27,000-odd copies in
December 1867 and again in June 1868,[43] the gross mounted to
a high of £2,398. 6s. 8d. and the net to £630. 12s. 5d.[44] Large
volume at big discounts: Frederic Chapman applied the formula
to books, and it worked.

v

There were still various difficulties with the journals, and various
experiments were attempted to solve them. To give *All the Year*

Fields lost for the time being the chance to work off their stock as a consequence of
the publicity attending another Dickens American tour. Perhaps anticipating such
a tour, the American writer and painter Thomas Buchanan Read, using an introduction he had obtained from Fields, requested permission to paint Dickens's
portrait, but Dickens refused him in Oct. 1860 (Altick, 'Dickens and America',
pp. 335–6).

[41] Frederic Chapman to Dickens, 10 Oct. 1861, MS. C & H, and Grubb, 'Some
Unpublished Correspondence', p. 118.

[42] Not to be confused with the Illustrated Library edition, issued by Chapman
and Hall from 1873; see Kathleen Tillotson's Introduction to the Clarendon
Twist, p. xxix; and Margaret Cardwell's Introduction to *Edwin Drood* (Oxford,
Clarendon Press, 1972), p. xxxii, n. 3.

[43] Ticknor and Fields laid in 2,000 sets of the edition, by now twenty-six
volumes with the inclusion of *A Tale of Two Cities*, *Great Expectations*, and the
two-volume *Our Mutual Friend*.

[44] Both Dec. 1867; reprints cut into profits the following year.

Round a boost even when it did not contain a continued narrative by him, Dickens composed occasional pieces under the title 'The Uncommercial Traveller'. A *6s.* crown 8vo volume of these essays appeared, in an edition of 1,500, and sold out by December 1860; a second edition of 1,000 and part of a third edition of 500 were sold by the end of 1861. Thereafter the book lay virtually dormant till 1870, although Dickens wrote several more essays in the series in 1863, and added it to the Cheap edition in 1865.[45]

A second problem was the back stock of *Household Words*, for which Chapman and Hall had paid Dickens £2,500. The *Bookseller*, reporting on Dickens's purchase at auction of the *Household Words* stock, 650,000 numbers plus the Christmas numbers and stereos, predicted that it had considerable commercial potential: 'As a set of books there will always be a demand for the work; and if at once offered at a moderate price, we have no doubt that 1,000 or 1,500 sets could be disposed of.'[46] Their view, alas, was too sanguine; the dust settled ever more thickly on the unsold sheets, decomposing in a warehouse. 'Have you any objection to our trying to sell the Household Words?' Frederic queried on 10 October 1861. 'We cannot make it move, and independent of the sum we gave for it we have now expended £800 in making the stock up and have not in all realized so much in sales.'[47] With the fierce competition from *All the Year Round*, *Once a Week*, and the *Cornhill*, it is no wonder that back issues of the now defunct journal were not selling briskly. One wonders why the *Bookseller* ever expected they would, since most of the fiction originally published in *Household Words* had subsequently been reprinted in some other form. Dickens, however, seems to have objected to Chapman's proposal; presumably he did not like the idea of seeing his old journal remaindered in bulk or scrapped in some degrading way. A year later, however, Chapman returned to the subject. 'I am anxious to have a few minutes talk with you when in town, as to the reissuing of the Household Words in half vols or some such form; for as it is we are doing but very little with it, in fact not enough to pay for the interest of the purchase—and I am most anxious not to do anything without your sanction.'[48] Apparently

---

[45] See the Nonesuch volume *Reprinted Pieces, The Uncommercial Traveller, and Other Stories* (Bloomsbury, Nonesuch Press, 1938).
[46] 25 May 1859, p. 924.
[47] Grubb, 'Some Unpublished Correspondence', pp. 118–19.
[48] Ibid., p. 120.

Dickens never sanctioned doing anything, though Ward, Lock, & Tyler published between 1868 and 1873 a cheap reissue in monthly parts and half-crown volumes 'printed from the original stereotyped plates', with the original announcements and advertisements omitted and some textual alterations.[49]

The most serious problem arising in connection with *All the Year Round* in the early 1860s was its fluctuating sales. Dickens knew that he had to continue publishing an original story in each issue, and took pains to inform his readers of this plan. At the conclusion of *A Tale of Two Cities*, in column one, page 95 of the 26 November 1859 issue, appears the following notice:

We purpose always reserving the first place in these pages for a continuous original work of fiction, occupying about the same amount of time in its serial publication, as that which is just completed. The second story of our series we now beg to introduce to the attention of our readers. It will pass, next week, into the station hitherto occupied by A Tale of Two Cities. And it is our hope and aim, while we work hard at every other department of our journal, to produce, in this one, some sustained works of imagination that may become a part of English literature.

Immediately thereafter Wilkie Collins's *The Woman in White* began. Dickens planned to follow Collins with a new novel by George Eliot;[50] but she decided against serializing her story and advertised it for sale by Blackwood's instead. Though she had definitely put out of mind writing anything for Dickens by 18 November 1859,[51] he was surprised to discover the following February that 'Adam (or Eve) Bede is terrified by the novel difficulties of serial writing' and was not going to 'be up to the scratch when Collins's sponge is thrown up' (N iii. 151). Consequently he asked Lever to jump into the breach with a new story beginning in July, and Lever complied. Collins's story occupied more space than expected: the penultimate instalment appeared in the 18 August issue, along with the beginning of Lever's tale and an explanation by Dickens of what was happening. Collins had the first page in the next issue, finishing his story at last; and Lever came along later in the number. But thereafter, starting with the

[49] Lohrli, p. 50.

[50] See his letter to George Henry Lewes, 14 Nov. 1859, in *The George Eliot Letters*, ed. Gordon S. Haight (7 vols., New Haven, Yale Univ. Press, 1954–5), iii. 203–4.

[51] *Journal* entry in *The George Eliot Letters*, iii. 205.

number for 1 September, *A Day's Ride: A Life's Romance* had
pride of place, serving as the lead story week after week.

It was deadly dull, and Dickens feared, then saw confirmed, a
drop in sales (N iii. 183–4). At the beginning of October he took
counsel and decided to do something drastic to arrest the slippage.
Everyone agreed that a new story by him was the only solution.
He had considered returning to the old twenty numbers, but concluded instead that he must recast his novel into weekly snippets,
and begin no later than the first of December, scarcely two months
away (N iii. 182). He explained his reasoning at length to Forster
on 6 October:

> The sacrifice of *Great Expectations* is really and truly made for myself.
> The property of *All the Year Round* is far too valuable, in every way, to
> be much endangered. Our fall is not large, but we have a considerable
> advance in hand of the story we are now publishing, and there is no
> vitality in it, and no chance whatever of stopping the fall; which on the
> contrary would be certain to increase. Now, if I went into a twenty-
> number serial, I should cut off my power of doing anything serial here
> for two good years—and that would be a most perilous thing. On the
> other hand, by dashing in now, I come in when most wanted; and if
> Reade and Wilkie follow me, our course will be shaped out hand-
> somely and hopefully for between two and three years. A thousand
> pounds are to be paid for early proofs of the story to America. (F IX.
> iii. 733–4)

And in a diplomatic letter of the same date, which must have been
tricky to write, Dickens informed Lever of his decision to run in
tandem. (In fact, *Great Expectations* supplanted *A Day's Ride* on the
first page of the journal.) As soon as he could, given the fact that
proofs were readied for America weeks in advance, Dickens announced his forthcoming story, in hopes of holding the audience
that he saw weekly slipping away.[52]

Thus though there are some indications that Dickens had been
thinking about the theme of *Great Expectations* for a while, both
the timing and the form of the story were once again determined
by economic considerations. 'From a strictly commercial point of
view', Edgar Rosenberg comments in his exuberant 'Preface to
Great Expectations', 'necessity, it would appear, was never more

---

[52] First notice in the issue of 27 Oct. 1860. Eager to reassure his readers, Dickens
announced the termination date of Lever's novel seven weeks early, on 9 Feb.
1861.

pressingly the mother of invention than in producing Pip and Magwitch and Joe: their incubation period seems to have been uniquely brief. If Dickens had any long-range premeditations about the novel, he kept them to himself; but there is no evidence that he had.'[53]

Dickens complained at least as much as usual about the labour of writing; and he suffered from ill health through most of the winter. Of such scraps of correspondence as have survived, Edgar Rosenberg reports, nearly half 'are little more than the self-satisfied noises of the buoyant merchandiser'.[54] To Mary Boyle in December Dickens writes: 'Pray read Great Expectations. I think it is very droll. It is a very great success, and seems universally liked' (N iii. 196). In January, February, and April 1861 he utters similar 'slightly shrill Odes to a Balance Sheet';[55] from all accounts the novel did succeed in arresting the slide and gaining new readers for *All the Year Round*. Whether Dickens's revised ending represents a concession to popular demand or more sensitively resolves the novel's themes is debatable; but it is difficult to see the grounds for the decision being economic, as the journal had already recovered its circulation well before the end of the novel, the manuscript of which in any case was completed ahead of time because of the American publishing agreements.

vi

Perhaps the most extraordinary testimony to the popularity of *Great Expectations* appears not in the ledgers of *All the Year Round*, nor even in the reviews, which hailed the restoration of Dickens's humour, but in the number, size, and kind of editions on both sides of the Atlantic that appeared within a few months of the novel's serialization. In the autumn of 1860 Tauchnitz evidently asked whether Dickens had plans to continue *The Uncommercial Traveller*, for in Dickens's reply he explains that the series had been brought to a close for now 'because I am about to produce in *All the Year Round* a new serial story of my own writing, which will be continued every week for nine months'. In another letter dated 21 November Dickens is able to be more explicit about the length

[53] Sub-titled 'The Pale Usher Dusts His Lexicons', *Dickens Studies Annual*, 2 (1972), 308.
[54] Ibid., p. 313.
[55] Ibid.

of his work: 'It will be four or five weekly numbers longer than *A Tale of Two Cities*.' Tauchnitz returned a hearty welcome at this news, and asked Dickens to name his price for advance sheets. But Dickens demurred. 'I cannot consent to name the sum you shall pay for *Great Expectations*', he replied on 22 December. 'I have too great a regard for you and too high a sense of your honourable dealing, to wish to depart from the custom we have always observed. Whatever price you put upon it will satisfy me. You have always proposed the terms yourself, on former occasions, and I entreat you to do so now.' On 4 January 1861 Dickens signed and returned a 'perfectly satisfactory' agreement, and *Great Expectations* then appeared in Tauchnitz's Series of English Writers.[56] In America the novel ran in *Harper's Weekly* from 24 November 1860 (a week ahead of *All the Year Round*, which technically jeopardized his English copyright)[57] to 3 August 1861, then was published by Harper's in two volumes, 12mo cloth, with illustrations by John McClenan; by James Gregory, also of New York, in a two-volume 'Household Edition'; and in two editions by T. B. Peterson and Brothers, the first a one-volume unillustrated paperback, and a later one-volume with McClenan's illustrations. Evidently Peterson had made arrangements with Harper's, since the paperback edition claims to have been 'Printed from the manuscript and early proof-sheets purchased from the author, for which Charles Dickens has been paid in cash, the sum of one thousand pounds sterling.'[58] The text, like all other foreign 1861 editions, follows *All the Year Round*.[59]

[56] All letters quoted in Kurt Otto, *Der Verlag Bernhard Tauchnitz, 1837–1912* (Leipzig [Tauchnitz], 1912), p. 56.

[57] Cf. Jones, p. 163: United States copyright law, by 1891, 'required that in order to secure American copyright the book had to be registered by deposit of the title-page before publication, and a copy of the book had to be deposited within a stated period after publication (between 1870 and 1891 within ten days after publication). However, in order to secure British copyright, first publication had to be in Britain, so that a publisher wishing to secure both British copyright for the English author, and American copyright for the American publisher to whom he had sold the rights, had to plan according to an extremely tight schedule.'

[58] See Herman Le Roy Edgar and R. W. G. Vail, 'Early American Editions of the Works of Charles Dickens', *Bulletin of the New York Public Library*, 33 (1929), 302–19. I cannot with any assurance identify this payment; the largest single deposit in the Coutts Account from Oct. 1860 to 31 Dec. 1861 is for £899. 19s. 9d., entered 13 Nov. 1860 'per Letter'.

[59] See Rosenberg, p. 376, n. 13.

In England, Chapman warily anticipated a small sale in bound form, ordering from Whiting's a printing of only 1,000 copies of the 'first edition' in three volumes, compared with 5,000 of the one-volume *Hard Times*. That appeared in July, and was quickly taken up; so was a second edition of 750 published in August; a third of like size in late August (N iii. 233); a fourth of 500 in September; and part of a fifth of 750 issued towards the end of October. Edgar Rosenberg, after collating three different editions, infers 'that these were all printed at a single impression and published by Chapman & Hall in the succeeding months with misleading title-pages, proclaiming them to be new editions in order to imply (and encourage) a rapid sale'. He goes on to speculate that 'Chapman may have deliberately overprinted the first edition but in view of the dubious market potential kept the publication of the early "editions" fairly small, supplying new bindings-up as the need for new issues arose'.[60] In the issues he collated, the same misprints persist.

Rosenberg's is but one in a long chain of hypotheses advanced by John C. Eckel, Winterich and Randall, John Carter, and Michael Sadleir to answer the question, 'Is there any sound explanation for the rarity of the first edition' of *Great Expectations* in three-volume form?[61] There may be no explanation other than chance for the lack of surviving copies for some of the editions, but the publishers' records quite clearly refute certain hypotheses, and general Victorian usage of the term 'edition' rescues Chapman from any imputation of dishonesty. After the type was reset for the first three-volume edition, Whiting's cast stereos; the charge for 'Composition, machining, & coldpressing' the first edition comes to £117. 10s. 1d.; thereafter Whiting's had only to machine and press for a new edition, so the charge drops to £37. 15s. 3d. for 750 copies, and to £26. 16s. 6d. for 500. Stereotyping was such a usual procedure with Dickens's works by this time that it may have been done without much consideration; on the other hand, the enthusiasm with which the serial had been greeted encouraged some hopes of a sustained volume sale. And though the subsequent editions were printed from these stereos, accounting for some at least of the deterioration in type between the first and fifth editions, Chapman and Hall's use of the word 'edition' has behind it the

[60] Rosenberg, p. 376, n. 13.
[61] See *The New Colophon*, 1 (1948), 402; 2 (1949), 84–5, 278–9.

sanction of Vice-Chancellor Page, who in deciding *Reade* v. *Bentley* in 1858 declared that 'A new "edition" is published whenever, having in his storehouse a certain number of copies, the publisher issues a fresh batch of them to the public'.[62] The flexible terminology of the time, Richard Altick observes, 'permitted publishers, especially in their advertising, to count every fresh impression, no matter how small, as a new edition'.[63]

There is one other feature of this issue of *Great Expectations* worthy of remark, and it explains the rarity of first editions. Three volumes post 8vo for 31*s.* 6*d.* is surely not a format predictable from anything which had gone before in Dickens's life. No other work of his had been issued in that form at that price. On the contrary, Dickens seems to have explored ways of producing his books in less expensive forms—the Cheap edition, the estimate for sixpenny numbers, the one-volume *Hard Times*. And if he was going to issue *Great Expectations* in some other format, why not the old monthly shilling numbers for which he originally designed the novel, and in which he continued to calculate?[64] Sadleir supposes, although it is 'the purest guesswork', that Chapman and Hall printed a large initial edition on the basis of Dickens's reputation and then 'found that the Dickens public looked for him in parts and then in a single 8vo volume and did not care for him as an illustrated three-decker'.[65] The great bibliographer and collector nods here: *Great Expectations* was *not* illustrated in 1861. John Carter comes nearer the mark with a rather more inspired guess: 'We may draw some deductions from the fact that *Great Expectations*, having been serialised in *All the Year Round*, was then put out not in part-issue form, for a large *buying* public, but as a three-decker, for the *borrowing* public—surely in itself (*pace* Mr. Sadleir) evidence of some lack of optimism in the author or his publisher.'[66] The distinction between the borrowing and the buying public is an important one, as this whole study has been at pains to show; but here their interests for once combined. John C. Eckel wins the prize with the correct answer, first offered in 1913 and reaffirmed in 1932, though obviously ignored by the

[62] Nowell-Smith, *International Copyright Law*, pp. 16–17.
[63] 'Nineteenth-Century English Best-Sellers: A Further List', *Studies in Bibliography*, 22 (1969), 199.
[64] See the long and interesting discussion by Edgar Rosenberg on this point, pp. 321–6.
[65] *New Colophon*, 2 (1949), 84.   [66] Ibid., p. 279.

other bibliographers: 'nearly the entire first edition was bought up by the libraries'.[67] The Chapman and Hall accounts record for the first time in their association with Dickens the impressive power of the circulating libraries, which were to dictate the format and content of fiction for the next thirty years. Fourteen hundred copies of the three-volume issue of *Great Expectations*, probably most of the first and over half of the second edition, were purchased by the Leviathan Mudie at 16*s*. 8*d*. a copy for a total of £1,166. 13*s*. 4*d*. It is likely that the three-volume format was selected solely because of Mudie's interest, and the novel's inclusion in 'the largest circulating library in the world', to quote an 1863 issue of the *Spectator*, significantly enlarged Dickens's readership, since Mr. Mudie estimated that 'every book finds, on an average, thirty readers—considerably more, in the majority of instances, as regards novels'.[68] No wonder that so many first editions are, in the words of Eckel, 'nothing but mutilated and badly soiled book waifs'.[69]

The enormous popularity of *Great Expectations*, then, can be measured by the fact that it sustained a large readership in *All the Year Round* (perhaps 100,000 copies sold weekly), then circulated (as few others of Dickens's works seem to have done) through the lending libraries, and still was in demand for an exceptionally high price as Dickens's serials go. And there are yet further editions published in England within two years of the novel's serialization: in November 1862 Chapman completely reset the type in one volume for the Library edition, post 8vo with vignette title for 7*s*. 6*d*., which sold 300 copies to George Robertson and Co. of Melbourne, the chief Australian wholesaler who maintained a London office, and 1,695 copies (25 as 24) for 5*s*. 6*d*. wholesale. For this edition Marcus Stone drew eight banal illustrations for £42, which Dalziel engraved for an additional £50. 8*s*.[70]

---

[67] *First Editions*, rev. and enl. (1932), p. 91. Percy Fitzgerald makes the same point in a note on p. 205 of *Memories of Charles Dickens* (Bristol, J. W. Arrowsmith Ltd.), which appeared in the same year as Eckel's original *First Editions* (1913), and since portions of Fitzgerald's text are close to articles appearing in the *Dickensian* as far back as 1907, he may deserve the palm. (Information kindly supplied by Edgar Rosenberg.)

[68] 'The Circulation of Modern Literature', p. 17.

[69] *First Editions* (1913), p. 91.

[70] The costs of these plates, £92. 8*s*., appear in the June 1863 accounts. On 8 Sept. Dickens told Chapman he had 'looked over the accounts of midsummer', and thought that the charge 'for the illustrations to the unpublished library

A crown 8vo cheap edition appeared in a printing of 5,000 in November 1863, but by that time demand was finally drying up: half the copies remained unsold at the end of the year.

vii

Whether in it for gain or not, Dickens's publishers, and Dickens himself, were having a good time.[71] Frederic Chapman complained about the 'wretched state of trade' (10 October 1861), claimed that the half-year to 30 June 1862 was 'about the worse [*sic*] in my recollection', fussed about the cost of reprints, fumed again in the autumn of 1866 about 'how bad business has been during the half year'.[72] But the balance sheets tell a very different story: from semi-annual payments of under £200 in the 1850s they rise to £300, then £500, and after June 1864 to more than £1,000. Dickens's expenses kept pace, of course: the cheques flew off in every direction, to pay for house bills, gas and water, Kate's quarterly allowance, wine and spirits at Justerini and Brooks, for rates, stabling, sundries, servants' wages, the children's allowances, for insurance policy premiums, for investments (mainly in 3 per cents), for club memberships at the Athenaeum and the Garrick, for charities, for taxes: 'For The Chancellor of the Exchequer. On account of Income Tax. By one who is sorry he ever did it.'[73] The deposits for the year ending 24 June 1864 mounted to just short of £10,000, and the expenses kept pace: they hovered at that level for the next four years, then crept up to £12,000 or £13,000.

'At the present day', Gladstone told his wife in 1864, 'money goes much further in three important items—books, clothes, and journeys.'[74] As far as books were concerned, a reduction of the import duty on foreign papers in 1860 led to a sudden increase in

edition of Great Expectations had best stand as it does' (N iii. 361). In the Dec. 1864 accounts there stands a charge for stereotyping the novel, and 1,000 copies of the text and eight engravings.

[71] So were others engaged in the trade. Charles Knight estimates 'literary returns' in 1864 at £4,000,000 (*Passages of a Working Life During Half a Century: With a Prelude of Early Reminiscences* (3 vols., London, Bradbury and Evans, 1864–5), iii. 183.

[72] Grubb, 'Some Unpublished Correspondence', pp. 118, 119 (8 Sept. 1862), and 122 (15 Sept. 1866).

[73] Unpublished, Huntington Library, dated 8 June 1864.

[74] Quoted in Philip Magnus, *Gladstone: A Biography* (New York, E. P. Dutton, 1954), pp. 145–6.

their importation; English manufacturers met the competition by reducing their own prices 10 per cent.[75] Then the paper duty was abolished, though Gladstone had a difficult time getting his bill through the Commons in 1860, and an equally difficult time getting it through the Lords in 1861. (When it was first defeated, Queen Victoria told the King of the Belgians that its rejection was '*a very good thing*'.) Announcing its abolition at the conclusion of *Great Expectations* in *All the Year Round*, Dickens promised that 'The repeal of the Duty on Paper will enable us greatly to improve the quality of the material on which All the Year Round is printed, and therefore to enhance the mechanical clearness and legibility of these pages. Of the Literature to which we have a new encouragement to devote them, it becomes us to say no more than that we believe it would have been simply impossible, when paper was taxed, to make the present announcement', namely, that a new romance by Bulwer (*A Strange Story*), and then a serial by Collins (*No Name*) were to follow. Whether Dickens could take advantage of the second of Gladstone's three items the record does not reveal, but photographs indicate that the splendid waistcoats and gorgeous velvets of an earlier period had given way to sober colours, baggy trousers, and stiffly starched white shirts. What he did to take advantage of the third, cheaper transportation, involves nearly every aspect of Dickens's career, and is completely bound up with the final decade of his life.

75 Plant, pp. 335–6.

15

'The End'

... the railway, and the telegraph, and the penny
postage, by bringing near to us a vast world beyond
our own limited circles, and giving us a present
interest in the transactions of the most distant regions,
enormously increase the number of readers, and of
themselves create a literature.

Blackwood's Edinburgh Magazine, January 1859[1]

i

IN THE LAST DECADE OF DICKENS'S LIFE, improvements
in transportation and communication contributed largely and
variously to his phenomenal popularity. To speak of the most
obvious improvement first, the ease of rail travel in the 1860s
made it possible for him to take his readings throughout the
British Isles and across America in a degree of comfort and regularity unknown a score of years earlier. Gone were the overheated
draughty carriages, the floors tessellated with phlegm, the plumes
of soot drifting into open windows, the unreliable schedules.
Though Dickens developed 'a now invincible dislike' to railway
travel after the Staplehurst accident in 1865 (F XII. i. 845), and
only consented to the last readings on the condition that no train
journeys be required (F XI. i. 805), he seems to have taken pretty
much for granted the increased mobility he and his friends enjoyed, and perhaps he never thought how much easier it was for
publishers to forward their wares to other cities now that railways
had come of age.

Transatlantic passages also became speedier, cheaper, and more

[1] 'Popular Literature—the Periodical Press', p. 98. I am extremely grateful to
my research assistant, Jean Eros, for bringing to my attention this important essay,
which appears in three consecutive instalments beginning in Jan. 1859.

dependable.[2] It was now possible for Wills to make arrangements for stereos of the numbers of *All the Year Round* to be shipped to America weekly, only a few weeks ahead of publication, and for American publishers, at the receiving end, to organize their whole effort around the regular receipt of those shipments. Dickens benefited from other improvements in communication in America during and after the Civil War: roads and rail lines were repaired and extended, more telegraph cable was strung, and by 1860 a transcontinental railway track was laid.[3] Commerce and communications were thus facilitated. The Boston to Washington corridor experienced a long boom between 1861 and 1873;[4] publishers, booksellers, newspapers, and authors shared in the general affluence. Harper's could shell out over a thousand pounds for a novel serialized elsewhere; others could outbid even Harper's. The Hon. Benjamin Wood, New York State Senator and newspaper publisher with a reputation for fast dealing, commissioned a short story, 'George Silverman's Explanation', in the spring of 1867. Dickens sent his manuscript to America with his reading tour Manager, George Dolby, who at the very moment he was about to leave New York finally received from Wood a bag supposedly containing the agreed-upon price, £1,000. Too hurried and suspicious to complete the transaction on the spot, Dolby turned over the manuscript and coins to Ticknor and Fields; something evidently went wrong, for the story eventually appeared in three instalments in the *Atlantic Monthly*, from January to March 1868. For the same sum, paid in full, Ticknor and Fields bought 'A Holiday Romance'; the series of four stories, purportedly written by children, ran in their children's magazine, *Our Young Folks*, in January, March, April, and May of the same year.[5]

It was not only to and in America that travel was easier. Exchange of persons and parcels throughout Europe increased at an

[2] See George Rogers Taylor, *The Transportation Revolution, 1815–1860*, The Economic History of the United States, vol. 4 (New York and Toronto, Rinehart, 1951), pp. 146–7.
[3] Dickens arranged to notify Ellen Ternan through Wills by means of a telegraph code if she could join him in America during his second reading tour (J, p. 1076).
[4] Edward C. Kirkland, *Industry Comes of Age*, The Economic History of the United States, vol. 6 (New York, Holt, Rinehart and Winston, 1961), pp. 2–4.
[5] See F IX. vi. 745; J, pp. 1071–2; and Herman Le Roy Edgar and R. W. G. Vail, 'Early American Editions of the Works of Charles Dickens', *Bulletin of the New York Public Library*, 33 (1929), 318.

ever accelerating rate. One consequence was the need for some kind of international copyright agreement to replace the plethora of complex and ill-assorted bilateral ones. We need not dwell on the long and complicated history of these agreements, clearly traced by Simon Nowell-Smith,[6] except to note that Dickens did become more and more aware of his foreign revenues, placing a notice reserving to himself the right of translation on the wrappers of all serials after *Copperfield*, as well as on the back page of his journals. Hachette and Tauchnitz were the principal foreign houses authorized to issue Dickens's works in translation; but there were many other translations, mostly unauthorized, and mostly published without any kind of payment to the original author.[7]

Frederic Chapman was quick to exploit the potential of these burgeoning foreign markets. In March 1866 he explained to Dickens that he had spent in the preceding half-year over £3,000 in reprints of the Cheap and Library editions: 'I find that it is necessary to keep a larger stock than we have been in the habit of keeping as I expect to receive frequent orders from America.'[8] The Library edition was sold in quantity throughout the sixties to Ticknor and Fields, Scribner's, Appleton, Little and Brown, and Lippincott. And this American demand was all the more remarkable when one recalls that in 1851 the Philadelphia firm of T. B. Peterson and Brothers bought from Carey, Lea and Blanchard, Stringer and Townsend, Jesper Harding, G. P. Putnam, and Harper's all the stereos, steels, and woodcuts 'that had ever been printed' in America, and had issued by 1867 twenty-three different uniform collected editions of Dickens's works ranging in price from twenty-five cents to $5.00 a volume.[9] Australia became a steady customer, not only for the Library edition, but for thousands of copies of the Charles Dickens edition, and Dickens's popularity down under led in 1862 to his considering a reading tour there by which he might clear £10,000 to £12,000 (F VIII. vi. 693 and n.). While Canada and India are not directly repre-

---

[6] *International Copyright Law*, *passim*, esp. ch. 3; see also the splendidly detailed story of the failure to obtain an Anglo-American agreement told by Barnes, *Authors, Publishers and Politicians*.

[7] As late as 1869 Dickens, in an unpublished letter in the Huntington Library, refused to deal with translators in countries that did not recognize his copyright.

[8] Grubb, 'Some Unpublished Correspondence', p. 122.

[9] Letter from Peterson to George W. Childs, published in the *Publishers' Circular* of 1 June 1867, and reprinted as an Appendix in Mackenzie, p. 4.

sented in the accounts, some copies of these editions surely found their way into bookshops there and elsewhere in the colonies, even granted all the problems about colonial sale; one recalls Dickens's 'splendid' reception in Toronto and Montreal as early as 1842.

Nearer at home, another aspect of railway travel contributed its share to Dickens's coffers. Literate Englishmen and women found themselves on trains for long stretches of time with nothing to do. What could be more reasonable than to pass the time reading a good book? So at least thought several enterprising businessmen in the later 1840s. Some of the railway companies pensioned off disabled employees by granting them the right to set up station stalls for vending books, papers, sweets, and other sundries. These establishments were often messy, and the men who ran them were frequently illiterate, but they made money: a Mr. Gibbs had Euston for £60 a year, and seems to have considered it a good bargain, though he may not have liked the competition that opened in 1848. In that year, W. H. Smith II offered for all the London and North Western stations at £1,500 per annum; in November the firm secured the stations of the Midland Company for £350 a year. There were obvious advantages to the railway companies in having one owner and uniform shops replacing the previous assortment of vendors. And there were immense possibilities for Smith, who within three years had expanded his thriving business to include railway advertising. A notice in the *Illustrated London News* of 22 March 1851 announced that the firm was willing to accept bills and advertisements for one, three, six, and twelve months, for one or more of the 188 stations on the London and North Western Railway, which carried around 6,000,000 passengers a year.[10]

An enterprising dealer in remainder stock named Routledge, 'Jack the Giant-Killer' as Henry Sotheran called him, also saw opportunity in the railway business. Routledge had started out as a rival to 'Napoleonic Bohn', the king of the Remainders; but after 1843 he found the semi-annual trade sales at the Albion poor bargains, so he went into publishing.[11] In the same year that Smith opened in Euston and elsewhere, Routledge issued the first volume of his Railway Library: James Fenimore Cooper's *The Pilot* in

[10] G. R. Pocklington and F. E. K. Foat, *The Story of W. H. Smith & Son* (London, printed for private circulation, 1937), pp. 10–13.

[11] Mumby, pp. 25–7.

fancy boards for a shilling. Within a few years novels especially published for sale at railway bookstalls were a thriving adjunct of several publishers' standard lines.[12] W. H. Smith, for instance, purchased the copyrights of Lever's novels in 1854 and began issuing them in 2s. reprints under Chapman and Halls' imprint.[13] By 1862, railway novels had spread to France; Dickens noticed his books in every station he entered.[14]

With his experience of publishing for Smith, it is not surprising that Frederic Chapman thought of exploiting the railway market for Dickens. In the spring of 1865 Chapman and Hall began issuing, monthly, reprints from stereotype plates of the Cheap edition. Virtue and Co. did the actual printing; and where the longer novels required dividing into two volumes, they sometimes had to reset the type at the point of division. The volumes were uniformly bound in green glazed boards, printed in black, with the title 'The People's *Pickwick*', 'The People's *Nickleby*', and so on, appearing on the back of the binding.[15] Thirty thousand copies of the two-volume *Pickwick*, then 25,000 of the one-volume *Twist*, were printed by 30 June 1865. The other books followed in sequence, and the sales held steady for over two and a half years. In 1865 over 135,000 volumes were sold; in 1866 nearly 117,000. Then the competition from the Charles Dickens edition killed the market. In the autumn of 1869, Chapman drastically reduced the wholesale price, from 17s. for a baker's dozen to 5d. apiece, and sold 82,100 volumes to Smith before the end of the year, plus another 11,400 to June 1870. All in all, the People's edition sold 382,317 volumes in Dickens's lifetime, more than 15,000 complete sets of the twenty-five volumes, and brought to Dickens as half-profit £3,300. It depended on large numbers of notices for its success: nearly 500,000 bills and 9,000 broadsides, largely distributed by Smith and Willing at the railway stations, plus notices in the papers and in the stationers' catalogues for a year. Yet despite this large-scale undertaking and its considerable rewards, there is no mention of the edition in either John Forster's or Edgar Johnson's biography. It was a successful commercial

---

[12] See Dalziel, ch. 8, ' "The Literature of the Rail" ', pp. 79–83.
[13] Griest, p. 32.
[14] F VII. v. 606 n.; see my Chapter 13 for a fuller discussion of Hachette's Railway Library.
[15] See the description in Nowell-Smith, 'The "Cheap Edition" of Dickens's Works', p. 250.

venture, but textually unimportant and certainly not presti-
gious.

Frederic Chapman kept lowering the price of others of Dickens's
works, too, with similar results. Take *Master Humphrey's Clock*.
The extraneous *Clock* material had supposedly been weeded out
shortly after publication, but the numbers containing *The Old
Curiosity Shop* and *Barnaby Rudge* continued to be sold in quantities ranging from 3,588 (December 1853) to a low of 611
(December 1861). After consolidating all the Dickens stock on his
own premises, Chapman slashed the price from 1s. 6d. per dozen
numbers to 3s. 10d. for each novel complete; that is a reduction
of about one-third, from just under 1½d. per number to around
1d., depending on which novel is used in the computation. Bohn
took 15,048 numbers (171 complete copies of each book) in the
half-year to December 1862, and came back regularly thereafter
for new supplies. A further cut was made in the price when
Chapman sold 100 volumes of each novel to Ticknor in 1868 for
3s. 3d. each. In terms of total novels thus sold, the results are not
impressive; but in terms of numbers of the *Clock*, which is what
the accounts record, the increase is dramatic: after 1862 the total
seldom fell below 6,000 per half-year, and climbed to a record
37,400 (425 books) in June 1868. Dickens's profits rarely exceeded
£20 per account, however; margins were slim and the costs of
reprinting heavy. But there were more encouraging signs than
profits: a surprisingly large number of copies of novels available
in several more convenient forms were sold, and when Chapman's
method was applied throughout the whole gamut of Dickens's
works, the increase in circulation and profits amounted to a great
deal.

ii

The timing and format of *Our Mutual Friend* were less influenced
by economic considerations than usual. Midsummer balances in
Dickens's account at Coutts's now showed healthy surpluses:
nearly £1,000 in 1862, over £800 the next year, and so on. With
the readings and Chapman's vigorous working of the copyrights
and back stock, Dickens enjoyed a substantial income and invested
periodically. A large contribution was made by *All the Year Round*,
whose circulation grew steadily. By the end of *Great Expectations*
its subscribers exceeded those for *The Times* by a few thousand,

and Bulwer's story attracted at least a thousand more (N iii. 218, 231). The Christmas number for 1862, containing *Somebody's Luggage*, sold 185,000 to 22 December; next year's did even better. 'The Christmas number has been the greatest success of all', Dickens told Wilkie Collins on 24 January 1864; it 'has shot ahead of last year; has sold about two hundred and twenty thousand; and has made the name of Mrs. Lirriper so swiftly and domestically famous as never was. I had a very strong belief in her when I wrote about her, finding that she made a great effect upon me; but she certainly has gone beyond my hopes' (N iii. 378). *Doctor Marigold's Prescriptions* (1865) reached 200,000 by New Year, and eventually topped a quarter of a million (N iii. 453; J, p. 1061); and the next year *Mugby Junction* sold out the entire printing of 265,000 within a month (N iii. 504). By 1869 the circulation of the Christmas number approached 300,000 (F VIII. v. 674).

Indeed, money delayed rather than hastened the appearance of the new novel. Dickens hit upon his title in 1861, but then he was engaged in *Great Expectations* and the struggle to halt the flight of subscribers from the journal. He hoped to begin his new novel in 1862, but 'Alas!' he moaned to Forster in April of that year, 'I have hit upon nothing for a story. Again and again I have tried.' He attributed his infertility to the 'odious little house' at 16 Hyde Park Gate South in which he was temporarily lodged, and which seemed 'to have stifled and darkened' his invention (F IX. v. 740–1). By August he had an idea; then other 'leading notions' began to crystallize: a young man feigning to be dead, two impecunious imposters marrying illusory wealth; 'bran-new' people; an uneducated father in fustian and an educated boy in spectacles; a good Jew to counterbalance Fagin. Dickens told Collins in August 1863, 'I am always thinking of writing a long book, and am never beginning to do it' (N iii. 360). Perhaps he might have started that month, but the new Christmas number demanded attention first. 'When I can clear the Christmas stone out of the road, I think I can dash into' the new twenty numbers, he reported to Forster (F IX. v. 741).

His resolve strengthened during September, and on the 28th of the month Dickens proposed terms to Chapman and Hall, who had no comprehensive agreement covering new serials:

In reference to a new work in 20 monthly Nos. as of old, I have carefully considered past figures and future reasonable possibilities. You have the means of doing the like in the main and no doubt will do so before replying to this letter.

I propose you to pay me £6000 for the half copyright throughout and outright at the times mentioned in your last letter to me on the subject. For that consideration I am ready to enter into articles of agreement with you securing you the publication of the work when I shall be ready to begin publishing and the half share.

As I must be rid of the Xmas No here and the Uncommercial Traveller before I can work to any great purpose, and as I must be well on before the first No. is published, I can not bind myself to time of commencement as yet. But I am really anxious to get into the field before next spring is out; and our interests cannot fail to be alike as to all such points, if we become partners in the story.

Of course, you will understand that I do not press you to give the sum I have here mentioned, and that you will not in the least inconvenience or offend me by preferring me to make other arrangements. If you should have any misgivings on this head, let my assurance that you need have none set it at rest.[16]

Acceding at all important points, Chapman signified his willingness to enter into the proposed agreement; two days later Dickens instructed Ouvry to draw up a contract;[17] and on 21 November 1863 it was signed by Edward and Frederic Chapman, and by Dickens.[18]

Dickens controlled his last twenty-part novel to an unprecedented extent. So certain was he of his power to make an agreement with any publisher that his offer to Chapman was very much on a 'take it or leave it' basis. His asking price for half-copyright during the serial run amounted to £300 per part: full copyright for serial publication only was thereby valued at £12,000! Moreover, the records indicate that the cost of buying this half-copyright, really a right to half the profits, was not charged against the gross income of the serial. Chapman risked the whole sum in advance without security, while Dickens guaranteed to himself £6,000, paid in instalments of £2,500 each on publication of the first and sixth parts, and £1,000 on publication of the final number, plus half of whatever the number sale netted, plus the whole

[16] Grubb, 'Some Unpublished Correspondence', pp. 120–1, transcribed from the Morgan Library MS. and not corrected by me.

[17] See the MS. memorandum for the agreement and letter to Ouvry, cited by J, p. 1010.

[18] The agreement is in the Berg Collection of the New York Public Library.

of whatever the novel produced following the first volume issue. The only certain income for Chapman, on the other hand, was the 5 per cent commission on gross sales, excluding payments for translation and advertising revenues. Two clauses gave the publishers scant comfort: if publication had not begun by the end of 1864 'through the default or neglect of the said Charles Dickens' then the Chapmans could void the agreement; and if Dickens died in mid serial his estate would owe compensation in an amount determined by Forster.

Dickens planned to start publication in the spring of 1864, spring having proved a propitious time for his serials. But he was determined not to begin until he had written five numbers. By mid October he saw perfectly 'the one main line on which the story is to turn', and feared that if he did not start writing 'while the iron . . . is hot, I shall drift off again, and have to go through all this uneasiness once more' (F IX. v. 741). He began readily enough, though his writing went much more slowly now, and his health was not up to the prolonged exertions of earlier years. By 25 January he had completed two numbers in 'a combination of drollery with romance which requires a great deal of pains and a perfect throwing away of points that might be amplified', but, he told Collins, 'I hope it is *very good*. I confess, in short, that I think it is.' None the less, he 'felt at first quite dazed in getting back to the large canvas and the big brushes; and even now, I have a sensation as of acting at the San Carlo after Tavistock House, which I could hardly have supposed would have come upon so old a stager' (N iii. 378-9).

While composing these first numbers, Dickens was also superintending the illustration and the all-important wrapper design. His artist this time was not the familiar Phiz, but rather Marcus Stone, and the illustrations were for the first time in Dickens's monthly serials to be engraved in wood by the Dalziels and W. T. Green. Many reasons have been advanced for the break with Browne. Arthur Allchin suggests that Browne's intensifying reserve rubbed Dickens the wrong way, especially as others of his companions supplied an unending stream of flattery and adulation. Browne himself said that he 'was about the last of those who knew [Dickens] in the early days with whom Dickens fell out, and considering the grand people he had around him and the compliments he perpetually received, it is a wonder we remained friends so long'.[19] Ley cannot accept this explanation as the whole truth, though Dickens may have interpreted Browne's increasing taciturnity as unfriendliness, and there is some evidence that Browne was not merely quiet, but quarrelsome.[20] Other causes advanced include Browne's working for Trollope and the rival *Once a Week*, his refusal to side with Dickens in the domestic split, and Dickens's fit of temper over Watt Phillips's play, which anticipated the climax of *A Tale of Two Cities* and caused Dickens to squabble with Browne among others. On learning that Stone was to replace him, Browne could offer no explanation to his partner Young: 'I don't know what's up any more than you do.' He speculated that 'Dickens probably thinks a new hand would give his old puppets a fresh look. . . . Confound all authors and publishers, say I; there is no pleasing or satisfying one or t'other. I wish I had never had anything to do with the lot.'[21] Undoubtedly the perfunctory character of some of Browne's drawings for *A Tale of Two Cities* contributed to Dickens's decision, though Browne would not admit the charge; and as Dickens's taste in art and style of writing both matured, Browne's tendency to caricature and comedy may have seemed inappropriate, jarring.

Dickens decided to drop Browne long before he thought of Stone.[22] He first became interested in the artistic ability of the son of his old friend Frank Stone during the writing of *Bleak House*. Marcus Stone, then aged twelve, having 'eagerly devoured' the fourth number, went to 'work upon an illustration of "Jo" the sweeps & the gateway of the graveyard where his kind friend the poor law writer had just been buried'. Dickens walked into the room, spied the drawing, and said, 'That's very good. You must give it to me when it is done.' In return, Dickens sent the boy proof of Browne's illustration that he 'might see how "Phiz" had treated the same locality'.[23] A year and a half later Dickens sent

[19] Both comments, as well as those which follow, are taken from J. W. T. Ley, *The Dickens Circle: A Narrative of the Novelist's Friendships*, 2nd edn. (London, Chapman and Hall, 1919), pp. 38–40.

[20] John Harvey, *Victorian Novelists and Their Illustrators* (New York, New York Univ. Press, 1971), p. 164.

[21] Frederic G. Kitton, *Dickens and His Illustrators*, 2nd edn. (London, George Redway, 1899), p. 113, prints a slightly different version of this letter.

[22] Ley, p. 150.

[23] Sister Lucile Carr, C.D.P., comp., *A Catalogue of the VanderPoel Dickens Collection at the University of Texas* (Austin, Texas: Humanities Research Center of the Univ. of Texas, 1968), item A 89, p. 13.

him a pre-publication copy of the completed *Child's History of England*. When Frank Stone died in 1859, Dickens busied himself in recommending the young artist to publishers, telling Thomas Longman IV: 'He is an admirable draughtsman, has a most dexterous hand, a charming sense of grace and beauty, and a capital power of observation. These qualities in him I know well to my own knowledge. He is, in all things, modest, punctual, and right, and I would answer for him, if it were needful, with my head.'[24] The opportunity for Dickens to commission Stone himself arrived quickly: Dickens got him to supply designs for Dalziel's woodcuts for the frontispiece to the Cheap edition of *Little Dorrit* (1861), and for the Library edition (1862) eight illustrations each for *Great Expectations*[25] and the *Child's History*, and four each for *Pictures from Italy* and *American Notes*. In 1864 Stone designed a second frontispiece, for the Cheap edition of *Two Cities*, and in February of that year Dickens took him on as an illustrator for the new serial,[26] imagining that Stone's qualities were well suited to Dickens's 'combination of drollery with romance' and the quiet restraint of his new work.

But the collaboration never succeeded. Dickens, despite his disaffection for some aspects of Browne's work, expected Stone to work in Browne's manner; perhaps the incident of the graveyard scene indicates, more clearly than Stone perceived, Dickens's preference in matters of treatment. Dickens took considerable care to coach Stone over the cover design:

I think the design for the cover *excellent*, and do not doubt its coming out to perfection. The slight alteration I am going to suggest originates in a business consideration not to be overlooked.

The word 'Our' in the title must be out in the open like 'Mutual Friend,' making the title three distinct large lines—'Our' as big as 'Mutual Friend.' This would give you too much design at the bottom. I would therefore take out the dustman, and put the Wegg and Boffin composition (which is capital) in its place. I don't want Mr. Inspector or the murder reward bill, because these points are sufficiently indicated in the river at the top. Therefore you can have an indication of the dustman in Mr. Inspector's place. Note, that the dustman's face should be

[24] Quoted in Ley, p. 40.

[25] Stone received £42 for drawing, and Dalziel £50. 8s. for engraving, these eight plates (MS. C & H).

[26] Harvey, p. 227, n. 10, based on an unpublished letter from Dickens to Stone, 14 Feb. 1864.

droll, and not horrible. Twemlow's elbow will still go out of the frame as it does now, and the same with Lizzie's skirts on the opposite side. With these changes, work away!

Mrs. Boffin, as I judge of her from the sketch, 'very good indeed.' I want Boffin's oddity, without being at all blinked, to be an oddity of a very honest kind, that people will like.

The doll's dressmaker is immensely better than she was. I think she should now come extremely well. A weird sharpness not without beauty is the thing I want. (N iii. 380)

But when in the course of publication Dickens found that Stone's figures were larger and his designs quite dissimilar, and that Stone could not work in Browne's style, he lost interest, allowing Stone to choose the subjects he liked, and neglecting even to inspect the illustrations before they went to the wood engravers.[27] Stone's illustrations in the end added little to the novel or its reputation, but in another way he was quite influential in shaping the book.

Shortly after hiring him, Dickens supplied Stone with enough hints for him to produce the wrapper design. Stone, for his part, kept a sharp eye on subjects that might contribute to Dickens's design, and a few days after finishing the wrapper he spied something of interest. Stone then rushed off to 57 Gloucester Place, Hyde Park Gardens, where Dickens was staying between February and June 'to be in town when my book is preparing and begins to come out' (N iii. 379). He found Dickens mulling over a rearrangement of the chapters and hunting for a new subject. At that moment, Dickens told Forster, 'Marcus . . . came to tell me of an extraordinary trade he had found out, through one of his painting requirements. I immediately went with him to Saint Giles's to look at the place, and found—' the establishment of Mr. Venus, which was written up and inserted at the end of Number II, displacing the earlier ending to the next number (F IX. v. 741). The anecdote indicates that Stone possessed some sort of understanding of the themes and materials of Dickens's projected book, and also shows anew Dickens's extraordinary

---

[27] Harvey, pp. 164–5, based on unpublished letters from Dickens to Stone; see also N iii. 435–6 to Stone asking for the subjects Stone will illustrate in Vol. II so that the printer can make up the list of illustrations, and suggesting that 'the frontispiece to the second volume should be the dustyard with the three mounds, and Mr. Boffin digging up the Dutch bottle, and Venus restraining Wegg's ardour to get at him. Or Mr. Boffin might be coming down with the bottle, and Venus might be dragging Wegg out of the way as described.'

capacity to perceive the connections among disparate things, and to weave them together at his story-teller's loom.

All parties expected a large sale for the new serial. That the illustrations were engraved in wood may be one indication, since woodcuts could stand up to 100,000 impressions; on the other hand, since Browne and Young had worked in tandem to produce the duplicate steel etchings, now that they had been replaced it may have been thought too complicated and risky to try to train a new team. And in any case, the sixties was *the* decade of wood engraving.[28] Dickens's £6,000 advance was another sign of great expectations. A third may be found in the records of advertising: Chapman carried on a far more extensive campaign than ever before, printing more than a million 8vo and 16mo bills, 145,000 demy 8vo catalogues, and plastering virtually the whole of England with posters. 'I have made all arrangements with Smith & Son as to placarding and also as to distributing 200,000 of the small bills', Chapman told Dickens on 15 March.[29] Eventually Smith distributed 300,000 bills; Chapman also rented '30 long frames [for] 4 months' for posters at Smith's major stands. Willing and Co. placed advertisements on 100 omnibuses; three-sheet posters were placed in the five stations in Birmingham and Bristol for a similar period; other posters were exhibited at Camberwell and Kennington Gates for two months; and, perhaps exploiting the importance of the Thames in the novel, 'Steamboats' were also posted. Almost £550 worth of advertising was taken in journals through the first six numbers. One result of all the optimism in Piccadilly was the exceptional size of the Advertiser: *Our Mutual Friend*, according to Hatton and Cleaver, contains the largest volume of the regular advertising sheet of any Dickens serial, and also includes eighty-nine insets and slips between the text and the rear wrapper.

For his last twenty-number serial Dickens selected as his printers not Bradbury and Evans, with whom he had severed connections except for the Library edition reprints, and not Charles Whiting, who turned out the weekly numbers of *All the Year Round* and the volume editions of *Great Expectations*, but rather William Clowes and Sons, a large printing firm with a huge stock of stereo plates and offices on both sides of the river near Charing Cross and Waterloo. Their initial printing for Number I was set at 40,000, of which 35,000 were stitched. Three days after publication the novel was in its 'thirtieth thousand, and orders flowing in fast' (F IX. v. 742); but demand peaked shortly thereafter. For the second number, Chapman reduced the print order to 35,000 and the stitching order to 31,000. The sales drop more than matched his fears. 'This leaves me going round and round like a carrier-pigeon before swooping on number seven', Dickens told Forster. According to Forster, 'the larger number was again reached, and much exceeded, before the book closed', but the records do not bear him out (F IX. v. 742). The print order declined steadily, to 30,000 (III–V), then to 28,000 (VI–XII), and finally to 25,000. Only 19,000 copies of the final double number were stitched into the green leaves.

Gamely, Chapman made good on his obligation to pay for half-rights. Bills for various sums, starting with £2,500 on 4 May 1864, and concluding with £500 on 29 September 1865, probably represent his payments, though Dickens's account in these last years is full of unidentified deposits for large amounts which may be interpreted when the pertinent volumes of the Pilgrim *Letters* appear.[30] The profits which Chapman so dearly bought did not equal his investment: to December 1865, a half-share returned only about £4,608. Chapman and Hall were also entitled to a commission, amounting in the aggregate to another £689. So Frederic Chapman spent £6,000 to get roughly £5,300. After 1865, all the profits reverted to Dickens, about £300 additional to his death; he also was paid £1,000 by Harper's for advanced proofs; and Tauchnitz purchased 'the right of reprinting in Germany' on his usual terms.[31] So altogether Dickens made well over £12,000 from a serial on which Chapman and Hall lost £700. But from another standpoint, the deal was a bargain: that £700 represented the cost of keeping Dickens and could be offset against the probable returns from selling other new works as well as back stock, worth £9,680

[30] Chapman and Hall's payments were apparently deposited as follows:

£2,500	4 May 1864
£1,500	14 Oct. 1864
£1,000	7 Dec. 1864
£500	28 Sept. 1865
£500	29 Sept. 1865 (MS. Coutts)

[31] Otto, p. 57.

wholesale at Christmas 1865, according to an estimate Chapman sent Dickens.

The relative commercial failure of *Our Mutual Friend* may have contributed its share to Dickens's evident depression during the summer of 1864. 'Although I have not been wanting in industry, I have been wanting in invention, and have fallen back with the book', he wrote to Forster. 'This week I have been very unwell; am still out of sorts; and, as I know from two days' slow experience, have a very mountain to climb before I shall see the open country of my work' (F IX. v. 742). In November of that year, John Leech died, putting Dickens out 'woefully. Yesterday and the day before I could do nothing; seemed for the time to have quite lost the power; and am only by slow degrees getting back into the track to-day' (F IX. v. 742).

One innovation in publishing the novel seems to have made little difference in sales, though it does demarcate the physical division of the work. At the end of Number X were included half-title, title, dedication, contents, and list of illustrations to Volume I, so that the first half could be bound up as a separate volume. Number XI begins with the pages renumbered, and the final number includes the same apparatus for Volume II as well as a Postscript in lieu of a Preface, since it was no longer possible to bind a Preface into the already cased copies of the first volume.

It is impossible to say who or what suggested this change in procedure. What is worthy of note is that Mudie's took at a discount 832 copies of the two-volume bound edition, and Smith 500. *Our Mutual Friend* must have been one of the few non-three-decker novels to find its way on to Mudie's shelves;[32] at the same time, it must have been one of the more cumbersome and expensive novels to sell at railway stalls. The fact is that shilling novels in monthly parts had pretty well run their course; they did not collect conveniently into three volumes for the lending libraries; they were too big for the commuter customers; they were a poor bargain for the average book buyer, who could get several stories for the same price or less by purchasing a shilling magazine, or a story complete in one instalment by ordering the Christmas number of

[32] Griest, p. 55, while conceding that some two-volume works did get stocked, notes that 'Two volumes instead of three might mean the difference between rejection and acceptance of a manuscript by an unknown author; for a writer with an established reputation it amounted to pounds, shillings, and pence.'

All the Year Round. Doctor Marigold's Prescriptions sold a quarter of a million copies where *Our Mutual Friend* sold 19,000.

iii

In June 1865 Dickens and Ellen Ternan were badly shaken in a railway accident near Staplehurst. 'I remember with devout thankfulness', Dickens told his readers in the Postscript to *Our Mutual Friend*, 'that I can never be much nearer parting company with my readers than I was then, until there shall be written against my life, the two words with which I have this day closed this book:— THE END.' We may never plummet the depths of his feeling about that terrible disaster, nor be able to say with certainty that there is any connection between this date, 9 June, and the day of his death exactly five years later. What is clear is that during the remaining five years the association of the end of a novel and the end of his life became more and more present to Dickens: almost every activity in which he was engaged after June 1865 had the aspect of a winding-up, a finale.

The death of his friends narrowed the circle of old intimacies: Arthur Smith and Henry Austin in 1861, Cornelius Felton and Angus Fletcher in 1862, Thackeray and Dickens's mother in 1863, his son Walter and John Leech in 1864, Paxton, who had bravely backed the *Daily News*, in 1865, Jane Carlyle in 1866, his brother Frederick in 1868, William Bradbury in 1869. The friendship with the other half of the firm, Pater Evans, sundered during the summer of 1858, was never repaired. On 22 July 1858 Dickens told Evans:

> I have had stern occasion to impress upon my children that their father's name is their best possession and that it would indeed be trifled with and wasted by him, if, either through himself or through them, he held any terms with those who have been false to it, in the only great need and under the only great wrong it has ever known. You know very well, why (with hard distress of mind and bitter disappointment), I have been forced to include you in this class. I have no more to say. (N iii. 33)

And he never relented, not even when Charley became engaged to Bessie, Evans's daughter, three years later. Dickens considered the match a product of Catherine's spite, 'because her hatred of the bride used to know no bounds'.[33] Beard, who was Charley's godfather, was invited to the wedding; Dickens wrote to him to express his 'earnest hope that it is not your intention to enter Mr. Evans's house on that occasion' (N iii. 249–50). Dickens himself refused to attend the wedding, but when Bessie produced a grandchild, the family came to Gad's Hill, where they spent at least one Christmas and probably more. Eventually Charley's six children born before Dickens's death consoled him somewhat for the loss of old companions.

In a jocular mood, Dickens once appointed 'William Hall and Edward Chapman of No. 186 Strand, their heirs, executors, administrators, and assigns, my periodical publishers, until I am advertised in the daily papers, as having been compressed into my last edition—one volume, boards, with brass plates' (P i. 189). Something of that finality hovers about the Charles Dickens edition, on which Dickens began working in 1866.[34] The format may have been suggested by Ticknor and Fields, though they were already in the throes of issuing the 'Diamond Edition' of Dickens's works in fourteen volumes with illustrations by Sol Eytinge, Jr., of which Dickens expressed public approval; print runs ranged from 12,000 of *Pickwick* down to 2,000 of many of the other books.[35] In the Charles Dickens edition each novel came out complete in a single volume, crown 8vo bound in red cloth-covered boards with a black design on the cover incorporating the intertwined initials 'CD' in an upper roundel and 'C & H' in a lower one, and with Dickens's signature stamped in gold to signify 'his present watchfulness over his own Edition'.[36] The texts, corrected and sometimes 'slightly revised' by Dickens,[37] were reset by Virtue and Co. within ruled boxes 'in a flowing open page, free from the

[33] Quoted in J, p. 997.
[34] In an 1866 reprint of the 1858 Cheap edition of *Bleak House* Dickens inscribed the descriptive headlines that, with a few minor changes, were used in the Charles Dickens edition of that novel. See Michael Slater, ed. and intro., *The Catalogue of the Suzannet Charles Dickens Collection* (London and New York, Sotheby Parke Bernet Publications and Trustees of the Dickens House, 1975), Catalogue item No. 111, p. 197; corroborated by a letter of 13 Sept. 1972 to me from Sylvère Monod.
[35] See statement of royalties paid to Dickens in the December 1867 accounts.
[36] Prospectus in the *Athenaeum*, 4 May 1867, p. 600.
[37] Tillotson, Introduction to the Clarendon *Twist*, p. xxx; see also Dickens's letter to Chapman and Hall, 7 May 1870, thanking Virtue's reader 'for his great care and attention' over proofs for the *Child's History* (Grubb, 'Some Unpublished Correspondence', p. 126).

objection of having double columns' as in the Cheap and People's editions; descriptive headlines which the Prospectus attributed to Dickens appear on each right-hand page. In addition, Dickens wrote new Prefaces. The longer works came out at 3s. 6d. apiece; the shorter ones, at 3s.; all included eight of the best illustrations except *A Child's History of England* and *The Uncommercial Traveller*, which had only four each. One volume appeared every month; the edition retained useful aspects of that system of periodical issue which had for so long been a constant and successful part of Dickens's publications.

The publicity campaign was immense. One million three hundred and fifty thousand prospectuses were printed. Smith and Son placarded their English and Irish stations for six months; Willing and Co. posted the London, Chatham, and Dover railway; Robertson covered Australia. In newspapers and magazines £764 worth of advertising was placed in the first six months, more than half the nearly £1,400 spent by the end of 1867. This edition clearly aimed at a wide assortment of readers: commuters, readers of *The Times* and the *Athenaeum*, the man in the street, whether that street be in Dublin, Melbourne, Dover, or Boston. Expectations were correspondingly large: 50,000 copies of *Pickwick*, 30,000 of *Chuzzlewit* and *Dombey*, and 25,000 of some of the others were initially printed. Within the year, *Pickwick*, *Nickleby*, and *Copperfield* had to be reprinted once, and *Chuzzlewit* twice.

Chapman sold copies in bulk at varying discounts: of the larger books, 20,332 as 18,768 to Bell and Daldy at 2s. 6d. less 12½ per cent; 26,767 to Routledge at 2s. 6d. less 10 per cent; 35,841 as 33,084 to agents at the same price; and 51,090 as 47,160 at 2s. 6d. without discount—all in the first half-year. The smaller volumes wholesaled for 2s. 1d. less the same range of discounts; and the eighteen (later twenty-one) volume sets went for 38s. 10d. By June 1870 over half a million volumes had been taken, for a total net profit in excess of £12,500 split equally between Dickens and his publishers.

In anticipation of this profit, Dickens arranged with Chapman before leaving on his American tour for the payment of an advance. The large sums that were owing to him each half-year were customarily diminished by some sort of monthly stipend, and often worked off by bills at several months' date. Confusions arose over the number of monthly stipends to be deducted from a particular account; the deposits sometimes came in irregularly, as in 1866 £300 was credited on 1 May, 12 June, and 21 July.[38] Dickens said in similar circumstances on a later occasion, 'I admit the soft impeachment concerning Mrs. Gamp: I likes my payments to be made reg'lar and I likewise likes my publisher to draw it mild' (N iii. 739–40). In December 1865 the calculations that Chapman submitted seemed muddled, but there is no indication that Dickens's handwritten alterations were made, and the December 1867 accounts were so incorrect that they had to be redrawn. To avoid such problems, Dickens set forth on 6 November 1867 in his own hand on the Midsummer accounts a memorandum detailing his arrangement about payments to be made for the second half of the year. Presumably the June 1867 accounts, 'left out as a guide to the next half year's account', were given to Forster, and the memorandum tacitly addressed to him, since Dickens would be in America when the accounts were drawn up. 'Said next half year's account is to be rendered on the 15th. of March, and the balance it shall show to be due to me is to be promptly paid, in money, and not in bills of any kind', Dickens minuted. 'But in consideration of Chapman and Hall's not having yet accounted at all for the Charles Dickens Edition, they have pre-paid *on account of the total balance to be stated on the 15th. of March, Fifteen Hundred Pounds*'. In fact, that sum, in three acceptances of £500 each credited to Dickens on 11 December, January, and February (MS. Coutts), had been enclosed in a letter from Chapman of 8 October. 'Note on the one hand', Dickens went on to explain, 'that Fifteen Hundred Pounds will therefore be deducted from the total balance due to me on the 15th. of March; and note on the other hand that the account then rendered of the Charles Dickens Edition is to comprise all profits yielded by it, from its beginning, to Christmas.'[39] It was that Christmas account which was so incorrect; but when finally approved, it showed that after deducting the £1,500 paid in advance and the £550 Ticknor and Fields paid directly to Dickens as royalties on the Diamond and

[38] MS. Coutts; see Dickens's letter to Wills of 7 Aug. 1866 referring to 'loose fish' and surmising that 'he', probably Chapman, has probably paid the balance owing, as he has been depositing £300 a month on account, 'since the last settlement' (N iii. 480–1). The June 1866 balance in Dickens's favour turned out to be £987. 4s. 7d. net of the three £300 earlier payments (MS. C & H); it was deposited on 4 Oct. (MS. Coutts).

[39] Grubb, 'Some Unpublished Correspondence', p. 124.

Charles Dickens editions, Chapman owed him only £254. 7s. 7d., which was paid into Coutts's on 26 March (MS. Coutts).

iv

Money was practically an obsession in these last years. 'Copyrights need be hereditary, for genius isn't', Dickens noted in his Diary apropos of Wordsworth's son whom he had met at a dinner given by the Revd. William Harness in February 1839 (P i. 639). Thirty years later, surveying his own large brood, Dickens must have come to nearly the same conclusion: Catherine, Georgina, the children and grandchildren, Ellen, seemed a large lot with small capacity among them all to support themselves. Forster, either genuinely ignorant or tactful, cannot say what 'pressed him on' in these last years, but whatever it was, 'his task . . . self-imposed, was to make the most money in the shortest time without any regard to the physical labour to be undergone' (F VIII. vii. 700). Forster never approved of the readings, but they made money: over £20,000 from America, £28,000 in a year and a half; £33,000 in all between 1866 and 1868 (F XI. i. 798, 800). And the readings sold books too, as Dickens predicted they would (N iii. 530): Ticknor and Fields did a land-office business ordering 1,000 sets (26,000 volumes) of the illustrated Library edition in the autumn of 1867 and placing a second order of equal size in the following spring (MS. C & H), and selling in quantity the Diamond edition, the Charles Dickens edition, and 'the only correct and authorized edition' of the readings. And other publishers, Little and Brown, Lippincott, Harper's, peddled their own copies with equal success. Indisputably in America as in England, 'the readings . . . opened up a new public who were outside before'; Dickens told de Cerjat as early as the beginning of February 1859 that 'his books have a wider range than they ever had, and his public welcomes are prodigious' (N iii. 92).

Dickens 'has got . . . some perman*t* nervous damage from that conquest of the £20,000 in Yankeeland', Carlyle told his sister, 'and is himself rather anxious now & then ab*t* it'.[40] Intimations of mortality came thick and fast. On 3 May 1869 Dickens executed a third will, leaving Ellen £1,000, Georgina £8,000, Catherine

[40] Quoted in K. J. Fielding, 'Carlyle and Dickens or Dickens and Carlyle?', *Dickensian*, 69 (1973), 118.

the interest on an equal sum, the servants each nine guineas. In July 1869 Anthony Trollope paid £10,000 for a third share in Chapman and Hall for his son Henry; Frederic had cleared the bargain with Dickens first, and Dickens in turn instructed Ouvry to make certain that all his agreements with Chapman were clearly set forth, possibly in a new Deed.[41] Nine months later Wills retired from *All the Year Round*; his share then fell to one-eighth, and Dickens gave over the business management to Charley with another eighth. At the same time, Dickens confirmed his supreme authority over every aspect of the enterprise, literary and other-wise.[42] By a codicil signed just one week before he died, Dickens bequeathed to Charley all his share and interest in the journal, including stereotypes and back stock (F, Appendix, p. 857). In every respect he was ordering his affairs, planning for a future he might not live to enjoy.

v

Not that he was wholly pessimistic, or suicidally inclined. Once the penultimate series of readings were out of the way, Dickens settled down at Gad's Hill to the planning of a new serial. About its precise format he was uncertain. Clearly the twenty-part novel no longer served. Various experiments had been tried to place serial parts on a par with the magazines: Smith, Elder issued *The Last Chronicle of Barset* in 6d. monthly numbers during 1866–7, but 'the enterprise was not altogether successful', Trollope recol-lected.[43] Even Mudie's was stumped by the opposition. When Anne Thackeray was negotiating with Smith, Elder about *The Village on the Cliff* (1866–7), Mudie's advised against issuing it as a three-decker following its appearance in the *Cornhill*. 'All the world, they said, reads the *Cornhill*, and the number of their subscribers who care to have the story apart from the magazine is comparatively few and would be nearly as well pleased if Mudie's gave them the bound volumes of the *Cornhill*.' Perhaps a cheap edition, to retail at twelve or thirteen shillings immediately upon completion of the magazine serialization, would answer; if

[41] Unpublished letters to Ouvry in the Huntington Library, dated 29 July, 13 Aug., and 22 Aug. 1869.
[42] Unpublished letter to Ouvry in the Huntington Library, dated 14 Apr. 1870.
[43] *An Autobiography*, p. 229.

Smith, Elder would try that expedient, Mudie's would take 500 copies. The publishers 'adopted the plan with good results'.[44]

The commercial reception of *Our Mutual Friend* bore out the general impression that the shilling part had had its day. So Dickens proposed two alternatives to Chapman: weekly instalments in *All the Year Round*, or twelve monthly numbers.[45] The smaller compass is probably not primarily related to Dickens's ill health. He did find the large canvas of his last serial disconcerting at first; he was now comfortable in more confined and compact instalments; he was anxious about his condition; but he was also being realistic about the market.

As far as Chapman was concerned, there was little to choose between the two. Weekly instalments in *All the Year Round* would shut him out entirely, and though profit may not have been the sole motive behind serving Dickens, it could not be entirely discounted. His advice was for the monthly parts; Dickens accepted it, and instructed Ouvry to draw up the contract.[46] That agreement breaks precedent in several ways. Chapman bought, for £7,500, the right to all the profits on the first 25,000 copies; thereafter he and Dickens shared equally. Uncertain what fortune awaited this new experiment, Dickens opted for a fat bird in the hand, while Chapman looked to the uncertain birds in the bush, counting on sales exceeding 25,000, since that volume in twelve numbers could hardly recoup his outlay. And there was a further provision similar to the agreement for *Our Mutual Friend*: if Dickens should die or otherwise become incapable of finishing the work, then Chapman was to be repaid some portion of his advance determined by Forster or, if he too was incapacitated, a nominee of Her Majesty's Attorney-General. It was an obvious proviso, given that Chapman was buying a manuscript before a word was written. How it was put into effect we do not know; there are payments of £4,000 in three large sums recorded in Dickens's account before his death that may represent Chapman's

44 Huxley, p. 91.

45 These options Dickens had also set forth to George W. Childs, proprietor of the *Public Ledger* and publisher of the *American Literary Gazette and Publishers' Circular*, on 31 July 1865, in encouraging him to offer 'for purchasing the exclusive right of having early proof sheets in America of the next story' he might write (N iii. 433).

46 See Cardwell's Introduction to the Clarendon *Drood*, pp. xv–xvi, citing an unpublished letter in the collection of N. C. Peyrouton, to Chapman, dated 20 Aug. 1869.

purchase money, and perhaps those are the only payments he was ever required to make. Anthony Trollope, in a letter to Frederic Chapman dated 25 September 1871, says: 'If J. Forster and Ouvry allow you £1875 for E Drood, I shall be very well contented.'[47] That could be the payment returned to Chapman as a consequence of Dickens's not finishing, but the date is late for such a settlement, and the comment which follows that the accountant 'Mr Harding expected more' may indicate that what was at issue was a valuation of Dickens's half of the stock in stereos, sheets, illustrations, and wrappers for *Drood* which Chapman was trying to buy back from the estate.

American rights to *Drood* involved Dickens in much needless controversy. His growing friendship with Fields led to an agreement signed 15 April 1867 appointing Ticknor and Fields his 'only authorized representatives in America'.[48] Harper's, Sampson Low, and T. B. Peterson resented the agreements, as well as Dickens's letter to Ticknor and Fields dated 16 April 1867 and subsequently published in the *Publishers' Circular* which claimed that 'In America the occupation of my life for thirty years is, unless it bears your imprint, utterly worthless and profitless to me.'[49] Their feelings were aired in the *Publishers' Circular* of Philadelphia on 1 June 1867. During his American tour, Dickens either forgot his agreement with Fields or believed that publication rights for a new serial might be split between two firms (especially if he issued it in weekly instalments in *All the Year Round*, as he had done with *Great Expectations*); he therefore intimated to Harper's that they could have advance sheets of any new work. By the end of October 1869 Dickens was urging Chapman to make his proposal for *Drood*, because 'I want to conclude an American negociation for simultaneous publication, and am pestered with offers of various sorts' (N iii. 748–9). When Harper's saw *Drood* announced in the London papers in November 1869, they offered on the twentieth of that month £2,000 for early sheets, 'assuming, of course, that it will be of the average length of *Our Mutual Friend* and *Great*

---

[47] *Letters*, no. 485.

[48] Letter from Dickens printed on verso title-page, Diamond edition, dated 2 Apr. 1867, quoted in Wilkins, *First and Early American Editions*, p. 45; the agreement between Dickens, Chapman and Hall, and Ticknor and Fields is in the Pierpont Morgan Library.

[49] See *Publishers' Circular* of 1 June 1867, reprinted in Mackenzie, Appendix, p. 1.

Expectations'. Since these two novels vary considerably in length, it is clear that Harper's were merely trying to establish whether they were buying a short story of twelve or twenty pages or a novel, be it a three-decker or a twenty-part serial. Gone for ever were the days when Dickens risked a loss of pay if he came up a few lines short of his contracted monthly budget of letterpress for Bentley. Moreover, Harper's nervously added, 'Should this offer not seem to you sufficient, we would be pleased to receive a proposition from you.'[50] It did seem sufficient, so Dickens accepted, though he declined to have anything to do with Harper's London agent, Sampson Low, whose letter in the *Publishers' Circular* he strongly resented. He communicated this decision to Fields, who was staying with Dickens that autumn. Biding his time, Fields remained silent then, but immediately on returning to Boston he looked up his old agreements, and found one specifically committing Dickens to his house for any new serial. When Dickens learned of this contract, he informed Harper's of the mistake, backing out of his agreement with them. For some reason, in late February or early March, Fields, Osgood wrote to Harper's expressing their chagrin that Dickens momentarily forgot his contract with them; Harper's then referred their correspondence to Dickens, adding 'Should they be unwilling to abide by their agreement with you for the publication of the story, we cheerfully renew our offer to you of the 20th November last.'[51]

By the beginning of the year, Fields, Osgood were also plagued with pirates who threatened competing editions of the new serial. They appealed to Dickens for help, but he declined: 'I cannot overcome my instinctive feeling that it would be a very unseemly thing for me to engage in any single combats with the Pirates. I have already announced my own connexion with your house; and it is for you, and not for me, to make all appeals or protests or other announcements connected with that association. I am quite clear as to my silent part.'[52] The Bostonians planned to issue the monthly parts of *Drood* in smaller portions in their weekly magazine *Every Saturday*, and since they would have the only set of advance proofs, to forestall the pirates they could even print ahead of publication in England on those occasions when a fifth Saturday preceded the last day of the month and the appearance

---

[50] Harper, pp. 261–2.   [51] Ibid., p. 262.
[52] Quoted by Cardwell, pp. xxxi–xxxii.

thereon of the next monthly part. When Harold Ticknor mentioned this solution in London during February, Dickens was adamant in contravening it: 'I told him that it was my business to know how the law stood in such a case, and that I *was certain* of the English copyright being lost as to any portion of Edwin Drood the publication of which should first take place in America, and that therefore I must positively prohibit such anticipation. I also told him that I knew there were people enough here, always on the watch, who would instantly avail themselves of my making so fatal a mistake' (N iii. 777). Probably at the same time, Dickens drafted a letter for Chapman and Hall to send 'as partners with him, in the English copyright of that book', confirming Dickens's statement and refusing to concede 'a privilege to you manifestly so absurd in the injury it would knowingly inflict upon his, and our, joint interests here'.[53] It must have been about this time that Harper's got word of the disagreement, and cheerfully renewed their offer of the preceding November; on 5 March 1870 Dickens told them that they might be 'quite sure that if I should find myself "free" to make a new arrangement concerning advance sheets of *The Mystery of Edwin Drood*, at any time during the issuing of the book in numbers, I will at once send them to you, and place myself in your hands'.[54]

Fields, Osgood evidently wrote to Dickens on 29 April once again requesting permission to publish portions in advance; in his reply of 14 May, Dickens recapitulated the history of this particular dispute, and enclosed an opinion from Ouvry that 'is quite final and conclusive' (N iii. 777). The Americans capitulated, deferring portions that would anticipate English publication until the succeeding week, Dickens received £1,000 for the advance proofs, Harper's ran the novel in a Monthly Supplement to their magazine *Harper's Weekly*, and thus the controversy ended.[55] German rights, by contrast, were quickly negotiated on 'quite satisfactory' terms with the always agreeable and liberal Tauchnitz.[56] And in addition Dickens received £50 for permitting Dr. Lehmann to translate *Drood* into German.[57]

---

[53] Grubb, 'Some Unpublished Correspondence', p. 125.
[54] Quoted in Harper, p. 263.
[55] This account is reconstructed from Cardwell, pp. xxx–xxxii; and Grubb, 'Some Unpublished Correspondence', pp. 125–6 and n. 99.
[56] Otto, p. 58.
[57] N iii. 771; deposited 23 Apr. (MS. Coutts).

Not only did Dickens change his American publishers in mid-stream; he also had to change his illustrator. In July and August 1869 Dickens formulated 'the idea of a story', providing Forster with tantalizing, but very incomplete, glimpses of his plans. Towards the end of September he was far enough along to think about a cover design and designer. Stone, if considered at all, was summarily rejected; but continuing in the pattern of helping young friends, Dickens agreed to give his son-in-law Charles Collins, the brother of Wilkie, a chance. He asked Frederic Chapman to send down to Gad's Hill, where Collins and Kate were staying, copies of the old green covers (N iii. 742). We cannot know for certain what Dickens wanted Collins to learn from Browne's wrappers: the general structure, perhaps, and the way in which Browne 'shadowed forth' the leading ideas of the book. That he wanted Collins to train from the old wrappers is yet another indication that although Dickens had severed connections with Browne the man, he had not altogether displaced him as an artist. When Collins had practised sufficiently, and understood the purposes and effect for which he was to work, Dickens gave him verbal instructions about the scenes, characters, and incidents he should depict. The result, completed by the end of October, Dickens thought 'excellent', 'charming'.[58] Frederic Chapman may have raised some questions about the rate of pay Collins should receive, for on the twenty-ninth of the month Dickens wrote that 'he must be paid what Marcus Stone was paid. I find that he knows how much that was, and as I hope he will do better—instead of worse—it would be unconscionable to offer him less. His cover is well worth £10. There can be no doubt about that. To offer him less would be absurd' (N iii. 748). But Collins's health failed him, as Dickens told Frederic Chapman one month later: 'Charles Collins finds that the sitting down to draw, brings back all the worst symptoms of the old illness that occasioned him to leave his old pursuit of painting; and here we are suddenly without an Illustrator! We will use his cover of course, but he gives in altogether as to further subjects' (N iii. 753).

The story of Dickens's selecting Luke Fildes to replace Collins is told in a letter from W. H. Chambers printed in Margaret Cardwell's Introduction to the Clarendon *Drood*. John Everett Millais, then staying at Gad's Hill, spied Fildes's powerful drawing

[58] To Forster (N iii. 754); to Fields (N iii. 760).

Houseless and Hungry' in the first issue of *The Graphic*, 4 December 1869, and burst into Dickens's room crying, 'I've got him.'
After looking at the picture, Dickens agreed that the young artist
might do, and so wrote soliciting other sketches: 'I see . . . that
you are an adept at drawing scamps, send me some specimens of
pretty ladies.' When these proved equally to answer to his purpose
—('I can honestly assure you that I entertain the greatest admiration for your remarkable powers' (N iii. 761), Dickens told
Fildes)—he engaged him, telling Fields afterwards that he had
been convinced by 'the very earnest representations of Millais' and
by 'a great number of [Fildes's] drawings' (N iii. 760). Fildes
jubilantly informed his best friend and future brother-in-law,
Henry Woods:

At last!
Congratulate me! I am to do Dickens's Story. Just got the letter
settling the matter. Going to see Dickens on Saturday.
Now for what I can do. This is the tide! Am I to be on the flood? My
heart fails me a little for it is the turning point in my career. I shall be
judged by this. But I shall try![59]

Fildes went to work quickly modifying Collins's cover design
(a proof of which Chapman sent him around 25 January), and
getting the illustrations for Part I, for which Dickens had supplied
him with page-proof, drawn, approved, engraved, and printed.
Clowes ran off enough quantities of the cover to last many months;
when unexpectedly the sixth number became the last, comprising
the usual front matter and two extra illustrations—vignette title,
and a portrait—the 'Price One Shilling' printed for the regular
numbers was covered by a pasted slip 'Price Eighteenpence'. But
Fildes was unhappy with the way his opening plates, engraved by
the Dalziels, turned out, and 'without complaining . . . or expressing himself otherwise than as being obliged' to the engraver 'for
his care of No. 1', told Dickens 'that there is a brother-student of
his, a wood-engraver, perfectly acquainted with his style and well
understanding his meaning, who would render him better' (N iii.
766). Part of the problem may have stemmed from the fact that
Fildes employed a new method, using photographic transfer, to
copy his design on to the block;[60] his 'brother-student', who 'has

[59] L. V. Fildes, *Luke Fildes, R.A.: A Victorian Painter* (London, Michael Joseph,
1968), p. 14.
[60] Ibid., p. 15. Among other advantages, Fildes was able to keep his original
drawings intact.

engraved Mr. Fildes' most successful drawings hitherto' (N iii. 766)
Dickens told Chapman, was undoubtedly more familiar with the
process, here used practically for the first time, than the Dalziels'
firm. In any case, Dickens accorded Fildes the honour of choosing
'whomsoever he knows will present him in his best aspect',
instructing Chapman to 'make the change' (N iii. 766). The plates
for Part II are unsigned by the engraver, but those for the remaining parts (though not the frontispiece, cut by I. [possibly Isaac L.]
Brown) are engraved by C. Roberts, presumably the 'brother-
student' Fildes recommended and possibly the same wood engraver who, on the faculty of the City and Guilds Technical Art
School, taught Charles Ricketts two decades later.[61] The whole
complex story of the illustrations for *Drood* indicates once again
that the old formulas, the familiar format and techniques, the
serviceable routines that had guaranteed success for thirty years,
no longer worked.

The wood engravings may show, as with *Our Mutual Friend*,
that Chapman and Hall hoped for a large circulation. The contract
which Chapman signed, guaranteeing to Dickens at least £625 per
part, clearly anticipated huge sales and profits, despite *Our Mutual
Friend*. Merchandisers expressed their optimism in very tangible
terms: the *Drood* Advertiser opens with thirty-six pages; Numbers
II, III, and V each contain twenty, IV rises to twenty-four, and the
final number drops to eighteen. It was a handsome tribute,
evidently not misplaced, since Forster reports that while Dickens
was still alive sales reached 50,000, but whether of the first number
or the third he does not say. 'We have been doing wonders with
No. 1', Dickens told Fields. '*It has very, very far outstripped every
one of its predecessors*' (N iii. 771), and was out of print within
a week.

Thoroughly professional, Dickens coped successfully with brand-
new illustrators and an unfamiliar format. When in early December
Clowes, the printers, reported that his first two numbers were
each six pages short, he went straight to work transposing one
chapter from the second to the first number and remodelling
the second altogether. Later on, he worked with great care to
bring on the events leading to the catastrophe at the appropriate
moment, dispersing his material so that the climax would come
at the right number, and the mystery develop and be resolved over

[61] See Muir, *Victorian Illustrated Books*, p. 190.

the whole twelve parts. Though rumours subsequently abounded that Dickens had trouble with the novel, and could not even see a way to solve the mystery himself, the last word we have, from Georgina and Mamie, is that he was 'in excellent spirits about his book'.[62]

Inevitably there were some mistakes, some misunderstandings. Dickens was anxious about Fildes's query concerning the importance of Jasper's long scarf, which Dickens confided was the murder weapon. Shortly before his death he asked Charley if he had 'let out too much of his story too soon'.[63] But these anxieties notwithstanding, the complex and painstaking business of writing, composing, proofing, printing, and selling a serial progressed on an even course. It could not have been accomplished had not the machinery been perfected over years of trial and error; it could not have been accomplished successfully without the assistance of countless minor figures, some of whose names appear at the head of the various compositors' 'takes' on the manuscripts, but most of whom have never been even so transiently memorialized. Towards the end of his life Dickens went out of his way to pay tribute to some of his silent collaborators: 'I am certain there are not in any branch of manual dexterity so many remarkable men as might be found in the printing trade', he told the Printers' Pension Society in 1864.

For quickness of perception, amount of endurance, and willingness to oblige, I have ever found the compositor pre-eminent. His labour is of a nature calling for the sympathy of all. Often labouring under an avalanche of work, carried through half the night—often through the whole night—working in an unnatural and unwholesome atmosphere produced by artificial light, and exposed to sudden changes from heat to cold, the journeyman printer is rendered peculiarly liable to pulmonary complaints, blindness, and other serious diseases.[64]

Dickens may have paid tribute to, but he also exacted his due from, these dextrous hands. He was one of those who might call unexpectedly for proof overnight, and he seldom if ever copied over a page, so that type was set from papers that became fouler, more interlineated, and more crabbed with each passing year. Yet

[62] *The Letters of Charles Dickens*, ed. by His Sister-in-Law and His Eldest Daughter [Georgina Hogarth and Mamie Dickens] (3 vols., London, Chapman and Hall, 1880 and 1882), ii. 446.

[63] Quoted by Charles Dickens, Jr., in his Introduction to the Macmillan edition of *Edwin Drood* (1923); see Cardwell, pp. xxvi–xxvii.

[64] *Speeches*, pp. 324–5.

he was exasperated beyond soothing by misreadings that were not only plausible but almost inevitable given the copy, the pressure of time, the quality of the working conditions. And proofs, when Dickens returned them, looked 'like an inky fishing-net' (N ii. 782). They were not perhaps quite so extremely revised as Balzac's, where 'From every character, every printed word, runs a line of ink soaring out like a rocket and bursting at the end into a luminous shower of phrases, adjectives, nouns, underlined, crossed through, mixed up, altered, overwritten ... four or five hundred arabesques of this sort, tangled, interwoven, climbing, running from one margin to the other and from south to north.'[65] But they were bad enough, and when Dickens corrected them, chopping here, adding there, rearranging paragraphs, adding or subtracting punctuation, capitalization, phrases, clauses, he did so usually without benefit of the original manuscript, and with an eye to filling all thirty-two pages with lively dialogue and description, and not to reproducing exactly whatever he had originally written. So he was grateful, and said so in public as chairman of a meeting of the Printers' Readers' Association in 1867, for the correctors of the press, those patient souls whose duties required 'much natural intelligence, much superadded cultivation, considerable readiness of reference, quickness of resource, an excellent memory, and a clear understanding'. After the loud cheers subsided, Dickens continued: 'And I most gratefully acknowledge that I have never gone through the sheets of any book that I have written without having had presented to me by the corrector of the press, some slight misunderstanding into which I have fallen, some little lapse I have made; in short, without having set down in black and white some unquestionable indication that I have been closely followed through my work by a patient and trained mind, and not merely by a skillful eye.'[66]

On 9 June 1870 all that came to an end. Struck down in the middle of a novel, Dickens died as he had lived, a writer; and many of the paintings that recorded Dickens's passing showed the artist at his desk. The estate which he garnered from a lifetime of

[65] Édouard Ourliac, quoted in André Maurois, *Prometheus: The Life of Balzac*, trans. Norman Denny (New York, Harper and Row, 1965), p. 281.
[66] *Speeches*, p. 367.

authorship amounted to £93,000, including a 'less than two years'' valuation of *All the Year Round* (F, Appendix, p. 860). Though perhaps as much as £45,000 had been earned in the final decade from readings, some of that money had been spent in living expenses over the same period, and even the money earned from the readings came in part because Dickens was a great writer. His estate was over twice that left by the haughty banker George Beadnell a few years earlier, the father who had once turned down the young writer as an eligible suitor for his daughter because he was obscure and poor.

Dickens's will stressed his desire to be buried without pomp or title, and to be mourned without scarves, cloaks, black bows, long hat-bands, 'or other such revolting absurdity'. It requested that no monument, memorial, or testimonial be created; though on that point the wishes of the nation revoked Dickens's testament. He preferred to rest his claims 'to the remembrance of my country upon my published works, and to the remembrance of my friends upon their experience of me in addition thereto' (F, Appendix, p. 859). The published works spoke, and speak, for themselves; Carlyle spoke for many of those friends: 'every new meeting ripened [my acquaintance] into more and more clear discernment of his rare and great worth as a brother man; a most cordial, sincere, clear-sighted, quietly decisive, just and loving man'. As for Dickens's death:

It is an event world-wide; a *unique* of talents suddenly extinct; and has 'eclipsed,' we too may say, 'the harmless gaiety of nations.' No death since 1866 has fallen on me with such a stroke. No literary man's hitherto ever did. The good, the gentle, high-gifted, ever-friendly, noble Dickens,—every inch of him an Honest Man.[67]

[67] Quoted in F XI. iii. 836.

16

The Audience Widens

I believe it to be a fact that of no English author has
the sale of the works been at the same time so large
and so profitable for the first half-dozen years after
his death as of Dickens . . .

ANTHONY TROLLOPE, 'Novel-Reading'[1]

IN THE THIRTY YEARS FOLLOWING DICKENS'S DEATH his
reputation suffered at the hands of those like the Stephen
brothers and Mrs. Oliphant who thought him vulgar,
critical of the educated and professional classes, and out of date.[2]
Forster's biography stirred up a good deal of reaction in the
leading journals, and brought forth some half-hearted defences
such as that by Richard Bentley's son George: 'As a novelist he is
distinguished, as a humorist he is unrivalled; but when he deals
with the larger spheres of morals, with politics, and with the
mechanism of state and official life, he is absurd.'[3]

Yet the denigration or dismissal of Dickens by intellectuals had
no effect on his popularity measured in sales. By 1863 Chapman
and Hall had disposed of 140,000 copies of *Pickwick* and 100,000 of
Nickleby.[4] During Dickens's lifetime his writings appeared in a
bewildering variety of editions, each designed to attract its own
class of customers, to work its special segment of the market.
Thus *Pickwick* could be obtained in shilling monthly numbers;
bound from the parts in cloth for 21*s*., half-morocco for 24*s*. 6*d*.,
or full morocco with gilt leaves for 26*s*. 6*d*.; in the Cheap edition
in 1½*d*. weekly numbers, 7*d*. monthly parts, as a set of unbound

---

[1] *The Nineteenth Century*, 5 (1879), 24.
[2] K. J. Fielding, '1870–1900: Forster and Reaction', *Dickensian*, 66 (May 1970),
86–8.
[3] *Temple Bar* (May 1873), quoted in Fielding, '1870–1900', p. 94.
[4] *Spectator*, 36 (1863), 17.

numbers for 4s., in wrappers for 4s. 6d., bound in cloth with full gilt back for 5s., or in 'half-morocco, marbled edges' for 7s. 6d.; in the Library edition of 1858, two volumes post 8vo bound in cloth at 6s. each; in the illustrated Library edition of 1861 at 7s. 6d. (later 8s.) each; in the People's edition of 1865, two volumes for 4s.; and in the Charles Dickens edition of 1867, one volume for 3s. 6d. *Oliver Twist*, originally serialized in *Bentley's Miscellany*, went through thirteen editions or variant issues by 1867.

G. H. Lewes pondered the discrepancy between Dickens's critical and popular receptions: 'There probably never was a writer of so vast a popularity whose genius was so little *appreciated* by the critics. . . . How are we to reconcile this immense popularity with this critical contempt?'[5] The real answer was, and to some extent still may be, that the discrepancy cannot be explained, though sales of Dickens's works in the 1960s to secondary school children and college undergraduates indicate the significant influence of a late academic appreciation in closing the gap between popular and critical appreciation. If anything, the discrepancy seems to be reversing, with intellectuals growing more responsive to Dickens while students flee from him.

Undaunted by the contempt towards Dickens expressed in the journals, Chapman and Hall went ahead with plans for the Household edition, which began appearing in 1871 in small quartos with vile woodcuts from new designs by the partly paralysed Browne. In this effort they may have been influenced by an obituary article in *The Graphic*, 13 June 1870, which noted that despite the bewildering array of inexpensive formats exploited by Dickens and his publishers to reach the masses,

there have never been in this country anything like those cheap popular editions which have secured to other writers so enormous a sale. For this reason the fame of Dickens is still chiefly confined to the middle and upper classes, while there cannot be any doubt that in the United States, owing to the low price at which his novels have been issued there, they have been read by a far greater number in proportion to population. With us, in fact, Dickens has yet to become, as he inevitably will become, the favourite of the poorer classes. . . . An edition of Thackeray in penny numbers would be certainly a doubtful experiment; but of an edition in that form of Dickens's works . . . what might not be expected? In other countries such editions of valuable

[5] 'Dickens in Relation to Criticism', *Fortnightly Review*, N.S. 11 (Feb. 1872), 143; and quoted in Fielding, '1870–1900', p. 93.

copyright works are common enough, even in the author's lifetime. The edition of Victor Hugo's great novel *Les Misérables* in penny numbers, with Brion's striking illustrations, is a case in point. Of the first issue of this publication it is said that 150,000 copies were sold, probably a greater number than has ever been circulated of the most successful of Mr Dickens's books.[6]

The writer was obviously mistaken in his surmise that no Dickens novel had approached the circulation of *Les Misérables*, but he was certainly correct in predicting great things from Dickens in penny numbers. The Household edition, which appeared in just such a format, as well as in monthly parts and volumes, got off to a hopeful start. Anthony Trollope wrote to Frederic Chapman that he had received conflicting reports from his son and Chapman about which format sold best: 'You say the greater sale is of the numbers,—which I should prefer as being the more likely to last. Harry says the greater sale is of the parts.' But, Trollope practically continued, 'in either case, 200,000 will do very well indeed. I shall be very anxious to hear what is the highest number reached, and also whether it is maintained.'[7] There is something incongruous about Trollope's profiting, in his later years, not only from his own writings but also from his investment in the firm that continued to circulate Dickens's works throughout the English-speaking world.[8] It is another indication of how far the status of writer had come from the bad old days.

In 1878 Chapman made another foray into bulk sales, concluding a complex set of agreements with George Routledge and Sons covering a variety of Dickens's properties. He sold the entire stock (106,000 copies, 30,000 of which were bound in boards) of the 2s. edition (the People's edition) of Dickens's works at 4d. per copy (covers for the remaining 76,000 being supplied), with the proviso that Chapman and Hall would buy back at the same price all copies unsold at the end of two years. At the same time Chapman guaranteed 'not to print any more copies, except to your order, at a less price than three Shillings retail, with the usual Trade allowances, till all these copies are disposed of'.[9]

[6] p. 674, quoted in Collins, *Dickens: The Critical Heritage*, pp. 16–17.

[7] *Letters*, no. 485.

[8] Another odd connection between Trollope and Dickens was established when Trollope's brother Thomas Adolphus married Ellen Ternan's sister.

[9] 27 Apr. 1878; *Publishers' Archives: George Routledge & Co. 1853–1900, Contracts 1850–78*, vols. 1 and 2 A–Q (Chadwyck-Healey Ltd. microfilms, reel 1).

In the same month of April a long agreement was reached[10] in which Routledge obtained from Chapman and Hall exclusive use of stereos and cover blocks for the 6*d.* edition of *Sketches by Boz* at a royalty of £1 per thousand copies. Routledge promised to print 20,000 copies by 1 May. Chapman and Hall were already committed to deliver 25,000 copies to F. Warne and Co., but otherwise agreed to sell *Sketches* only to Routledge. They also covenanted to sell 10,000 copies of the 1*s.* edition of *Oliver Twist* and 5,000 of *Sketches*, both in quires for 4½*d.* per copy, to give Routledge exclusive use of the *Twist* stereos in order to produce a 25,000 copy first edition of a sixpenny version by New Year's Day, and to refuse permission to print an edition at that price for any other firm. In the same agreement Chapman and Hall further promised to 'print at once' 20,000 copies of the 2*s. Chuzzlewit* and to sell that to Routledge at 9*d.* each in sheets, along with copies of the 2*s. Pickwick, Sketches, Twist,* and *Nickleby* at the same price in sheets or 11*d.* in boards. Again, Routledge became the exclusive distributor of that edition. Five hundred sets of the twenty-one-volume Charles Dickens edition were to be supplied through Routledge for America at 18*s.* per set, with the right to renew at the same terms indefinitely. Another 10,000 volumes of that edition were to be supplied at half retail price, again with the right to buy more 'at the usual trade price less fifteen per cent. discount'. Routledge was not to wholesale these books to W. H. Smith, Simpkin Marshall, Hamilton, or W. Kent, the only markets Chapman and Hall reserved for themselves, but otherwise they were at liberty to sell to anyone. Finally, Chapman and Hall agreed to sell the Household edition to Routledge at half retail price on special order, with the customary provisions for future orders. In September Routledge offered £200 for 20,000 of *Twist* '6th Ed. quires only & no Wrapper', and £600 for 30,000 *Pickwick*s in 'two parts quires only'.[11]

These agreements document the continuing expansion of Dickens's sales. Twelve years after his death no fewer than 4,239,000 volumes had been purchased in England alone.[12] But Dickens was not just sold; his works were given away as

[10] Memorandum of an Agreement, 16 Apr. 1878, Routledge *Archives.*
[11] 21 Sept. 1878, Routledge *Archives.*
[12] Mowbray Morris, 'Charles Dickens', *Fortnightly Review,* N.S. 32 (Dec. 1882), 762; rpt. in Collins, *Dickens: The Critical Heritage,* p. 599.

incentives to customers. Two instances of these 'free' Dickens books have survived, the first related by Trollope in 1879, the second only recently brought to light in *Notes and Queries* (1973).

Trollope records:

There has grown up a custom of late, especially among tea dealers, to give away a certain number of books among their poorer customers. When so much tea has been consumed, then shall be a book given. It came to my ears the other day that eighteen thousand volumes of Dickens's works had just been ordered for this purpose. The book-seller suggested that a little novelty might be expedient. Would the benevolent tea-dealer like to vary his presents? But no! The tradesman, knowing his business, and being anxious above all things to attract, declared that Dickens was what he wanted. He had found that the tea-consuming world preferred their Dickens.[13]

And in the nineties Richard Edward King of Curtain Road, E.C., obtained plates of the Charles Dickens edition from which he ran off reprints. King produced a *Pickwick* with his own imprint in September 1893; early in 1894 he pressed another set with the imprint of Faudel Phillips, wholesalers of embroidery silks, who used the copies as 'free gifts' to lure customers; and a third *Pickwick* was 'Published by C. Boardman', a furniture firm, for similar purposes.[14] Once, the shilling novels in monthly parts had been good places in which to advertise; now they were themselves advertisements.

On 2 July 1892 the *Publishers' Circular* commented that 'A total of close upon seven hundred thousand copies assuredly proves that Dickens is by far the most popular modern writer, with the single exception of Scott. Mr. Chapman, indeed, avers that "no author sells within sight of Dickens," but probably he had forgotten the author of "Waverley."' Perhaps, but in the twentieth century Dickens far outpaced his closest rival. Chapman and Hall alone sold 2,000,000 copies of his works between 1900 and 1906,[15] and in the latter year James Milne published an article entitled 'How Dickens Sells: He Comes Next to the Bible and Shakespeare'.[16] *John o' London's Weekly* conducted a survey in 1920 to determine

[13] 'Novel-Reading', pp. 32–3.
[14] See *Notes and Queries*, 218 (1973): query by J. M. Harries (p. 100) and reply by P. G. Scott (p. 341).
[15] Arthur Waugh in an interview in the *Book Monthly*, Aug. 1906, according to the *Dickensian*, 2 (1906), 228.
[16] *Book Monthly*, 3 (1906), 773–6.

if Dickens was still popular; the consensus among public lib-
rarians was overwhelmingly affirmative.[17] J. M. Dent's reported
in 1928 that he was a bestseller in their Everyman's Library
series; *Copperfield* led both the Everyman and the Collins Illustrated Classics series in 1935, perhaps because of M.G.M.'s film,
one of many based on Dickens's writings which are yet another
testimony to his universal popularity.[18] One second-hand book
dealer in 1931 explained the absence of any Dickens title in his
shop: 'He is so popular . . . that as soon as I get in a copy of any
single one of his books it is snapped up.'

Foreigners took to Dickens in ever increasing numbers too.
'For the last eleven years', Trinarch Ivansvitch Wredenskii told
Dickens in 1849, 'your name has enjoyed a wide celebrity in
Russia, and from the banks of the Neva to the remotest parts of
Siberia you are read with avidity. Your Dombey', he concluded
grandly, 'continues to inspire with enthusiasm the whole of the
literary Russia' (F VI. iv. 509–10). The influence of Dickens on
Russian authors has been much debated; even after the Revolution he continued his hold on the people. *Izvestia* recorded in
1937 that Dickens 'has become one of the most beloved authors
with Soviet readers', instancing the 166,000 copies of *Pickwick*,
Dombey, *Hard Times*, and *Bleak House* purchased in Moscow
bookshops within one week.[19]

Between 1858 and 1863 Hachette may have sold nearly
100,000 copies, and in the hundred years that followed by actual
tally they disposed of 777,101. In their series the two least popular
titles have proved to be *Barnaby Rudge* (18,819) and *Les Grandes
Ésperances* (18,144), neither of which was reprinted after World
War I. On the other hand, since 1939 there have been several re-
impressions of the best sellers: *Contes de Noël* (119,845), *David
Copperfield* (100,036), *Oliver Twist* (83,897), and *Aventures de Mr.
Pickwick* (75,712).[20]

In 1944 Dean Mott, an authority on popular literature in

[17] For this and the following three examples I am indebted to Michael Slater,
'1920–1940: "Superior Folk" and Scandalmongers', *Dickensian*, 66 (May 1970),
125–7.
[18] Dilys Powell, 'Postscript: Dickens on Film', *Dickensian*, 66 (May 1970),
183–5; and the continuing series of articles on and lists of films based upon
Dickens's works in the *Dickens Studies Newsletter*.
[19] Slater, '1920–1940', p. 127.
[20] Mistler, *La Librairie Hachette*, p. 162.

America, estimated that 2,000,000 copies of the *Carol*, and between 500,000 and 1,000,000 copies of each of the sixteen other works, had been sold, making Dickens 'the best-selling author in the history of American publishing'.[21] George Ford, surveying American circulation of Dickens's works in the single year 1968, arrived at the estimates of total sales given below.[22]

Estimate of Total Sales of Dickens's Works in the United States during 1968

	Title	Total sales
1.	Tale of Two Cities	293,060
2.	Great Expectations	238,670
3.	Oliver Twist	162,955
4.	Hard Times	106,050
5.	A Christmas Carol	97,440
6.	David Copperfield	60,970
7.	Bleak House	42,860
8.	Pickwick Papers	26,573
9.	The Mystery of Edwin Drood	11,485
10.	Our Mutual Friend	9,939
11.	Martin Chuzzlewit	8,525
12.	Dombey and Son	7,320
13.	Old Curiosity Shop	6,045
14.	Nicholas Nickleby	3,300
15.	Magic Fishbone	3,215
16.	The Cricket on the Hearth	3,105
17.	Little Dorrit	1,665
18.	Barnaby Rudge	1,625
19.	Christmas Stories	1,060
20.	American Notes	280
21.	Sketches by Boz	265
22.	A Child's History	80
23.	The Uncommercial Traveller	80
	TOTAL	1,086,567

Finally, there are so many paperback editions—more than seventy-five different printings of fifteen titles spread among twenty-four publishers—that *Dickens Studies Newsletter* has since September 1971 been running a kind of Consumer Report to help the befuddled buyer. But there is no sign that the flood is about to abate, or that future generations will be less responsive than the preceding ones have been to the vigour, humour, and humanity of Dickens.

[21] *Dickensian*, 40 (Mar. 1944), 56.
[22] 'Dickens in the 1960s', *Dickensian*, 66 (May 1970), 170–1.

It is the quality of Dickens's imagination, after all, that causes people to buy and read his works. The specialist perspective may seem to have created throughout this study the notion that format alone was the key to Dickens's success. Nothing could be further from the truth. His works were as certain to be read as bread to be eaten, as *The Economist* put it. Had he written exclusively in three-deckers, or for the theatre, undoubtedly Dickens could have adapted his vision and values to those genres and audiences. Indeed, what is apparent at the outset of his career is only that he wanted to be a writer; it was a series of accidents, or perhaps more accurately, contingent opportunities of which he took advantage, that steadied his ambition, channelling it into writing novels.

Nevertheless, those contingent opportunities were for Dickens, in the case of certain aspects of the whole business of publishing books—legal, financial, social, mechanical—newly available, and did contribute in multiple and significant ways to the pheno-menon (no lesser word will do) that Dickens became and still remains. Some fairly exact analogies with more recent develop-ments in the mass media may illustrate this contention better. Unquestionably films, and more recently television productions, made from Dickens's novels, Christmas Books, even from his life, have contributed significantly to the maintenance and ex-pansion of his audience. Conversely, noted film makers of several eras have borrowed ideas and techniques from Dickens's craft for translation into moving images. Public acknowledgement of that debt has provided yet another avenue of access to his works. Dickens's own readings must have functioned in a similar way. People more accustomed to the stage than the page were sent back to the printed word by what they had seen and heard; and Dickens's contemporaries, as well as those of a later generation like Emlyn Williams, Philip Collins, Robert Garis, and William Axton, found in his theatricality new dimensions of art.

Even closer parallels are apparent between the growth of paperback publishing in the post-war era, and the growth of serial fiction in the decades following the Treaty of Paris.[23] Oscar Dystel, president and chief executive officer of Bantam Books,

<hr>

[23] Allen Lane got Penguin into paperbacks well before the war (1935), but his was until the 1940s a pioneering, rather than characteristic, operation. Pocket Books began in 1939, Avon in 1941, Popular Library in 1942, and Bantam in 1945.

recently reviewed the three 'key factors' responsible for creating 'a mass market paperbound book industry'.[24] They are 'the availability of editorial material', 'the introduction of the rubber plate rotary press', and 'the advent of the magazine wholesaler as the distribution arm'. Those same factors—the availability of literary material, new technology, and expanded distribution—converged in the nineteenth century to revolutionize publishing through serial issue. Before good popular material could be written expressly for and bought at good prices by Victorian publishers, it was necessary to make legal and financial arrangements whereby the author shared in the productions of his pen. Once that was accomplished, publishers could pay incentive prices, sums that themselves created the stimulus to write. And authors were encouraged to write (and behave, in some cases) in ways that captured widespread attention, so that publishers could recoup their investment.

Revolutions in the hardware of publishing, from paper-making to binding, from composition to illustration, allowed those publishers to produce books in large numbers quickly, more or less uniformly, and cheaply, exactly what the rubber rotary press did for our modern age: 'those huge, fast presses which, for the first time, enabled publishers to print paperbacks like magazines, ordering large, economical quantities at a unit cost of pennies.'[25]

The third factor involves enlargement of distribution and markets. In the eighteenth century there were perhaps half a dozen streets in London where publishers were congregated, and in the rest of the British Isles only a few other firms engaged in publishing; with the exception of university towns, there were scarcely any good retail bookshops either. But in 1836, when Chapman and Hall launched *Pickwick*, they sold copies not only in the Strand but all over the realm, and not only through the outlets clustered around St. Paul's but also by means of pedlars, provincial shops, and the Royal mail. By 1870 individual novels and collected editions of the works could be had at W. H. Smith's stores and other shops selling sundries, tobacco, sweets, stationery, and magazines as well as a few books.

[24] 'The Paperback & the Bookstore', special advertising supplement to the *New York Times*, 25 May 1975, pp. 16–17; used by permission of Bantam Books, Inc.
[25] Ibid., p. 17.

It is not difficult to discern the comparable effect that paperback distribution has had on publishing:

While most of the traditional booksellers continued to concentrate on the hardcover market, paperback book sales were being tended to by a new kind of bookseller—the wholesaler, his driver salesman, and the newsstand-drugstore operator, whose establishment typified a totally new kind of book outlet. Most importantly, this expanded distribution was creating a new kind of book audience, a hungry audience of millions of people of all ages who perhaps had never before bought a book, or had been in a bookstore, but who were now flocking to the newly installed wire book racks, attracted by the paperback's friendly appearance, convenience, compactness and low price, as well as its editorial content.[26]

The revolutionary distribution system, Dystel says, *created* a new audience, one that had perhaps never bought a book, and who now sought out the attractive, convenient, compact, cheap, and entertaining paper-covered texts. How similar to the feeling we know Dickens's green leaves inspired among millions of his countrymen, who might for the first time own a book, or at least a portion of one, complete with text and illustrations and a puzzling but enticing wrapper design for a few pennies.

People bought Dickens who couldn't even read, and therefore clubbed together to purchase the parts and take them to the corner tobacconist to be read aloud. The episode Forster recounts of the elderly charwoman who exclaimed upon meeting Dickens that she thought 'three or four men must have put together *Dombey*' has often been instanced as testimony to Dickens's prodigality of invention, to the 'phenomenon' of Dickens as I called it earlier. The story is equally, if not more, interesting for what it reveals about the strategies ordinary people devised to obtain Dickens's writing, and valuable because so little testimony from illiterates survives:

Being pressed farther to what her notion was of this mystery of a *Dombey* (for it was known she could not read), it turned out that she lodged where there were several other lodgers; and that on the first Monday of every month there was a Tea, and the landlord read the month's number of *Dombey*, those only of the lodgers who subscribed to the tea partaking of that luxury, but all having the benefit of the reading. (F V. vii. 454)

(The story also, incidentally, confirms the affinity noted earlier between the Inimitable and Tea.)

That Dickens issued the writings which made him famous serially is therefore a fact of paramount importance. Serialization does not explain the character of his imagination; it only partly accounts for the structures of his fiction; it is not the only cause of his unprecedented popularity and success. It bears approximately the same relation to his work as the Globe Theatre does to Shakespeare's, establishing the physical arena for the art, defining the scope and class of audience, connecting in an exceptionally direct way the author to his public, the performance to his purse. *As You Like It* need not be played in a replica of the Globe, any more than Dickens need be read in parts. But a fuller understanding of the opportunities and constraints that shaped each work may be gained from an awareness of the circumstances of their first appearance.

Serial publication supplied Dickens with both opportunities and constraints. In the early years the cornucopia spewed forth pounds and parts in a never-ceasing stream. The reception of *Pickwick* took everyone by surprise. It was so unprecedented that it provoked immediate strains in every dimension of publishing: illustrations had to be duplicated because no steel plate could stand the number of impressions demanded; repeated cash binds forced Chapman and Hall to revise their payment schedules, while at the same time increasing their stipends to Dickens; contractual agreements that did not and probably could not have been expected to anticipate such a reception had to change to represent what was, all things considered, a new enterprise— based on lots of preceding experience and experiments, to be sure, but new in scale and in scope.

Those very opportunities so effectively exploited by all concerned also entailed constraints that eventually proved too restrictive. It is difficult to defend the exact pretexts Dickens chose for quarrelling with Bentley and Macrone, equally difficult not to sympathize with them for trying, and failing, to ride on the back of the tiger.[27] They fell off for different reasons, Macrone for being

---

[27] See Ley's notes 101 and 102 in his edition of Forster (pp. 98–100), where he

opportunistic and flexible enough to try to reissue the *Sketches* in yet another serial format identical to the one which had just proved so popular, Bentley for being opportunistic but conventional in hiring Dickens as editor and then trying to confine him to standard novel contracts. Dickens may not have behaved like a gentleman; he certainly broke his word; but then, as the courts recognized, how do you force an artist to write against the grain? And how could it not go against the grain to spend months writing a book for pennies a page whose copyright would unquestionably fetch thousands of pounds for its owner, the publisher?

Chapman and Hall deserve credit for keeping up with Dickens as long as they did. More payments for *Pickwick*, then *Nickleby*, than originally promised; a wholly new venture in weekly parts with the *Clock*; a year-long vacation for their author financed against probable future books; unexpectedly a highly controversial travelogue in two volumes instead of the expected fiction; then an unsuccessful novel issued at the height of a traumatic and transatlantic depression in publishing; and finally an expensive, wonderful Christmas Book whose design and manufacture were peremptorily removed from their control. Yet their capacity to stay in the saddle had its limits too. Again serial publication revealed a serious constraint: the author's sale of outright copyright, even his lease for the duration of the serial run, gave him an income only during the months he wrote and published. No green leaves meant no green notes, or else a mortgaged future. And the only security on the mortgage was the hope of future leaves unfolding from who knows what mysterious reservoir of genius and energy.

Dickens recognized not only the economic constraint of serial publication, but also its artistic drawbacks. He thrashed about in the early forties for some other equally rewarding way of writing: weekly parts to foil the pirates, perhaps a three-decker issued all at once, maybe a series of travel books composed of letters possibly published first in a newspaper or magazine, occasional political and social commentary in a leading organ of public opinion. The most successful alternative ironically precipitated the break with Chapman and Hall, namely the Christmas Books, which

concludes that with respect to all Dickens's disputes with his publishers, 'not in a single one had Dickens fair play on his side'.

in one form or another became a central component in the phenomenon of Dickens until his death. Issuing the *Carol* in the same year as the first Christmas card, originated by Henry Cole and designed by John Calcott Horsley, R.A., Dickens became associated with the Christmas season, with 'la philosophie de Noël', and with a complex and peculiarly English December festival comprising food, drink, theatre, presents, charity, celebration, family, and worship.

The break with Chapman and Hall involves many ironies. It was ostensibly precipitated by the *Carol* profits, over which they had no control and could hardly, in fairness, be blamed. Its origins can be traced back to Hall's understandable, if ill-advised, recommendation that something further be done to secure repayment of the firm's advances. That *Chuzzlewit* was not reducing the debt fast enough was nobody's fault. Times were bad for books. That there was a debt to be repaid stemmed from Dickens's legitimate need for a break from constant writing. And that he had to write constantly was the disadvantageous side of the serial coin.

Moreover, the move to Bradbury and Evans produced other ironies. The firm that developed serialization saw its former printing subcontractor collect at least double their annual income from Dickens's serials and magazine in the forties and fifties. At the same time Chapman and Hall remained legally allied to Dickens through shared copyrights so that they could not get divorced. And though serials put novel-owning within the means of poorer classes, it did not reach low enough, nor were the monthly parts permanent. Hence the Cheap edition, which at the same time made Dickens's work less expensive and, in bound form, more permanent. It was the first in a series of collected editions published during Dickens's lifetime that aimed at different markets and resulted in wider sales and continued profits from previously published works. Though few of those editions are textually significant, in terms of the audiences to which they were directed and the steady profits they generated (excepting, for three years, the Library edition), they were immensely important to Dickens, to his publishers, and to his readers.

In the fifties strains intensified once more. For the most part they were related to Dickens's personal and imaginative life, and not to his publications. But the break with Bradbury and Evans was ultimately caused by two different understandings of the relation between a popular author's public and private life. Dickens shaped his public image to his audience, his age, and his philosophy. No one reading his letters can remain unaware of how often Dickens's choice was governed by what seemed fitting, even expedient, for such a popular figure: he will not give to every writer of begging letters, but he will lend his name, his pen, his presence, even his voice, on behalf of International Copyright, indigent authors and widows, the dignity of literature. He will not meet the Queen in farcical costume, nor stand for Parliament on the basis of his fame; but he will play before Her Royal Highness and use every public forum to propagandize for certain reforms. At each point he tries to discriminate between being famous, like Scott, and being notorious, like Byron. Unfortunately by 1856 some of his human needs were not met within the family, and demanded fulfilment with an urgency he could no longer deny. Dickens entered into his protracted liaison with Ellen Ternan no more lightly than George Eliot joined Lewes at Weimar, though some of the later criticism of his separation from Kate and alliance with Ellen seems to imply a casual heartlessness. Having determined on that momentous step, Dickens took extraordinary care, in his way, to make the public division (the addition always remaining private) as compatible as possible with that long-nurtured public image of the genial humourist, the champion of the poor, the apostle of the home. Bradbury and Evans, so right from every standpoint connected narrowly with the publication of *Punch*, were none the less fatally wrong in judging how important to the phenomenon of Dickens it was for them publicly to associate themselves with his defence. Once again, the constraints imposed by serial publication were more fully appreciated by Dickens than by others.

The return to Chapman and Hall further ramified the ironies of Dickens's relations with his publishers. For the firm had already lost its junior partner by death, and was shortly to lose its senior one through retirement. There is both more continuity with the Strand and less than meets the eye: more, because the 1844 break was never decisive and complete like the 1858 one,[28] less because the partners in the firm had completely changed by 1860. More-

---

[28] In seven accounting periods between 1846 and 1861, Chapman and Hall's earnings for Dickens exceeded those from Bradbury and Evans.

over, though Chapman and Hall had developed serial fiction, Bradbury and Evans had enjoyed its fruits. When Dickens returned to his old firm the twenty-part serial no longer commanded the same place in the market: the 2s. and later 1s. magazines, and the three-decker, were gradually supplanting it.[29] So Dickens once again thrashed about searching for a new formula: in weekly parts and three volumes, in twenty numbers or twelve.

By the sixties, it seems fair to say, Dickens's independence of the circulating libraries was a distinctly mixed blessing. *Vanity Fair*, issued concurrently with *Dombey* in twenty numbers by Bradbury and Evans, had been taken up by Mudie's after the serial run, and by 1863 was fourth in popularity there.[30] At the same time Thackeray's reputation rose among the literati, making the *Cornhill* under his editorship a more exciting and significant journal than *All the Year Round*. No book by Dickens appears in Mudie's list of the ten most popular novels, though evidently the Leviathan stocked various collections beginning with the Cheap edition, and bought substantial numbers of *Great Expectations* and *Edwin Drood*. More and more in the last decade of his life the three-decker consolidated its claim to being *the* form for fiction. And adoption by Mudie's seemed, in the words of Mrs. Oliphant, 'a sort of recognition from heaven'.[31] That Dickens continued to eschew three volumes probably encouraged critics to condemn him as vulgar and low class, Cockney, though the plots and characters of many of Mudie's staples were in fact infinitely more trivial and common, dealing chiefly with a decidedly bourgeois conception of romantic love.

If the theatre and Christmas Books were a way out in the forties, the readings offered an escape in the fifties and sixties. They gave Dickens an opportunity to discharge huge quantities of psychic tension in the most personal and direct of encounters with his auditors, they reinforced the sense of a powerful authorial

---

[29] Trollope refers in a letter to Frederic Chapman to 'the old fashioned mode of publishing' he employed with *Rachel Ray*, issued in October in two volumes (*Letters*, no. 210, 9 Nov. 1863). At the same time *The Small House at Allington* was running serially in the *Cornhill*. Starting Jan. 1864 *Can You Forgive Her?* appeared in monthly parts, and *The Belton Estate* ran in the *Fortnightly Review* before coming out as a three-decker. Griest, pp. 44, 239–40, n. 20.

[30] *Spectator*, 36 (1863), 17–18.

[31] *Annals of a Publishing House: William Blackwood and his Sons* (3 vols., Edinburgh, Blackwood, 1897), ii. 458; quoted in Griest, p. 25.

presence connecting and energizing all his works, they enlarged and renewed his audience. But the *format* of the readings was essentially theatrical and oral; the publications issued in connection with various engagements in England and America never amounted to much. Readings stimulated sales of books and editions, but not of themselves.

Likewise the weekly journals, *Household Words* and *All the Year Round*, provided vehicles for escape from the constraints of serial fiction. Bradbury and Evans did well by the first, then lost everything and probably more in trying to establish a rival *Once a Week*. Chapman and Hall, who had backed *Master Humphrey's Clock* without much success, never got another chance to share in a Dickens periodical. But Dickens, who absolutely consolidated his editorial and financial control over his last magazine, eventually lost interest in it, finally turning over much of the management to Charley, whose competence had for years been questionable.

Throughout it all, there is no doubt that, to return to the point raised in the opening chapter, Dickens's muse was often 'given a final push by his bank manager'.[32] Indeed, one other small irony is the fact that his bank manager was Miss Coutts, for and with whom Dickens exerted himself prodigiously over three decades.[33] If anyone would have forgiven him his debts, it was she; but that very friendship made it imperative that he not overdraw his account at her bank. It is true that during the thirties Dickens had to write, furiously and continuously, to keep in the black; but that was also the time when his vitality and imagination, his optimism and cleverness, his manic gaiety and sense of power, were at their peak to spur him on. The timing of works throughout the forties was likewise affected by his balance sheet, and the contracts he signed throughout the first decade of his professional life carried forward previous debts to be cancelled by future surpluses.

Yet there is little evidence to support any contention that money alone motivated Dickens, or that he pandered to the pound. Sending Martin to America, even if it was done solely to boost sales (which seems doubtful) didn't work; killing Nell and

[32] Philip Collins, 'A Tale of Two Novels: *A Tale of Two Cities* and *Great Expectations* in Dickens' Career', *Dickens Studies Annual*, 2 (1972), 339.
[33] Johnson, *The Heart of Charles Dickens*, passim.

Paul and Dora were artistic decisions, not financial ones. However shrill Dickens's odes to the balance sheet, money helped shape the format and determine the timing of his works, and that was all—except for the readings, which do seem to have been to an unusual extent inspired by visions of pots of gold at the ends of provincial rainbows.

If Midsummer balances sometimes prompted Dickens and his publishers to new ventures, they also, after the forties, permitted him respites. The fifties show no let-up in Dickens's productivity: *Bleak House, Hard Times, Little Dorrit, A Tale of Two Cities, A Child's History of England, Household Words, All the Year Round,* and a succession of Christmas numbers, plus readings and plays. But his income evens out: there are no longer the awful dry spells between serials, because now his resources are strengthened by back sales, by new collected editions, by new markets on the Continent and in America, by the biannual profits of the journal, and by investments. Thus in the sixties there was not the necessity to write which was so urgent at an earlier time. True, Dickens sought money more than ever before, but the relative scarcity of new literary ventures may be partly attributable to the absence of earlier kinds of financial pressure. This apparent contradiction does not lessen the mystery of those final years; if anything it increases the obscurity of the causes which forced such a hectic baffled pace. The absence during Dickens's last decade of an economic necessity to write new works is, especially in contrast to earlier periods, a fact worth noting. None the less an imagined, and to some extent real, concern about the future financial security of his family impelled a succession of new editions, bulk sales of old ones, negotiations for foreign rights, and reading tours, more than the composition of further novels. Such shifts to make money underscore the significance, and the insignificance, of Dickens's publishing relations to his artistic productivity.

One point about foreign rights needs to be stressed. All things considered, Dickens did not do badly from countries that had no reciprocal copyright agreements with England. Several publishers behaved with model rectitude and consideration: Carey and Lea in the thirties, Harper's from the forties on, Tauchnitz from 1843, Hachette after 1856. Counting only direct payments to Dickens or his publishers from American firms, he received nearly £10,000, more if the annual payments for *All the*

Year Round were regularly received. And that excludes royalties on sales of editions Ticknor and Fields issued in connection with the second American tour, and all profits from those readings, which would not have been so enormously lucrative had there not been for decades thousands of cheap copies of all Dickens's writing circulated in every possible format from Maine to the banks of the Mississippi. It was more pique than truth that led Dickens to allege in 1867 that until that year 'In America the occupation of my life for thirty years is . . . utterly worthless and profitless to me.'[34]

The conditions of publishing, then, had much to do with Dickens's career. What seems puzzling from a literary perspective —the poor sales of *Chuzzlewit*, for instance—may be explained by conditions in the trade. And what looks like a falling-off of popularity and talent in the sixties, measured by critical reception, sales, and numbers of new works, seems very different when one examines publishers' records and totals all the different editions shipped off in thousands of copies to Boston, New York, Ireland, Australia, France, Germany, and the terminals of the great British railway system. His continued sales are ultimately even more important than the initial figures: the staggering fact about *Pickwick* or the *Carol* or *Copperfield* is not the number of copies sold at the start, but the progressive *increase* in circulation with each succeeding year, edition, and generation of readers. In countless ways, though the source of Dickens's popularity must always be acknowledged to be his literary achievement, that circulation was both originally and subsequently affected by the various relations into which he entered with his publishers.

What we have witnessed, buried beneath the masses of Gradgrindian 'facts and calculations' and the colourful anecdotes, is nothing less than a revolution in publishing, brought about by attendant revolutions in literacy, real wages, urbanization, industrialization, technology, commerce, finance, transportation, and law, to be sure, but at critical points fuelled and sparked by one writer, Charles Dickens. Working closely with a succession of enterprising publishers at home and abroad, Dickens democratized fiction. At the same time, he achieved through popular patronage a status as professional writer that no one before him, and few since, have enjoyed. Serial publication was for Dickens what the

[34] Mackenzie, Appendix, p. 1.

Globe Theatre was for Shakespeare. That Dickens wrote for money should be at the very least a neutral fact, and not a reason for calling his artistry or integrity in question. How it became possible for Dickens to write for money, on the other hand, takes us into the very heart of nineteenth-century culture and into all the intimately reciprocal connections between the artist and his age.

Appendices

INTRODUCTION

THESE appendices digest the information contained in the account books rendered to Dickens every six months from 1846 to 1870 by his two principal English publishers, Bradbury and Evans (1844–61) and Chapman and Hall (1836–70). They constitute the most detailed and complete record of a major author's publications that has yet been published, offering an unparalleled history of the biannual fluctuations in sales experienced by each of Dickens's literary ventures. One can infer from their perusal the continuing popularity of *Pickwick*, the effect of the Crimean War on the book trade, and the development during the sixties of significant relations between Dickens's publishers and the discount houses of Bohn, Routledge, and Smith and Son. It is possible to ascertain the number of parts of *David Copperfield* or the Cheap edition sold during Dickens's lifetime, and to calculate his, and his publishers', total income by year or through the duration of the accounts (Appendix C). These records, confirmed and supplemented by Bradbury and Evans's 'Paper and Print' ledgers for 1844–63, comprise the basis for much of the preceding narrative.

Upon the voluminous material of the account books, which run to over 1,100 folio pages, I have imposed grids which enable us to capture major features of Dickens's publishing career. The accounts themselves were made up twice a year in order to show Dickens the status of each of his titles in each of their editions. The clerks frequently used abbreviations of all sorts, because they were dealing with a man who knew his way around a printing house, and who was intimately familiar with press room charges, trade allowances, wholesale dealers, and international markets.[1] Every account principally reflects the conditions prevailing at the time it was composed; to a lesser extent, it takes its place in a chain of accounts, using as the base figure for each title the number remaining unsold at the end of the preceding accounting period, and carrying over to the next the amount of unsold stock and the occasional deferred charge or deficit.

---

[1] For evidence of Dickens's early interest in the minutiae of publishers' accounts, see his two-part article on 'Scott and his Publishers' in *The Examiner*, 31 Mar. and 29 Sept. 1839, reprinted in Waugh *et al.*, eds., *Collected Papers*, The Nonesuch Dickens (Bloomsbury, The Nonesuch Press, 1937), 127–42.

But the accounts were made up by clerks who came and went— there are at least ten changes of handwriting in the Chapman and Hall records—for firms whose partners changed, and for titles whose copyright shares might be altered from time to time or whose commissions might be reduced, increased, or eliminated. There was little energy expended in keeping them consistent over a quarter of a century. Moreover, though the accounting methods of the two firms are roughly comparable, the reports were made up by two entirely different publishing houses, one with sixteen years' experience publishing, wholesaling, and retailing serials, books, and editions, the other a printing concern that got into publishing first through a humour magazine and then, reluctantly, took over the publishing as well as the printing of their most famous client. It is unlikely that Bradbury and Evans's clerks ever saw Chapman and Hall's accounts, or vice versa, except perhaps when the firms shared the copyright in such works as the Cheap edition *Oliver Twist*.

Consequently the amount of variation in procedures and categories makes these ledgers difficult to use verbatim, even if the handwriting were always legible, which it is not. Therefore, I have selected certain categories and attempted to establish accurate, consistent figures for them throughout the whole period. This effort has involved much winnowing of information, much condensation or digestion of data, and some modification of the written record where other sources indicate it to be necessary. These tables are not substitutes for the original records; they organize and summarize them according to elementary classifications: sales, profits, printing orders. In their very form they are an act of interpretation.

Every effort has been made, therefore, to make the figures themselves reliable. But errors of interpretation, inconsistencies in nomenclature, even errors of computation so riddle the originals that inevitably some considerable margin for mistake threatens anyone who attempts to systematize or interpret these accounts. In dealing with individual line items all students should be advised that the discrete data do not always represent the same thing, though they may seem to. In some, but not all, Bradbury and Evans accounts, for example, the figure for commission includes their payments of agents' commissions; by checking the 'Paper and Print' ledgers or otherwise calculating the likely division of commission, I have arrived at an approximation of the publishers' share. Thus in some cases my figure will not agree with the MS. account. Also, sometimes for both publishers the commission is deferred until a later accounting period: my figures usually indicate when the sum was due, rather than when it was paid. And there are hundreds of other cases where my transcription varies from the original; they are mostly trifling and mostly deliberate, but they add up to a whole that should be more reliable than, but unfaithful to, the MS. accounts themselves.

For each appendix the titles are listed in alphabetical order. Since there are so many different titles and title-pages for Dickens's works, I have employed the customary forms, rather than exact titles from, say, the printed title-page of the first bound edition. *The Life and Adventures of Martin Chuzzlewit* will be found under *Martin*, *The Posthumous Papers of the Pickwick Club* under *Pickwick*. *The Old Curiosity Shop* and *Barnaby Rudge* are hidden under the title *Master Humphrey's Clock*, for Chapman and Hall continued to account in numbers of the *Clock* even when only the sections containing the novels were reprinted and sold.

Novels and other works sometimes seem to disappear; there is an especially large sump hole in 1861. Bradbury and Evans account for their works title by title, and thus until the final transfer of all stock in 1861 to Chapman and Hall there is an account for each of their Christmas Books and their volumes in the Cheap, Library, and reading editions. Chapman and Hall, on the other hand, tend to consolidate titles: the Cheap edition appears in their records in four different collective accounts: weekly numbers and parts, volumes at 3s., volumes at 3s. 6d., and volumes at 5s. It is not therefore possible to trace the history of any title in that edition, since after 1861 its individuality is collectivized according to economic criteria. A similar fate met the Christmas Books in their original 5s. editions, the five reading editions, and the Library edition.

Identification of the precise edition of any text to which the record refers has also been difficult. The publishers tend to head their pages by a brief title and some identification of format: 'crown 8vo numbers' or 'demy 8vo parts'. These paper sizes do not always tally with the descriptions offered in the publishers' advertisements, or in the *English Catalogue*. The many alternative forms of *Oliver Twist* have confused everyone: Chapman, Dickens, Bradbury and Evans, and Gerald Grubb.

Numbers are notoriously untrustworthy, and these numbers deserve a special place in the museum of notoriety. They can be made to say many things that are not quite true, some that are quite false, and they cannot be made quite to yield the simple answers we all seek. How much did Dickens make from his books? The records only start in 1846, ten years after his first, huge, successes; they do not consistently record payments from foreign publishers; they do not include his profits from *Household Words* or *All the Year Round*. How much did his publishers make? Were his complaints about their enriching themselves at his expense valid? Again, the records are incomplete in various ways. How many copies did he sell? Depending on what one means by copies (do you count incompleted runs of a serial or the Cheap edition numbers? do you include copies of newspapers that serialized the story?), the records again fail to be complete or even helpful. One can say that the demand for some titles kept up at a level far higher than for some other titles; equally, one cannot explain issuing two different new editions of *Dombey* in 1858 on the grounds of demand—they came out in the same year to fill gaps in the Cheap and Library editions.

Whatever one asks of these records, the answer ought to be qualified by 'about', 'approximately', 'nearly', 'almost', 'in the neighbourhood of', and all those other 'weasel' words scholars employ and the public deplores. Whether it was worth going through so much to get to so little, as Tony Weller remarked about the alphabet, is a matter of taste.

Appendix A

SALES AND PROFITS OF DICKENS'S WORKS
1846–70

THESE tables record the cost and sales of Dickens's works from 1846 to June 1870. Below each title I have supplied several pieces of information. The first item, missing in some instances, indicates the number of numbers, parts, or volumes containing the title, as the publisher accounts for that work. The Library edition did not reach its full complement of twenty-six volumes until 1867 with the addition of the two-volume *Our Mutual Friend*. And all the '20 parts as 19' novels came out in bound form with covers ranging from cloth to full morocco and at prices ranging from 21s. to 26s. 6d. So the figure is there merely to indicate to what format the account usually, or at some important point, refers. Where no figure is given, as in the Cheap edition in numbers and parts, it is because the information might mislead more than help: the numbers were serially printed for several years and did not reach their end until the 209th, containing the conclusion of the last Christmas Book, appeared in 1852. Moreover, the seventeen numbers of the Cheap edition Christmas Books received a separate accounting through 1861.

The next piece of information is the name of the publisher. It is not always, however, the name of the publisher who published the book. On the title-page of a first edition of *The Chimes* Chapman and Hall are identified as publishers, but in fact Bradbury and Evans printed and accounted for it. Because Dickens shared copyrights with two different publishers, the collected editions until 1861 reflected the split, some volumes being accounted for by one firm, some by the other. Thus I have chosen to indicate the publisher's account from which the table is drawn; though even here, in the case where the book is transferred to Chapman and Hall for the sixties, my practice necessarily differs from my principle.

The date that follows, and the price that follows the date, refer to the format identified at the beginning of the line. For the most part, the price at which one of Dickens's books was first sold was the price at which it could be obtained throughout his lifetime; often, of course, titles were remaindered at lesser sums. But there was virtually no inflation between 1836 and 1870: *Our Mutual Friend* and *Edwin*

Drood sold for a shilling a number just as *Pickwick* had three decades before, and *Pickwick* could still be purchased bound for 21*s*. in 1870.

For most of the tables, the presentation is the same. The left-hand column records the accounting period: June (J) or December (D), followed by the year. Next comes the column of sales, in quantity. Usually the quantity is stated in terms of the format specified at the top of the page: *Nickleby* by parts, the Cheap edition by numbers and parts, the Christmas Books by volumes, and the Charles Dickens edition by separate volumes and sets of eighteen. For *Oliver Twist* and *Great Expectations* in three volumes, the sales figures are for the title complete. Since Victorian publishers sold copies in a bewildering variety of ways for incredibly confusing ranges of discounts and free books, I have included in these figures all books allowed as discounts or free copies, but excluded books given away free by the publishers to Dickens to distribute among his friends, or sent out as review copies or to the depository libraries. Technically, therefore, this column only partly reflects *sold* books. Where the publisher was giving a discount to an exporter or retailer or dealer in remainders, the book may or may not be considered to have been sold. It was sold, if at all, to another book dealer, not to a customer. Generally there are no returns from these sales, but whether the individual retailer actually disposed of each title in his stock, or threw some out that got dirty, torn, or tired, these accounts do not specify. On the other hand, in addition to acting as book wholesalers, Chapman and Hall sometimes sold quantities—even large quantities—of copies on their own as retailers. Or at least they account for a large number of copies in some accounts sold at the highest of the publishers' prices, without any discount, and I infer from this that these are the copies which they disposed of without assistance through their network of shops and associates. Not one of these prices, it will be observed, comes close to equalling the retail cost of the book; the discounts get deeper and deeper in the sixties, as Frederic Chapman concentrates on expanding volume. In J66 all remaining copies of the two-volume edition of *American Notes*, which retailed for 21*s*., were sold for 1*s*. 6*d*. per volume, and in the last two accounting periods (D69, J70), Chapman disposed of 93,500 copies of the People's edition to Smith and Son at 5*d*. apiece.

Profits at least ought to be simple to determine. But unfortunately the figures in these columns are as much subject to qualification and interpretation as any others. The customary, but not inevitable, practice for both publishing houses was to account for the individual titles separately, and then on the cash account or general account or balance sheet to list the sums owing to Dickens. Bradbury and Evans usually figure the profit split on the individual account and carry that forward; Chapman and Hall after 1861 tend to carry forward the net profit, add all the nets together, and divide by two, since after Dickens's return to them they split fifty/fifty all profits and losses. Even in such straight-forward procedures there are mistakes—figures mis-carried or mis-calculated. But there were also special provisions governing certain books. Warehousing and insurance for the numbers of *Master Humphrey's Clock* was a joint expense to be deducted from net profits; for some titles, notably *Pickwick*, the split was not fifty/fifty but two-thirds/one-third, Dickens getting the smaller share. And where there were losses, the accounts differ in their treatment. Sometimes, usually in the case of Bradbury and Evans, the losses are appropriately divided in the same way profits are, and carried forward to the cash account. In such cases it is possible to add up the columns and arrive at net profits for Dickens and his publishers. In other cases, more often with Chapman and Hall, the losses are not divided, sometimes not brought forward to the balance sheet to be cancelled by other profits, but carried forward to the next account of the individual title and so on until the profits on that book wipe out the deficit. If the loss is carried forward then, either on the individual account or the general one, it must not be added time after time, as it is only a loss carry-forward, not a new deficit.

It may seem inexplicable that the same volume of business in two different years should produce such different results. Ten thousand copies of *Pickwick* sold during the J65 period yielded a scant £9. 6s. 8d. as half-profit, yet six months later on the same volume Dickens's net increased almost seven-fold to £62. 9s. The difference can be attributed largely to the cost of reprinting numbers to increase or equalize stock, and thus the first two appendices work together to provide the history of Dickens's publications.

Publishers' commissions were customarily figured as a percentage of the gross sales. They ranged from 15 to 5 per cent; after 1858 Bradbury and Evans's was cut to 5 per cent on all titles in their possession. In a few cases the publishers shared in the profits, but received no com-mission; this was regularly done on many titles after 1861. Conversely, in at least one other case, *A Christmas Carol*, Chapman and Hall had no part of the copyright or profits, only a commission. It has been diffi-cult to dig out of these records the figures for commissions, but it became apparent early in my study that simply noting the division of profits did not fairly reflect the income enjoyed respectively by the copyright partners. Half-profits plus a 5 per cent commission on gross sales could mean that Chapman and Hall received considerably more than Dickens; the *Pickwick* split tilts even more towards the publishers when one adds to their two-thirds' share of the profits their commission income.

Then there are all the exceptions to these rules and practices, most of which are separately footnoted. One kind of note concerns mistakes in computation committed by the publishers' clerks; some of these Dickens caught, some slipped by. The D67 accounts were very sloppy; the whole set had to be corrected. At other times there was no account supplied at all, or at most a laconic notation that the account was still in arrears or that there had been no sales. When Bradbury and Evans totalled up their books in preparation for transferring all their shares to Chapman and Hall in 1861, they recorded the quantities. Since technically all these items were sold, I have listed those figures in the appropriate column, but in parenthesis for two reasons: one, the books were not sold in the same sense as other sales; two, Chapman and Hall could not confirm Bradbury and Evans's figures, coming up with considerably fewer numbers of some titles, more of others, and eventually forcing an adjustment in the terms of sale among all parties.

Because so much business was done in bulk during the sixties, I have tried to note the kinds of bargains Frederic Chapman concluded, and their quantities. His clerks are not consistent in their information, and I have not tried to fill their lacunae. For the most part the firms listed in these notes are familiar to students of Victorian publishing; I have given them all a name and stuck with it, no matter how often the firm itself altered its name during the period. Thus Ticknor and Fields remains Ticknor and Fields even after 1868, when it became Fields, Osgood, and Co.

On these bulk sales the reader who wants to check the computations should beware of the phrase 'per dozen'; predictably, in view of all the other confusions we have found, it does and does not mean what it says. In the phrase '52 as 48 at 6s. per dozen' it means per every twelve copies, the thirteenth already being signified by '52 as 48'. But usually '1,001 parts at 6s. per dozen' means 'per thirteen parts': 1,001 divided by 13 equals 77 exactly. There is no absolute consistency in phrasing, so every price has to be confirmed separately, to ascertain how many a dozen might be.

The figure in parentheses under 'Sales, quantity' beneath the J70 account indicates the number of copies remaining as of 30 June 1870.

AMERICAN NOTES FOR GENERAL CIRCULATION[1]

2 vols., Chapman and Hall, 1842, 21s.

	Sales, quantity[2]	Sales, receipts			Profit, Dickens			Profit, C & H			Commission,[3] C & H		
		£	s.	d.	£	s.	d.	£	s.	d.	£	s.	d.
J46	12	9	0	0	4	15	8	1	11	0		9	0
D46	13	9	15	0	1	5	11		8	8		9	9
J47	15	10	10	0	6	6	6	2	2	2		10	6
D47	6	4	10	0	2	2	9		14	3		4	6
J48	10	7	10	0	4	8	2	1	9	4		7	6
D48	2	1	10	0		17	3		5	9		1	6
J49	8	6	0	0	3	17	8	1	5	10		6	0
D49	3	2	5	0	1	6	5		8	10		2	3
J50	5	3	15	0	2	7	0		15	9		3	9
D50	2	1	10	0		17	8		5	10		1	6
J51													
D51													
J52	4	3	0	0	1	16	9		12	3		3	0
D52													
J53	4	3	0	0	1	16	0		12	0		3	0
D53	3	2	5	0	1	6	5		8	10		2	3
J54													
D54	4	3	0	0	1	18	3		12	9		3	0
J55	4	3	0	0	1	16	0		12	0		3	0
D55													
J56													
D56	5	3	15	0	2	2	2		14	1		3	9
J57	3	2	5	0	1	12	0		10	9		2	3
D57													
J58	5	3	15	0	1	15	7½	1	15	7½		3	9
D58													
J59													
D59	6	4	10	0	1	17	9	1	17	9		—	
J60													
D60	10	7	10	0	3	3	9	3	3	9		7	6
J61													
D61													
J62													
D62													
J63													
D63													
J64													
D64													
J65													
D65													
J66	91[4]	6	16	6	3	4	10	3	4	10		6	10

[1] See also *Pictures from Italy* and *American Notes*, Library edition.
[2] Figures are for the two-volume set.
[3] 5 per cent throughout; equal profits from J58.
[4] All remaining stock sold at 1s. 6d. each; no reprints through J70.

Appendix A

THE BATTLE OF LIFE A LOVE STORY

1 vol., Bradbury and Evans, 1846, 5s.

	Sales, quantity	Sales, receipts			Profit, Dickens			Profit, B & E			Commission, B & E		
		£	s.	d.	£	s.	d.	£	s.	d.	£	s.	d.
D46	24,450[1]	4,030	11	6	1,281	15	4	427	5	1	403	1	2
J47	264		44	9	0		6	7		2	2	4	6	5
D47	18		3	3	0	1	0	10		6	11		6	3
J48														
D48	2			7	0		4	9		1	7			8
J49	2			7	0		4	9		1	7			8
D49	4			14	0		8	6		2	10		1	4
J50														
D50														
J51	2			7	0		4	9		1	7			8
D51	6		1	1	0		12	7		4	2		2	1
J52	2			6	0		4	1		1	4			7
D52														
J53	3			10	6		7	1		2	5		1	0
D53	5			17	6		10	6		3	6		1	9
J54														
D54	2			7	0		4	3		1	5			8
J55														
D55	3			10	6		6	6		2	3		1	1
J56	9		1	11	6	1	1	3		7	1		3	2
D56	3			10	6		7	1		2	5		1	0
J57	6		1	1	0		6	8		2	3		2	1
D57	5			17	6		11	0		3	8		1	9
J58	15		2	12	6	1	16	10		12	4		1	8[2]
D58	3			10	6		6	9		2	2			6
J59	9		1	11	6	1	0	0		7	0		1	7
D59	10		1	15	0	1	4	11		8	4		1	9
J60	12		2	2	0	1	0	11		7	0		2	1
D60	9		1	10	6	1	0	9		6	10		1	6
J61	24		4	0	6	2	13	7		17	11		4	0
D61	(515)[3]													

[1] Includes one copy to The Hague for £4.0.0, and one copy to 'Williams & [illeg.]', 'price not fixed'.
[2] Commission reduced to 5 per cent.
[3] Transferred to Chapman and Hall 'Christmas Books'.

BLEAK HOUSE

20 parts as 19, Bradbury and Evans, 1852–3, 20s.

	Sales, quantity	Sales, receipts £ s. d.	Advertising receipts £ s. d.	Profit, Dickens £ s. d.	Profit, B & E £ s. d.	Commission, B & E £ s. d.
J52	163,285	5,652 3 9	636 15 11	2,224 0 9	741 7 0	628 18 0
D52	202,724	7,017 7 6[1]	654 13 6	3,106 13 6	1,035 11 2	767 4 1
J53	191,268	6,620 17 0[2]	648 6 6	2,760 1 6	920 0 6	726 18 4
D53	129,576	4,485 6 9[3]	227 19 5	2,067 19 11	689 6 8	471 6 8
J54	13,371	462 17 3		245 6 7	81 15 7	46 5 9
D54	5,057	175 1 0		87 18 5	29 6 2	17 10 1
J55	7,425	257 0 6		122 8 0	40 16 0	25 14 0
D55	2,308	79 18 3		41 16 9	13 18 11	7 19 10
J56	2,309	79 19 0		33 14 1	11 4 9	7 19 11
D56	1,624	56 5 0		25 13 8	8 11 3	5 12 6
J57	2,323	80 8 9		47 9 6	15 16 6	8 0 10
D57	1,801	62 7 3		16 19 11	5 13 3	6 4 9
J58	2,493	86 6 6		43 0 3	14 6 9	4 6 4[4]
D58	283	9 16 6		6 14 10	2 4 11	4 9 10
J59	648	22 9 3		14 6 4	4 15 5	1 2 6
D59	214	7 8 6		—1 13 11	— 11 4	7 5
J60	396	13 14 6		8 16 1	2 18 9	13 9
D60	368	12 15 0		8 6 2	2 15 5	12 9
J61	115	4 0 3		2 2 6	14 2	4 0

[1] Plus £120 for advance proofs to the United States of Numbers V–X.
[2] Plus £120 for advance proofs to the United States of Numbers XI–XVI.
[3] Plus £80 for advance proofs to the United States of Numbers XVII–XX.
[4] Commission reduced to 5 per cent.

BLEAK HOUSE (cont.)

	Sales, quantity	Sales, receipts £ s. d.	Advertising receipts £ s. d.	Profit, Dickens £ s. d.	Profit, B & E (C & H) £ s. d.	Commission, B & E (C & H) £ s. d.
D61	(6,819)[5]	9 10 0[6]		3 14 6	3 14 6	9 6
J62	312[6]	69 5 0[7]		14 3 9	14 3 9	9 3
D62	4,180[7]	40 12 6[8]		14 5 9	14 5 8	1 1
J63	2,600[8]					
D63						
J64						
D64	5,500[9]	85 18 9[9]		12 14 0	12 14 0	4 6 0
J65	1,000[10]	15 12 6[10]		1 3 6	1 3 6	15 6
D65	3,000[11]	46 17 6[11]		— 15 9	4	2 6 10
J66	2,500[12]	39 1 3[12]		14 2 1½	14 2 1½	1 19 0
D66	1,500[13]	23 8 9[13]		7 2 2	7 2 2	1 3 5
J67[14]						
D67	12,000	187 10 0		43 17 0	43 17 0	9 7 6
J68						
D68	3,000[15]	41 17 6[15]		2 17 10	2 17 10	2 1 0
J69	800	12 10 0		3 14 3	3 14 3	12 6
D69	2,000[16]	31 5 0		14 16 10½	14 16 10½	1 11 3
J70	3,020	47 3 9		— 24 8 5	5	2 7 2
	(8,810)					

5 Transferred to Chapman and Hall.
6 Includes 130 at 6s. 9d. per dozen = £3.7.6; 182 at 8s. 9d. per dozen = £6.2.6.
7 Includes 3,920 = 196 vols. to Bohn at 6s. 3d. per volume = £61.5.0; 260 at 8s. per dozen = £8.0.0.
8 All to Bohn, 130 vols. at 6s. 3d. per volume.
9 All to Bohn, 275 vols. at 6s. 3d. per volume.
10 All to Bohn, 50 vols. at 6s. 3d. per volume.
11 All to Bohn, 150 vols. at 6s. 3d. per volume.
12 All to Bohn, 125 vols. at 6s. 3d. per volume.
13 All to Bohn, 75 vols. at 6s. 3d. per volume.
14 Reprinting.
15 Includes 2,000 = 100 vols. to Ticknor and Fields at 5s. 3d. per volume; [1,000] = 50 vols. at 6s. 3d. per volume.
16 Plus 700 wasted.

BLEAK HOUSE, Cheap Edition

1 vol., Bradbury and Evans, 1858, 5s.

	Sales, quantity	Sales, receipts			Profit, Dickens			Profit, B & E			Commission, B & E		
		£	s.	d.	£	s.	d.	£	s.	d.	£	s.	d.
D58	3,692	619	12	6	20	17	0	6	19	0	30	19	8
J59	400	57	15	0	26	16	11	8	19	0	2	17	9
D59	413	68	14	6	37	5	3	12	8	5	3	8	9
J60	547	91	10	0	5	5	6	1	15	2	4	11	6
D60	159	26	12	6	9	9	5	3	3	2	1	6	8
J61	320	53	12	0	26	16	8	8	18	11	2	13	7
D61	(467)[1]												

[1] Transferred to Chapman and Hall 'Cheap Edition'.

BLEAK HOUSE, Library Edition, XVIII and XIX

2 vols., Bradbury and Evans, 1859, 6s. each

	Sales, quantity	Sales, receipts			Profit, Dickens			Profit, B & E			Commission, B & E		
		£	s.	d.	£	s.	d.	£	s.	d.	£	s.	d.
J59	959	191	17	6	−220	7	0	−73	9	0	9	11	10
D59	1,159	131	17	6	72	5	1	24	1	9	6	11	10
J60	100	19	19	2	11	17	11	3	19	3	1	0	0
D60	48	9	6	8	6	7	7	2	2	7		9	4
J61	37	7	10	0	4	19	4	1	13	2		7	6
D61	(1,663)[1]												

[1] Transferred to Chapman and Hall 'Library Edition'.

Appendix A

CHARLES DICKENS EDITION

Chapman and Hall, 1867–8, 3s. each[1]

	Sales, quantity	Sales, receipts			Net Profit			Commission, C & H		
		£	s.	d.	£	s.	d.	£	s.	d.
D67	60,307[2]	5,364	7	7[2]	1,351	14	9	268	0	0
J68	66,898[3]	5,847	13	8[3]	688	8	5	292	7	8
D68	42,549[4]	3,731	15	4[4]	848	17	6	186	11	9
J69	13,481[5]	1,226	17	6[5]	441	5	2	61	6	10
D69	17,108[6]	1,560	0	0[6]	878	13	6	78	0	0
J70	12,467[7]	1,096	12	6[7]	209	19	0	54	16	6
	(47,358)									

[1] Includes *Sketches by Boz, Oliver Twist, The Old Curiosity Shop, Barnaby Rudge, Christmas Books, American Notes* and *Reprinted Pieces, Hard Times* and *Pictures from Italy, A Tale of Two Cities, The Uncommercial Traveller,* and *Great Expectations.*

[2] 8,840 as 8,160 to Bell and Daldy at 2s. 1d. less 12½ per cent = £743.15.0; 2,431 as 2,254 to Melbourne at 2s. 1d. less 15 per cent = £199.11.7; 14,651 as 13,524 to Routledge at 2s. 1d. less 10 per cent = £1,267.17.6; 15,925 as 14,700 to agents at 2s. 1d. less 10 per cent = £1,378.3.6; 18,460 as 17,040 at 2s. 1d. = £1,775.0.0.

[3] 16,185 as 14,940 to Routledge at 2s. 1d. less 10 per cent = £1,400.12.6; 9,893 as 9,132 to Bell and Daldy at 2s. 1d. less 12½ per cent = £832.7.0; 2,808 as 2,592 to Melbourne at 2s. 1d. less 15 per cent = £229.10.0; 17,225 as 15,900 to agents less 10 per cent = £1,490.12.6; 20,787 as 18,188 at 2s. 1d. = £1,894.11.8.

[4] 25,623 as 23,652 to Routledge at 2s. 1d. less 10 per cent = £2,217.7.6; 4,472 as 4,028 to Bell and Daldy at 2s. 1d. less 12½ per cent = £367.2.10; 3,484 as 3,216 to Melbourne less 15 per cent = £284.15.0; 8,970 as 8,280 at 2s. 1d. = £862.10.0. In addition, 12,000 volumes went to make up 1,200 sets.

[5] 884 as 816 to Melbourne at 2s. 1d. less 15 per cent = £72.5.0; 5,889 as 5,436 to agents at 2s. 1d. less 10 per cent = £509.12.6; 6,708 as 6,192 at 2s. 1d. = £645.0.0.

[6] 390 as 360 to Melbourne at 2s. 1d. less 15 per cent = £31.17.6; 8,255 as 7,620 to agents at 2s. 1d. less 10 per cent = £714.7.6; 8,436 as 7,812 at 2s. 1d. = £813.15.0. In addition, 2,500 volumes went to make up 250 sets.

[7] 156 as 144 to Melbourne at 2s. 1d. less 15 per cent = £12.15.0; 4,004 as 3,696 to Warne and Co. at 2s. 1d. less 12½ per cent = £336.17.6; 5,382 as 4,968 to agents at 2s. 1d. less 10 per cent = £465.15.0; 2,925 as 2,700 at 2s. 1d. = £281.5.0. In addition, 7,000 volumes went to make up 700 sets.

CHARLES DICKENS EDITION

Chapman and Hall, 1867–8, 3s. 6d. each[1]

	Sales, quantity	Sales, receipts			Net profit			Commission, C & H		
		£	s.	d.	£	s.	d.	£	s.	d.
D67	138,086[2]	14,847	3	0[2]	2,627	11	0	742	7	0
J68	41,041[3]	4,461	19	6[3]	667	6	4	223	2	0
D68	37,414[4]	4,123	12	3[4]	625	14	0	206	3	8
J69	21,697[5]	2,321	8	0[5]	848	10	7	116	1	6
D69	17,186[6]	1,885	5	6[6]	457	8	6	94	5	3
J70	24,557[7]	2,589	13	3[7]	687	3	7	129	9	9
	(32,187)									

[1] Includes *Pickwick Papers, Nicholas Nickleby, Martin Chuzzlewit, Dombey and Son, David Copperfield, Bleak House, Little Dorrit,* and *Our Mutual Friend.*

[2] 20,332 as 18,768 to Bell and Daldy at 2s. 6d. less 12 per cent = £2,052.15.0; 4,056 as 3,744 to Melbourne at 2s. 6d. less 15 per cent = £397.16.0; 26,767 as 24,708 to Routledge at 2s. 6d. less 10 per cent = £2,779.13.0; 35,841 as 33,084 to agents at 2s. 6d. less 10 per cent = £3,721.19.0; 51,090 as 47,160 at 2s. 6d. = £5,895.0.0.

[3] 12,532 as 11,568 to Routledge at 2s. 6d. less 10 per cent = £1,301.8.0; 6,318 as 5,832 to Bell and Daldy at 2s. 6d. less 12½ per cent = £637.17.6; 2,184 as 2,016 to Melbourne at 2s. 6d. less 15 per cent = £214.4.0; 20,007 as 18,468 at 2s. 6d. = £2,308.10.0.

[4] 11,427 as 10,548 to Routledge at 2s. 6d. less 10 per cent = £1,186.8.6; 2,067 as 1,908 to Bell and Daldy at 2s. 6d. less 12½ per cent = £208.13.9; 1,820 as 1,680 to Melbourne at 2s. 6d. less 15 per cent = £178.10.0; 22,100 as 20,400 at 2s. 6d. = £2,550.0.0. In addition, 9,600 volumes went to make up 1,200 sets.

[5] 1,248 as 1,152 to Melbourne at 2s. 6d. less 15 per cent = £122.8.0; 13,910 as 12,840 to agents at 2s. 6d. less 10 per cent = £1,444.10.0; 6,539 as 6,036 at 2s. 6d. = £754.10.0.

[6] 585 as 540 to Melbourne at 2s. 6d. less 15 per cent = £57.7.6; 7,592 as 7,008 to agents at 2s. 6d. less 10 per cent = £788.8.0; 9,009 as 8,316 at 2s. 6d. = £1,039.10.0. In addition, 2,000 volumes went to make up 250 sets.

[7] 208 as 182 to Melbourne at 2s. 6d. less 15 per cent = £19.6.9; 6,838 as 6,312 to Warne and Co. at 2s. 6d. less 12½ per cent = £690.7.6; 12,181 as 11,244 to agents at 2s. 6d. less 10 per cent = £1,264.19.0; 5,330 as 4,920 at 2s. 6d. = £615.0.0. In addition, 5,600 volumes went to make up 700 sets.

CHARLES DICKENS EDITION

Chapman and Hall, 1867–8, sets of 18 volumes, £2. 18s. 0d.

	Sales, quantity	Sales, receipts			Net profit			Commission, C & H		
		£	s.	d.	£	s.	d.	£	s.	d.
J68	(1,200)[1]									
D68	918[2]	1,616	18	10[2]	974	9	10	80	17	0
J69	160[3]	267	19	0[3]	254	11	0	13	8	0
D69	208[4]	344	17	0[4]	210	12	3	17	4	9
J70	767[5]	1,300	3	0[5]	907	11	0	65	0	0
	(97)									

[1] Complete sets printed.

[2] 13 as 12 to Routledge at 38s. 10d. less 10 per cent = £20.19.6; 15 as 14 to Bell and Daldy at 38s. 10d. less 12½ per cent = £23.15.10; 45 as 42 to Melbourne at 38s. 10d. less 15 per cent = £69.6.6; 65 as 60 to agents at 38s. 10d. less 10 per cent = £104.17.0; 780 as 720 at 38s. 10d. = £1,398.0.0.

[3] 108 as 100 to agents at 38s. 10d. less 10 per cent = £174.15.0; 52 as 48 at 38s. 10d. = £93.4.0.

[4] 156 as 144 at 38s. 10d. less 10 per cent = £251.13.0; 52 as 48 at 38s. 10d. = £93.4.0.

[5] 416 as 384 to agents at 38s. 10d. less 10 per cent = £671.1.0; 351 as 324 at 38s. 10d. = £629.2.0.

CHEAP EDITION

Chapman and Hall, 1847–, 1½d. weekly numbers, 7d. monthly parts

	Numbers Sales, quantity	Numbers Sales, receipts £ s. d.	Parts Sales, quantity	Parts Sales, receipts £ s. d.	Profit, Dickens £ s. d.	Profit, C & H £ s. d.	Commission, C & H £ s. d.
D47	727,155	2,796 15 0	164,190	2,947 0 0	132 11 4	132 11 3	287 3 9
J48	265,980	1,023 0 0	83,967	1,507 2 0	462 13 7	462 13 6	126 10 1
D48	248,183	954 11 0	52,754	946 17 4	371 9 9	371 9 8	95 1 5
J49	232,258	893 6 0	56,264	1,009 17 4	299 11 5	299 11 5	95 3 2
D49	227,591	875 7 0	43,264	776 10 8	300 5 2	300 5 2	82 11 11
J50	221,689	852 13 0	48,191	864 19 4	300 17 10¹	300 17 9¹	85 17 8
D50	256,672	987 4 0	30,654	550 4 0	307 13 7	307 13 7	76 13 4
J51	166,491	640 7 0	2,691	48 6 0	265 12 8	265 12 8	34 8 8
D51	128,479	494 3 0	2,717	48 15 4	227 14 4	227 14 4	27 2 10
J52	136,968	526 16 0	3,510	63 0 0	233 5 3	233 5 2	29 9 10
D52	178,477	686 9 0	884	15 7 4	204 3 10	204 3 9	35 2 4
J53	188,435	724 15 0	1,950	35 0 0	227 19 6	227 19 6	37 19 9
D53	184,990	711 10 0	2,730	49 0 0	242 11 5	242 11 4	38 0 6
J54	125,463	482 11 0	1,950	35 0 0	102 3 3	102 3 3	25 17 6
D54	136,253	524 1 0	39	14 0	31 19 6	31 19 6	26 4 9
J55	148,473	571 1 0	481	8 12 8	88 17 11	88 17 10	28 19 8
D55	119,886	461 2 0	442	7 18 8	87 0 5	87 0 5	23 9 0
J56	126,711²	454 4 9²	793	14 4 8	134 18 0	134 18 0	23 8 5
D56	146,497³	529 18 6³	273	14 18 0	160 7 6	160 7 5	26 14 9

¹ General account gives £297.17.10.

² Includes 20,904 sold in New Orleans for £54.5.0, and 7,241 sold in New York at 9d. per dozen for £20.17.9 = 28,145 numbers for £75.2.9.

³ Includes 19,201 sold to 'Parry for America' for £50.17.0, and 10,946 sold in New York for £31.11.6 = 30,147 numbers for £82.8.0.

CHEAP EDITION (cont.)

	Numbers Sales, quantity	Numbers Sales, receipts £	s.	d.	Parts Sales, quantity	Parts Sales, receipts £	s.	d.	Profit, Dickens £	s.	d.	Profit, C & H £	s.	d.	Commission, C & H £	s.	d.
J57	138,398[4]	518	4	3[4]	260	4	13	4	50	7	5	50	7	5	26	0	0
D57	173,680	668	0	0	182	3	5	4	76	10	6	76	10	6	33	11	3
J58	80,431	309	7	0	26		9	4	82	15	7	82	15	7	15	19	0
D58	134,277	516	9	0	91	1	12	8	82	11	11	82	11	11	25	18	0
J59	119,470	459	10	0	143	2	11	4	126	15	9[5]	126	15	9[5]	23	2	0
D59	165,016[6]	642	7	0	39		14	0	204	14	4	204	14	4	32	3	0[7]
J60	169,039	650	3	0	104	1	17	4	208	6	5	208	6	5	32	12	0
D60	145,210	558	10	0	117	2	2	0	66	9	6	66	9	6	23	0	6
J61	72,046	277	2	0	143	2	11	4	69	5	1	69	5	1	13	19	8
D61	121,030	465	10	0					87	5	9	87	5	9	23	5	6
J62	160,121	615	17	0					119	13	3	119	13	3	30	15	9
D62	122,564	471	8	0					126	10	9	126	10	9	23	11	6
J63	180,999	696	3	0					88	18	9	88	18	9	34	16	0
D63	188,396	724	12	0					233	6	4	233	6	4	36	4	6
J64	185,146	712	2	0					141	18	9½	141	18	9½	35	12	0
D64	172,900	665	0	0					150	13	6	150	13	6	33	5	0
J65	212,601	817	14	0					200	5	1	200	5	1	40	13	9
D65	417,774[8]	1,519	9	8[8]					326	4	6½	326	4	6½	75	19	6
J66	288,002	1,107	14	0					305	19	1½[9]	305	19	1½[9]	55	7	9
D66	217,802	837	14	0					227	6	1	227	6	1	41	17	9
J67	101,400	390	0	0					137	3	5[9]	137	3	5[9]	19	10	0

4 Includes 6,279 consigned to Singapore, Jamaica, etc. at 5d. per dozen for £10.1.3.

5 Duties received from colonies amount to £8.9.4.

6 Erroneously reckoned as = 12,847 dozen numbers, when actually only = 12,693; correction charged against expenses, J60.

7 Less 7s. 8d. error corrected in J60.

8 Includes 104,500 = 500 sets to Lippincott at 12s. 7d. = £314,11,8; 313,274 at 1s. per dozen = £1,204.18.0.

9 Insurance and warehousing deducted = £18.0.0.

CHEAP EDITION (cont.)

	Numbers		Parts		Profit, Dickens	Profit, C & H	Commission, C & H
	Sales, quantity	Sales, receipts £ s. d.	Sales, quantity	Sales, receipts £ s. d.	£ s. d.	£ s. d.	£ s. d.
D67	2,600	10 0 0			4 12 6	4 12 6	10 0
J68							
D68							
J69	2,080	8 0 0			3 16 0	3 16 0	8 0
D69							
J70	60,820[10]	123 11 3			58 13 10½	58 13 10½	6 3 6
	(241,672)						

[10] All to Smith and Son: 13,950 = 450 *Pickwick Papers*
10,880 = 340 *Nicholas Nickleby*
8,000 = 250 *Martin Chuzzlewit*
7,200 = 300 *Barnaby Rudge*
6,600 = 300 *The Old Curiosity Shop*
4,750 = 250 *Oliver Twist*
4,500 = 225 *Sketches by Boz*
3,740 = 220 *Christmas Books*
1,200 = 100 *American Notes*

Appendix A

CHEAP EDITION

Chapman and Hall, 1847–, vols. at 5s.[1]

	Sales, quantity	Sales, receipts			Profit, Dickens			Profit, C & H			Commission, C & H		
		£	s.	d.	£	s.	d.	£	s.	d.	£	s.	d.
D61	4,200	705	12	0	51	6	1½	51	6	1½	35	5	6
J62	2,575	436	19	6	70	10	0	70	10	0	21	17	0
D62	2,300	386	8	0	87	12	0	87	12	0	19	6	6
J63	2,225[2]	364	19	6[2]	79	5	2	79	5	2	18	5	0
D63	2,275	382	4	0	83	17	5½	83	17	5½	19	2	2
J64	2,900	487	14	0	128	0	7	128	0	7	24	7	8
D64	4,400	739	4	0	68	12	7	68	12	7	36	19	2
J65	2,200	369	12	0	123	4	3	123	4	3	18	9	6
D65	6,797[3]	981	7	4[3]	171	1	5½	171	1	5½	49	1	4
J66	4,399[4]	735	0	0[4]	130	2	2	130	2	2	36	15	0
D66	4,025[5]	663	12	0[5]	177	16	9½	177	16	9½	35	14	0
J67	1,950	315	0	0	113	2	6	113	2	6	15	15	0
D67	2,132	344	8	0	27	2	6	27	2	6	17	4	3
J68	260	42	0	0	19	19	0	19	19	0	2	2	0
D68													
J69													
D69													
J70	1,700[6]	106	5	0[6]	50	9	4½	50	9	4½	5	6	3
	(3,872)												

[1] Includes *Dombey and Son*, *David Copperfield*, *Bleak House*, *Little Dorrit*, *Our Mutual Friend*, and *Barnaby Rudge* by 1865.

[2] Includes 525 as 504 to Robertson at 3s. 6d. less 10 per cent = £79.7.6; 1,700 as 1,632 at 3s. 6d. = £285.12.0.

[3] Includes 1,000 vols. quires to Lippincott at 1s. 7d. = £79.3.4; 1,000 vols. cloth to Lippincott at 2s. = £100; 572 as 528 vols. at 'Sale Cate' at 3s. 6d. = £92.8.0; 4,225 as 4,056 at 3s. 6d. = £709.16.0.

[4] Includes 624 as 576 at 3s. 6d. = £100.16.0; 3,775 as 3,624 at 3s. 6d. = £634.4.0.

[5] Includes 1,950 as 1,800 at 3s. 6d. = £315.0.0; 2,075 as 1,992 at 3s. 6d. = £348.12.0.

[6] All to Smith and Son at 1s. 3d.

CHEAP EDITION

Chapman and Hall, 1847–, vols. at 3s. 6d.[1]

	Sales, quantity	Sales, receipts			Profit, Dickens			Profit, C & H			Commission, C & H		
		£	s.	d.	£	s.	d.	£	s.	d	£	s.	d.
D65	3,236[2]	333	0	0[2]				−76	13	2	16	13	0
J66	742[3]	88	10	0[3]	31	7	9	31	7	9	4	8	0
D66	885[4]	103	10	0[4]	35	19	3	35	19	3	5	3	6
J67	611	70	10	0	17	19	9	17	19	9	3	10	6
D67	104	12	0	0	5	14	0	5	14	0		12	0
J68	208	22	15	0	10	16	1½	10	16	1½	1	2	9
D68	104	12	0	0	3	6	0	3	6	0		12	0
J69													
D69													
J70	550[5] (2,779)	13	15	0[5]	6	10	7½	6	10	7½		13	9

[1] Includes *Pictures from Italy*, *Hard Times*, and *Great Expectations*.
[2] Includes 500 vols. quires to Lippincott at 1s. 4d. = £33.6.8; 500 vols. cloth to Lippincott at 1s. 8d. = £41.13.4; 2,236 as 2,064 at 2s. 6d. = £258.0.0.
[3] Includes 117 as 108 at 2s. 6d. = £13.10.0; 625 as 600 at 2s. 6d. = £75.0.0.
[4] Includes 585 as 540 at 2s. 6d. = £67.10.0; 300 as 288 at 2s. 6d. = £36.0.0.
[5] All to Smith and Son at 6d.

CHEAP EDITION

Chapman and Hall, 1847–, vols. at 3s.[1]

	Sales, quantity	Sales, receipts			Profit, Dickens			Profit, C & H			Commission, C & H		
		£	s.	d.	£	s.	d.	£	s.	d.	£	s.	d.
D65	5,004	453	15	0				−48	18	3	22	13	9
J66	994[2]	97	18	4[2]	27	17	5	27	17	5	4	18	0
D66	845[3]	82	10	0[3]	23	6	9	23	6	9	4	2	6
J67	585	56	5	0	16	16	4½	16	16	4½	2	16	3
D67	156	15	0	0	7	2	6	7	2	6		15	0
J68	234	22	10	0	10	13	9	10	13	9	1	2	6
D68	91	8	15	0	4	3	1½	4	3	1½		8	9
J69													
D69													
J70	390[4] (1,695)	9	15	0[4]	4	2	7½	4	2	7½		9	9

[1] Includes *A Tale of Two Cities*, *The Uncommercial Traveller*.
[2] Includes 169 as 156 at 2s. 1d. = £16.5.0; 825 as 784 at 2s. 1d. = £81.13.4.
[3] Includes 520 as 480 at 2s. 1d. = £50.0.0; 325 as 312 at 2s. 1d. = £32.10.0.
[4] All to Smith and Son at 6d.

A CHILD'S HISTORY OF ENGLAND

3 vols., Bradbury and Evans, I: 1852, II: 1853, III: 1854, 10s. 6d.

	Sales, quantity	Sales, receipts (£ s. d.)	Profit, Dickens (£ s. d.)	Profit, B & E (£ s. d.)	Commission, B & E (£ s. d.)
J52	2,101[1]	252 2 6	−24 16 6	− 8 5 6	25 4 3
D52	237[1]	28 10 0	7 3 0	2 7 9	2 17 0
J53	374[1]	45 0 0	22 4 11	7 8 4	4 10 0
D53	938[2]	112 12 6	35 8 5	11 16 2	11 5 3
J54	971[2]	116 12 6	58 3 1	19 7 9	11 13 3
D54	485[3]	58 5 0	4 11 5	1 10 5	5 16 6
J55	1,036	124 7 6	40 15 9	13 12 0	12 8 9
D55	249	30 0 0	14 19 6	4 19 9	3 0 0
J56	603	72 7 6	35 16 5	11 18 10	7 4 9
D56	149	18 0 0	−10 11 4	−3 10 6	1 16 0
J57	548	65 17 6	32 2 8	10 14 3	6 11 9
D57	251	30 2 6	−6 7 8	−2 2 7	3 0 3
J58	522	62 15 0	32 15 9	10 18 7	3 2 9
D58	129	15 10 0	7 4 0	2 8 0	15 6
J59	352	42 5 0	−6 2 1	−2 0 8	2 2 3
D59	181	21 15 0	10 3 1	3 7 8	1 1 9
J60	274	33 0 0	3 19 8	1 6 7	1 13 0
D60	218	26 5 0	13 13 7	4 11 2	1 6 3
J61	97 (759)[4]	11 15 0	6 9 7	2 3 2	11 9
				C & H	C & H
D61	100	16 16 0	5 4 7½	5 4 7½	16 9
J62	125	15 0 0	4 7 6	4 7 6	15 0
D62	150	18 0 0	6 3 9	6 3 9	18 0
J63	150	18 0 0	7 10 5	7 10 4	18 0
D63	50[5]	6 0 0	2 3 6	2 3 6	6 0
Vol. II					
J53	1,602	192 5 0	−30 18 2	−10 6 1	19 4 6
Vol. III					
J54	1,776	213 2 6	−47 18 7	−15 19 7	21 6 3

[1] Vol. I only.
[2] Vols. I and II.
[3] Vols. I, II, and III from this date on.
[4] Transferred to Chapman and Hall: I: 368, II: 181, III: 160 in quires; 50 bound.
[5] No account thereafter.

A CHILD'S HISTORY OF ENGLAND

1 vol., Chapman and Hall, 1863, 6s.

	Sales, quantity	Sales, receipts			Profit, Dickens			Profit, C & H			Commission, C & H		
		£	s.	d.	£	s.	d.	£	s.	d.	£	s.	d.
J63	700	1											
D63													
J64	990	253	12	0	17	2	7½	17	2	7½	12	13	6
D64													
J65													
D65	368[2]	72	10	0[2]	−0	14	11				3	12	6
J66	125	25	0	0	9	7	0	9	7	0	1	5	0
D66	114[3]	22	10	0[3]	8	18	3	8	18	3	—		
J67													
D67	100	20	0	0	8	2	0	8	2	0	1	0	0
J68													
D68	500	96	5	0	17	2	6	17	2	6	4	16	3
J69	141[4]	27	2	6[4]	11	9	9	11	9	9	1	7	0
D69	230[5]	42	10	0[5]	16	13	9	16	13	9	2	2	6
J70	184[6] (0)	35	8	4[6]	14	7	5	14	7	5	1	15	6

[1] 'not sufficient to pay the cost'.

[2] Includes 143 as 132 to Simpkin sale account at 4s. 2d. = £27.10.0; 225 as 216 at 4s. 2d. = £45.0.0.

[3] Includes 39 as 36 at 4s. 2d. = £7.10.0; 75 as 72 at 4s. 2d. = £15.0.0.

[4] Includes 41 as 38 at 4s. 2d. less 10 per cent = £7.2.6; 100 as 96 at 4s. 2d. = £20.0.0.

[5] Includes 130 as 120 at 4s. 2d. less 10 per cent = £22.10.0; 100 as 96 at 4s.2d. = £20.0.0.

[6] All at 4s. 2d.

THE CHIMES

1 vol., Bradbury and Evans, 1844, 5s.

	Sales, quantity	Sales, receipts			Profit, Dickens			Profit, B & E			Commission, B & E[1]		
		£	s.	d.	£	s.	d.	£	s.	d.	£	s.	d.
J46	667	107	19	6	−93	11	6[2]	−31	3	11	10	16	0
D46	126	21	3	6	14	2	3	4	14	1	2	2	4
J47													
D47	8	1	8	0		18	11		6	3		2	10
J48	2		7	0		4	9		1	7			8
D48	10	1	15	0	1	2	1		7	4		3	6
J49	4		14	0		9	6		3	2		1	4
D49	9	1	11	6	1	1	3		7	1		1	7
J50													
D50	4		14	0		8	6		2	10		1	4
J51													
D51	3		10	6		6	8		2	2		1	0
J52	2		6	0		4	1		1	4			7
D52	2		6	6		4	4		1	6			8
J53													
D53													
J54													
D54	8	1	8	0		17	11		5	11		2	10
J55													
D55	4		14	0		9	0		2	11		1	5
J56	10	1	15	0	1	3	7		7	11		3	6
D56	5		17	6		11	4		3	9		1	9
J57	9	1	11	6		15	8		5	2		3	2
D57	5		17	6		11	0		3	8		1	9
J58	23	4	0	6	2	7	7		15	10		4	0[3]
D58	12	2	2	0		17	1		5	9		2	1
J59	11	1	18	6	1	5	6		8	6		1	11
D59													
J60	4		14	0		9	9		3	3			8
D60	11	1	17	6	1	0	8		6	11		1	10
J61	9	1	11	6		19	0		6	4		1	7
	(2,092)[4]												

[1] Commission frequently includes agents' commission in accounts; pro rated to reflect publishers' percentage.

[2] Error; should be −£93.11.8. Account includes all costs and sales since 18 Jan. 1845.

[3] Commission altered to 5 per cent.

[4] Transferred to Chapman and Hall 'Christmas Books'.

THE CHIMES

1 vol., Bradbury and Evans, 1858, 1s.

	Sales, quantity	Sales, receipts			Profit, Dickens			Profit, B & E			Commission, B & E		
		£	s.	d.	£	s.	d.	£	s.	d.	£	s.	d.
J58	1,988	65	0	6	−15	7	4	−5	2	5	3	5	0[1]
D58	2,228	72	17	0	17	17	11	5	19	4	3	12	10
J59	557	18	4	9	11	7	6	3	15	10		18	3
D59	202	6	12	6	3	18	5	1	6	2		6	7
J60	112	3	12	0	1	15	1		11	9		3	7
D60	145	4	14	11	2	16	7		18	11		4	9
J61	27		17	9		8	2		2	9			10
	(202)[2]												

[1] At 5 per cent throughout.
[2] Transferred to Chapman and Hall 'Readings 1/-'.

CHRISTMAS BOOKS

5 vols., Chapman and Hall, Bradbury and Evans, 1843–8, 5s. each[1]

	Sales, quantity	Sales, receipts			Profit, Dickens			Profit, C & H			Commission, C & H		
		£	s.	d.	£	s.	d.	£	s.	d.	£	s.	d.
D61	33	5	12	0	1	17	5	1	17	5		5	8
J62	50	8	8	0	3	4	4	3	4	4		8	4
D62	75	12	12	0	3	19	3	3	19	3		12	6
J63	75	12	12	0	5	12	0	5	12	0		12	6
D63	50	8	8	0	3	12	4	3	12	4		8	4
J64	100	16	16	0	6	3	7½	6	3	7½		16	9
D64	100	16	16	0	6	17	1½	6	17	1½		16	9
J65	150	25	4	0	9	16	4	9	16	5	1	5	3
D65	50	8	8	0	3	19	10	3	19	10		8	4
J66	75	12	12	0	5	19	9	5	19	9		12	6
D66													
J67[2]													
D67[3]													

[1] Includes *A Christmas Carol, The Chimes, The Cricket on the Hearth, The Battle of Life, The Haunted Man.*
[2] Reprinting?
[3] No further accounts.

CHRISTMAS BOOKS

1 vol., Chapman and Hall, 1869, 12s.

	Sales, quantity	Sales, receipts			Advertising receipts			Profit, Dickens			Profit, C & H			Commission, C & H		
		£	s.	d.	£	s.	d.	£	s.	d.	£	s.	d.	£	s.	d.
D69	1,904[1]	648	15	9[1]	15	0	0	109	0	0	109	0	0	32	8	9
J70	(84)															

[1] Includes 100 to Ticknor and Fields in quires at 3s. = £15.0.0; 400 to Ticknor and Fields in cloth at 4s. 6d. = £90.0.0; 150 to Appleton and Co. at 6s. = £45.0.0; 104 to Melbourne at 8s. 6d. less 15 per cent = £34.13.9; 325 as 300 at 8s. 6d. = £127.10.0; 825 as 792 at 8s. 6d. = £336.12.0.

CHRISTMAS BOOKS, Cheap Edition[1]

1 vol., Chapman and Hall, 1852, weekly numbers at 1½d.; monthly Parts 1–3 (= XLIX–LI of Cheap edition, 4 numbers each) at 7d., Part 4 (= LII, 5 numbers) at 8½d.; cloth at 3s. 6d.

	Numbers		Parts 1, 2, and 3		Part 4			Commission, C & H
	Sales, quantity	Sales, receipts £ s. d.	Sales, quantity	Sales, receipts[2] £ s. d.	Sales, quantity	Sales, receipts[3] £ s. d.	Net profit £ s. d.	£ s. d.
J53	108,420	417 0 0	5,252	94 5 4	1,560	34 0 0	−90 16 1	28 10 6
D53								
J54	19,604	75 8 0	52	18 8	13	5 8	−26 16 3	3 16 8
D54								
J55	146,237	562 9 0	5,408	97 1 4	1,599	34 17 0	27 9 9	35 19 6
D55	8,568[4]	31 14 6[4]					26 8 4	1 11 9
J56	9,035[5]	33 16 3[5]					24 11 5	1 13 10
D56	10,621[6]	39 12 6[6]			13	5 8	32 5 11	2 0 9
J57	9,204	35 8 0	52	18 8			29 0 10	1 15 6
D57	9,191[7]	35 7 0[7]	13	4 8			60 5 8[8]	3 17 10
J58	8,255[9]	31 15 0[9]	52	18 8			63 2 1[8]	4 0 6
D58			39	14 0	13	5 8		

1 Often called 'Christmas Carols' in the accounts.

2 Publisher's price 4s. 8d. per dozen.

3 Publisher's price 5s. 8d. per dozen.

4 Includes 1,275 numbers = 98 doz. sold in New York for 9d. per dozen = £3.13.6, and 7,293 = 561 doz. at 1s. = £28.1.0.

5 Includes 975 numbers = 75 doz. sold to Bangs at 9d. per dozen = £2.16.3, and 8,060 = 620 doz. at 1s. = £31.0.0.

6 Includes 546 numbers to 'Singapore etc' at 5d. per dozen = £0.17.6.

7 Excludes 12,000 numbers used to make 3,550 'Readings'; 190 "Readings" done up from folded stock' sold to Mr. Hindland at 6d. ea. = £4.15.0, 182 'Readings' at 6d. = £4.4.0, and 2,041 'Readings' = 157 doz. sold at 4s. 2d. per dozen = £32.14.2.

8 Includes profits from 'Readings'.

9 Excludes 8,000 numbers used to make 2,200 'Readings'; 2,977 = 229 doz. sold at 4s. 2d. per dozen = £47.14.2.

CHRISTMAS BOOKS, Cheap Edition (*cont.*)

Numbers	Sales, quantity	Sales, receipts £ s. d.	Parts 1, 2, and 3 Sales, quantity	Sales, receipts £ s. d.	Part 4 Sales, quantity	Sales, receipts £ s. d.	Net profit £ s. d.	Commission, C & H £ s. d.
J59	11,011	42 7 0					35 17 6	2 2 6
D59	10,205	39 5 0					6 18 6	1 19 3
J60	8,125	31 5 0					25 1 9	1 11 3
D60	7,943	30 11 0					24 15 6	1 10 6
J61	7,839	30 3 0					4 5 0	1 10 0
D61	6,799	26 3 0					22 11 10	1 6 2
	(22,250)							

CHRISTMAS BOOKS, Library Edition

1 vol., Bradbury and Evans, 1859, 6s.

	Sales, quantity	Sales, receipts			Profit, Dickens			Profit, B & E			Commission, B & E		
		£	s.	d.	£	s.	d.	£	s.	d.	£	s.	d.
D59	555[1]	110	19	2[1]	−85	4	3	−28	8	1	5	10	11
J60	569[2]	63	16	8[2]	35	5	9	11	15	3	3	3	10
D60	25[3]	4	19	7[3]	2	10	4		16	9		5	0
J61	16	3	6	8		16	1		5	5		3	4
	(818)												

[1] Includes 4 sold in quires at 3s. 9d., and 551 as 529 at 4s. 2d.

[2] Includes 500 sold in America in quires at 2s. ea., 6 sold in quires at 3s. 9d., and 63 as 61 at 4s. 2d.

[3] Includes 11 sold in quires at 3s. 9d., and 14 at 4s. 2d.

A CHRISTMAS CAROL

1 vol., Chapman and Hall,[1] 1843, 5s.

	Sales, quantity	Sales, receipts			Profit, Dickens			Profit, B & E			Commission, B & E		
		£	s.	d.	£	s.	d.	£	s.	d.	£	s.	d.
J46	694[2]	113	18	8[2]	28	7	6	9	9	2	11	7	10
D46	363	59	3	0	22	1	4	7	7	1	5	18	3
J47	96[3]	16	1	9[3]	10	9	1	3	9	8	1	12	2
D47	64[4]	10	13	3[4]	3	16	5	1	5	6	1	1	4
J48	119	18	18	0	11	19	9	3	19	11	1	17	10
D48	112	18	0	6	8	18	9	2	19	7	1	16	0
J49	45	7	14	0	—11	15	10	—3	18	8		15	4
D49	41	7	0	0	3	10	11	1	3	8		14	0
J50	76	12	15	6	5	4	9	1	14	11	1	5	6
D50	22	3	17	0	2	9	11		16	7		7	8
J51	32	5	8	6	1	10	3		10	1		10	10
D51	38	6	9	0	4	5	6	1	8	6		12	11
J52	66	11	2	6	4	9	6	1	9	10	1	2	3
D52	13	2	5	0		11	7		3	11		4	6
J53	30	5	1	6	2	14	1		18	1		9	10
D53	45	7	14	0	2	0	7		13	6		15	4
J54	48	8	4	6	3	12	3	1	4	1		16	5
D54	35	5	19	0	2	18	2		19	5		11	10
J55	45	7	14	0	—9	8	10	—3	2	11		15	5
D55	41	6	16	6	3	8	3	1	2	9		13	8
J56	73	12	8	6	5	8	3	1	16	1	1	4	10
D56	48	8	4	6	3	3	5	1	1	2		16	5
J57	44	7	3	6	4	3	4	1	7	10		14	4
D57	79	13	6	0	5	11	9	1	17	3	1	6	6
J58	44	7	10	6	3	16	7	1	5	7		7	6[5]
D58	61	10	6	6	4	12	2	1	10	9		10	4
J59	49	8	11	6	5	10	2	1	16	9		8	7
D59	22	3	17	0	1	7	10		9	4		3	10
J60	50	8	8	0	—12	0	4	—4	0	1		8	5
D60	14	2	5	6		6	7		2	2		2	3
J61	45	7	14	0	4	9	0	1	9	8		7	8
	(431)[6]												

[1] Published on commission and transferred to Bradbury and Evans in 1844.

[2] Includes 40 as 39 in quires at 2s. 10½d. = £5.12.2; 644 as 619 cloth at 3s. 6d. = £108.6.6. Account goes from 4 Dec. 1845, when 469 copies in quires and 42 in cloth were transferred from Chapman and Hall.

[3] Includes 6 in quires at 2s. 10½d. = £0.17.3; 90 as 87 cloth at 3s. 6d. = £15.4.6.

[4] Includes 6 in quires at 2s. 10½d. = £0.17.3; 58 as 56 cloth at 3s. 6d. = £9.16.0.

[5] Commission reduced to 5 per cent.

[6] Transferred to Chapman and Hall 'Christmas Books'.

A CHRISTMAS CAROL, Reading Edition

1 vol., Bradbury and Evans, 1857, 1s.

	Sales, quantity	Sales, receipts			Profit, Dickens			Profit, B & E			Commission, B & E		
		£	s.	d.	£	s.	d.	£	s.	d.	£	s.	d.
D57	4,158	135	19	0	−2	14	1	−	18	1	13	11	10
J58	2,740	89	12	6	22	7	1	7	9	1	4	9	8
D58	5,955	194	13	0	49	9	11	16	10	0	9	14	8
J59	1,586	51	17	0	9	10	10	3	3	8	2	11	10
D59	1,343	43	18	4	25	0	5	8	6	10	2	3	11
J60	473	15	9	9	−6	7	8	−2	2	7		15	6
D60	254	8	6	6	5	2	7	1	14	3		8	4
J61	280 (684)[1]	9	3	5	4	11	10	1	10	7		9	2

[1] Transferred to Chapman and Hall 'Readings 1/-'.

THE CRICKET ON THE HEARTH

1 vol., Bradbury and Evans, 1845, 5s.

	Sales, quantity	Sales, receipts			Profit, Dickens			Profit, B & E			Commission, B & E[1]		
		£	s.	d.	£	s.	d.	£	s.	d.	£	s.	d.
J46	3,074	514	17	6	294	6	5	98	2	1	51	9	9
D46	467	77	3	6	38	15	3	12	18	5	7	14	4
J47	—1												
D47	7	1	4	6		16	7		5	6		2	5
J48	23	3	13	6	2	3	8		14	6		7	4
D48	6	1	1	0		12	9		4	3		2	0
J49	3		10	6		7	1		2	4		1	1
D49	4		14	0		8	8		2	11		1	5
J50	8	1	8	0		17	3		5	9		2	10
D50	6	1	1	0		13	2		4	5		2	1
J51	14	2	5	6	1	8	4		9	6		4	6
D51	4		13	6		8	7		2	11		1	4
J52	19	3	5	6	1	18	4		12	10		6	6
D52	3		10	6		6	10		2	4		1	0
J53	3		10	6		7	2		2	4		1	0
D53	8	1	8	0		16	9		5	7		2	10
J54	16	2	16	0	1	15	2		11	9		5	7
D54	18	3	3	0	2	0	8		13	7		6	4
J55	17	2	16	0	1	17	10		12	7		5	7
D55	14	2	9	0	1	11	9		10	7		4	11
J56	25	4	4	0	2	13	2		17	8		8	4
D56	18	3	3	0	2	2	6		14	2		6	4
J57	8	1	8	0		11	4		3	10		2	10
D57	6	1	1	0		13	1		4	5		2	1
J58	41	7	0	0	3	17	5	1	5	10		7	0[2]
D58	13	2	5	6	1	10	10		10	4		2	3
J59	18	2	19	6	1	8	9		9	7		3	0
D59	6	1	1	0		14	5		4	9		1	1
J60	19	3	6	6	1	2	3		7	5		3	4
D60	22	3	12	6	2	11	4		17	2		3	8
J61	5		17	6		11	8		3	11			10
	(392)[3]												

[1] Commission frequently includes agents' commissions in accounts; pro rated to reflect publishers' percentage.
[2] Commission altered to 5 per cent.
[3] Transferred to Chapman and Hall 'Christmas Books'.

THE CRICKET ON THE HEARTH
1 vol., Bradbury and Evans, 1858, 1s.

	Sales, quantity	Sales, receipts			Profit, Dickens			Profit, B & E			Commission, B & E		
		£	s.	d.	£	s.	d.	£	s.	d.	£	s.	d.
J58	2,058	67	6	0	−14	12	1	−4	17	5	3	7	3
D58	1,701	55	12	1	25	5	10	8	8	8	2	15	7
J59	336	11	0	4	−4	6	1	−1	8	9	11	0	
D59	182	5	19	0	1	18	8		12	11		5	11
J60	121	3	19	6	1	16	0		12	0		4	0
D60	210	6	17	6	4	2	6	1	7	6		6	10
J61	76 (304)[1]	2	10	3		8	10		2	11		2	6

[1] Transferred to Chapman and Hall 'Readings 1/-'.

DAVID COPPERFIELD

20 parts as 19, Bradbury and Evans, 1849–50, 20s.

	Sales, quantity	Sales, receipts			Advertising receipts			Profit, Dickens			Profit, B & E			Commission, B & E		
		£	s.	d.	£	s.	d.	£	s.	d.	£	s.	d.	£	s.	d.
J49	59,218	2,049	17	3	393	19	6	611	14	5	203	18	1	244	7	8
D49	121,888	4,219	4	0	454	9	6	1,724	5	3	574	14	5	467	7	4
J50	121,585	4,208	14	9	408	14	6	1,730	4	7	576	14	10	461	14	11
D50	128,017	4431	7	6	273	17	6	1,992	5	1	664	1	9	470	10	6
J51	6,811	235	16	0				119	0	8	39	13	7	23	11	7
D51	4,035	139	13	9				82	6	7	27	8	10	13	19	4
J52	5,700	197	6	6				87	4	2	29	1	5	19	14	8
D52	6,012	208	2	6				95	16	11	31	19	0	20	16	3
J53	4,293	148	12	3				61	6	6	20	8	9	14	17	3
D53	3,237	112	1	0				62	9	10	20	16	8	11	4	1
J54	3,344	115	15	3				54	17	7	18	5	11	11	11	6
D54	2,519	87	4	6				14	2	0	4	14	0	8	14	6
J55	3,171	109	15	3				63	14	3	21	4	9	10	19	6
D55	3,034	105	0	9				55	18	8	18	12	10	10	10	0
J56	2,985	103	7	0				23	8	4	7	16	0	10	6	8
D56	2,104	72	16	6				39	10	3	13	3	5	7	5	8
J57	3,121	108	0	9				58	7	4	19	9	1	10	16	1
D57	1,749	60	11	3				30	13	5	10	4	6	6	1	1
J58	2,885	99	18	0				52	1	11	17	7	4	4	19	11[1]
D58	418	14	9	6				—			—			14	6	
J59	1,038	35	19	3				23	8	9	7	16	3	1	16	0
D59	412	14	5	9				5	12	4	1	17	6	14	3	
J60	958	33	3	9				13	8	11	4	9	7	1	13	2
D60	789	27	6	9				13	10	1	4	10	0	1	7	4

	Volumes			C & H	C & H
J61	342	11 17 0	7 16 2	2 12 1	11 10
D61	(7,762)²				
J62	221	7 8 9	3 1 3	3 1 3	7 5
D62	5,524³	95 15 3³	23 3 11	23 3 12	4 15 9
J63	6,240⁴	97 10 0⁴	19 4 6	19 4 6	4 17 6
D63	2,080⁵	32 10 0⁵	10 19 6	10 19 6	1 12 7
J64	8,240⁶	128 15 0⁶	23 3 6	23 3 6	6 8 9
D64					
J65	5,000⁷	78 2 6⁷	31 5 2	31 5 2	3 18 2
D65	2,000⁸	31 5 0⁸	—36 3	3 4	1 11 3
J66	6,000⁹	93 15 0⁹	36 6 8½	36 6 8½	4 13 9
D66	2,000⁸	31 5 0⁸	12 10 1	12 10 1	1 11 3
J67¹⁰					
D67	12,000	187 10 0	28 12 9	28 12 9	9 7 6
J68	1,500	23 8 9	11 2 8	11 2 8	1 3 5
D68	3,000¹¹	41 17 6¹¹	11 2	11 2	2 1 10
J69	1,200	18 15 10	6 11 5½	6 11 5½	18 9
D69					
J70	5,080 (9,607)	79 7 6	2 10 3	2 10 3	3 19 4

¹ Commission reduced to 5 per cent.
² Transferred to Chapman and Hall.
³ Includes 4,900 parts = 245 volumes to Bohn at 6s. 3d. per volume = £76.11.3; 624 at 8s. per dozen = £19.4.0.
⁴ All to Bohn, 312 volumes at 6s. 3d. per volume.
⁵ All to Bohn, 104 volumes at 6s. 3d. per volume.
⁶ All to Bohn, 412 volumes at 6s. 3d. per volume.
⁷ All to Bohn, 250 volumes at 6s. 3d. per volume.
⁸ All to Bohn, 100 volumes at 6s. 3d. per volume.
⁹ All to Bohn, 300 volumes at 6s. 3d. per volume.
¹⁰ Reprinting.
¹¹ Includes 2,000 = 100 volumes to Ticknor and Fields at 5s. 3d. per volume = £26.5.10; 1,000 = 50 volumes at 6s. 3d. per volume = £15.12.6.

Appendix A

DAVID COPPERFIELD, Cheap Edition

1 vol., Bradbury and Evans, 1858, 5s.

	Sales, quantity	Sales, receipts			Profit, Dickens			Profit, B & E			Commission, B & E		
		£	s.	d.	£	s.	d.	£	s.	d.	£	s.	d.
D58	4,709	789	15	6	114	15	6	38	5	2	39	9	9
J59	1,090	182	5	0	22	19	7	7	13	2	9	2	3
D59	720	120	7	0	−4	9	7	−1	9	11	6	0	4
J60	714	119	14	0	66	3	6	22	1	2	5	19	8
D60	501	87	9	6	46	19	9[1]	15	13	2[1]	4	7	6
J61	530 (1,726)[2]	88	19	0	−49	9	0	−16	9	9	4	9	0

[1] Net profit listed at £62.13.0; 1d. unaccounted for in division.
[2] Transferred to Chapman and Hall 'Cheap Edition'.

DAVID COPPERFIELD, Library Edition

2 vols., Bradbury and Evans, 6s. per volume

	Sales, quantity	Sales, receipts			Profit, Dickens			Profit, B & E			Commission, B & E		
		£	s.	d.	£	s.	d.	£	s.	d.	£	s.	d.
J59	1,246	249	6	8	−202	16	0	−67	12	0	12	9	4
D59	1,131[1]	126	4	2[1]	85	19	10	28	13	4	6	6	3
J60	99	19	15	0	11	15	5	3	18	6		19	9
D60	55	10	16	8	7	11	7	2	10	6		10	10
J61	40 (1,395)[2]	8	2	6	4	5	7	1	8	7		8	1

[1] Includes 1,000 sold in America at 2s. ea. = £100.0.0; 12 in quires at 3s. 9d. and 119 as 115 in cloth at 4s. 2d. = £26.4.2.
[2] Transferred to Chapman and Hall.

DOMBEY AND SON

20 as 19 parts, Bradbury and Evans, 1846–8, 20s.

	Sales, quantity	Sales, receipts			Advertising receipts			Profit, Dickens			Profit, B & E			Commission, B & E		
		£	s.	d.	£	s.	d.	£	s.	d.	£	s.	d.	£	s.	d.
D46	122,035	4,106	19	2	556	17	6	1,498	4	8	499	8	2	466	7	8
J47	197,110	6,633	10	5	593	4	6	2,773	19	9	924	13	2	722	13	6
D47	188,940	6,358	11	0	525	19	0	2,635	2	11	878	7	7	688	9	0
J48	159,274	5,360	3	6	351	0	0	2,258	4	6	752	14	10	571	2	4
D48	4,746	159	14	5				94	4	8	31	8	3	15	19	5
J49	1,484	49	18	11				29	16	0	9	18	8	4	19	10
D49								−14	17	11	−4	19	4			—
J50	734	24	14	4				15	9	9	5	3	3	2	9	5
D50	862	29	0	5				18	7	10	6	2	7	2	18	0
J51	877	29	10	7				19	10	2	6	10	1	2	4	4
D51	671	22	10	9				12	7	0	4	2	3	2	5	0
J52	2,083	70	2	3				41	18	8	13	19	7	7	0	3
D52	2,288	77	0	0				47	19	1	15	19	8	7	14	0
J53	3,247	109	6	0				62	17	10	20	19	4	10	18	7
D53	1,208	40	13	9				11	11	6	3	17	2	4	1	4
J54	1,638	55	2	6				29	0	2	9	13	4	5	10	3
D54	1,845	62	2	6				29	12	1	9	17	5	6	4	3
J55	2,020	67	19	10				38	12	0	12	17	4	6	16	0
D55	1,806	60	16	3				36	7	10	12	2	8	6	1	7
J56	2,022	68	1	6				34	5	0	11	8	4	6	16	2
D56	1,319	44	8	1				18	14	4	6	4	9	4	8	9
J57	3,090	103	19	7				41	16	11	13	19	0	10	8	0
D57	1,570	52	17	3				31	0	7	10	6	11	5	5	9

DOMBEY AND SON (cont.)

	Sales, quantity	Sales, receipts £ s. d.	Advertising receipts £ s. d.	Profit, Dickens £ s. d.	Profit, B & E £ s. d.	Commission, B & E £ s. d.
J58	2,402	80 17 6		44 18 1	14 19 4	4 0 10[1]
D58	233	7 17 6		1 18 3	12 9	7 10
J59	561	18 17 9		11 15 9	3 18 6	18 10
D59	264	8 17 11		5 8 7	1 16 2	8 11
J60	304	10 5 0		6 17 2	2 5 9	10 3
D60	639	21 10 3		11 2 3	3 14 1	1 1 6
J61	427	14 8 0		9 10 7	3 3 7	14 5
	(4,972)[2]				C & H	C & H
D61	234	7 17 6		3 4 11	3 4 11	7 10
J62						
D62						
J63	8,320[3]	130 0 0[3]		18 19 3	18 19 3	6 10 0
D63	2,080[4]	32 10 0[4]		13 2 10½	13 2 10½	1 12 6
J64	7,400[5]	115 12 6[5]		18 12 3	18 12 3	5 15 8
D64						
J65						
D65	2,000[6]	31 5 0[6]		9 2 2	9 2 2	1 11 3
J66						
D66	5,500[7]	85 18 9[7]		3 5 5	3 5 5	4 5 10

J67[8]	10,000	156 5 0	32 4 6	32 4 6	7 16 2
D67	1,500	23 8 9	8 16 9½	8 16 9½	1 3 5
J68	3,000[9]	41 17 6[9]	18 0 0	18 0 0	2 1 9
D68	800	12 10 0	2 9 11	2 9 11	12 6
J69					
D69					
J70	3,320	51 17 6	−20 13 1		2 11 9
	(9,578)				

[1] Commission reduced to 5 per cent.
[2] Transferred to Chapman and Hall.
[3] All to Bohn, 416 volumes at 6s. 3d. per volume.
[4] All to Bohn, 104 volumes at 6s. 3d. per volume.
[5] All to Bohn, 370 volumes at 6s. 3d. per volume.
[6] All to Bohn, 100 volumes at 6s. 3d. per volume.
[7] All to Bohn, 275 volumes at 6s. 3d. per volume.
[8] Reprinting.
[9] 2,000 = 100 volumes to Ticknor and Fields at 5s. 3d. per volume; 1,000 = 50 volumes at 6s. 3d. per volume.

DOMBEY AND SON, Cheap Edition

1 vol., Bradbury and Evans, 1858, 5s.

	Sales, quantity	Sales, receipts			Profit, Dickens			Profit, B & E			Commission, B & E		
		£	s.	d.	£	s.	d.	£	s.	d.	£	s.	d.
J58	4,044	679	10	6	−24	2	7	−8	0	10	33	19	6
D58	2,002	334	15	0	61	7	4	20	9	1	16	14	9
J59	255	42	17	6	6	7	1	2	2	5	2	2	10
D59	227	37	11	6	16	0	9	5	6	11	1	17	7
J60	545	91	7	0	51	0	0	17	0	0	4	11	4
D60	437	73	7	0	40	3	9	13	7	11	3	13	4
J61	437	73	4	0	38	6	9	12	15	7	3	13	2
	(1,046)[1]												

[1] Transferred to Chapman and Hall 'Cheap Edition'.

DOMBEY AND SON, Library Edition

2 vols., Bradbury and Evans, 1858, 6s. per volume

	Sales, quantity	Sales, receipts			Profit, Dickens			Profit, B & E			Commission, B & E		
		£	s.	d.	£	s.	d.	£	s.	d.	£	s.	d.
D58	586	118	6	8	−99	15	9	−33	5	3	5	18	4
J59	1,789	257	18	4	−22	12	1	−7	10	9	12	17	11
D59	90	17	19	2	10	17	9	3	12	7	18	0	
J60	80	16	0	0	9	6	6[1]	3	2	2[1]	16	0	
D60	34	6	14	2	4	12	10	1	11	0	6	9	
J61	8	1	13	4	16	3		5	5		1	8	
	(1,375)[2]												

[1] Error of 4d. in division of net profits of £12.8.4; should be Dickens: £9.6.3, Bradbury and Evans: £3.2.1.
[2] Transferred to Chapman and Hall.

GREAT EXPECTATIONS

3 vols., Chapman and Hall, 1861, 31s. 6d.

	Sales, quantity[1]	Sales, receipts			Profit, Dickens			Profit, C & H			Commission, C & H		
		£	s.	d.	£	s.	d	£	s.	d.	£	s.	d.
30 Jan. 62	3,429[2]	3,194	8	7[2]	1,927	10	4	—			239	11	6[3]
J62	32	34	17	6	24	2	0	—			2	12	3
D62	12[4]	13	2	6[4]	5	19	3	5	19	3	1	4	0[5]
J63	27[6]	9	9	0[6]	3	18	1	3	18	0		9	6[7]
D63													
J64													
D64													
J65													
D65													
J66	247[8]	27	15	9[8]	13	4	0	13	4	0	1	7	9

[1] Figures are for three-volume sets.
[2] Includes 1,400 to Mudie at 16s. 8d. = £1,166.13.4; 130 to Tinsley at 20s. = £130.0.0; 160 as 154 to Tinsley at 20s. 3d. = £155.18.6; 62 as 60 to America and Australia at 20s. 3d. = £60.15.0; 590 as 567 to agents at 22s. 6d. less 10 per cent = £574.1.9; 1,025 as 984 at 22s. 6d. = £1,107.0.0.
[3] At 7½ per cent on gross sales receipts.
[4] Includes 3 to Tinsley at 15s. = ? £3.0.0; 9 at 22s. 6d. = £10.2.6.
[5] Includes allowances to agents.
[6] Includes 25 as 24 to Robertson, Melbourne at 6s. = £7.4.0; 2 at 22s. 6d. = £2.5.0.
[7] At 5 per cent.
[8] All remaining stock at 2s. 3d.

GREAT EXPECTATIONS, Library Edition

1 vol., Chapman and Hall, 1862, 7s. 6d.

	Sales, quantity	Sales, receipts			Profit, Dickens			Profit, C & H			Commission, C & H		
		£	s.	d.	£	s.	d.	£	s.	d.	£	s.	d.
D62	1,995[1]	503	5	2[1]	100	8	0	100	8	0	25	3	2
J63	325	83	4	0	6	1	6	6	1	6	4	3	2
D63	175[2]	21	8	0[2]	9	16	10	9	16	10	1	1	4
J64													
D64													
J65													
D65	[3]				−12	3	3[4]	—				12	9[4]

[1] Includes 300 as 288 to Robertson, Melbourne at 5s. 4d. less 10 per cent = £69.2.6; 1,695 as 1,628 at 5s. 4d. = £434.2.8.
[2] Includes 150 copies in quires to Ticknor and Fields at 2s. = £15.0.0.
[3] 225 copies in quires from D63 account transferred to Library Edition D65.
[4] Number in cloth sold overstated by 50, account therefore shows a deficiency.

GREAT EXPECTATIONS, Cheap Edition

1 vol., Chapman and Hall, 1863, 3s. 6d.

	Sales, quantity	Sales, receipts			Profit, Dickens			Profit, C & H			Commission, C & H		
		£	s.	d.	£	s.	d.	£	s.	d.	£	s.	d.
D63	2,443[1]	288	0	0[1]	6	0	6	6	0	6	14	8	0
J64	400	48	0	0	15	7	6	15	7	6	2	8	0
D64	425	51	0	0	17	15	3	17	15	3	2	11	0
J65	500	60	0	0	18	14	3	18	14	3	3	0	0
D65	(1,225)[2]												

[1] Includes 1,325 as 1,272 at 2s. 6d. = £159.0.0; 1,118 as 1,032 at 2s. 6d. = £129.0.0.

[2] 1,000 in quires, 225 in cloth, transferred to Chapman and Hall 'Cheap Edition'.

HARD TIMES

1 vol., Bradbury and Evans, 1854, 5s.

	Sales, quantity	Sales, receipts			Profit, Dickens			Profit, B & E			Commission, B & E		
		£	s.	d.	£	s.	d.	£	s.	d.	£	s.	d.
D54	5,616	943	12	0	208	5	11	69	8	8		—	
J55	318	53	11	0	36	1	7	12	0	6		—	
D55	170	28	14	0	17	14	0¹	5	18	0¹		—	
J56	46	7	17	6	4	16	6	1	12	2		—	
D56	68	11	11	0	7	5	10	2	8	8		—	
J57	101	16	19	6	9	11	7	3	3	10		—	
D57	15	2	12	6	1	13	3		11	1		—	
J58	52	8	15	0	4	16	5	1	12	2		8	9
D58	43	7	7	0	3	13	0	1	4	4		7	4
J59	44	7	10	6	4	13	0	1	11	0		7	6
D59	11	1	18	6		17	5		5	9		1	11
J60	40	6	16	6	4	4	10	1	8	4		6	10
D60	87	14	14	0	7	18	6	2	12	10		14	8
J61	28	4	13	8	3	1	7	1	0	7		4	8
	(1,295)²								C & H			C & H	
D61	25	4	4	0	1	13	2	1	13	2		4	2
J62	9³												
D62	3	2	2	0		17	4		17	3		2	1
J63	62⁴	9	13	8⁴	3	10	0	3	10	0		9	8
D63	50⁵	6	16	1⁵	2	19	2	2	19	2		6	9
J64	100⁶	13	12	2⁶	5	7	4	5	7	4		13	6
D64	75	12	12	0	4	17	9	4	17	9		12	6
J65	25	4	4	0	1	11	2	1	11	1		4	2
D65	50	8	8	0	3	8	10	3	8	10		8	4
J66	25	4	4	0	1	19	11	1	19	11		4	2
D66³													

¹ Overstated by 2d.; actual net profit was £23.11.10.
² Transferred to Chapman and Hall.
³ No further account.
⁴ Includes 50 as 48 to Robertson at 3s. 6d. less 10 per cent = £7.11.8; 12 at 3s. 6d. = £2.2.0.
⁵ Includes 25 to Bohn at 2s. 1d. = £2.12.1; 25 as 24 at 3s. 6d. = £4.4.0.
⁶ Includes 50 to Bohn at 2s. 1d. = £5.4.2; 50 as 48 at 3s. 6d. = £8.8.0.

THE HAUNTED MAN

1 vol., Bradbury and Evans, 1848, 5s.

	Sales, quantity	Sales, receipts			Profit, Dickens			Profit, B & E			Commission, B & E[1]		
		£	s.	d.	£	s.	d.	£	s.	d.	£	s.	d.
D48	17,776	2,931	17	6	793	5	11	264	8	8	293	3	9
J49	479	79	9	0	45	10	1	15	3	4	7	18	10
D49													
J50	10	1	15	0		6	0		2	0		3	6
D50	6	1	1	0		12	7		4	3		2	1
J51													
D51													
J52	7	1	3	0		14	9		4	11		2	3
D52													
J53													
D53	4		14	0		9	0		3	0		1	5
J54													
D54	3		10	6		6	5		2	1		1	0
J55													
D55													
J56	3		10	6		6	10		2	4		1	0
D56	3		10	6		7	1		2	4		1	1
J57													
D57	6	1	1	0		13	11		4	7		2	1
J58	2		7	0		4	6		1	6			4[2]
D58	3		10	6		7	1		2	4			6
J59	3		10	6		5	5		1	9			6
D59	3		10	6		6	9		2	3			6
J60													
D60	6	1	0	0		9	4		3	2		1	0
J61	13	2	5	6	1	8	9		9	7		2	3
	(1,564)[3]												

[1] Commission frequently includes agents' commissions in accounts; pro rated to reflect publishers' percentage.

[2] Commission altered to 5 per cent.

[3] Transferred to Chapman and Hall 'Christmas Books'.

LIBRARY EDITION

26 vols., Bradbury and Evans, Chapman and Hall, 1858–,
6s. per volume; illustrated, 1861–, 7s. 6d. per volume[1]

	Sales, quantity	Sales, receipts			Profit, Dickens			Profit, C & H			Commission, C & H		
		£	s.	d.	£	s.	d.	£	s.	d.	£	s.	d.
J58	11,300[2]	1,910	0	0[2]				−305	12	9	78	0	0
D58	4,500[3]	700	0	0[3]				−727	17	6	35	0	0
J59	250	50	0	0				−706	15	6	2	10	0
D59	400	80	0	0				−661	3	6	4	0	0
J60	275	55	0	0				−628	10	0	2	15	0
D60	675[4]	115	0	0[4]				−545	7	0	5	15	0
J61	6,450[5]	1,640	0	0[5]	56	10	0	56	10	0	82	0	0
D61	3,475[6]	885	8	0[6]	144	17	8	144	17	8	44	5	0
D61	500[7]	128	0	0	38	4	1½	38	4	1½	6	8	0
J62	4,300[8]	1,096	12	0[8]	233	14	0	233	14	0	54	16	8
D62	4,127[9]	1,024	3	8[9]	183	10	7	183	10	7	50	14	2
J63	1,818[10]	444	17	2[10]	61	2	2	61	2	2	22	4	9
D63	3,526[11]	632	2	0[11]	61	15	11½	61	15	11½	31	12	0
J64	2,476[12]	620	14	0[12]	189	10	6	189	10	6	31	1	0
D64	2,600	665	12	0	128	10	9	128	10	9	33	15	6
J65	2,200	563	4	0	91	19	8	91	19	9	28	3	2
D65	11,508[13]	1,778	1	2[13]	117	17	7	117	17	7	88	18	0

[1] Includes, from Chapman and Hall, *Pickwick Papers* (2 vols., 1858), *Nicholas Nickleby* (2 vols., 1858), *The Old Curiosity Shop* (2 vols., 1858), *Barnaby Rudge* (2 vols., 1858), *Martin Chuzzlewit* (2 vols., 1858), *Sketches by Boz* (1 vol., 1858), *A Tale of Two Cities* (1 vol., 1866), *Great Expectations* (1 vol., 1866), *Our Mutual Friend* (2 vols., 1867), and the eleven volumes transferred from Bradbury and Evans in 1861.

[2] Includes 3,500 volumes to Ticknor and Fields at 2s. per volume = £350.0.0; American titles and vignettes supplied.

[3] Includes 2,000 volumes to Ticknor and Fields at 2s. per volume = £200.0.0.

[4] Includes 100 each of *Pickwick* I and II to Ticknor and Fields at 2s. per volume = £20.0.0.

[5] Includes 200 as 192 to New York at 4s. 2d. = £40.0.0.

[6] Includes 75 as 72 to America at 4s. 2d. = £15.0.0.

[7] Volumes transferred from Bradbury and Evans and amalgamated hereafter.

[8] Includes 4,225 as 4,056 at 5s. 4d. = £1,081.12.0; 75 as 72 at 4s. 2d. = £15.0.0.

[9] Includes 492 to Scribner at 4s. 2d. = £102.10.0; 60 as 58 without illustrations at 4s. 2d. = £12.1.8; 3,475 as 3,336 at 5s. 4d. = £889.12.0; 100 volumes in quires to Ticknor and Fields at 2s.

[10] Includes 326 to Scribner at 4s. 2d. = £67.18.4; 92 as 89 without illustrations at 4s. 2d. = £18.10.10; 1,400 as 1,344 at 5s. 4d. = £358.8.0.

[11] Includes 276 to Scribner at 4s. 2d. = £57.10.0; 1,600 as 1,536 at 5s. 4d. = £409.12.0; 1,650 volumes in quires to Ticknor and Fields at 2s. = £165.0.0.

[12] Includes 276 to Scribner at 4s. 2d. = £57.10.0; 2,200 as 2,112 at 5s. 4d. = £563.4.0.

[13] Includes 6,000 volumes in quires = 250 sets to Appleton at 2s. 6d. less 7½ per cent = £693.15.0; 480 volumes in quires = 20 sets to Little and Brown at

390 · *Appendix A*

LIBRARY EDITION (*cont.*)

	Sales, quantity	Sales, receipts			Profit, Dickens			Profit, C & H			Commission, C & H		
		£	s.	d.	£	s.	d.	£	s.	d.	£	s.	d.
J66	10,210[14]	1,639	0	0[14]	284	19	6½	284	19	6½	81	19	0
D66	2,376[15]	630	2	8[15]	144	15	11½	144	15	11½	31	10	0
J67	6,954[16]	1,331	12	4[16]	303	3	10	303	3	10	66	11	6
D67	27,250[17]	2,398	6	8[17]	315	6	2½	315	6	2½	119	18	0
J68	27,025[18]	2,337	2	8[18]	238	2	0[19]	238	2	0[19]	116	17	1
D68	4,325[20]	722	13	0[20]	158	5	4½	158	5	4½	36	2	6
J69													
D69	16,950[21]	2,083	17	1[21]	291	18	8½	291	18	8½	104	3	9
J70	1,670[22]	433	12	4[22]	79	10	7½	79	10	7½	21	13	8
	(9,740)												

2s. 6d. = £60.0.0; 600 volumes cloth = 25 sets to Lippincott at 3s. = £90.0.0; 720 volumes cloth = 30 sets to Little and Brown at 3s. = £108.0.0; 1,320 volumes cloth = 55 sets to Johnstone at 3s. 6d. = £231.0.0; 288 as 277 volumes cloth to Scribner at 4s. 2d. = £57.14.2; 2,100 as 2,016 at 5s. 4d. = £537.12.0.

[14] Includes 600 volumes in quires to Lippincott at 2s. 8d. = £80.0.0; 1,200 volumes cloth to Lippincott at 3s. = £180.0.0; 2,400 volumes cloth to Ticknor and Fields at 3s. = £360.0.0; 2,400 volumes in quires to Ticknor and Fields at 2s. = £240.0.0; 600 volumes in quires to Little and Brown at 2s. 6d. = £75.0.0; 100 as 96 to Scribner at 4s. 2d. = £20.0.0; 960 volumes cloth to Johnstone at 3s. 6d. = £168.0.0; 900 as 864 at 5s. 4d. = £230.8.0; 1,050 as 1,008 at 5s. 8d. = £285.12.0.

[15] Includes 676 as 624 at 5s. 8d. = £176.16.0; 1,700 as 1,632 at 5s. 8d. = £453.6.8.

[16] Includes 2,000 to Appleton at 2s. 6d. less 7½ per cent = £231.5.0; 300 volumes without illustrations to Ticknor and Fields at 2s. 2d. = £32.10.0; 200 volumes to Ticknor and Fields at 3s. 2d. = £31.13.4; 1,062 to Little and Brown at 2s. 6d. = £132.15.0; 107 volumes in cloth to Lippincott at 3s. = £16.1.0; 585 as 540 at 5s. 8d. = £153.0.0; 2,700 as 2,592 at 5s. 8d. = £734.8.0.

[17] Includes 1,250 as 1,200 at 5s. 8d. = £340.0.0; 26,000 to Ticknor and Fields at 1s. 7d. = £2,058.6.8.

[18] Includes 26,000 to Ticknor and Fields at 1s. 7d. = £2,058.6.8; 1,025 as 984 at 5s. 8d. = £278.16.0.

[19] Adjustment of £110.12.0 for overcharges J67 included in expenses.

[20] Includes 2,500 to Ticknor and Fields at 1s. 7d. = £197.18.4; 1,825 as 1,752 at 5s. 8d. = £524.14.8.

[21] Includes 725 as 696 at 5s. 8d. less 10 per cent = £177.9.9; 3,225 as 3,096 at 5s. 8d. = £877.4.0; 13,000 volumes = 500 sets to Ticknor and Fields at 1s. 7d. = £1,029.3.4.

[22] Includes 766 as 736 at 5s. 8d. less 10 per cent = £187.13.8; 904 as 868 at 5s. 8d. = £245.18.8.

LITTLE DORRIT

20 parts as 19, Bradbury and Evans, 1855–7, 20s.

	Sales, quantity	Sales, receipts £ s. d.	Advertising receipts £ s. d.	Profit, Dickens £ s. d.	Profit, B & E £ s. d.	Commission, B & E £ s. d.
D55	63,393	2,194 7 9	369 19 6	890 13 11	296 18 0	—
J56	204,402	7,075 9 3[1]	642 1 0	3,601 17 7	1,200 12 7	—
D56	180,725	6,255 18 0[2]	616 8 6	3,252 0 8	1,084 0 3	—
J57	197,576	6,839 2 0[3]	461 11 0	3,612 9 3	1,204 3 1	—
D57	14,377	497 14 0[4]		359 12 3	119 17 6	—
J58	3,006	104 1 3		55 16 1	18 12 0	5 4 0
D58	1,098	38 0 6		24 13 2	8 4 5	1 18 0
J59	1,068	36 19 6		25 9 10	8 9 11	1 17 0
D59	300	10 7 9		4 14 4	4 11 5	10 4
J60	580	20 2 0		13 15 9	4 11 11	1 0 1
D60	332	11 10 3		5 1 1	1 13 9	11 6
J61	355	12 7 0		7 11 5	2 10 5	12 4
	(9,924)[5]			C & H	C & H	C & H
D61	260	8 15 0		3 12 7½	3 12 7½	8 9
J62						
D62	4,000[6]	62 10 0[6]		17 10 0	17 10 0	3 2 6
J63						
D63						
J64	4,940[7]	77 3 9[7]		2 16 9	2 16 9	3 17 0

1 Plus £75.0.0 for early proofs of I–VI to America, and £25.0.0 each from Mr. Krause and Mr. Heber.
2 Plus £75.0.0 for early proofs of VII–XII to America.
3 Plus £50.0.0 for early proofs of XIII–XVI to America.
4 Plus £50.0.0 for early proofs of XVII–XX to America.
5 Transferred to Chapman and Hall.
6 All to Bohn, 200 volumes at 6s. 3d.
7 All to Bohn, 247 volumes at 6s. 3d.

LITTLE DORRIT (cont.)

	Sales, quantity	Sales, receipts £ s. d.	Advertising receipts £ s. d.	Profit, Dickens £ s. d.	Profit, C & H £ s. d.	Commission, C & H £ s. d.
D64	2,000[8]	31 5 0[8]		14 16 10½	14 16 10½	1 11 3
J65	2,000[9]	31 5 0[9]		9 12 3	9 12 3	1 11 4
D65	2,720[10]	42 10 0[10]		19 12 1½	19 12 1½	2 2 6
J66						
D66						
J67[11]						
D67	12,000	187 10 0		7 7 4	7 7 4	9 7 6
J68	1,500	23 8 9		11 2 8	11 2 8	1 3 5
D68	2,600[12]	35 12 6[12]		16 18 6	16 18 6	1 15 6
J69	800	12 10 0		2 0 0½	2 0 0½	12 6
D69	2,000[13]	31 5 0		12 4 7	12 4 7	1 11 3
J70	1,360	21 5 0		−53 1 3		1 1 3
	(11,132)					

8 All to Bohn, 100 volumes at 6s. 3d.
9 All to Bohn, 100 volumes at 6s. 3d.
10 All to Bohn, 136 volumes at 6s. 3d.
11 Reprinting.

12 Includes 2,000 = 100 volumes to Ticknor and Fields at 5s. 3d. = £26.5.0; 600 = 30 volumes at 6s. 3d.
13 Plus 860 parts wasted.

LITTLE DORRIT, Library Edition

2 vols., Bradbury and Evans, 1859–, 6s. per volume

	Sales, quantity	Sales, receipts			Profit, Dickens			Profit, B & E			Commission, B & E		
		£	s.	d.	£	s.	d.	£	s.	d.	£	s.	d.
D59	1,099	219	16	8	−210	4	9	−70	1	7	10	19	10
J60	1,144	128	13	4	86	19	1	28	19	9	6	8	8
D60	138	27	9	2	16	13	1	5	11	0	1	7	5
J61	65	13	2	6	7	8	6	2	9	6		13	2
	(1,520)[1]												

[1] Transferred to Chapman and Hall.

MARTIN CHUZZLEWIT

20 parts as 19, Chapman and Hall, 1843–4, 20s.

	Sales, quantity	Sales, receipts			Profit, Dickens			Profit, C & H			Commission, C & H		
		£	s.	d.	£	s.	d.	£	s.	d.	£	s.	d.
J46	1,378	42	8	0	14	18	9	14	18	8	2	2	5
D46	3,484	107	4	0	44	6	2	44	6	1	5	7	3
J47	1,963	60	8	0	22	7	2	22	7	2	3	0	6
D47	520	16	0	0	5	11	10	5	11	9		16	0
J48	1,170	36	0	0	15	2	7	15	2	6	1	16	0
D48	1,131	34	16	0	13	8	6	13	8	6	1	14	9
J49	1,014	31	4	0	12	6	3	12	6	2	1	11	3
D49	273	8	8	0	2	8	11	2	8	11		8	5
J50	325	10	0	0	3	9	0	3	9	0		10	0
D50	702	21	12	0	9	3	7	9	3	6	1	1	7
J51	416	12	16	0	4	8	3	4	8	2		12	10
D51	442	13	12	0	5	13	8	5	13	8		13	8
J52	429	13	4	0	4	6	8	4	6	8		13	2
D52	494	15	4	0	5	8	10	5	8	10		15	2
J53	390	12	0	0	5	1	1[1]	5	1	0[1]		12	0
D53	585	18	0	0	6	10	0	6	10	0		18	0
J54	741	22	16	0	8	18	7	8	18	6	1	2	10
D54	702	21	12	0	7	14	8	7	14	9	1	1	8
J55	637	19	12	0	8	14	3	8	14	3		19	6
D55	585	18	0	0	6	8	0	6	8	0		18	0
J56	507[2]	13	14	0[2]	5	14	6	5	14	6		13	6
D56	1,508[3]	37	16	0[3]	13	1	8	13	1	8	1	17	9
J57	1,196[4]	32	10	0[4]	7	3	8	7	3	7	1	12	6

[1] Chapman and Hall credited with the extra 1d. in the cash account.
[2] Includes 247 to New York at 6s. per dozen = £5.14.0.
[3] Includes 1,118 to Bangs at 6s. per dozen = £25.16.0.
[4] Includes 559 to Bangs at 6s. per dozen = £12.18.0.

MARTIN CHUZZLEWIT (*cont.*)

	Sales, quantity	Sales, receipts			Profit, Dickens			Profit, C & H			Commission, C & H		
		£	s.	d.	£	s.	d.	£	s.	d.	£	s.	d.
D57	1,027	31	12	0	13	9	3	13	9	3	1	11	6
J58	1,079	33	4	0	14	1	0	14	1	0	1	13	0
D58	676	20	16	0	7	18	5	7	18	4	1	0	9
J59	390	12	0	0	4	19	0	4	19	0		12	0
D59	1,053	32	8	0	—0	7	6				1	12	6
J60	390	12	0	0	4	10	9	4	10	9		12	0
D60	1,469	45	4	0	15	11	11	15	11	10	2	5	3
J61	260	8	0	0	3	3	0	3	3	0		8	0
D61	156	4	16	0	2	0	0	2	0	0		4	0
J62	455[5]	12	16	0[5]	5	2	2	5	2	1		12	9
D62	5,408[6]	87	13	0[6]	30	10	5	30	10	5	4	7	8
J63	4,160[7]	65	0	0[7]	26	8	6	26	8	6	3	5	0
D63													
J64	13,540[8]	211	11	3[8]	31	10	4½	31	10	4½	10	11	6
D64													
J65													
D65	4,000[9]	62	10	0[9]	24	2	6	24	2	6	3	2	6
J66													
D66	7,220[10]	112	16	3[10]	15	16	0	15	16	0	5	12	9
J67[11]													
D67	10,000	156	5	0	13	8	7½	13	8	7½	7	16	3
J68	1,500	23	8	9	11	2	8	11	2	8	1	3	5
D68	3,000[12]	41	17	6[12]	17	13	4	17	13	4	2	1	10
J69	1,200	18	15	0	6	13	7½	6	13	7½		18	9
D69	2,000[13]	31	5	0[13]	12	12	4½	12	12	4½	1	11	3
J70	3,020 (9,353)	47	3	9	—24	8	5				2	7	2

[5] Includes 156 at 6s. per dozen = £3.12.0; 299 at 8s. per dozen = £9.4.0.
[6] Includes 5,200 parts = 260 volumes to Bohn at 6s. 3d. per volume = £81.5.0; 208 at 8s. per dozen = £6.8.0.
[7] All to Bohn, 208 volumes at 6s. 3d.
[8] All to Bohn, 677 volumes at 6s. 3d.
[9] All to Bohn, 200 volumes at 6s. 3d.
[10] All to Bohn, 360 volumes at 6s. 3d.
[11] Reprinting.
[12] Includes 2,000 = 100 volumes at 5s. 3d.; 1,000 = 50 volumes at 6s. 3d.
[13] Plus 2,800 parts wasted.

MASTER HUMPHREY'S CLOCK

88 weekly numbers, Chapman and Hall, 3*d.* per number[1]

	Sales, quantity	Sales, receipts			Profit, Dickens			Profit, C & H			Commission, C & H		
		£	s.	d.	£	s.	d.	£	s.	d.	£	s.	d.
J46	6,305	48	10	0	36	11	11[2]	36	11	10[2]	2	8	6
D46	8,086	62	4	0	20	5	3	20	5	3	3	2	3
J47	6,643	51	2	0	17	5	7[3]	17	5	7	2	11	1
D47	4,680	36	0	0	16	1	8	16	1	8	1	16	0
J48	4,797	36	18	0	10	10	6	10	10	6	1	16	11
D48	3,601	27	14	0	12	8	8	12	8	7	1	7	9
J49	1,534	11	16	0		7	11		7	10		11	9
D49	1,040	8	0	0	3	8	3	3	8	3		8	0
J50	1,053	8	2	0	3	6	11½[4]	3	6	11½		8	1
D50	1,131	8	14	0	3	13	7	3	13	6		8	9
J51	1,391	10	14	0	4	5	5[4]	4	5	5		10	8
D51	1,261	9	14	0	3	5	10	3	5	9		9	8
J52	1,443	11	2	0	4	13	9[4]	4	13	8		11	1
D52	2,080	16	0	0	6	18	6	6	18	6		16	0
J53	2,145	16	10	0	7	5	9	7	5	9		16	6
D53	3,588	27	12	0	7	7	0	7	7	0	1	7	6
J54	1,053	8	2	0	3	6	6	3	6	6		8	0
D54	2,106	16	4	0	6	4	8	6	4	7		16	3
J55	1,612[5]	11	7	6[5]	3	10	1	3	10	1		11	4
D55	871	9	2	0[6]	3	18	0	3	18	0		9	0
J56	2,951[7]	21	3	0[7]	7	8	6	7	8	6	1	1	0
D56	3,770[8]	22	17	6[8]	9	8	1	9	8	1	1	2	10
J57	2,383[9]	17	14	4[9]	3	2	10	3	2	10		17	9
D57	1,135[9]	8	2	4[9]	2	19	8	2	19	8		8	0
J58	3,159	24	6	0	10	2	9	10	2	9	1	4	6
D58	3,198	24	12	0	10	3	4	10	3	4	1	4	7
J59	2,119	16	6	0	6	18	0	6	18	0		16	4
D59	1,560	12	0	0	4	11	6	4	11	6		12	0
J60	910	7	0	0	2	14	0	2	14	0		7	0

[1] 45 numbers of *The Old Curiosity Shop* and 43 numbers of *Barnaby Rudge* = 88 numbers of the *Clock*. Despite Dickens's statement that the miscellaneous pages (Numbers 1–3, 5–6) were set aside as wastage, Chapman and Hall always account as if all of the first 45 numbers contained the *Shop*. The *Clock* was also sold in monthly parts containing 4 numbers at 1*s.*, or 5 numbers at 1*s.* 3*d.*, and in three volumes: I (15 Oct. 1840) and II (*c.* 10 Apr. 1841) for 8*s.*, III (15 Dec. 1841) for 10*s.* 6*d.*

[2] Includes half-payment from Tauchnitz of £30.0.0.

[3] Cash account figure differs—£17.6.1—and correctly states half-profit.

[4] Dickens's half-share of the cost of warehousing and insurance (£4.17.6) deducted in the cash account.

[5] Includes 533 numbers sold in New York at 1*s.* 6*d.* per dozen = £3.1.6.

[6] Error for £6.14.0, not corrected until J56.

[7] Includes 806 numbers sold in New York at 1*s.* 6*d.* per dozen = £4.13.0.

[8] Includes 2,730 numbers to Bangs at 1*s.* 5*d.* per dozen = £14.17.6.

[9] Includes 264 numbers to New York at 1*s.* 5*d.* per dozen = £1.8.4.

Appendix A

MASTER HUMPHREY'S CLOCK (cont.)

	Sales, quantity	Sales, receipts			Profit, Dickens			Profit, C & H			Commission, C & H		
		£	s.	d.	£	s.	d.	£	s.	d.	£	s.	d.
D60	2,015	15	10	0	5	12	9	5	12	9		15	6
J61	949	7	6	0	2	16	4	2	16	4		7	4
D61	611	4	14	0	1	18	7½	1	18	7½		4	9
J62													
D62	15,048[10]	65	11	0[10]	31	2	9	31	2	9	3	5	6
J63	13,780[11]	59	16	0[11]	5	16	9	5	16	10	2	19	10
D63	4,902[12]	21	9	4[12]	10	4	0	10	4	0	1	1	4
J64	12,496[13]	54	8	8[13]	12	4	3	12	4	3	2	14	4
D64													
J65	13,200[14]	57	10	0[14]	2	16	8	2	16	7	2	17	6
D65	9,925[15]	43	2	6[15]	19	6	0	19	6	0	2	3	0
J66	8,800[16]	38	6	8[16]	16	6	2	16	6	2	1	18	4
D66	7,725[17]	33	10	10[17]	15	18	8	15	18	8	1	13	6
J67													
D67													
J68	37,400[18]	162	18	4[18]	4	11	1	4	11	1	8	2	10
D68	12,320[19]	47	16	8[19]	22	14	6	22	14	6	2	7	8
J69	2,640[20]	11	10	0[20]	5	9	3	5	9	3		11	6
D69	4,665[21]	20	2	6[21]	9	11	3	9	11	3	1	0	0
J70	7,900[22]	34	10	0[22]	16	7	9	16	7	9	1	14	6
	(24,608[22])												

[10] Includes 7,695 numbers = 171 OCS to Bohn at 3s. 10d. = £32.15.6; 7,353 numbers = 171 BR to Bohn at 3s. 10d. = £32.15.6.

[11] Includes 8,190 numbers = 182 OCS to Bohn at 3s. 10d. = £34.17.8; 5,590 numbers = 130 BR to Bohn at 3s. 10d. = £24.18.4.

[12] Includes 1,935 numbers = 43 OCS to Bohn at 3s. 10d. = £8.4.10; 2,967 numbers = 69 BR to Bohn at 3s. 10d. = £13.4.6.

[13] Includes 6,390 numbers = 142 OCS to Bohn at 3s. 10d. = £27.4.4; 6,106 numbers = 142 BR to Bohn at 3s. 10d. = £27.4.4.

[14] Includes 6,750 numbers = 150 OCS to Bohn at 3s. 10d. = £28.15.0; 6,450 numbers = 150 BR to Bohn at 3s. 10d. = £28.15.0.

[15] Includes 5,625 numbers = 125 OCS to Bohn at 3s. 10d. = £23.19.2; 4,300 numbers = 100 BR to Bohn at 3s. 10d. = £19.3.4.

[16] Includes 100 each OCS and BR to Bohn at 3s. 10d.

[17] Includes 4,500 numbers = 100 OCS to Bohn at 3s. 10d. = £19.3.4; 3,225 numbers = 75 BR to Bohn at 3s. 10d. = £14.7.6.

[18] Includes 425 dozen numbers each OCS and BR at 3s. 10d. = £81.9.2 each.

[19] Includes 4,300 numbers = 100 BR to Ticknor and Fields at 3s. 3d.; 4,500 numbers = 100 OCS to Ticknor and Fields at 3s. 3d.; 1,720 numbers = 40 BR at 3s. 10d.; 1,800 numbers = 40 OCS at 3s. 10d.

[20] Includes 30 dozen numbers each OCS and BR at 3s. 10d. = £5.15.0 each.

[21] Includes 75 dozen numbers OCS at 3s. 10d. = £14.7.6; 30 dozen numbers BR at 3s. 10d. = £5.15.0.

[22] Includes 80 dozen numbers OCS at 3s. 10d. = £15.6.8; 100 dozen numbers BR at 3s. 10d. = £19.3.4.

NICHOLAS NICKLEBY

20 parts as 19, Chapman and Hall, 1838–9, 20s.

	Sales, quantity	Sales, receipts £ s. d.	Profit, Dickens £ s. d.	Profit, C & H £ s. d.	Commission, C & H £ s. d.
J58	832	25 12 0	−31 12 3		1 5 6
D58	598	18 8 0	−16 14 7		18 4
J59					
D59					
J60	611	18 16 0	3 4	3 4	18 9
D60	260	8 0 0	2 7 0	2 7 0	8 0
J61	299	9 4 0	3 12 8	3 12 7	9 3
D61	182	5 12 0	2 7 3	2 7 3	5 6
J62	234	7 4 0	3 0 2	3 0 1	7 3
D62	7,438[1]	121 6 9[1]	16 3 8	16 3 7	6 1 4
J63					
D63	7,240[2]	113 2 6[2]	4 14 9	4 14 9	5 13 2
J64	3,640[3]	56 17 6[3]	21 5 0	21 5 0	2 16 9
D64	6,000[4]	93 15 0[4]	39 17 0½	39 17 0½	4 13 9
J65	1,000[5]	15 12 6[5]	2 15 1	2 15 1	15 2
D65	4,000[6]	62 10 0[6]	22 6 0	22 6 0	3 2 6
J66	3,500[7]	54 13 9[7]	9 18 0	9 18 0	2 14 9
D66	2,000[8]	31 5 0[8]			1 11 2

[1] Includes 7,100 = 355 vols. to Bohn at 6s. 3d. = £110.18.9; 338 at 8s. per dozen = £10.8.0.
[2] All to Bohn, 362 volumes at 6s. 3d.
[3] All to Bohn, 182 volumes at 6s. 3d.
[4] All to Bohn, 300 volumes at 6s. 3d.
[5] All to Bohn, 50 volumes at 6s. 3d.
[6] All to Bohn, 200 volumes at 6s. 3d.
[7] All to Bohn, 175 volumes at 6s. 3d.
[8] All to Bohn, 100 volumes at 6s. 3d.

NICHOLAS NICKLEBY (cont.)

	Sales, quantity	Sales, receipts			Profit, Dickens			Profit, C & H			Commission, C & H		
		£	s.	d.	£	s.	d.	£	s.	d.	£	s.	d.
J67[9]													
D67	10,000	156	5	0	14	13	4½	14	13	4½	7	16	3
J68	2,000	31	5	0	14	16	10½	14	16	10½	1	11	3
D68	3,200[10]	45	0	0[10]	18	15	6	18	15	6	2	5	0
J69	1,000	15	12	6	4	16	6	4	16	6		15	6
D69													
J70	4,700	73	8	9	−3	4	9	3	4	9	3	13	6
	(8,466)												

[9] Reprinting.
[10] Includes 2,000 = 100 volumes at 5s. 3d.; 1,200 = 60 volumes at 6s. 3d.

OLIVER TWIST

3 vols., Richard Bentley, Chapman and Hall, 1838, 25s.

	Sales, quantity[1]	Sales, receipts			Profit, Dickens			Profit, C & H			Commission, C & H		
		£	s.	d.	£	s.	d.	£	s.	d.	£	s.	d.
J46	25	21	18	0	17	16	1	—			1	1	11
D46	7	6	7	9	6	1	4	—				6	5
J47													
D47	2	1	16	6	1	14	8	—			1		10
J48													
D48													
J49	4	3	13	0	3	9	4	—				3	8
D49	3	2	14	9	2	7	6	—				2	9
J50													
D50													
J51	4	3	13	0	3	3	4	—				3	8
D51	4	3	13	0	3	1	10	—				3	8
J52	4	3	13	0	2	18	10	—				3	8
D52													
J53	2	1	16	6	1	14	8	—			1		10
D53	5	4	11	3	3	16	3	—				4	6
J54													
D54													
J55	5	4	11	3	4	6	9	—				4	6
D55													
J56	2												
D56	12[3]	6	15	8[3]	3	13	5	—				6	9
J57													
D57													
J58	5	4	11	3	4	6	9	—				4	6
D58													
J59													
D59													
J60													
D60													
J61													
D61													
J62													
D62													
J63													
D63													
J64													
D64													
J65													
D65													
J66	377[4]	56	11	0	26	17	1½	26	17	1½	2	16	6

[1] Figures are for the three-volume set.
[2] 25 copies sent to America; no returns until Mar. 1857.
[3] Includes 8 at 7s. 10d. = £3.2.8.
[4] All remaining stock; not reprinted.

OLIVER TWIST
10 parts, Bradbury and Evans, 1846, 10s.

	Sales, quantity	Sales, receipts £ s. d.	Advertisements, receipts £ s. d.	Profit, Dickens £ s. d.	Profit, B & E £ s. d.	Commission, B & E £ s. d.
J46	23,836	844 3 10	44 13 0	81 7 2	81 7 2	84 8 5
D46	14,303	469 11 1	19 17 6	97 10 10	97 10 9	46 19 1
J47	1,441	47 2 1		20 10 3	20 10 2	4 14 2
D47	1,003	32 15 11		13 7 11	13 7 10	3 5 7
J48	969	31 13 3		13 5 4	13 5 3	3 3 4
D48	604	19 15 3		7 13 9	7 13 9	1 19 6
J49	447	14 12 6		6 9 1	6 9 0	1 9 3
D49	508	16 12 2		7 4 6	7 4 6	1 13 3
J50	813	26 11 7		10 19 2	10 19 1	2 13 2
D50	77	2 11 0		1 0 0	1 0 0	5 0
J51	119	3 17 11		1 10 2	1 10 1	7 8
D51	159	5 4 1		2 2 9	2 2 9	10 5
J52	279	9 2 9		3 16 1	3 16 0	18 3
D52	234	7 13 0		2 12 1	2 12 0	15 4
J53	563	18 8 4		7 8 7	7 8 7	1 16 10
D53	105	3 8 9		1 8 7	1 8 7	6 10
J54	340	11 2 5		2 13 5	2 13 4	1 2 3
D54	278	9 2 0		3 17 5	3 17 4	18 2
J55	635	20 15 1		8 0 7	8 0 6	2 1 6
D55	217	7 2 4		11 4	11 3	14 2
J56	387	12 13 7		4 17 4	4 17 4	1 5 4
D56	248	8 2 3		2 8 5	2 8 5	16 3
J57	738	24 3 1		9 16 10	9 16 10	2 8 3
D57	125	4 2 2		1 6 5	1 6 4	8 2

Period	Volumes	£ s. d.	£ s. d.	C & H £ s. d.	C & H £ s. d.
J58	554	18 2 8	6 10 3	6 10 3	18 2[1]
D58	95	3 2 4	1 6 2	1 6 1	3 2
J59	564	18 9 0	8 14 4	2 18 2	18 5
D59	108	3 10 10	2 2 10	14 4	3 6
J60	374	12 2 3	6 15 7	2 5 3	12 1
D60	398	13 0 8	8 9 11	2 16 8	13 0
J61	470	15 7 5	7 18 0	2 12 8	15 4
	(1,869)		C & H	C & H	C & H
D61					
J62					
D62	3,450[2]	54 12 6[2]	8 4 3	8 4 3	2 14 7
J63					
D63	4,700[3]	74 8 4[3]	18 9	18 9	3 14 4
J64					
D64	1,500[4]	23 15 0[4]	8 17 3½	8 17 3½	1 3 9
J65	750[5]	11 17 6[5]	2 8 6	2 8 6	11 8
D65	1,500[6]	23 15 0[6]	9 13 5	9 13 5	1 3 9
J66			7		
D66					
J67					
D67					

[1] Commission reduced to 5 per cent.
[2] All to Bohn, 345 volumes at 3s. 2d.
[3] All to Bohn, 470 volumes at 3s. 2d.
[4] All to Bohn, 150 volumes at 3s. 2d.
[5] All to Bohn, 75 volumes at 3s. 2d.
[6] All to Bohn, 150 volumes at 3s. 2d.
[7] Deficiency of £18.7.5 carried to J68.

OLIVER TWIST (cont.)

	Sales, quantity	Sales, receipts	Advertisements, receipts	Profit, Dickens	Profit, C & H	Commission, C & H
		£ s. d.	£ s. d.	£ s. d.	£ s. d.	£ s. d.
J68	5,500	87 1 8		5 6 7½	5 6 7½	4 7 0
D68	1,500[8]	21 13 4[8]		10 5 10	10 5 10	1 1 8
J69	1,000	15 16 8		7 10 5	7 10 5	15 10
D69	1,000[9]	15 16 8		5 18 3	5 18 3	15 9
J70	1,070	16 18 10		6 8 8½	6 8 8½	17 0
	(1,277)					

8 1,000 = 100 volumes to Ticknor and Fields at 2s. 9d.; 500 = 50 volumes at 3s. 2d.
9 Plus 742 parts wasted.

OLIVER TWIST, Cheap Edition

19 weekly numbers, Chapman and Hall, 1849–50, 1½d. weekly numbers,
7d. monthly parts

	Sales, numbers, quantity	Sales, quires, receipts			Sales, parts, quantity	Sales, parts, receipts			Profit, Dickens and partners		
		£	s.	d.		£	s.	d.	£	s.	d.
D49	33,332	128	4	0	6,071	108	19	4	−27	18	6
J50											
D50											
J51	14,222	54	14	0	234	4	4	0	52	0	8
D51											
J52	20,228	77	16	0	156	2	16	0	72	12	2
D52											
J53											
D53	34,190	131	10	0	273	4	18	0[1]	32	19	2[1]
J54	5,850	22	10	0	52		18	8	20	13	4
D54											
J55											
D55											
J56	12,129[2]	43	16	6[2]					38	18	6
D56	13,949[3]	50	4	9[3]					43	19	6
J57	12,730[4]	47	11	0[4]					41	6	6[5]
D57	12,207	46	19	0					−91	16	8
J58											
D58											
J59	31,889	122	13	0	65	1	3	4	17	10	6
D59[6]											

[1] Accounts give 'Parts-profit = £41.18.0' instead of correct amount, £4.18.0. Net profit adjusted to correct error. D53 includes J53 account.

[2] Includes 1,898 in New Orleans for £4.18.6; 468 in New York at 9d. per dozen = £1.7.9.

[3] Includes 1,898 to Parry for £4.18.6; 1,079 to Bangs at 9d. per dozen = £3.2.3.

[4] Includes 627 to Singapore, etc., at 5d. per dozen = £1.0.0.

[5] Cash account deducts '¼ share' to be paid to B & E = £10.6.7.

[6] No further accounts.

OLIVER TWIST, Library Edition

1 vol., Bradbury and Evans, 1858, 6s.

	Sales, quantity	Sales, receipts			Profit, Dickens			Profit, B & E			Commission, B & E		
		£	s.	d.	£	s.	d.	£	s.	d.	£	s.	d.
D58	689	137	18	4	−145	13	4	−48	11	2	6	17	11
J59	594	68	18	9	36	2	7	12	0	10	3	8	11
D59	43	8	12	11	5	9	3	1	16	5		8	8
J60	56	11	2	6	7	14	1	2	11	5		11	2
D60	24	4	18	4	3	8	2	1	2	9		4	11
J61	3		12	6		8	10		3	0			8
	(573)												

OUR MUTUAL FRIEND

20 parts as 19, Chapman and Hall, 1864-5, 20s.

	Numbers		Bound Vols.		Advertising receipts	Profit, Dickens	Profit, C & H	Commission, C & H
	Sales, quantity	Sales, receipts	Sales, quantity	Sales, receipts				
		£ s. d.		£ s. d.	£ s. d.	£ s. d.	£ s. d.	£ s. d.
24 Oct.	136,422[1]	4,480 9 6[1]			1,033 8 6	1,173 19 0	1,173 19 0	224 0 6
D64	60,554[2]	2,011 0 3[2]			460 7 6	803 5 6[3]	803 5 6[3]	100 11 0
J65	87,685[4]	2,885 13 6[4]			772 19 6	942 8 3	942 8 2	144 5 8
D65	84,357[5]	2,778 5 6[5]	5,385[6]	1,864 13 0[6]	483 17 4	1,689 2 0½	1,689 2 0½	239 18 9
J66	10,153[7]	342 18 0[7]	350	130 4 0		400 5 6	—	23 13 0
D66	676	23 8 0	175	65 2 0		76 13 6	—	4 8 6
J67	520	18 0 0	150	55 16 0		65 9 0	—	3 13 0
D67	312	10 16 0	25	9 6 0		38 2 0[8]	—	2 0 0
J68	299	9 12 0	40	15 2 3		25 9 3		

[1] Includes 31,200 at 8s. 9d. per dozen = £1,040 [sic, should be £1,050]; 58,305 at 9s. per dozen = £1,816.8.6; 46,917 at 9s. per dozen = £1,624.1.0.

[2] Includes 13,663 at 8s. 9d. per dozen = £459.16.3; 20,787 at 9s. per dozen less 10 per cent = £647.12.0; 26,104 at 9s. per dozen = £903.12.0.

[3] Includes £150.0.0 from Australia.

[4] Includes 24,752 at 8s. 9d. per dozen = £833.0.0; 36,335 at 9s. per dozen less 10 per cent = £1,131.19.6; 26,598 at 9s. per dozen = £920.14.0.

[5] Includes 24,128 at 8s. 9d. per dozen = £812.0.0; 34,255 at 9s. per dozen less 10 per cent = £1,067.3.6; 25,974 at 9s. per dozen = £899.2.0.

[6] Includes 1,664 as 1,536 to Mudie's = £595.4.0; 1,000 as 960 to Smith and Son at 7s. 9d. less 10 per cent = £334.16.0; 221 as 204 subscribed, 13 as 12, at 7s. 9d. = £79.1.0; 2,500 as 2,208 at 7s. 9d. = £855.12.0.

[7] Includes 4,160 at 8s. 9d. = £140.0.0; 1,313 at 9s. per dozen less 10 per cent = £40.18.0; 4,680 at 9s. = £162.0.0.

[8] Includes £20.0.0 for one set of electrotype plates sold to an Italian paper.

OUR MUTUAL FRIEND (cont.)

	Numbers		Bound Vols.		Advertising receipts	Profit, Dickens	Profit, C & H	Commission, C & H
	Sales, quantity	Sales, receipts	Sales, quantity	Sales, receipts				
		£ s. d.		£ s. d.	£ s. d.	£ s. d.	£ s. d.	£ s. d.
D68	4,052[9]	64 4 0[9]	84[10]	30 11 0[10]		90 0 3	—	4 14 9
J69	2,052[11]	32 19 0[11]	30	11 4 9		41 19 6	—	2 4 3
D69	1,639[12]	26 5 6[12]				24 19 3	—	1 6 3
J70	2,160	33 15 0				32 1 3	—	1 13 9
	(94,334)							

[9] Includes 4,000 = 200 volumes at 6s. 3d. = £62.10.0; 52 as 48 at 8s. 6d. per dozen = £1.14.0.

[10] 4 at 7s. 9d. = £1.11.0; 80 sold soiled to Smith and Son at 7s. 3d. = £29.0.0.

[11] Includes 2,000 = 100 volumes at 6s. 3d. = £31.5.0; 52 as 48 at 8s. 6d. per dozen = £1.14.0.

[12] Includes 1,600 = 80 volumes at 6s. 3d. = £25.0.0; 39 as 36 at 8s. 6d. per dozen = £1.5.6.

PEOPLE'S EDITION

27 vols., Chapman and Hall, 1865, 2s. per volume

	Sales, quantity	Sales, receipts[1]			Profit, Dickens			Profit, C & H			Commission, C & H		
		£	s.	d.	£	s.	d.	£	s.	d.	£	s.	d.
J65	57,200	3,366	0	0	314	14	4	314	14	4		—	
D65	78,325	4,609	2	6	600	3	7½	600	3	7½		—	
J66	57,122	3,351	8	2	546	2	5½	546	2	5½		—	
D66	59,800	3,519	0	0	472	4	9½	472	4	9½		—	
J67	28,080	1,652	8	0	373	18	8	373	18	8		—	
D67	4,745	279	4	6	139	12	3	139	12	3		—	
J68	2,873	169	1	6	84	10	9	84	10	9		—	
D68													
J69	672[2]	40	7	2[2]	17	6	5	17	6	5	2	0	4
D69	82,100[3]	1,710	8	4[3]	643	10	8	643	10	8	85	10	6
J70	11,400[4] (16,664)	237	10	0[4]	108	10	9	108	10	9	11	17	6

[1] From J65 to J68, net of 10 per cent discount.
[2] Includes 100 at 1s. = £5.0.0; 312 as 24 dozen at 17s. less 10 per cent = £18.7.2; 260 as 20 dozen at 17s. = £17.0.0.
[3] All at 5d.
[4] All to Smith and Son at 5d.

Appendix A

THE PICKWICK PAPERS

20 parts as 19, Chapman and Hall, 1836–7, 20s.

	Sales, quantity	Sales, receipts			Profit, Dickens			Profit, C & H			Commission, C & H		
		£	s.	d.	£	s.	d.	£	s.	d.	£	s.	d.
J46	2,379	73	4	0	20	18	1	41	16	2	7	6	5
D46	3,978	122	8	0	33	8	8	66	17	4	12	4	10
J47	3,406	104	16	0	29	14	3	58	8	5	10	9	8
D47	1,456	44	16	0	12	5	6	24	10	11	4	9	7
J48	1,131	34	16	0	9	12	2	19	4	3	3	9	7
D48	819	25	4	0	6	19	11	13	19	8	2	10	5
J49	377	11	12	0	3	0	5	6	0	11	1	3	2
D49	585	18	0	0	4	19	10	9	19	8	1	16	0
J50	1,001	30	16	0	8	14	0	17	8	0	3	1	6
D50	1,235	38	0	0	10	15	0	21	10	0	3	16	0
J51	689	21	4	0	5	14	7	11	9	1	2	2	4
D51	1,274	39	4	0	11	3	9	22	7	4	3	18	5
J52	1,482	45	12	0	13	1	8	26	3	2	4	11	2
D52	1,508	46	8	0	13	5	11	26	11	9	4	12	10
J53	936	28	16	0	8	1	0	16	2	0	2	17	6
D53	1,560	48	0	0	12	2	0	24	4	0	4	16	0
J54	1,456	44	16	0	12	11	6	25	2	11	4	9	6
D54	1,508	46	8	0	12	8	9	24	17	6	4	12	9
J55	2,223[1]	62	14	0[1]	16	11	1	33	2	3	6	5	4
D55	1,690	52	0	0	−17	6	6	−34	13	0	5	4	0
J56	1,768[2]	52	10	0[2]	14	18	4	29	16	8	5	5	0
D56	3,666[3]	100	4	0[3]	28	9	3	56	18	5	10	0	4
J57	3,055[4]	90	2	0[4]	25	12	0	51	4	0	9	0	0
D57	4,056	124	16	0	−63	11	6				12	9	6
J58	2,561[5]	71	2	0[5]		4	3		4	3	3	11	0[6]
D58	2,587	79	12	0	35	5	6	35	5	5	3	19	7
J59	1,144	35	4	0	15	2	0	15	2	0	1	15	0
D59	2,171	66	16	0	29	7	7	29	7	7	3	6	10
J60	1,976	60	16	0	26	11	8	26	11	7	3	0	9
D60	2,184	67	4	0	26	6	5	26	6	4	3	7	3
J61	1,950	60	0	0	25	2	0	25	2	0	3	0	0
D61	611	18	16	0	8	10	7	8	10	7		18	10
J62	1,612[7]	44	18	0[7]	19	4	4	19	4	4	2	4	10
D62	10,493[8]	179	18	0[8]	40	6	2	40	6	1	8	19	10

[1] Includes 741 sold in New York at 6s. per dozen = £17.2.0.
[2] Includes 247 sold in New York at 6s. per dozen = £5.14.0.
[3] Includes 1,638 to Bangs, New York at 6s. per dozen = £37.16.0.
[4] Includes 507 to Bangs, New York at 6s. per dozen = £11.14.0.
[5] Includes 1,001 sold to exporters at 6s. per dozen = £23.2.0.
[6] Commission reduced to 5 per cent.
[7] Includes 611 at 6s. per dozen = £14.2.0; 1,001 at 8s. per dozen = £30.16.0.
[8] Includes 9,440 parts = 472 volumes to Bohn at 6s. 3d. per volume = £147.10.0; 1,053 at 8s. per dozen = £32.8.0.

THE PICKWICK PAPERS *(cont.)*

	Sales, quantity	Sales, receipts			Profit, Dickens			Profit, C & H			Commission, C & H		
		£	s.	d.	£	s.	d.	£	s.	d.	£	s.	d.
J63	10,400[9]	162	10	0[9]	15	12	9	15	12	8	8	2	6
D63	15,000[9]	234	7	6[9]	44	4	9	44	4	9	11	14	3
J64	5,000[9]	78	2	6[9]	31	2	6	31	2	6	3	18	1
D64	5,000[9]	78	2	6[9]	31	2	0	31	2	0	3	18	1
J65	10,000[10]	156	5	0[10]	9	6	8	9	6	8	7	16	3
D65	10,000[10]	156	5	0[10]	62	9	0	62	9	0	7	16	4
J66			11										
D66	11,900[12]	185	18	9[12,13]	10	0	2	10	0	2	9	6	0
J67[14]													
D67	13,000	203	2	6	21	0	1½	21	0	1½	10	3	1
J68	2,500	39	1	3	16	2	9½	16	2	9½	1	19	0
D68	4,500[15]	65	6	3[15]	31	0	6	31	0	6	3	5	3
J69	3,000	46	17	6	16	3	3	16	3	3	2	6	11
D69	2,000	31	5	0	12	8	6	12	8	6	1	11	4
J70	2,500	39	1	3	—33	9	4				1	19	0
	(11,905)												

[9] All to Bohn at 6s. 3d. per volume.

[10] All to Bohn, 500 volumes at 6s. 3d.

[11] 50 sets of plates on India paper sold to Hurd and Houghton for £40.0.0, less £22.12.0 cost of reprinting; proceeds in cash account.

[12] All to Bohn, 595 volumes at 6s. 3d.

[13] 50 sets of plates on India paper sold to Hurd and Houghton for £38.0.0, less £14.0.0 cost of reprinting; proceeds in cash account.

[14] Reprinting.

[15] Includes 2,000 = 100 volumes to Ticknor and Fields at 5s. 3d.; 2,500 = 125 volumes at 6s. 3d.

Appendix A

PICTURES FROM ITALY

1 vol., Bradbury and Evans, 1846, 6s.

	Sales, quantity	Sales, receipts			Profit, Dickens			Profit, B & E			Commission, B & E[1]		
		£	s.	d.	£	s.	d.	£	s.	d.	£	s.	d.
J46	4,911	928	5	10	304	15	6	101	11	10	98	4	7
D46	501	100	4	2[2]	53	9	4	17	16	5	10	0	5
J47	123	24	11	8	15	9	3	5	3	1	2	9	2
D47	41	8	6	8	4	18	3	1	12	9		16	8
J48	9	1	17	6		—			—			—	
D48	14	2	18	4	1	17	10		12	7		5	10
J49	17	3	8	9	2	0	3		13	5		6	10
D49	4		16	8		10	4		3	5		1	8
J50	34	6	17	6	3	15	10	1	5	3		13	9
D50	12	2	10	0	1	5	11		8	7		5	0
J51	37	7	10	0	3	15	0	1	4	11		15	0
D51	4		16	8		10	0		3	4		1	8
J52	17	3	10	10	1	15	10		12	0		7	1
D52	24	5	0	0	3	0	8	1	0	2		10	0
J53	55	11	0	10	6	4	2	2	1	4	1	2	1
D53	8	1	13	4	1	1	10		7	4		3	4
J54	42	8	10	10	4	4	9	1	8	3		17	1
D54	12	2	10	0	1	6	11		9	0		5	0
J55	18	3	15	0	2	0	1		13	5		7	6
D55	12	2	10	0	1	12	1		10	8		5	0
J56	8	1	13	4	1	0	1		6	8		3	4
D56[3]													

[1] Commission frequently includes agents' commissions in accounts; pro rated to reflect publishers' percentage.

[2] Plus £17.0.0 from Tauchnitz.

[3] No further accounts.

PICTURES FROM ITALY AND AMERICAN NOTES, Library Edition

1 vol., Bradbury and Evans, 1859, 6s.

	Sales, quantity	Sales, receipts			Profit, Dickens			Profit, B & E			Commission, B & E		
		£	s.	d.	£	s.	d.	£	s.	d.	£	s.	d.
J59	517	103	10	10	−111	0	8	−37	0	3	5	3	6
D59	59	11	15	5	7	2	9	2	7	7		11	9
J60	594	68	16	8	46	2	3	15	7	5	3	8	10
D60	62	12	5	5	8	4	0	2	14	8		12	3
J61	23	4	15	10	2	7	11		16	0		4	9
	(727)[1]												

[1] Transferred to Chapman and Hall.

THE POOR TRAVELLER: BOOTS AT THE HOLLY-TREE INN: AND MRS. GAMP

1 vol., Bradbury and Evans, 1858, 1s.

	Sales, quantity	Sales, receipts			Profit, Dickens			Profit, B & E			Commission, B & E		
		£	s.	d.	£	s.	d.	£	s.	d.	£	s.	d.
D58	6,175	201	17	6	16	15	4	5	11	10	10	1	10
J59	719	23	10	4	14	6	1	4	15	5	1	3	6
D59	301	9	17	0	—	15	4	—	5	2		9	10
J60	153	5	1	0	2	12	0		17	4		5	0
D60	150	4	18	6	2	16	11		19	0	4	11	
J61	164 (306)[1]	5	7	8	2	2	9		14	3		5	4

[1] Transferred to Chapman and Hall, 'Readings 1/-'.

READINGS

5 vols., Bradbury and Evans, Chapman and Hall, 1858, 1s. per volume[1]

	Sales, quantity	Sales, receipts			Profit, Dickens			Profit, C & H			Commission, C & H		
		£	s.	d.	£	s.	d.	£	s.	d.	£	s.	d.
D61	1,595	48	17	6	12	10	11½	12	10	11½	2	8	10
J62													
D62													
J63	2,106	68	17	0	4	0	11	4	0	11	3	8	10
D63													
J64	2,080	68	0	0	5	10	6	5	10	6	3	8	0
D64	1,053	34	8	6	8	16	11½	8	16	11½	1	14	6
J65	728	23	16	0	9	11	7	9	11	8	1	3	9
D65	1,144	37	8	0		19	4		19	4	1	17	4
J66													
D66	1,027	33	11	6	6	8	3	6	8	3	1	13	6
J67	806	26	7	0	10	7	0	10	7	0	1	6	0
D67													
J68	1,300	42	10	0	6	15	11	6	15	11	2	2	6
D68	1,612	52	14	0	20	1	3	20	1	3	2	12	9
J69													
D69													
J70	338 (4,096)	11	1	0	—9	2	0				11	0	

[1] Includes *A Christmas Carol*, *The Chimes*, *The Cricket on the Hearth*, *The Story of Little Dombey*, and *The Poor Traveller: Boots at the Holly-Tree Inn: and Mrs. Gamp*.

Appendix A

SKETCHES BY BOZ

20 monthly parts, Chapman and Hall, 1837-9, 20s.

	Sales, quantity	Sales, receipts			Profit, Dickens			Profit, C & H			Commission, C & H		
		£	s.	d.	£	s.	d.	£	s.	d.	£	s.	d.
J58	884	27	4	0				−47	15	0[1]	1	7	0
D58	312	9	12	0				−39	17	6		9	6
J59													
D59													
J60													
D60										2			
J61										2			
D61										2			
J62										2			
D62													
J63	9,286[3]	157	6	0[3]	16	14	11	16	14	10	7	17	3
D63	1,400[4]	21	17	6[4]	8	3	4	8	3	4	1	1	10
J64	3,880[5]	60	12	6[5]	24	7	0	24	7	0	3	0	6
D64	3,000[6]	46	17	6[6]	14	2	1	14	2	1	2	6	10
J65	2,000[7]	31	5	0[7]	9	5	8	9	5	7	1	11	3
D65	2,000[7]	31	5	0[7]	10	17	7½	10	17	7½	1	11	3
J66													
D66	3,000[6]	46	17	6[6]	9	4	1	9	4	1	2	6	10
J67													
D67													
J68	10,500	164	1	3	16	19	7½	16	19	7½	8	4	0[8]
D68	2,600[9]	35	12	6[9]	12	16	6	12	16	6	1	15	6
J69	1,400	21	17	6	8	3	4½	8	3	4½	1	1	9
D69	1,000[10]	15	12	6	7	8	6	7	8	6		15	6
J70	2,000	31	5	0	11	10	1½	11	10	1½	1	11	3
	(5,268)												

[1] Heavy printing expenses because Chapman and Hall had no stock.

[2] Accounts 'in arrear' throughout this period.

[3] Includes 8,480 parts = 424 volumes to Bohn at 6s. 3d. per volume = £132.10.0; 806 at 8s. per dozen = £24.16.0.

[4] All to Bohn, 70 volumes at 6s. 3d.

[5] All to Bohn, 194 volumes at 6s. 3d.

[6] All to Bohn, 150 volumes at 6s. 3d.

[7] All to Bohn, 100 volumes at 6s. 3d.

[8] Commission not deducted until following account.

[9] Includes 2,000 = 100 volumes to Ticknor and Fields at 5s. 3d.; 600 = 30 volumes at 6s. 3d.

[10] Plus 2,460 parts wasted, including 2,000 of II.

THE STORY OF LITTLE DOMBEY

1 vol., Bradbury and Evans, 1858, 1s.

	Sales, quantity	Sales, receipts			Profit, Dickens			Profit, B & E			Commission, B & E		
		£	s.	d.	£	s.	d.	£	s.	d.	£	s.	d.
J58	2,252	73	12	9	−22	0	5	−7	6	10	3	13	8
D58	3,546	115	19	1	18	5	8	6	1	10	5	15	11
J59	590	19	6	0	12	4	8	4	1	7		19	3
D59	471	15	8	2	7	16	9	2	12	3		15	5
J60	110	3	12	6	1	14	1		11	5		3	8
D60	148	4	17	0	2	13	9		17	11		4	10
J61	203 (139)[1]	6	13	2	3	1	0	1	0	4		6	8

[1] Transferred to Chapman and Hall 'Readings 1/-'.

A TALE OF TWO CITIES

8 parts as 7, Chapman and Hall, 1859, 8s.

	Parts		Bound Vols.		Advertising receipts	Gross income	Gross expenses	Commission, C & H
	Sales, quantity	Sales, receipts	Sales, quantity	Sales, receipts				
		£ s. d.		£ s. d.	£ s. d.	£ s. d.	£ s. d.	£ s. d.
Aug. 59	15,691	543 3 0			132 15 6	675 18 6	530 4 10[1]	40 14 8
Nov. 59	16,406	567 18 0			144 1 3	711 19 3	457 9 0[1]	42 11 9
Mar. 60	533	18 9 0	2,456[2]	756 10 6[2]		774 19 6[3]	424 14 0[4]	58 2 6
Jun. 60	39	1 7 0	400	123 4 0		124 11 0[3]	91 13 0	9 6 9

[1] Does not include Chapman and Hall's commission.
[2] 25 as 24 at 6s. 5d. per volume.
[3] Includes advertising income.
[4] Includes Chapman and Hall's commissions to date.

A TALE OF TWO CITIES (cont.)

Parts	Sales, quantity	Sales, receipts £ s. d.	Profit, Dickens £ s. d.	Profit, C & H £ s. d.	Commission, C & H £ s. d.
D60					
J61					
D61					
J62					
D62	1,136[1]	18 18 8[1]	7 12 3	7 12 3	18 8
J63	936[2]	15 12 0[2]	6 1 6	6 1 6	15 6
D63	680[3]	11 6 8[3]	5 7 8	5 7 8	11 4
J64	1,008[4]	16 16 0[4]	7 19 7	7 19 7	16 10
D64	800[5]	13 6 8[5]	5 11 1	5 11 1	13 4
J65					
D65	1,000[6]	16 13 4[6]	7 0 6	7 0 6	16 9
J66					
D66	1,488[7]	24 16 0[7]	6 5 4	6 5 4	1 4 8
J67					
D67	2,400	40 0 0	6 10 6	6 10 6	2 0 0
J68	400	6 13 4	3 3 4	3 3 4	6 8
D68	1,000[8]	14 11 8[8]	6 18 7	6 18 7	14 6
J69	560	9 6 8	3 10 7½	3 10 7½	9 4
D69					
J70					

[1] All to Bohn, 142 volumes at 2s. 8d.
[2] All to Bohn, 117 volumes at 2s. 8d.
[3] All to Bohn, 85 volumes at 2s. 8d.
[4] All to Bohn, 126 volumes at 2s. 8d.
[5] All to Bohn, 100 volumes at 2s. 8d.
[6] All to Bohn, 125 volumes at 2s. 8d.
[7] All to Bohn, 186 volumes at 2s. 8d.
[8] Includes 800 = 100 volumes to Ticknor and Fields at 2s. 3d. = £11.5.0;
200 = 25 volumes at 2s. 8d. = £3.6.8.

THE UNCOMMERCIAL TRAVELLER

1 vol., Chapman and Hall, 1860, 6s.

	Sales, quantity	Sales, receipts			Profit, Dickens			Profit, C & H			Commission, C & H		
		£	s.	d.	£	s.	d.	£	s.	d.	£	s.	d.
D60	1,450	290	0	0	106	7	3	—			21	15	0
J61	1,000	200	0	0	100	12	6	—			15	0	0
D61	175	35	0	0	4	13	6	—			2	12	6
J62	25	5	0	0	3	7	6	—				7	6
D62													
J63													
D63													
J64													
D64													
J65	50	10	0	0	3	14	0	3	14	0		10	0
D65	25	5	0	0	1	16	6	1	16	6		5	0
J66[1]													

[1] No further accounts.

Appendix B

THE PRINTING HISTORY OF DICKENS'S
MONTHLY SERIALS, 1846–70

THESE charts record the printing and stitching orders, and the sales of Dickens's monthly serials from 1846 to 1870. There are some unexpected entries. *Oliver Twist*, published in *Bentley's Miscellany* and in volumes, appears because it came out in ten monthly parts (Jan.–Oct. 1846). And there are omissions, too: no account of *Edwin Drood*, since Chapman and Hall bought the copyright for the first 25,000 copies of the serial run. Inexplicably, there are no accounts for *Sketches by Boz* (20 numbers, 1837–9) or *Nicholas Nickleby* (20 in 19, 1838–9) until 1858, when they were reprinted by Chapman and Hall 'according to the new arrangements' (MS. C & H).

Dickens's publishers often printed more copies of the letterpress of a part than they did illustrations or wrappers, which were proportionately more expensive. If sales went well, additional copies of the plates and wrappers could be printed on their special papers and the numbers stitched up, but if the parts were not wanted immediately, then the letterpress could be reserved for making up the first volume edition. The stitching run is therefore a closer index to monthly sales than the printing run, though after the first accounting the separate charges for the parts that required more wrappers stitched on tended to get lumped together. Sometimes parts were wrappered years after the initial production; thus late stitching runs also indicate that the work was still available then for purchase in numbers.

Although Dickens's publishers continue to account in monthly numbers throughout his life, it seems clear that in the sixties reprintings were for volume issue. For example, there were 'numbers various' of *David Copperfield* stitched to December 1861; thereafter there are five accounting periods in which all the numbers were reprinted, but the print order is with one exception uniform for all twenty numbers, and there is no charge for stitching. The parts were evidently sold as unbound quires. Yet even here there are exceptions: the D55 accounts show that 500 copies of *Pickwick* I–XX were reprinted—and sold as 130 dozen numbers.

In most cases the accounting periods were the usual half-yearly ones ending 30 June and 31 December. But for *A Tale of Two Cities* and *Our Mutual Friend* different intervals were selected during initial publication. In J67 Chapman and Hall informed Dickens that all the 'original editions' were in the course of being reprinted. Thus in that year, for the most part, reports of costs and sales were held over until the end of the year.

BLEAK HOUSE

	June 1852		Dec. 1852		June 1853	
	Printed	Stitched	Printed	Stitched	Printed	Stitched
I. March 1852	38,500	34,043	2,500			
II. April	36,000	30,000	2,500			
III. May	35,500	33,000	1,500			
IV. June	35,000	34,000	1,500			
V. July	35,000	34,000			1,000	
VI. August			35,000	34,000		
VII. September			35,000	33,500		
VIII. October			35,000	33,500		
IX. November			35,000	33,000		
X. December			34,500	32,500		
XI. January 1853			34,000	32,500		
XII. February					34,000	32,200
XIII. March					34,000	32,000
XIV. April					34,000	32,000
XV. May					34,000	31,500
XVI. June					34,000	31,700
XVII. July					34,000	31,500
XVIII. August						
XIX. } September XX. }						
Numbers various, stitched		14,329				11,788

	Dec. 1853		June 1854	Dec. 1854	June 1855	Dec. 1855
	Printed	Stitched	Printed	Printed	Printed	Printed
I. March 1852	2,500				750	
II. April	1,500		1,000			
III. May	1,500		1,000			
IV. June	1,500		1,000			
V. July	1,500				1,000	
VI. August	1,500		1,000			
VII. September	750		1,000			
VIII. October			1,000			
IX. November					1,000	
X. December			1,000			
XI. January 1853			1,000			
XII. February				750		
XIII. March					750	
XIV. April						
XV. May						
XVI. June						
XVII. July						500
XVIII. August	34,000	31,500			1,000	
XIX. } September XX. }	34,000 34,000	31,500 31,500				
Numbers various, stitched		5,848	3,200	775	850	575

Appendix B

BLEAK HOUSE (cont.)

	June 1856 Printed	Dec. 1856 Printed	June 1857 Printed	Dec. 1857 Printed	June 1858 Printed	Dec. 1858 Printed
I. March 1852						
II. April	500					
III. May	500					
IV. June				500		
V. July						
VI. August				500		
VII. September				500		
VIII. October				500		
IX. November						
X. December					500	
XI. January 1853				500		
XII. February			500			
XIII. March						
XIV. April		750				
XV. May	500				500	
XVI. June	500					
XVII. July				500		
XVIII. August						
XIX. } Septem-	500				500	
XX. } ber	500				500	
Numbers various, stitched	873	502	318	448	432	136

	June 1859 Printed	Dec. 1859 Printed	June 1860 Printed	Dec. 1860 Printed	June 1861 Printed	Dec. 1861 No a/c
I. March 1852		500				
II. April						
III. May						
IV. June						
V. July						
VI. August						
VII. September						
VIII. October						
IX. November						
X. December						
XI. January 1853						
XII. February						
XIII. March						
XIV. April						
XV. May						
XVI. June		500				
XVII. July						
XVIII. August		500				
XIX. } September						
XX. }						
Numbers various, stitched	108	120	180	108	84	

BLEAK HOUSE (cont.)

	June 1862 Printed	Dec. 1862 Printed	June 1863 Printed	Dec. 1863 No a/c	June 1864 No a/c	Dec. 1864 Printed
I. March 1852						
II. April						
III. May						
IV. June						
V. July						
VI. August						
VII. September						
VIII. October						
IX. November						
X. December						
XI. January 1853						
XII. February						
XIII. March						
XIV. April						
XV. May						
XVI. June						
XVII. July						
XVIII. August						
XIX. } September						
XX. }		3,470[1]				5,633[1]
Numbers various, stitched	182					

	June 1865 Printed	Dec. 1865 Printed	June 1866 Printed	Dec. 1866 Printed	June 1867[2] Printed	Dec. 1867 Printed
I. March 1852		500				500
II. April		500				500
III. May		500				500
IV. June		500				500
V. July		500				500
VI. August		500				500
VII. September		500				500
VIII. October		500				500
IX. November		500				500
X. December		500				500
XI. January 1853		500				500
XII. February		500				500
XIII. March		500				500
XIV. April		500				500
XV. May		500				500
XVI. June		500				500
XVII. July		500				500
XVIII. August		500				500
XIX. } September		500				500
XX. }		500				500
Numbers various, stitched						

[1] Numbers various.
[2] 'The Original Editions all have been reprinted during the half year.'

BLEAK HOUSE (*cont.*)

	June 1868 No a/c	Dec. 1868 Printed	June 1869 Printed	Dec. 1869 Printed	June 1870 Printed
I. March 1852		250			500
II. April		250			500
III. May		250			500
IV. June		250			500
V. July		250			500
VI. August		250			500
VII. September		250			500
VIII. October		250			500
IX. November		250			500
X. December		250			500
XI. January 1853		250			500
XII. February		250			500
XIII. March		250			500
XIV. April		250			500
XV. May		250			500
XVI. June		250			500
XVII. July		250			500
XVIII. August		250			500
XIX. } September		250			500
XX. }		250			500

Numbers various,
  stitched

DAVID COPPERFIELD

	June 1849		Dec. 1849		June 1850	
	Printed	Stitched	Printed	Stitched	Printed	Stitched
I. May 1849	30,000	26,000				
II. June	24,000	20,000				
III. July	24,000	19,000				
IV. August			24,000	19,000		
V. September			24,000	19,300		
VI. October			22,000	19,300		
VII. November			22,000	19,300		
VIII. December			22,000	19,700		
IX. January 1850			22,000	19,700		
X. February					22,000	19,700
XI. March					22,000	19,800
XII. April					22,000	19,800
XIII. May					22,000	20,000
XIV. June					22,000	20,100
XV. July					22,000	20,100
XVI. August						
XVII. September						
XVIII. October						
XIX. } November						
XX. }						
Numbers various, stitched				7,700		4,900

	Dec. 1850		June 1851	Dec. 1851	June 1852	Dec. 1852
	Printed	Stitched	Printed	Printed	Printed	Printed
I. May 1849						
II. June						750
III. July						
IV. August						
V. September						
VI. October			1,250			
VII. November			500			750
VIII. December					500	750
IX. January 1850			1,250			
X. February						750
XI. March					750	
XII. April					750	
XIII. May					500	
XIV. June					500	
XV. July				500		750
XVI. August	22,000	20,100		500		750
XVII. September	22,000	20,100		500		750
XVIII. October	22,000	20,200			500	750
XIX. } November	22,000	20,300			500	
XX. }	22,000	20,300			500	
Numbers various, stitched		8,500	2,575	1,000	1[1]	687

[1] Unspecified number.

DAVID COPPERFIELD (cont.)

	June 1853 Printed	Dec. 1853 Printed	June 1854 Printed	Dec. 1854 Printed	June 1855 Printed	Dec. 1855 Printed
I. May 1849						
II. June			500			
III. July	750					
IV. August				500		
V. September				1,000		
VI. October	750					
VII. November			500			
VIII. December						
IX. January 1850				1,000		
X. February			500			500
XI. March			750			
XII. April		500			500	
XIII. May	1,000					
XIV. June	1,000					
XV. July				500		
XVI. August				500		
XVII. September				500		
XVIII. October				1,000		
XIX. ⎫ Novem-	1,000					
XX. ⎭ ber	1,000					
Numbers various, stitched	750	500	412	318	453	378

	June 1856 Printed	Dec. 1856 Printed	June 1857 Printed	Dec. 1857 Printed	June 1858 Printed	Dec. 1858 Printed
I. May 1849						
II. June	750					
III. July	750					
IV. August	500					500
V. September						
VI. October	750					
VII. November	750					
VIII. December	500					500
IX. January 1850						
X. February				500		
XI. March	500				500	
XII. April			500			
XIII. May	750					
XIV. June	750					
XV. July	750					500
XVI. August	500				500	
XVII. September	500				500	
XVIII. October						500
XIX. ⎫ Novem-	750					
XX. ⎭ ber	750					
Numbers various, stitched	264	372	300	132	213	242

DAVID COPPERFIELD (cont.)

	June 1859 Printed	Dec. 1859 Printed	June 1860 Printed	Dec. 1860 Printed	June 1861 Printed	Dec. 1861 Printed
I. May 1849						
II. June			500			
III. July			500			
IV. August						
V. September				500		
VI. October						
VII. November						
VIII. December						
IX. January 1850			500			
X. February						
XI. March						
XII. April						
XIII. May						
XIV. June			500			
XV. July						
XVI. August						
XVII. September						
XVIII. October						
XIX. ⎱ Novem-		500				
XX. ⎰ ber		500				2,000[1]
Numbers various, stitched	156	72	132	132	72	221

	June 1862 No a/c	Dec. 1862 Printed	June 1863 Printed	Dec. 1863 Printed	June 1864 Printed	Dec. 1864 No a/c
I. May 1849					500	
II. June					500	
III. July					500	
IV. August					500	
V. September					500	
VI. October					500	
VII. November					500	
VIII. December					500	
IX. January 1850					500	
X. February					500	
XI. March					500	
XII. April					600	
XIII. May					500	
XIV. June					500	
XV. July					500	
XVI. August					500	
XVII. September					500	
XVIII. October					500	
XIX. ⎱ Novem-					500	
XX. ⎰ ber		4,450[1]	6,080[1]		500	
Numbers various, stitched						

[1] Numbers various.

DAVID COPPERFIELD (cont.)

	June 1865 Printed	Dec. 1865 Printed	June 1866 Printed	Dec. 1866 Printed	June 1867[1] Printed	Dec. 1867 Printed
I. May 1849		500				750
II. June		500				750
III. July		500				750
IV. August		500				750
V. September		500				750
VI. October		500				750
VII. November		500				750
VIII. December		500				750
IX. January 1850		500				750
X. February		500				750
XI. March		500				750
XII. April		500				750
XIII. May		500				750
XIV. June		500				750
XV. July		500				750
XVI. August		500				750
XVII. September		500				750
XVIII. October		500				750
XIX. ⎫ Novem-		500				750
XX. ⎭ ber		500				750

Numbers various, stitched

	June 1868 Printed	Dec. 1868 Printed	June 1869 Printed	Dec. 1869 No a/c	June 1870 Printed
I. May 1849		250			500
II. June		250			500
III. July		250			500
IV. August		250			500
V. September		250			500
VI. October		250			500
VII. November		250			500
VIII. December		250			500
IX. January 1850		250			500
X. February		250			500
XI. March		250			500
XII. April		250			500
XIII. May		250			500
XIV. June		250			500
XV. July		250			500
XVI. August		250			500
XVII. September		250			500
XVIII. October		250			500
XIX. ⎫ November		250			500
XX. ⎭		250			500

Numbers various, stitched

[1] 'The Original Editions all have been reprinted during the half year.'

DOMBEY AND SON

	Dec. 1846		June 1847		Dec. 1847	
	Printed	Stitched	Printed	Stitched	Printed	Stitched
I. October 1846	34,000	34,000	4,000	2,750		
II. November	32,000	32,000	2,000	2,000	1,000	900
III. December	32,000	30,750	2,000	2,000		
IV. January 1847	32,000	30,000		2,000	1,000	800
V. February			32,000	32,000	2,000	800
VI. March			33,000	32,000		
VII. April			33,000	32,000		
VIII. May			33,000	32,000		
IX. June			33,000	31,500		
X. July			33,000	31,500		
XI. August					32,000	32,000
XII. September					32,000	31,500
XIII. October					32,000	31,500
XIV. November					32,000	31,500
XV. December					32,000	31,500
XVI. January 1848					33,000	31,500
XVII. February						
XVIII. March						
XIX. } April						
XX. }						
Numbers various, stitched						4,500

	June 1848		Dec. 1848	June 1849	Dec. 1849	June 1850
	Printed	Stitched	Printed	Printed	Printed	Printed
I. October 1846	2,750					
II. November	2,750					
III. December	2,750					
IV. January 1847	3,000					
V. February	1,750					
VI. March	3,000					
VII. April	2,500					
VIII. May	1,500					
IX. June	2,000					
X. July	2,000					
XI. August	1,500					
XII. September	1,500					
XIII. October	1,500					
XIV. November	2,500					
XV. December	2,500					
XVI. January 1848	1,500					
XVII. February	34,000	32,000				
XVIII. March	34,000	32,000				
XIX. } April	35,000	32,000				
XX. }	35,000	32,000				
Numbers various, stitched	5,700[1]		1,291	882	650	566

[1] [I] 650; [II] 450; [III] 450; [XVIII] 500; [Numbers various] 3,650.

Appendix B

DOMBEY AND SON (*cont.*)

	Dec. 1850 Printed	June 1851 Printed	Dec. 1851 Printed	June 1852 Printed	Dec. 1852 Printed	June 1853 Printed
I. October 1846						
II. November						
III. December						
IV. January 1847						
V. February						
VI. March						
VII. April						
VIII. May						
IX. June						
X. July						
XI. August						
XII. September				250		
XIII. October						
XIV. November						
XV. December						
XVI. January 1848						
XVII. February						
XVIII. March						
XIX. ⎫ XX. ⎬ April						
Numbers various, stitched	404	675	325	576	60	362

	Dec. 1853 Printed	June 1854 Printed	Dec. 1854 Printed	June 1855 Printed	Dec. 1855 Printed	June 1856 Printed
I. October 1846						500
II. November						
III. December						
IV. January 1847						
V. February						
VI. March						
VII. April						
VIII. May			500			
IX. June						
X. July						
XI. August	750					
XII. September	500					
XIII. October	500					
XIV. November						
XV. December						
XVI. January 1848						
XVII. February			500			
XVIII. March	500					
XIX. ⎫ XX. ⎬ April						
Numbers various, stitched	236	365	341	204	287	240

DOMBEY AND SON (*cont.*)

	Dec. 1856 Printed	June 1857 Printed	Dec. 1857 Printed	June 1858 Printed	Dec. 1858 Printed	June 1859 Printed
I. October 1846					500	
II. November		500				
III. December		500				
IV. January 1847		500				
V. February						
VI. March						
VII. April						
VIII. May		500				
IX. June						
X. July						
XI. August		500				
XII. September	500					
XIII. October	500					
XIV. November						
XV. December						
XVI. January 1848			500			
XVII. February		500				
XVIII. March	500					
XIX. } XX. } April						
Numbers various, stitched	240	144	280	108	252	48

	Dec. 1859 Printed	June 1860 Printed	Dec. 1860 Printed	June 1861 Printed	Dec. 1861 Printed	June 1862 No a/c
I. October 1846						
II. November						
III. December						
IV. January 1847						
V. February			500			
VI. March						
VII. April						
VIII. May						
IX. June						
X. July						
XI. August						
XII. September						
XIII. October						
XIV. November						
XV. December						
XVI. January 1848						
XVII. February						
XVIII. March						
XIX. } XX. } April						
Numbers various, stitched	144					

DOMBEY AND SON (*cont.*)

	Dec. 1862 No a/c	June 1863 Printed	Dec. 1863 Printed	June 1864 Printed	Dec. 1864 No a/c	June 1865 No a/c
I. October 1846				500		
II. November				500		
III. December				500		
IV. January 1847				500		
V. February				500		
VI. March				500		
VII. April				500		
VIII. May				500		
IX. June				500		
X. July				500		
XI. August				500		
XII. September				500		
XIII. October				500		
XIV. November				500		
XV. December				500		
XVI. January 1848				500		
XVII. February				500		
XVIII. March				500		
XIX. } April				500		
XX. }				500		
Numbers various, stitched		9,700[1]				

	Dec. 1865 Printed	June 1866 No a/c	Dec. 1866 Printed	June 1867[2] Printed	Dec. 1867 Printed	June 1868 Printed
I. October 1846					500	
II. November					500	
III. December					500	
IV. January 1847					500	
V. February					500	
VI. March					500	
VII. April					500	
VIII. May					500	
IX. June					500	
X. July					500	
XI. August					500	
XII. September					500	
XIII. October					500	
XIV. November					500	
XV. December					500	
XVI. January 1848					500	
XVII. February					500	
XVIII. March					500	
XIX. } April					500	
XX. }					500	
Numbers various, stitched			9,490[1]			

[1] Numbers various.
[2] 'The Original Editions all have been reprinted during the half year.'

DOMBEY AND SON (*cont.*)

	Dec. 1868 Printed	June 1869 Printed	Dec. 1869 No a/c	June 1870 Printed
I. October 1846				500
II. November				500
III. December				500
IV. January 1847				500
V. February				500
VI. March				500
VII. April				500
VIII. May				500
IX. June				500
X. July				500
XI. August				500
XII. September				500
XIII. October				500
XIV. November				500
XV. December				500
XVI. January 1848				500
XVII. February				500
XVIII. March				500
XIX. } April				500
XX. }				500

Numbers various, stitched

LITTLE DORRIT

	Dec. 1855		June 1856		Dec. 1856	
	Printed	Stitched	Printed	Stitched	Printed	Stitched
I. December 1855	38,000	36,280	2,000		1,000	
II. January 1856	35,000	32,000	2,000			
III. February			36,500	34,800		
IV. March			35,000	34,000		
V. April			36,000	34,500		
VI. May			36,000	34,000		
VII. June			35,000	33,000		
VIII. July			34,000	32,000		
IX. August					33,000	31,500
X. September					32,000	30,500
XI. October					32,000	30,500
XII. November					31,500	30,250
XIII. December					31,500	30,250
XIV. January 1857					31,500	30,000
XV. February						
XVI. March						
XVII. April						
XVIII. May						
XIX. } June						
XX. }						
Numbers various, stitched				10,764		1,550

	June 1857		Dec. 1857	June 1858	Dec. 1858	June 1859
	Printed	Stitched	Printed	Printed	Printed	Printed
I. December 1855	2,000					
II. January 1856	2,000					
III. February	1,000					
IV. March	2,000					
V. April						
VI. May						
VII. June						
VIII. July						
IX. August						
X. September			1,000			
XI. October						
XII. November	1,000					
XIII. December						
XIV. January 1857						
XV. February	31,000	29,750	1,000			
XVI. March	31,000	29,500		750		
XVII. April	31,000	29,500				
XVIII. May	31,000	29,250				
XIX. } June	31,000	29,250				
XX. }	31,000	29,250				
Numbers various, stitched		1,400	1,150	550	875	450

LITTLE DORRIT (*cont.*)

	Dec. 1859 Printed	June 1860 Printed	Dec. 1860 Printed	June 1861 Printed	Dec. 1861 Printed	June 1862 No a/c
I. December 1855						
II. January 1856						
III. February						
IV. March						
V. April						
VI. May						
VII. June						
VIII. July						
IX. August						
X. September						
XI. October	500					
XII. November						
XIII. December						
XIV. January 1857						
XV. February						
XVI. March						
XVII. April						
XVIII. May			500			
XIX. } June						
XX. }					1,000[1]	
Numbers various, stitched	349	250	175	325	260	

	Dec. 1862 Printed	June 1863 No a/c	Dec. 1863 No a/c	June 1864 Printed	Dec. 1864 Printed	June 1865 Printed
I. December 1855						
II. January 1856						
III. February						
IV. March						
V. April						
VI. May						
VII. June						
VIII. July						
IX. August						
X. September						
XI. October						
XII. November						
XIII. December						
XIV. January 1857						
XV. February						
XVI. March						
XVII. April						
XVIII. May						
XIX. } June						
XX. }	1,300[1]				6,913[1]	
Numbers various, stitched						

Numbers various.

Appendix B

LITTLE DORRIT (*cont.*)

	Dec. 1865 Printed	June 1866 No a/c	Dec. 1866 No a/c	June 1867[1] Printed	Dec. 1867 Printed	June 1868 Printed
I. December 1855					1,000	
II. January 1856					1,000	
III. February					1,000	
IV. March					1,000	
V. April					1,000	
VI. May					1,000	
VII. June					1,000	
VIII. July					1,000	
IX. August					1,000	
X. September					1,000	
XI. October					1,000	
XII. November					1,000	
XIII. December					1,000	
XIV. January 1857					1,000	
XV. February					1,000	
XVI. March					1,000	
XVII. April					1,000	
XVIII. May					1,000	
XIX. ⎫ June XX. ⎭	35[2]				1,000 1,000	
Numbers various, stitched						

	Dec. 1868 Printed	June 1869 Printed	Dec. 1869 Printed	June 1870 Printed
I. December 1855				500
II. January 1856				500
III. February				500
IV. March				500
V. April				500
VI. May				500
VII. June				500
VIII. July				500
IX. August				500
X. September				500
XI. October				500
XII. November				500
XIII. December				500
XIV. January 1857				500
XV. February				500
XVI. March				500
XVII. April				500
XVIII. May				500
XIX. ⎫ June XX. ⎭				500 500

Numbers various, stitched

[1] 'The Original Editions all have been reprinted during the half year.'
[2] Numbers various.

MARTIN CHUZZLEWIT

	June 1846 Printed	Dec. 1846 Printed	June 1847 Printed	Dec. 1847 Printed	June 1848 Printed	Dec. 1848 Printed
I. January 1843						
II. February						
III. March						
IV. April						
V. May						
VI. June						
VII. July						
VIII. August						
IX. September						
X. October						
XI. November						
XII. December						
XIII. January 1844						
XIV. February						
XV. March						
XVI. April						
XVII. May						
XVIII. June						
XIX.⎫ July XX.⎭						
Numbers various, stitched	975	750			850[1]	1,150	900

	June 1849 Printed	Dec. 1849 Printed	June 1850 Printed	Dec. 1850 Printed	June 1851 Printed	Dec. 1851 Printed
I. January 1843						
II. February						
III. March						
IV. April						
V. May						
VI. June						
VII. July						
VIII. August						
IX. September						
X. October						
XI. November						
XII. December						
XIII. January 1844						
XIV. February						
XV. March						
XVI. April						
XVII. May						
XVIII. June						
XIX.⎫ July XX.⎭						
Numbers various, stitched	975	50	500	525		500

[1] Total for year.

MARTIN CHUZZLEWIT (cont.)

	June 1852 Printed	Dec. 1852 Printed	June 1853 Printed	Dec. 1853 Printed	June 1854 Printed	Dec. 1854 Printed
I. January 1843						
II. February						
III. March						
IV. April		250				
V. May						
VI. June						
VII. July						
VIII. August						
IX. September						
X. October						
XI. November						
XII. December						
XIII. January 1844						
XIV. February						
XV. March						
XVI. April						
XVII. May						
XVIII. June						
XIX. } July						
XX. }						
Numbers various, stitched	100	50	150	100		

	June 1855 Printed	Dec. 1855 Printed	June 1856 Printed	Dec. 1856 Printed	June 1857 Printed	Dec. 1857 Printed
I. January 1843						
II. February						
III. March						
IV. April						
V. May						
VI. June						
VII. July						
VIII. August						
IX. September						
X. October						
XI. November						
XII. December						
XIII. January 1844						
XIV. February						
XV. March						
XVI. April						
XVII. May						
XVIII. June						
XIX. } July						
XX. }						
Numbers various, stitched				609[1]		
				300		

[1] Numbers various.

MARTIN CHUZZLEWIT (cont.)

	June 1858 Printed	Dec. 1858 Printed	June 1859 Printed	Dec. 1859 Printed	June 1860 Printed	Dec. 1860 Printed
I. January 1843						
II. February						
III. March						
IV. April				500		
V. May				500		
VI. June						
VII. July				500		
VIII. August						
IX. September						
X. October				500		
XI. November				500		
XII. December						
XIII. January 1844						
XIV. February						
XV. March						
XVI. April						
XVII. May						
XVIII. June						
XIX. } July				500		
XX. }				500		
Numbers various, stitched						

	June 1861 Printed	Dec. 1861 Printed	June 1862 Printed	Dec. 1862 Printed	June 1863 Printed	Dec. 1863 Printed
I. January 1843						
II. February						
III. March						
IV. April						
V. May						
VI. June				500		
VII. July						
VIII. August						
IX. September						
X. October						
XI. November						
XII. December						
XIII. January 1844						
XIV. February						
XV. March						
XVI. April						
XVII. May						
XVIII. June						
XIX. } July						
XX. }						8,500[1]
Numbers various, stitched						

[1] Numbers various.

MARTIN CHUZZLEWIT (*cont.*)

	June 1864 Printed	Dec. 1864 No a/c	June 1865 No a/c	Dec. 1865 Printed	June 1866 No a/c	Dec. 1866 Printed
I. January 1843						
II. February						
III. March						
IV. April						
V. May						
VI. June						
VII. July						
VIII. August						
IX. September						
X. October						
XI. November						
XII. December						
XIII. January 1844						
XIV. February						
XV. March						
XVI. April						
XVII. May						
XVIII. June						
XIX. } July						
XX. }	10,800[1]					9,008[2]
Numbers various, stitched						

	June 1867[3] Printed	Dec. 1867 Printed	June 1868 Printed	Dec. 1868 Printed	June 1869 Printed	Dec. 1869 Printed
I. January 1843		750				
II. February		750				
III. March		750				
IV. April		750				
V. May		750				
VI. June		750				
VII. July		750				
VIII. August		750				
IX. September		750				
X. October		750				
XI. November		750				
XII. December		750				
XIII. January 1844		750				
XIV. February		750				
XV. March		750				
XVI. April		750				
XVII. May		750				
XVIII. June		750				
XIX. } July		750				
XX. }		750				
Numbers various, stitched						

[1] [I–XX] 500 each; [numbers various] 800.   [2] Numbers various.
[3] 'The Original Editions all have been reprinted during the half year.'

MARTIN CHUZZLEWIT (cont.)

	June 1870 Printed
I. January 1843	500
II. February	500
III. March	500
IV. April	500
V. May	500
VI. June	500
VII. July	500
VIII. August	500
IX. September	500
X. October	500
XI. November	500
XII. December	500
XIII. January 1844	500
XIV. February	500
XV. March	500
XVI. April	500
XVII. May	500
XVIII. June	500
XIX. } July	500
XX. }	500

Numbers various, stitched

NICHOLAS NICKLEBY

	June 1858 Printed	Dec. 1858 Printed	June 1859 Printed	Dec. 1859 Printed	June 1860 Printed	Dec. 1860 Printed
I. April 1838	250					
II. May	250					
III. June	250					
IV. July	250					
V. August	250					
VI. September	250					
VII. October	250					
VIII. November	250					
IX. December	250					
X. January 1839	250					
XI. February	250					
XII. March	250					
XIII. April	250					
XIV. May	250					
XV. June	250					
XVI. July	250					
XVII. August	250					
XVIII. September	250					
XIX. } October	250					
XX. }	250					

	June 1861 Printed	Dec. 1861 Printed	June 1862 Printed	Dec. 1862 Printed	June 1863 Printed	Dec. 1863 Printed
I. April 1838				500		750
II. May				500		750
III. June				500		750
IV. July				500		750
V. August				500		750
VI. September				500		750
VII. October				500		750
VIII. November				500		750
IX. December				500		750
X. January 1839				500		750
XI. February				500		750
XII. March				500		750
XIII. April				500		750
XIV. May				500		750
XV. June				500		750
XVI. July				500		750
XVII. August				500		750
XVIII. September				500		750
XIX. } October				500		750
XX. }				500		750

NICHOLAS NICKLEBY (cont.)

	June 1864 Printed	Dec. 1864 Printed	June 1865 Printed	Dec. 1865 Printed	June 1866 Printed	Dec. 1866 Printed
I. April 1838				750		
II. May				750		
III. June				750		
IV. July				750		
V. August				750		
VI. September				750		
VII. October				750		
VIII. November				750		
IX. December				750		
X. January 1839				750		
XI. February				750		
XII. March				750		
XIII. April				750		
XIV. May				750		
XV. June				750		
XVI. July				750		
XVII. August				750		
XVIII. September				750		
XIX. } October				750		
XX. }				750		

	June 1867[1] Printed	Dec. 1867 Printed	June 1868 Printed	Dec. 1868 Printed	June 1869 Printed	Dec. 1869 No a/c
I. April 1838		750				
II. May		750				
III. June		750				
IV. July		750				
V. August		750				
VI. September		750				
VII. October		750				
VIII. November		750				
IX. December		750				
X. January 1839		750				
XI. February		750				
XII. March		750				
XIII. April		750				
XIV. May		750				
XV. June		750				
XVI. July		750				
XVII. August		750				
XVIII. September		750				
XIX. } October		750				
XX. }		750				

[1] 'The Original Editions all have been reprinted during the half year.'

NICHOLAS NICKLEBY (*cont.*)

	June 1870 Printed
I. April 1838	500
II. May	500
III. June	500
IV. July	500
V. August	500
VI. September	500
VII. October	500
VIII. November	500
IX. December	500
X. January 1839	500
XI. February	500
XII. March	500
XIII. April	500
XIV. May	500
XV. June	500
XVI. July	500
XVII. August	500
XVIII. September	500
XIX. } October	500
XX. }	500

OLIVER TWIST

	June 1846		Dec. 1846		June 1847	Dec. 1847
	Printed	Stitched	Printed	Stitched	Printed	Printed
I. January 1846	5,000	5,000	1,000			
II. February	5,000	4,390				
III. March	5,000	4,000				
IV. April	5,000	4,000				
V. May	5,000	3,750				
VI. June	5,000	3,750				
VII. July	5,000	3,250				
VIII. August			5,000	3,250		
IX. September			5,000	3,250		
X. October			5,000	3,250		
Numbers various, stitched						[IV] 20

	June 1848	Dec. 1848	June 1849	Dec. 1849	June 1850	Dec. 1850
	Printed	Printed	Printed	Printed	Printed	Printed
I. January 1846						
II. February						
III. March						
IV. April						
V. May						
VI. June						
VII. July						
VIII. August						
IX. September						
X. October						
Numbers various, stitched				24		

	June 1851	Dec. 1851	June 1852	Dec. 1852	June 1853	Dec. 1853
	Printed	Printed	Printed	Printed	Printed	Printed
I. January 1846						
II. February						
III. March						
IV. April						
V. May						
VI. June						
VII. July						
VIII. August						
IX. September						
X. October						
Numbers various, stitched		128	[1]	148		12

[1] Unspecified number.

OLIVER TWIST (*cont.*)

	June 1854 Printed	Dec. 1854 Printed	June 1855 Printed	Dec. 1855 Printed	June 1856 Printed	Dec. 1856 Printed
I. January 1846						
II. February	500					
III. March						
IV. April						
V. May				500		
VI. June						
VII. July						
VIII. August						
IX. September						
X. October						
Numbers various, stitched	12	[III] 24	[VII] 12	45	48	

	June 1857 Printed	Dec. 1857 Printed	June 1858 Printed	Dec. 1858 Printed	June 1859 Printed	Dec. 1859 Printed
I. January 1846						
II. February						
III. March			250			
IV. April					500	
V. May						
VI. June						
VII. July						
VIII. August						
IX. September						
X. October						
Numbers various, stitched	58	56	36	[V] 12	80	

	June 1860 Printed	Dec. 1860 Printed	June 1861 Printed	Dec. 1861 Printed	June 1862 No a/c	Dec. 1862 Printed
I. January 1846			500			
II. February						
III. March						
IV. April						
V. May						
VI. June						
VII. July						
VIII. August						
IX. September						
X. October						4,350[1]
Numbers various, stitched	12	106				

[1] Numbers various.

OLIVER TWIST (cont.)

	June 1863 No a/c	Dec. 1863 Printed	June 1864 No a/c	Dec. 1864 Printed	June 1865 Printed	Dec. 1865 Printed
I. January 1846		750				
II. February		750				
III. March		750				
IV. April		750				
V. May		750				
VI. June		750				
VII. July		750				
VIII. August		750				
IX. September		750				
X. October		750				
Numbers various, stitched						

	June 1866 No a/c	Dec. 1866 No a/c	June 1867[1] Printed	Dec. 1867 No a/c	June 1868 Printed	Dec. 1868 Printed
I. January 1846					500	
II. February					500	
III. March					500	
IV. April					500	
V. May					500	
VI. June					500	
VII. July					500	
VIII. August					500	
IX. September					500	
X. October					500	
Numbers various, stitched						

	June 1869 Printed	Dec. 1869 Printed	June 1870 Printed
I. January 1846			
II. February			
III. March			
IV. April			
V. May			
VI. June			
VII. July			
VIII. August			
IX. September			
X. October			
Numbers various, stitched			

[1] 'The Original Editions all have been reprinted during the half year.'

OUR MUTUAL FRIEND

	Oct. 1864		Dec. 1864		June 1865	
	Printed	Stitched	Printed	Stitched	Printed	Stitched
I. May 1864	40,000	35,000				
II. June	35,000	31,000				
III. July	30,000	27,000				
IV. August	30,000	25,000				
V. September	30,000	25,000				
VI. October	28,000	24,000				
VII. November			28,000	24,000		
VIII. December			28,000	24,000		
IX. January 1865			28,000	24,000		
X. February					28,000	
XI. March					28,000	
XII. April					28,000	
XIII. May					25,000	} 40,000
XIV. June					25,000	
XV. July					25,000	
XVI. August						
XVII. September						
XVIII. October						
XIX. } November						
XX. }						

	Dec. 1865		June 1866	Dec. 1866	June 1867	Dec. 1867
	Printed	Stitched	Printed	Printed	Printed	Printed
I. May 1864						
II. June						
III. July						
IV. August						
V. September						
VI. October						
VII. November						
VIII. December						
IX. January 1865						
X. February						
XI. March						
XII. April						
XIII. May						
XIV. June						
XV. July						
XVI. August	25,000					
XVII. September	25,000	} 59,000				
XVIII. October	25,000					
XIX. } November	25,000	} 19,000				
XX. }	25,000					

OUR MUTUAL FRIEND (*cont.*)

	June 1868 Printed	Dec. 1868 Printed	June 1869 Printed	Dec. 1869 Printed	June 1870 Printed
I. May 1864					
II. June					
III. July					
IV. August					
V. September					
VI. October					
VII. November					
VIII. December					
IX. January 1865					
X. February					
XI. March					
XII. April					
XIII. May					
XIV. June					
XV. July					
XVI. August					
XVII. September					
XVIII. October					
XIX. } November					
XX. }					

PICKWICK PAPERS

	June 1846 Printed	Dec. 1846 Printed	June 1847 Printed	Dec. 1847 Printed	June 1848 Printed	Dec. 1848 Printed
I. April 1836						
II. May						
III. June						
IV. July						
V. August						
VI. September						
VII. October						
VIII. November						
IX. December						
X. January 1837						
XI. February						
XII. March						
XIII. April						
XIV. May						
XV. July						
XVI. August						
XVII. September						
XVIII. October						
XIX. ⎱ Novem-						
XX. ⎰ ber						
Numbers various, stitched			1,150			

	June 1849 Printed	Dec. 1849 Printed	June 1850 Printed	Dec. 1850 Printed	June 1851 Printed	Dec. 1851 Printed
I. April 1836						
II. May						
III. June						
IV. July						
V. August						
VI. September						
VII. October						
VIII. November						
IX. December						
X. January 1837						
XI. February						
XII. March						
XIII. April						
XIV. May						
XV. July						
XVI. August						
XVII. September						
XVIII. October						
XIX. ⎱ Novem-						
XX. ⎰ ber						
Numbers various, stitched						

PICKWICK PAPERS (cont.)

	June 1852 Printed	Dec. 1852 Printed	June 1853 Printed	Dec. 1853 Printed	June 1854 Printed	Dec. 1854 Printed
I. April 1836				250		
II. May						
III. June						
IV. July						
V. August						
VI. September						
VII. October						
VIII. November						
IX. December						
X. January 1837						
XI. February						
XII. March						
XIII. April						
XIV. May						
XV. July						
XVI. August						
XVII. September						
XVIII. October						
XIX. ⎫ Novem-						
XX. ⎭ ber						
Numbers various, stitched						

	June 1855 Printed	Dec. 1855 Printed	June 1856 Printed	Dec. 1856 Printed	June 1857 Printed	Dec. 1857 Printed
I. April 1836		500				1,000
II. May		500				1,000
III. June		500				1,000
IV. July		500				1,000
V. August		500				1,000
VI. September		500				1,000
VII. October		500				1,000
VIII. November		500				1,000
IX. December		500				1,000
X. January 1837		500				1,000
XI. February		500				1,000
XII. March		500				1,000
XIII. April		500				1,000
XIV. May		500				1,000
XV. July		500				1,000
XVI. August		500				1,000
XVII. September		500				1,000
XVIII. October		500				1,000
XIX. ⎫ Novem-		500				1,000
XX. ⎭ ber	245[1]	500				1,000
Numbers various, stitched						

[1] Numbers various.

Q

PICKWICK PAPERS (cont.)

	June 1858 Printed	Dec. 1858 Printed	June 1859 Printed	Dec. 1859 Printed	June 1860 Printed	Dec. 1860 Printed
I. April 1836						
II. May						
III. June						
IV. July						
V. August						
VI. September						
VII. October						
VIII. November						
IX. December						
X. January 1837						
XI. February						
XII. March						
XIII. April						
XIV. May						
XV. July						
XVI. August						
XVII. September						
XVIII. October						
XIX. ⎱ November						
XX. ⎰ ber						
Numbers various, stitched						

	June 1861 Printed	Dec. 1861 Printed	June 1862 Printed	Dec. 1862 Printed	June 1863 Printed	Dec. 1863 Printed
I. April 1836				500	750	1,000
II. May				500	750	1,000
III. June				500	750	1,000
IV. July				500	750	1,000
V. August				500	750	1,000
VI. September				500	750	1,000
VII. October				500	750	1,000
VIII. November				500	750	1,000
IX. December				500	750	1,000
X. January 1837				500	750	1,000
XI. February				500	750	1,000
XII. March				500	750	1,000
XIII. April				500	750	1,000
XIV. May				500	750	1,000
XV. July				500	750	1,000
XVI. August				500	750	1,000
XVII. September				500	750	1,000
XVIII. October				500	750	1,000
XIX. ⎱ November				500	750	1,000
XX. ⎰ ber				500	750	1,000
Numbers various, stitched						

PICKWICK PAPERS (cont.)

	June 1864 Printed	Dec. 1864 Printed	June 1865 Printed	Dec. 1865 Printed	June 1866 No a/c	Dec. 1866 Printed
I. April 1836			1,000			
II. May			1,000			
III. June			1,000			
IV. July			1,000			
V. August			1,000			
VI. September			1,000			
VII. October			1,000			
VIII. November			1,000			
IX. December			1,000			
X. January 1837			1,000			
XI. February			1,000			
XII. March			1,000			
XIII. April			1,000			
XIV. May			1,000			
XV. July			1,000			
XVI. August			1,000			
XVII. September			1,000			
XVIII. October			1,000			
XIX. ⎱ November			1,000			
XX. ⎰ ber			1,000			21,644[1]
Numbers various, stitched						

	June 1867[2] Printed	Dec. 1867 Printed	June 1868 Printed	Dec. 1868 Printed	June 1869 Printed	Dec. 1869 Printed
I. April 1836		1,000				
II. May		1,000				
III. June		1,000				
IV. July		1,000				
V. August		1,000				
VI. September		1,000				
VII. October		1,000				
VIII. November		1,000				
IX. December		1,000				
X. January 1837		1,000				
XI. February		1,000				
XII. March		1,000				
XIII. April		1,000				
XIV. May		1,000				
XV. July		1,000				
XVI. August		1,000				
XVII. September		1,000				
XVIII. October		1,000				
XIX. ⎱ November		1,000				
XX. ⎰ ber		1,000				
Numbers various, stitched						

[1] Numbers various.
[2] 'The Original Editions all have been reprinted during the half year.'

PICKWICK PAPERS (*cont.*)

	June 1870 Printed
I. April 1836	500
II. May	500
III. June	500
IV. July	500
V. August	500
VI. September	500
VII. October	500
VIII. November	500
IX. December	500
X. January 1837	500
XI. February	500
XII. March	500
XIII. April	500
XIV. May	500
XV. July	500
XVI. August	500
XVII. September	500
XVIII. October	500
XIX. } November	500
XX. }	500

Numbers various, stitched

SKETCHES BY BOZ

	June 1858 Printed	Dec. 1858 Printed	June 1859 No a/c	Dec. 1859 No a/c	June 1860 No a/c	Dec. 1860 No a/c
I. November 1837	850					
II. December	850					
III. January 1838	850					
IV. February	850					
V. March	850					
VI. April	850					
VII. May	850					
VIII. June	850					
IX. July	850					
X. August	850					
XI. September	850					
XII. October	850					
XIII. November	850					
XIV. December	850					
XV. January 1839	850					
XVI. February	850					
XVII. March	850					
XVIII. April	850					
XIX. May	850					
XX. June	850					

	June 1861 Printed	Dec. 1861 No a/c	June 1862 No a/c	Dec. 1862 No a/c	June 1863 Printed	Dec. 1863 Printed
I. November 1837					395	
II. December					395	
III. January 1838					395	
IV. February					395	
V. March					395	
VI. April					395	
VII. May					395	
VIII. June					395	
IX. July					395	
X. August					395	
XI. September					395	
XII. October					395	
XIII. November					395	
XIV. December					395	
XV. January 1839					395	
XVI. February					395	
XVII. March					395	
XVIII. April					395	
XIX. May					395	
XX. June					395	

SKETCHES BY BOZ (*cont.*)

	June 1864 Printed	Dec. 1864 Printed	June 1865 Printed	Dec. 1865 Printed	June 1866 No a/c	Dec. 1866 Printed
I. November 1837						125
II. December						125
III. January 1838						125
IV. February						125
V. March						125
VI. April						125
VII. May						125
VIII. June						125
IX. July						125
X. August						125
XI. September						125
XII. October						125
XIII. November						125
XIV. December						125
XV. January 1839						125
XVI. February						125
XVII. March						125
XVIII. April						125
XIX. May						125
XX. June				750[1]		125

	June 1867[2] Printed	Dec. 1867 No a/c	June 1868 Printed	Dec. 1868 Printed	June 1869 Printed	Dec. 1869 Printed
I. November 1837			1,000			
II. December			1,000			
III. January 1838			1,000			
IV. February			1,000			
V. March			1,000			
VI. April			1,000			
VII. May			1,000			
VIII. June			1,000			
IX. July			1,000			
X. August			1,000			
XI. September			1,000			
XII. October			1,000			
XIII. November			1,000			
XIV. December			1,000			
XV. January 1839			1,000			
XVI. February			1,000			
XVII. March			1,000			
XVIII. April			1,000			
XIX. May			1,000			
XX. June			1,000			

[1] Numbers various.
[2] 'The Original Editions all have been reprinted during the half year.'

SKETCHES BY BOZ (*cont.*)

June
1870
Printed

I. November 1837
II. December
III. January 1838
IV. February
V. March
VI. April
VII. May
VIII. June
IX. July
X. August
XI. September
XII. October
XIII. November
XIV. December
XV. January 1839
XVI. February
XVII. March
XVIII. April
XIX. May
XX. June

A TALE OF TWO CITIES

	Aug. 1859 Printed	Aug. 1859 Stitched	Nov. 1859 Printed	Nov. 1859 Stitched	Mar. 1860 Printed	June 1860 Printed
I. June 1859	15,000					
II. July	10,000	22,000				
III. August	7,000					1,000
IV. September			5,000		1,500	1,500
V. October			5,000		1,500	1,000
VI. November			5,000	21,000	1,500	1,000
VII. } December			5,000		1,500	1,000
VIII. } December			5,000		1,500	1,000
Volumes, bound from parts					2,500	400

	Dec. 1860 No a/c	June 1861 No a/c	Dec. 1861 No a/c	June 1862 No a/c	Dec. 1862 Printed	June 1863 Printed
I. June 1859						
II. July						
III. August						
IV. September						
V. October						
VI. November						
VII. } December						
VIII. } December						
Volumes, bound from parts						

	Dec. 1863 Printed	June 1864 Printed	Dec. 1864 Printed	June 1865 No a/c	Dec. 1865 Printed	June 1866 No a/c
I. June 1859						
II. July						
III. August						
IV. September						
V. October						
VI. November						
VII. } December						
VIII. } December						
Volumes, bound from parts						

A TALE OF TWO CITIES (cont.)

	Dec. 1866 Printed	June 1867[1] Printed	Dec. 1867 Printed	June 1868 Printed	Dec. 1868 Printed	June 1869 Printed
I. June 1859						
II. July						
III. August						
IV. September						
V. October						
VI. November						
VII. VIII. } December	1,340[2]		3,125[2]			
Volumes, bound from parts						

	Dec. 1869 No a/c	June 1870 No a/c
I. June 1859		
II. July		
III. August		
IV. September		
V. October		
VI. November		
VII. VIII. } December		
Volumes, bound from parts		

[1] 'The Original Editions all have been reprinted during the half year.
[2] Numbers various.

Appendix C

INCOME FROM DICKENS'S WORKS FOR DICKENS, BRADBURY AND EVANS, AND CHAPMAN AND HALL, 1846–70

THE term 'profit' in the following tables covers a multitude of sources of income: advertising revenue from serials, payments for early proofs, 'royalties' from America, 'colonial duties', adjustments of previous accounts, and receipts from the sales of extra copies of the plates. It excludes direct payments to Dickens, such as the £1,000 paid for the first serial rights to *Hard Times*. Moreover, the gross income for any accounting period has been reduced not only by the usual printing and sales costs, but also by charges for warehousing and insurance, for books and parts wasted, and for adjustments of previous accounts. Since the two publishing firms kept their books differently, I have shown that difference in these tables, and where different accounting periods were supplied (*Great Expectations* in 3 volumes, *A Tale of Two Cities* in numbers, and *Our Mutual Friend* to October 1864), the totals have been added to the applicable half-year's account. In each case, publishers' commissions are listed in a separate column. It would be easy enough to ascertain the publishers' income in any six-month interval by adding their net profit to their commission. It would also be possible to obtain what might look like precise totals for income throughout all the accounting periods. But since these figures themselves rest on so many prior assumptions and interpretations about what constitutes profit and commission, I have refrained from appending totals that might be misleadingly exact.

INCOME FROM DICKENS'S WORKS FOR DICKENS AND BRADBURY AND EVANS, 1846-61

| | Dickens | | | Bradbury and Evans | | | |
	– £ s. d.	+ £ s. d.	Total £ s. d.	– £ s. d.	+ £ s. d.	Total £ s. d.	Commission £ s. d.
J46	93 11 6	722 12 1	629 0 7	31 3 11	290 10 3	259 6 4	256 6 7
D46			3,005 19 0			1,067 0 0	942 3 3
J47			2,820 14 11			953 18 3	735 15 5
D47			2,660 1 10			895 12 4	694 4 1
J48			2,285 18 0			770 16 1	576 11 6
D48			908 0 6			307 16 0	313 10 8
J49	11 15 10	696 11 2	684 15 4	3 18 8	236 9 7	232 10 11	260 0 10
D49	14 17 11	1,737 9 5	1,722 11 6	4 19 4	583 19 6	579 0 2	470 0 7
J50			1,766 17 4			596 5 1	469 3 1
D50			2,017 3 0			673 1 0	474 11 8
J51			146 19 4			49 19 10	27 14 7
D51			102 19 8			35 14 11	17 13 9
J52	24 16 6	2,366 6 3	2,341 9 9	8 5 6	791 6 3	783 0 9	683 14 8
D52	30 18 2	2,923 11 10	3,264 8 0			1,089 17 6	800 2 10
J53			2,892 13 8	10 6 1	979 9 8	969 3 7	779 19 5
D53			2,183 16 11			728 18 2	499 8 10
J54	47 18 7	399 13 0	351 14 5	15 19 7	135 0 0	119 0 5	99 8 4
D54			356 1 7			121 5 5	40 11 2
J55	9 8 10	313 10 1	304 1 3	3 2 11	109 17 1	106 14 2	59 8 3
D55			1,065 9 7			355 10 7	29 11 8
J56			3,750 8 5			1,253 7 10	35 17 0
D56	10 11 4	3,352 4 7	3,341 13 3	3 10 6	1,119 0 7	1,115 10 1	21 5 9
J57			3,817 11 1			1,279 1 8	39 7 4
D57	9 1 9	449 6 7	440 4 10	3 0 8	150 13 2	147 12 6	36 6 0

INCOME FROM DICKENS'S WORKS FOR DICKENS AND BRADBURY AND EVANS, 1846–61 (*cont.*)

| | Dickens | | | | | | Bradbury and Evans | | | | | | Commission | | |
| | − | | | + | | | Total | | | − | | | + | | | Total | | | | | |
	£	s.	d.	£	s.	d.	£	s.	d.	£	s.	d.	£	s.	d.	£	s.	d.	£	s.	d.
J58	76	2	5	274	8	9	198	6	4	25	7	6	95	16	7	70	9	1	72	16	4
D58	245	10	10	377	17	10	132	7	0	81	17	1	126	16	9	44	19	8	137	13	1
J59	567	3	11	237	13	11	−329	10	0	189	1	5	79	4	9	−109	16	8	73	16	3
D59	302	7	10	306	7	5	3	19	7[1]	100	16	1	102	2	8	1	6	7	50	10	10
J60	18	8	0	399	18	1	381	10	1	6	2	8	133	6	5	127	3	9	40	6	2
D60							237	3	1							79	1	3	21	10	11
J61	49	9	0	151	10	4	102	1	4	16	9	9	50	10	6	34	0	9	18	10	1

[1] Not paid until the J60 accounts.

INCOME FROM DICKENS'S WORKS FOR DICKENS AND CHAPMAN AND HALL, 1846-70

	Dickens Profits			Chapman and Hall Profits			Commission		
	£	s.	d.	£	s.	d.	£	s.	d.
J46	95	0	6	94	18	6	13	8	3
D46	105	7	4	131	17	4	21	10	6
J47	75	14	0	100	3	4	16	11	9
D47	170	7	9	179	9	10	294	11	8
J48	502	7	0	509	0	1	134	0	1
D48	405	4	1	411	12	2	100	15	10
J49	322	13	0	319	12	2	98	19	0
D49	314	16	1	316	10	10	85	9	4
J50	318	14	9½	325	17	5½	90	1	0
D50	332	3	5	342	6	5	82	1	2
J51	283	4	3	285	15	4	37	18	2
D51	250	19	5	259	1	1	32	8	3
J52	260	2	11	269	0	11	35	11	11
D52	229	17	1	243	2	10	41	6	4
J53	251	17	11	257	0	3	42	10	7
D53	273	13	1	281	1	2	73	19	3
J54	126	19	10	139	11	2	31	15	10
D54	60	5	10	71	9	1	36	15	1
J55	123	16	1	134	16	5	37	3	4
D55	124	16	2	97	6	5	65	19	6
J56	174	18	7	143	4	8	31	19	8
D56	241	13	6	239	9	8	42	0	0
J57	120	3	10	112	8	7	39	13	3
D57	122	0	3	92	19	5	49	15	9
J58	173	11	8	108	19	2	106	16	1
D58	199	1	3	135	18	11	72	11	3
J59	189	12	3	153	14	9	30	17	10
D59	647	13	7	240	11	2	43	13	7
J60	650	11	5	242	6	1	192	12	5
D60	250	14	1	119	11	1	59	4	6
J61	265	6	7	160	9	0	116	14	3
D61	383	14	6	379	1	0	119	15	2
J62	2,430	13	10	462	10	1	354	18	4
D62	703	18	1	703	17	11	159	7	0
J63	383	2	11	383	2	7	121	16	1
D63	501	7	9	501	7	8	130	10	5
J64	682	2	8	682	2	8	150	19	10
D64	2,490	8	10	2,490	8	9	452	18	11
J65	1,784	12	5	1,784	12	4	631	12	1
D65	2,965	15	8½	2,965	15	8½	527	16	6
J66	1,887	1	7	1,486	16	1	224	19	4
D66	1,309	6	6	1,208	4	7	153	5	2
J67	1,038	0	7	972	11	6	113	2	3
D67	2,304	7	7	2,241	5	7	1,216	0	6
J68	1,027	9	4	1,002	0	0	653	14	8
D68	1,476	1	5	1,386	1	2	552	15	9
J69	829	17	9	787	18	3	206	11	9
D69	1,799	6	2	1,774	6	10	423	18	1
J70	1,220	3	2	1,188	1	11	321	12	10

Appendix D

INCOME FROM *HOUSEHOLD WORDS* AND *ALL THE YEAR ROUND*

THE following tables indicate the biannual receipts from Dickens's publishing ventures, *Household Words* (where his partners were Bradbury and Evans, John Forster, and W. H. Wills) and *All the Year Round* (where Wills was, until 1870, the only sharer in the copyright). Income from these sources has been segregated because for the most part it derives not from Dickens's own writings, but from his proprietorship and editing of the journals, and is thus in some respects like income produced by his other financial speculations.

In the Philip H. and A. S. W. Rosenbach Foundation Museum, receipts based on verified accounts, showing the division of profits and signed by Dickens, exist for *All the Year Round* to 1867, and for its predecessor to 1859, excepting those for the half-years ending 31 March 1852 and 31 March 1854.[1] The missing figures have been supplied from the Author's Ledger in the possession of Bradbury, Agnew & Co., transcribed and annotated by William E. Buckler.[2] Through 1855, the Ledger entries do not differ significantly from the receipts, though there are discrepancies ranging from a farthing to a penny. However, the Bradbury Ledger, and thus Buckler's transcription, fail to redistribute the income following Forster's withdrawal in the mid-fifties. A Memorandum about the 10 January 1854 meeting of the partners, which Forster did not attend, recorded a resolution to instruct the solicitors to prepare a legal endorsement to the Deed of Partnership specifying that Forster, 'being unable to render the literary services referred to in the Deed', was released on payment of a £1,100 note of hand at two years' date. That sum was not to be construed as the worth of Forster's eighth share, but merely an amount agreed to by the partners in this instance. Further, if Forster did not take up his note by its expiration, his share reverted to the other partners. The exact legal resolution was enacted six weeks later, on 22 February. Forster relinquished his share by not paying the note, so on 23 February 1856 his

---

[1] For permission to use these receipts, as well as the Memoranda and Agreements cited hereafter, I am grateful to the Rosenbach Foundation and its Director, Clive E. Driver.

[2] 'Dickens's Success with *Household Words*', *Dickensian*, 46 (1950), 197–203.

eighth interest in *Household Words* was available to the other partners. In a Memorandum of resolutions by the partners, dated 13 May 1856, that share was declared to belong to Dickens during his life. In turn, he made over to Wills, so long as he continued as Sub-Editor, one-half of that eighth to add to Wills's own one-eighth share. Thus Dickens thereafter received nine-sixteenths, and Wills three-sixteenths, of the income. A further resolution provided that at Wills's retirement or death his additional one-sixteenth share reverted to Dickens, 'who will then exercise his own discretion as to retaining it or bestowing it, or any part of it upon any future Sub Editor; as he may think most advantageous to the interests of Household Words, and the efficiency of his own connexion with it'. At Dickens's death, Forster's whole eighth share became the joint property of Dickens's heirs and the surviving *Household Words* partners, 'in trust, honourably to employ it according to their discretion in rewarding future Editors or Sub Editors or both, with an interest, beyond and above a salary, in the character and success of Household Words'.

A 28 December 1853 Agreement stipulated that Dickens was to receive £1,000 in two instalments to write a novel the length of five single numbers of *Bleak House* which would run weekly in *Household Words*. That payment was not to be counted as an expense of the journal, but rather constituted 'the personal venture of the four partners [Bradbury, Evans, Forster, and Wills] . . . with a view to the enlargement of the circulation of Household Words and the consequent enhancement of the value of their several shares'. Dickens retained the copyright of his novel, which became *Hard Times*. Buckler lists payment of £1,000 in his transcription of the Author's Ledger for 31 December 1854, along with small sums to the other partners. Actually, Dickens received the money in two equal portions as the Agreement prescribed, on publication of the first and last instalments. These payments have been excluded from this table, since they represent money from writing rather than publishing; the other partners' shares do not appear in the Rosenbach receipts, possibly because the Ledger merely notes accrued profits from the last accounting which were included in and disbursed at the next biannual audit.

I do not know why the Rosenbach lacks the *All the Year Round* receipts for 31 October 1864 and for all years after 1867.

INCOME FROM *HOUSEHOLD WORDS*, 1850-9

	Dickens			B & E			Forster			Wills			Total		
	£	s.	d.	£	s.	d.	£	s.	d.	£	s.	d.	£	s.	d.
30 Sept. 50	263	2	7	131	11	3	65	15	8	65	15	8	526	5	2
31 Mar. 51	594	6	9	297	3	4	148	11	8	148	11	8	1,188	13	5
30 Sept. 51	558	3	7	279	1	9	139	10	11	139	10	11	1,116	7	2
31 Mar. 52	453	4	5	226	12	4	113	6	2	113	6	2	906	8	10
30 Sept. 52	482	8	7	241	4	3	120	12	2	120	12	2	964	17	2
31 Mar. 53	651	10	5	325	15	2½	162	17	7¼	162	17	7¼	1,303	0	10
30 Sept. 53	263	17	11	131	18	11	65	19	6	65	19	6	527	15	10
31 Mar. 54	196	13	7	98	6	10	49	3	5	49	3	5	393	7	2
30 Sept. 54	466	8	10	233	4	5	116	12	2½	116	12	2½	932	17	8
31 Mar. 55	472	15	0	236	7	6	118	3	9	118	3	9	945	10	1
30 Sept. 55	236	17	6½	118	8	9½	59	4	4½	59	4	4½	473	15	1
31 Mar. 56	468	0	11	208	0	5				156	0	3	832	1	7
30 Sept. 56	216	7	2	96	3	3				72	2	4	384	12	9
31 Mar. 57	575	9	6	255	15	4				191	16	6	1,023	1	4
30 Sept. 57	377	12	2	167	16	6½				125	17	4½	671	6	1
31 Mar. 58	605	4	3	268	19	10				201	14	8	1,075	18	9
30 Sept. 58	343	18	10	152	17	2				114	12	11	611	8	11
31 Mar. 59	604	19	6	268	17	7				201	13	2	1,075	10	3

INCOME FROM *ALL THE YEAR ROUND*, 1859-67

	Dickens			Wills			Total		
	£	s.	d.	£	s.	d.	£	s.	d.
31 Oct. 59	469	13	2	156	11	1	626	4	3
30 Apr. 60	1,246	13	7	415	11	2	1,662	4	9
31 Oct. 60	1,365	15	3	455	5	1	1,821	0	4
30 Apr. 61	509	8	9	169	16	4	679	5	1
31 Oct. 61	310	1	8	103	7	2	413	8	10
30 Apr. 62	1,320	0	4	440	0	1	1,760	0	5
31 Oct. 62	1,417	5	11	472	8	8	1,889	14	7
30 Apr. 63	2,069	14	0	689	18	0	2,759	12	0
31 Oct. 63	1,000	13	9	333	11	3	1,334	5	0
30 Apr. 64	2,142	16	6	714	5	5	2,857	1	11
31 Oct. 64				Missing					
30 Apr. 65	1,370	9	9	456	16	7	1,827	6	4
31 Oct. 65	1,203	11	5	401	3	10	1,604	15	3
30 Apr. 66	1,540	8	2	513	9	5	2,053	17	7
31 Oct. 66	1,135	14	4	378	11	5	1,514	5	9
30 Apr. 67	1,873	10	5	624	10	1	2,498	0	6
31 Oct. 67	778	13	3	259	11	1	1,038	4	4

Select Bibliography

In addition to the following sources I have consulted other sources not listed: unpublished letters by and to Dickens, individual and small collections of letters by Dickens dispersedly published since the last collected edition (1938), and the runs of numerous periodicals, including *The Bookman* and the *Publisher's Circular*.

I. WRITINGS BY CHARLES DICKENS

A. Works: *Twentieth-Century Editions Consulted*

The Christmas Books. Ed. Michael Slater. 2 vols., Penguin, Harmondsworth, Middlesex, 1971.

Dombey and Son. Ed. Alan Horsman. The Clarendon Dickens, Clarendon Press, Oxford, 1974.

Hard Times. Ed. George Ford and Sylvère Monod. Norton Critical Edition, W. W. Norton, New York, 1966.

Charles Dickens' Uncollected Writings from Household Words, 1850–59. Ed. Harry Stone. 2 vols., Indiana University Press, Bloomington and London, 1968.

The Mystery of Edwin Drood. Ed. Margaret Cardwell. The Clarendon Dickens, Clarendon Press, Oxford, 1972.

The Mystery of Edwin Drood. Intro. Charles Dickens, Jr. Macmillan, New York, 1923.

Oliver Twist. Ed. Kathleen Tillotson. The Clarendon Dickens, Clarendon Press, Oxford, 1966.

The Posthumous Papers of the Pickwick Club. Ed. Robert L. Patten. Penguin, Harmondsworth, Middlesex, 1972.

Pictures from Italy. Ed. David Paroissien. André Deutsch, London, 1973.

The Public Readings. Ed. Philip Collins. Clarendon Press, Oxford, 1975.

Reprinted Pieces, The Uncommercial Traveller, and Other Stories. Gen. eds. Arthur Waugh, Hugh Walpole, Walter Dexter, and Thomas Hatton. The Nonesuch Dickens, Nonesuch Press, Bloomsbury, 1938.

B. *Correspondence and Speeches*

Charles Dickens as Editor: Being Letters Written by Him to William Henry Wills His Sub-Editor. Ed. R. C. Lehmann. Sturgis &Walton, New York, 1912.

The Heart of Charles Dickens. Ed. Edgar Johnson. Duell, Sloan and Pearce, New York; Little, Brown and Co., Boston, 1952.

The Letters of Charles Dickens. Ed. Walter Dexter. 3 vols., The None-such Dickens, Nonesuch Press, Bloomsbury, 1938.

The Letters of Charles Dickens. Ed. His Sister-in-Law and His Eldest Daughter [Georgina Hogarth and Mamie Dickens]. 3 vols., Chapman and Hall, London, 1880 and 1882.

The Letters of Charles Dickens. Vols. i (1820–39) and ii (1840–1), ed. Madeline House, Graham Storey; vol. iii (1842–3), ed. Madeline House, Graham Storey, and Kathleen Tillotson. The Pilgrim Edition, 3 vols. to date, Clarendon Press, Oxford, 1965, 1969, and 1974.

Mr. and Mrs. Charles Dickens: His Letters to Her. Ed. Walter Dexter. Constable, London, 1935.

The Speeches of Charles Dickens. Ed. K. J. Fielding. Clarendon Press, Oxford, 1960.

II. GENERAL BIBLIOGRAPHY

ADRIAN, ARTHUR A. *Mark Lemon: First Editor of Punch*. Oxford University Press, London, New York, and Toronto, 1966.

ALDIS, H. G. 'Book Production and Distribution, 1625–1800.' In *The Cambridge History of English Literature*, ed. A. W. Ward and A. R. Waller, xi. 344–79. G. P. Putnam's Sons, New York; Cambridge University Press, Cambridge, 1914.

ALLEN, CLARENCE E. *Publishers' Accounts*. Gee & Co., London, 1897.

ALTICK, RICHARD D. 'Dickens and America: Some Unpublished Letters.' *The Pennsylvania Magazine of History and Biography*, 73 (1949), 326–36.

—— *The English Common Reader: A Social History of the Mass Reading Public 1800–1900*. University of Chicago Press, Chicago and London, 1957.

—— 'English Publishing and the Mass Audience in 1852.' *Studies in Bibliography*, 6 (1954), 3–24.

—— 'Nineteenth-Century English Best-Sellers: A Further List.' *Studies in Bibliography*, 22 (1969), 197–206.

ARNOLD, FREDERICK. *The Public Life of Lord Macaulay*. Tinsley Brothers, London, 1862.

The Author's Printing and Publishing Assistant. 2nd edn., Saunders and Otley, London, 1839.

BALZAC, HONORÉ DE. *Lost Illusions*. Trans. Ellen Marriage. The Novels of Balzac, Centenary Edition, vol. 6. John D. Morris and Co., Philadelphia, n.d.

BARNES, JAMES J. *Authors, Publishers and Politicians: The Quest for an Anglo-American Copyright Agreement, 1815–1854.* Ohio State University Press, Columbus, 1974.

—— *Free Trade in Books: A Study of the London Book Trade since 1800.* Clarendon Press, Oxford, 1964.

BAY, J. C. *Fortune of Books: Essays, Memories and Prophecies of a Librarian.* W. M. Hill, Chicago, [1941].

BELL, [HENRY THOMAS] MACKENZIE. *A Forgotten Genius: Charles Whitehead.* T. Fisher Unwin, London, 1885.

BENTLEY, RICHARD, AND SON. *A List of the Principal Publications Issued from New Burlington Street during the Year* . . . Richard Bentley and Son, privately printed, London, various dates.

BEVINGTON, DAVID M. 'Seasonal Relevance in *The Pickwick Papers*.' *Nineteenth-Century Fiction*, 16 (1961), 219–30.

BLAKE, ROBERT. *Disraeli.* St. Martin's Press, New York, 1967.

BLAKELY, DOROTHY. *The Minerva Press, 1790–1820.* Oxford University Press, Oxford, for the Bibliographical Society, London, 1939 (for 1935).

BOSWELL, JAMES. *Boswell's Life of Johnson, Together with Boswell's Journal of a Tour to the Hebrides and Johnson's Diary of a Journey into North Wales.* Ed. George Birkbeck Hill, rev. and enl. L. F. Powell. 6 vols., Clarendon Press, Oxford, 1934.

BOURNE, HENRY R. FOX. *English Newspapers.* Chatto and Windus, London, 1887.

BRACHER, PETER. 'The Lea & Blanchard Edition of Dickens's *American Notes*, 1842.' *Publications of the Bibliographical Society of America*, 63 (1969), 296–300.

—— 'The New York *Herald* and *American Notes*.' *Dickens Studies*, 5 (1969), 81–5.

BRIGGS, ASA, ed. *Essays in the History of Publishing in Celebration of the 250th Anniversary of the House of Longman, 1724–1974.* Longman, London, 1974.

BROWNE, EDGAR A. *Phiz and Dickens as They Appeared to Edgar Browne.* Dodd, Mead & Co., New York, 1914.

BUCKLER, WILLIAM E. 'Dickens's Success with *Household Words*.' *Dickensian*, 46 (1950), 197–203.

BUTT, JOHN. 'The Composition of *David Copperfield*.' *Dickensian*, 46 (1949–50), 90–4, 128–35, 176–80; 47 (1950–1), 33–8.

—— '*David Copperfield* from Manuscript to Print.' *Review of English Studies*, N.S. 1 (1950), 247–51.

BUTT, JOHN. 'Dickens's Notes for His Serial Parts.' *Dickensian*, 45 (1949), 129–38.

—— and TILLOTSON, KATHLEEN. *Dickens at Work*. Methuen, London, 1957.

CALHOUN, PHILO, and HEANEY, HOWELL J. 'Dickens' *Christmas Carol* after a Hundred Years: A Study in Bibliographical Evidence.' *Publications of the Bibliographical Society of America*, 39 (1945), 271–317.

CAREY, HENRY C. *Letters on International Copyright*. A. Hart, late Carey and Hart, Philadelphia, 1853.

CARLTON, WILLIAM J. 'Dickens's Debut in America.' *Dickensian*, 55 (1959), 55–6.

—— 'Dickens's Insurance Policies.' *Dickensian*, 51 (1955), 133–7.

CARR, SISTER MARY CALLISTA. 'John Forster: A Literary Biography to 1856.' Ph.D. dissertation, Yale University, 1956.

—— [SISTER LUCILE CARR, C.D.P.]. *A Catalogue of the VanderPoel Dickens Collection at the University of Texas*. Humanities Research Center, Austin, Texas, 1968.

CARTER, JOHN. *Binding Variants in English Publishing, 1820–1900*. Constable, London; R. Long & R. R. Smith, New York, 1932.

—— *Books and Book Collectors*. World Publishing Co., Cleveland and New York, 1957.

—— 'Further Answers to Appeal 24, *Great Expectations*.' *New Colophon*, vol. 2, part 7 (1949), 278–9.

—— ed. *New Paths in Book Collecting: Essays by Various Hands*. Constable, London, 1934.

CHAPMAN, JOHN. *Cheap Books, and How to Get Them*. John Chapman, London, 1852.

CHARVAT, WILLIAM. *The Profession of Authorship in America, 1800–1870: The Papers of William Charvat*. Ed. Matthew J. Bruccoli. Ohio State University Press, Columbus, 1968.

CHESTERTON, G. K. *Charles Dickens: A Critical Study*. Dodd Mead, New York, 1906.

CHURTON, EDWARD. *The Author's Handbook: A Complete Guide to the Art and System of Publishing on Commission*. 3rd edn., E. Churton, London, 1845.

CLENDENING, LOGAN. *A Handbook to Pickwick Papers*. Alfred A. Knopf, New York and London, 1936.

'The Circulation of Modern Literature.' *Spectator*, 36 (Supplement, 3 Jan. 1863), 16–18.

COHEN, JANE R. ' "A Melancholy Clown"—The Relationship of

Robert Seymour and Charles Dickens.' *Harvard Library Bulletin*, 19 (1971), 250–79.

COHN, ALBERT M. *George Cruikshank: A Catalogue Raisonné.* Office of 'The Bookman's Journal', London, 1924.

COLERIDGE, S[AMUEL] T[AYLOR]. *Biographia Literaria.* Ed. J. Shawcross. 2 vols., Oxford University Press, Geoffrey Cumberledge, London, 1907.

COLLINS, A. S. *Authorship in the Days of Johnson: Being a Study of the Relation between Author, Patron, Publisher and Public, 1726–1780.* Robert Holden, London, 1927.

—— *The Profession of Letters: A Study of the Relation of Author to Patron, Publisher, and Public, 1780–1832.* George Routledge, London, 1928.

COLLINS, PHILIP. 'The *All the Year Round* Letter Book.' *Victorian Periodicals Newsletter*, no. 10 (Nov. 1970), pp. 23–9.

—— 'Dickens and *Punch.*' *Dickens Studies*, 3 (1967), 4–21.

—— 'A Tale of Two Novels: *A Tale of Two Cities* and *Great Expectations* in Dickens' Career.' *Dickens Studies Annual*, 2 (1972), 336–51.

—— ed. *Dickens: The Critical Heritage.* Barnes and Noble, New York, 1971.

'The Condition of Authors in England, Germany, and France.' *Fraser's Magazine*, 35 (1847), 285–95.

CONSTABLE, THOMAS. *Archibald Constable and His Literary Correspondents.* 3 vols., Edmonston and Douglas, Edinburgh, 1873.

COOLIDGE, ARCHIBALD CAREY, JR. 'Serialization in the Novels of Charles Dickens.' Ph.D. dissertation, Brown University, 1956.

COX, HAROLD, and CHANDLER, JOHN E. *The House of Longman, 1724–1924.* Longmans, Green, and Co., London, 1925.

CRUSE, AMY. *The Victorians and Their Books.* George Allen & Unwin, London, 1935.

CURWEN, HENRY. *A History of Booksellers.* Chatto and Windus, London, [1873].

DALZIEL, MARGARET. *Popular Fiction 100 Years Ago.* Cohen and West, London, 1957.

DARWIN, BERNARD. *The Dickens Advertiser: A Collection of the Advertisements in the Original Parts of Novels.* Elkins Matthews & Marrot, London, 1930.

DAVIS, EARLE. *The Flint and the Flame: The Artistry of Charles Dickens.* University of Missouri Press, Columbia, 1963.

DELATTRE, FLORIS. *Dickens et la France.* Librairie Universitaire, Paris, 1927.

DeVries, Duane. *Dickens's Apprentice Years: The Making of a Novelist.* Harvester Press, Sussex, 1976.

Dexter, Walter. 'The "Library", "Peoples", and "Charles Dickens" Editions.' *Dickensian*, 40 (1944), 186–7.

—— 'The *Metropolitan Magazine* and Dickens's Early Work.' *Dickensian*, 33 (1937), 93–6.

—— and Ley, J. W. T. *The Origin of Pickwick: New Facts Now First Published in the Year of the Centenary.* Chapman and Hall, London, 1936.

Dibdin, Thomas Frognall [pseud. Mercurius Rusticus]. *Bibliophobia. Remarks on the Present Languid and Depressed State of Literature and the Book Trade. In a Letter Addressed to the Author of the Bibliomania.* Notes by R. Heber [pseud. Cato Parvus]. Henry Bohn, London, 1832.

Dickens, Sir Henry F. *Memories of My Father.* Victor Gollancz, London, 1928.

Dickens, Mary [his eldest daughter]. *Charles Dickens.* Cassell, London, 1885; rpt. 1911.

—— *My Father as I Recall Him.* Roxburghe Press, Westminster, 1897; rpt. E. P. Dutton, New York, n.d.

'Dickens and His French Publishers.' *Dickensian*, 29 (1932–3), 7–10.

Dickinson, Violet, ed. *Miss Eden's Letters.* Macmillan, London, 1919.

Duffy, Sir Charles Gavan. *Conversations with Carlyle.* Sampson Low, Marston, and Company, London, 1892.

Dystel, Oscar. 'The Paperback & the Bookstore.' In a special advertising supplement to the *New York Times*, 25 May 1975, pp. 16–17, 23.

Eckel, John C. *The First Editions of the Writings of Charles Dickens and Their Values: A Bibliography.* 1st edn., Chapman & Hall, London, 1913.

—— *The First Editions of the Writings of Charles Dickens: Their Points and Values.* Rev. and enl. edn., Maurice Inman, New York; Maggs Bros., London, 1932.

—— *Prime Pickwick in Parts: Census with Complete Collation, Comparison and Comment.* Foreword A. Edward Newton. Edgar H. Wells, New York; Charles H. Sawyer, London, 1928.

Eddy, Spencer L., Jr. *The Founding of The Cornhill Magazine.* Ball State Monograph no. 19, Publications in English, no. 13. Ball State University, Muncie, Indiana, 1970.

Edgar, Herman Le Roy, and Vail, R. W. G. 'Early American Editions of the Works of Charles Dickens.' *Bulletin of the New York Public Library*, 33 (1929), 302–19.

ELIOT, GEORGE. *The George Eliot Letters.* Ed. Gordon S. Haight. 7 vols., Yale University Press, New Haven, 1954-5.

ELLIS, S. M. *William Harrison Ainsworth and His Friends.* 2 vols., John Lane, Bodley Head, London; John Lane Co., New York, 1911.

EXMAN, EUGENE T. *The Brothers Harper: A Unique Publishing Partnership and Its Impact upon the Cultural Life of America from 1817 to 1853.* Harper and Row, New York, 1965.

FIELDING, K[ENNETH] J. ' "American Notes" and Some English Reviewers.' *Modern Language Review,* 59 (1964), 527-37.

—— 'Bradbury *v.* Dickens.' *Dickensian,* 50 (1954), 73-82.

—— 'Carlyle and Dickens or Dickens and Carlyle?' *Dickensian,* 69 (1973), 111-18.

—— *Charles Dickens: A Critical Introduction.* 2nd edn. rev. and enl., Riverside Studies in Literature, Houghton Mifflin Co., Boston, 1964.

[——] ' "David Copperfield" and Dialect.' *Times Literary Supplement,* 30 Apr. 1949, p. 288.

—— 'Dickens and International Copyright.' *Bulletin of the British Association for American Studies,* N.S. no. 4 (Aug. 1962), 29-35.

—— '1870-1900: Forster and Reaction.' *Dickensian,* 66 (May 1970), 85-100.

—— 'The Monthly Serialisation of Dickens's Novels.' *Dickensian,* 54 (1958), 4-11.

—— 'The Weekly Serialisation of Dickens's Novels.' *Dickensian,* 54 (1958), 134-41.

—— and GRUBB, GERALD G. 'New Letters from Charles Dickens to John Forster.' *Boston University Studies in English,* 2 (1956), 140-93.

FILDES, L. V. *Luke Fildes, R.A.: A Victorian Painter.* Michael Joseph, London, 1968.

FITZGERALD, PERCY. 'Boz's Publishers.' *Dickensian,* 3 (1907), 10-14.

—— 'Boz and His Publishers.' *Dickensian,* 3 (1907), 33-7, 70-3, 93-6, 126-9, 158-61.

—— *The History of Pickwick: An Account of Its Characters, Localities, Allusions, and Illustrations; With a Bibliography.* Chapman and Hall, London, 1891.

—— *Memories of Charles Dickens: With an Account of 'Household Words' and 'All the Year Round' and of the Contributors thereto.* J. W. Arrowsmith, Bristol; Simpkin, Marshall, Hamilton, Kent & Co., London, 1913.

FOAT, F. E. K., and POCKLINGTON, G. R. *The Story of W. H. Smith & Son.* Privately printed, London, 1937.

FORD, GEORGE. *Dickens and His Readers: Aspects of Novel-Criticism since 1863.* Princeton University Press, Princeton, 1955.

—— 'Dickens in the 1960s.' *Dickensian*, 66 (May 1970), 163–82.

—— 'Self-Help and the Helpless in *Bleak House*.' In *From Jane Austen to Joseph Conrad: Essays Collected in Memory of James T. Hillhouse*, ed. Robert C. Rathburn and Martin Steinmann, Jr., pp. 92–105. University of Minnesota Press, Minneapolis, 1958.

—— 'The Titles for *Bleak House*.' *Dickensian*, 65 (1969), 84–9.

FORSTER, JOHN. *The Life of Charles Dickens.* Ed., annot. and intro. J. W. T. Ley. Doubleday, Doran, and Co., New York, [1928].

—— Review of *Jack Sheppard. Examiner*, 3 Nov. 1839, pp. 691–3.

GASKELL, PHILIP. *A New Introduction to Bibliography.* Oxford University Press, New York and Oxford, 1972.

GERRING, CHARLES. *Notes on Printers and Booksellers with a Chapter on Chap Books.* Simpkin, Marshall, Hamilton, Kent & Co., London, 1900.

GETTMANN, ROYAL A. *A Victorian Publisher: A Study of the Bentley Papers.* Cambridge University Press, Cambridge, 1960.

GIMBEL, RICHARD. 'The Earliest State of the First Edition of Charles Dickens' *A Christmas Carol*.' *Princeton University Library Chronicle*, 19 (1958), 82–6.

GISSING, GEORGE R. *Charles Dickens: A Critical Study.* Blackie & Son, London, Glasgow, and Dublin, 1898.

—— *Critical Studies of the Works of Charles Dickens.* Greenberg, New York, 1924.

—— *The Private Papers of Henry Ryecroft.* E. P. Dutton, New York, 1903.

GORDAN, JOHN D. 'Reading for Profit: The Other Career of Charles Dickens; An Exhibition from the Berg Collection.' *Bulletin of the New York Public Library*, 62 (1958), 425–42, 515–22.

GREAT BRITAIN, *Parliamentary Papers*, vol. 89 (1887), pp. 580, 583, and 584.

—— *Parliamentary Papers*, vol. 68 (1890), pp. 632–3.

—— Public Record Office, C. 15. 596/B–76. X/K. 2107.

—— Public Record Office, C. 31. 1392/1608. X/K. 2107.

—— Public Record Office, C. 31. 1392/1635. X/K. 2107.

—— Public Record Office, C. 33/1058.

GRIEST, GUINEVERE L. *Mudie's Circulating Library and the Victorian Novel*. Indiana University Press, Bloomington and London, 1970.

GROSS, JOHN. *The Rise and Fall of the Man of Letters: Aspects of English Literary Life Since 1800*. Weidenfeld and Nicolson, London, 1969.

GRUBB, GERALD G. 'The American Edition of "All the Year Round".' *Publications of the Bibliographical Society of America*, 47 (1953), 301–4.

—— 'Dickens and the *Daily News*: The Origin of the Idea.' In *Booker Memorial Studies: Eight Essays on Victorian Literature in Memory of John Manning Booker*, ed. Hill Shine, pp. 60–77. University of North Carolina Press, Chapel Hill, 1950.

—— 'Dickens and the "Daily News": Preliminaries to Publication.' *Nineteenth-Century Fiction*, 6 (1951–2), 174–94.

—— 'Dickens and the "Daily News": The Early Issues.' *Nineteenth-Century Fiction*, 6 (1951–2), 234–46.

—— 'Dickens and the "Daily News": Resignation.' *Nineteenth-Century Fiction*, 7 (1952–3), 19–38.

—— 'Dickens' Pattern of Weekly Serialization.' *English Literary History*, 9 (1942), 141–56.

—— 'Personal and Business Relations of Charles Dickens and Thomas Coke Evans.' *Dickensian*, 48 (1952), 106–13, 168–73.

—— annot. 'Some Unpublished Correspondence of Dickens and Chapman and Hall.' *Boston University Studies in English*, 1 (1955), 98–127.

HAIGHT, GORDON S. *George Eliot: A Biography*. Clarendon Press, Oxford, 1968.

HARPER, HENRY J. *The House of Harper: A Century of Publishing in Franklin Square*. Harper and Brothers, New York and London, 1912.

HARRIES, J. M. Query. *Notes and Queries*, 218 (1973), 100.

HARVEY, JOHN. *Victorian Novelists and Their Illustrators*. New York University Press, New York, 1971.

HATTON, THOMAS, and CLEAVER, ARTHUR H. *A Bibliography of the Periodical Works of Charles Dickens*. Chapman and Hall, London, 1933.

HAWES, DONALD. 'Marryat and Dickens: A Personal and Literary Relationship.' *Dickens Studies Annual*, 2 (1972), 39–68.

HEPBURN, JAMES. *The Author's Empty Purse and the Rise of the Literary Agent*. Oxford University Press, London, New York, and Toronto, 1968.

HINDLEY, CHARLES. *History of the Catnatch Press*. Charles Hindley, London, 1886.

HINDLEY, CHARLES. *Life and Times of James Catnatch.* Reeves and Turner, London, 1878; reissue Singing Tree Press, Detroit, 1968.

HODDER, GEORGE. *Memories of My Time.* Tinsley Brothers, London, 1870.

HONE, PHILIP. *The Diary of Philip Hone, 1828–1851.* Ed. and intro. Allan Nevins. 2 vols., Dodd, Mead and Co., New York, 1927.

HOPKINS, TIGHE. 'The "Tauchnitz" Edition: The Story of a Popular Publisher.' *Pall Mall Gazette*, 25 (Oct. 1901), 197–208.

HOWE, ELLIC, ed. *The London Compositor, 1785–1900.* The Bibliographical Society, London, 1947.

HUXLEY, LEONARD. *The House of Smith Elder.* Privately printed, London, 1923.

JAMES, G. P. R. 'Some Observations on the Book Trade, as Connected with Literature, in England.' *Journal of the [Royal] Statistical Society*, 6 (1843), 50–60.

JAMES, LOUIS. 'An Artist in Time: George Cruikshank in Three Eras.' In *George Cruikshank: A Revaluation*, ed. Robert L. Patten, pp. 157–68. Princeton University Library, Princeton, 1974.

JAMES, PHILIP. *English Book Illustration, 1800–1900.* King Penguin Books, London, 1947.

JAQUES, E. T. *Charles Dickens in Chancery: Being an Account of His Proceedings in Respect of the 'Christmas Carol' with Some Gossip in Relation to the Old Law Courts at Westminster.* Longmans, Green and Co., London, 1914.

JENNETT, SEÁN. *The Making of Books.* Faber and Faber, London, 1956.

JOHNSON, EDGAR. *Charles Dickens: His Tragedy and Triumph.* 2 vols., Simon and Schuster, New York, 1953.

—— *Sir Walter Scott: The Great Unknown.* 2 vols., Macmillan, New York, 1970.

JONES, ANNABEL. 'Disraeli's *Endymion*: A Case Study.' In *Essays in the History of Publishing in Celebration of the 250th Anniversary of the House of Longman, 1724–1974.* Ed. Asa Briggs, pp. 141–86. Longman, London, 1974.

KASER, DAVID, ed. *The Cost Book of Carey & Lea, 1825–1838.* University of Pennsylvania Press, Philadelphia, 1963.

KIRKLAND, EDWARD C. *Industry Comes of Age. The Economic History of the United States*, vol. 6. Holt, Rinehart and Winston, New York, 1961.

KITTON, FREDERIC G. *Charles Dickens by Pen and Pencil.* 3 vols., Frank T. Sabin, London, 1890–2.

—— *Charles Dickens, His Life, Writings, and Personality.* 1902; 2 vols., Caxton Publishing Co., London, n.d.

—— *Dickens and His Illustrators.* 2nd edn., George Redway, London, 1899.

—— *The Minor Writings of Charles Dickens.* Elliott Stock, London, 1900.

—— *The Novels of Charles Dickens: A Bibliography and Sketch.* Elliott Stock, London, 1897.

—— *'Phiz' (Hablot Knight Browne) A Memoir; Including Selections From His Correspondence and Notes on His Principal Works.* George Redway, London, 1882.

KNIGHT, CHARLES. *The Old Printer and the Modern Press.* John Murray, London, 1854.

—— *Passages of a Working Life During Half a Century: With a Prelude of Early Reminiscences.* 3 vols., Bradbury & Evans, London, 1864–5.

—— *Shadows of the Old Booksellers.* Bell and Daldy, London, 1865.

—— *The Struggles of a Book against Excessive Taxation.* 2nd edn., London, 1850.

KUNZLE, DAVID. *The Early Comic Strip: Narrative Strips and Picture Stories in the European Broadsheet from c. 1450 to 1825. History of the Comic Strip,* vol. 1. University of California Press, Berkeley, Los Angeles, and London, 1973.

—— *'Mr. Lambkin*: Cruikshank's Strike for Independence.' In *George Cruikshank: A Revaluation,* ed. Robert L. Patten, pp. 169–87. Princeton University Library, Princeton, 1974.

LAUTERBACH, CHARLES E., and LAUTERBACH, EDWARD S. 'The Nineteenth Century Three-Volume Novel.' *Publications of the Bibliographical Society of America,* 51 (1957), 263–302.

LEWES, G. H. 'Dickens in Relation to Criticism.' *Fortnightly Review,* N.S. 11 (1872), 141–54.

LEY, J. W. T. *The Dickens Circle: A Narrative of the Novelist's Friendships.* 2nd edn., Chapman & Hall, London, 1919.

—— 'Robert William Buss: A Tribute to an Unlucky Artist.' *Dickensian,* 6 (1910), 33–7, 71–5.

LOHRLI, ANNE, compiler. *Household Words.* University of Toronto Press, Toronto, 1973.

MACAULAY, THOMAS BABINGTON. *Prose and Poetry.* Ed. G. M. Young. Rupert Hart-Davis, Reynard Library, London, 1967.

MCCARTHY, JUSTIN, and ROBINSON, JOHN R. *'The Daily News' Jubilee, A Political and Social Retrospect of Fifty Years of the Queen's Reign.* Sampson Low & Co., London, 1896.

MACKENZIE, R. SHELTON. *Life of Charles Dickens*. T. B. Peterson and Bros., Philadelphia, 1870.

MACKINNON, SIR FRANK. 'Notes on the History of English Copyright.' In *The Oxford Companion to English Literature*, ed. Sir Paul Harvey, pp. 921–31, 4th edn., Clarendon Press, Oxford, 1967.

MACREADY, WILLIAM CHARLES. *The Diaries of William Charles Macready, 1833–1851*. Ed. William Toynbee. 2 vols., G. P. Putnam's Sons, New York, 1912.

MAGNUS, PHILIP. *Gladstone: A Biography*. E. P. Dutton, New York, 1954.

A Manual of Book-keeping for Booksellers, Publishers, and Stationers . . . by a Bookseller. Simpkin and Marshall, London, 1850.

MARKHAM, VIOLET R. *Paxton and the Bachelor Duke*. Hodder & Stoughton, London, 1935.

MASSON, DAVID. *British Novelists and Their Styles*. Macmillan, London, 1859.

MAUROIS, ANDRÉ. *Prometheus: The Life of Balzac*. Trans. Norman Denny. Harper & Row, New York, 1965.

MAYO, ROBERT D. *The English Novel in the Magazines 1740–1815: With a Catalogue of 1375 Magazine Novels and Novelettes*. Northwestern University Press, Evanston; Oxford University Press, London, 1962.

MEIDINGER, M. HENRY. 'An Historical and Statistical Account of the Book Trade.' *Journal of the Statistical Society of London*, 3 (1840–1), 161–90, 376–86.

MEYNELL, ALICE. 'How *Edwin Drood* Was Illustrated.' *Century Magazine*, 27 (1884), 522–8.

MILNE, JAMES. 'How Dickens Sells: He Comes Next to the Bible and Shakespeare.' *Book Monthly*, 3 (1906), 773–6.

MINNEGERODE, MEADE. *The Fabulous Forties, 1840–1850*. G. P. Putnam's Sons, New York, 1924.

'Mr. Charles Dickens and His Late Publishers.' *Once a Week*, May 1859, pp. 3–4.

MISTLER, JEAN. *La Librairie Hachette de 1826 à nos jours*. Hachette, Paris, 1964.

MONOD, SYLVÈRE. *Dickens the Novelist*. University of Oklahoma Press, Norman, 1968.

MORGAN, CHARLES. *The House of Macmillan, 1843–1943*. Macmillan Co., New York, 1944.

MORRIS, MOWBRAY. 'Charles Dickens.' *Fortnightly Review*, N.S. 32 (1882), 762–79.

MOTT, FRANK LUTHER. *Golden Multitudes: The Story of Best Sellers in the United States.* Macmillan, New York, 1947.

[Mudie's Select Library.] *Mudie's Select Library: Principal Works of Fiction in Circulation, 1848, 1858, 1869.* Catalogues arranged and indexed by Sara Keith. University Microfilms, Ann Arbor, Michigan, 1955.

—— *Mudie's Select Library: Title Index to Principal Works of Fiction in Circulation in 1848, 1858, 1869, with Their Occurrence in the Mudie Catalogues for 1876 and 1884.* Arranged and indexed by Sara Keith. Denver, Colorado, 1955; University Microfilms, London, 1960.

—— *Mudie's Select Library, 1876 and 1884: New Titles not Appearing in the Lists for 1848–1869.* Arranged and indexed by Sara Keith. University Microfilms, London, 1960.

MUIR, P[ERCY] H. 'Note No. 53. The Tauchnitz *David Copperfield*, 1849.' *Book Collector*, 4 (1955), 253–4.

—— 'Note No. 55. Dickens and Tauchnitz.' *Book Collector*, 4 (1955), 329.

—— *Victorian Illustrated Books.* B. T. Batsford, London, 1971.

MUMBY, F[RANK] A[RTHUR]. *The House of Routledge, 1834–1934: With a History of Kegan Paul, Trübner, and Other Associated Firms.* George Routledge, London, 1934.

—— *Publishing and Bookselling. A History from the Earliest Times to the Present Day.* 4th edn., Jonathan Cape, London, 1956.

MURRAY, JOHN, IV. *John Murray III, 1808–1892.* John Murray, London, 1919.

NEUBERG, VICTOR E. *Chapbooks: A Bibliography.* Vine Press, London, 1964.

NISBET, ADA. 'The Mystery of "Martin Chuzzlewit".' In *Essays Critical and Historical Dedicated to Lily B. Campbell by Members of the Departments of English, University of California*, pp. 201–16. English Studies I. University of California Press, Berkeley and Los Angeles, 1950.

NOBLE, THOMAS A. *George Eliot's Scenes of Clerical Life.* Yale Studies in English, vol. 159. Yale University Press, New Haven and London, 1965.

NOWELL-SMITH, SIMON. 'The "Cheap Edition" of Dickens's Works [First Series] 1847–1852.' *The Library*, 5th ser., 22 (1967), 245–51.

—— *The House of Cassell: 1848–1958.* Cassell, London, 1958.

—— *International Copyright Law and the Publisher in the Reign of Queen Victoria.* Clarendon Press, Oxford, 1968.

OLIPHANT, MRS. [MARGARET]. *Annals of a Publishing House: William Blackwood and His Sons; Their Magazine and Friends.* 2 vols., William Blackwood & Sons, Edinburgh and London, 1897.

The Opinions of Certain Authors on the Bookselling Question. John W. Parker and Son, London, 1852.

[OTTO, KURT.] *Der Verlag Bernhard Tauchnitz, 1837–1912: Mit einem Anhang enthaltend Auszüge aus den Briefen englischer und amerikanischer Autoren der Tauchnitz Edition.* [Tauchnitz], Leipzig, 1912.

PALMER, A. H. *The Life and Letters of Samuel Palmer, Painter and Etcher.* New edn., intro. Raymond Lister, pref. Kathleen Raine. Eric and Joan Stevens, London, 1972.

PAROISSIEN, DAVID. '*Pictures from Italy* and Its Original Illustrator.' *Dickensian,* 67 (1971), 87–90.

PARRISH, M. L., and MILLER, ELIZABETH V. *Wilkie Collins and Charles Reade.* London, 1940; rpt. Burt Franklin, Bibliography and Reference Series No. 186, New York, 1968.

PARSONS, IAN. 'Copyright and Society.' In *Essays in the History of Publishing in Celebration of the 250th Anniversary of the House of Longman, 1724–1974,* ed. Asa Briggs, pp. 29–60. Longman, London, 1974.

PASTON, GEORGE [pseud. of E. M. Symonds]. *At John Murray's: Records of a Literary Circle, 1843–1892.* John Murray, London, 1932.

PATTEN, ROBERT L. 'Dickens Time and Again.' *Dickens Studies Annual,* 2 (1972), 163–96.

—— 'The Fight at the Top of the Tree: *Vanity Fair* Versus *Dombey and Son.*' *Studies in English Literature,* 10 (1970), 759–73.

—— '*Pickwick Papers* and the Development of Serial Fiction.' *Rice University Studies,* 61 (Winter 1975), 51–74.

—— 'Plot in Charles Dickens' Early Novels, 1836–1841.' Ph.D. dissertation. Princeton University, 1965.

—— ' "The Story-Weaver at His Loom": Dickens and the Beginning of *The Old Curiosity Shop.*' In *Dickens the Craftsman: Strategies of Presentation,* ed. Robert B. Partlow, Jr., pp. 44–64. Southern Illinois University Press, Carbondale and Edwardsville, Illinois; Feffer & Simons, Inc., London and Amsterdam, 1970.

—— ' "A Surprising Transformation": Dickens and the Hearth.' In *Nature and the Victorian Imagination,* ed. Ulrich C. Knoepflmacher and Georg B. Tennyson, pp. 153–70. University of California Press, Berkeley and Los Angeles, 1977.

PATTERSON, LYMAN RAY. 'Copyright and Author's Rights: A Look at History.' *Huntington Library Bulletin,* 16 (1968), 370–84.

—— *Copyright in Historical Perspective.* Vanderbilt University Press, Nashville, Tennessee, 1968.

PEACOCK, CARLOS. *Samuel Palmer: Shoreham and After.* John Baker, London, 1968.

The Perils of Authorship; An Enquiry into the Difficulties of Literature. 'By an Old and Popular Author.' Published for the Author, London [1840?]. BM. No. 12331. de. 8 (4).

PETHERAM, JOHN. *Reasons for Establishing an Author's Publication Society.* John Petheram, London, 1843.

PHILLIPS, WALTER C. *Dickens, Reade, and Collins, Sensation Novelists: A Study in the Conditions and Theories of Novel Writing in Victorian England.* 1919; reissue Russell & Russell, Inc., New York, 1962.

PLANT, MARJORIE. *The English Book Trade: An Economic History of the Making and Sale of Books.* R. R. Bowker Co., New York, 1939.

POLLARD, GRAHAM. 'Novels in Newspapers: Some Unpublished Letters of Captain Mayne Reid.' *Review of English Studies*, 18 (1942), 72–85.

—— 'Serial Fiction.' In *New Paths in Book Collecting*, ed. John Carter, pp. 245–77. Constable, London, 1934.

'Popular Literature—the Periodical Press.' *Blackwood's Edinburgh Magazine*, 85 (1859), 96–112, 180–95.

POWELL, DILYS. 'Postscript: Dickens on Film.' *Dickensian*, 66 (May 1970), 183–5.

RANDALL, DAVID A. 'Answer to Appeal 24: *Great Expectations.' New Colophon*, vol. 2, part 5 (Jan. 1949), 84–5; vol. 2, part 7 (Sept. 1949), 279.

—— 'Charles Dickens and Richard Bentley.' *Times Literary Supplement*, 12 Oct. 1946, p. 496.

RAY, GORDON N. *Thackeray. The Age of Wisdom, 1847–1863.* McGraw Hill Book Co., Inc., New York, Toronto, and London, 1958.

—— *Thackeray. The Uses of Adversity, 1811–1846.* McGraw Hill Book Co., Inc., New York, Toronto, and London, 1955.

—— 'Trollope at Full Length.' *Huntington Library Quarterly*, 31 (1968), 313–40.

REID, T. WEMYSS. *The Life, Letters, and Friendships of Richard Monckton Milnes, First Lord Houghton.* 3rd edn., 2 vols., Cassell, London, 1891.

REITLINGER, GERALD. *The Economics of Taste: The Rise and Fall of Picture Prices 1760–1960.* Barrie and Rockliff, London, 1961.

ROBINSON, HENRY CRABB. *Henry Crabb Robinson on Books and Their Writers.* Ed. Edith J. Morley. 3 vols., J. M. Dent, London, 1938.

ROSENBACH, A. S. W. *A Catalogue of the Writings of Charles Dickens in the Library of Harry Elkins Widener*. Privately printed, Philadelphia, 1918.

ROSENBERG, EDGAR. 'A Preface to *Great Expectations*: The Pale Usher Dusts His Lexicons.' *Dickens Studies Annual*, 2 (1972), 294–335.

ROUTLEDGE, GEORGE AND SONS. *Publishers' Archives: George Routledge & Co. 1853–1900, Contracts 1850–78*. Microfilm, Chadwyck-Healey, London, n.d.

RUST, S. J. 'At the Dickens House: Legal Documents Relating to the Piracy of *A Christmas Carol*.' *Dickensian*, 34 (1938), 41–4.

SADLEIR, MICHAEL. 'Bibliographical Aspects of the Victorian Novel.' Typescript of Sandars Lectures, Cambridge University, November 1937.

—— *Bulwer: A Panorama*. 2 vols., Constable & Co., London, 1931.

—— *XIX Century Fiction: A Bibliographical Record*. 2 vols., 1951; rpt. Cooper Square Publishers, Inc., New York, 1969.

—— 'Yellow-Backs.' In *New Paths in Book Collecting: Essays by Various Hands*, ed. John Carter, pp. 125–61. Constable, London, 1934.

SAINTSBURY, GEORGE E. B. 'Dickens.' In *Cambridge History of English Literature*, ed. A. W. Ward and A. R. Waller, xiii. 336–76. G. P. Putnam's Sons, New York; University Press, Cambridge, 1917.

SALA, GEORGE A. H. F. *Charles Dickens*. George Routledge and Sons, London, 1870; rpt. Gregg International Publishers, Ltd., Westmead, Farnborough, Hants, 1970.

SARGENT, GEORGE H. 'Dickensiana in America.' *Bookman's Journal*, N.S. 5 (1922), 23–4.

[SAWYER, CHARLES J., and DARTON, F. J. HARVEY.] *Dickens v. Barrabas, Forster Intervening: A Study Based upon Some Hitherto Unpublished Letters*. Charles J. Sawyer, London, 1930.

SCOTT, P. G. Reply: 'Pickwick Papers'. *Notes and Queries*, 218 (1973), 341.

SCOTT, SIR WALTER. *The Letters of Sir Walter Scott*. Ed. H. J. C. Grierson. Centenary Edition, 12 vols., Constable, London, 1932–7.

SEYMOUR, MRS. [ROBERT]. *An Account of the Origin of the 'Pickwick Papers'*. 1854; rpt. for the author, London, 1901.

'Seymour's Unpublished Sketches for *Pickwick*.' *Dickensian*, 27 (1931), 146–7.

SHAYLOR, JOSEPH. *The Fascination of Books, with Other Papers on Books and Bookselling*. Simpkin Marshall & Co., London, 1912.

—— *Sixty Years a Bookman*. Selwyn & Blount, London, 1923.

SHILLINGSBURG, PETER. 'The First Edition of Thackeray's *Pendennis*.' *Papers of the Bibliographical Society of America*, 66 (1972), 35–49.

SLATER, MICHAEL. *The Composition and Monthly Publication of Nicholas Nickleby*. Scolar Press, Menston, Yorkshire, 1973.

—— '1920–1940: "Superior Folk" and Scandalmongers.' *Dickensian*, 66 (May 1970), 121–42.

SMILES, SAMUEL. *A Publisher and His Friends: Memoir and Correspondence of John Murray, with an Account of the Origin and Progress of the House, 1768–1843*. Condensed and ed. Thomas Mackay. John Murray, London, 1911.

SMITH, GRAHAME. *Dickens, Money and Society*. University of California Press, Berkeley and Los Angeles, 1968.

SOUTHTON, J. Y. 'Authorised Leipzig Edition of Dickens.' *Dickensian*, 8 (1912), 181–3.

SPEDDING, JAMES. *Publishers and Authors*. John Russell Smith, London, 1867.

SPIELMANN, M. H. *The History of 'Punch'*. Cassell, London, Paris, and Melbourne, 1895.

STANG, RICHARD. *The Theory of the Novel in England, 1850–1870*. Columbia University Press, New York; Routledge & Kegan Paul, London, 1959.

STEVENSON, LIONEL. *Dr. Quicksilver: The Life of Charles Lever*. 1939; reissue Russell & Russell, New York, 1969.

—— *The Showman of Vanity Fair*. Charles Scribner's Sons, New York, 1947.

STONEHOUSE, J. H., ed. *Catalogue of the Library of Charles Dickens from Gadshill Reprinted from Sotheran's 'Price of Current Literature' Nos. CLXXIV and CLXXV*. Piccadilly Fountain Press, London, 1935.

STOREY, GLADYS. *Dickens and Daughter*. Frederick Muller, London, 1939.

SUCKSMITH, H. P. 'Dickens at Work on *Bleak House*: A Critical Examination of His Memoranda and Number Plans.' *Renaissance and Modern Studies*, 9 (1965), 47–85.

SUTHERLAND, JOHN A. *Victorian Novelists and Publishers*. Athlone Press, London, 1976.

SYMONDS, *see* Paston, George.

TANSELLE, G. THOMAS. 'The Sales of Melville's Books.' *Huntington Library Bulletin*, 17 (1969), 195–215.

TAYLOR, GEORGE ROGERS. *The Transportation Revolution, 1815–1860*. *The Economic History of the United States*, vol. 4. Rinehart & Co., Inc., New York and Toronto, 1951.

THACKERAY, WILLIAM MAKEPEACE. *The Letters and Private Papers of William Makepeace Thackeray.* Ed. Gordon N. Ray. 4 vols., Harvard University Press, Cambridge, Massachusetts, 1945–6.

[——] 'A Pictorial Rhapsody: Concluded. And Followed by a Remarkable Statement of Facts by Mrs. Barbara.' *Fraser's Magazine,* 22 (1840), 112–24.

TILLOTSON, KATHLEEN. *Novels of the Eighteen-Forties.* Clarendon Press, Oxford, 1954.

—— 'Oliver Twist in Three Volumes.' *The Library,* ser. 5, 18 (1963), 113–32.

TIMPERLEY, C. H. *A Dictionary of Printers and Printing.* London, 1839.

TINSLEY, WILLIAM. *Random Recollections of an Old Publisher.* 2 vols., Simpkin, Marshall & Co., London, 1900.

TODD, WILLIAM B. 'Dickens's *Battle of Life*: Round Six.' *Book Collector,* 15 (1966), 48–54.

TOMPKINS, J. M. S. *The Popular Novel in England, 1770–1800.* Constable, London, 1932.

TREDREY, F. O. *The House of Blackwood, 1804–1954.* William Blackwood & Sons Ltd., Edinburgh and London, 1954.

TROLLOPE, ANTHONY. *An Autobiography.* Ed. Bradford Allen Booth. University of California Press, Berkeley and Los Angeles, 1947.

—— *The Letters of Anthony Trollope.* Ed. Bradford Allen Booth. Oxford University Press, London, New York, and Toronto, 1951.

—— 'Novel-Reading.' *The Nineteenth Century,* 5 (1879), 24–43.

TWYMAN, MICHAEL. *Printing 1770–1970: An Illustrated History of Its Uses and Development in England.* Eyre & Spottiswoode, London, 1970.

VIVIAN, CHARLES H. 'Dickens, the "True Sun", and Samuel Laman Blanchard.' *Nineteenth-Century Fiction,* 4 (1949–50), 328–30.

WALLIS, PHILIP. *At the Sign of the Ship: Notes on the House of Longman, 1724–1974.* Longman Group Ltd., London, 1974.

WARD, MRS. HUMPHRY [MARY AUGUSTA]. *A Writer's Recollections.* W. Collins, London, 1918.

WAUGH, ARTHUR. *A Hundred Years of Publishing: Being the Story of Chapman & Hall, Ltd.* Chapman & Hall, London, 1930.

WEISS, HARRY B. 'Hannah More's Cheap Repository Tracts in America.' *Bulletin of the New York Public Library,* 50 (1946), 539–49, 634–41.

WELSH, ALEXANDER. *The City of Dickens.* Clarendon Press, Oxford, 1971.

WHITE, GLEESON. *English Illustration, 'The Sixties': 1855–70.* 1897; rpt. Kingsmead Reprints, Bath, 1970.

WILES, R. M. *Serial Publication in England before 1750.* University Press, Cambridge, 1957.

WILKINS, W. GLYDE. 'Dickens and His First American Publishers.' *Dickensian,* 9 (1913), 257–61.

—— 'Early Foreign Translations of Dickens's Works.' *Dickensian,* 7 (1911), 35–7.

—— 'First and Early American Editions of the Works of Dickens.' *Dickensian,* 3 (1907), 186–8.

—— *First and Early American Editions of the Works of Charles Dickens.* 1910; rpt. Burt Franklin, Bibliography and Reference Series No. 151, New York, 1968.

WOODMAN, R. E. G. 'Dickens and His Publishers.' *Times Literary Supplement,* 25 Jan. 1947, p. 51.

WORDSWORTH, WILLIAM and DOROTHY. *The Letters of William and Dorothy Wordsworth: The Later Years,* ed. Ernest de Selincourt. 3 vols., Clarendon Press, Oxford, 1939.

YATES, EDMUND. *Edmund Yates: His Recollections and Experiences.* 2 vols., Richard Bentley and Son, London, 1884.

Index

Compiled by FRANK T. DUNN